Hardwood Heroes

Celebrating a Century of Minnesota Basketball

by
Ross Bernstein

Nodin Press

"Hardwood Heroes: Celebrating a Century of Minnesota Basketball"
by Ross Bernstein
(WWW.BERNSTEINBOOKS.COM)

Cover Painting by Duluth Artist Tim Cortes: (218) 525-4953

Published by Nodin Press,
(A division of Micawber's Inc.)
525 North Third Street
Minneapolis, MN 55401

Midwest Distribution by: The Bookmen (612) 341-3333

Printed in Minnesota by Printing Enterprises

Edited by Joel Rippel

ISBN 0-931714-93-1
Library of Congress Control Number: 2001096221

Photo Credits:
University of Minnesota: 6, 7, 10, 11, 36, 65-96, 173-176, 215
Eric Miller: 44-60
David Sherman: 189-191, 216
Minnesota State High School League: 117-167, 193-209
Minnesota Historical Society: 5, 12, 13, 192, 193
Dick Jonckowski Archives: 14-35, 37-44, 187-188
Vern Mikkelsen: 97-9, 210-211
Janet Karvonen: 209
Tim Cortes: 4
University of Minnesota-Duluth: 107-108, 184-187
St. Cloud State University: 36, 114-116, 180-182
Minnesota State University, Mankato: 113-114, 183-184
Bemidji State University: 111, 186
Southwest State University: 110, 185
UM-Crookston: 108
UM-Moorhead: 108-109
Augsburg College: 100-101, 177, 179
St. John's University: 104-105
University of St. Thomas: 99,178-180
Hamline University: 97
Concordia College: 179
Gustavus Adolphus College: 103
Macalester College: 105
St. Olaf College: 178
St. Ben's: 177-178
Carleton College: 102, 177

Acknowledgements:
I would really like to thank all of the people that were kind enough to help me in writing this book. In addition to the countless pro,
college and university Sports Information Directors that I hounded throughout this project I would like to sincerely thank all of the men
and women that allowed me to interview them. In addition, I would particularly like to thank my publisher, and friend, Norton Stillman.

Tim Cortes	Ardie Eckhart	Tim Kennedy	Andy Johnson	Mike Cristaldi	Bob Nygard	Madge Makowske
Vern Mikkelsen	Karen Zwach	Howard Voigt	Mike Mohalis	Gene McGivern	Mike Hemmesch	Judy Strohmeyer
Kevin McHale	Anne Abicht	Paul Allen	Dave Wright	Larry Scott	Brian Curtis	Stacy Deidric
Dick Jonckowski	Tim Trainor	Paul Thompson	Ron Christian	Andy Bartlett	Mike Herzberg	Eric Miller
Joel Rippel	Bob Snyder	Chris Owens	Jim Larson	Steph Reck	Eric Sieger	Julie Arthur Sherman
Ann Johnson	Kent Wipf	Chris Blisette	Ron Christian	Kelly Loft	Jim Cella	Randy Royals
Randy Johnson	Don Stoner	Kurt Daniels	Tom Clark	Julie Nagel	Dan McMahon	Toddler Rendahl
Ed Kalafat	Greg Peterson	Paul Allen	John Griffin	Jim Cella	David Sherman	Johnny Lindy
Mike Miernicki	Tom Jones	Bob Nygaard	Matt Pederson	Don Nadeau	Jim Hastings	*H.J. Pieser*

For Sara, my wife and best friend...
I love you more than ever

Cover Painting by Artist Tim Cortes

I would especially like to express my gratitude to Minnesota sports artist, Tim Cortes, for allowing me the privilege of showcasing his new hard-court masterpiece entitled: *"Nothing but Net"* on the cover of my new book. I couldn't be more pleased with the final product and simply can't thank him enough for all of his hard work. He is not only an amazing artist, he is also a wonderful friend. *(Contact Tim directly if you would like to purchase a signed, numbered, limited edition print of the cover painting — he even has multiple framing and matting options and can ship anywhere in the world.)*

One of the nation's premier photo realism artists, Cortes uses colored pencils as his preferred medium. Hundreds of his collectible lithographs have been sold throughout North America and his clients are a venerable who's-who of American sports. From Shaquille O'Neal to Mark McGwire and from Wayne Gretzky to Troy Aikman, Cortes has been commissioned to create countless commemorative works of art over the past decade.

Randy Moss

His paintings have also been featured in numerous venues around the world, including: the US Hockey Hall of Fame, Franklin Mint, Kelly Russell Studios and Beckett's Magazine, as well as on trading cards, pro sports teams' game-day programs, and in various publications. Known for his impeccable detail, Cortes has dedicated his life to the pursuit of celebrating the life and times of many of the world's most famous athletes and the sporting events in which they play.

Cortes grew up in Duluth, where he later starred as a hockey goaltender at Duluth East High School. After a brief stint in the United States Hockey League, Cortes went on to play between the pipes for two seasons in the mid-1980s for the University of Minnesota's Golden Gophers. Cortes then decided to pursue his passion of art and sports full-time, and enrolled at the prestigious Minneapolis College of Art and Design. He has been painting ever since!

Today Tim lives in Duluth with his wife Kathy and their two children. He continues to play senior hockey and also gives back by coaching both youth football and hockey.

If you would like to purchase a signed, limited edition print of "Nothing but Net," or any other of Tim's hundreds of works of art, please check out his web-site or contact his new studio in Duluth, where you, too, can own a piece of sports history.

Troy Aikman

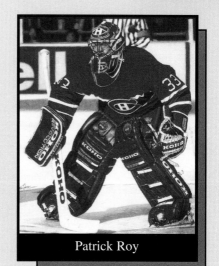

Patrick Roy

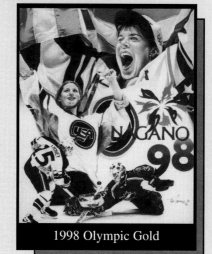

1998 Olympic Gold

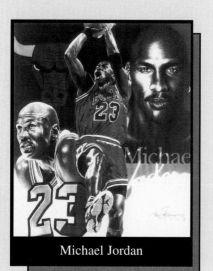

Michael Jordan

Table of Contents

6.   Foreword by Kevin McHale

8.   Introduction

9.   In the Beginning

12.   The History of Pro Hoops in Minnesota

14.   The Minneapolis Lakers

37.   The ABA's Minnesota Muskies & Pipers

44.   The NBA's Minnesota Timberwolves

62.   The CBA and IBA

65.   The Golden Gophers

97.   The Minnesota Intercollegiate Athletic Conference (MIAC)

106. The Northern Sun Conference Basketball (NSIC)

112. The North Central Conference Basketball

117. The Boy's State Tourney

173. The History of Women's Basketball in Minnesota

173. The Lady Gophers

177. The Women's Minnesota Intercollegiate Athletic Conference (MIAC)

180. The Women's North Central Conference (NCC)

184. The Women's Northern Sun Conference Basketball (NSIC)

187. The Evolution of the Women's Pro Game

189. The WNBA's Minnesota Lynx

192. The Girls' State Tourney

210. Afterword by Vern Mikkelsen

216. About the Author

Foreword by Kevin McHale

Kevin McHale is without question the greatest basketball player ever to hail from the state of Minnesota. With his patented fade-away jumper and silky smooth touch, he was simply unstoppable in the low post. His hoops legacy was in fact a rather unique form of basketball artistry. From jump-hooks to baseline reverse lay-ins, McHale was a true artist whose canvas was the hardwood.

After an amazing Hall of Fame career with the Boston Celtics, Minnesota was blessed when its most prodigal of native sons decided to return home for good to begin his second career as an executive with the upstart Timberwolves. An avid outdoorsman, Kevin couldn't wait to get back to the Land of 10,000 Lakes to resume fishing and hunting, which, outside of the basketball court, is where he probably feels most at home.

McHale's story is a long and fascinating one though, which has roots that extend all the way up to Hibbing, where he grew up learning the values of a strong work ethic from a father who was a miner on the great Mesabi Iron Range. It was up in the great northwoods where this kid learned to love and appreciate the power of sports. At first, Kevin played them all. And who knows? Had it not been for that lanky six-foot-ten frame of his, perhaps he would've gone on to greatness as a winger for the North Stars instead!

But fortunately for us, he decided to pursue his calling on the hardcourt, where he has certainly made us all so very proud. From what began as a hobby at Green Haven Elementary School, became an obsession for a kid who dreamt of one day playing for his beloved University of Minnesota Golden Gophers. As a youngster Kevin would oftentimes even go down to the Hibbing library to read about the Gophers in the Minneapolis Newspapers. He had to have his fix, and it made him even hungrier to pursue his dreams.

Kevin worked hard as a prepster and went on to earn All-State honors as a junior at Hibbing Senior High. He led his club to the post-season that year as well, only to get upset in the first round of the playoffs by Little Falls. Then, as a senior, he led his Blue Jackets to the 1976 Class AA State Basketball Tournament title game against Bloomington Jefferson. They ultimately lost that big game to the Jaguars, but not before making believers out of every "David vs. Goliath" fan in the state. And, when Kevin outplayed Jefferson's All-State big man, Steve Lingenfelter, many of the nation's top collegiate recruiters knew that they were witnessing something special.

Kevin, who went on to win the coveted "Mr. Basketball Minnesota" award after his senior season, modestly turned away all of the scholarship offers though, and opted to instead pursue his dream of wearing the maroon and gold at the U of M. Gopher fans everywhere rejoiced when they heard the news, and tabbed him as the savior of a program that was on the rebound. McHale then came in and simply took Gold Country by storm, becoming an instant fan-favorite.

From there the team went through its share of ups and downs, with one of the highlights perhaps coming in Kevin's final game as a Gopher when he led the team to the NIT Finals, where the team ultimately lost to All-American Center Ralph Sampson and Virginia. Kevin became synonymous with Minnesota basketball though, and from 1977-1980, he averaged 15.2 points and 8.5 rebounds per game, while accumulating an incredible 1,704 points — then second all-time in school history. A two-time All-Big 10 selection, McHale was also the U's career record holder in blocked shots with 235, and had also amassed the second most rebounds of all-time with 950 as well.

After his illustrious career in Gold Country, he was selected with the third overall pick of the first round of the 1980 NBA Draft by the Boston Celtics. Before he joined the club though, he played on a pair of U.S. gold medal-winning Pan-Am teams in both Puerto Rico and Mexico.

Kevin then headed east to join one of the greatest teams in all of sports, the Celtics. He would help make up one of the most formidable front-lines in the history of the game, alongside of Larry Bird and Robert Parrish. He made an impact his first season, leading the team to the NBA title, en route to making the All-Rookie team. He led Boston to two more championships in both 1984 and 1986, as well as five Eastern Conference titles and eight Atlantic Division crowns. He was given the NBA's Sixth-Man Award both in 1984 and 1985, and among his seven trips to the All-Star game, he was selected to the All-NBA First Team in 1987. He was also named to the NBA All-Defensive First Team in 1986, 1987, and 1988.

Over his incredible 13-year NBA career he scored 17,335 points, while averaging 17.9 points, 7.3 rebounds, and 1.7 assists per game. He ranks 10th all-time in the NBA in career field goal percentage with .554, and also shot a remarkable 79.8 percent from the free-throw line. Twice he led the league in field-goal percentage, and he remains the only player in NBA history to shoot over 60 percent from the field and 80 percent from the free throw line in the same season when he did it in 1987. And, his 56-point effort against the Detroit Pistons on March 3, 1985 still ranks second all-time in Celtics' single-game history.

In 1993 Kevin quietly retired from the game. Perhaps famed Boston Globe writer Bob Ryan put it best: "The long-armed wonder from Minnesota's Mesabi Iron Range won his way into the hearts of Beantowners with his lunch-bucket approach to the game and his uncanny ability to play Tonto to Larry Bird's Lone Ranger."

"He's the best post-up player since Kareem," said Robert Parrish. "And no forward could guard him. No one." Danny Ainge, McHale's former teammate laughingly called him "the black hole," because once you got a pass to him inside, the ball was not coming back out. "He just struck fear in the hearts of the defenders," he said. "During the height of his career he was easily the best power forward playing the game, and I'd rate him in the top three of all time," said former Celtics great Bob Cousy. "Kevin was a great college player but I think he turned out to be a better pro player. As a low-post player he's the best I've ever seen," added Larry Bird.

Kevin came home to his beloved Minnesota in 1993 and began working with the Minnesota Timberwolves. For two years he worked as the assistant G.M. and also served as a TV analyst on Wolves' games. In May of 1995, he took over the team, becoming their general manager as well as vice president of basketball operations. In that role, McHale has become responsible for the franchise's entire basketball op's department — overseeing player personnel decisions, scouting and the coaching staff. One of his first moves with the Wolves was selecting high-school phenom Kevin Garnett with the fifth-overall pick in the 1995 NBA Draft. He wasted little time in retooling the entire Wolves roster and soon made his presence felt. In 1997, the team made its first-ever playoff appearance under McHale's former Gopher teammate and pal, Head Coach Flip Saunders. Since then the Wolves have made four consecutive post-season appearances and have emerged as one of the league's brightest teams.

McHale's legacy will include many things. Most importantly though, will perhaps be his reputation as the most unstoppable NBA low-post scorer of his era. His hard work and desire to win, coupled with his creativity with the ball down in the paint truly revolutionized the game for generations to come. His list of honors and accolades is even more impressive than his stats. In 1997 McHale was named as one of the NBA's Top 50 Players for the league's first half-century, and in 1999 he was immortalized forever when he was inducted into the prestigious Basketball Hall of Fame in Springfield, Mass. In addition, in 1995, Kevin was even honored as the best player in 100 years of Gopher Basketball history, as his No. 44 was officially retired up into the rafters of Williams Arena.

Today Kevin continues his never-ending quests of shooting that perfect round of golf, landing a 10-pound Walleye, watching and hoping that his Vikings will someday win the Super Bowl, and most importantly, getting his T-Wolves to the promised land of NBA champions. He is happy to be home though, pursuing both of his passions of the great outdoors and basketball with his wife and their five children.

So who better than to talk about the last century of Minnesota basketball as well as the future state of the state of this great game, than "Mr. Basketball" himself, our very own Kevin McHale:

In the Beginning...

While the game of basketball was officially invented back in 1891 by Dr. James A. Naismith, in Springfield, Mass., the sports' roots can be traced back much further in time. In fact, the concept of throwing a round object through a hoop is quite ancient. In one instance archaeologists even unearthed an ancient Mayan city in the Yucatan Peninsula which was discovered to have had an enclosed "arena," complete with stone grandstands, for just such an activity. There were even wall carvings which depicted seven-man teams throwing a ball through vertical rings which were roughly 12 feet high.

And, if that weren't enough proof, according to "The Amazing Basketball Book," similar games were being played throughout the millennium by all sorts of different cultures. One of them was the 16th-century Aztecs, who, according to the book: "played a particularly tough brand of ball and hoop called Ollamalitzli. The player who made a shot was entitled to the clothing of all the spectators; the captain of the losing team often had his head chopped off."

While it is not known for sure whether or not Dr. Naismith had the same intentions of lopping off his opponents' melons, the game he created was no doubt an amalgam of many games of agility and athleticism. Naismith has long been considered as the "father of basketball," having invented the game he so dearly loved more than 110 years ago. His story is an interesting one to say the least. A remarkably versatile and humble man, there was no way he could've ever imagined that his little game would achieve such global popularity and ultimately be played by more people than any game in the world. After all, he was just seeking to find an indoor activity for his restless students on those long, cold New England winter days.

So, at the International YMCA Training School (now Springfield College) in Springfield. Mass., Naismith, a physical education instructor, assembled the pieces that would become the game of "Basket Ball" — it would three more decades before it would be shortened to just one word. Naismith had the school janitor nail two peach baskets to each end of the gymnasium balcony, and then had the school's secretary type his original 13 rules. The kids then came in and he explained to them how it was played.

"I selected two captains and had them choose sides," Naismith said years later. "I placed the men on the floor. There were three forwards, three centers and three backs on each team. I chose two of the center men to jump, then threw the ball between them. It was the start of the first basket ball game and the finish of trouble with that class."

The early caged court

Despite the fact that the game ended in a no-doubt thrilling 1-0 victory, by all accounts it was a big success. The students found the new game to be fun and before long news of its popularity quickly spread throughout the campus. Within a few months kids and adults alike across the United States were playing basket ball. One of the big reasons for the game's rapid growth was due to the fact that the YMCA had a publication, the Triangle, which was regularly sent out to its network of nationwide affiliates. Naismith's original 13 rules were printed in one of those issues, and with it, so began the genesis of one of the world's greatest games.

Leagues quickly sprang up from coast-to-coast. Rules and the style of play varied from town to town, but for the most part, courts were 40-by-60 feet, and, in many cases, were enclosed with chicken-wire fencing, or netting, that served to keep the ball from going out of bounds. Before long the players themselves were referred to as "cagers." They played the game anywhere they could, finding refuge in YMCA's, school gymnasiums, local armories, Masonic temples and even hotel ballrooms.

The first professional basketball game took place on November 7, 1896, when the Trenton (NJ) Basketball Team defeated the Brooklyn YMCA squad, 16-1. The teams, which played at a local Masonic Temple, charged admission and agreed to split the profits.

A Canadian by birth, Dr. James A. Naismith, a physician and minister with degrees in Philosophy, Religion, Education and Psychology, originally invented the game of basketball as a way to provide entertainment for his Springfield, Mass., students during the wintertime. A humanitarian who cared deeply about the well-being of others, Naismith never profited from the sport he invented, promoting it rather for the love of the game. A star athlete at Montreal's McGill University, Naismith championed the importance of physical education and athletics, living by the motto: "a sound mind is a sound body." An avid sports fan and innovator, he also invented the football helmet.

He coached briefly at the University of Kansas, but focused instead on his life's calling of helping others. He became famous for creating this wonderful game, a stroke of genius that never brought him fame or fortune during his lifetime, but enormous recognition following his passing in 1939. He was, however, afforded a glimpse of the game's potential appeal in 1936 when he attended the Berlin Olympics, where basketball was played as a medal sport for the first time. One historical textbook even listed Naismith as No. 4 of the 100 most influential sports figures in America during the 20th century. For his historic invention, Naismith's name adorns the world's only Basketball Hall of Fame, a tribute that forever makes the good doctor synonymous with the game, sport and lifestyle of basketball.

Dr. James Naismith

Dr. Naismith's Original 13 Rules:

The object of the game is to put the ball into your opponent's goal. This may be done by throwing the ball from any part of the grounds, with one or two hands, under the following conditions and rules:

1. The ball may be thrown in any direction with one or both hands.
2. The ball may be batted in any direction with one or both hands.
3. A player cannot run with the ball. The player must throw it from the spot on which he catches it, allowances to be made for a man who catches the ball when running if he tries to stop.
4. The ball must be held by the hands. The arms or body must not be used for holding it.
5. No shouldering, holding, pushing, tripping or striking in any way the person of an opponent shall be allowed; the first infringement of this rule by any player shall come as a foul, the second shall disqualify him until the next goal is made, or, if there was evident intent to injure the person, for the whole of the game, no substitute allowed.
6. A foul is striking the ball with the fist, violation of Rules 3, 4, and such as described in Rule 5.
7. If either side makes three consecutive fouls it shall count as a goal for the opponents.
8. A goal shall be made when the ball is thrown or batted from the grounds into the basket and stays there, providing those defending the goal do no touch or disturb the goal. If the ball rests on the edges, and the opponent moves the basket, it shall count as a goal.
9. When the ball goes out of bounds, it shall be thrown into the field of play by the person touching it. He has a right to hold it unmolested for five seconds. In case of a dispute the umpire shall throw it straight into the field. The thrower-in is allowed five seconds; if he holds it longer it shall go to the opponent. If any side persists in delaying the game the umpire shall call a foul on that side.
10. The umpire shall be the judge of the men and shall note the fouls and notify the referee when three consecutive fouls have been made. He shall have power to disqualify men according to Rule 5.
11. The referee shall be judge of the ball and shall decide when the ball is in play, in bounds, to which side it belongs, and shall keep the time. He shall decide when a goal has been made and keep account of the goals, with any other duties that are usually performed by a referee.
12. The time shall be two fifteen-minute halves, with five minutes rest between.
13. The side making the most goals in that time shall be declared the winner. In the case of a draw the game may, by agreement of the captains, be continued until another goal is made.

The Trenton players received $15 each, with the $1 that was left over going to team captain, Fred Cooper, who immediately became pro basketball's "highest paid player."

From there, the game began to grow at nearly every level, including at high schools, college and universities, as well as professionally. In the pro ranks, however, there were different rules than in college. The pro's allowed its players to make a series of two-handed, single-bounce dribbles, while the prepsters preferred the continuous dribble. At first the game was somewhat barbaric, with a football-like presence taking over. In addition to that, the players also had to be aware of other obstacles, such as hot stoves, steam pipes, and even posts or structural columns sometimes located in the middle of their courts. And, if that weren't enough, in addition to worrying about injuring themselves while slamming into the cage itself, the visiting players also had to watch out for drunk fans who found humor in ramming knitting needles and throwing lit cigarettes and even hot rivets at them through the wire mesh as they were shooting free-throws.

The "cage" game all but dried up in the 1920s, but pro basketball plowed ahead with a series of leagues rising and falling along the way. The great teams of this era were Harlem's Renaissance (an all-black team also known as the "Rens" which played well into the late 1940s before disbanding with an amazing record of 2,588 wins and 529 losses), the Original Celtics and the Philadelphia SPHAs (South Philadelphia Hebrew Association). These teams survived and even prospered because they barnstormed for money, playing as many as two hundred games per season.

Another successful league was the American Basketball League, which was formed in 1925 by Joe Carr, who was also the president of the

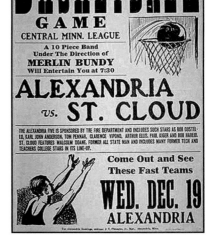

upstart National Football League. The first league of any significance, the ABL, was a "national" league with franchises that stretched from New York to Chicago. The league was instrumental in advancing the game in several ways, including: signing its players to exclusive contracts that prevented them from constantly changing teams, making back-boards mandatory in each arena, eliminating the wire cages from around the courts, and also adopting new rules which ultimately sped up the game and increased the scoring.

By the early 1930s, many basketball promoters found they could attract a decent crowd if they combined the games with a big-band dance following the game. This proved to be the perfect

The Basketball Hoop

When Dr. Naismith invented the game of basketball back in 1891, he mounted a pair of peach baskets on the walls. It was affective, but still required someone to physically climb up there and get the ball down after every basket. A couple of years later, when the game grew in popularity, baskets began to emerge that were made out of wire. By the turn of the century, the Narragansett Machine Company in Providence, RI, invented a basket with an iron rim holding that supported the net. It too had a bottom, but in this version there was a chain attached that could be pulled to open the trap-door and let the ball fall out. It wouldn't be until 1906 when the open-bottomed basket was conceived, and it didn't become commonplace until around 1910.

date-night out for couples everywhere, and really helped to promote the game. Back then, the game was played in three periods, with the teams playing a period, followed by the fans dancing awhile, and so on. One of the big problems with this though was all the dance wax which was put on the hardwood floors. In fact, it wasn't uncommon to see players "slide and shoot" as they made their way across the court.

The culmination of all the regional pro leagues back in the 1930s and '40s, was the Chicago Herald American tournament. Simply known as the "world tournament," this helped to promote the game as well, with teams of all ethnicity's coming to the Windy City every year to do battle. Among the early dynasties of this era were the Harlem Globetrotters, who, with their crowd-pleasing antics and dazzling ball-handling displays, won several world crowns en route to becoming the most famous team of all time.

The National Basketball League was formed in 1937, and over the next decade the NBL would emerge as the best of the bunch.

Max Exner

Basketball first came to Minnesota when a gentleman by the name of Max Exner, a former roommate of James Naismith, moved to Minnesota from Massachusetts in 1892 to become Carleton College's Director of Physical Culture. While there, he quickly saw the winter-time void left in the wake of football and baseball, so he decided to introduce the game, which he had learned just a year earlier, to the students of Northfield. The rest, they say, is history!

One of the reasons for its success was due to its connection with businesses and industrial companies who sponsored teams. Colorful clubs such as the Akron Good Year Wingfoots, Toledo Jim White Chevrolets, Chicago Gears, Fort Wayne Zollner Pistons and Anderson Packers were all sponsored by companies who would entice the top players from around the country to play for them by giving them lucrative jobs working at their factories during the day-time, while they played ball at night.

Naismith was the honorary referee at the Williams Arena Dedication Game on Feb. 4, 1928

Athletic Union teams were also in hot pursuit of big-time talent. As was the case for Oklahoma A&M All-American Center Bob Kurland, who decided to take a swanky desk job in Bartlesville, Oklahoma, where he proudly played for the Phillips (Petroleum) 66 "Oilers" squad. The same was true for future Minneapolis Lakers Hall of Famer, Jim Pollard, who, at first turned down the pro's to take a cushy job with the AAU's Oakland Bittners, a grocery chain.

Before long the pro's and colleges were competing big-time for talent and for the fans' entertainment dollars. In 1938 the National Invitational Tournament (NIT) was created at Madison Square Garden, a venue big enough to attract big sponsors and big crowds. Soon thereafter large arenas around the country were playing host to pro and college games as the sport began to grow by leaps and bounds. By the end of WWII, waves of young men returned home from overseas and essentially flooded the market with new money. They wanted to be entertained, particularly in the wintertime, and basketball seemed to be the answer.

In 1946 the Basketball Association of America was founded by arena owners who wanted to fill their venues when their hockey teams were on the road. The hoop game was the perfect fit. Before long the BAA and the NBL fought over the best talent from the amateur and professional ranks, with both sides struggling to stay afloat. Eventually the upstart leagues, tired of feuding and raiding one another, made a merger of sorts, with the National Basketball Association rising from the ashes. Our very own Minneapolis Lakers, with their superstar George Mikan, were right smack-dab in the middle of all of this, and were a huge reason why today the NBA is the greatest show on earth.

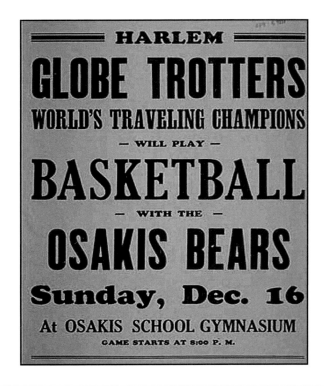

Pro Hoops in Minnesota

Minnesota has a long and storied professional and semi-professional basketball history. In as far back as the early 1910s, fully pro independent teams from such locales as Red Wing and Chaska were playing throughout the Midwest and even on the East Coast. Into the 1920s and '30s semi-pro teams sprouted up throughout the state, giving former college kids the opportunity to keep playing the game that they loved. The sport was even growing in Northern Minnesota, where the round-ball was making some headway in the heart of hockey country. One of the early stars up on the Iron Range was former Duluth Eskimos (NFL) and Brooklyn Dodgers (MLB) star, Wally Gilbert, who played for a semi-pro traveling all-star team out of Two Harbors as well as for the Duluth Tank Corps.

By the mid-1930s one of the area's better teams was the Galloping Gophers, an all-star team led by Gopher Football All-American and Faribault native Bud Wilkinson, that traveled around the Midwest playing mostly independent semi-pro teams. Once, in the late 1930s, they even beat the famed Harlem Globetrotters.

One of our first pro teams was the Minneapolis Sparklers. The Sparklers, also known as the Rock Spring Sparklers of Shakopee, were a local semi-pro team which played briefly in the post WWII era. They had several local stars who played on the squad including, former Gophers Johnny Kundla, Tony Jaros, Warren Ajax, Clarence Hermsen, Ken Exel, Don Smith and Willie Warhol. In 1943 the Sparklers landed a berth in the World Pro Tournament in Chicago, an invitational tournament staged by the Chicago Herald American, which, from 1939 to 1948, crowned the World Champions of Basketball. There, the Sparklers wound up finishing fourth, just behind the Harlem Globetrotters. They managed to win their first game over the Chicago Ramblers, 45-41, before getting crushed in the quarterfinals by an all-black team, the Washington (D.C.) Bears, 48-21, who went on to claim the world title.

Our next team was the St. Paul Saints, and here is their story. Professional basketball was going through its share growing pains in the late 1940s and Minnesota was right smack dab in the middle of it all. In 1946 the Basketball Association of America (BAA) was organized as a rival league to the existing National Basketball League (NBL). Then, in 1947, the Professional Basketball League of America was established by Maurice White. White, who was then-owner of the NBL's world champion Chicago Gears, got greedy and decided to create a new league. Comprised mainly of cities in the Midwest and South, his new league would feature his Gears as the marquis team. The reason for this was because his Gears were led by a giant six-foot-10 center out of DePaul University by the name of George Mikan, whom White felt could single-handedly carry the entire league on his back and eventually run the NBL out of business. With three pro circuits now competing for talent and dollars in America, it was a truly wild time for pro hoops.

While the PBLA would prove to be a short-lived league, it did make the Twin Cities one the premier basketball out-posts in the country during this era. When the PBLA was created, it wanted to make sure it had a franchise in Minnesota. They knew that the upstart Lakers, which came into existence when a group headed by Sid Hartman purchased the NBL's Detroit Gems, had just announced that they would be renaming the club and playing in Minneapolis that year as members of the NBL. The PBLA wanted to make sure that they had a team of their own to compete with the Lakers, and so were born the St. Paul Saints.

Managed by Phil Gallivan and led by player-coach Bruce Hale, the St. Paul Saints were one of 16 teams in the PBLA. Other teams included the: Atlanta Crackers, Birmingham Skyhawks, Chattanooga Majors, Chicago American Gears, Grand Rapids Rangers, Houston Mavericks, Kansas City Blues, Louisville Colonels, New Orleans Hurricanes, Oklahoma City Drillers, Omaha Tomahawks, St. Joseph Outlaws, Springfield Squires, Tulsa Rangers and Waterloo Pro-Hawks.

The Saints' first home game late that October ended in a 59-49 loss to the Chicago Gears, before 3,100 St. Paul Auditorium fans. The star of the Gears was, of course, the best player in all of basketball — Center George Mikan, who scored 17 points in the win. It would be big George's first-ever game in Minnesota, but certainly not his last.

The season was plugging along without a hitch early-on, until financial problems hit like a ton of bricks. The reason was due to the fact that White was insisting on running the circuit out of his Chicago offices. White, who owned all the teams in the new league, was single-handedly managing all the salaries, transportation logistics and scheduling for every team, and simply couldn't keep up. With that,

The Old Minneapolis Auditorium

The Lakers enjoyed a home-court advantage in that their playing floor at the Minneapolis Auditorium was actually several feet narrower than the standard 50-foot court width.

"When Mikan, Mikkelsen and Pollard stretched their arms across that narrow court, nobody could get through," joked Syracuse National's player-coach Al Cervi. "Those three made every court look narrow," added Nat's guard Paul Seymour.

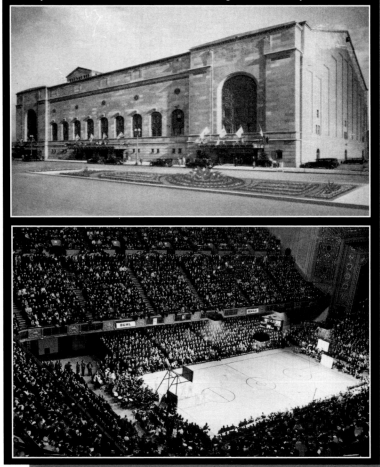

on November 13, 1947, and after just two and a half weeks of play, the PBLA was disbanded. (Ironically, White then immediately applied for his Chicago Gears to be readmitted back into the National Basketball League. One could only assume that the NBL's league owners were smiling when they unanimously rejected his application.)

The Saints, which were led by Guard Bruce Hale and Forward Jack Dwan, both of whom were averaging 16 and 14 points per game, respectively, posted a respectable 6-3 record during that short-lived campaign — good for second place in the Northern Division behind the Gears, before closing up shop forever.

With that, the players from the disbanded league became subject to an NBL dispersal draft. The Minneapolis Lakers, by virtue of having the worst record in the league the previous year as the Detroit Gems, were then given the first choice. There was little suspense over whom they would select... Welcome to Minnesota Mr. Mikan!

The Early "Cagers" and Their Sometimes Unsavory Venues...

Pro basketball's early venues and arenas were anything but glamorous. Back in the day, teams had to make do with facilities, which, by today's standards, would be unthinkable. Because the early game had developed a rather unsavory reputation for its overly aggressive nature (not to mention the rowdy and unruly fans who came to watch the contests), many teams had to barnstorm from place to place just to find a home. As a result, many of the early clubs were forced to rent high school or college gymnasiums, convention halls, armories, renovated auditoriums, ballroom dance floors or even a trolley car barn — which was where the Baltimore Bullets played, in order to stage a game. (In some instances, the basketball game was just a warm-up for a concert, circus or dance, which might be held afterwards.) Folding chairs were brought in and the players oftentimes helped to set them up while the coaches sold tickets and tied up loose ends. Many of the venues even had netting or wire caging (hence the nickname "cagers") surrounding the playing court, which kept the balls inbounds while also preventing drunk fans from either tossing chairs or simply joining in on the action at center court.

What gave the early game such character though, was its fabulous playing venues. From big cities to small towns, each locale had its own signature characteristics which made it unique. Let's see, there was Syracuse's State Fair Coliseum, a musty, dimly-lit arena which was famous for its guide-wires that supported the basket. Those wires then extended into the crowd, where the fans would shake them, causing the basket to shimmy, just as an opposing player was about to shoot a free-throw. Or how about Fort Wayne's "Snake Pit," which was an old high school gymnasium with a sunken floor surrounded by six-foot high concrete walls. With almost no area between the wall and the floor, the fans, who sat on the bleachers directly above that wall, were right on top of the players during the game! The Pittsburgh Ironmen played on a hardwood floor that had huge gaps between the floor boards; while at Waterloo's arena, there was a giant heating unit at the end of the court which mysteriously kicked on to blow hot air all over the visiting team as they were running up court.

In Rochester's Edgerton Park Sports Arena, there was a big set of double doors directly behind the basket — which occasionally saw a driving player charge through and into an awaiting snowbank. And in Midland, Flint's Dow Chemical team had a set of swinging "in and out" doors behind the basket which oftentimes saw players get pushed through, only to return to the action via the other side. The grand-daddy of them all though was St. Louis's Kiel Auditorium, which served as both a basketball arena and a theatre. There, the two stages backed up against each another and were separated by just a partition. If a player made a wrong turn coming out of the locker room, he might end up stage-left.

"They'd sometimes have the ballet going on at the same time as a basketball game," recalled Vern Mikkelsen in Stew Thornley's 1989 book: "Basketball's Original Dynasty." "We always had to make sure we went the right direction or we could have ended up right in the middle of Swan Lake!"

Another short-lived professional basketball team which played in Minnesota was the St. Paul Lights, which played just 20 games during the 1950-51 season as members of the National Professional Basketball League. The NPBL came into existence as a result of the NBA's growth. (The NBA came into existence when the NBL and BAA merged in 1948.) During this era of pro hoops, the pro teams were starting to gain in popularity and thus began playing in larger venues. Soon the smaller cities, which didn't have the financial resources or arenas, began dropping out. So, several of them, including the Sheboygan Redskins, Anderson Packers and Waterloo Hawks, got together under the leadership of former NBL commissioner, Doxie Moore, and revived the old National Basketball League for the 1950-51 season. They renamed the new Midwestern circuit as the National Professional Basketball League, and tried to give the NBA a run for its money. Needless to say, it would be a short run.

The NPBL, which, in addition to its three ex-NBA entries, then also added the Lights, Louisville Alumnites, Grand Rapids Hornets, Evansville Agogans, Denver Refiners and Kansas City Hi-Spots. The league was looking good, but never really made it off the ground. Shortly into their inaugural season a whole host of logistical and financial problems came to the forefront, and before long teams were folding. Among them were the local Lights, who had appealed in vain for an NBA franchise — but were repeatedly denied. The Lakers were the big show in town at that time, and they weren't about to welcome any direct competition from just across the river.

The Lights, which were owned by Dick Headley and coached by former Hamline star, Howie Schultz, played their home games at the local St. Paul Auditorium. There, the Blue & White Lights played to decent sized crowds and made believers out of scores of St. Paulites who came out to root them on. The team was led by a couple of NBPL All-Stars in Guard Stan Miasek and Forward Wally Osterkorn, who both averaged 13 points per game that season. In addition, there were several local stars, including: Hamline's Howie Schultz, Rollie Seltz and Hal Haskins, as well as Kenny Mauer from St. Thomas. The Lights, however, after posting a very respectable 12-8 record, folded after just two months of play — disbanding midway through the season. Incidentally, the Sheboygan Redskins, who finished with a league-best 29-16 record, were crowned as league champs.

The NPBL was going through its share of problems, but, ironically, what was keeping it afloat was the NBA. You see, because the NBA was continuing its shake-out of franchises, dropping from 11 teams in 1950 to just eight in 1954, scores of good young players were welcomed into the league — giving it much-needed credibility and an infusion of talent.

The next big-time professional team Minnesota would get would go down as one of the greatest sports franchises in the history of modern sports — and they're still going strong. I am speaking, of course, of our very own Minneapolis Lakers.

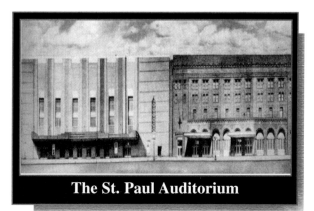

The St. Paul Auditorium

Shaquille O'Neal, Kobe Bryant, Magic Johnson, Wilt Chamberlain and Jerry West — all household names for a legendary California sports institution better known as the Los Angeles Lakers. But for those of us in the Land of nearly 20,000 watering holes, we know better. There are about as many lakes in Southern California as there are Hollywood stars in Minnesota. That's right, basketball's original dynasty started out as our very own Minneapolis Lakers, and before they were shipped off to Tinseltown, in 1960, they were the hoop game's first really big deal.

This is a story about a franchise that literally rescued pro basketball from a dull, boring existence, and turned it into pure magic. Our Minneapolis Lakers, with the game's first giant — George Mikan, first jumping jack — Jim Pollard, and first power forward — Vern Mikkelsen, brought six world championships to the Gopher State — in a style all their own. They were, in a word, simply awesome.

The Lakers journey is a long and fascinating one that actually takes us first to the Motor City in the post-war mid-1940s, where the lowly Detroit Gems had earned the distinction of becoming the worst team in a fledgling league called the National Basketball League, or NBL. The NBL, which had been around since the late 1930s, was comprised of both big city as well as small towns teams scattered throughout the Midwest and East Coast, and was in a constant struggle to keep its head above water financially. Interest in the game was growing however, and many of the team's owners were trying to figure out how to make more money. Many of them owned hockey franchises and liked the thought of having basketball teams to fill up their venues when their skaters were on the road.

Now, it was an interesting time for pro sports in Minnesota during this era. While the great outdoors still reigned supreme, and the Gopher Football team ruled the covers of the local sports pages, fans were steadily becoming more and more interested in following the pro game. They already had a pair of Class AAA baseball teams in the Minneapolis Millers and St. Paul Saints, both farm clubs of the major league Brooklyn Dodgers and Boston Red Sox. And there were also a couple of Central Hockey League teams in the Minneapolis Bruins and St. Paul Rangers, both minor league affiliates of the NHL's Boston Bruins and New York Rangers. Sure Gopher Basketball was solid during this era, and so were the Hamline Pipers, but would pro hoops thrive in this winter sports market? Why not? It was the post World War II boom and there was a new sense of optimism and wealth.

Minnesota got its first taste of big-time pro ball in 1946 when a group of local businessmen decided to host an NBL game at the Minneapolis Auditorium between the Oshkosh All-Stars and Sheboygan Redskins. Spearheading the group was a 26-year-old sportswriter named Sid Hartman, who had convinced his friend Ben Berger, a Polish immigrant who owned several local restaurants and movie theaters, to sponsor the contest as a sort of trial-run to see if pro basketball could be a viable business venture in the Twin Cities.

Their plan worked. More than 5,500 hoop fans showed up that December 1st to watch Oshkosh beat Sheboygan, 56-42. Adding to the spectacle were a couple of local boys starring for Oshkosh named Don Smith and Kenny Exel, both of whom had starred at the University of Minnesota as well as at Minneapolis Roosevelt High School. In addition, the contest's referees were a couple of well-known coaches from the area in John Kundla, of St. Thomas College, and Frank Cleve, of Minneapolis Henry High School.

Upon seeing the success of their little experiment, Hartman then convinced Berger and another associate, Morris Chalfen, a fellow restauranteur (he owned the Nankin) and ice-show promoter, to acquire a franchise. In July of 1947 the trio made it official when they plunked down $15,000 to buy the Detroit Gems — the bottom feeders of the NBL that season. Perhaps you're wondering why they would want the league's worst team? You see, Hartman had done his homework, and knew that because they had finished with the worst record, they would be entitled to the number one overall dispersal draft pick that next season. And that could only mean one thing, Hartman had his eyes set on Depaul University's All-American Center George Mikan, who had been playing for the soon-to-be defunct Chicago Gears of the NBL.

The Gems had been started on a whim by a local Detroit jewelry store owner named Maury Winston, an avid fan who figured that buying a basketball franchise would help to promote his business. Poor Maury couldn't have been more wrong! You see, at the time pro basketball had few fans and the press treated it like it was the plague. College hoops were all the rage back in the day, while the pro game was just trying to stay afloat.

It was a unique era in pro basketball at this time, as teams were seemingly popping up everywhere. While the NBL had expanded to 11 clubs by 1946, another rival pro circuit, the Basketball Association of America (BAA), which featured 12 teams of its own, was also formed that same year. It was a very competitive environment for pro sports in general, and making money was not the easiest thing to do.

Ben Berger

Born in Ostrowiec, Poland in 1897, Ben Berger came to America at the age of 16 in search of a better life. His family, who stayed behind, was later killed during the Holocaust. Determined to make it, Berger worked hard and built a local movie theatre empire which numbered nearly two dozen at its peak. He also operated the popular Schiek's Cafe in downtown Minneapolis, among other restaurant interests.

Berger, who was the initial owner of the Lakers, sold the team in 1957 to a group led by local trucking magnate, Bob Short. After selling the team, Berger bought the minor-league Minneapolis Millers of the International Hockey League. He was also very involved in civic and philanthropic endeavors. In addition to serving as a commissioner on the Minneapolis Park Board, he also founded Amicus, an organization that helped ex-convicts to adjust to life after incarceration. Sadly, Berger died in 1988 at the age of 90. He was one of Minnesota's first sports pioneers.

Pro hoops were played mostly in blue-collar factory towns, primarily sponsored by local companies anxious to promote their goods and services. Many of the players had to work regular nine-to-five jobs (average salaries at this time were usually around a couple thousand bucks per season), and simply played the game for the fun of it. It was a bygone era for the game though. Colorful teams such as the: Fort Wayne Zollner Pistons, Akron Goodyear Wingfoots, Firestone Non-Skids, Toledo Jim White Chevrolets, Anderson Duffy Packers, Toledo Jeeps, Cleveland Chase Brass, St. Louis Bombers, Chicago Stags, Indianapolis Olympians and Youngstown Bears came and went through the years, paving the way for what we know today as the NBA.

Meanwhile, Winston's Gems went on to amass an unbelievably horrible 4-40 record that season (the worst in modern pro basketball), which by all standards was a huge flop. So bad was the team that one night just six paying customers showed up to see the team play at a local high school gymnasium. Winston, who knew he was in way over his head, even gave the half-dozen die-hards a refund because he was so embarrassed. He lost tens of thousands of dollars in the disaster, and was eager to cut his losses by selling the franchise to anyone who was interested.

Don "Swede" Carlson

Enter Sid and the boys. Hartman called Winston after the season and arranged to meet him in the Detroit Airport to purchase the team for the whopping sum of $15,000. Sid flew in, handed him a check and signed the papers. The entire deal took all of 15 minutes. All he got was a piece of paper and a bunch of old, smelly, red, white and blue uniforms — not even a basketball was included in the deal.

The NBL even went ahead and assigned all of the Gems' players to other teams in the league. Winston was thrilled to cut his losses, while Hartman knew he had gotten a bargain. There were several franchises for sale at the time, but Sid knew that with the worst record, his new franchise would get the first crack at signing Mikan that upcoming season. Hartman knew that the Chicago American Gears were in serious financial trouble. Their owner, Maurice White, had plans to break away from the NBL and form his own rival league to showcase his budding young star, George Mikan. His new league took a nose-dive that next season though, and with it the Gears went broke.

Max Winter

So, the group went ahead and assembled a team for the 1947-48 season. Their first step was to hire both a general manager and coach. At first Chalfen and Berger wanted Hartman to serve as the GM, but Sid wanted to keep more of a behind-the-scenes low profile to be able to wheel-and-deal. He had a great gig going at the newspaper and didn't want give that up. In addition, Sid had a million contacts in the world of sports and knew almost every coach personally. This would afford him a huge advantage when it came to recruiting, scouting and drafting players for the upstart team. (Sid's early confidantes were a literal who's-who of college basketball, including: DePaul Coach Ray Meyer, Kentucky Coach Adolph Rupp, Oklahoma State Coach Hank Iba, Cal Coach Pete Newell and Michigan State Coach Fordy Anderson.)

"When I broke into the newspaper business many years ago, conditions were a lot different than today," Hartman would later recall. "Everybody in the sports department worked on the side as a publicity man for one of the local teams or promoters. How things have changed! Nothing like that happens today, because of conflict-of-interest concerns, but that was a different era. Back then, I watched members of the sports department make a few bucks on the side, so I got the idea of starting a pro basketball team. Minnesota didn't have any major league sports at the time, so Charlie Johnson, the executive sports editor, encouraged me to pursue pro basketball. There was an understanding, however, that I wouldn't write anything about the Lakers."

With that, the group hired former boxing promoter and local tavern owner, Max Winter, to serve as the GM. (Winter would later form the group that founded the Minnesota Vikings in 1960, and he served as that team's president for nearly 30 years.) So, Winter would focus on the business and operations side of the team, while Hartman focused on player personnel. Then, they went ahead and asked legendary Hamline University Coach Joe Hutton Sr., who had built the Pipers into a small-college power nationally, to be their head coach. But Hutton was leery of pro ball and respectfully declined. So they turned to St. Thomas College's first-year Head Coach, Johnny Kundla, a 31-year-old kid, who, after starring at Minneapolis Central High School, went on to guide the Gophers to a Big-l0 title in 1937. Kundla, whose prior coaching experience consisted of a brief stint as a Gopher assistant, as well as leading De LaSalle High School to a State Catholic League title, at first said no to the offer. But Hartman kept hounding him and when he offered him a three-year $9,000 contract — twice what he was making at St. Thomas, he said yes, instantly making him the youngest coach in the league.

Jim Pollard and George Mikan emerged as Minnesota's first two big professional stars

Winter's first task was to promote a newspaper contest to name the team. After hundreds of submissions, the Lakers were chosen in honor of Minneapolis being nicknamed as the "City of Lakes." It was also decided that the colors of the Swedish Flag, light blue and golden yellow, would best represent Minnesota's ethnic Scandinavian heritage. Winter, ever the promoter, then went out and made his new team the first in pro hoops to sport its very own cheerleaders, the Lakerettes, a bunch of modestly dressed high school gals from the suburbs. He even hired an orchestra to play the team's new fight-song and entertain the fans before the games. (Later, Winter would even have crews available after games on cold nights to jump-start fans' cars out in the parking lot.)

By now it was mid-August and Hartman was focused on filling his roster. He started by purchasing the contracts of a couple of local boys from the rival BAA's Chicago Stags for the sum of $15,000. The two veterans, Tony Jaros and Don "Swede" Carlson, both of whom had previously starred at the U of M as well as at Minneapolis Edison High School, gave the club instant credibility. Jaros, who

Johnny Kundla

The Original "Coach K"

John Kundla was born on July 3, 1916, in Star Junction, Pa., and grew up in Minneapolis, where he attended Central High School. After a great prep career, he went on to play basketball under coach Dave MacMillan at the University of Minnesota. John also played baseball at Minnesota, but his main sport was hoops. In basketball, he earned three varsity letters and led the Gophers to the Big Ten co-championship in 1937. He captained the Gophers in 1939, and in addition to earning All-Big Ten Conference honors, was even selected as the winner of the prestigous Conference Medal of Honor for scholastic and athletic proficiency.

Following graduation, he played one season of professional baseball with Paducah in the Class C Kitty League. Kundla also stayed active as a player as well during this time, even leading his Rock Spring Sparklers, of Shakopee, to the 1943 World Pro Tournament in Chicago.

Kundla then returned to Minnesota and served as a basketball assistant to MacMillan before accepting the head coaching job at De LaSalle High School in downtown Minneapolis, where he coached the Islanders to a Minnesota State Catholic League Championship in 1944. Following a two-year stint in the Navy during World War II, Johnny decided to get back into coaching, this time at St. Thomas, where he coached the Tommies to a modest 11-11 record in 1947.

By this time, the Minneapolis Lakers had come to town. Originally, they had offered the head coaching position to coaching legend, Joe Hutton, who had been Hamline's coach since 1931 and had built the Pipers into a national small-college power. But, when Hutton politely declined, the Lakers decided to hire the 31-year-old Kundla as their first coach. He thus left the security of St. Thomas and signed a three-year deal with Minnesota's fledgling professional basketball franchise for a whopping $3,000 per year.

In 11-plus years as the Laker head coach, Kundla compiled an impressive record of 466-319 for Minneapolis. At the time of his retirement, only the legendary Red Auerbach of the Celtics had more pro coaching wins. Johnny also won 70 playoff games while losing just 35, a record that translated into an amazing six world championships for the state of Minnesota. In addition to coaching four NBA All-Star Games (1951-54), he also became one of only three coaches in NBA history to have guided teams to three consecutive world titles.

"I've seen a lot of great teams, at least on paper, that won nothing," said Boston's legendary Coach, Red Auerbach. "Sure Kundla had a great team, but he did great things with them."

In 1958-59, tired of the stress and travel demands, Kundla stepped down as coach of the "New Lakers," as they were now called, and became the teams' general manager. In his first move as G.M., he hired George Mikan to be his coaching predecessor. It was a short-lived move though, as Kundla found himself back on the bench just a short while later.

In 1959, the day after the Lakers lost to the Celtics in the NBA Finals, Kundla announced his resignation, in order to return to his alma matter as head basketball coach. After 11 seasons of coaching the Gophers, Ozzie Cowles decided to step down, and Kundla jumped in to take over. Johnny coached the Gophers from 1959 to 1968, earning 110 career wins against 105 losses in nine seasons with the maroon and gold. He also guided the U.S Nationals into international competition in 1964-65, and served on the NCAA Rules Committee. In 1968, University of North Dakota head coach Bill Fitch took over for the Gophers, and Kundla went over to the U's St. Paul campus, where he served as the University's Physical Education Director. He was later inducted into the Pro Basketball Hall of Fame in 1995, alongside his star pupil, Vern Mikkelsen, making it the first time a coach and player were enshrined with one another.

"I can still remember Ray Meyer walking me down the aisle in Springfield, at the Hall of Fame, it was such a thrill," Kundla recalled. "My family was all there, and I don't think I will ever experience anything any better than that."

Kundla, a humble and quiet man, always kept an even demeanor on the court. Even as a young coach, he displayed sound judgement and always stuck to his beliefs that defense and discipline were the keys to success. A tremendous tactician, his greatest asset as a coach might have been in recognizing the strengths of his players, and then utilizing them. He somehow managed to keep three superstars: Mikan, Mikkelsen and Pollard, all happy and content — a feat nearly impossible by today's standards. He was a "players coach" and for that his men loved him. He will forever be remembered as one of the game's greatest.

"I was very lucky to be a Laker, and there is no greater thrill than winning a world championship," said Kundla. "The national recognition we got for the state of Minnesota was such a thrill for me to see. I was very proud of our Laker teams and I owe it all to my players. I'm grateful to Mikan, Mikkelsen, Martin, Pollard, Skoog, Grant, and all the others. We had players with such character, team spirit, and a will to win. I was just very lucky to be their head coach."

A Quartet of Hall of Famers

Johnny and his wife Marie later settled down in Minneapolis where they had six wonderful children and many grandchildren.

"John Kundla is one of the greatest coaches of all time," said Vern Mikkelsen. "He's never been given the proper credit simply because everyone said that anyone could've coached our championship teams. I sort of look at John similarly today as I did with the Chicago Bulls head coach, Phil Jackson. Like Jackson, John was wonderful at coaching each of us at our own individual levels, and that really motivated us to play for him and win. I am just very grateful for the fact that he gave me the opportunity to play with the Lakers."

"John is just an excellent guy," added George Mikan. "He had a great way about him, and he could keep the players focused on the game. He also had the ability to help you when things weren't going your way. He could critique your game and correct any problems that you had to get you back out there. He was great at analyzing team defenses and he was a master at setting up plays to would help us excel. He is a wonderful person and a great coach."

had also starred for the Minneapolis Millers baseball club, was a six-foot-three forward, while Carlson was a smaller playmaker and defensive specialist.

Herm Schaeffer

Hartman's ultimate goal though was to somehow sign former Stanford Forward Jim Pollard, who, after playing for the Coast Guard squad, had gone on to become a star in the Amateur Athletic Union (AAU) with the Oakland Bittners. (On the East Coast, pro basketball was the big deal, but on the West Coast, there were only AAU leagues — which, although sponsored by industrial companies, were every bit as good as their eastern counterparts.) Nearly every team in both the BAA and NBL had tried to sign the speedy forward, but he was content on staying put, instead keeping his eye on playing for Team USA in the 1948 Olympics. The six-foot-six Pollard had earned the nickname of the "Kangaroo Kid," for his amazing leaping ability — making him one of the first above-the-rim "Michael Jordan-like" players.

Sid kept after him though and eventually won him over with his charm and youthful exuberance. Pollard took a liking to Sid and even turned down more money to eventually sign with Minneapolis for the sum of $12,000 a year, plus a $3,000 signing bonus — big dough in those days. The one catch was that he had a few buddies from the Bittners that he insisted come with him to Minneapolis. Hartman reluctantly agreed, and with that the Kangaroo Kid had become a Laker. The signing was a huge deal. News of it even resulted in a panicked phone call from Oakland Mayor Joe Smith, who pleaded with the local star to stay put. Hartman fondly recalled what happened next in his 1997 book entitled appropriately enough, "Sid!"

"We were at a meeting in Chicago, and commissioner Doxie Moore was lecturing the owners on the big money teams were starting to pay players," recalled Sid. "He said, 'I know everyone wants Pollard, but we shouldn't be getting into bidding wars and driving up salaries.' The same thing — escalating salaries — that commissioners and owners are talking about today is what they were talking about in 1947. I was a 27-year-old kid, representing a new team and attending one of my first league meetings. I raised my hand in the middle of the conversation and said: 'Commissioner, I would like to announce that the Minneapolis Lakers have signed Jim Pollard...' You could have heard a pin drop in that room."

Incredibly, Pollard became the tallest player on the Minneapolis squad. The team did add another player of similar height in Bob Gerber, but was still searching for that elusive big-man. Their roster was then rounded out by a couple more ex-Gophers in Don Smith, Warren Ajax and Ken Exel — a move that was certain to put more of the locals' butts in the Minneapolis Auditorium's nearly 10,000 seats.

The team held its first training camp at a community center in northwest Minneapolis which was affectionately nicknamed the "Nuthouse." Kundla tried to get his new recruits to work together, but it was going to be tough. (Later, Hartman would arrange to have legendary Coach Adolph Rupp conduct preseason workouts for the Lakers at the University of Kentucky. Back then the NCAA didn't have any rules against the pros training with college kids, so Rupp would help Kundla to workout his players and whip them into game-shape.)

Finally, after weeks of training, the team boarded a chartered DC-3 to fly to their first game against the Oshkosh All-Stars on November 1, 1947. Led by their star center, Leroy "Cowboy" Edwards, a veteran who had become famous for his ability to make hook-shots with either hand, the All-Stars came out strong. But the underdog Lakers had history on their side in that first-ever game, with Pollard, who led the Lakers with 10 points, battling Edwards all night long down in the paint. Minneapolis jumped out to a 26-18 half-time lead and then hung on to win, 49-47, thanks to Swede Carlson's thrilling game-winner in the game's final seconds.

The team arrived home to a heroes welcome at the airport as Hartman and Winter, along with the players' wives, celebrated by all going down to the Rainbow Cafe for dinner and cocktails. The Lakers went on to post a 3-1 record over that next week before an event took place which forever changed not only the franchise's history, but pro basketball's in general — the miraculous signing of George Mikan. Here's how the whole saga went down.

The Chicago American Gears, which had dropped out of the NBL after having won the league title the year before, had broken away from the NBL thanks to team owner Maurice White's wild idea to form his own rival league, the Professional Basketball League of America. He figured that with six-foot-ten rookie Center George Mikan as his drawing card, it was going to be a slam-dunk money maker. But, the 24-team league, which franchised teams throughout the South in new areas such as Atlanta, Houston and New Orleans, quickly went broke and the PBLA folded just two weeks into the 1947-48 season. White, who was drinking heavily and insisted on controlling the entire league's payroll, scheduling and transportation logistics out of his Chicago office, lost a cool $600,000 — a decent chunk of change back in the day. White then immediately applied for readmission back into the NBL, but the other owners smugly rejected his application. So, players from the disbanded league then became subject to an NBL dispersal draft.

As a result, Mikan, already considered the best player in the pro ranks at that time, was free to negotiate a new deal with another team. And, while every team wanted him, it was the Lakers, by virtue of having the worst record the year before, who had the first crack at signing him. Winter and Hartman quickly flew the big man into Minneapolis to talk shop. George was familiar with the Twin Cities, having just scored 17 points the week before to lead his Gears to a 59—49 victory over the upstart St. Paul Saints (one of the PBLA franchises that had recently gone belly-up), and liked the area.

After spending the day negotiating a potential contract, Mikan's agent, Stacy Osgood, advised his client to reject their proposal and see what the other clubs had to offer. Osgood was also eager to finish up their meeting due to the fact that they had to catch the last plane out to Chicago. Big George had a lot of options. He could either return to Chicago to sign with the rival Chicago Stags, or he could simply complete his law studies at Depaul University and become a lawyer.

"He wanted $12,000 to sign, which was a ton of money in 1947,"

1948 -- WORLD CHAMPION LAKERS -- 1948
NATIONAL PROFESSIONAL BASKETBALL LEAGUE
Left to Right: Herm Schaefer, Don Carlson, Paul Napolitano, Tony Jaros, Don Smith, John Jorgensen, Jack Dwan, Jim Pollard, George Mikan.

Jim Pollard

The Kangaroo Kid

Jim Pollard will always be remembered for the spring in his legs and his amazing jumping ability, hence the nickname: "The Kangaroo Kid." In fact, he had such leaping ability that he became the first bona fide "dunker" in pro basketball, although his acrobatic dunks were done mostly in practice — because dunking during a game in those days was thought to be ungentlemanly! They didn't measure the players' vertical leaping ability back then, but if they would have, Pollard's would've certainly been astonishing, even by today's standards. He was truly the Michael Jordan of his day.

Born on July 9th, 1922, Jim Pollard's roots were formed in Oakland Calif., where he starred on the Oakland Technical High School basketball team. Full of promise and potential, the young Pollard took his talents to Stanford University, where the All-American led the Indians to the 1942 NCAA championship. From there he joined the U.S. Coast Guard and played on several service teams over the next three years, followed by a couple of semi-pro AAU squads as well.

Pollard's story of how he became a Laker is as interesting as the man himself. Just before the Lakers first season in 1947-48, GM Sid Hartman was assembling the pieces to put together a winning team. Specifically, they were trying hard to land a young six-foot-five jumping jack out of the California Industrial league named Jim Pollard, who was playing for the local AAU Oakland "Bittners." (On the East Coast, pro basketball was all the rage, but on the West Coast, there were only the AAU leagues, and they were every bit as good as the eastern pros.) In fact, a lot of pro teams had previously tried and failed to sign Pollard, who had been training for a spot on the coveted 1948 Olympic team.

But somehow, someway, Sid was able to persuade the young star to forego his Olympic dreams and move to the tundra. The news spread quickly that somebody had finally talked him into signing. Oakland Mayor Joe Smith even called Pollard and pleaded with him not to go. But Jim liked the tenacious Hartman and agreed to sign a Laker contract. There was one catch though. In addition to his $12,000 a year, plus a $3,000 signing bonus, Pollard made Sid agree to bring along three of his Bittner teammates. He reluctantly agreed, and went on to become one of the game's all-time great ones. The rest, they say, is basketball history.

"We used to know when Pollard had been in the building," recalled Washington Capitols star, Horace "Bones" McKinney, in Roland Lazenby's 1993 book, "The Lakers: A Basketball Journey," "because the tops of the backboards would be clean where he raked them. Pollard was fast, too. You couldn't press him either. He was too good moving with the ball. He'd get by you in a cat-lick."

Pollard was the ying to Mikan's yang, and complimented the big-man for several years. He revolutionized the jump-shot and earned a reputation as a rebounding-machine. He was also an upstanding citizen in Minnesota, becoming a big fan-favorite along the way. In addition, because he only completed just one year at Stanford, he also went to night school and in 1953 received his degree from the University of Minnesota as well.

In 1955, Jim Pollard announced his retirement from the Lakers to accept the head coaching position at LaSalle College in Philadelphia, where he posted a modest 48-28 record. Then on January 2, 1960, after a three-year stint in Philly, Pollard rejoined his beloved Lakers, this time as their coach, taking over the reigns in midseason from John Castellani. He would have his work cut out for him though. The Lakers were 11-25 at that point, and things were not looking good. Minneapolis would finish the season at 25-50, and while they did upset Detroit in the first round of the playoffs, they ultimately lost to the St. Louis Hawks in the Division Finals. That season would be Pollard's last, as well as the last for the Lakers in Minneapolis. (He would later go on to coach the Chicago Packers, an NBA expansion team run by Sid Hartman in 1961-62, the ABA's Minnesota Muskies in 1967-68, as well as the Miami Floridians from 1968-70 — when the Muskies franchise was relocated to Miami.)

Pollard, the team's first captain, was the last of the original Lakers. A fabulous rebounder and all-around team player, he would finish his illustrious eight-year career with 6,522 points — good for a 13.1 points per game scoring average. He also grabbed 2,487 (5.0 rpg) rebounds from 1950-55 as well (rebounds were not tracked until the 1950 season).

Along with George Mikan, he was the only Laker to be a member of all six championship teams. And, while Big George had been named the "Best Basketball Player of the First Half Century" by the Associated Press, two years later, all of the players who had been in the league since its inception were given another poll as to who they thought was the greatest player ever. This time they chose Jim Pollard.

The four-time NBA All-Star, who was the high scorer of the 1954 All-Star Game in Madison Square Garden with 23 points, was inducted into the Basketball Hall of Fame in 1977. Sadly, he died in 1993 at the age of 71.

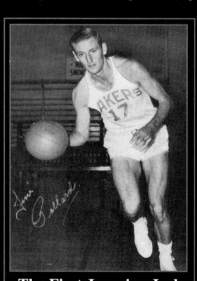

The First Jumping Jack

Here is what a few of his former teammates had to say about him:

"We were very close friends and roommates for several years," said Vern Mikkelsen. "He was probably the best athlete that I have ever played with or against. He was a very moody player, but on the floor, he played way above his head. He was just a marvelous athlete and a great friend. I miss him."

"Jim Pollard was probably the most graceful ball-player that I ever had," said John Kundla. "He could do everything: run, pass, shoot, jump or whatever. He was the creator of the jump-shot. He was so graceful and smooth with everything. He could be playing today. When they put the press on, Jim would bring the ball down the court and nobody could guard him. We didn't keep track of assists back then, but he had a ton of them — most of them going to George! He was an excellent all-around ball-player with and without the ball."

"The Kangaroo Kid, he was one fabulous ballplayer," said George Mikan. "He was just an extraordinarily fine basketball player who could do it all. He could run like a deer, and had a great ability to pass the ball. His pin-point passes were just amazing. What can I say, he was just a tremendous leaper, a great ballplayer and a fine person."

"He was one of those guys that could do everything," said Bud Grant. "Just like Julius Erving, he could take off at the top of the circle and glide into the basket and lay it in. He could hang in the air and shoot with different hands. He was special."

recalled Sid in his book of the same name. "Mikan was scheduled to fly back to Chicago that night on the last flight out. Max and I talked it over and figured that if Mikan got on that flight, he was gone for good. We assumed the BAA was going to give the Chicago Stags the right to sign Mikan, rather than lose him to the Lakers and the NBL. So I drove Mikan to the airport, and I made sure to get lost on the way. I drove north toward Anoka, rather than south toward the airport. After Mikan missed his flight, we put him up in a downtown hotel, then brought him to the Lakers office in the Loeb Arcade the next morning and agreed to give him the $12,000."

The acquisition of Mikan was a huge deal, and immediately made the upstart Lakers one of the league's favorites to win it all. With Big George now taking over at center, this also allowed Pollard to move back to his natural forward position. Hartman then signed Jack Dwan of the disbanded St. Paul Saints, and then added the speedy ball-handler Herm Schaefer, a six-foot-one point guard from the Indianapolis Kautskys. The master of the pick and roll, Schaefer would now be able to run the floor with a couple of future Hall of Famers on his side.

Mikan joined the squad for their fifth game of the season, and needless to say, things didn't go as rosy as one might think. He did manage to score 16 points in his debut, a 56-41 loss to Sheboygan, but his welcome into the new league was anything but hospitable.

Chuck Mencel

"When we got out on the floor, we threw him the ball and said, 'Show us what you can do...,' " said Jim Pollard in Roland Lazenby's 1993 book, "The Lakers: A Basketball Journey." "I played with that big horse for every game for seven years, and that's the only time I ever heard him say, 'Please don't throw me the ball; they're killing me!' The rest of us just threw him the ball and stood there. They ganged up on him and kicked the hell out of George that first night."

The Lakers went on to lose four of their first five games with Mikan as their center. The team soon began to gel though, and came out of the slump in a big way — winning 39 of their last 50 games to take the NBL's Western Division title by 13 games over the second-place Tri-Cities Blackhawks. It wasn't easy though. Pollard and Mikan were each stars and had to learn how to play and co-exist together out on the court. Pollard was a slasher who loved to drive the lane, while Big George clogged up the middle, making it difficult for him to operate. They eventually formed a chemistry together though, and went on to dominate. Coach Kundla even coined a phrase for their new pick-and-roll routine called the "J&G (Jim and George) Play," something that over time would prove to be virtually unstoppable.

"George was great if he stayed on his side of the lane," added Pollard. "But a lot of times, as soon as I got the ball on the wing, he would come over to my side of the lane. I would tell him, 'Stay over there a minute.' But that wasn't his style of play. When we first started playing together, I couldn't very well go to the middle because he was there. When I started to drive, he'd go to the basket. So he'd bring his man, six-eight, six-ten, down to the basket where they'd kick the hell out of me. At that time, George didn't know what I could do. He'd go to the basket, and I'd flip the ball to him and he'd miss it. I kept telling him, 'You better get your hands up because nine out of ten passes are going to hit you right in the face.' After a while, he learned to give me that one count, to give me that step and give me room to drive, and then he could come in. If his man switched off on me, I'd flip him the ball. It made it easier for George, too. But we had to learn that. It took us a while."

The bespectacled giant, Mikan, did have moments of greatness that first year though. One of which came on January 18th, in a 75-73 win over the Rochester Royals. The big guy's bucket with just three seconds left broke a 73-73 tie and also gave him 41 points, breaking the league's single-game scoring record by one point. (Not bad for just 40-minute games!) Later that season Winter arranged a game with Abe Saperstein's world famous Harlem Globetrotters, at the Chicago Stadium. A record 17,823 fans (many of whom slept outside overnight to get tickets) showed up to see the Trotters, who, at the time, played the game pretty seriously with only a few antics — usually when they were way ahead. The Trotters, who were led by legendary players Goose Tatum, Nat "Sweetwater" Clifton and dribbler-extraordinaire Marques Haynes, were riding a 103-game winning streak, but didn't take the Lakers lightly. Minneapolis jumped out to a 32-23 half-time lead, but the Globetrotters came back to win the game, 61-59, on a miraculous last second shot.

By the time the regular season had ended, the Lakers had posted an amazing 43-17 record. They then breezed through the quarterfinals against Oshkosh, three games to one, and then swept Tri-Cities in the semifinals to advance to the NBL Finals against the Eastern Conference champion Rochester Royals. Before the Finals though, the Lakers accepted an invitation to play in the annual World Professional Tournament in Chicago. (Believe it or not, at that time winning the WPT was considered a bigger deal than an NBL or a BAA title.) There the Lakers rolled over the Wilkes-Barre Barons, 98-48, in the opening round, and then knocked off the Anderson Packers by three points in the semifinals. They then took on the defending champion New York Rens, all-black barnstorming team, in the title game, and led by Mikan, who set a tournament record with 40 points, the Lakers beat the Rens, 75-71, to win the World Pro Crown.

Minneapolis now had just one day of rest before taking on Rochester in their best-of-five series at the Minneapolis Armory (Their usual arena, the Minneapolis Auditorium, was full of campers and fishing boats for the annual Sportsman's Show, so they incredibly had to find another locale!). The Royals, led by a pair of guards from Seton Hall, Bob Davies and Bobby Wanzer, were a finesse squad, while the Lakers had garnered a reputation as a bunch of bruisers. The big news for Rochester though, was the fact that their six-foot-nine All-Star Center, Arnie Risen, had suffered a broken jaw and would miss the entire

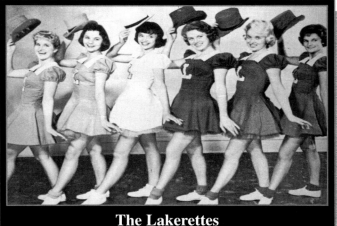

The Lakerettes

championship series — a real break for Minneapolis.

The series opened to a jam-packed Armory with the Lakers taking Games One and Two. It then shifted to New York for the remaining games, as the Royals came back to take Game Three, 74-60, despite Mikan's 32-point performance. Then, in Game Four, the Lakers came out and dominated. They led from the opening buzzer and thanks to 27 points from Mikan and another 19 from Pollard, the Lakers cruised to an impressive 75-65 win — taking the NBL Crown in just their first year in the league.

"After we won, we had to hustle to catch a train out of Rochester," Pollard would later recall. "On the way out, we picked up a couple of six-packs and put em in the stainless-steel sink in the men's room on the train. Then we sat there and celebrated our first championship with the train rattling all around and the wheels rolling underneath."

For the season Mikan finished with a record 1,195 points, (nearly doubling the league's old mark), while averaging 21.3 points per game and leading the NBL in virtually every offensive category. For his efforts he was named as the league's MVP. In addition, he and Pollard were both named to the NBL's All-Star team. The worst-to-first Lakers were now kings of the court, and quietly, a new sports dynasty was born.

The Lakers then made a major decision during that off-season when they, along with the Rochester Royals, Fort Wayne Pistons and Indianapolis Jets, opted to jump ship and defect from the NBL to Maurice Podoloff's upstart Basketball Association of America — which had just completed its second year of operation. The BAA was already an eight-team circuit that featured franchises in several major markets including: New York, Philadelphia, Boston, Baltimore, St. Louis and Chicago. Now, the four new NBL teams, which took up residence in the BAA's Western Division along with Chicago and St. Louis, would make up a perfectly balanced 12-team league. The addition of the four clubs really bolstered the BAA's reputation. It already had the marquis arenas in the major markets, but this gave it the big-name players it needed. The biggest of those names, of course, was George Mikan — who was very excited to now get the chance to showcase his talents in big venues such as New York's Madison Square Garden.

Minneapolis opened the 1948-49 season in Baltimore against the defending BAA-champion Bullets as Laker Forward Herm Schaefer's 23 points led the way to a 84-72 victory. There were several new faces on the roster that season, including Johnny Jorgensen, a former teammate of Mikan's at DePaul, Mike Bloom, a former All-American forward at Temple and Guard Earl Gardner from Depaw. (During the season the Lakers would also add University of Utah Forward Arnie Ferrin, as well as NYU's Don Forman and DePaul's Whitey Kachan.)

On November 24, the Lakers set a single-game BAA scoring record when they dumped the Providence Steamrollers, 117-89. Mikan then made history a few weeks later when he unloaded for 48 points to set another new BAA mark. Mikan topped the 40-point plateau on seven different occasions that season while twice surpassing 50, ultimately fending off Philadelphia's Joe Fulks to win the league scoring crown with 28.3 points per game.

By now George had become almost "Paul Bunyan-like" in his infamy. One night, at the "Basketball Mecca," Madison Square Garden, the marquee out front advertised his appearance as "Geo. Mikan vs. Knicks." And he lived up to the billing, scoring 48 points en route to leading the Lakers past New York, 101-74. (At that time, the 101 points were the most ever accumulated by one club on the Garden floor!)

Minneapolis also continued its series against the Harlem Globetrotters, this time splitting the home-and-home battle. Both Jim Pollard and Swede Carlson sat out the away game in Chicago, but returned to lead the Lakers past the Trotters, 68-53, in front of a record 10,122 fans at the Auditorium. In the game, Laker Guard Don Forman decided to perform some crowd-pleasing antics of his own, including a dazzling dribbling exhibition that brought the crowd to its feet.

The team wound up finishing the regular season with a 44-16 record, good for runner-up in the Western Division, one game behind their old nemesis, the Rochester Royals. The playoffs opened that March with the Lakers sweeping the Chicago Stags on Big George's two-game, 75-point effort.

From there Minnie took on Rochester in another best-of-three series in the Western Division Finals. And, while Royals Center Arnie Risen had been absent in the '48 Finals, he was rarin' to go this time around. The series opened in New York with the Lakers watching their 17-point lead wither away behind an amazing rally which gave the Royals a two-point advantage with just under a minute to go in the game.

Tony Jaros

That's when Tony Jaros nailed what proved to be the game-winning basket with just 18 ticks on the clock as the Lakers hung on for a dramatic 80-79 win. Back at the St. Paul Auditorium for Game Two, the Lakers went on to outscore the Royals 18-3 in the fourth quarter as they cruised to a 67-55 victory and a berth in the BAA Finals.

Next up for Minneapolis were the Eastern Division champs from Washington. The Capitols, who were guided by legendary Coach Red Auerbach, were led by six-foot-nine Center Bones McKinney, Forwards Bob Feerick and Kleggie Hermsen, and Guards Freddie Scolari and Sonny Hertzburg. The best-of-seven series opened at the Minneapolis Auditorium, and behind Mikan's 42-point performance, the Lakers hung on to take Game One, 88-84 — thanks to a pair of last-second free-throws by Carlson. They remained hot in Game Two as well. Auerbach's strategy of isolating his defense to blanket Mikan worked, holding the big-man to just 10 points. But the rest of the Lakers lit it up with Carlson and Schaeffer each tallying 16 and 13 points, respectively — as Minneapolis took a 2-0 lead with a 76-62 win. The series then shifted to Washington's tiny Uline Arena (with a seating capacity of about 4,000) for Game Three, where Mikan poured in 35 points to lead the Lakers to a 94-74 win and a commanding 3-0 lead.

The Caps came out strong in Game Four though, beating Minneapolis by the final of 83-71. Bones McKinney played Mikan tough throughout the game, but George hung in there to score 27 points — despite chipping a bone in his wrist early in the game on a flagrant foul by Kleggie Hermsen that knocked him into the first row of seats.

Mikan recalled the play in Roland Lazenby's 1996 book, "The NBA Finals: A 50 Year Celebration:" "Red told them to drag me off the court and get the game going," he said. "Hermsen made sure he fouled out quick after that. There's such a thing as retribution in sport. You didn't necessarily have to get back at someone because your teammates would." (Hermsen, a former Gopher from Minnesota, feared that if the series shifted back to Minneapolis, the hometown crowd might want to lynch him for his tackle of Big George!)

So tough was Mikan that he scored 22 points in Game Five with a huge cast on his right wrist. He played on though, despite being hacked at by the Caps throughout the game. "I can remember playing with my broken arm held up in the air during that game," said Mikan, "and on one play in particular, the Washington players were going for my arm and not the ball — which was on my other hand!"

The Caps were too much in the end and won the game, 74-66, to bring the series to three game to two. And, despite the obvious attempts by the Caps to hack at his injured wrist, Big George kind of liked having the cast as part of his artillery. His opponents were already fearful of his powerful drop step and this just added to the fun.

1949 -- WORLD CHAMPION LAKERS -- 1949
PROFESSIONAL BASKETBALL ASSOCIATION OF AMERICA
Left to Right: Don Forman, Herm Schaefer, Don Carlson, Don Smith, Tony Jaros, John Jorgensen, Earl Gardner, Arnie Ferrin, Jack Dwan, Jim Pollard, George Mikan.

"That cast was hard as a brick; it fit right in with his elbows," Bones McKinney would later recall. "It would kill you. And it didn't bother his shooting a bit."

The Lakers got serious in Game Six (now back at the St. Paul Auditorium because of the annual sportsman's show), however, as Mikan scored 29 points to lead the Lakers to a 77-56 victory. The more than 10,000 screaming fans loved every minute of it as the defending NBL champs were now the BAA champs as well.

Mikan, who scored an unthinkable 303 points in 10 playoff games, again led the league in nearly every offensive category, only bolstering his reputation as the game's biggest star. He was a fierce competitor who hated to lose. Teammate Jim Pollard recalled what it was like to play with "Mr. Basketball" that season in Roland Lazenby's 1993 book, "The Lakers: A Basketball Journey."

"Toward the end of a ball game, if we were ahead by 20, George would come over to the bench and say, 'Let's beat 'em good. Let's kick the hell out of 'em so they don't want to play us ever again.' " "George gloried in that 'I am number one' feeling," Pollard added. "That's why he was so successful. He wanted that spot, wanted to be number one, wanted you to be a little bit fearful of him on the court."

And, while Mikan averaged a league-best 28.3 points per game, Pollard, who was often left wide open thanks to George's double and triple-teaming, also averaged 15 points. In addition, Guard Herm Schaefer averaged 10.4 points and Swede Carlson chipped in 9.5 as well. By now the team was selling tickets like crazy, and was operating in the black. A big part of that success came from the team's booster club, the "Laker Clubhouse" (one of the first organized booster organization's in pro sports), which was a group of civic leaders who helped to promote and sell season tickets.

By now the BAA had severely crippled the NBL financially, and a truce of sorts was called in 1949 when the two rival leagues decided to merge. The result was the newly created National Basketball Association, or NBA, and BAA head honcho Maurice Podoloff was then named as the new league's first president. The league's 17 charter members included the BAA's: Minneapolis Lakers, Baltimore Bullets, Boston Celtics, Fort Wayne Pistons, Washington Capitols, Rochester Royals, Philadelphia Warriors, Chicago Stags, New York Knickerbockers and St. Louis Bombers. The NBL then provided the: Anderson Packers, Syracuse Nationals, Indianapolis Olympians, Tri-Cities Blackhawks, Denver Nuggets, Waterloo Hawks and Sheboygan Redskins.

It was a wild time for pro basketball at this juncture with many of the clubs joining the upstart circuit literally teetering on the verge of bankruptcy. Trying to arrange the travel logistics and coordinate the scheduling all of those games was a huge headache as teams were suddenly scrambling just to find local gyms and arenas to play their games in. The Lakers, now playing in their third league in just three seasons, were placed in the Central Division along with Chicago St. Louis, Rochester and Fort Wayne. The others were then divided into both the Eastern and Western Divisions.

The Lakers, who were showing some signs of aging and wanted to get a little bit younger, made a couple of huge roster additions that off-season in picking up Askov (Minn.) native Vern Mikkelsen, a six-foot-seven forward out of Hamline University. They also added University of Texas All-American Guard Slater Martin, along with Gopher great, Bud Grant. (A couple of pretty good pick-ups considering all three would go on to become Hall of Famers — Mikkelsen and Martin in basketball, and Grant in football, as the coach of the Vikings!) University of Michigan Guard Bob "Tiger" Harrison was also picked up and would fit in nicely with Martin in the back court.

Slater Martin, a quick ball handler, would go on to become known as a prototypical "point guard," while the big, strong and agile Mikkelsen would be molded into the original "power forward." Now, with Mikan leading the charge down the middle, the Lakers had really become the model for all the modern teams that came later. Kundla even installed what he termed as a "double pivot" offense with both Mikan and Mikkelsen at the four and five (power forward and center) positions. At first this was quite an adjustment for Mikkelsen, whose new role was primarily to rebound, set screens, and set picks, but he learned quickly and evolved into one of the game's preeminent defenders. In addition, Mik, who

Vern Mikkelsen

Dunkin' Donuts

Back in the day, slam-dunking was almost unheard of. In fact, few players could dunk, and the ones who could, like Jim Pollard, didn't dare do it in a game for fear of retaliation. It was considered "hot-dogging" and very ungentlemanly, so players, who didn't want to embarrass another team or player, simply did lay-up's or tip-in's instead. It wasn't until the 1950s, when Wilt "The Stilt" Chamberlain hit the scene, that dunking became popular.

Bob Harrison

was now learning to play the game while facing the basket, also went on to master a two-handed over-head set-shot, something that helped to keep the defenders honest.

The Lakers kicked off the opening game of the NBA's first season against the Philadelphia Warriors and their star Joe Fulks, who owned pro basketball's all-time single-game scoring record of 63 points. Jim Pollard was the hero in this one though as he scored 30 points in the 81-69 Minneapolis victory. There were many highlights of this season, including two big wins over the Harlem Globetrotters: 76-60 at the Chicago Stadium in February and 69-54 at the St. Paul Auditorium in March. It was yet another terrific season for the Lakers though as they went on to finish the season tied for first place in the Central Division. With that they played a one-game playoff tie-breaker against Rochester, whom they finished tied with at identical 51-17 records, ultimately beating the Royals by the final score of 78-76 to claim the divisional title. Led by Mikan's 35 points, the Lakers, who were down by six points with just three minutes to go, came from behind to win the game on a dramatic last-second jumper by Tony Jaros.

Minneapolis had become the talk of pro hoops. With Mikan (who captured another scoring title, with 27.4 points per game), Pollard and Mikkelsen, the Lakers now had the most formidable front line in the league. The trio could of defenders was even more lethal on their home court at the Minneapolis Auditorium, where the floor was actually some four feet narrower than that of a normal court. The result — just one home loss that entire season.

The Lakers then went on to sweep the Chicago Stags, Fort Wayne Pistons and Anderson Packers in the first three rounds of the playoffs to advance to the NBA Finals. There, they would face the Syracuse Nationals, who were led by player-coach Al Cervi and six-foot-seven Forward Dolph Schayes. The Nats, who also only lost one home game that season, played against a much easier schedule in the East, and as a result, wound up with the home-court advantage in the best-of-seven Finals series.

Game One opened at Syracuse's State Fair Coliseum with the Lakers finding themselves down 66-64 with just a minute to go in the game. That's when a surprised Bud Grant found himself on the receiving end of a Jim Pollard pass that resulted in a dramatic game-tying hook shot. The Nats rolled right back behind Cervi's long jumper, but Mikan swatted it away and Grant scooped up the rebound. He then tossed it to a streaking Harrison, who, in turn drained a thrilling 40-footer at the buzzer to ice the game for Minnie, 68-66.

The Nats put up a smoke screen in Game two, literally. You see, Big George made a mistake in the locker room after Game One when he accidentally told some of the newspaper reporters that he was allergic to all the smoke in the arena. "That next night all the fans came out smoking cigars," Mikan would later jokingly say. "You could hardly see across the floor!"

Despite George's 32 points the Nats rebounded to take Game Two, 91-85. The series then shifted back to the Twin Cities, where the Lakers returned home to find the Minneapolis Auditorium once again filled with campers, RV's and fishing boats for the annual Sportsman's Show. After going to the Armory, which was also occupied, they finally turned to the Gophers' home, Williams Arena. But thanks to a recent ruling that prohibited pro teams from playing in Big Ten facilities, Gopher Athletic Director Frank McCormick, nervous about the competition, now had all the ammo he needed to simply say no thanks. So, the Lakers ultimately ended up playing Games Three and Four in the St. Paul Auditorium.

There, Syracuse tried all kinds of tactics to slow down Mikan, including fouling him before he could even shoot. Now, even though the rules of the day allowed for only one free throw on a non-shooting foul, Mikan, an 80% free-throw shooter, still made them pay dearly. More than 10,000 fans showed up to watch the Lakers dominate the two games, 91-77 and 77-69, as they cruised to take a three games to one lead in the series. Syracuse then won Game Five back in New York, 83-76, to get it back to three games to two.

Now, for Game Six, the Minneapolis Auditorium was available, and the Lakers knew that they would feel right at home to on their old floor. They were right. Minneapolis played tough in this one, literally! Jim Pollard and Paul Seymour got into a brawl in the slug-fest, and the police even had to be called in to break it up. So too did Slater Martin and Swede Carlson, who both mixed it up with Billy Gabor. By the fourth quarter Syracuse's Al Cervi had been ejected from the game and no less than four Lakers had fouled out as well. In between all of that nonsense though, Mikan managed to score 40 points and Pollard, despite being covered like a bad suit by Paul Seymour, added another 16 of his own in a 110-95 Laker blow-out. It was the team's third consecutive championship, and first NBA title. They were officially a dynasty.

"We had won a championship in all three different leagues at that point," said Coach Kundla following that 1950 season. "That was really a wild series. I remember Harrison sinking that 40-footer to win the first game at the fairgrounds. Then, in the final game, I remember Seymour was guarding Mikan, and he was pinching George every time he got the ball. Finally George got so upset that when he went up for a shot, he gave him an elbow right to his forehead, giving Seymour a giant knot right on the noggin. George blew his top and I had to take him out of the game, but he did make the shot and the ref even called a foul on Seymour. Cervi, the player-coach, was really a mean competitor, and his teams would fight anybody. That series was a real brawl because at the time, our teams didn't like each other very much. It was a great series, and it is always special winning a championship, particularly that one, because it was our first NBA title."

Mikan once again led the league in scoring during the regular season with 27.4 points per game (only one other player topped 20.0 ppg), and even stepped it up a notch in the post-season by averaging an amazing 31.3 points per contest as well. In addition, for the first time, African-American players were allowed to compete in the league. One of the first black stars was Nat "Sweetwater" Clifton, who had spent several years as the Harlem Globetrotters star center and leading scorer.

"Playing the Globetrotters was tough because as players we didn't get a nickel," recalled Vern Mikkelsen. "Winter and Saperstein cleaned up on those games and it was in our contracts that we had to play. Playing in Chicago that year against the Trotters was historic because it was the first televised game back in Minnesota. I can also remember during the game when Rollie Johnson came down and whispered into Kundla's ear to take a time-out. Pollard then ripped into Kundla about taking a break at that point because the team was on a real roll. Kundla then explained that he had to, because the television advertisers told him that they needed to take a break for a com-

The Big Three: Pollard, Mikan & Mik

Slater Martin

At just 5-foot-10 and just 165 pounds, Slater "Dugie" Martin, was not the prototypical NBA ball player. And while he might have been diminutive in stature, his status on the basketball court was enormous. Many thought he was simply too small to play in the NBA, but the flashy point guard made a living by proving them all wrong.

Born on October 22, 1925, in Elmira, Texas, Martin went on to lead his Davis High School team to a pair of Texas state titles. Then, after serving a brief stint in the Navy, Martin went on to earn All-American honors at the University of Texas. From there Dugie was drafted by the Lakers in 1949. Considered by many to have been the first true "point guard," Martin went on to lead the Lakers to four world championships from 1950-54, and then earned another when he joined Hall of Famers Bob Pettit, Ed Macauley and Cliff Hagan with the St. Louis Hawks in 1956.

At first Martin was intimidated by the Lakers' big stars. He was used to running an up-tempo offense in college, not the methodical, slow-paced NBA game that the Lakers were famous for. Before long, the veteran Herm Schaeffer had stepped aside and was teaching the young rookie how to run the team. And in no time the lightning quick defender was taking great pride in his unique ability to distribute the ball within the Lakers' lumbering offense. Martin dished out assists and orchestrated plays for Mikan, Mikkelsen and Pollard, ultimately becoming one of the NBA's all-time great ones. Consistently rated as the best "small-man" defender in the league by his peers, Dugie played a huge role in building the NBA's first true dynasty.

Upon his retirement in 1960, Martin ranked sixth all-time in the NBA for games played (745), fifth in minutes (21,889), fourth in assists (3,160) and seventh in fouls (2,238). Incredibly, he missed just four games in seven years with Minneapolis. An excellent play-maker, the scrappy guard played in the NBA for 11 seasons, scoring 7,337 points (9.8 ppg) while dishing out 3,160 assists. A seven-time All-Star, Martin, who also served as the ABA's Houston Mavericks Head Coach & GM from 1967-68, was inducted into the Basketball Hall of Fame in 1982.

mercial. And so was born the first 'TV-Time-Out' ever."

The league was also going through a transformation period of its own, as six of the league's original clubs (Denver, St. Louis, Chicago, Sheboygan, Waterloo and Anderson) folded with the remaining teams scrambling to claim the players who were cut loose. The NBA was now consolidated into 11 teams and realigned into two divisions. The Western Division featured the Lakers, Rochester Royals, Fort Wayne Pistons, Indianapolis Olympians and Tri-Cities Blackhawks, while the Eastern Division consisted of the New York Knicks, Boston Celtics, Philadelphia Warriors, Syracuse Nationals, Washington Capitols (who would fold later in the season) and Baltimore Bullets. (Incidentally, several of the teams which dropped out of the NBA joined the National Professional Basketball League, an upstart circuit that included the St. Paul Lights, which were coached by former Hamline star Howie Schultz. The Lights were "dimmed" however, just two months into their inaugural season.)

The season got underway without a pair of familiar faces in the lineup. Herm Schaefer retired to become a Laker assistant coach and scout, while Don "Swede" Carlson also retired and later went on to become the basketball coach and A.D. at suburban Columbia Heights High School. The Lakers got off to another terrific start, proving to be nearly invincible yet again on their home court. But that all changed on November 22, 1950, when the Auditorium played host to the Fort Wayne Zollner Pistons, a team which came to town with a serious game plan that would forever change the game of basketball.

The game got underway with the Pistons controlling the opening tip, and their game plan becoming blatantly obvious from the onset. By the time the Lakers got set up in their defensive positions, they realized that Fort Wayne was going to be taking their sweet time. In fact, Piston Center Larry Foust simply stood at mid-court with the ball on his hip, and forced the Lakers to come out and play him man-to-man. The Pistons would occasionally make a pass or two, but it was clear that they wanted to control the tempo of the game. By the end of the first quarter Fort Wayne had an ugly 8-7 lead, and their stall tactics kept up through half-time, with the Lakers taking an incredible 13-11 edge. The 7,021 fans booed and stomped their feet in protest, but the Pistons were dead set on beating the bigger Lakers they only way they saw fit. The strategy worked for the most part, and even got the Lakers good and frustrated. They would eventually make stupid lunges to steal the ball and got burned in the process.

Minneapolis had scored only one point in the fourth quarter but still held an 18-17 lead. Fort Wayne's Curly Armstrong then in-bounded the ball with just under 10 seconds to go in the game to a breaking Foust, who laid one in over Mikan and Mikkelsen to give his club a 19-18 lead. The Lakers then ran the ball upcourt only to see Slater Martin's desperation shot clank off the rim as the buzzer sounded. The result: the lowest-scoring game in NBA history. The fans, and players alike, were shocked. Most declared it an outrage and that something had to be done. League President Maurice Podoloff called an emergency meeting to discuss the game, and while rule changes were discussed, none were implemented until a few years later when the 24-second shot-clock was introduced — thus limiting the amount of time a team could take without taking a shot.

The Lakers went on to play well that season, despite Pollard's fractured cheekbone which sidelined him for more than two weeks. Upon his return, the team surpassed Rochester to retake the lead in the Western Division. At mid-season a wonderful new tradition was started: the NBA's first All-Star game, which was played at the Boston Garden. Mikan, Mikkelsen and Pollard were all invited, as was John Kundla, who coached the Western squad to a 111-94 loss to Joe Lapchick's Eastern team.

Later that season Mikkelsen sprained his ankle and was forced to miss four games. (Incredibly, they were the only games he would ever miss in his 10-year career!) He came back strong though, and Minneapolis finished the regular season with the best record in the NBA. Once again Big George won the league's scoring title, but in the second-to-last regular-season game, he broke his ankle. This ultimately spelled doom for the Lakers as they headed into the playoffs. They beat Indianapolis, two games

Bud Grant

George Mikan: "Mr. Basketball"

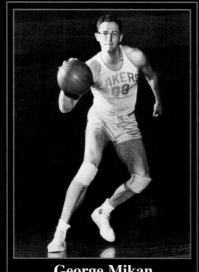

George Mikan

The first dominant big man in pro basketball and the game's first true superstar, George Mikan, was, at times, a man among men out on the hardcourt. Never before in history had someone come along and made such a lasting impact on his or her sport the way Big George did. Mikan was six-foot-ten when few else were and the game had simply not yet evolved to account for a man of his sheer size and stature. He was, in a word, unstoppable.

George Lawrence Mikan Jr. was born in 1924, in Joliet, Illinois. A tall, lanky kid, George grew up loving sports. His boyhood hero was none other than Babe Ruth, who he got to meet when he was 10 years old, after winning the Will County Marble Championship. "The reward for winning was tickets to a White Sox game against the Yankees," George recalled. "After the game I got to meet the Babe and he even gave me an autographed baseball."

George went on to attend Joliet Catholic High School., where, incredibly, he was cut from his freshman basketball team. "You just can't play basketball with glasses on," his coach told him, "you better turn in your uniform." George was determined though, and, after transferring to Quigley Prep School, emerged as a real prep star. Upon graduating in 1941, George decided that he wanted to pursue a life in the priesthood. The war was on by this time but George was too tall and had too poor eyesight for active service, so he opted for college. He desperately wanted to attend the University of Notre Dame, but financially knew it was impossible. Knowing that a schol-arship would pay for his education, he then opted for DePaul. He still managed to sneak down to South Bend during his freshman year though to try-out for Notre Dame's legendary Coach, George Keogan (a native of Detroit Lakes, Minn.). There, after a miserable try-out, Keogan mer-cilessly told the clumsy, uncoordinated kid, that he should "Go back to DePaul, where he'd make a better scholar than a basketball player…"

Now, more determined than ever, George worked hard with DePaul's famed Coach Ray Meyer on acquiring the skills that would eventually make him the most dominant player in basketball. Meyer worked his prized pupil mercilessly, putting him on a regimen which greatly improved his agility, quickness and coordination, with drills that included skipping rope, throwing the medicine ball, shadowbox-ing and even ballet dancing. He would even tell George to try and dance with the shortest and smallest girls he could find at school dances, forcing him to either improve his footwork, or never get a date! Then, at the end of each practice, he would make him take 250 right-hand-ed hooks followed by another 250 with the left — a grueling repetition which would later become known simply as the "Mikan Drill" in basketball "how-to" manuals everywhere.

George worked to develop and refine his soon-to-be famous signature hook shot, which Laker Coach Johnny Kundla later jokingly said looked more like a "shot-put!" It may not have been pretty, but it was good enough to make him a three-time All-American and become the nation's leading scorer in his junior and senior seasons. Mikan, who's brother Eddie later played for the Blue Demons as well, went on to become the nation's biggest college star, leading the Demons to the 1945 NIT title along the way.

Following his playing days at DePaul, George entered the then uncertain world of professional basketball, first with his hometown Chicago American Gears of the National Basketball League, and then with the Minneapolis Lakers, where he would lead his team to six world championships. His journey from the Windy City to the City of Lakes would be a wild one to say the least.

After signing an unprecedented five-year, $62,000 contract in the spring of 1946, Mikan wound up sitting out nearly half of the team's games that season when the cash-strapped club started cutting his paychecks short. They eventually got it worked out though, and George came back to lead his club to the NBL championship. Then, Gears owner, Maurice White, got the crazy idea to start his own 24-team circuit, the League of America, primarily to showcase his new superstar to the entire country. It quickly flopped though, and waiting in the wings were the soon-to-be formed Minneapolis Lakers, who had recently purchased the defunct Detroit Gems earlier that season. And why, might you ask, would the group from Minnesota, led by famed sports writer Sid Hartman, want to buy the league's worst team? Simple. The Gems had the rights to the first pick in the NBL's dispersal draft that next year — which they just so happened to use to select Big George.

Team Owner Max Winter then flew the young center to Minneapolis with the hopes of hammering out a contract with him. George and the Lakers were unable to come to terms though, so he decided to return home to Chicago. But Hartman, who would serve as the team's general manager, saved the day by mysteriously getting lost while driving George to the airport. Mikan, of course, missed his flight and was forced to stay one more night. The next day, George sat down with Winter and Hartman again, this time inking a deal.

With his new contract, George joined the Lakers for their fifth game of the 1947-48 season, at Sheboygan. The rest, they say, is his-tory. Mikan soon began to revolutionize the game. Whereas in the past, guards and occasionally forwards had been the games' stars, Mikan redefined the center position. While most teams used them only to rebound and set picks, because most big men were considered too awk-ward to shoot, George quickly changed the rules. With his wide shoulders and firm elbows, he began to dominate the game like no other before him.

With future Hall of Famer Jim Pollard feeding him the ball, the Lakers went on to win the Western Division title by 13 games that year, and didn't look back until they had beaten the Rochester Royals for the NBL championship.

"We were being judged on whether or not we could make it in the world of professional basketball," said Mikan, who was named as the league's MVP, "and the excitement of winning that first Laker championship was just fantastic. It put us on the map, because at the time, big cities looked at Minneapolis as a tiny hick town. Well, we 'hicked' them all-right, we became league champions!"

In a very "Jordanesque" way, George was the big draw for the new league. Fans came from all over the Upper Midwest to see the gentle giant.

One time, in 1951, the Lakers were playing New York at Madison Square Garden, and the marquee in front of the Garden advertising that night's game read: "GEO. MIKAN vs. KNICKS." As game time neared, Mikan found himself to be the only player dressed for the game in the locker room. So, finally he said, "Come on, gentlemen, we have a ballgame to play." His teammates then jokingly replied back: "No, George. You have a ballgame to play, and we can't wait to see how you do against the Knicks!"

Opposing teams soon found out that the best way to beat the Lakers was to simply try to keep the ball away from Mikan. In 1950, Fort Wayne refused to shoot the ball and dared not give up their possession, ultimately just sitting there and stalling out an unbelievable 19-18 victory. (That was the lowest scoring game in NBA history and ultimately resulted in the creation of the 24-second clock.)

And that wasn't the only rule change in basketball that was a direct result of Mikan. You see, George did most of his damage down in the lane, which, at the time, was only six feet wide. This allowed him to set up right in the low post right next to the basket, making him virtually impossible to stop. So, in 1951, the league doubled the width of the foul lane to 12 feet. This move was aimed at big men in general, but Mikan in particular. (The league, in an attempt to level the playing field, even tried raising the basket to 12 feet. Luckily though, the experiment lasted for just one game before cooler heads prevailed.)

On September 24, 1954, Mikan, who by now had received his law degree from the U of M, announced his plans to open his own law practice and retire as an active NBA player. Financially, he was set, and the game's first bigger-than-life star had a bunch of endorsement deals lined up for everything from sneakers to beer to chewing gum. Regularly featured on magazine covers and on television, George was famous and wanted to settle down to raise his large family. So Winter, wanting to focus his attention on landing an NFL franchise for Minnesota (the Vikings), then sold his stock to Mikan, announcing that he would succeed him as the team's general manager. George attempted a comeback in 1956, but struggled, eventually becoming the Laker's coach in 1957-58. But with a 9-30 record, Coach Mikan once again left the game he loved.

Simply Unstoppable

A Laker from 1948-54, and again in 1955-56, his statistics were incredible. The seven-time world champ became the first player in history to score 10,000 points, ultimately finishing with 11,764. (At the time of his retirement, the next closest player, Joe Fulks, was more than 3,700 points behind him.) A perennial seven-time all-star, four times he led the league in scoring. Amazingly, George missed only two games in his career with Minneapolis. He was the Lakers leading scorer 348 out of the possible 458 regular-season games that he played in, finishing with career averages of 22.9 points and 13.4 rebounds per game.

He did return to basketball again in the next decade. When the American Basketball Association was formed in 1967, George became its first commissioner. With their trademark red, white, and blue ball, the new rebel league distinguished itself from the mighty, but conservative, NBA. Mikan was influential in creating many of the innovations that are commonplace in the game today such as the three-point shot as well as non-basketball halftime and on-court entertainment for the fans. When the ABA moved its headquarters to New York City in 1969, Mikan resigned.

Although Chamberlain, Russell, Abdul-Jabbar and O'Neal would follow, Mikan was the NBA's first truly dominant pivot man and the first big man capable of carrying his entire team. In 1950, Mikan was named the "Greatest Basketball Player for the First Half of the 20th Century" by the Associated Press, and 46 years later, as part of the NBA's 50th Anniversary Celebration, George was named one of the "50 Best Players" in league history. In 1959, he was inducted as a charter member of the Basketball Hall of Fame.

After basketball, Mikan, who ran a very successful law firm in the Twin Cities, also got into real-estate as well as the travel business. He resurfaced onto the hardwood once again in the mid-1980s as the head of a task force which ultimately brought professional basketball back to Minneapolis — in the form of the expansion Minnesota Timberwolves. A tremendous family man, George and his wife Pat raised six children (One of George's sons, Larry, a former Golden Gopher, also played briefly in the NBA in the early 1970s.), and presently reside in Scottsdale, Ariz.

But for George, who recently had his right leg amputated just below the knee due to complications from diabetes, his greatest honor might have come at the Minneapolis Target Center on April 8th, 2001, when he was honored in a "Celebration at Center Court" during halftime of a game between the LA Lakers and Timberwolves. There, in front of dozens of his former teammates, George was presented with a life-size bronze sculpture — which will stand forever in the arena's lobby. Fittingly, it depicted a 6-foot-10 legend with his back-to-the-basket and his arm extended into the pose of a hook shot — George's signature move, as he is about to score the game-winning basket.

It was a larger-than-life tribute to a larger-than-life man who has certainly made us all very proud. A true gentleman, George Mikan's contributions to the sport and his impact on the NBA still loom as large as his six-foot-ten frame. The cornerstone of the league's first dynasty, George was simply the best. Here's what a few of his former teammates had to say about their comrade:

"He was in a class by himself," said Vern Mikkelsen. "He never hazed the rookies, and when he went out for dinner and a movie, he invited everybody along. There was never any sign of him being a superstar around us. He would be on our backs something fierce when he needed to be, and he had an unbelievable faith in his ability to get the job done. He instilled an attitude in all of us that even if we were down, we weren't going to get beat, and that we could always win the game. He was a great player and is a great person. He went from being my idol in high school, to my opponent in college, to my teammate with the Lakers, to my great friend. He is a heck of a guy and I feel very lucky to be his friend."

"He was the greatest competitor that I ever played with, in any sport," said Bud Grant. "And, although he was no gazelle, he could run the floor for a big man. He used to play the whole game, and the tougher the game, the more he wanted the ball."

"You had to be alive during Mikan's day to realize what a phenomenon he was," said Slater Martin. "He was the big man of his era with remarkable tenacity and strength. He had the ability to pursue his own rebounds and no one could keep him off the boards."

"In my lifetime I have only seen two centers who could just take charge of a game, who could put so much fear in other players that they stayed away from him in the middle," said Jim Pollard. "One was Bill Russell, the other, and he was even more dominant, was George Mikan. Once he stationed himself under the basket, he was tough to push out. For rival players it must have been like trying to move the Statue of Liberty."

"He was the greatest competitor and a team player I ever had," said John Kundla. "He made the Minneapolis Lakers, and made this town a major-league city. I remember Wilt Chamberlain and Bill Russell telling George that he was their idol growing up, and the two said that he was partially responsible for much of their success in the NBA. He brought big league basketball to Minneapolis, and did so much for Minnesota. He is Mr. Basketball, and I owe all my success to him. He was the greatest."

George & Vern Just Jammin'...

Arnie Ferrin

to one, in the first round of the post-season, but then lost to Hall of Famer Bob Davies and the Rochester Royals in the Conference Finals, three games to one. Mikan, who played with a cast and used ethyl chloride to numb his pain, insisted on playing. And, despite his bum hoof, he tallied 41 points in Game One against the Olympians, but just couldn't hold up, scoring a career-low two points in Game Two. The Lakers had officially been dethroned.

For the first time in George Mikan's pro career, he was not a champion — and that made him mad. He would retaliate by taking out his frustrations on the rest of the league in 1952, something that scared the hell out of opposing players and coaches from coast to coast.

Something else happened during that era which forever changed the fan's perception of the pro game though. You see, at the time college basketball was still more popular than the NBA was, but in 1951 that all changed when a nationwide point-shaving and game-fixing scandal was uncovered. After a lengthy investigation, it had been revealed that many of the fixed games took place at Madison Square Garden, where several schools, including the City College of New York (which had won the NCAA and NIT tournaments the year prior), Long Island University and New York University played their games.

By the time the smoke had cleared, nearly 40 players from schools coast to coast had been implicated. Even legendary Kentucky Head Coach Adolph Rupp, who had once boasted that "Gamblers couldn't reach my team with a ten-foot pole," found himself victimized by two of his former players, Alex Groza and Ralph Beard, who were later found to have taken part in the rigging of Wildcat games. The fall-out was severe, as both Groza and Beard, who had gone on to become big stars with the NBA's Indianapolis Olympians, were quickly banished for life by the league for their involvement. Other players would also get the boot, including Kentucky's seven-foot big man, Bill Spivey, who had just led the Wildcats to the NCAA Championship over Kansas State at Williams Arena in Minneapolis.

All in all it was a big black eye for basketball as a whole, but the pro game somehow emerged smelling like a rose — something that greatly helped its popularity into the future. Meanwhile, the Lakers returned to action in 1952 with some new rule changes that were clearly meant to slow down Big George and Minneapolis' nearly unstoppable offense. With that, the league's Rules Committee, determined to even the playing field, decided to widen the lane from six feet to 12, thus preventing Mikan from simply setting up shop under the basket and scoring at will. (The three-second rule would now force him to set up outside the lane, opening it up for everyone else.) Max Winter was furious about the rule change and even threatened to take drastic measures. "We shall never widen our lane in Minneapolis, and teams may play games here under protest if they care to," said Winter in Stew Thornley's 1989 book: "Basketball's Original Dynasty." "If lanes are widened in other arenas, I shall advertise in advance of our games in those towns that George Mikan will not appear on the floor."

Winter eventually caved in, but the ruling did cost Mikan his first NBA scoring crown that season — despite a very respectable 24-point average. The fall-out of the rule change also meant that Pollard and Mikkelsen got a few more looks at the hoop, which resulted in both players averaging more than 15 points per game that season.

"Actually, the rule change opened up the lane and made it more difficult for them to defense me," said Mikan in Roland Lazenby's 1993 book: "The Lakers: A Basketball Journey." "Opposing teams couldn't deter our cutters going through the lane. It moved me out and gave me more shot selection instead of just short pivots and hooks. I was able to dribble across the lane and use a lot more freedom setting the shot up."

(Opponents also got upset with Mikan's spectacles, which were a quarter-inch thick and would often fog up, causing stoppages in play while he wiped the lenses dry. For Big George, who once joked that trying to see without them was like "driving a car without wipers during a rainstorm…", these breaks in action gave him a much needed rest. But teams got tired of this, and after he had dominated the league for a couple of years, they complained that if he wanted to wipe off his glasses, then the Lakers should be forced to call a time-out. The league agreed, but Johnny Kundla, who often-times tossed his center a clean pair of spare specs out his coat pocket on the fly, out-smarted them all!)

But the Lakers knew that they were going to need more outside shooting, and Sid Hartman had an idea of just where to find it — on Rochester's bench, where the six-foot-two, two-handed set-shot sniper, Pep Saul, had been sitting. Sid knew that Rochester would never trade him to the Lakers though, so he went to the struggling Baltimore Bullets, where he finagled a deal which had Bullets Coach Clair Bee purchase Saul from Rochester and then promptly sell him to Minneapolis for a few thousand bucks. The Royals were furious and protested, but Sid's deal was legit, and it ultimately proved to be a great move for the team's offense.

Ed Kalafat

In addition, the Lakers also added a couple of local homers in former Gopher star Whitey Skoog, who had perfected the jump-shot, and a pair of Hamline stars in Joe Hutton Jr. and Howie Schultz. While Hutton was the son of Hamline's legendary basketball coach, Joe Hutton Sr., Schultz, a St. Paul Central High School star who had played center for Hamline from 1940-43, also played pro baseball for the Brooklyn Dodgers as well. (Schultz would ultimately lose his starting position to a promising young rookie first baseman named Jackie Robinson!) The three would prove to be great players for Minneapolis in the years to come.

The Lakers got off to a good start that season, eventually finishing in second place in the West with a record of 40-26, one game back from rival Rochester. There were some highlights along the way too, including Mikan's 61-point performance in a double-overtime win over the Royals. He also set an NBA record by hauling in 36 rebounds in one game, beating Syracuse's Dolph Schayes old mark of 35. The Laker's big three of Mikan, Pollard and Mikkelsen each topped the 1,000 point mark that year, giving the team its most balanced scoring attack ever. So dominant were the trio that famed Basketball commentator, John Devaney, noted that "standing shoulder to shoulder, Mikan, Mikkelsen and Pollard looked like a ragged row of alpine mountains…"

By the end of the season Skoog was sidelined with a bum knee, something the team would have to work around. In the playoffs Minneapolis breezed past Indianapolis in the opening round, then headed to Rochester for the start of a best-of-five semi-final series against the defending champion Royals.

There, the Lakers lost Game One by 10, despite Mikan's 47-point effort, but came back to take

Game Two. Minneapolis then took Game Three back home, and thanks to Pollard's last-second game-winning stuff-in, was able to also take the deciding Game Four, 82-80, to win the series. From there the Lakers prepared to do battle with the New York Knicks, who, under Coach Joe Lapchick, were making their second consecutive trip to the NBA Finals. Led by such stars as Max Zaslofsky, Sweetwater Clifton, Al & "Tricky Dick" McGuire, Connie Simmons, Ernie Vandeweghe, Harry Gallatin and Vince Boryla, the Knicks were a formidable opponent.

Dick Garmaker

The Finals opened in St. Paul, at the Auditorium, where Jim Pollard led the way with 34 points in a 83-79 win. The game wasn't without controversy though, as Al McGuire had a basket go in that wasn't counted. Amazingly, the refs, who gave him two foul shots on the play, didn't see the ball go in, and despite protests, refused to count it. The 10,000 fans there that night saw it go in, but didn't complain too hard when the overtime game ended with their Lakers victorious. The Knicks rebounded to take game two, 80-72, only to see Minneapolis steal Game Three, 82-73. The game was played in New York's 69th Regiment Armory because Madison Square Garden was being occupied by the circus. Game Four was another overtime thriller with the Knicks, who held big No. 99 to just 11 points, etching out a 90-89 win. Pollard, who had injured his back in the game, was replaced by Bob Harrison. Game Five, which saw Mikan and Pollard each tally 32, was all Minneapolis, 102-89, while Game Six went to the Knicks, 76-68, setting up a decisive Game Seven back in the Minneapolis Armory — a place the Knicks had never won a game in. There, thanks to Mikan's 22 points and Pollard's 10 down the stretch, the Lakers blew out New York, 82-65, to capture their fourth championship in five years. For their efforts, the team received a whopping $7,500 bonus.

The Lakers were moving to more of a perimeter game that next season, something that was just fine with Mikan. Tired of taking a pounding on nearly every play, Big George, who, because of the NBA's rule changes, lost the scoring crown to Philadelphia Warrior's young jump shot specialist, Paul Arizin, was still the league's best player. He was eager to keep the Laker machine rolling along in 1953 — a team which saw only new face on its roster that year — Jim Holstein, a six-three guard from Cincinnati.

"We had offensive plays for all of the players back then," said Vern Mikkelsen. "There was the 'J&G Play' for Jim and George, the 'California' which was for Pollard, the 'Texas' for Slater Martin and the 'Michigan' for Bobby Harrison. Then one day Kundla came up with the 'Askov,' and Kundla would diagram it like this: 'Vern, you come over to the left side and set a pick, then go over to the right side and set a pick, and then after that you go get the rebound.' After that I knew that I had finally arrived!"

The team cruised to yet another brilliant season, with one of the highlights coming that January, at the All-Star game in Fort Wayne, where Kundla guided the Western squad to its first win, 79-75, thanks to game MVP George Mikan's 22 points and 16 rebounds. Once again, the season came down to a dog-fight against Rochester, with Minneapolis ultimately winning the division crown with an impressive 48-22 record. The team then swept Indianapolis, followed by a five-game series victory over Fort Wayne to breeze through the Western Division play-offs. For their efforts, they would once again face the New York Knicks in the NBA Finals. One bright spot of the playoffs came with the addition of former Ohio State All-American, Dick Schnittker, who, after serving a brief military stint, became the property of Minneapolis when the Washington Capitols folded a few years prior.

The series got underway in Minneapolis with the Knicks surprising the Lakers by taking Game One, 96-88, to jump out to a 1-0 lead. The Lakers then held on to take Game Two, 73-71, and salvage a split before heading out to the Gotham City. Once again, because the circus was in town, the Knickerbockers were kicked out of Madison Square Garden and forced to play the next three games at the 69th Regiment Armory — taking away a serious home court advantage. The Knick players were pumped up heading back to New York, convinced that they would finally win the title back on their home turf. Many of the players boldly predicted that the series would be over in four games, and boy were they right. It was going to be over in four, but not quite the way they were hoping for!

Slater Martin's stifling defense handcuffed Ernie Vandeweghe and held Dick McGuire to just two points, while Pollard and Mikan each hit for 19 and 20 respectively, as the Lakers took Game Three, 90-75. Then, as an insurance policy, Sid Hartman brought in famed DePaul University Head Coach, Ray Meyer, for the playoffs. Meyer, who had a tremendous rapport with Mikan from being his college coach, could tell Big George things that his teammates simply couldn't. So, in Game Four in New York, after Mikan took a jump shot in the first half that missed the mark, Meyer said, "Take that jump shot of yours and stick it in your ear." Mikan, who was upset, opted to dish the ball off to Whitey Skoog instead. Big George wound up fouling out of this one with just a few minutes to go and the score tied at 67-67. Skoog then recaptured the lead on a nice drive into the paint, and then gave the Lakers the lead for good just moments later when he grabbed Jimmy Holstein's missed

Whitey Skoog

Flanked by the "Tall Timbers" front line of Mikan, Pollard and Mikkelsen, was one of the true lunch-pail players of the Laker dynasty, Guard Myer "Whitey" Skoog. And, although he never made an NBA All-Star team and rarely cracked the starting lineup, Whitey, a former Golden Gopher star from Brainerd, was one of the team's all-time fan favorites.

Sure, he averaged less than double figures in scoring throughout his half dozen or so seasons in the pro ranks, and rarely struck fear into the hearts of his opponents, but was a solid player who could be counted on by his teammates whenever they needed him. An oftentimes underappreciated journeymen, Whitey was a role player who will go down as one of the good guys.

After his career with the Lakers in 1957, Whitey went on to become a coaching legend at Gustavus Adolphus College, in St. Peter. Skoog guided the Gusties for 24 seasons and racked up a whopping 292 victories along the way. He also led his boys to a pair of conference titles as well as a NAIA National Tournament appearance in 1976.

free-throw and put it back in to seal a 71-69 victory.

After the game Coach Kundla gave the boys the next day off to relax, so they toured Broadway's clubs after the game. Well rested, the team came back hard and ready to play. Game Five was a thriller as the Lakers opened a 44-35 lead at the intermission, only to see the Knicks go into a full-court press, and eventually cut the Laker lead was down to 84-82 with under a minute to go. Then, up by one, Mikkelsen sank a free throw, and on the ensuing jump, tapped the ball to Mikan who scored on a three point play to seal the deal at 91-84. The series was over and once again, the Lakers were the best team in basketball — a real dynasty.

"After we split Games One and Two in Minneapolis, said Vern Mikkelsen, "Sweetwater Clifton razzed me as we were walking off the court and said 'Hey Mik we're not coming back to Minnie, this series will be all over in New York!.' Then, after we swept them in three straight I grabbed him after the game and said 'Yah, you were right Sweet-Sweet, we're definitely not going back to Minnie!' Afterwards we all went out and had a big victory celebration at the famous Copa Cabanna restaurant in the Big Apple. Those were great times!"

Big Mik

Mikan, now known affectionately as the "Monster of the Midway," was unstoppable. National television exposure had made him even larger than life and seemingly everyone in the country knew who he was. He was the Babe Ruth of basketball, and the league's biggest draw. He was also getting up there in years, and, despite his 21 points and 14 rebounds per game average, the Lakers knew that he needed an understudy. With that, the team went ahead and drafted Kansas All-American Center, Clyde Lovellette, the man set to be groomed as the heir apparent to a legend. Lovellette, who had spent a year playing in AAU competition for the Phillips 66ers, would go on to become a one of the best, eventually being inducted into the Hall of Fame alongside fellow teammates George Mikan, Vern Mikkelsen, Jim Pollard and Slater Martin — not a bad starting lineup, eh?

But Lovellette's arrival in Minneapolis didn't come without its share of controversy. Sid Hartman recalled how it all went down in his 1997 book: "Sid!" "The league draft meeting was held in Milwaukee that year," said Sid. "We had won another title, so we were drafting last. Max Winter kept bugging me, asking who we were going to draft? Max liked to go out in the hall during breaks and talk to his buddies in the league about the choice we were going to make. I kept telling Max, 'Leave me alone. We'll see what happens.' My guess was the other teams would pass on Lovellette because they figured he was locked into the Phillips 66ers. We had our team coming back intact, so I was thinking long-term — post-Mikan. No one took Lovellette. When our turn came, I said, 'The Lakers take Clyde Lovellette.' Ned Irish of the New York Knicks started screaming bloody murder. 'The Lakers have Mikan, they have Mikkelsen, they have Pollard,' Irish said. 'They can't have Lovellette. We won't have a league.' I got up and said: 'This is a free country. I read the NBA constitution. I read the U.S. Constitution. There are no rules against the Lakers drafting Lovellette.' "

One of the highlights, or lowlights as some saw it, of the 1954 season happened on March 7th, in a game against the Milwaukee Hawks at the Minneapolis Auditorium, which was played with a couple of experimental rules. The league, anxious to try out some new playing scenarios, raised the baskets from 10 feet to 12 during the game, to see how the players would react. Many people thought that with players like Mikan dominating the game underneath, the league needed to raise the baskets to even the playing field. The Lakers went on to shoot a miserable 28% that night, but still managed to beat the Hawks, 65-63. By all accounts the players hated it and the fans felt the same way. Said Kundla after the game: "It was a screwy game. Nobody could hit the darn thing. The guys who couldn't shoot hit the most and the big guys still got the rebounds." In addition, to address the problem of free throws taking too long and slowing up the tempo of the game, no foul shots were taken during the regular playing time and instead, were held and shot at the end of the two halves. Needless to say, both rule changes were promptly killed after the game. The players, however, later confessed that it took them a few weeks after the disastrous game to find their shooting touches again.

Ah... the Luxuries of Train Travel Back in the '50s

"Train travel back then was just brutal," recalled Vern Mikkelsen. "It was always a seven hour ride to Chicago before we could then transfer on to places such as New York, Philly, Detroit, Rochester or wherever. Logistically it was awful. One time we were playing a game in Rochester, and we had to take the train back to Minneapolis for a game that next night. Now, the New York Central Railway came through Rochester at precisely 10:22 p.m., but our game that night went into overtime, so we didn't even get a chance to shower. We just threw on our overcoats over our uniforms, and we ran to all catch cabs to the train depot. Now, to make it worse someone screwed up our advance reservations, and we couldn't get our usual "roomettes." Instead, we had to spend the night in old-fashioned Pullman cars, which had the smaller, double bunks. By the time we got on board, all that was left were the coffin-like upper bunks, because the people on board who had already been sleeping for several hours had taken the lower ones. So here we are with our stinky uniforms that we had to air out for our game that next night. We had to hang our uniforms all over the car and in the morning, with that steam heat, the place stunk worse than anything I have ever been around! Those people sleeping below us got a good-morning wake-up call like you wouldn't believe! Our train got in at 6:00 p.m. that next night, and we went straight to the Auditorium to play another game. It was tough. We spent more time on trains than we did at home. We knew every schedule, every porter, every dining car waiter — it was not a very glamorous lifestyle for anyone!"

That season, in an attempt to grow fan interest and generate additional revenue, more and more Laker games were played on neutral courts throughout the Midwest in such locales as: Rochester, Hibbing and Moorhead, as well as Des Moines, Grand Forks and LaCrosse, to name a few. Minneapolis went on to finish the regular season four games ahead of Rochester in the Western Division — good enough for the NBA's best record at 46-26. Mikan, who was slowed by a pair of bad knees, was relied upon less and less as Jim Pollard and Vern Mikkelsen continued to dominate the front line, while Whitey Skoog and Slater Martin ran the Lakers' backcourt.

They entered the playoffs with the league finally mandating that they also remove some tables from around their home Auditorium floor, as well as widen their court from 46 to the regulation 50 feet. Both were seen as moves to give opposing teams at least a fighting chance in one of the league's toughest venues.

The Lakers went on to take care of the Fort Wayne Pistons and Rochester Royals, in a (round robin) best-of-three playoff series, to advance to the NBA Finals against the Syracuse Nationals.

Clyde Lovellette

The first player in history to play on an NCAA, Olympic and NBA championship team, Clyde Lovellette was born on September 7, 1929, in Petersburg, Indiana. After garnering all-state honors at Garfield (IN) High School, six-foot-nine center went on to lead the Kansas Jayhawks to the 1952 NCAA title over St. John's en route to capturing MVP honors. The three-time All-American, who led the Big Seven in scoring in each of his three seasons playing under legendary Coach "Phog" Allen, was also named as the College Player of the Year in 1952.

Lovellette's power down in the paint then landed him a spot on the 1952 Olympic team which brought home the gold in Helsinki. From there the big center was drafted by the Minneapolis Lakers, and after playing a season at the AAU level with the Phillips 66ers, joined the team as an understudy to George Mikan.

At the pro level, Lovellette became one of the first players to be able to move outside and utilize the one-handed set shot — a move that greatly extended his shooting range. As a result, the versatile big man was able to play either the small forward, power forward or center positions, forcing the opposition to stay honest.

After a couple of seasons in Minnesota, Clyde was dealt to the Cincinnati Royals and later played with the St. Louis Hawks and Boston Celtics. In 704 NBA games stretching over 11 seasons, Lovellette scored 11,947 points (17.0 ppg) and grabbed 6,663 rebounds (9.3 rpg). (He also had six seasons of averaging 20 or more points, including 23.4 ppg in 1957-58.) A three-time All-Star, Clyde won championships in both Minneapolis (1954) and Boston (1963, 1964).

One of the first physical and high-scoring centers, the journeyman will be remembered for his solid roles as backup to several of the game's most memorable starting centers, starting with Big George in Minneapolis, followed by Bob Pettit in St. Louis, and finally Bill Russell in Boston. For his efforts the gentle giant was elected to the Basketball Hall of Fame in 1988.

(Indianapolis folded, thus leaving just nine teams.) There, the Nats, who were without Guard Billy Gabor, and had their star, Dolph Schayes, playing with a broken right wrist in a cast, lost to Minneapolis in Game One, 79-68. Game Two, which was nationally televised by NBC, saw Syracuse prevail, 62-60, thanks to Paul Seymour's dramatic jump-shot from half-court in the final seconds to even the series. The home loss stunned the crowd of 6,277, making it the first time the Lakers had lost a playoff game in the Minneapolis Auditorium, a streak that covered seven seasons. The Lakers then won two of three out in Syracuse's War Memorial Auditorium, only to see the Nats take Game Six on Jim Neal's thrilling last-second 25-footer at the buzzer. Staying calm, the Lakers, behind Pollard's 21 points, then held off Syracuse in Game Seven, 87-80, to once again stake their claim as the league's best. Incredibly, it was their sixth championship in seven years: four in the NBA, one in the BAA, and one in the NBL.

Big George, now 30 years old, abruptly ended one of pro sports' greatest rides after that season by announcing his retirement. Mikan, who was making a whopping $35,000 annual salary, had graduated from law school and was ready to take open his own law practice. Sure, there had been some grumblings about a contract dispute, but the league's all-time leading scorer was tired of the pounding (Mikan's list of battle scars included a pair of broken legs, broken bones in both feet, as well as fractures of his wrist, nose, thumb, and three fingers — not to mention nearly 175 stitches!), and clearly not looking forward to the league's newest rule, the 24-second shot clock — a change definitely not suited to his slow style of play. For Mikan, who used to methodically grab rebounds, and then lumber down the court while his teammates waited for him on the other end, this was not the style of basketball he could dominate. He was used to camping under the basket, waiting patiently for a lob pass, and then, while elbowing his would-be defenders aside, dropping in an easy lay-up or hook-shot. Many critics felt the rule was specifically meant to run him out of the game. "The 24-second clock discriminates against George Mikan," said an outraged Max Winter. "It's like baseball legislating against Babe Ruth."

Teams knew that in order to stop George they had to play him physical. "Nobody gave George anything," Pollard once said, "he earned his baskets." The beatings had clearly taken a toll on his game. But, the game went on, and without their superstar the Lakers forged ahead. Max Winter was able to convince Mikan to come back mid-way through the season though, this time in a new capacity. You see, Max, who wanted desperately to land a professional football franchise for the area (he would eventually be a part of the Minnesota Vikings ownership group in 1960), resigned and worked out a deal which had Mikan purchasing his stock as well as succeeding him as Vice President and General Manager of the team. (Sid Hartman still ran the operations of the team though — negotiating contracts, signing players, and running the club.) The team went on to finish with a 42-30 record in 1955, good for just third best in the now eight-team league (the Baltimore Bullets also disbanded that year).

The league was changing though and along with the new shot clock rule, the league also instituted a new foul limit rule as well (a limit of six team fouls per quarter was instituted, after which every foul thereafter would result in two penalty free throws), in order to curb the ever-growing number of fouls in the game. With the two new changes the game sped up rapidly and lended itself to an entirely new style of play. That season the league's scoring average rose by nearly 14 points per game, and 100-point games became commonplace. The Lakers, who were anything but a "run-and-gun" quick-strike offensive team, found themselves to be like a fish out of water at times. They did manage to beat Rochester in the first round of the playoffs, but then lost to the Fort Wayne Pistons in the Western Conference Finals to end their season.

The Pistons, which featured veteran guards Andy Phillip and Frankie Brian, forwards George Yardley and Mel Hutchins and rugged center Larry Foust, were all the Lakers could handle. Minneapolis lost Games One and Two out in Fort Wayne, with the latter coming on an overtime free throw by Max Zaslofsky to give the Pistons a 98-97 win. Minneapolis then took Game Three at home, 99-91, behind Whitey Skoog's

The Lakerettes Band

Bob Leonard

24 points, but then lost the series that next night when Fort Wayne out-muscled the Lakers, 105-96.

For the season, Vern Mikkelsen, the team's new captain, led the Lakers with 19.4 points and 10 rebounds per game, while Center Clyde Lovellette, who filled in nicely for Big George, averaged 18.7 points and 11.5 rebounds per contest as well. In addition, Slater Martin laid in 13.6 points and six rebounds per game, while his backcourt partner, Whitey Skoog, averaged 11 of his own. The big blow occurred following the season though when Forward Jim Pollard, who, after enduring a sub-par year of averaging just 11 points and eight rebounds per game, decided to retire in order to take the head coaching job at LaSalle College in Philadelphia. Known as the "Kangaroo Kid" for his off-the-chart leaping ability, Pollard would go down as one of the NBA's all-time great ones. The last of the original Lakers, he averaged in double figures in scoring during each of his eight years with the Lakers, and was the only player to be a member of all six Laker championship teams.

With the retirement of Pollard, Dick Schnittker moved into the vacated forward spot along-side Mikkelsen. Several local boys joined the squad that year as well, including ex-Gophers Ed Kalafat, a big strong forward from Montana, Chuck Mencel, who had just been named as the Big Ten's MVP, and Dick Garmaker, a six-foot-three shooting guard from Hibbing who held eight scoring records at the U of M. The Laker roster also featured its first black player, Bob Williams, from Florida A & M, who later went on to play with the Harlem Globetrotters.

After starting out horribly, including suffering their worst loss ever, a 119-75 drubbing in Boston, the Lakers quickly found themselves in the Western Conference cellar. The big news that year came after the all-star break, when it was announced that Mikan was getting in shape to make a comeback. That's right, bad knees and all, the new councelor had decided to get back into the action and rejoin his old mates midway through the season. The team had slipped into last place in the division, and George, who had already been named "Basketball Player of the Half Century" by the Associated Press, wanted desperately to show the world that he could still play. With his return came a resurgence in attendance, as well as a boost in team morale. On Saturday, January 14, 1956, a season-high crowd of over 7,100 jammed into the Armory to see the game's greatest player score 11 points in 12 minutes as the Lakers beat Fort Wayne, 117-94.

One of the highlights of the second half of the season came against the Syracuse Nationals, when, after three overtimes, the Lakers were able to win by the final score of 135-133. Lovellette paced the Lakers with 30 points, while Mikkelsen had 25 and Martin added 20 in the historic contest which set an NBA record for its combined total of 168 points.

Despite finishing below .500 for the first time in franchise history with a 33-39 record, Minneapolis was able to resurrect their season and work their way back into second place behind Fort Wayne in the Western Division. From there, thanks to Slater Martin's 28-points, the Lakers went on to beat the St. Louis Hawks, with whom they were tied with at the end of the regular season, in a one-game playoff. The two teams then immediately turned around and played each other in the first round of the playoffs, and, despite the fact that the Lakers outscored the Hawks by 56 points in the best-of three series, St. Louis wound up advancing to the Finals thanks to Al Ferrari's game-winning basket in Game Three. (Minneapolis beat St. Louis, 133-75, in Game Two, even setting a record for the largest margin of victory in NBA history, with 58!)

Mikan, who did average 10.5 points and 8.3 rebounds in 37 games, once again called it quits, this time for good. He knew that Lovellette, who averaged 21.5 points, fourth in the league, and 14 rebounds, was forging his own identity and didn't want to stand in his way. So, in 1957, the Lakers front office decided that they needed to put their heads together to try and figure out how they were going to get back to being a championship caliber club. Sid Hartman then began to ponder the thought of how his team could somehow lose just enough games that year in order to be in a position to earn the No. 1 draft pick that next season. After all, the best player to come out of college basketball since Mikan, University of San Francisco Center Bill Russell, a tenacious defender who was six-foot-nine and fast as hell, was just the big-man the Lakers needed to get back on top. And, by all accounts, he had indicated that he wanted to succeed his idol, George Mikan, as the team's center.

In order to finish in the cellar though, the Lakers would have to end up in last place — which ultimately meant that they would have to get rid of perennial all-star, Vern Mikkelsen, who in his seventh season had become a rebounding and scoring force in the NBA. Hartman had reportedly struck a deal with the Celtics in which Minneapolis would send Big Mik packing in exchange for Boston's rights to three Kentucky players — Cliff Hagan, Frank Ramsey and Lou Tsiropoulas — who were all in the service but would be available for the next season. It was a move which would have all but guaranteed them the lousiest record in the league. But, just before the transaction could go down, Celtics owner Walter Brown asked Lakers' owner Ben Berger if he could back out of the deal — which Berger let him do. The move infuriated Sid.

In fact, so upset was Sid that he ultimately quit. "It was at that time that I had to decide whether to stay with the newspaper or go full-time with the Lakers," he said in Stew Thornley's 1989 book, 'Basketball's Original Dynasty.' "When Berger called off the Mikkelsen deal, I told him, 'I'm done. Get somebody else to run the team.' I finished out the rest of the season and then I was gone."

(Who knows, had the deal gone down, maybe a new dynasty might have been born? Maybe the Lakers, and not the Celtics, would have won 11 NBA championships in 13 seasons over the next two decades under Bill Russell? Ironically, the Celtics wound up acquiring Russell's draft rights from St. Louis, who, as the NBA's only all-white team, had serious reservations about him being accepted by their fans, in a year which saw the top two teams pass on him because of his high salary demands. In fact, Minneapolis was in line to draft him at No. 3, but Boston stepped up and traded the Hawks for their draft

Lakers All-Time No. 1 (NBA) Draft Picks:

1949 Vern Mikkelsen (Hamline)
1950 Kevin O'Shea (Notre Dame)
1951 Whitey Skoog (Minnesota)
1952 Tam Ackerman (West Liberty)
1953 Jim Fritsche (Hamline)
1954 Ed Kalafat (Minnesota)
1955 Bill Banks (SW Texas)
1956 Jim Paxson (Dayton)
1957 Jim Krebs (SMU)
1958 Elgin Baylor (Seattle)
1959 Tam Hawkins (Notre Dame)

Joe Hutton Jr.

pick at the last minute. One can only speculate, but if that did happen you can bet that the Lakers certainly wouldn't have moved to Los Angeles three years later and their would probably be no Boston Celtics mystique like we know today!)

So, with the deal dead, the Lakers set out to do battle in 1957 under Head Coach Johnny Kundla. Kundla made several changes to his lineup that season, which included trading future Hall of Famer Slater Martin to the New York Knicks for seven-foot center Walter Dukes. (Martin would later be traded to St. Louis, where he would play on an-other championship team.) With Dukes in the middle, that now allowed Clyde Lovellette to move to forward — a move which would ultimately make the team a better one. But, when Minneapolis lost Whitey Skoog to a back injury early in the season, things did not look good. Dick Garmaker did step in as the club's playmaker, as he, along with guard Bob Leonard, averaged 16 and 11 points, respectively, that season. Meanwhile, in the frontcourt, Lovellette averaged 20.8 points and 13.5 rebounds, Mikkelsen put in 13.7 points and 8.8 rebounds, and Dukes added 10 points and 11 rebounds as well.

The Lakers posted a modest 34-38 record, which, in the weak Western Division, was somehow good enough to share first place honors with St. Louis and Fort Wayne. They then went on to face the Pistons in the divisional semifinals where Minneapolis prevailed with a two-game sweep. From there the Lakers met up with the Bob Pettit-led St. Louis Hawks, who cruised past Minneapolis in three straight playoff games, ending yet another disappointing season for the Lakers. St. Louis took Game One by nine, only to squeak by in Game Two, 106-104. Then, in Game Three, St. Louis simply out-lasted Minneapolis down the stretch, winning, 143-135, in double overtime to take the sweep.

Larry Foust

The Lakers problems weren't always on the court though as the ownership's cash problems came to the forefront in 1957. Ben Berger, who had bought out Mikan by this point, and owned two-thirds of the team, wanted to sell the franchise. (Berger, who became owner of the Minneapolis Millers of the International Hockey League, had threatened to move the club to Kansas City, but later decided to sell to local interests.) So, in an effort to give the struggling club some much needed financial stability, a civic fund drive, led by Minneapolis Star Sports Editor, Charlie Johnson, was formed. It ultimately raised $200,000 to buy out Berger, but, with 117 new "investors" now calling the shots, along with a 15-member board, headed by lawyer and trucking magnate Bob Short, the Lakers were nothing short of a mess. It was the beginning of a rebuilding process that would ultimately spell doom for the franchise.

By now Johnny Kundla was tired of the coaching pressures, and decided to become the team's GM. His first move was to then name George Mikan to succeed him as coach. Big George, who was left with a hodge-podge group of veterans and kids both coming and going, had no idea what he was in for. The result was a team with no chemistry that won only nine of its first 39 games. One of the big blows came early on that season when all-star Forward Clyde Lovellette, who had worn out his welcome with the new ownership group, was shipped off to the Cincinnati Royals. (The team did receive a first round draft pick for old Clyde, however, which turned out to be University of West Virginia sharp-shooter, "Hot Rod" Hundley. The new owners figured that Hundley, a dribbling showboat who was famous for his behind-the-back no-look passes, would be entertaining for the fans and ultimately increase the team's faltering attendance.) In addition, Kundla, who was forced to start unloading salaries in an effort to save money, traded Walter Dukes to Detroit for Center Larry Foust and Guard Corky Devlin. And, if that weren't enough, Whitey Skoog retired at the age of 30 because of his nagging knee and back problems. It was the beginning of a downward spiral that didn't bode well for Minnesota basketball.

The team was losing and no one seemed to care. The players were enjoying the post-game poker games on the buses and bar-hopping even more than the games themselves, and nothing positive seemed to be happening out on the hardcourt. Just how bad did it get? Well, in his first pro game, rookie forward McCoy Ingram got the ball after the opening tip and promptly shot it into the opponent's goal. The fans stayed away in droves, as the 10,000-seat Auditorium sat no more than 900 lonely spectators on many nights. By mid-season management decided to make a change by flip-flopping Mikan to GM and putting Kundla back on the bench to finish coaching out the season. After trading jobs so to speak (Mikan really decided to just go back to his law practice after that), the Lakers went 10-23 down the stretch to finish with a miserable 19-53 record, good for worst in the league. Incredibly, it was the first time in franchise history that the Lakers failed to make the playoffs. One highlight did occur late in the season when the team beat the Harlem Globetrotters in what would prove to be the final meeting of a truly great rivalry. The crafty veteran Mikkelsen paced the Lakers with 17.3 points and 11.2 rebounds per game that season while Larry Foust contributed 16.8 points and 12.2 rebounds as well.

Before long the club faced several legal judgments and court actions totaling more than $40,000, forcing Short to call an investors' meeting at the team's offices. There, he then asked the other investors if they wanted to buy a block of the team's stock that had been authorized but unissued to cover the debts. When none came forward, Short reportedly pulled out a cashier's check for $40,000 and made the purchase himself. With that, Short became the majority owner, while successfully diluting the other investors' holdings. (A group of investors would later sue Short over the move, but he won and ultimately became the team's sole owner.)

By now most of the NBA teams had moved to major metropolitan areas (Fort Wayne had moved to Detroit and Rochester to Cincinnati), and the Laker ownership group got worried about being able to survive in a small market. The team, whose name had now officially been changed from the "Minneapolis Lakers" to the "New Lakers," complete with slick new dark blue jerseys and a logo which featured stars on it (the owners thought this would create a broader appeal to new fans — go figure…), was in dire straights, and in desperate need of help. Short, who dictated that nearly one third of the team's games be played on the road at neutral sites that year, in an attempt to generate more money for the cash-strapped franchise, knew that his team was on the verge of going broke. He even raised the cheap ticket prices from .90¢ to $2.50, with the better seats going for nearly $5.00. And, if that weren't enough, Short also decided to do some interior decorating to the Lakers' official new homecourt, the

George and the Fellas

Minneapolis Armory, by adding a new floor and new seats.

The only good thing that came from the team finishing in the cellar, was that they would now get the first choice in the 1958 college draft. They needed a miracle, and, incredibly, that's just what they got. Their savior, was noneother than Elgin Baylor, a flashy young six-foot-five rookie small forward out of the University of Seattle, who, as the nation's leading rebounder, had just taken his Seattle Chieftains to the NCAA Finals, where they eventually lost to Kentucky. Blessed with the ability to somehow hang in mid-air, he would become known as the league's first real sky-walker, long before the likes of Julius Erving and Michael Jordan.

It was not going to be easy to sign the kid though. Baylor had publicly stated his intention to complete his senior year at Seattle and not enter the NBA draft. But with draft day nearing, and the Minneapolis franchise's future in doubt, team owner Bob Short opted to gamble and drafted Baylor with his first pick, eventually signing him after month of negotiating. Short was later quoted as saying that if Baylor had turned him down, the club would have "gone out of business and declared bankruptcy." The NBA had put the Lakers on financial probation and specified that if the club didn't average at least $6,600 in gate receipts for home games, the league would have the power to take over the team. All that changed, however, as the fans poured into the Minneapolis Auditorium to see the "new" Lakers new phenom.

Baylor, who started opposite Forward Vern Mikkelsen, was joined by Center Larry Foust and Guards Dick Garmaker and "Hot Rod" Hundley to give Johnny Kundla's Lakers a solid starting five. Baylor was also joined by new teammates Alex "Boo" Ellis, and the six-foot-eight Steve Hamilton, who would later go on pitch for the New York Yankees as their ace-lefty out of the bullpen. The Lakers came together late in the season to post a marginal 33-39 record — good enough for second place in the West and a trip to the post-season.

Baylor wasted little time in making his presence known in the NBA by becoming the first rookie ever to garner MVP honors at the All-Star Game. Another highlight from the regular season came near the tail end, when the Lakers played Boston in a real barn-burner. By the time the dust had settled in this one, the Celtics had beaten Minneapolis by the final score of 173-139 — which was good for a new NBA record in total points.

From there they beat Detroit, two games to one, in the first round of the playoffs. Now, the 1959 NBA Finals were supposed to feature the two best teams in the NBA that year, Boston and St. Louis, in what would've been their third-straight meeting for the championship. However, in the West, the Baylor-led Lakers knocked off the defending world champs from St. Louis in the conference finals. The Hawks had won two of three to start the series against the Lakers, but Minneapolis won the final three by the scores of: 108-98, 98-97 (in overtime at St. Louis), and 106-104 back in Minneapolis, to set the stage for the mighty Celtics. It wouldn't be easy though, as the team had lost 18 straight against the Beantowners, and, to make matters worse, Elgin was nursing a badly bruised knee.

The rejuvenated Lakers quickly realized that Red Auerbach's squad, which featured Bill Russell, Bob Cousy, Tommy Heinsohn, Bill Sharman and Frank Ramsey, was going to be a handful. Owner Bob Short even tried to motivate his players by offering them presents such as new sets of tires and sport coats if they won the championship. While that might have spared Johnny Kundla from any Knute Rockne-like motivational speeches that he had to deliver to get his players ready to play the mighty Celtics, it certainly didn't help.

With that, the Celtics came out and sent a message to Minneapolis right out of the gates, spanking them in Games One and Two, 118-115 and 128-108, respectively. By the time the series had returned back to Minneapolis, it was all but over. The Celtics were dominant and took no prisoners. After a Celtics' victory in Game Three back in Minnie, 123-110, the Lakers decided to make Game Four interesting. Two nights later, on April 9th, Baylor and Bob Leonard combined to give the Lakers a brief 95-93 lead early in the fourth quarter, but Boston clinched the series with a 118-113 victory thanks to Guard Bill Sharman's phenomenal outside shooting. Baylor had 30 points, while Leonard finished with 21, but it was too little too late. Even though they kept the margins of victory to within less than five points for three of the games, the Celtics were able to sweep the Championship Series four games to none. It was the first time ever that an NBA Finals would end in a sweep, and for the Celtics, it was their first of eight straight world titles.

For the season Mikkelsen averaged 13.8 points and 7.9 rebounds while Foust contributed 13.7 points and 8.7 rebounds, but Baylor was the real star, leading the team in nearly every offensive category en route to averaging 25 points, 15 rebounds and four assists per game. For his amazing efforts he was named as the NBA's Rookie of the Year and earned a roster spot on the coveted All-Pro Team. He also finished third, behind Bill Russell and Bob Pettit, in the Player of the Year voting as well.

"My rookie year with the Lakers was a great one for me," said Elgin. "Being the number one player chosen in the draft, playing on the NBA all-star team, and just to be playing in the NBA was wonderful. The reception by my teammates in Minneapolis was great, and I was accepted and treated like one of them right away. The year before the team had finished in last place, so it was a thrill because no one thought we would get close to the Finals. We beat the defending world champion St. Louis Hawks to win the West, and we were all very proud of our accomplishments that season. Minneapolis had a good year, made a great run, and a lot of wonderful things happened that season, but the Celtics had a better team, and they beat us."

Then, the day after the Celtic sweep, Coach Kundla announced his retirement and accepted the newly-vacated head basketball coaching position with the University of Minnesota Golden Gophers, replacing Ozzie Cowles. (The future Hall of Famer had compiled a 466-319

Elgin Baylor

Sometimes being the worst team in the NBA isn't necessarily a bad thing, especially when your prize for futility is a superstar. In 1958, the Minneapolis Lakers got to choose first in the annual college draft as the result of their appalling losing performance in the 1957-58 season. The Laker selection was Elgin Baylor, and he did not disappoint the Minneapolis fans. In his first year Elgin became the NBA's Rookie of the Year, the all-star Game MVP, and a first team All-Pro. More importantly, Baylor led his team to the NBA Finals.

Although the top-rated senior in college basketball was Indiana's Archie Dees, Seattle University's Elgin Baylor was the player every team wanted. Elgin, who led the nation in rebounding in 1957, had taken his Seattle Chieftains to the 1958 NCAA finals before eventually losing to Kentucky.

Born in Washington, D.C., Baylor, who starred at Washington's Springarn High School, opted to first attend the College of Idaho in 1954 (on a football scholarship believe it or not!). There, after being noticed by the school's basketball coach, he led the hoops team to a 23-4 record while averaging 31 points and 20 rebounds per game. The following season, Elgin transferred to Seattle University and, after sitting out the year because of the NCAA transfer rule, led Seattle to a 22-3 record. Elgin, who pulled down 508 rebounds and averaged 30 points per game that year, averaged 32.5 points per game and grabbed 559 boards the next.

The All-American had publicly stated his intention to complete his senior year at Seattle and not enter the NBA draft. But with draft day nearing, and the Minneapolis franchise's future in doubt, team owner Bob Short opted to gamble and drafted Baylor with his first pick, eventually signing him after a month of negotiating.

The Big E

Elgin won the Rookie of the Year Award in 1959, averaging nearly 25 points, 15 rebounds, and four assists, while leading the down-trodden Lakers all the way back to the NBA Finals, where the ultimately lost to the Boston Celtics.

"My last year with the Lakers was Elgin's first, and we were kind of a rag-tag bunch when he came in as a rookie," recalled Vern Mikkelsen. "Coach Kundla wanted me, as team captain, to teach Elgin about how to play the pro game. He didn't need any teaching. Elgin had a pocket full of press clippings, and he was the best there was to came out of college at that time. I could tell he was in a class by himself. He had all the ability in the world and became such a fabulous player. He had a wonderful career with the Lakers, both in Minneapolis and Los Angeles, and he is a great person."

Baylor may be best remembered most for his unbelievable driving, twisting, lay-ups which featured spectacular mid-air antics. The terms "hang time" and "body control" became synonymous with him. He was also known for following his own shot, and it has been said that if that statistic would have been kept, he may very well hold the NBA record for scoring the most points off of his own put-backs. Often, during the course of a tight game, when the Lakers really needed him, he would switch from the forward to the center or guard position when the situation warranted. When the opposition was engaged in a full-court press , Baylor was the only one trusted to bring the ball upcourt.

Elgin has been called the father of the modern aerodynamic game. Boston Celtic great Bob Cousy remembers: "Elgin was the first one who would go up for the jump shot, hang up there for 15 seconds, have some lunch and a cup of coffee, and [then] decide to shoot the thing. Elgin was that spectacular. He was the first guy who literally couldn't be stopped."

Baylor was more than the first of the great skywalkers, he was an explosive scorer whose career scoring average is exceeded only by Wilt Chamberlain and Michael Jordan. Baylor used his body control and unbelievable creativity like no other before him. His Laker career stats from 1958-1972 included averaging: 27.4 PPG, 13.5 RPG, 4.3 APG, and he was a 10-time All-NBA first teamer. He is also considered among the greatest rebounders for his size the NBA has ever known, posting-up any big man. He could pass and dribble with the best guards in the league, and his amazing speed made him a stellar defender.

"I can't say enough about Elgin," said John Kundla. "He could play an entire game without getting a little tired because he had more stamina than any player I ever saw. He was a tremendous all-around ballplayer. He could just hang up in the air and he could do it all — passing, shooting, dribbling, jumping, and defending. He was just great. His first year with us was so terrific, and right away I knew he was one of the best all-around athletes I ever saw play the game of basketball. One time, he scored 50 points in a game off of only two field goals he shot from the outside. His other points came off of rebounds and put-backs. He was a truly special player."

During his career, he appeared in 11 All-Star games and was named the co-MVP in 1959. He also still holds the NBA All-Star game record for most career free throws attempted (98) and made (78). Baylor was named to the NBA's 35th Anniversary All-Time Team in 1980 and was enshrined in the Basketball Hall of Fame in 1976.

Baylor, who teamed with Jerry West to form one of the most feared scoring duos in NBA history, retired early in the 1971-72 season due to nagging knee injuries. Ironically, the Lakers won the NBA championship that year, an achievement that somehow eluded him over his amazing career. He was undoubtedly the greatest NBA player never to win a title. His Los Angeles teams lost in the Finals seven times in 11 years; three of those Finals were decided in seventh games with the Celtics, which the Lakers lost by a combined total of seven points.

"It was really exciting for me to be a Minneapolis Laker," said Baylor. "In college I never thought about playing professionally. The only thing I thought about was being able to go to college. Growing up, I knew my family could not afford to send me to college, so I really hoped that I could just get a scholarship either in football or basketball. Then, to be able to play for Minneapolis was very special to me. The honor, the pride, and the glory of just being a professional in the sport of basketball was great. Playing with and against the best players in the world was tremendous. All the traveling, meeting people, and making friends was all very special to me. I loved the city of Minneapolis. It still is a great city, and the people there were great to me."

After basketball Elgin went on to become the Head Coach of the Utah Jazz before settling down as the long-time General Manager of the Los Angeles Clippers. Elgin and his wife Elaine have two daughters and a son and reside in the Los Angeles area.

The Original Skywalker

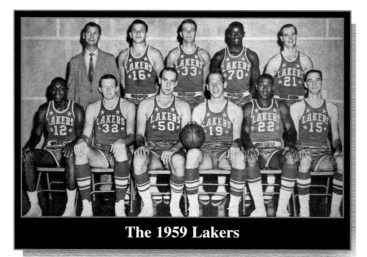

The 1959 Lakers

regular season record during his 12 years with the Lakers, which included six world championships.) Replacing Kundla as the new head coach was John Castellani, who had been Baylor's coach at Seattle University. Regarding the speculation in Minneapolis that Castellani's hiring was a move to keep Baylor happy, Elgin replied: "John was a great person, and I had a great relationship with him. When they hired him, I was happy."

In 1959, Baylor fulfilled his military commitment by joining the Army Reserve Medical Corps training program at Fort Sam Houston, in San Antonio, Tex. Because Short didn't want him to fall behind in practice, he moved the entire team's training camp to San Antonio to be with their star. Amazingly, Private Baylor played soldier by day and exhaustedly joined his Lakers for games by night, where several thousand soldiers would pile into the base's gymnasium to watch the action. Castellani was soft on his players and let them do as they wished. So, for the fellas, who stayed in some nearby barracks, it was a real vacation — playing poker all night and occasionally slipping into Mexico to mingle with the local senioritas.

Short was optimistic about his team's outlook that year. Sure, future Hall of Famer Vern Mikkelsen had retired, but his club had risen from the dead, and Baylor had emerged as the most exciting player in the league. So, he signed Baylor to a long-term contract worth an incredible $50,000 per year. The elated Baylor responded by having a great second season for the Lakers as well. In the season opener against the Detroit Pistons, he scored 52 points. Against the Celtics, Baylor scored an NBA single-game record of 64 points in a 136-115 victory, breaking Jumpin' Joe Fulks' 10-year old record by one point. Incredibly, it was the first victory for the Lakers over Boston in 22 games stretching nearly four years. Before long the Lakers became one of the league's biggest draws, with fans lining up to catch a glimpse of Elgin Baylor.

But, by midseason, the team was just 11-25, so Short decided to take some drastic measures. He knew that Castellani, who had a good

Just Plane Scary...

Now, air travel back in the day was always an adventure. It was a luxury to not have to take the train, but flying then was nothing like it is today. In fact, sometimes, if there were severe head winds, four fuel stops during a 12-hour trip from Boston to Minneapolis were not uncommon. In some instances the pilots would even have to circle around a small town airport to wake up someone in order to have them bring out a gas truck to refuel the plane. There were many travails along the way, but none of them could compare to what happened on January 18, 1960, on the way home from a game against St. Louis. That's when the team's charter plane, an old two-engine DC-3 prop transport, (a rebuilt World War II C-47) which team owner Bob Short had purchased to alleviate some of the travel schedule problems, got caught up in a good ol' fashioned Midwestern blizzard.

After the game, the plane, which was delayed due to some mechanical problems, took off at about 8:30 p.m. that night from Lambert Field. But, somewhere over Iowa freezing drizzle started to come down hard, limiting visibility to next to zero. To make matters worse, shortly after takeoff the electrical system went dead, knocking out radio communications, as well as the heating and defrosting system, forcing the pilot to fly with the cockpit windows open. If that weren't bad enough, the compass even went out, making it nearly impossible to see a thing. The pilot, Vern Ullman, a marine veteran who now had a flashlight as his only source of light in the cockpit, then took the plane high above the clouds and proceeded to navigate towards Minneapolis by way of the North Star.

By now everyone on board was cold, nervous and downright afraid. After witnessing the copilot open his cockpit window to reach out and scrape the ice from the windshield, they knew that this was no laughing matter. They wrapped themselves in blankets and tried to control their breathing in the unpressurized plane. For team minority owner, Frank Ryan, who decided to bring his wife and kids along on the trip, it was unbearable. The players, who had frequently gone into the cockpit to screw around with the pilots on previous flights, knew that it was going to take a miracle to bring her down. And, to make matters worse, a few days earlier Jimmy Krebs's new Ouija board had warned that the plane would crash — something that freaked everybody out.

Finally, about five hours later, miles off course and nearly out of gas somewhere over western Iowa, Ullman started to frantically search for an airport. When he realized that there was no airport nearby, he decided that he was going to have to put her down and hope for the best. The players all said a little prayer, tightened their seat belts and assumed crash positions. Some of them could be heard making public vows, including Jimmy Krebs, who promised to quit cheating at cards and to throw away that damned Ouija board.

The blowing snow was ferocious, but somehow Ullman was able to guide the big bird down through the muck, narrowly missing some telephone wires and a grove of trees, and, after a couple of tries, land safely in a cornfield. He killed the power and floated her in to the uncut corn, which was covered with three feet of soft snow, for a picture perfect landing. The relieved players cheered and then promptly jumped from the plane into knee-deep snow. A local quickly came over and welcomed the crew to Carroll, Iowa, and before long a snowball fight ensued. When they all got off the plane they hiked down the road about a mile to an awaiting hearse, along with a bunch of rescue vehicles.

"That landing was so smooth you could have held a cup of coffee and not spilled a drop," Pollard said, in Roland Lazenby's 1993 book, "The Lakers: A Basketball Journey." "But when I saw that hearse I got the shakes… The guy driving it was the village undertaker."

Safe and sound, the group retreated to an old hotel in town which housed a bunch of senior citizens. There they brewed some hot coffee and raided the liquor cabinet. It wasn't long before someone broke out a deck of cards, and before they knew it, a poker game broke out. And on this particular night even Coach Jim Pollard, who had previously banned the game, didn't mind playing a little five-card-stud!

rapport with Baylor, just wasn't the man for the job. His practices were, at times, merely pick-up games, and many of the players didn't respect him. It was a recipe for disaster. So, one day, after a practice, Short came into the lockerroom and asked the players to take a vote on who they wanted to be their coach. Castellani was promptly voted out, 8-1, in favor of former Laker great, Jim Pollard. With that, Short brought back the "Kangaroo Kid," who, with his low-key style and hard work ethic, he figured would be able to turn the team around.

Ironically, one of Pollard's first moves was to outlaw the players from playing poker, and in particular, to prevent "Slick" Leonard and Dick Garmaker from taking all of Baylor's money. "We were pretty much divvying up Elgin's money," Hundley admitted in Roland Lazenby's 1993 book, "The Lakers: A Basketball Journey." "But Pollard couldn't stop us completely. We'd still play."

"At first, Elgin was kind of a loner, and we couldn't really get him into being a part of our bunch," recalled Vern Mikkelsen. "But later we got him to join the poker-playing group of players called the 'dead-enders,' which consisted of Dick Garmaker, Hot Rod Hundley, Slick Leonard and I. Garmaker used to say that he would pick Elgin up at his house and bring him to the airport for the road games because he didn't want any chance of him missing the plane. Dick said that he made more money off Elgin in poker than he made in his salary!"

Hot Rod Hundley

Pollard also convinced Baylor to take some rests throughout the game so that his batteries would be charged in the fourth quarter, when the game was on the line. But the team had other, bigger problems, including the lack of a big man in the middle. Foust was out and the team was relying on six-foot-eight swingman Jimmy "Boomer" Krebs, out of SMU, to do all the banging underneath, and it just wasn't working. Krebs, who tired easily, just wasn't getting the job done and as a result, Baylor was having to help out too much down low — killing the team's offensive break-out.

Add to all of this, the fact that because the Lakers were still playing their games in several local arenas, rotating between the Armory, the Minneapolis and St. Paul Auditoriums and even at Hamline's Norton Fieldhouse, that once, Baylor nearly missed a home game because he drove to the wrong arena. It all ultimately spelled the end for the Lakers, who wound up finishing the season with a 25-50 record. Despite their horrible record, they did make the playoffs because they had the third-best record in a four-team division. Led by Baylor's 35 points and 16 rebound average in the series, the Lakers swept the second-place Detroit Pistons in the divisional semifinals, and then headed to St. Louis for the Western Division Finals. There, Minneapolis surprisingly jumped out in front of the Hawks, three games to two, but St. Louis avoided embarrassment for a second straight season by posting a 21-point victory in Game Six and then crushed the Lakers for good with a 97-86 thrashing in Game Seven.

Baylor, who averaged 29.6 points per game, the third best in the league, was the lone bright spot for the Lakers that season. He did receive some scoring help, however, from Dartmouth Forward Rudy LaRusso, who averaged 14 points and 9.6 rebounds as well. But sadly, the writing was already on the wall for the franchise. That's because Short, who had been threatening to move the team throughout the season, arranged to have several "home" games played away from the Twin Cities, including two in Los Angeles, to test the interest of West Coast fans. The league had already given him permission to move, and figured the franchise would be better off in a major market with new fans.

"We should have won that series," Pollard said. "We played better basketball. I think it was just a case of wanting too badly to win. I always felt that if we had beaten St. Louis that year the Laker franchise would have remained in Minneapolis. The money we'd have made in the World Series with Boston would have kept us in business."

It wasn't the first time Los Angeles had been discussed in relocation talks either. In fact, former minority owner Maurice Chalfen wanted to move there after the Brooklyn Dodgers moved there in 1957, but Ben Berger shot the idea down. For Short, the choice was much easier though. The team stunk and the bills were piling up everywhere he looked.

He did give it one final shot, in 1959, when, because of the team's lack of a suitable, revenue-making venue, he asked the University of Minnesota if he could rent out their spacious Williams Arena. They said no. But Short, ever persistent, even made one last ditch effort by offering to purchase an iron lung machine for the university's hospital. But the school, fearing the competition, again said no thanks.

With that, Short attended a league owners meeting at the Roosevelt Hotel in New York to formally ask for permission to move to Los Angeles. He had already reached a tentative agreement for the club to play its home games that next season in the newly constructed LA Sports Arena, and figured the owners' vote was going to be a slam dunk. That was his first mistake. During the morning session of the meeting, a vote was taken in which seven owners voted to approve the move, while one, the New York Knicks, said no. The Knicks, who, in addition to complaining about the increased travel costs from New York to L.A., were also guilty of wanting to kill the move in order to claim Baylor — by virtue of being the league's worst team, when the Lakers folder. For whatever the reasons, the vote did not pass and the Lakers were told that they would either have to make a go of it in Minnie, or else close up shop.

That afternoon something miraculous happened. While walking back from lunch to the afternoon session of the meeting, Short grabbed a newspaper at the hotel gift shop. In it he saw a story which announced that Harlem Globetrotters' Owner Abe Saperstein had formed a rival circuit to compete with the NBA called the American Basketball League. Saperstein, who for years had wanted an NBA franchise in California, but was denied, had finally decided to make a go of it on his own. By now the league owners were scared of the would-be competition on the uncharted left coast, so that afternoon they decided to have a re-vote — this time unanimously ruling that the Lakers could indeed go ahead with their move to LA. The one concession that the owners insisted upon making though was that Short agree to pay each team's extra travel costs out to the West Coast. "That'll break us," said Short to his business partner, Frank Ryan, in Roland Lazenby's 1993 book: "The

You Should Be in Pictures...

The Lakers were the first sports organization to have an annual team film made up. After each season, Max Winter called in a producer from New York to make a promotional film about the club's season which provided steady material for the newsreels of the era. Minneapolis, winning championship after championship, proved to be good not only for the film makers, but also for the team — which used the footage to study their opponents.

The Harlem Globetrotters

Osborne Lockhart & Reggie Perkins played at the U of M and St. Cloud State

The Harlem Globetrotters, arguably the most celebrated basketball team in American history, are today owned by former Minneapolis businessman Mannie Jackson. Their rich history and tradition is a long and storied adventure that takes us all the way back to 1927, when a then 23-year-old Chicago promoter by the name of Abe Saperstein, assembled a basketball team comprised of young African American men which he named as the "Savoy Big Five." (The team played its home games at Chicago's Savoy Ballroom, where dances would be held following the games in order to drum up more business.)

Saperstein booked the team throughout the Midwest and made money on appearance fees when they played local town teams, semi-pro clubs and all-star quintets. Within a few years he decided to change the team's name to the Harlem Globetrotters, figuring that "Harlem" would identify the players as Black and "Globe Trotters" would suggest exotic world travel.

They soon became famous for their pre-game warm-up "circle," which included humorous entertainment accompanied by precision ball-handling skills to the smooth sounds of "Sweet Georgia Brown." Their humor was said to be a means of deflecting the occasional ugly racial overtones that the players would encounter from time to time in opposing arenas. An added bonus of the team's funny antics meant that if the crowd was having a good time, and laughing, they didn't seem to mind when their team got whipped by 50 points. As a result, they usually got invited back, which was good for Saperstein's bottom line.

While the Trotters are today world renown for their humor and dazzling ball-handling routines, in the early days the team played it straight. In fact, in the beginning the team was downright serious about winning. In the 1939 season alone the Trotters posted an amazing 148-13 record, and in 1940 the club went on to beat George Halas' NBL's Chicago Bruins to win the prestigious "world tournament."

One night during that 1939 season, the Globetrotters were leading a local opponent by the score of 112-5. So, in an effort to not run up the score any further, the players began to clown around out on the court. The crowd loved it. After the game, Saperstein told his players that the antics were great, but only when they had a safe lead on the board. Inman Jackson served as the team's first "Clown Prince," a role which would become legendary for future generations of Trotters.

With their new-found celebrity, the team made a switch to their now trademark red-white-and-blue uniforms. They had arrived. And, while Sonny Boswell, Hillery Brown, Inman Jackson, Babe Pressley and Bernie Price, were the team's early stars, the team skyrocketed to even higher heights of superstardom when they signed Reece "Goose" Tatum, out of Arkansas, and Marcus Haynes, who Saperstein recruited following a loss to his Langston (Oklahoma) University team one night. They later added former New York Knicks star "Sweetwater" Clifton as well as "Showboat" Hall to make an extremely formidable line-up. Tatum, with his never-ending routine of gimmicks and gags was hilarious, and extremely entertaining for the fans.

It was now the post-war era and people wanted to escape — this was the perfect outlet. The traveling comedy club was being booked around the country and the fans were eating it up. But, in order to keep their reputation as the world's best, they had to play the top pro teams straight-up. Enter the Minneapolis Lakers.

The Lakers had many encounters with the Trotters, beating them on several occasions along the way. When the Trotters beat the world champion Lakers in 1948 and 1949, however, Lakers' Coach Johnny Kundla grumbled that Saperstein had used his own refs. After that they each got to bring their own officials. The 1948 match was a heart-breaker for the Lakers, as Globetrotter standout Elmer Robinson won the game on a last second, two-handed 20-footer at the buzzer.

The fact of the matter was that no pro team wanted to lose to them, regardless of the fact that the scores didn't count towards their regular season standings. In addition, many of the Lakers hated to play the Trotters not only of their antics, but because the games weren't part of the schedules – which meant that they didn't get paid for them either.

In 1949, the Lakers played the Trotters for the third time, and this one was all Minneapolis. More than 10,000 fans crammed into the Minneapolis Auditorium to watch the home-town boys win, 68-53. The Lakers even swept them in 1950, with the second game coming in front of nearly 22,000 fans at the Chicago Stadium. That game was significant for several reasons. First, the sheer number of fans who showed up was amazing, and secondly, it marked the first time that the Lakers were broadcast on television.

One funny incident from that game which involved WCCO's Rollie Johnson, who did the play-by-play, ultimately led to the first-ever "TV-Time-out." Midway through the game with the Lakers up by 10, Rollie realized that he was going to need to take some time for one of his advertisers' commercials to air. So he walked down to Johnny Kundla on the court and asked him to please take a time-out. So, just as Jim Pollard was speeding up-court en route to an easy basket, Kundla called for time.

"Jim came over to the bench with this look on his face and asked me what was the matter," Kundla recalled in Stew Thornley's 1989 book: "Basketball's Original Dynasty." "I told him Rollie needed a time-out. He got so mad at me he wouldn't go back in the game."

The Lakers swept the series' again in 1951 and 1952, with the last game of '52 at Chicago Stadium ending in a 84-60 Laker rout. That was all Saperstein could take of the Lakers, as he "mysteriously" cut his ties with the NBA champs from Minnesota after that.

Throughout this era several marquis players joined the club, including Meadowlark Lemon and Wilt "the Stilt" Chamberlain. Ball-handler extraordinaire Curly Neal would come later. In 1968 the team finally played a game in Harlem, New York, some 41 years after the team's original debut back in 1927 in Hinckley, Illinois. From there they have simply become legendary. Their popularity got so huge that before long, four separate teams were on tour, playing seven days a week around the world. By 1972 they had their own television musical-variety series, "The Harlem Globetrotters Popcorn Machine," and shortly thereafter they had negotiated an exclusive agreement with ABC-TV for exclusive network coverage on the prestigious "Wide World of Sports."

The Trotters have since gone on to become one of the most celebrated sports franchises on the planet. They have performed throughout the world to countless fans both young and old alike, entertaining them all along the way. In the later years, however, instead of playing legitimate teams, they stuck to beating up their regular arch-rivals, the Washington Generals, who, for some reason, just couldn't find a way to beat those guys. (In 1995 the Generals were retired and replaced with the NY Nationals, who are still trying to find a way to win!)

Through it all the Globetrotters have been real role-models. They got their start by boosting the morale in the black communities across the country in a time when things were not even close to being on an equal playing field. They have also featured women, as was the case in 1985 when four-time University of Kansas All-American and Olympic star Lynette Woodard became the first lady to play for the Trotters — an event which signaled a major breakthrough for women's hoops.

They have always had a close tie with Minnesota as well, first touring here in as far back as the mid-1930s against local amateur and all-star teams from around the state, and later with the Lakers. Never wanting to become complacent, the team is always looking to add to their mystique. As was the case in 2001, when Michael "Wild Thing" Wilson set a new world-record in the vertical slam dunk category when he slammed a ball through a hoop set 12 feet high.

The Trotters are an American institution, having played nearly 25,000 games in 115 countries before more than 100 million fans around the world. According to 1996 "Q" ratings, which measures the marketability of athletes and celebrities, the Globetrotters are the most popular and well-liked professional entertainment team in the world. They continually play to standing-room-only crowds, still bring smiles to the faces of kids everywhere, and are without question the undisputed "Greatest Show on Earth."

Lakers: A Basketball Journey." "We're already broke…" he replied. And so went the Minneapolis Lakers to La-La land.

The final nail in the coffin was hammered home on April 28, 1960, when Short publicly announced that the Minneapolis Lakers were officially moving to Los Angeles. "When you are in trouble, you have the choice of selling, taking bankruptcy, or operating your way out," said Short, who obviously chose the latter option.

The Lakers, who were going to be run by one of Short's buddies, Lou Mohs, a former St. Thomas College star and longtime newspaper man from Minneapolis, were then blessed with the second pick in the 1960 draft, which promptly landed them a skinny, six-foot-two forward out of West Virginia by the name of Jerry West. Along with Baylor, West would then be joined shortly by Wilt "The Stilt" Chamberlain, and before long the trio of future Hall of Famers would lead the Lakers into becoming a national power once again.

It was nonetheless the end of a truly wonderful era of hardwood heroes in Minnesota. Six world championships in 13 glorious seasons of professional basketball in the Land of 10,000 Lakes gave the Lakers, like the New York Yankees, Cleveland Browns and Montreal Canadiens before them, the distinction of being their sport's first dynasty. They had established a standard of excellence by which professional basketball was soon to be measured, and when it was all said and done — they had made Minnesota very proud indeed.

Minnesota sports fans would be pacified that next year though by Murray Warmath's Golden Gopher Football team, which went on to win a National Championship and Rose Bowl, easing the pain of the Lakers defection just a bit. Soon the expansion Vikings and Twins came to life that next season as well, followed by the North Stars just a short time later — making Minnesota a real sports hot-bed. The Lakers had paved the way for big-time pro sports in Minnesota all right, but pro basketball, meanwhile, wouldn't make its return to the Gopher State for another 29 years, when the expansion Timberwolves were born in 1989. And, do you know who helped spearhead the effort to bring pro ball back after nearly three decades? None other than George Mikan and Vern Mikkelsen, a couple of real, old fashioned Minnesota sports heroes.

From What Originally Cost $15,000

The Lakers were originally purchased in 1947 for $15,000. Bob Short, who paid $150,000 10 years later, went on to sell the franchise to Jack Kent Cooke in 1965 for $5.2 million. Cooke then sold it to Jerry Buss in 1979 for $67.5 million. Today the Lakers are probably worth more than $300 million. Go figure!

The ABA's Muskies & Pipers

When the Minneapolis Lakers left town back in 1960, most thought that big-time pro basketball was finished in the Land of 10,000 Lakes. But, just seven years later, the upstart American Basketball Association opened up shop right in our own backyard. That's right, the ABA was originally headquartered in Minneapolis (the league office was located downtown in the old Farmers and Mechanics Bank Building), thanks to former Laker Hall of Famer George Mikan, who was asked to serve as its first commissioner. Minnesota would be right in the mix of the fray too, by sporting a couple of early franchises called the Muskies, which came in 1969, and the Pipers, which arrived a year later. Both would stay for just a season, but they left us with a ton of wonderful memories that have lingered here ever since.

With its trademarked red-white-and blue ball, the ABA, in many ways revolutionized the game of basketball — ultimately helping to make it the fastest and most exciting game on the planet. Slam-dunks, three-pointers and free-wheeling entertainment were staples of the new circuit, all things later adopted by the rival NBA.

To fully understand the ABA, however, we have to go back to its genesis, 1967, when a maverick businessman by the name of Dennis Murphy (yeah, the same guy who later founded the upstart "blue-pucked" World Hockey Association), got a wild idea about giving the mighty NBA a serious run for its money. Back then, the NBA had only 10 teams. The Philadelphia 76ers, and their star Center, Wilt Chamberlain, were the defending champions at the time, but pro basketball was not anything like it is today. This was still the era of granny-shots and short-shorts. It was primarily a game for the purists, and probably ranked a distant fourth behind baseball, football and even hockey, in terms of popularity among most sports fans.

Getting fans into the arenas was another story. Few games were sellouts and even fewer were televised. By this time the average NBA player was earning around $10,000 per year, and that didn't even count his sneakers — which he had to purchase himself. About the last thing the sports world needed at this point was another pro basketball league. But Murphy, who originally wanted to start a rival football league, but was beaten to the punch when the AFL was formed, was dead-set on playing with the big boys. So, he rounded up some investors and started making calls. It was amazingly unscientific to say the least. There were no focus groups, no market research, no discussions about corporate sponsorship and licensing opportunities, nothing. Just a guy with a dream, which sometimes, is all it takes.

The NBA, on the other hand, thought the entire saga was a joke. They were already struggling, and couldn't imagine another league coming in and doing any better. Sure, there had been other rival leagues that had come and gone through the years, but none of them had a salesman like Murphy burning the midnight oil.

With that, Murphy asked George Mikan to serve as the league's first commissioner. Big George had a lot of credibility at the time and was a household name in the world of basketball. George, now 43-years-old and thriving as a lawyer and owner of a travel agency in Minneapolis, agreed, but under a

Mel Daniels

Irv Inniger

couple of conditions. He wanted the league to be headquartered in the Twin Cities, and he also wanted to give the league a signature point of differentiation — something that really made it stand out from the NBA. His idea: a red, white and blue basketball.

"We were trying to get the network television contract, and I thought the typical brown ball was very hard to see in a large auditorium," said Mikan in an NBA.com interview. "I decided on a ball with different-colored panels of red, white, and blue for three reasons. First, it was patriotic; second, the TV viewability was just fantastic; and third, because of the saleability of the ball. The young kids really liked it."

And, while the NBA just laughed at the "clown ball," it would prove to be a stroke of genius for a league that clearly wanted to be very different from its big brother in every possible way. So the group got started by assembling what would turn out to be 11 inaugural teams. Getting those teams together and assembling front-offices was another story. Many of the new ownership groups had money along with a genuine passion for the game. But what they did not have, was a clue.

Take the Dallas Chaparrals for instance. This franchise got its name at the first ownership meeting, which was held at the "Chaparral Conference Room" of the Dallas Sheraton hotel. When the topic of discussion turned to naming the team, one of the marketing rocket scientists simply looked at the nameplate above the door and suggested the nickname "Chaparrals." Where the Chaparrals truly became a part of ABA lore was at the 1967 draft, however. You see, team GM Max Williams, a former hoops star at SMU, had assembled a list of what he determined to be the best college prospects. But, because he wanted to save money on travel expenses, he sent an associate to the draft instead of going himself. The associate, armed with Williams' list, thought that he was supposed to draft the players listed on the sheet in order of talent. But, what he didn't realize was that the list was written in alphabetical order. As a result, the Chaparrals first five picks were: 1) Matt Aitch, 2) Jim Burns, 3) Gary Gray, 4) Pat Riley and 5) Jim Thompson.

The league was full of characters, and Mikan, who served as the league's top boss until 1969, was very liberal with regards to who he let in. Take for instance Connie Hawkins, Roger Brown and Doug Moe, all of whom had been banned from the NBA because of their alleged involvement during the college basketball scandals of the early 1960s. This was shoring up to be the "second chance" league for players either cut or banished from the NBA. After all, in 1967, there were only about 120 men playing pro ball, which meant that there were a lot of other talented players out there who just never got an opportunity to showcase their skills. For whatever the reasons, the league didn't care. They just wanted to get it off the ground and worry about the details later.

As a result of the rival league, players quickly realized that they now had options, as well as leverage. If a player was drafted by both an NBA as well as an ABA team, he could sit back and let a bidding war ensue. While this was good for the players, it was bad for the leagues — ultimately resulting in a ton of frivolous lawsuits. It didn't take long for the two sides to declare war on one another, both for players as well as for respect. Take future Hall of Famer Rick Barry, who, after just dethroning Wilt Chamberlain as the NBA scoring champion, decided to jump ship across the Bay from the NBA's San Francisco Warriors to the ABA's Oakland Oaks. A lawsuit ensued and as a result, Barry, expected to be the ABA's biggest star, was forced to sit out the league's entire first season.

Agents also began to play major roles. You see, prior to the advent of the ABA, it had always just been assumed that college players would graduate before turning pro, something the NBA referred to as the "four-year rule." Even Wilt Chamberlain, perhaps the biggest star of all-time, was not allowed into the NBA when he quit the University of Kansas after his junior year, back in 1958. They made him wait a year, ultimately forcing him to play with the Harlem Globetrotters for a season, before allowing him to join to the Philadelphia Warriors. The ABA didn't care about those old stuffy rules though. They didn't want to penalize players who might not be good students, and hey, let's be real… they needed the talent and were going to do just about anything they had to do in order to beat the NBA at its own game.

With that, the underdog ABA just started to draft and sign players. The NBA, of course, was furious. They filed lawsuits, but to no avail. The final blow came when the ABA signed junior college star Spencer Haywood, declaring him as a "hardship case," by basically saying that the NBA was depriving him of his right to support his mother and nine brothers and sisters. These early signings infuriated both the NBA as well as the NCAA, which had always been the league's farm system, but there was nothing to do to stop it.

The players themselves were the characters in this league: guys like controversial talk-show host Morton Downey, Jr., who was a part-owner of the New Orleans franchise, or how about Denver Rockets Guard, Lefty Thomas, who played with rings on all 10 of his fingers. It was also full of guys with great nicknames, like: "Dr. J," "The Iceman," "Slick," "Fatty," "Goo," "Magnolia Mouth," "Mr. Excitement," "Hawk" and "Bad News." The league was seemingly never without a dull moment. But there were also a whole bunch of guys who would go on to stardom as well, including guys like: Julius Erving, Wilt Chamberlain, George Gervin, Moses Malone, Rick Barry, Bobby Jones, Connie Hawkins, Artis Gilmore, Billy Cunningham, Maurice Lucas and Dan Issel, to name just a few.

Errol Palmer

Many great coaches would come out of the league too, such as Larry Brown, K.C. Jones, Doug Moe, Hubie Brown and Lou Carnesecca — not to mention a quartet of Hall of Famers in Slater Martin and Jim Pollard, both former Laker greats who coached the Houston Mavericks and Minnesota Muskies, respectively, as well as Dallas player-coach Cliff Hagan, and Max Zaslofsky, who guided New Jersey.

It was also a unique time in American history. The Civil Rights Movement was going on and the Vietnam War was about to explode. Sex, drugs and rock and roll were all the rage, and people were just rebelling for the sake of rebelling. It was also the dawn of big bell-bottoms, wide lapels, six-inch heeled boots and huge Afros. Somehow, someway, the ABA got caught up in all of this and kind of just rode the wave. The NBA, on the other hand, was all about the establishment. They had the money, the television exposure, and they had the power. The ABA was about freedom, and about having fun. Authority figures, such as coaches, were not revered in the same light as they are today. Hey, some guys even refused to acknowledge the National Anthem before games — so they sure as heck weren't about to be ordered around out on the court.

Through it all, the first season got underway with mixed reviews. Attendance was low, but entertainment was high. The fans were looking for cheap amusement and this was definitely it. The games and the players had flair, a real commodity back in the day. There was a lot of running and gunning with fast breaks, big windmill dunks and in-your-face trash-talking. They wanted to be innovative and different, and they succeeded. The three-point shot and 30-second shot-clock were big hits, as was the fact that players could not foul-out in the ABA either — all subtle nuances that directly contradicted the stuffy NBA. (And, in addition to creating half-time entertainment, they even later came up with the Slam-Dunk Contest, an event which proved to be enormous hit with the fans.)

But after a while the lack of funds started to erode the already fledgling fan-base. In some instances, there were literally less than 100 fans in attendance for games. With no TV exposure and no money for marketing, it was an uphill battle of gigantic proportions. The media, at times, treated the ABA like a bastard step-child, and never gave it its proper due.

Before long teams were making wild trades and selling players like fast-food. Franchises were opening and closing faster than McDonalds, and players were holding their breath every time they cashed a check. Teams came and went, but overall the league found a niche. Before long the talent in the ABA was nearly as good as the NBA's — although the NBA would never dare admit it.

By the end of the 1975-76 season, the ABA was on its last legs. Franchises in Baltimore, San Diego, Utah and Virginia were all dead and buried, and the six remaining: New York, San Antonio, Indiana, Denver, Kentucky and St. Louis were on life-support. With that, the league approached big-brother and offered them a proposition. They wanted to join forces and merge. The NBA, tired of losing money and its dignity, reluctantly agreed — but with some stipulations. They agreed to allow four ABA clubs: the New York Nets, San Antonio Spurs, Indiana Pacers and Denver Nuggets, to pay a $3

Dick Jonckowski

One of the funniest human beings you will ever meet, Dick "The Polish Eagle" Jonckowski has spent a life-time making others laugh. He is also one Minnesota's biggest sports fanatics. In fact, the basement of his Shakopee home is a venerable fire hazard, because it is crammed so full of wonderful pieces of sports memorabilia. Full of signed pictures, programs and random treasures, it is a collection like no other, and truly shows the passion he has towards the world of sports.

A graduate of New Prague High School in 1961, Dick went on to play one season of professional baseball in the St. Louis Cardinals farm system, in Salisbury, NC. (*I assure you, it was nothing like Doc. Moonlight Graham's infamous "cup of coffee" from the movie "Field of Dreams!"*) After studying at Brown Institute, Jonckowski worked for three years as a sportscaster: serving as the Sports Director for both WLDY, in Ladysmith, Wis., in 1964, as well as for KSMM, in Shakopee, where he has been ever since, hosting his sports radio show, "The Coaches Round Table," now in its 35th year.

In 1967, Jonckowski joined the upstart Minnesota Muskies basketball club of the ABA, working in the team's public relations department. When the Muskies moved to Miami that off-season, Dick then became Assistant Public Relations Director for the Minnesota Pipers, yet another ABA club which immediately moved in from Pittsburgh when the Muskies left town. Dick continued his work in the world of pro basketball when he became the P.A. announcer for the upstart Minnesota Fillies, a pro women's team which played for a few seasons back in the late 1970s.

Since then, the "Polish Eagle" has become one of the Midwest's top after-dinner speakers, emceeing roasts and banquets from coast-to-coast along the way. In addition, he has gained much notoriety as the voice of the Gophers, serving as the program's long-time public address announcer for both basketball and baseball games. In fact, Dick replaced the legendary Jules Perlt, who had served as the team's P.A. announcer for some 60 years, and has filled in wonderfully ever since.

A true living legend, (*Hey, just ask him...*), Dick is a true Minnesota Sports Sacred Cow! Living large by his now infamous motto: "Laugh and Live Longer," Dick is a true friend to the game of basketball.

"I started out as a Boy Scout ushering games at old Williams Arena and my love for the game of basketball just grew from there," said Dick. "I saw my first Laker game in 1955 when I was 12 years old and really fell in love with those guys. Since then I have been a huge Gopher Basketball fan and to be a part of that team means the world to me. I mean to be able to help out in a small way, like getting the crowd going with the microphone, is very gratifying. From the Muskies to the Pipers and from the Fillies to the Timberwolves, I have always been a fan, and that is what it is all about."

million "induction" fee, thus raising the NBA's total number of teams to 22. They agreed. The two remaining franchises were bought out, and the remaining ABA players were then placed into a special dispersal draft.

As a result, the financially pinched clubs had to sell everything but the kitchen sink in order to come up with the buy-out fee. One such cash-strapped club was the Nets, who even had to sell their star, Dr. J., to Philadelphia in order to just get into the league. (The good doctor responded by leading the Sixers to the NBA Finals that next year, and a championship in 1983.) A few years later the NBA adopted the ABA's three-point line, and also its coveted All-Star Game "Slam-Dunk Contest" — both of which proved to be huge in growing the league into what we know it as today.

Just how good was the old American Basketball Association? Well, of the 84 players who competed in the ABA in its final season, 63 went on to play in the NBA. And, if that weren't enough, nearly half of the players in the first NBA All-Star following the merger were former ABA players.

The free-wheeling ABA truly changed the game as we know it today, and helped to make it the most exciting game on the planet. It was a real wild ride in the annals of pro basketball history all right, and Minnesota was right in the mix of it all. But, to fully understand our role in the upstart league, let's go back in time and take a closer look at our two franchises: the Muskies and the Pipers.

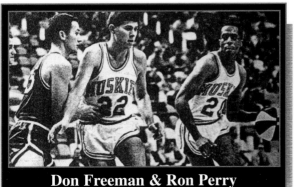

Don Freeman & Ron Perry

The Minnesota Muskies

The Minnesota Muskies (named after the elusive muskellunge, a large pike native to the state's many lakes and rivers) became charter members of the upstart ABA on February 2nd, 1967, when the league's inception was officially announced. The new franchise was purchased for $30,000 by Larry Shields (President of the Shields Development Company), Eddie Holman (owner of the Holman Oil and Gas Drilling Corp.) and Phil Barrett, with Shields serving as President and Holman as GM. The first thing the new group did was to hire former Laker great Jim Pollard to serve as the team's first coach, a position he graciously accepted.

"I had to give it a lot of thought," said Pollard at that time. "Coaching is seldom a long-term proposition. They come and go. This was a new league, which meant there would be a new product to sell. But it was professional basketball, and it meant coming back to Minnesota. I took the offer and I'm delighted I did."

"The NBA was taking up only about 10 or 12 college boys a year," Pollard added. "There's a lot more capable of playing pro ball. We're proving it in the ABA right now. I think we have a solid franchise in Minnesota, one that will put the state on the map again as a great center of professional basketball."

The Muskies, along with the Pittsburgh Pipers, Indiana Pacers, Kentucky Colonels and New Jersey Americans, would comprise the Eastern Division, while the Dallas Chaparrals, New Orleans Buccaneers, Denver Rockets, Houston Mavericks, Anaheim Amigos and Oakland Oaks, made up the West. The team, which sported Blue and Gold uniforms, was set to open play in the newly constructed 15,500-seat Metropolitan Sports Center in Bloomington — home of the NHL's expansion North Stars, which also came into existence that same year. Now all they needed were some players.

Owner Eddie Holman & Coach Jim Pollard

The team's first-ever draft pick was six-foot-ten New Mexico Center Mel Daniels, who, despite already being drafted in the first round by the NBA's Cincinnati Royals, took a gamble on the new league and signed with the Muskies. Minnesota also signed six-foot-three Illinois Guard Donnie Freeman, as well as Forward Les "Big Game" Hunter, a member of Loyola's 1963 NCAA championship — all of whom would play in the ABA's All-Star game that year in Indianapolis. Other signees included Virginia Tech Guard Ron Perry, Kentucky Wesleyan Forward Sam Smith, and former Gopher Guard, Terry Kunze, from Duluth. (In addition, the team also drafted future Chicago Bulls Hall of Fame Coach, Phil Jackson, who signed instead with the New York Knicks.) One other pick was a "homer" selection, in former Gopher All-American Lou Hudson, who had just averaged 18.4 points per game as a rookie with the NBA's St. Louis Hawks. But, Hudson got into some contract issues with his former club and the courts prohibited him from coming to the ABA.

With that, the Muskies came out of the gates quickly with their very talented young lineup. They opened the season at home against Kentucky on Sunday, October 22nd, 1967, in front of 8,104 fans, only to fall to the Colonels, 104-96. Sam Smith tallied 24 points in the loss while Daniels added 19 before being ejected in the third quarter for fighting with Kentucky's Ken Rhine.

The team struggled a bit though, dropping their next three games. Finally, after a humiliating 115-99 loss to Anaheim, GM Eddie Holman fined each man $25, because of "complacency, lackadaisical work and lack of effort."

"I had to show these guys that the people of Minnesota will not tolerate such basketball," said Holman of the fines.

From there the team got hot and by early November, following a 125-75 blowout win over Kentucky, they had improved their record to 9-4. Then, on Thanksgiving day, Minnesota beat the tough Indiana Pacers, 121-99, on Don Freeman's 26 points, to jump into first place in the East.

By December the team was still in first place, an accomplishment which gave Jim Pollard the honor of being named as the coach of the Eastern Squad at the first annual ABA All-Star Game, which was to be held in Indiana. There, the "Kangaroo Kid" was joined by Daniels, Freeman, and Hunter, who represented the Muskies proudly. Daniels led the way with 22 points and 15 rebounds, while Freeman added 20 and Hunter pitched in seven points and nine rebounds of his own, en route to leading the East to a 126-120 victory.

Meanwhile, the slow-starting Pittsburgh Pipers, who had gone on a 15-game winning streak, got hot and bumped the fish out of the top spot and into second place. From there the Pipers only got stronger, and despite several nice runs, the Muskies, who ended the season with league's second-best overall record of 50-28, finished the season four games behind Pittsburgh. With that, the team was headed to the post-season, where they hosted Kentucky in the first round of the playoffs. It was a wild ride for the Colonels, however, who made it there on the heels of a fire-storm.

Here's what went down: The New Jersey Americans and Kentucky Colonels both finished tied for the fourth and final playoff spot and were set to meet in a tie-breaker game in an old arena in Commack, New York, due to the fact that the Americans' home arena was unavailable. But, when it was determined that the hardwood floor at the old dump was riddled with holes and cracks, the two teams deemed it "unfit to play." As a result, both teams apparently agreed to move the tie-breaker game to Minnesota, where it would be played at the Met. But, when Kentucky arrived in town, they learned that Commissioner Mikan had already issued them a forfeited victory. At that point Americans' Owner Art Brown went nuts and vowed to file a lawsuit declaring the act illegal. (While the legal action turned out to be a veiled threat, probably because he didn't have the money to pursue a long, drawn out court-case,

Terry Kunze

Minnesota Muskies All-Time Roster	
No.	Player
20	Don Freeman
22	Ron Perry
23	Dick Clark
24	Irv Inniger
32	Errol Palmer
33	Terry Kunze
34	Mel Daniels
35	Les Hunter
50	Skip Thoren
51	Gary Keller
52	Sam Smith

he did, however, vow to "seek Mikan's ouster as commissioner.")

Arvesta Kelly

With that all out of the way, the Muskies went on to beat Kentucky in the Eastern Division Semifinals, three games to two. Minnesota took Game One, 115-102, lost Game Two, 100-95, rebounded to take Game Three, 116-107, got blown out in Game Four, 88-54, but came back to take the fifth and final game, 114-108, to advance to the Finals, where they would face their old nemesis, the Pittsburgh Pipers. Interestingly, just prior to the series, GM Eddie Holman resigned. So, Pollard called his old pal, fellow Laker great, Vern Mikkelsen, to replace him.

Big Mik's pep-talk didn't inspire the team though, as they came out and got smoked by the Pipers four games to one. The series, which opened in the Steel City, was marred by controversy even before it began. That evening, April 4th, Martin Luther King was assassinated. And despite many calls to cancel the game, it was played anyway, with the Pipers overcoming a nine-point half-time deficit to beat the Muskies, 125-117. Minnesota won two days later, 131-123, to tie the series, but Game Three, in Bloomington, would be delayed for three days for Dr. King's funeral. From there the Pipers, behind the league's MVP, Connie Hawkins, cruised, taking both games at the Met, 101-99 & 117-108, before closing the series out back in Pittsburgh, 114-105. The Pipers would then go on to beat New Orleans in the Finals, four games to three, for the inaugural ABA championship.

For the Minnesota Muskies, it was a sad ending to an otherwise solid season — at least on the court that was. Freeman ended up averaging 16.3 points per game, while Hunter contributed 17.6 points as well. But the big story was Mel Daniels, who was named as the ABA's Rookie of the Year that season by averaging 22.2 points per game and leading the league in rebounds, with 15.6.

Little did they know it, however, that that game would be the franchise's final one ever. Despite posting the second-best record in the league that year — not to mention playing in a beautiful new arena — the team averaged a measly 2,500 fans per game that season (Believe it or not, they had just 100 season ticket holders!), and was in serious debt. Couple that with the fact that team owner Larry Shields apparently didn't enjoy spending his winters in balmy Minnesota, and the writing was on the wall. Efforts were made to bolster attendance that next season by scheduling many of the team's home games on the road, in neutral cities, and they had even secured a lucrative television contract, but it was too little too late. It was curtains.

With that, the Minnesota Muskies became the Miami Floridians, where, in 1968-69, they finished in second place in Eastern Division and went on to beat the Minnesota Pipers in the playoffs, four games to three, before losing to Indiana in the Division Finals, four games to one. Wait a minute. Did you say Minnesota Pipers? That's right, that off-season, the defending ABA champion Pittsburgh Pipers moved to Minnesota, where they dared to take up where the now-defunct Muskies left off. Just when you thought big-time pro hoops were gone and dead in Minnie, the Pipers come marching into town. Who'da thunk it?

(Incidentally, the Floridians sold Mel Daniels that off-season to the Indiana Pacers in order to pay off some of the team's ever-mounting debts. It went down as one of the worst deals in ABA history, as Daniels would go on to become a perennial All-Star! Oh, and as far as the Floridians franchise, it was purchased by the league in 1972 and later disbanded.)

The Minnesota Pipers

On June 28th, 1968, Gabe Rubin, announced that he was moving his defending ABA champion Pittsburgh Pipers to Minnesota. He claimed that, like the Muskies, poor attendance had wreaked financial havoc on his club, so he figured a move was in order. Hey, why not pack up and move to a small-market city which just had a team leave for those very reasons? Go figure. Anyway, Rubin came in and sold a controlling interest of the club to Bill Erickson, a Northfield attorney who had also served as legal counsel for the ABA, but would remain as chairman of the board. "I'm provincial," said Erickson. "And I'm just provincial enough to think that basketball can succeed in Minnesota."

One of the first things that the new organization did was to hire "The Great Dane" Vern Mikkelsen as the team's new GM. The former Laker great, who had served as the GM of the Muskies prior to their move, was excited about being a part of the new franchise.

"I saw it as a great opportunity," Vern would later say. "My insurance business was doing well, but I wanted to get back into the game just a little bit. Here we were with the defending champs from the league, and it was a really exciting time for Minnesota basketball. I thought it would be fun to get back into it and overall it was a good experience. The only bad thing about it was the fact that my alma mater, Hamline, was none too pleased that I had taken up with another Minnesota team named the Pipers!"

The team then named Jim Harding as its new head coach. Harding, a 39-year-old who had compiled a 93-28 record in five seasons at LaSalle College in Philadelphia, was a fiery, disciplined coach who was known for working his players extremely hard. He also had a shadow cast over him with regards to several alleged NCAA violations during his coaching career. Nonetheless, he was hired to lead the defending champs to yet another ABA title.

The big prize for Minnesota in all of this though, was the fact that they were getting the ABA's biggest star: Connie "The Hawk" Hawkins, the league's leading scorer (26.8 ppg) and reigning MVP. Hawkins, who grew up to become a legend on the playgrounds of New York City, had been banned from play-

Tom Washington

Chico Vaughn

Connie "The Hawk" Hawkins

Cornelius "Connie" Hawkins was born on July 17, 1942, in the Bedford-Stuyvesant section of Brooklyn. By the age of 11 he could dunk a basketball and from there he simply grew up to become a playground legend on the streets of New York City. "I played 24 hours a day," Hawkins would later say. "There wasn't anything else I was interested in, so I spent all my time at it."

One of seven children, Hawkins went on to become a high school All-American, even receiving more than 250 college scholarship offers. He decided to go to school in the Midwest though, to play at Iowa, far, far away from the slums of the Big Apple. There, as a freshman, his collegiate career was cut short when his name became involved in a gambling and point-shaving scandal that rocked the entire basketball world.

Hawkins was not arrested, indicted, or even directly implicated. But it was suggested that he had introduced other players to a man convicted of fixing games, and as a result of being "linked" to the scandal, he was black-balled by Iowa. So, he turned to the NBA, who also said "No Way." With that, he attempted to exonerate his reputation by playing with the fledgling American Basketball League's Pittsburgh Rens, where, at just 19, he was named as the league's MVP. That next year the league died though, and the Hawk this time decided to see the world as a member of the famed Harlem Globetrotters.

"When the league folded, Abe Saperstein let some of us try out for the Globetrotters," said Hawkins. "I played for the Trotters for four years. It was a great experience. I learned how to travel and play games daily. This is the most important thing a pro player can learn and you learn quickly with the Trotters because they travel far and fast."

Finally, he caught a break when the upstart ABA welcomed him in as a member of the Pittsburgh Pipers for their inaugural 1967-68 season. How good would he do playing with the big boys? Not bad by most accounts. He led the team to the championship and was named as the league's MVP! From there he joined the Minnesota Pipers, when the team was relocated there that next season, and electrified the crowds by soaring through the air like none before him. And, although he was hampered by injuries for much of that season, he emerged as one of the league's biggest stars.

But, when the Pipers moved back to Pittsburgh that next year, the Hawk, who had averaged 28.2 points and 12.6 rebounds in his two years in the ABA, finally got his wish when he was reinstated back into the NBA. The Hawk, now 27, would at last get to soar with the big birds as a member of the Phoenix Suns.

Having found redemption, Hawkins poured in 24.6 points per game that year (sixth in the NBA), and also dished out five assists while hauling in 10.4 rebounds. For his efforts the six-foot-eight swingman was named to the All-NBA First Team along with Willis Reed, Walt Frazier, Jerry West and Billy Cunningham. He had emerged as an awesome offensive force with creativity around the basket never seen before. He was quick, agile, and could leap out of the building.

"He was the first guy on that Dr. J. or Michael Jordan level," said former ABA star Doug Moe in a Sports Illustrated article. "Long strides. Hold it in one hand. Wheel it around. Nobody could match him for that."

Hawkins' numbers dipped slightly over the next two seasons, averaging 20.9 and 21.0 points in 1971 and 1972, respectively, but he still remained one of the league's biggest draws. By 1973 the forward's skills were beginning to fade a bit, but he was still able to tally 16.1 points per game. Then, early into the 1973-74 season, he was traded to the Los Angeles Lakers, where his scoring average dropped to 12.6 points per game — still solid numbers by most accounts. He would average just 8.0 points that next year, before moving on to Atlanta, where he once again contributed 8.2 points per contest. Finally, at age 33, the Hawk decided to hang up the sneakers for good after that season. In his seven years in the NBA, however, he averaged an impressive 16.5 points and 8.0 rebounds per game.

One of the league's first above-the-rim players, capable of not only swooping and soaring to the hoop, but also for being able to throw-down monster dunks, Hawkins was full of style, flash and cool. He overcame a lot of adversity in his career, and for that, he will go down as one of the great ones. Finally, in 1992 he was inducted into the Basketball Hall of Fame. For Hawkins, who had always maintained his innocence in the betting scandal, it was sweet vindication. He almost single-handedly proved that not all of the world's greatest basketball was being played on the NBA hardcourts, and luckily for us, he had just enough juice left in the tank to become a star in the NBA — even when he was well beyond his prime.

ing in the NBA because of an alleged connection with gamblers as a freshman at the University of Iowa. (Even though it was never proven that Hawkins accepted any money, Iowa expelled him and the NBA blacklisted him.) So, the six-foot-eight swingman instead played for the Pittsburgh Rens, of the old American Basketball League, and later with the Harlem Globetrotters.

The 1968 Pipers

Along with the Hawk, the Pipers had Chico Vaughn, a veteran guard who had played for the NBA's St. Louis Hawks and the Detroit Pistons, All-ABA Guard Charlie Williams, Forward Art Heyman, and Forward Tom Washington, who, like Hawkins, had allegedly been banned from the NBA for failing to rat out a teammate who had been offered a bribe while at Seattle University.

The team had learned a lot that first year in the league, and wanted to make sure it didn't repeat the same mistakes. They knew that the Muskies had played in front boat-loads of fans who were disguised as empty seats at the Met Center too, so they knew that if they were going to be successful they were going to have to be able to draw fans out to see them play. So, in an attempt to establish more state-wide support, it was decided that the Pipers, in addition to playing their home games at the Met, would also play 10 games in Duluth, at the newly-constructed Duluth Arena (now called the DECC). And, while Duluth had played host to several big-time teams in the past, including the Duluth football Eskimos (who later became the Washington Redskins) and minor league hockey's Hornets and baseball's Dukes, it would be the Zenith City's first foray into big-time pro basketball.

In addition, not only did the Pipers embark on a massive promotional campaign which saw players visit more than 100 communities on a 10,000-mile tour, they also planned a direct mail campaign to target more than 10,000 churches, bars, restaurants, fraternal clubs, and chambers of commerce to sell tickets. (Much of this effort was spearheaded by a tenacious young sports fanatic by the name of Dick "The Polish Eagle" Jonckowski, the Pipers' Public Relations Director, who would go on to become a Minnesota sports broadcasting legend!) They even managed to get 10 of their games televised on

Art Heyman

WTCN- Ch. 11, while KSTP agreed to broadcast their games on the radio. They were covered!

Ironically enough, the team's first opponent that year was the former Muskies themselves, the Miami Floridians. On October 27th, 1968, just 1,943 fans showed up at the Met Center to watch the Pipers, decked out in Orange and Blue short-short uniforms, roll the former fish in the season opener, 126-94. Behind Hawkins' great play, the Pipers did leapfrog to the top of the Eastern Division standings though, and open up a comfortable lead over the second-place Floridians.

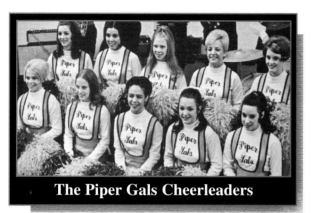

The Piper Gals Cheerleaders

Hawkins dazzled the Minnesota fans with a variety of creative scoop shots and slam dunks. On November 27th, he set an ABA record by lighting up the New York Nets for 57 points, followed by a 53-point outing against the Denver Rockets just a week later. Meanwhile, on the West Coast, another player was tearing it up: Oakland's Rick Barry, who was battling the Hawk for the league scoring title. Their much anticipated match-up, however, never materialized due to the fact that Hawkins ruptured a blood vessel in his arm and had to sit out the Oakland game. With Hawkins on the bench, Barry tallied 45 points en route to leading the Oaks to a 127-122 victory.

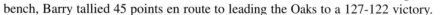

Charlie Williams

After spending a week on the sidelines, the Hawk returned to find his team in disarray. Coach Harding was constantly feuding with his men about the way to run the team and the players were displeased with their treatment on the court. Emotions finally came to a climax when Harding and Center Tom Hoover got into a public altercation one evening. The press jumped all over it and the team was forced to deal with the huge distraction. Shortly thereafter, Harding began to experience some heart problems and his doctor ordered him to take an indefinite leave of absence. With that, GM Vern Mikkelsen was named as the team's interim coach until it could all be sorted out. Big Mik would guide the Muskies to a marginal 6-13 mark over the stretch, but the team still maintained its lead in the West.

Harding was back on the bench after a few weeks of R&R, and returned to watch his star player, Hawkins, tear the cartilage in his right knee. The injury would require surgery and the Hawk would miss the next three weeks of play, including the upcoming All-Star Game. By the All-Star break the Muskies were really banged up. In addition to Hawkins, Art Heyman, who suffered a pulled groin, also had to give up his spot on the Eastern All-Stars. So, in addition to Coach Harding, the lone representatives for the big game would instead be Charlie Williams and Tom Washington.

Then, at the All-Star weekend in Louisville, Kentucky, Harding, who was upset with Williams and Washington for skipping a banquet the night before the game, decided to fine both players a cool $500. But, when team officials overruled him, he instead went to plead his case with Pipers' Chairman, Gabe Rubin. That's when all hell broke loose. Later that night, the two got into a brawl that left Rubin with a big lump on his noggin, and Harding with a scratched-up face.

With that, Commissioner Mikan immediately relieved Harding of his All-Star coaching duties, and a few days later, the Pipers canned him. It was all one big mess.

Mikkelsen took over the team for a while, until Gus Young, the team's Director of Special Promotions, was named as the new head coach. Young, a former coach at Carleton College and Gustavus Adolphus University, was thrown into a snake pit. Not only did he have a team in disarray, he also didn't have its biggest star, Connie Hawkins. In the midst of all the chaos, the team lost five of its first six right out of the gates, and by mid-February, had been bumped out of the top spot in the East. Hawkins did eventually return, but he was slowed due to the injury.

If that weren't enough, snowy weather in Minneapolis and Duluth severely hurt attendance. But even when the weather was nice, the team still had trouble drawing fans. On March 6th, the team even lowered all of its ticket prices to just two bucks, in an attempt to get people to come out and see them. It was a disaster. There was even a supermarket promotion which offered fans the opportunity to purchase two tickets for just 29¢, which also flopped.

From there the team made a few jumps back into first place, but ultimately finished the regular season at No. 4 with a very disappointing 36-42 record. They did make the post-season though, where they would face the 43-35 Miami Floridians, in the Eastern Division Semifinals. The Pipers were looking good at this point, and Hawkins was finally finding his old groove. In fact, he averaged 30.2 points (second in the ABA to Rick Barry) and 11.4 rebounds (fifth in the league), while shooting .503 from the field that season.

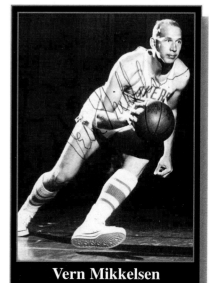

Vern Mikkelsen

Steve Vacendak

The series was a back and forth affair which finally came down to a dramatic Game Seven. Miami took Game One, 119-110, in Miami, only to see the Pipers rebound to take Game Two, 106-56. They then went up two games to one by beating the Floridians in Game Three, 109-93, only to lose the next two, 116-109 & 122-107. Minnesota did rally to take Game Six, in a close one, 105-100, but was edged out in the deciding final Game Seven, 137-128, to end its season.

With the season now over, the ownership group assessed its losses… and it wasn't pretty. The team had averaged just over 2,000 fans per game that year — not the kind of numbers necessary to sustain a pro ball club. The answers were right in front of them though. The Vikings were in the Super Bowl that year, the Twins made it to the American League Championship Series, and the upstart North Stars were still in their honeymoon phase. All in all, there was too much other "stuff" going on in the Twin Cities for the fans to care about a mediocre basketball team. All in all, the ABA was failing to draw fans and most of the big name stars were either in the NBA, or on their way to the NBA — something that was just too hard for many of the smaller markets to compete with.

By the time the dust had settled the team had lost an estimated $400,000 that year, and many speculated that the franchise would relocate to Jersey City. Instead, they once again did what everybody least expected — they moved back to Pittsburgh. Go figure. It would be a tough move though. The fans had never really forgiven them for leaving in the first place, and if that weren't enough, Hawkins left the troubled team to sign with the NBA's Phoenix Suns — which had reinstated him back into the league. As for the Pipers? After relocating back to the Iron City in 1970, where they finished with a paltry 29-55 record and missed the playoffs, the team renamed itself as the Pittsburgh Condors for 1971. It didn't help either, as the team was later purchased by the league and disbanded.

Yep, that was it. Minnesota's involvement with the ABA was officially dead. Mikan gave up his commissionership that next year and the league offices were packed up and moved to New York. The league hung around for another seven years or so, before finally merging four of its clubs into that elite fraternity known as the NBA. But hey, it was one helluva wild ride, and a truly fascinating sidebar to Minnesota's wonderful basketball history.

The Minnesota Timberwolves

When the six-time world champion Minneapolis Lakers packed up and left town back in 1960 for L.A., no one could've possibly imagined that the return of big-time professional basketball to the Land of 10,000 Lakes would take nearly 30 years. To be exact, it was a 29-year hiatus that the NBA took, a time which saw Minnesota gain professional franchises in football, baseball and hockey. Sure, we had a brief taste of the upstart ABA in the late 1960s, with the Muskies in 1968 and Pipers in 1969, but that was a mere cup of coffee for the die-hard hoops fan. But the desire for basketball was always strong in Minnie, both at the prep and collegiate levels, and it was just a matter of time before the wheels got turning with regards to getting a pro team back to the Twin Cities.

The push to bring pro basketball back actually got jump-started on January 12, 1984, when then-Minnesota Governor Rudy Perpich appointed a 30-member task force, headed by ex-Laker Hall of Famer George Mikan, to lobby for a new team. By 1986 a pair of multimillionaire Minneapolis businessmen, Harvey Ratner and Marv Wolfenson, had gotten involved in the process. "Harv and Marv," as they would become known, had worked as partners for decades in both the real-estate business as well as in building a successful chain of health clubs (Northwest Swim and Racquet) throughout the Twin Cities area. They were both avid hoops fans and wanted desperately to try to lure a team to Minnesota.

Pooh Richardson

At first they initially made offers to buy the Milwaukee Bucks, San Antonio Spurs and Utah Jazz — all of which were for sale at the time. But, when those deals fell through, the group was left without any options. Then, in 1987, the NBA voted to expand by adding four teams to the league over the next two seasons. The NBA Expansion Committee spent nearly a year listening to offers from rival cities, and when it was all said and done, Charlotte and Miami were added for the 1988-89 season, and Orlando and Minnesota were added for 1989-90. Harv and Marv had gotten their team.

With that, the dynamic duo put together an investment group to help raise the $32 million needed to purchase the expansion franchise. They then got the wheels turning to begin the sale of 10,000 season tickets — a requirement set forth by the league in order to secure the deal. In addition, they also began working with the City of Minneapolis, as well as the State of Minnesota, to secure the necessary financing for what would turn out to be one of the few privately funded arenas in the nation — the new Target Center, which would be located on First Avenue North between Sixth and Seventh Streets in downtown Minneapolis.

Now, Ratner and Wolfenson, both well into their 60s, knew that they needed to recruit some big-time help to make this all happen. So, they hired Wolfenson's son-in-law, Bob Stein, a former academic and athletic All-American Linebacker at the University of Minnesota who, after playing for eight seasons in the NFL, had become a successful attorney and sports agent. Stein would serve as the president and run the day-to-day operations of the new organization. (Stein even had to give up representing NBA players to avoid a conflict of interest. Among the St. Louis Park native's NBA clients were former Gophers Randy Breuer and Jim Petersen.) He then began to make preparations for the team's arrival. His first order of business was to oversee the logistics of building a new basketball arena in the heart of downtown Minneapolis. He also had to make sure that the team had somewhere to play in 1989, while this new 18,000-seat arena was being constructed. With that, it was determined that the Wolves would play their first season in the Metrodome, the home of the Vikings and Twins.

Before long a contest, which included 1,284 different nicknames, was held to determine the team's new name. When it was over, the name "Timberwolves" had beaten out the "Polars" by a 2-to-1 margin in a vote held by 842 City Councils throughout the state. By July of 1988 Billy McKinney was named as the team's Director of Player Personnel, and the search was on for the team's first coach. Several candidates emerged as the front-runners, including Bill Fitch, George Karl and Bob Weiss, with the most intriguing choice being that of Bill Musselman.

Tony Campbell

Musselman, who coached the University of Minnesota to a Big Ten title back in 1972, before leaving in the midst of both 128 NCAA violations as well as the infamous "Ohio State Brawl," had just led the Albany Patroons to a CBA crown. He also had big-time pro experience, both with the ABA as well as the NBA, where he coached the Cleveland Cavaliers. Musselman also had a local following and the fans knew that he was a winner — all things that impressed Stein. Stein figured that his philosophy of hard work and hustle on defense, combined with discipline and patience on offense, was the ideal system for an upstart expansion team.

"It reinforced that he's an excellent coach," said Stein of Musselman in Bill Heller's 1989 book, "Obsession: Timberwolves Stalk the NBA." "To take four separate teams and just about start from scratch each year and win four straight championships anyplace is real tough and it's real impressive. (He won CBA titles with Sarasota, Tampa Bay, Rapid City and Albany.) Then the record Albany had that year (48-6, the best single-season winning percentage ever recorded by a pro basketball club in the United States) was unbelievable. And I thought he handled the players real well. He won the championship (in Albany) after losing his four top players. There were just a lot of elements that were real impressive to me. Then I talked to people who had been assistant coaches for him. I talked to agents who had dealt with him about how he handled their players when he coached them and in terms of being unselfish and helping them move up to the NBA. I talked to players. I talked to players' wives. What I saw was just a totally different impression than the one I started out with."

It was controversial, but on August 23, 1988, a press conference was held announcing that Musselman had indeed been signed to a four-year contract to serve as the team's first head coach. There, Musselman described what he envisioned his team would be like: "Visualize a cold, dark night in the state of Minnesota. A pack of timberwolves stalking and waiting for its prey. And the prey — the opposition — is fearful of what might happen. World War III will take place. In lighter terms, the prey is in for a tough night and the battle of its life."

With that, Musselman immediately went to work. And work he did — like a man possessed. Before the 1988-89 season would begin that next Fall he would scout several hundred NBA, college and CBA games, all with the intent of being prepared for the upcoming college and league expansion drafts.

"You want people that know how to play the game," said Musselman of the type of player he wanted for his team. "Game intelligence is very important. A lot of people play the game; very few know how to play it. I think intelligence and character are important. You also have to get players that other people like to play with, and you have to find competitors. We want good people with character and work habits who'll be playing in the league for eight to 10 years, providing they don't get hurt."

(It is interesting to note that Musselman tried to bring pro basketball back to Minnesota in a little-known episode just a decade earlier, in 1976. You see, after he left the Gopher program, he met with former Minneapolis Lakers Owner, Ben Berger, about either trying to land an NBA expansion franchise, or to try and lure an existing NBA or ABA team looking to relocate. Musselman, who knew that the ABA was going to either fold or merge the NBA, wanted to land a franchise quickly. He had even spoke of going after the ABA's Virginia Squires, who were in financial trouble at the time. Berger was interested, but that next year the ABA closed up shop, with just four of its clubs being absorbed into the NBA, thus killing the idea. Pro ball in Minnie would have to wait.)

By the time the draft rolled around, Musselman and his coaching staff were ready. Here's how it went down. In the 1989-90 expansion draft, each NBA team would be allowed to protect eight of the 12 players on its roster, leaving four to be selected by either Minnesota or Orlando — the other expansion franchise. The Timberwolves went in optimistic, but figured they would mostly be getting a bunch of washed-up veterans and bench warmers.

Ty Corbin

Orlando chose first and selected Sidney Green, a power forward from the New York Knicks. With that, the Timberwolves pounced on "Bad Boy" Rick Mahorn, the tough power forward for the newly crowned NBA champion Detroit Pistons. Mahorn was stunned to hear the news, finding out while he was attending the team's victory celebration on their Palace Arena floor. The six-foot-ten, 255-pound enforcer, who averaged 7.3 points and 6.9 rebounds, in addition to leading the NBA in fines, was not exactly thrilled to learn of his team's decision to let him go.

Musselman was then pleasantly surprised to wind up with Phoenix Forward Tyrone Corbin, who averaged 8.2 points and 5.2 rebounds for the Suns, with the second pick.

"He's the epitome of a tremendous role player, said Musselman. "We're looking for over-achiev-ers. To be the leading offensive rebounder at six-foot-six on a great team, that tells you something."

From there Minnesota took Centers Steve Johnson of Portland and Brad Lohaus of Sacramento, Guards David Rivers of the Lakers, Mark Davis of Milwaukee and Maurice Martin of Denver, and

Scott Brooks

Forwards Scott Roth of San Antonio, Shelton Jones of the 76ers and Eric White of the Clippers.

"We had a helluva expansion draft," Musselman said. "Hey, we got a starter off a world championship team (Mahorn) and a starter (Corbin) off a team that won 55 games."

The team had little time to rejoice though, as the college draft was less than two weeks away. Musselman, who had spent months scouting, was exhausted. He was also being inundated by rival teams posturing for better position — with more than a dozen alone calling to try and make a deal for Corbin. Musselman stayed put though, hoping instead that the team's three picks, 10th, 34th, and 38th, would produce the nucleus of what would become a future playoff-caliber team.

Finally, on draft day, the Wolves were ready to do some damage. There was a lot of speculation as to what Musselman would do, but all indications pointed to him selecting a point guard — something he had always made a top priority of at every level he had coached at. When the draft got underway, just one guard, Florida State's George McCloud (taken by Indiana with the No. 7 pick) went before Minnesota's selection. The draft gurus had then pegged the Timberwolves to take either Stanford's Todd Lichti, one of the nation's best shooting guards, or point guards Tim Hardaway of UTEP or B.J. Armstrong of Iowa. Musselman surprised them all, however, when he went a completely different direction and picked six-foot-one UCLA Point Guard Jerome "Pooh" Richardson.

Just then, the network (TBS) switched over to a live remote at the Minneapolis Convention Center, where more than 12,000 rabid Wolves fans had gathered for the "Miller Beer Genuine Draft Party" — billed as the NBA's biggest-ever draft day bash. There, the highly liquored crowd, which had been watching old Minneapolis Lakers footage all afternoon, promptly went nuts. It was not known at the time if Pooh, who many of the prognosticators felt was a second-rounder at best, was being praised or razzed. As one writer put it, it was one part "Pooh," one part "Boo" and another part "Who?" All anyone could hear was a muttered "OOOHHHH!!!" Either way, it would turn out to be a great pick. Musselman was impressed by the way the guard handled himself on and off the court, and knew he would fit in.

"He likes to lead," said Musselman. "He makes decisions on the court as well as anybody. He's an extremely confident kid. He has an attitude about him that just reeks of confidence. And he knows the game. You sit down and talk to him, and he talks the game much beyond his age."

With their second-round picks, the Timberwolves drafted seven-foot-one Missouri Center Gary Leonard, and swingman Doug West from Villanova. It wasn't long before the scribes were having a field day by criticizing the Woofies' picks. Musselman didn't care though. He had the men he wanted and was anxious to introduce his new boys to the media. So, he called a press conference that next day, where he also used the opportunity to unveil the team's new uniforms, which featured a midnight blue timberwolf outlined in forest green and silver.

"It's a great opportunity," said Pooh to the media horde. "You get to learn a lot by playing a lot. I feel great about going there. I want to be depended on, I like the challenge."

Meanwhile, Musselman was working tirelessly to fill out the rest of his roster. So, with the draft over, he turned to his old stomping grounds — the CBA, where he grabbed several former players, including Forward Sam Mitchell, journeyman Guard Sidney Lowe, as well as Los Angeles Lakers Guard Tony Campbell — an absolute steal who would turn out to be the team's first star. The coach also reluctantly traded Rick Mahorn, who simply refused to play for the expansion team, to the Philadelphia 76ers for several future draft picks.

In October the team opened its first training camp at the 98th Street Northwest Health Club in Bloomington. Three weeks later they embarked on a six-game pre-season schedule with their first contest coming against the Los Angeles Lakers — Minneapolis' former NBA team. A Metrodome crowd in excess of 20,000 came out to watch the upstart Wolves lose a close one, 100-90. Then, on November 3rd, the team played its inaugural regular-season game against the SuperSonics, in Seattle. The opening day starting lineup consisted of Sam Mitchell and Tod Murphy at the forwards, Brad Lohaus at center, and Tony Campbell and Sidney Lowe at Guards. Mitchell earned the dubious honor of scoring the first points in club history by sinking a pair of free throws at 11:15 of the first quarter. He also scored the team's first field goal a few minutes later, but the T-Wolves lost, 106-94.

Five nights later they were welcomed home to their temporary arena, the Metrodome, where more than 35,000 fans showed up to watch the Wolves take on mighty Chicago. Michael Jordan was his usual dazzling self though, scoring 45 points in the 96-84 Bulls win. The Wolves finally registered their first victory on November 10th at the Dome, a 125-118 overtime thriller against Charles Barkley and the Philadelphia 76ers, with Campbell and Corbin each hitting for 38 and 36 points, respectively. The original voice of the Timberwolves, broadcaster Kevin

Luc... had some issues

Harlan, gave a stirring rendition of the game's final moments: "Barkley holds it ... Barkley holds it ... Go Crazy! Go Crazy! Go Crazy! Wolves Win!"

The team then earned its first road victory in Miami a few weeks later, when they beat the Heat, 105-100. The team did surprisingly well that inaugural season, with several highlights coming along the way. Among them was a 27-point victory over Cleveland in December, as well as a nice run in February which saw the team compile a very respectable 6-7 record, including a club-high four-game winning streak. Tony Campbell had the hot hand over that stretch, even recording a team-record 44-point, 14-rebound masterpiece in a 116-105 victory over Larry Bird, Kevin McHale and the Boston Celtics, in front of more than 35,000 screaming fans at the Metrodome.

Six weeks later, on March 20th, Lowe set the club record for assists in a game with 17 against the Golden State Warriors. And, despite some big-time low-lights, including a nine-game losing skid early in the year, the Timberwolves played tough defense — at one point even ranking fifth in the NBA. Throughout it all the fans came out in droves to see the return of NBA basketball to Minnesota. In March, more than 43,000 fans came to see the Timberwolves nearly upset Magic Johnson and the L.A. Lakers, while in April, 49,551 people attended a game between Minnesota and the Denver Nuggets — making it the third-largest single-game attendance total in league history.

Later that month, 45,458 fans watched the Wolves beat the fellow expansion Orlando Magic, 117-102, giving the team its 22nd victory of the season, the most among the league's four expansion teams. In the end the Timberwolves ended the season with a modest 22-60 record, finishing 6th in the relatively weak Midwest Division — 19 wins behind their closest rival, fifth-place Houston. But the biggest news wasn't the team's success on the court, but rather, off of it —where Minnesota wound up setting an NBA single-season attendance record by drawing more than one million crazed fans.

Musselman was earning the respect of his players by preaching tenacity on defense and patience on offense. As far as the team's performance on the court, they could hold their heads high in knowing that they ended the season ranked among the league leaders in team defense, having allowed only 99.4 points per game. On the other end of the court, Tony Campbell led the team in scoring, reaching double figures every time out, and averaging 23.2 points per game. In addition, Pooh Richardson, who proved to be an all-around playmaker by dishing out 554 assists and averaging nearly 12 points per game, was named to the NBA All-Rookie First Team.

Minnesota's first year in the NBA was solid and overall the team had a lot to build on for the future. The state was thrilled to have a team again, and the fans showed that they were in this thing for the long haul. Expectations would be higher that next year though, and Coach Musselman knew that he would have to get even better. That off-season the team used its first-round "lottery pick" in the 1990 college draft to take seven-foot Center, Felton Spencer, out of the University of Louisville. Spencer would give the team more of a presence in the middle, but was still raw by NBA standards.

Felton Spencer

The team kicked off the 1990-91 season by christening the brand-spanking new Target Center in a 102-96 exhibition loss to the Philadelphia 76ers. Leading the charge for the Sixers was former Vikings All-Pro Wide Receiver-turned TV personality, Ahmad Rashad, who, while filming a segment for NBC's Inside Stuff, suited up and even drained a 20-foot jumper during the game. And, despite the fact that the facilities' state-of-the-art scoreboard didn't work for the first half, it was still a momentous occasion in the world of Minnesota basketball — finally giving the team an identity of its own.

They rebounded two weeks later to win their regular season-opener, 98-85, over the Dallas Mavericks at the Target Center before a sellout crowd of 19,006. From there the Timberwolves went up and down early in the season, humbled by a seven-game losing streak in December. The team was clearly struggling and looking for answers. With that, Musselman decided to abandon his methodically controlled defensive game plan and replaced it with an up-tempo offensive strategy. Musselman, who was starting to fall out of favor with his players, had always believed the only way the Wolves could be competitive was to play a half-court game — relying on tough defense to win — but he gave in and decided to try something different.

The result saw the low-scoring Wolves, which had averaged less than 87 points per contest (nearly 20 points below the league average), immediately respond by waxing Seattle, 126-106. Pooh Richardson was elated to be running a much more free-spirited offense, and he quickly emerged as one of the team's leaders. From there they scored at least 100 points over their next eight games, highlighted by a mid-January three-game road winning streak.

The club continued to gel under the new game-plan and in April, they even posted a 7-5 record — the organization's first-ever winning month. One of the highlights along the way came on April 4th when they set a team scoring record by torching the Denver Nuggets for a whopping 134 points. The Timberwolves even went on a late-season tear, winning six of its final eight games to finish with 29 victories — seven more than in their inaugural season.

Tony Campbell once again led the team in scoring with 21.8 points per game, and rookie Center Felton Spencer added eight rebounds per game en route to earning a spot on the NBA All-Rookie second team. In addition, Pooh Richardson chipped in 17.1 points and nine assists per game, while Ty Corbin added 18 points as well.

Even though the team had done much better than anyone might have predicted, finishing with an expansion-best 29-53 record, Coach Musselman was canned after the season. Musselman wanted to win right now, while the organization wanted to play younger players more often and build for the future. Management and the fiery coach differed on how to develop the young club, and in the end, management simply won out. With that, former Boston Celtics Head Coach Jimmy Rodgers was hired to take over.

"I'm not here to do anything but win," said Rodgers. "But I do understand that to move along, you have to take care of the franchise's building blocks, your young players. And, oh yes, we will run with the basketball."

That was more than welcome news for the players, who were chomping at the bit to play a quicker style of basketball. The team added yet another seven-footer in that year's expansion draft, Australian-born Luc Longley, out of the University of New Mexico. Luc wasn't the most gifted of athletes, but he was, among other things… tall — a criteria that apparently merited him as a first-round draft pick. Go figure. They also pulled off their first big trade early in the season by shipping Tyrone Corbin to the Utah Jazz for aging six-foot-eleven Power Forward Thurl Bailey — a move which they felt would shore up a weak interior.

Randy Breuer

Rodgers came in with high expectations, and believe it or not, really messed things up in his first year at the helm. Sure, he introduced a new a free-wheeling offense, which his players loved, but the team lacked discipline and leadership. Couple that with the fact that there just wasn't that much talent on the roster and it was a recipe for disaster.

Ironically, Rodgers' inaugural game behind the Wolves' bench would prove to be an omen of things to come. You see, the team's opening game of the 1991 campaign was a record-setting night. Not for the team, however, but for city of Minneapolis, which experienced its all-time heaviest one-day snowfall of 24 inches in just 24 hours — a huge blizzard even by Minnesota standards. As a result, less than 7,000 fans showed up to watch the Wolves lose to the Utah Jazz, 112-97. From there the team went 1-13 and people just knew that it was going to be a long, cold winter.

Injuries plagued the team, sidelining nearly everybody at one point or another, including: Felton Spencer, Gerald Glass, Tod Murphy, Tom Garrick, Tony Campbell and former Gopher Center, Randy Breuer, who was acquired after a lengthy career with the Milwaukee Bucks. They did manage to win three of their first six games in January, but then free-fell into a pair of 10-game and 16-game losing streaks.

Sam Mitchell

Sam Mitchell grew up in Columbus, Georgia, loving the game of basketball. After leading Columbus High School to the state semifinals in 1981, Sam went on to graduate from tiny Mercer College, in Macon, GA, as the school's all-time leading scorer. From there he opted to join the Army, but his love of basketball proved to be too much. So, he was granted a discharge and wound up playing for clubs in both the CBA and the USBL, where he dreamt of one day playing in the NBA. One of his coaches in the CBA, the Tampa Bay Thrillers, was Bill Musselman. Musselman knew that Sam had potential and when he became the T-Wolves head coach in 1989, he began to assemble his roster. He wanted young, hard working kids who would be good team-players. So he sent Billy McKinney, the Timberwolves' director of player personnel, to see if the six-foot-seven forward was NBA material. As soon as McKinney saw Mitchell, he pulled him out of a pre-game lay-up drill and asked him if he would be willing to sign with the Timberwolves. Mitchell, so excited about his dream finally coming true, grabbed the contract, slapped it on McKinney's back, and signed it right there on the spot. And, while the contract wasn't for millions, it did offer a kid facing long odds a chance to finally showcase his talents at the highest level.

"It's a dream come true to play in this league, and especially for an organization like the Timberwolves," said Mitchell. "When you grow up you dream about playing in the NBA, and to make it is something very special to me. I don't take it for granted, that's for sure."

Since then Sam has spent the better part of his 12-year NBA career in Minnesota, with the exception of his brief three-year hiatus in Indiana, where he and Pooh Richardson were shipped off to back in 1992 in a trade for Chuck Person and Micheal Williams. He came back a few years later though, after deciding to play a couple of seasons in France, and recently re-signed with the Wolves yet again in 2001. The 38-year-old crafty veteran has become one of the team's all-time biggest fan-favorites and has been embraced by the community. Prior to Kevin Garnett, he was also the team's all-time leading scorer, having averaged nearly 10 points per game throughout his steady career. A tireless worker and truly positive influence in the lockerroom, Sam's been a tremendous part of the organization since its inception. And, as his career winds down, perhaps we will be seeing him on the sidelines in a different capacity.

"He has the skills, the knowledge, to be in a front-office," said Coach Saunders. "He sees the big picture. But I've told him I think he should coach. Sam's a people person. You can see from what he does with our players, being available to them and telling them things sometimes before I can. Being a GM or president, you're into it but you're removed from the game. I think Sam can handle the rigors of practice, the rigors of the road, and get through to a team every day. His communication skills are the best, his knowledge of the game is excellent and I just think that's what coaching is all about."

Overall, he has enjoyed his time in Minnesota and is glad to be back for another campaign. He wants dearly to give the fans a championship, and has found that by working with the younger players, he can make a difference both on and off the court.

"Minnesota has some great loyal fans, and they have been good to me," said Mitchell. "I think that as long as you go out and play hard every night, they will respect you. They are knowledgeable and really understand the game, and I hope we can get them a title here before it is all said and done."

In the end the Timberwolves took three giant leaps backwards, finishing with a league-worst 15-67 record – cutting the team's number of wins nearly in half. Rodgers had a team in disarray and didn't know quite what to do. In his defense, the team's draft picks of Spencer and Longley had turned out to be awful. Spencer was injured more often than not and Longley, who had serious issues, held-out for an entire month before reporting to camp. Both were big projects and neither was contributing — it was a bad situation all the way around.

That next season the team was poised to finally get a stud in the NBA's Draft Lottery. They were the worst team in the league after all, and deserved the No. 1 pick. Team mascot, Crunch, even camped out for days on a downtown Minneapolis billboard in anticipation. But, in the end, the ping-pong balls bounced in the favor of Orlando and Miami instead. And, with those first two picks they got a pair of future Hall of Famers in Shaquille O'Neal and Alonzo Mourning. The Wolves, meanwhile, got door No. 3, the third pick, and with it newly appointed GM Jack McCloskey selected the NCAA Player of the Year, six-foot-eleven Center Christian Laettner. Yeah, he wasn't as sexy as Shaq and Zo, but most felt he was the best available pick at the time. After all, Laettner, an Olympic "Dream Teamer," was the first player ever to start in four Final Fours, and he had just led the Duke Blue Devils to a pair of NCAA titles in both 1991 and 1992 — with the latter one taking place at the Metrodome.

Laettner's combination of size and speed made him a perfect fit as the team's power forward of the future. He also had an amazing desire to win, something that the Timberwolves hoped would be infectious. They figured that his winning attitude and fiery competitiveness would inject new life into the franchise, but others feared a much different scenario.

"Laettner gives Minnesota a talent they can build around," said NBA and Olympic Dream Team Coach Chuck Daly. "He's a tough kid, but I don't know if he'll be able to handle the losing he's going to experience right away."

"Trader Jack" as he was better known as back with the Detroit Pistons (for his frequent wheelings and dealings), then got busy. Knowing that he needed to replace the scoring punch lost by Tony Campbell's departure to the New York Knicks, McCloskey went ahead and pulled the trigger on a deal that sent Pooh Richardson and Sam Mitchell to the Indiana Pacers for the "Rifleman" Chuck Person and

Micheal Williams. It was, as they say, a blockbuster.

At first the deal looked good. The team started the 1992-93 season with six new faces in the lineup, jumping out to a 4-7 record that November. Person led the team in scoring with 20 points and 8.5 boards per game over the stretch, while Laettner averaged 19.5 points and 8.1 rebounds as well. In addition, Guards Doug West and Michael Williams were distributing the ball nicely and playing good defense. Williams did well in replacing Richardson at the point, even ending the season with 84 consecutive free throws — breaking an all-time league mark held by Calvin Murphy.

This is where the story, unfortunately, gets ugly. That December the team went 1-12, highlighted by the worst defeat in franchise history — a 37-point drubbing on December 5th by the Seattle SuperSonics. The team was in trouble. Laettner, who was being looked upon to be a team leader, had suddenly experienced more losses in three weeks with the Timberwolves then he had in four years at Duke. Frustrated and angry, Laettner, who had a big ego and an even bigger salary, lashed out at both the front office as well as at his teammates With no team chemistry, the team self-destructed. Players were playing for themselves, everybody wanted to shoot the ball, and in the end, there just weren't enough basketballs to go around.

A few weeks later Rodgers was canned and former T-Wolves Guard Sidney Lowe, then an assistant with the club, was named as the interim head coach. It was a mess. The youngest head coach in the league, at just 33, Lowe jumped right in and guided the hapless Timberwolves to a 13-40 record over the rest of the year. The team improved under Lowe but still struggled to finish with a paltry 19-63 overall record. It was baptism by fire for the rookie skipper, as he suffered through a 12-game losing streak in April — the second-longest dry spell in franchise history. And, while, Person and Williams played well in their first year with the team, averaging 16.8 and 15.1 points per game, respectively, the team still lacked a big-time star. Doug West, the lone holdover from the original Timberwolves roster, led the team in scoring with 19.3 points per game, while Laettner, who added 18.2 ppg that season, was also named to the NBA All-Rookie First Team.

By the start of the 1993-94 season it was safe to say that Minnesota's "honeymoon" was officially over. The fans were tired of all the losing and were growing impatient. The other expansion teams were all playing very well (Orlando would later make it to the NBA Finals), and the Wolves were seemingly getting worse. They needed help. So, in an attempt to alleviate the team's volatile chemistry situation, the Wolves went ahead and used their No. 5 overall lottery pick to draft six-foot-five UNLV Guard, Isaiah Rider. Rider, who would prove to be the biggest headache in franchise history, was an explosive scorer, but had an attitude that clashed with seemingly everything it came in contact with. It was, as they say, not the best decision.

Doug West

Minnesota lost its first five games that season but was sitting at an improved 14-27 by midseason. In retrospect, the only true highlight of the year came at that point, when the NBA's 44th annual All-Star Game was held at the Target Center. Highlighting the weekend's festivities was the rookie Rider, who, with his series of spinning jams, wound up beating Seattle's Shawn Kemp on a spectacular between-the-legs, one-handed jam (which he called the "East Bay Funk"), to win the coveted "Gatorade Slam Dunk" title.

And, while the dunk was awesome (Charles Barkley said it may have been the best dunk he'd ever seen) in a classic "Rider-esque" moment after the contest, he told the national viewing audience on TNT that he wanted to thank himself for winning and coming through on his prediction.

From there things got ugly though as the team went just 6-35 for the second half of the year, finishing the season on a horrible 10-game losing skid. Even the league's worst club, the Dallas Mavericks, embarrassed the Wolves by beating them for their only two wins over their first 30 games, with both wins coming at the Target Center nonetheless. Laettner did manage to average 16.8 points and 8.6 rebounds per game, while Rider averaged 16.6 points, 4.0 rebounds and 2.6 assists, to earn a spot on the NBA All-Rookie First Team.

After the season the franchise was dealt an even bigger blow when rumors began to circulate that the team was on the auction block. That's right, despite the fact that nearly 20,000 nightly patrons jammed into the posh Target Center Arena to witness the teams' continued marathon of losing, it was later announced that the franchise was being sold to "Top Rank of Louisiana." The group of investors, with ties to both the boxing and also the casino and gaming industries, wanted to relocate the fledgling club to New Orleans, where it could be renamed and overhauled. Team owners Harv and Marv had had enough and repeatedly claimed that due to an unfair lease arrangement at the Target Center, they were losing boat-loads of cash. Luckily, the NBA Board of Governors stepped in and vetoed the sale, however, clearing the path for another ownership group to emerge — this one led by former Minnesota State Senate Minority Leader, Glen Taylor, a billionaire who had made his fortune in the printing business. (Taylor is CEO of the Mankato-based Taylor Companies, which, with more than 12,000 employees, is the nation's largest printer of wedding invitations, among other things.)

T-Wolves All-Time Records:

Season	W	L
2000-01	47	35
1999-00	50	32
1998-99	25	25
1997-98	45	37
1996-97	40	42
1995-96	26	56
1994-95	21	61
1993-94	20	62
1992-93	19	63
1991-92	15	67
1990-91	29	53
1989-90	22	60

Taylor vowed to resurrect the franchise, thus ending the darkest period in team history. But it wasn't going to be easy. Here's what legendary scribe Sid Hartman had to say about the entire saga in his 1997 book entitled: "Sid!": "The biggest mistake was that Marv and Harv should have stayed in the Metrodome for another season, continued to draw those huge crowds, and allowed the contractors to build Target Center at a reasonable pace. Instead, they fast-tracked Target Center, kept making improvements on the fly, and a building that was supposed to cost $80 million came in at $104 million. Marv and Harv also lost their financing — and a bundle of money — when Hal Greenwood's savings and loan, Midwest Federal, collapsed."

"Attendance was excellent, but Wolfenson and Ratner were in trouble financially," he added. "The city of Minneapolis had a chance to take over Target Center and have both the Timberwolves and the North Stars as tenants. The politicians screwed it up, of course, and finally Wolfenson and Ratner made a deal to sell the team to a New Orleans group. They did not want to see the team move, but Marv and Harv had to do something to wake up the politicians. The team would have been gone, just like the hockey club, if was not for NBA Commissioner David Stern."

The 1994-95 season was ushered in with a new sense of optimism. The team had a new owner and he wanted to turn this ship around. With that, Lowe was let go and Bill Blair was hired as the team's new head coach. In addition, former Gopher and Boston Celtics' legend, Kevin McHale, who had been doing the team's television analysis, was hired to serve as the team's assistant general manager. His insight and experience would prove to be invaluable.

Thurl Bailey

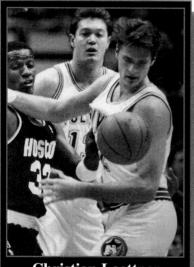

Christian Laettner

On the court, Chuck Person proved to be the odd-man out with regards to strong personalities, and was released. Then, the team went ahead and drafted talented forward Donyell Marshall from the University of Connecticut with yet another lottery pick. Marshall, the Big East Player of the Year, was tabbed as a team-player, something this squad was in desperate need of. Optimism was running high, but unfortunately, the talent level wasn't.

The season got underway with the team struggling to fit into Blair's new offensive system. Laettner and Rider were playing well, but made no bones about how they felt about each other. There was tension, and it was not a good environment for the rookie, Marshall, to be in. As a result, his game suffered. On a team that had little time to develop potential players, Marshall, who was a big disappointment in the eyes of management, was dealt at mid-season to the Golden State Warriors in exchange for Forward Tom Gugliotta. The "Googs" deal would prove to be the best move in franchise history.

"I was happy to come to Minnesota because I knew they wanted me here and I finally felt at home after all the trades," said Gugliotta, who, after playing two great seasons for the Washington Bullets, had been traded to Golden State for All-Star Forward Chris Webber.

The versatile six-foot-ten sharp-shooter provided an instant spark for the team, contributing 14.4 points, 7.2 rebounds and 4.5 assists per game that season. But it was too little too late because in the end the team just plain stunk. To make matters worse, Point Guard Micheal Williams missed all but one game with a foot injury. At 21-61 and in last place in the Midwest Division, the Wolves even set an NBA record by losing at least 60 games for the fourth consecutive season. They needed help everywhere. The Wolves ranked 26th in offensive production at 94.2 points per game, even breaking the old franchise record low of 95.2 points per contest set back in 1990. They were out-rebounded by an average of 6.1 boards per game, the largest margin in the league, and won only a single game against a club with a winning record.

After the season Kevin McHale took over as the team's vice president of basketball operations, replacing GM Jack McCloskey. In addition, his former Gopher teammate and longtime friend, Phil "Flip" Saunders, who had gone on to coach in the CBA, where he eventually won two championships, was named as the team's GM. McHale promised fans that he would make some bold moves to shake things up when he took over, and he wasted little time in making good on that promise. On June 28, 1995, in Toronto's SkyDome, the Wolves, after patiently watching Joe Smith, Jerry Stackhouse, Antonio McDyess, and Rasheed Wallace go in the first four picks of the draft, selected a high-school phenom by the name of Kevin Garnett, from Chicago's Farragut Academy.

The basketball establishment was astonished to say the least. After all, it had been 20 years since a player had been drafted directly out of high school into the NBA. (There had only really been four players that had successfully made the transition from high school directly to the NBA — Moses Malone in 1974, Darryl Dawkins and Bill Willoughby in 1975, and Shawn Kemp in 1989, who did play briefly at the collegiate level.) But hey, these Wolves had nothing to lose. Now entering their seventh sad year of mediocrity and tired of being the league's doormat, they gambled, and it would prove to be the biggest and best move in franchise history.

Timberwolves on the All-NBA Rookie Team

2000	Wally Szczerbiak	(1st team)
1997	Stephon Marbury	(1st team)
1996	Kevin Garnett	(2nd team)
1994	Isaiah Rider	(1st team)
1993	Christian Laettner	(1st team)
1991	Felton Spencer	(2nd team)
1990	Pooh Richardson	(1st team)

Sports Illustrated even featured the kid on their cover with the headline: "Ready or Not." The seven-foot beanpole was a terrific all-around talent, maybe the best athlete in the draft, the magazine reported. Described as a cross between Reggie Miller and a kinder, gentler version of Alonzo Mourning, he could run, leap like crazy, block shots, monster-dunk, handle the ball like a guard, and shoot 20-footers with ease. He represented the most elusive of all commodities for the league's bottom-feeders, and that was hope. Some members of the media hyped him as a "savior," and even the "next Michael Jordan."

Would he dominate and revolutionize the game of professional basketball? Or would he join a long line of NBA casualties crushed by fame, too much money, and the groupies? To be sure, there are countless young men who play professional hockey and baseball at even younger ages. But this was different — this was the NBA.

"Is he a franchise player?" retorted Timberwolves Coach Bill Blair at a press conference. "I can't say that but this kid does some things that excite you. From a maturity level? No way he can be ready. He's not ready for the airplanes, the four games in six days, and for the free time he's now possessing. Those things we have to help him with. You just hope he's so interested in basketball, you hope he wants to be the best player in the league."

Reaction around the basketball world was mixed. "He's a genetic freak," said Detroit head coach Doug Collins. "All the great ones are." Said McHale: "Garnett is a basketball junkie. He's the kind of guy we'll have to chase off the court, rather than worry he's not spending enough time on it." Former Seattle general manager Bob Whitsitt, who drafted Shawn Kemp said: "The team that takes Garnett has to commit its entire organization. Ownership, coaches, other players, everyone has to realize this is a 24-hour-a-day process. You have to be willing to spend the years, not the days, the years, to make this work." Russ Granik, the NBA's deputy commissioner, even put in his two cents worth: "If it were up to us, we'd prefer not to see someone come into the league at that tender age, but the courts say otherwise."

Why the Timberwolves?

- There are about 1,200 wolves in Minnesota, making up the vast majority of the species' population in the continental U.S.
- Wolves mostly reside in the northern third of Minnesota with most being found in the least accessible forested areas.
- The state is home to the International Wolf Center, a comprehensive research center and wolf exhibit area, located in Ely.
- The Twin Cities-based Minnesota Zoo and the Science Museum of Minnesota both have exhibits highlighting the rare animals.
- The Endangered Species Act of 1973 prohibited the public taking of wolves, and Minnesota's population has remained stable since then.
- Although the wolf is on the federal Endangered Species List in the 48 contiguous states, it is classified as only "threatened' in Minnesota.

Less than a month removed from his senior prom, Garnett, the most highly recruited high school player of all-time, was about to become a superstar in the Land of 10,000 Lakes. But drafting a 19-year-old was no easy task. The nay-sayers were out in force, and if the Wolves wanted to keep up any fan base at all, Garnett would have to deliver. The Minnesota fans were skeptical because few had ever seen the lad play, making him a real enigma. Garnett also carried some baggage with him that would raise some questions. The move from South Carolina his senior year to Chicago came in large part as a result of an incident in which he and several friends were charged with assaulting a student. His police record was later cleared, but there were many genuine concerns about Garnett's maturity, social skills, stamina, sense of responsibility, friends, and even his diet. He was more than a typical NBA "project," and he needed a lot of T.L.C. As one reporter put it, "People in Minnesota hear the word project, and they break out in a Luc Longley-sized rash." Over time Garnett would prove them all wrong though. Dead wrong.

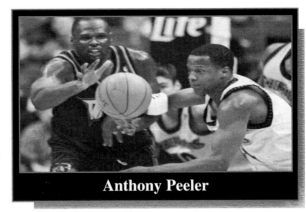
Anthony Peeler

Shortly thereafter Kevin was flown to Minneapolis for a press conference. The media was everywhere, as everyone was anxious to hear from the youngster who had quickly garnered the new nickname of "Da Kid." They wanted to hear from the man who was about to be awarded a fat three-year $5.6 million contract. As he sat proudly next to McHale, KG began to answer the seemingly endless array of questions from the onslaught of reporters. As McHale presented him with his new No. 21 jersey (ending any speculation that it was going to be retired due to the brilliant performance of its previous owner, Stacey King), Garnett just smiled proudly.

"Mr. McHale can give me a lot of good advice," said Garnett at the press conference. "Mr. McHale had a lot of success... in his day and age." McHale, now smiling, said: "I wish you'd left out that age part!"

"I'm not gonna rush nothing," added Garnett. "I'm not going to do anything I know I can't do. I can't wait to get in the gym with Mr. McHale, and learn some of those dazzling moves he has." He went on to add: "The one thing that bothers me is everybody thinking I just got into this without thinking it over. I thought about it a lot, and I think I'm ready."

Knowing that it was going to be a full-time job, developing and grooming the young player into his new surroundings, the Timberwolves took some steps to protect their investment. GM Flip Saunders called the steps "safety nets," and laid out the groundwork to ease his transition. He would suddenly go from playing less than 30 games to more than 90, and his new friends and colleagues were going to be 10 and even 20 years his elder. Culture shock was going to set in and teams knew that while he had amazing potential, there was also some serious baggage. Fame and fortune were going to change this kid, but determining just how much was the $5.6 million dollar question.

One of the biggest steps was going to be surrounding him with teammates which would help him grow and mature. They got scared when they heard Garnett's response to being asked whether he was looking forward to playing with the notorious Isaiah Rider, who had already gotten into his fair share of trouble with the team, as well as the law, over the years. "I really look up to J.R. and respect him as a player," said Garnett. When Coach Blair was asked about the comment he sarcastically replied: "We're gonna get him another role model..."

McHale and Saunders wanted to build the team around Garnett, and were well on their way to doing just that. Garnett was still pretty skinny at this point, and that off-season the Wolves got him on an extensive weight training program to put some meat on his bones. He would need to prepare for the pounding he was about to get by all of the wide-bodies in the NBA.

He reported to the team's training camp that summer with a lot of confidence and hit it off immediately with his new teammates. They loved his bubbly, energetic personality, and before long were treating him like just one of the guys. He bonded with his new friends and was excited about hitting the court against some real competition. Another key part of his learning curve came when McHale brought in both Terry Porter and Sam Mitchell, a pair of savvy NBA veterans, who would serve as mentors to Garnett in the locker room.

The Wolves were building for the future and, in 1995, big things were happening at the Target Center. Shortly after the season got underway, Coach Bill Blair was replaced by Saunders. Later in the season, McHale made a big trade, sending Christian Laettner and Center Sean Rooks to the Atlanta Hawks in exchange for Andrew Lang and Spud Webb. Laettner had been openly critical of Garnett's abilities and also his big contract, creating a level of animosity in the lockerroom. Wanting to finally create some good chemistry, McHale waved good-bye to Christian. With that, KG cracked the starting lineup, impressing everyone — especially Coach Saunders.

"He's the most versatile player in the game," said Flip. "He has the ability to defend anyone, and offensively, he can score, but he's also willing to pass."

Later, in March, in a game against Philadelphia, he tied the franchise rookie record with 19 rebounds. Then, three weeks later, he had a career-high 33 points against Boston. The Timberwolves even went 8-8 in March, marking only the second time in franchise history that the team had finished a month with a .500 or better record. Things were going well for the rookie. The Wolves finished strong that year, posting their second-best record ever at 26-56 — good enough for fifth in the Midwest Division. Garnett had emerged as a huge fan-favorite, making him one of Minnesota's biggest sports celebrities in just his first season. He averaged a modest 10.4 points, 6.3 rebounds and 1.8 assists per game that year and even broke Felton Spencer's club record for blocked shots in a season, with 131. For his efforts, he was named to the NBA's All-Rookie Team.

After the season Rider and all of his baggage were sent packing to the Portland Trailblazers in exchange for Guard James Robinson, Forward Bill Curley, and future considerations. An amazing athletic talent, Rider's strong personality proved to just be too much in the end. His run-ins with the law and his continued off-court problems were a constant distraction. From breaking team rules to missing team planes and meetings, Rider was seemingly always in the dog house. (Once, while arguing a technical foul with a referee, Rider was even joined on the court by his screaming mother, who had been sitting in a courtside seat!) By now the Wolves had weeded out the bad apples and hedged all their bets by rebuilding their team around Kevin Garnett.

That June, at the 1996 NBA draft, the Wolves were designated to pick fifth in the lottery. Now KG, who was pals with Georgia Tech Point Guard Stephon Marbury, really wanted McHale to draft him. The Milwaukee Bucks, however, who had the

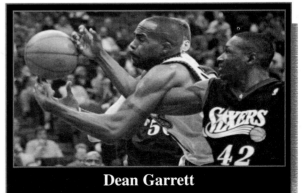
Dean Garrett

Kevin Garnett

Da Kid

On May 19, 1976, Kevin Maurice Garnett was born to O'Lewis McCullough and Shirley Garnett in Greenville, South Carolina. There Kevin quickly grew to love playing sports. He later moved to the town of Mauldin, just outside of Greenville, where, because he wasn't allowed to have a basketball hoop in the family driveway, he found himself spending most of his free time on the basketball courts at nearby Springfield Park.

By the time high school rolled around, Kevin was six-foot-seven. He desperately wanted to go out for the basketball team, but was concerned that his mom would think it would distract him from his studies in school. Kevin's mom, a practicing Jehovah's Witness, was a stern disciplinarian and wanted to make sure that her son got his education and then went on to college. He went ahead and tried out though, and stood out right away.

"I knew he was going to be very, very good even when he was a freshman," said Mauldin High School Coach James "Duke" Fisher. "He was a phenom right from the get-go. He showed so many amazing skills out on the basketball court that you could just tell that you were witnessing something special. Prior to that I knew nothing about him, so it was a real surprise for us as coaches to see this phenom just sort of appear out of thin air. I mean he had become a sort of playground legend I guess, but we knew nothing about him until he showed up for practice."

Garnett played hard during his freshman campaign for the Mauldin Mavericks and even worked his way into the starting lineup before the year was over. When it was all said and done, the center had averaged about 13 points, 14 rebounds and seven blocks per game. Pretty soon everybody knew who "KG" was, and he quickly became the big man on campus.

"Kevin absolutely worked his tail off that summer and came into that next season more determined than ever," said Coach Fisher. "That year he became our team's leader on and off the court. He would leave our practice and then head to the playground to practice again, he became obsessed with improving his game and with winning."

After that season, Kevin got a phone call from a kid in Brooklyn, New York. The 15-year-old kid, like Kevin, was also a prep basketball star. His name was Stephon Marbury, and he had heard a lot about Kevin from his high school all-star camp coaches. He figured that he had a lot in common with him and decided to just give him a call. The two hit it off right out of the gates and quickly became phone-buddies. They shared many of the same on and off-court problems, pressures and concerns, and found comfort in talking with each other. After a while Kevin's mom threatened to pull the plug, literally, on their long-distance phone calls — which by now were starting to cost a fortune. Kevin even got a job at the local Burger King just to help pay for the phone bills.

Marbury wanted Kevin to come to New York that summer to play with him in an all-star camp, but Mrs. Garnett wasn't too keen on her son going off alone to the Big Apple. Kevin did, however, play on a couple of local teams in South Carolina, and also got to go to Chicago to play in an All-Star camp as well. His experiences there with Coach William Nelson made a lasting impression.

By Kevin's junior year the media and the recruiters were everywhere, following his every move. Little kids even hounded him for autographs, he was the town's biggest celebrity. On the basketball court Kevin really stepped it up a notch during his junior year. By now tickets to Mauldin Mavericks' games were sell-outs, and fans treated him like a rock star. They even crowded into the hallways around the gymnasium just to listen to the games and be close to the action. Kevin handled the pressure as best as he could though, and emerged as one of the nation's elite prep players.

"Coaches from around the nation were knocking on my door to take a look at Kevin," said Coach Fisher, "it was a real circus. You name it and they were there: UNLV, Connecticut, Cincinnati, Michigan, North Carolina, North Carolina State, South Carolina, and on and on and on. They all knew that he was going to be the next great one."

Garnett averaged 27 points, 17 rebounds and seven blocks per game during his junior campaign, and for his efforts was named as Mr. Basketball South Carolina. By now, Kevin was sitting on top of the world. Surely no one could've ever imagined that it would be his last game ever in a Mauldin Mavericks uniform. An unfortunate incident would lie ahead that would forever change KG's life.

You see, on a typical Spring day later that May, a fight broke out at the high school. Several kids were involved in the brawl, and when it was all said and done, a couple of black students were hurt and a white student broke his ankle. Garnett, who was just walking by when the fight broke out, somehow got accused of being one of the instigators. Despite maintaining that he was merely an innocent bystander in the whole mess, he was now right in the middle of a full-blown racial incident. Some of the kids who were at the scene even proclaimed that Garnett was involved in the fight, and it became his word against theirs. At nearly seven-feet tall, I guess Kevin was easy to pick out of the crowd.

Like it or not, he was being charged with "second-degree lynching," a charge that in the South Carolina judicial system translated into simple assault. Shortly thereafter, his arrest made all of the local newspaper headlines. Luckily though, after a brief stay at the police station, Kevin and the four other boys who had been arrested, were merely ordered to participate in an intervention program and the charges against them were dropped.

After the incident, Kevin felt like his teachers were treating him differently. Once an icon, he sadly began to feel like an outsider who had been badly betrayed. Meanwhile, his mother was upset about her son being involved with the police and also about his slumping grades. She knew that there needed to be a change, and it needed to be sooner than later.

That summer Kevin headed back to Chicago to play in a Nike All-Star basketball camp. There, he played and studied under the tutelage of Coach William Nelson, a math teacher and Head Coach at Farragut Academy, a public school in suburban Chicago. Farragut was a basketball powerhouse in the Windy City, and Kevin knew that he could learn a lot from the coach Nelson. The two hit it off that summer, and Kevin stepped up his game to an even higher level.

"My first impression of Kevin could be described in one word: skinny," said Coach Nelson jokingly. "He must have only been about 200 pounds when I first met him at summer camp. But he was raw and had so much talent and energy. I knew right away that he was going to be special."

Kevin confided in the coach, and revealed to him that he and his mother thought that a change of scenery might be in his best interests. Nelson passionately agreed, and conferred with Kevin's mom that her son would be far better off playing in such a marquis high school program. He insisted that he could work with Kevin both on the court and in the classroom, to make sure that he would be able to get a college scholarship and one day maybe even have a chance at playing in the NBA.

When the camp was over Kevin and his mom discussed their options. He told her that he wanted to move to Chicago, but was also interested in going to New York, to play with his new friend, Stephon Marbury, at Brooklyn's Lincoln High School. Convinced that Kevin needed more discipline in his academics and less distractions, she decided that Chicago would be a better move. Now, all that was left to do was to tell everyone back at Mauldin High School that their superstar was transferring to Illinois for his senior year. It wasn't going to be easy.

With that, Kevin, his mom Shirley, who was now separated from her husband, and his younger sister, Ashley, packed up, said their good-bye's and headed north. It wasn't going to be an easy move, that was for sure. Moving from the rural and scenic rolling hills of South Carolina to the harsh inner city of Chicago's west-side was going to be an adjustment to say the least.

Once there, the three rented a one bedroom apartment on the 12th floor of a complex on Ashland Avenue, right across from the University of Illinois at Chicago Medical Center. And, even though they didn't know anyone once they got there, they did take comfort in knowing one neighbor, Coach Nelson, who also lived in the same apartment building. To support her family, Shirley began working two jobs — both at a pharmaceutical company and also at a housing development management office. The cost of living was much higher in Chicago, and Kevin's mom was making the ultimate sacrifice for her son to be able to pursue his dreams.

Kevin also soon found that he couldn't just go outside like before and shoot hoops in the neighborhood. Crime, gangs and guns were all prevalent in the area surrounding his new home, making for a tough situation. Night games, which were part of his life down in Mauldin, were now out of the question. The local gyms were also overcrowded with all of the other kids who wanted to play, so court-time now became a precious commodity. As a result, Coach Nelson sometimes drove him to community college gyms to play. There he could also battle with kids much bigger and older to toughen him up.

Soon Kevin started school at Farragut Academy, where he looked forward to learning the game under the tutelage of Coach Nelson. There, the coach was able to teach his new prodigy a more physically demanding style of basketball than he had been used to down in South Carolina. The prep competition was fierce in the Chicago area, with many kids going on to the ranks of Division One basketball year in and year out.

"As a coach I had to ask myself 'what can I do to help him?'," said Nelson. "It was pretty obvious that he was already going to help my team. So, I took it upon myself to toughen him up and try to improve on his toughness down in the paint. To get him ready, I brought in some big football players to bang him around underneath the basket. I mean there were no seven-footers around to challenge him, so this was the next best thing I guess."

The Farragut Admirals were a basketball power in the Windy City, and Kevin was poised to help lead his new team to the state championship. He wasted little time in making a name for himself either. The team got off to a quick start and Kevin stepped up his game to an entirely different level. People were amazed at his ability to run the floor with such speed and grace and at how well he could dribble and pass the ball. For a big man he was unlike anything they had ever seen. Kevin, who had now grown to six-foot-eleven, could absolutely do it all. Sometimes the big center played like a much smaller point guard, bringing the ball up the court through traffic, while at other times he played like a small forward, draining three-pointers from well beyond the arc. He could also play like a power forward as well, cleaning up the boards like a rebounding machine.

The Wolves' "Alpha-Male"

He was the complete package, and before long everyone was coming out to see this phenom. TV stations started to follow the team, and highlights of Farragut's games were shown not only on the local Chicago channels, but often-times on national sports shows, like ESPN, as well. Pretty soon pro scouts were coming to their games, and rumors began to circulate that this kid might even be ready for the NBA. He quickly became the most famous prep player in the country.

"It didn't take me long to figure out that I needed to let the offense revolve around Kevin," said Nelson. "He was so versatile and such a dominant player, that it didn't take long for him to become the most feared player in the country that year. His reputation grew pretty quickly and when we started to see all of the scouts at our games, we knew that he had the potential to be playing in the pro's that next year."

Back on the home-front, Kevin, his mom and sister, were slowly adjusting. It wasn't easy. Their car was stolen on more than one occasion and money was tight. But they hung in there and made the best of it. "Bug," his best friend from back home came up to say hello from South Carolina, and Stephon Marbury also came to town to visit as well. When he and Kevin finally met it was like magic. They immediately headed for the nearest basketball court and put on a show like no one had seen before. It was amazing. They were hitting on perfectly timed no-look alley-oop slam-dunks, and playing like they were seasoned NBA veterans. Their chemistry and timing was incredible, and they knew that had something special. They both had a blast and spent the rest of the day dreaming about one day playing with each other on the same team in the NBA.

The Admirals continued to play well that season, and were even projected as the odds-on favorites to win the Illinois state title. Unfortunately though, in the latter part of the season, the team's star guard, Ronnie Fields, was injured in a car accident, ending his season prematurely. With Ronnie out, Kevin was now constantly double and triple teamed down the stretch run. Garnett, normally a very unselfish player, was now being asked to do it all by his coaches. It was too much though, and Farragut, which had posted a stellar 28-2 record, was upset in the state tournament quarterfinals.

It was a disappointing way to end an otherwise spectacular senior season. His unbelievable stats of 26 points, 18 rebounds, 7 assists, and 7 blocked shots per game, as well as his gaudy .666% shooting percentage, were good enough to land him the title of "Mr. Basketball Illinois" though. And if that weren't enough he was also named as the National Player of the Year by USA Today, as well as being named as a member of Parade Magazine's prestigious First Team All-American squad.

Then, after the season, Garnett, whose four-year high school basketball totals included: 2,533 points, 1,807 rebounds and 739 blocked shots, was named the Most Outstanding Player of the McDonald's All-America Game. There, against the nations best college prospects, he posted 18 points, 11 rebounds, 4 assists and 3 blocked shots. The nationally televised game earned Garnett an NBA "sure thing" reputation among the scouts and recruiters, a label that was almost unheard of for a kid his age.

At that point, not knowing whether or not if he had passed his final attempt on the ACT, Kevin weighed his options for one last time. If he failed to score high enough on his entrance exams he figured he could always go to a college as a "Proposition 48" student. That meant that he would simply have to sit out his freshman season, being allowed to play if and when he passed the test. But, the two schools he had supposedly narrowed it down to, either the University of Michigan or University of North Carolina, were very expensive, and without a scholarship, he didn't know if he could even afford to go. Another avenue was the junior college route where he could play basketball immediately, and then transfer to a major college when he passed his test for his sophomore year. But, if he got injured, it could all be over in a heartbeat.

The only other option was to do the unthinkable: skip college altogether and declare himself eligible for the 1995 NBA draft. Could it be possible for an 18-year old kid to make the jump to the big-time without any seasoning at the collegiate ranks? After all, there hadn't been a player in more than 20 years to go directly from high school to the NBA. It proved to be great drama, and everyone in the world of sports quickly ate it up. Everyone — except the NBA that was.

"If it were up to us, we'd prefer not to see someone come into the league at that tender age, but the courts say otherwise," said NBA Deputy Commissioner Russ Granik, who didn't want to see Garnett's move encourage an influx of future kids to declare themselves eligible for the draft instead of going to college.

That summer, after being selected to play on the USA Junior Select Team which won the 1995 Hoop Summit in Springfield, Mass., Kevin decided to roll the dice and enter the draft. Many pre-draft predictions had him projected to be an early first round pick, and that was enough to give him the confidence he needed to take such a big step. He had also talked about it extensively with his mother, coach and friends, and they all supported his decision as well. His buddy Stephon, who had scored well on his ACT, was also highly recruited and ultimately decided to attend Georgia Tech University, which had one of the nation's premier college basketball programs. He knew that Kevin was a special talent, and also supported his decision to go pro.

Kevin then hired an agent and filled out the necessary paperwork. Incredibly, just a few days before the June draft, Kevin learned that he had finally passed the ACT. After all that, he was now eligible for a scholarship to the college of his choice. But, it was too late though, because Mr. Garnett had already made up his mind to go pro. He was about to make history.

Kevin worked hard that Spring to get into game shape. He knew that he was about to boldly go where just a handful of young men had dared go before him — the trek to the NBA directly from high school. In fact, prior to KG there had only really been four players that had successfully made the transition from high school directly to the NBA: Moses Malone in 1974, Darryl Dawkins and Bill Willoughby in 1975, and Shawn Kemp in 1989 (who did actually attend a year of college). At the same time, Sports Illustrated fed the media frenzy by featuring Garnett on their cover with the headline: "Ready or Not."

"Wherever I go, it'll be an opportunity," said Garnett. "Millions of kids want to play pro basketball, and here I am getting the chance early. I learned one thing though, never hate a positive option."

On the other side of the aisle were the NBA teams themselves, who found the entire Garnett situation to be nerve-racking to say the least. On one hand they knew that the kid had the potential to be a franchise player. But on the other hand they also knew that he might be a bust, and they could come out of the draft with a "project" which could set them back for years. The teams' general managers and executives, the ones who were responsible for drafting players, knew that taking an unproven 19-year-old was not going to be easy.

One of those executives was former Boston Celtic's Hall of Fame Forward Kevin McHale, who, after retiring from the NBA, was now in charge of turning the Minnesota Timberwolves into winners. Minnesota, which entered the league as an expansion team back in 1989, had been a perennial doormat in the league, and McHale knew that he needed to get his franchise back on the winning track in order to get the fans back into the seats. The club finished the 1994 season with a dismal 20-62 record, and needed to take some chances — it was safe to say that they were desperate. There was a lot of pressure on McHale, who would be selecting the fifth overall "lottery" pick in the draft, to turn their program into a winning tradition, and he knew that he needed to select a player who was going to help them accomplish those lofty goals.

The word on Garnett come draft day was that he was a 6'11" beanpole with terrific all-around talent. Sports Illustrated even went as far as saying that he just might be the best athlete in the draft. He was described as a cross between Indiana Guard Reggie Miller and a kinder, gentler version of Miami Center Alonzo Mourning. He could run, leap like crazy, block shots, monster-dunk, handle the ball like a guard, and shoot 20-footers with ease. He represented the most elusive of all commodities for the league's bottom-feeder's, and that was hope. Some members of the media even hyped him up as a "savior," while others quickly tabbed him as the "next Michael Jordan."

There were genuine concerns though about his maturity, social skills, stamina, sense of responsibility, friends, and even his diet. They were also worried about how long it was going to take him to fill out his six-foot-eleven frame. At just 220 pounds, he was tiny by NBA big-man standards. He was more than a typical NBA "project" though and prospective GM's knew that this kid was going to need a lot of T.L.C. Whoever selected him was going to have to realize that he was going to need supervision in nearly every aspect of his life both on and off the court. He would suddenly go from playing less than 30 games to more than 90, and his new friends and colleagues were going to be 10 and even 20 years his elder. Culture shock was going to set in and teams knew that while he had amazing potential, there was also some serious baggage. Fame and fortune were going to change this kid, but determining just how much was the million dollar question.

Finally, on June 28, 1995, in Toronto's SkyDome, with the eyes of the sports world upon him, Kevin Garnett sat patiently amongst the nation's top collegiate players

Howlin' Wolf

who were all waiting to see where they would be drafted. The wait was agonizing as NBA Commissioner David Stern slowly introduced the lottery picks. First went Joe Smith, to Golden State, then Jerry Stackhouse, to Philly, followed by Antonio McDyess, who was taken by the L.A. Clippers, and Rasheed Wallace, who was next taken by Washington. Minnesota was up next, and to Kevin's surprise, Commissioner Stern calmly announced that the Timberwolves had indeed selected him with their pick. The crowd went wild as Kevin grinned from ear to ear.

He then stood up, hugged his family and friends who were with him, and proudly walked up to the podium to shake the hands of both Commissioner Stern and his new boss, Kevin McHale. When McHale presented Kevin with his brand new No. 21 jersey, Kevin had to pinch himself to make sure it all wasn't just a dream. He had done it. Less than a month removed from his senior prom, he had officially made it to the NBA. He was going to be a millionaire.

The reaction back in Minnesota was mixed. While most were ecstatic, and others just willing to withhold judgement about their new prize until they could see him out on the hardcourt, others were downright skeptical. Everyone was anxious to see what this kid could do though, and the expectations were at an all-time high. It also seemed like everybody had an opinion on the situation as well.

"Is he a franchise player?" retorted (then) Timberwolves Head Coach Bill Blair at a press conference. "I can't say that but this kid does some things that excite you. From a maturity level? No way he can be ready. He's not ready for the airplanes, the four games in six days, and for the free time he's now possessing. Those things we have to help him with. You just hope he's so interested in basketball, you hope he wants to be the best player in the league."

Shortly thereafter Kevin was flown to Minneapolis for a press conference. The media was everywhere, as everyone was anxious to hear from the youngster who had quickly garnered the new nickname of "Da Kid." They wanted to hear from the man who was about to be awarded a fat three-year $5.6 million contract. As he sat proudly next to McHale, KG began to answer the seemingly endless array of questions from the onslaught of reporters.

"I'm not gonna rush nothing," said Garnett of his outlook on the upcoming season. "I'm not going to do anything I know I can't do. I can't wait to get in the gym with Mr. McHale, and learn some of those dazzling moves he has. Mr. McHale can also give me a lot of good advice. Mr. McHale had a lot of success in his day and age."

McHale, now smiling, said: "I wish you'd left out that age part! Garnett is a basketball junkie," he added. "He's the kind of guy we'll have to chase off the court, rather than worry he's not spending enough time on it."

"The one thing that bothers me is everybody thinking I just got into this without thinking it over," Garnett went on to say. "I thought about it a lot, and I think I'm ready."

The T-Wolves, knowing that it was going to be a full-time job developing and grooming their budding new superstar into his new surroundings, took some steps to protect their investment. Kevin also decided to have his best friend Bug move in with him into his two-bedroom apartment, along with three dogs as well. In fact, many of his friends from the "OBF" (Kevin's posse, which he called the Original Block Family) back home would come to stay with him for long periods of time in Minnesota. Kevin was very close to his friends, and they would serve a vital role in his transition into his new surroundings. The Wolves understood this and later would occasionally even allow some of them to travel with Kevin to certain road games on the team airplane, just to make him feel more comfortable.

From there he has just been amazing. In his six NBA seasons he has averaged 18.5 points, 9.5 rebounds, 3.9 assists and 1.8 blocks per game, while also amassing the longest current streak of double figure games in the league at 210 straight games. In addition, he ranked #3 in the NBA in 2001 for double-doubles, with 54. A perennial All-Star, he is among the league's very best all-around players.

Full of high octane energy and high flying slam dunks, Kevin Garnett has become the prototypical NBA forward. He is seven-feet tall, but plays like a point guard. Just what makes this kid the game's preeminent player? He is the rarest of big men with an incredible array of skills who just might very well be the most complete all-around player in the league. He is also a fun-loving kid, raw with passion and emotion, and full of charm and wit — something that has made him one of the game's most endeared athletes of all-time. The fans love him and watch with awe as he carries the future hopes of the T-Wolves in his every leap.

Technically speaking, Garnett is a freak of nature. He has fabulous running ability, stamina and agility. He can play like a small forward, yet can be just as dominant in the post-up game underneath the basket. He can also handle the ball, pass off the dribble and shoot from the perimeter. Defensively, he is a perfectionist who can rebound like an animal, block shots, and guard much quicker players who are half his size. He is truly the complete package. He is unselfish and exemplifies the term "team player." In just six short seasons this top dog has earned the nicknames of the "Big Ticket" as well as "The Franchise" — and make no mistake about it, he is the "alpha male" on this team.

Even if Kevin Garnett wasn't paid a cent, he would probably still be out shooting hoops somewhere just for the fun of it — probably well into the night. Basketball is his obsession, as well as his escape, and he has never forgotten where he came from. In fact, KG has brought his posse, the "OBF" into both his personal and professional life. So down to earth is Garnett that he has even put many of his family members and friends on the payroll. They stay with him at his new home and he treats them like family. He is an incredibly generous person and his friends adore him for his kindness.

The OBF has big plans, including the launching of a premium line of urban-inspired men's apparel and accessories, appropriately called "OBF by Kevin Garnett." The business is even talking about the development of a Fox-TV comedy sitcom loosely based on the group's interactions with an NBA superstar. The group also manages Kevin's daily affairs and helps to coordinate his many endorsement deals, his business meetings, his fan-club mail and his TV appearances.

The group also helps to coordinate his summer basketball camps, his charities and his random acts of kindness — like when he gives away coats to underprivileged kids or rents suites at the Target Center so young cancer patients can see Wolves' games in person. He even had his old hometown playground court at Springfield Park resurfaced and renovated for all of the kids in the neighborhood to enjoy. (The dedication of the park was even marked by the untying of a giant shoelace along with several free cookouts that Kevin arranged.)

The OBF even attends to his fleet of snowmobiles, go-karts, and sports cars (Bug's favorite is a canary-yellow Range Rover nicknamed "the bus"), as well as his nine dogs at his palatial home in suburban Minnetonka, just outside of Minneapolis. The OBF provides Garnett with a support system that has kept him out of trouble and well on his way to being a world class role-model to countless kids everywhere. Kevin even rewards his group at the end of every season when "Operation Go-Hard" kicks in. That's when they all go on vacation together to places like Australia, Japan or Las Vegas to enjoy the sites and just have fun together.

Kevin is also bettering himself as a person. He has vowed to one day obtain a college degree, and has also enrolled for a business-correspondence course through the University of Minnesota. He has become computer savvy, enjoys the internet and even studies the stock market.

"I think I've changed, but the one thing I've always tried to be is myself," said Garnett in an SI article. "I think people respect a genuine person. I think I've become more of a leader. I think I've become more hungry about basketball and wanting to win. I think I've become more direct with people. I think we all change as we get responsibility, as we grow."

Overall, Garnett has accepted the responsibility of being the leader of the Timberwolves and hopes to pass along his passion and commitment for winning on to his teammates. That mentality, along with his diligent work ethic, has won him the respect of his teammates and adoration of his fans. He gives great interviews to the media, never shies away from giving an autograph and shows great respect to his teammates, opponents, and even the referees. His sportsmanship both on and off the court have become the standard for all kids to look up to. From his "poster-dunks" to his wonderful boyish smile, the 6'11" forward (who is actually about seven-foot-one now, but doesn't want to be known as a seven-footer) is the real deal. Fans seem to live vicariously through him on the hardcourt, while his teammates seem to just be in awe of him.

"This is an iffy league," said Garnett in a USA Today article. "Today you can be sunshine, and tomorrow you can be rain. I just do the best I can. I'm the product of an environment. I'm a player just like anybody else. My goal is to bring this franchise a championship, and I can best do that by playing to have fun and by playing to win. Every night I try to make the fans and management understand that they have something special here, and I'm going to give everything I have, whether I'm feeling great or have a 102-degree temperature. I might be limping, but as long as I can run, I'm with you. That's just the way I was brought up — to have loyalty and respect for the game."

In the six years before Garnett arrived, Minnesota had never won more than 29 games and they were the only team in NBA history to lose at least 60 games in four straight seasons. Since his arrival, the Wolves are a perennial playoff team poised on taking the next step into the world of NBA champions. Leading the charge will no doubt be No. 21, who, no matter how old he is, will always be "Da Kid!"

fourth pick in the draft, selected Marbury, and forced McHale to do some wheeling and dealing. The Wolves then took Connecticut Guard Ray Allen and promptly turned around and offered the Bucks both Allen and a future number one draft pick in exchange for Marbury. They agreed and the T-Wolves now had the "perfect compliment" to Garnett. Throw in Gugliotta, and these kids had the potential to make it big-time.

When the season got underway that year, there was a renewed sense of optimism in Minnesota. Never before had the team looked so promising and the fans could sense that they were witnessing something special. With KG and Gugliotta hitting the floor at the forward posts and "Steph" running the offense from the point, the team got off to a fast start by winning its first three home games. Kevin also brought something to the team that it had never had before, a sense of fun out on the court. Even though he was a fierce competitor, he was smiling and seemingly having a ball during the games. He and Marbury were hooking up on alley-oop slam dunks and the fans were loving every minute of it.

There were several highlights throughout the season. One of which came in mid-December when Wolves went on their best "hot-streak" in franchise history, riding an 8-2 wave. Over that stretch they knocked off three straight playoff opponents starting with Shaq and the Lakers, 103-88, led by Garnett's 23 points; followed by Marbury's 33-point, 8-assist effort in a 107-98 victory over Utah; finalized with a 16-point comeback rally to beat the Knicks, 88-80.

Terrell Brandon

Marbury was hot. So hot that he was named as the NBA Rookie of the Month for January, averaging 16.9 points, 8.1 assists and 2.1 steals, en route to leading the Timberwolves to a 9-6 record. Then, on February 21st Garnett had an unofficial coming out party in a 120-101 home upset of the two-time defending champion Houston Rockets. Garnett dominated the second half by tallying 17 points and grabbing 12 rebounds en route to sparking a 15-2 Minnesota run. Said Tom Gugliotta after the game: "It was the best performance I've ever seen from a teammate."

At midseason the Wolves were all the buzz of the NBA and to top it off, KG and Googs were invited to play in the NBA All-Star Game — the first two players in franchise history ever to be so honored. By April the T-Wolves were shooting for their first-ever trip to the post-season, and Kevin was leading the charge. They beat some solid teams down the home stretch including, Milwaukee, 122-112, on April 18th to make it to an impressive 40 wins. With that they had secured their best-ever record, and a much deserved trip to the playoffs.

The players were ecstatic about being in their first-ever playoff series, but knew that they would have their hands full against their first round opponents, the top-ranked Houston Rockets. Led by All-Stars Charles Barkley, Clyde Drexler and Hakeem Olajuwon, the Rockets came out tough and won the first two games in Houston, 112-95 and 96-84. Highlighting the action was a brief skirmish which broke out between Houston thug Kevin Willis and Minnesota's classy veteran, Sam Mitchell. After enduring several cheap shots from Willis throughout the first two contests, Mitchell finally went after him before having to be restrained by his teammates. And, although he was ejected, Mitchell had sent a clear message to the rest of the league that this young team wasn't going to be pushed around.

Down two games to none the Wolves hung tough though. They came home to face the Rockets in front of a packed house at the Target Center, featuring more than 19,000 home-town fans going wild. Minnesota came out strong in the game, matching the Rockets point for point throughout the game. It was 59-59 at the half, and then 81-81 after the third. Garnett kept the Wolves in the game, and even led them to a one-point lead late in the contest on a nice jumper from the top of the key. Center Dean Garrett, the league's oldest rookie at age 31, also played great by scoring 26 points and 15 rebounds against Hakeem Olajuwon. It was too little too late though, as Clyde Drexler and Sir Charles took over down the stretch to lead the Rockets past the T-Wolves, 125-120, and sweep the three-game series. After the game, Barkley even huddled with Garnett and Marbury out on the court, commending them on a great series and assuring them that their day would come.

It was a tough loss for Minnesota, but they knew that they had the nucleus of a great team in Garnett, who averaged 17 points and 8 rebounds per game, Marbury, who averaged 16 points and 8 assists, and Gugliotta, who netted 21 points and 9 boards as well. In addition, Garnett led the team in minutes played, showing his durability and world-class conditioning. Just how good was he? After the season, a poll of NBA coaches and GMs asked who they thought was going to be the star player of the next decade. Garnett was their overwhelming choice.

The 1997-98 Wolves came out of the gates with a new look. Literally. That's because they unveiled a new logo and new uniforms that year, going this time with the trés chic black on black, with a hint of green-look. Gone was the timid Siberian Husky puppy logo and in was an in-your-face psycho wolf that looked like he wanted to devour your children. This new-look team was mean, and meant business.

That season was also a pivotal one off the court as well because Kevin Garnett was forced to decide what he wanted to do for the long-term of his future. You see, Kevin's three-year contract was in its final season, and under its terms he could either play his third year with the Timberwolves, and then simply go to whatever team would pay him the most money as a free-agent, or he could sign a long-term contract with Minnesota. It was a hairy situation that summer in Minnie as Kevin showed the world that he had a poker-face. Timberwolves Owner Glen Taylor did not want to risk losing his star player, but also knew that he only had so much money to spend as well. What transpired was history in the making, literally.

That July, Taylor offered Garnett a contract worth more than $103 million over six years. Garnett's agent, Eric Fleisher, who also represented Stephon Marbury, scoffed at the offer, even telling the people of Minnesota that his client would definitely not be back with the team when his contract was up that next season. Many, many Minnesotans were outraged, and it

Wally Szczerbiak

An All-American at Miami of Ohio who ranked third in the country in scoring his senior season with 24.2 points per game, Wally Szczerbiak was also a member of the 1998 USA Basketball Goodwill Games team that captured the gold medal — averaging a team-high 17.2 ppg. The first-round draft pick of the Wolves has some pretty good basketball lineage in his family as well. His father, Walt, played professionally for the Pittsburgh Condors of the ABA and for Real Madrid in Spain. Wally has emerged as one of the game's top up and coming players, and will only get better as he matures and develops.

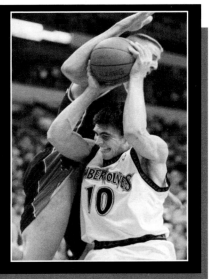

LaPhonso Ellis

sparked a national debate across the country. Garnett's agent held firm though, and shortly thereafter the two sides announced that they had signed an unbelievable six-year $126 million contract, which averaged nearly $21 million per season. It was the single-largest contract in sports history — fully four times the amount that the team's original owners, Marv Wolfenson and Harvey Rattner, paid for the franchise back in 1987 — $32.5 million. It was safe to assume that after signing the deal Kevin's identity changed from "Da Kid" to "Da Franchise."

"Kevin Garnett is a great kid," said McHale. "He is a tremendous, tremendous young man. I really like him, and I think he is going to go down as one of the all-time really great NBA players. He just has a love of the game and he plays it with such a sense of enjoyment. He is truly a unique kid, and I think we're really fortunate here in Minnesota to have him."

"The fact is, if we had let Kevin play this season, there were teams out there who were willing to pay that type of money," added McHale. "We couldn't afford to be like Orlando. They lost Shaq (O'Neal – to free agency), and you don't recover easily from something like that."

For KG, who just wanted to get it all over with and get back to playing basketball, he was glad it was finally all over. He knew that a lot of people were disgusted that a 21-year-old kid was going to make more in one game than many of them would make in a lifetime. He needed to get past it.

"I'm happy to be here and I'm glad it's over," said Garnett modestly. "I was going to play like KG whether I was playing for a dollar or for three quadrillion. It wasn't a money issue."

Kevin also knew that a lot of other players in the league would be envious and downright resentful of his fat contract — players who had won championships and had paid their dues through the years. That made him work even harder. By the time the season began Kevin was a full-fledged superstar in the world of sports. He was starring in Nike sneaker commercials, endorsing countless products and making a real name for himself. He was also a role-model for millions of kids everywhere, something he really enjoyed. He didn't drink, didn't smoke and didn't do drugs, so he had no problem with kids looking up to him.

"He's so mature, it's scary," said NBA TV analyst David Aldridge. "For a guy to be the first to come out of high school in 20 years and be successful living 1,000 miles away from home, then sign the richest contract and still not get into any trouble, shows great maturity and class. He was obviously raised well."

The season kicked off with expectations yet again running high in Minnesota. Now that their T-Wolves had tasted the fruits of the postseason, they wanted their squad to make a run at the title. The team started out red-hot, opening the season with an 11-14 record, and going on to win 14 of its next 16 games. On Dec. 23rd Minnesota won 112-103 at Seattle to end a streak of 26 straight losses to the Sonics, fueled by Marbury's team-record eight three-pointers and 35 points. That next week Michael Jordan and the world champion Chicago Bulls finally fell to the Wolves, ending a 16-game losing streak against Chicago — the last team Minnesota had yet to beat. In front of a standing-room only crowd of 20,097, the T-Wolves came back from six down at the half behind Googs and Steph, each of whom tallied 23 points in the 99-95 win. Marbury concluded the climactic ending as he intercepted Chicago's last gasp inbound pass, before hurling the ball into the stands and rolling on the court — even kissing the center court team logo.

That February long-time Timberwolf Doug West was dealt to Vancouver in exchange for Anthony Peeler, who had his career resurrected in Minnesota — averaging a much-needed 13 points off the bench in 30 games with the team. Later that month Garnett was voted by the fans to start in the 1998 All-Star Game, the first time a Minnesota player had received such an honor. He didn't disappoint either, scoring 12 points and 4 rebounds in the contest, which was held in New York Cities' Madison Square Garden.

Garnett's national exposure at the All-Star Game fueled a second-half explosion of productivity. Some of his highlights included: posting 25 points, 17 rebounds and 4 assists in a 100-95 overtime victory over the Houston Rockets on February 20th; hitting the game-winning jumper with 1.2 seconds left, registering 26 points, 12 rebounds and 7 assists, in a 115-113 double-overtime win over the Detroit Pistons on March 1st; and tallying a season-high 32 points, while adding 14 rebounds, 6 assists and 4 steals, in a 104-96 victory over the Sacramento Kings on March 29th.

Then, the Wolves were struck with some horrible news when Tom Gugliotta suffered a season-ending ankle injury. Without Googs, and his 20.1 points and 8.7 rebounds in the lineup, Minnesota fell into an 8-15 tailspin. Garnett was now double-teamed virtually every time he touched the ball. He hung in there though, and at times carried the team on his back down the homestretch. On April 7th he garnered team-highs of 27 points, 14 rebounds, 4 blocked shots and 3 assists in a 92-89 win over the Miami Heat. He then followed that up with a 26-point, 16-rebound performance in a 107-102 win over the Philadelphia 76ers just three days later.

Joe Smith

Minnesota finished with 12 wins in their final 16 games to earn the seventh seed in the Western Conference playoffs. With that, the T-Wolves had made the playoffs for the second straight year, improving to a 45-37 record. This time they would face the heavily favored Seattle SuperSonics, who were led by their fiery point guard, Gary Payton. The best-of-three series opened in Seattle, and despite KG's 18 points and 18 rebounds, the Wolves got crushed by the final score of 108-83.

Game Two was a whole other ball game though as Stephon Marbury played like a champ, dumping in 25 points, while Terry Porter added 21 and Anthony Peeler chipped in 14 rebounds, as the Wolves evened up the series at one game apiece, 97-93. Nearly a decade after its inception, the team finally had its first-ever playoff victory. Saunders had tactically decided to go with a smaller, quicker lineup for the game and it paid off in spades. But, without their three big men: Tom Gugliotta, Stanley Roberts and Cherokee Parks, who were all injured, the team knew it had to be sharp.

Game Three was held at the friendly confines of the Target Center and it was a memorable one. What started with future Minnesota Governor Jesse Ventura rapelling from the rafters, concluded with a monstrous Kevin Garnett dunk that sent shock waves through the arena. KG, who scored 19 points, grabbed 8 rebounds, had 6 assists and blocked 3 shots, led a 31-18 point charge in the fourth quarter as Minnesota made history with its first home playoff win, 98-90. Anthony Peeler was also red-hot, scorching the Sonics for four three-pointers, while veterans Sam Mitchell and Terry Porter added 19 and 18, respectively, as well.

Seattle, on the brink of elimination, rallied in Game Four though, despite Garnett's 20 points and 10 rebounds, to win by the final of 92-88. Now, with the series tied at two-two, Game Five headed back to Seattle. There, seldom used Guard Reggie Jordan banked in a long three-pointer to give Minnesota an early lead at the end of the first quarter. Anthony Peeler lit it up in the first half by hitting five of six three pointers, and even jammed home a hellacious baseline dunk en route to a 29-point effort. But Minnesota's depleted bench couldn't answer the call down the stretch, as the experienced Sonics pulled away late, 97-84, to win the opening round playoff series. Garnett, who had scored in double figures in 86 straight games, let his emotions get to him in the big game and simply got frustrated, scoring just seven points while committing a costly 10 turnovers. It was an ugly way to end an otherwise promising season.

The upcoming 1998-99 season came to a screeching halt before it even started. You see, because of the escalating salaries that the players were demanding (particularly that of Garnett), the NBA owners decided to lock-out their players in an attempt to create a much-needed salary cap. The cap would ensure that all of the teams had the same amount of money to spend on their rosters, thus creating a sense of financial parody in the league. The players were opposed to the lock-out, but in the end, the two sides came together after a two month work-stoppage in an attempt to do what was best for the league. (Translation: They knew the fans were getting angry, so they settled!)

However, under the new system teams had to keep their payrolls in check. So, if they paid one player a lot of money, like KG, they would have less to pay the others. Such was the case with Wolves' stars Gugliotta and Marbury. McHale and Taylor were worried about being able to afford the contracts of the pair, which were almost up. They knew that they only had so much money to offer them under the new arrangement, and that they could leave as free-agents to sign elsewhere if they wanted.

Googs, who was disappointed with his situation in Minnesota as the "third option" behind KG and Steph, decided that it was time to go and promptly left to play for the Phoenix Suns. He even took several million less just to get out of town — a move that really ticked off

Flip Saunders

Born on February 23, 1955 in Cleveland, Ohio, Phil "Flip" Saunders went on to become an All-American Guard at Cuyahoga Heights High School in Cleveland. In his senior season, 1973, he was even named Ohio's Class A Player of the Year after averaging a state-high 32.0 points per game. From there Flip continued his basketball career at the University of Minnesota, where he started 101 of his 103 career contests and became one of the program's all-time biggest fan-favorites. As a senior, he teamed up with Kevin McHale to lead the Gophers to a then all-time school-best 24-3 record.

Upon graduation Saunders began his successful coaching career at Golden Valley Lutheran College, where he compiled a 92-13 record, including a perfect 56-0 mark at home, over four seasons. In 1981, he joined the coaching staff at the University of Minnesota, as an assistant, and helped coach the Golden Gophers to the 1982 Big Ten championship. After five seasons in Gold Country, Flip moved on to become an assistant coach at the University of Tulsa, where he worked for two seasons before heading off to coach in the Continental Basketball Association. In the CBA Saunders achieved an amazing record of coaching success. In fact, he still ranks third all-time in the league with 253 victories.

He began his pro career in 1988 with the Rapid City Thrillers, then moved on to the La Crosse Catbirds for five seasons, before coaching the Sioux Falls Skyforce for one year. (From 1991-94 he also served as GM and team president of the Catbirds.) Saunders' impressive coaching resume includes seven consecutive seasons of 30-or-more victories, two CBA championships (1990 & 1992), two CBA Coach of the Year honors (1989 & 1992) and 23 CBA-to-NBA player promotions.

In May of 1995 Flip got his big break when he was hired by his old pal, Kevin McHale, to serve as the Assistant GM of the Timberwolves. But his stay in the front-office was short-lived though, because just six months later he replaced Bill Blair as the team's head coach. Since then Saunders has been instrumental in developing young talent and also in changing in the team's attitude both on and off the court. In his first full season as the team's head coach, 1996-97, Saunders became the all-time winningest coach in franchise history, leading the team to a then all-time best record of 40-42 and its first-ever playoff appearance. He has since led the club to five consecutive post-season appearances and is well on his way to leading the team to an NBA championship.

With an overall record of 227-213, Flip, who recently signed a five-year $20 million contract extension in the summer of 2001, currently resides in the Twin Cities with his wife, Debbie, and their four children.

When recently asked how he would describe his coaching style, Saunders happily replied: "It's a combination of things. It's some X's and O's, but I think it's really about understanding what players can and can't do. Getting them to maximize what they can do as far as reaching their potential and giving players enough rope to hang themselves. In situations both offensively and defensively, I'm more of teacher and let them carry out game plans. On game day, I'm more of a field general, fielding situations and adjusting on the fly more."

the fans. As a result, the Wolves were able to sign Forward Joe Smith to fill Gugliotta's spot. But, shortly thereafter, in a shocking move, Marbury decided that he too wasn't happy and wanted to play closer to his friends and family back in New York City. So, midway through the season the Timberwolves were forced to trade him to the New Jersey Nets in exchange for point guard Terrell Brandon and a future first-round draft pick. Ironically, both Googs and Steph opted to go elsewhere for much less money than was offered to them by Minnesota. (In the end, each of the players wanted to be the star of their own team, knowing that as long as KG was with the Wolves, he was going to always be the main attraction.)

The NBA played a shortened 50-game schedule that season, with the new-look Wolves again emerging as one of the elite teams in the Western Division. The team chemistry was totally different this season, as KG learned to play with his new teammates. He worked his magic though, and pulled the new group together. On January 17th he recorded 23 points, 9 rebounds and 9 assists, in a 116-102 victory over the Houston Rockets; followed by a 22-point, 19 rebound gem that beat the Sacramento Kings, 102-90, just a few days later. He then hit a milestone on March 9th when he scored his 4,000th career point, on a night which saw him tally 22 points, 16 rebounds, 6 assists and 4 blocked shots, in an 85-84 win over Seattle. For his efforts he was even named as the NBA Player of the Week.

The T-Wolves finished with a 25-25 record and again found themselves in the playoffs for the third straight year. There they would

Rasho Nesterovic

face the twin-towers of Tim Duncan and David Robinson, and the very tough San Antonio Spurs in the first round. The underdog Wolves lost Game One down in Texas by the final of 99-86, but came back behind Kevin's 23 points and 12 rebounds to take Game Two, 80-71. Game Three was held at the Target Center in Minneapolis, but despite Garnett's 23 points and 12 rebounds, the Wolves played poorly and wound up on the short end of an 85-71 ball-game. They came out with their backs against the wall in the pivotal Game Four, and Kevin knew that he would have to take over in order for his team to have a chance. He did manage to score 20 points and 16 rebounds, but in the end the Spurs once again prevailed, 92-85.

The players were devastated. They could not seem to get past the first round of the playoffs and it was getting frustrating. For the season KG, who tallied 25 double-doubles in just 50 games, solidified his status as one of the NBA's brightest stars, averaging nearly 21 points and 11 rebounds per game and also ranking among the league leaders in blocks and steals. In addition, Forward Joe Smith averaged 13.7 points and 8.2 rebounds, helping to fill the void left by Gugliotta, while two-time All-Star Terrell Brandon contributed 14.2 points and 9.8 assists in the 21 games he spent with the Timberwolves as well.

That off-season Coach Saunders signed a new multi-year contract extension, while his top assistant, Randy Wittman, departed to become the head coach of the Cleveland Cavaliers. The team was shaping up to look pretty good though. The new "trio" of KG, Smith and Brandon had gelled that season, and were poised to do some damage in 1999-2000. Adding to the mix was the team's newest draft pick, sharp-shooting Small Forward Wally Szczerbiak, out of the University of Miami of Ohio. (Szczerbiak, the fifth overall lottery pick, was compensation from New Jersey in lieu of the Marbury deal.) The team also added another first round pick in Duke Guard Will Avery as well.

With that the team opened the season in Tokyo, Japan vs. the Sacramento Kings, ultimately coming up on the wrong side of a 100-95 loss at the Tokyo Dome. They rebounded back to take a 114-101 victory that next night though, to even the mini-series at one apiece. From there the team headed back to the states to do battle with the rest of the league.

The Wolves jumped out to a quick 5-2 record to start the season. Garnett was carrying the team on his back, as evidenced by his amazing 35-point performance in a 93-90 win over the New York Knicks, which earned him the NBA's Player of the Week honors for mid-November. The team went on a roller-coaster ride in December though, losing eight straight, only to rally back and win eight of nine right afterwards. KG was named Player of the Week yet again in late December, when he averaged 23 points and 15 rebounds over a stretch that also saw him grab a career-high 23 rebounds in a 107-105 win in Orlando.

The team then lit it up after the holidays. Flip Saunders was even named NBA Coach of the Month for January after guiding the Wolves to a franchise-record 12-3 mark. (The club posted a 6-1 record on the road, and was 8-3 against .500+ opponents.) So hot was KG that he was also named NBA Player of the Month that January, averaging 25.8 points and 10.5 rebounds per game.

Garnett was again named as a starter in the NBA All-Star Game, where this time he lit it up for 24 points and 10 rebounds. Later, in March, he kept it going by tallying 38 points and 8 rebounds in a 116-115 OT win over his old pal Steph at New Jersey, and then recorded a career-high 40 points in a 109-106 win at Boston later that same week. The team went 5-3 over its last eight games to finish with a franchise-best record of 50-32. With that, they were once again part of the post-season festivities — this time as a sixth-seed against the Portland Trailblazers.

The first-round series opened in Portland's Rose Garden Arena with the Blazers, who were led by All-Star Forwards Scottie Pippen and Rasheed Wallace, taking Game One, 91-88, in a nail-biter. Forward Malik Sealy led the Wolves with 23 points while KG added 10 rebounds in the loss. Game two was also a close one that could've gone either way. Garnett played valiantly, tallying 23 points and 10 boards in the heart-breaking 86-82 loss. Game Three then shifted back to Minnesota, where 19,006 fans crammed into the Target Center to watch their Wolves try and mount a rally. They came out smoking too, taking a 47-40 half-time lead, and they didn't look back. Behind Brandon's 28 points, they went on to win the game by the final of 94-87, renewing the hopes of hoops fans everywhere in the Gopher State. Then, with the series at two games to one, the Wolves came out and laid an egg in Game Four. KG's 17 points, 10 rebounds and 9 assists were simply not enough in this one as Portland came back to outscore the Wolves 28-13 in the fourth quarter and went on to win, 85-77. Once again, the season had ended prematurely in the first round with the players wondering why.

Chauncey Billups goes up against Khalid El-Amin

KG did set a milestone that year though, becoming only the ninth player in NBA history to average at least 20 points, 10 rebounds and 5 assists per game in a single season. At season's end he had also scored in double figures in 210 consecutive games, giving him the longest current streak in the NBA. For his efforts he was named to the prestigious All-NBA and All-NBA Defensive First Teams, recognizing him as the best player at his position in the entire league. It didn't mean a lot to Kevin though, because all he wanted was to win a championship. He had all the money and recognition that he needed, he just wanted to take that off-season and focus on getting his club past the first-round and deep into the playoffs.

"When you get into this league it's all about winning," reflected Garnett. "It's not about how good of a one-on-one player you are or how good of an individual player you are or how you shoot the ball. Some people get caught up in the points and stuff. But if you don't win it doesn't mean anything. Round one is getting a little boring. I'm getting tired of these early vacations. Every year I come in with the mindset that we have a chance at being one of the best teams in the league. That's how we have to think."

That summer Kevin returned home triumphantly from the Olympic games in Sydney, Australia, with a shiny new gold medal around his neck. It was an incredible achievement that got shoved to the back-burner later that summer though, when tragedy suddenly struck the Timberwolves family.

First, on May 5th, the franchise's first coach, Bill Musselman, who was now an assistant coach with Portland, died of cancer, ending the life of a brilliant man. Then, just two weeks later, one evening while driving home from KG's birthday party, teammate Malik Sealy was tragically killed in a car accident by a drunk driver near downtown Minneapolis. For the players, the news was absolutely devastating. Malik was one of the team's most popular and well-respected players, and he would dearly be missed. The team rallied around the misfortunes though and focused on the upcoming season. They knew that "Leak" and "Coach Muss" would've wanted the team to play hard and that's just what they were going to do.

Then, if that weren't enough, another unfortunate incident took place just prior to the start of the 2000-01 season involving Forward Joe Smith. Here's what happened: Smith had signed with the team earlier that season but wanted to ink a long-term contract to finish his career in Minnesota. But, because of the salary cap, the team could only offer so much immediately, with the promise of more in the future — almost to the tune of $70 million. However, when his agent stupidly put the new deal into writing (when the wink-wink turned to ink-ink…), it was considered to be a "secret contract" and thus violated the NBA's new salary cap rules. The illegal deal was big news in the basketball world and as a result, NBA Commissioner David Stern threw the book at the Wolves. By the time the smoke had cleared Smith was wearing a Detroit Pistons uniform, while Wolves owner Glen Taylor and Vice President Kevin McHale found themselves serving one-year suspensions. And, if that weren't enough, the team was penalized to the tune of losing four future first-round draft picks along with a $3.5 million fine.

Through all of this adversity, however, the Wolves somehow pulled through. They signed several free agents including, Forward LaPhonso Ellis, as well as Guards Chauncey Billups and Felipe Lopez — all of whom would pick up the slack big-time. The squad did manage to overcome a sluggish 7-13 start to post a 43-19 (.694) finish — third-best in the entire league. The run was fueled by a tenacious defense that limited opponents to just 96.0 points per game (11th in the NBA) and 44.5 percent shooting (10th).

Malik Sealy

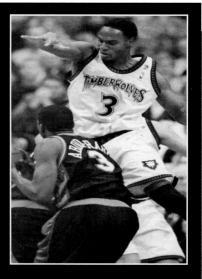

On May 20, 2000, the Minnesota sports world was shocked and saddened to learn that Timberwolves Forward Malik Sealy had been tragically killed by a drunk driver while driving home from teammate Kevin Garnett's birthday party. Sealy, one of the most popular and well-liked players on the team, was just 30 years old.

A native of New York, Malik attended St. John's University, where because of his smooth offensive skills and adaptability on the court, he earned the nickname "Silk". There, he led the Redmen to several post-season appearances and as a senior was named as an All-American. After graduating from St. John's with a Bachelor's Degree in business in 1992, Malik was the 14th overall draft pick by the NBA's Indiana Pacers. He spent three years with the Pacers, two years with the Los Angeles Clippers and one year with the Detroit Pistons before joining Minnesota as a free agent in 1999. A member of the Timberwolves for just two seasons, Sealy was coming off one of his finest seasons of his eight-year NBA career in 1999-00, having played in all 82 games, the last 60 as a starter, and averaging better than 11 points and 4 rebounds per game en route to helping the team to its first 50-win season.

A self described "Renaissance Man," Sealy was much more than a basketball player. He started a men's accessories company, "Malik Sealy XXI, Inc.," designing and selling neckties. He opened Baseline Recording Studios in Manhattan, and even enjoyed acting, appearing in the movie "Eddie" as well as making guest appearances on television's "The Sentinel" and "Diagnosis Murder." He was also actively involved in a wide variety of charities including serving an the board of Wheelchair Charities Inc. and the Bronx Police Athletic League. He was a regular visitor to the Ronald McDonald House in Minneapolis, took an active role in various school programs and also ran basketball clinics in conjunction with the Refugee Project at the Camp Hill Summer program in North Carolina.

A wonderful player and truly great person, Malik will forever be missed. He was survived by his wife Lisa and their three-year old son, Malik Remington.

There were a lot of highlights during the season for KG though, including being named as the NBA Player of the Week for November 19th when he led the Wolves to a 3-0 record by averaging 27 points, 11 rebounds, 4 assists, 2 blocks and 2 steals per game. There was also his season-high 20-rebound outing against Indiana on December 16th, as well as a career-high 40-point performance against the Western Conference leading Sacramento Kings on February 7th. In addition, KG also made history on November 9th when his three-pointer in the closing seconds of a game against Philly pushed him past teammate Sam Mitchell and into first place on the Timberwolves' all-time scoring chart with 8,143 career points. Da Kid was now the franchise's all-time leading scorer.

KG was again named to the All-Star team, this time after leading the team to an impressive 11-game winning streak. But they lost their first five out of the break, only to fade back once again to the middle of the pack. Then, as the season wore down, there were a few key games that helped to solidify the team's stranglehold on the eighth and final playoff spot. One of them came on April Fool's Day when they beat the Portland Trailblazers, in Portland, thanks to Felipe Lopez's last-second game-winning three-pointer as the Wolves held off a last second charge to win 95-90. Terrell Brandon had 30 points and 11 assists, while Garnett added 16 points and 10 rebounds in the big win. The team was gelling at the right time and getting help from everybody, including McHale's project, seven-foot Center Rasho Nesterovic, who was finally beginning to show that he belonged in the NBA, and also former Gopher Guard Bobby Jackson, who also played well at the No. 2 guard spot.

The team rounded out the year by going 9-7 and posted a very solid 48-win season, good enough to seal that coveted eighth and final playoff spot. It was their fifth straight post-season berth, and the team was anxious to finally make a run. Determined to make it out of the first round of the play-offs, the Wolves suited up to do battle with the San Antonio Spurs — and this time it was personal.

The series opened up at the Alamodome in San Antonio with the Wolves losing Game One, 87-82, as a series of mistakes and mishaps did in the Timberwolves in the final two minutes of their playoff opener. After digging out of a 14-point hole by halftime, they managed to rally back. Then, after outscoring the Spurs 28-12 in the third quarter, the Wolves took an 80-79 lead on Brandon's jumper with 2:27 left. That would be Brandon's last shot of the game though, as he sprained his left ankle on the

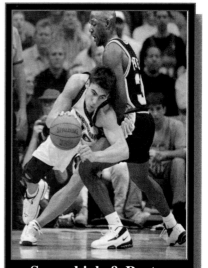

Szczerbiak & Porter

1989
Pooh Richardson (1st round — 10th overall)
Gary Leonard (2nd round)
Doug West (2nd round)

1990
Felton Spencer (1st round — 6th overall)
Gerald Glass (2nd round)

1991
Luc Longley (1st round — 7th overall)
Myron Brown (2nd round)

1992
Christian Laettner (1st round – 3rd overall)
Marlon Maxey (2nd round)
Chris Smith (2nd round)
Tim Burroughs (2nd round)

1993
Isaiah Rider (1st round – 5th overall)
Sherron Mills (2nd round)

1994
Donyell Marshall (1st round — 4th overall)
Howard Eisley (2nd round)

1995
Kevin Garnett (1st round — 5th overall)
Mark Davis (2nd round)
Jerome Allen (2nd round)

1996
Ray Allen (1st round — 5th overall)

1997
Paul Grant (1st round — 20th overall)
Gordon Malone (2nd round)

1998
Rasho Nesterovic (1st round — 17th overall)
Andrae Patterson (2nd round)

1999
Wally Szczerbiak (1st round — 6th overall)
William Avery (1st round -— 14th overall)
Louis Bullock, Jr. (2nd round)

2000
Igor Rakocevic (2nd round — 51st overall)

2001
Loren Woods, Arizona
(2nd round– 46th overall)

Our Governor... The No. 1 Wolves Fan!

ensuing play. Without his ability to bring the ball up court, the team floundered, turned the ball over, and lost it down the stretch.

Game Two was ugly as San Antonio's stifling, league-best defense proved to be the difference in a 86-69 defeat. Already ahead at halftime, 50-36, the Spurs scored 12 unanswered points early in the third quarter and held the Wolves to just one field goal in the first seven minutes of the period. KG tallied 16 in the loss, but Brandon, who somehow played, just wasn't himself.

Minnesota came back though, and rebounded to win Game Three, 93-84, back in Minneapolis. In that game the Wolves got a balanced scoring attack: Garnett led the way with 22, Brandon scored 21, Szczerbiak added 18 and Peeler pitched in with 13 of his own. It was a huge win for the franchise and it gave everyone hope that finally they might have a chance to get into the second round.

With that, they rallied to try and even the series at two games apiece in Game Four. But, as usual, they came up short, 97-84, to yet again be eliminated from the first round of the best-of-five NBA playoff series. The fans thought the Wolves might have a chance when Anthony Peeler's three consecutive three-pointers cut the Spurs' eight-point lead to 75-73 with 5:29 left, but the Spurs ran away with it down the stretch. The Wolves turned over the ball twice, missed a couple of key shots and left San Antonio Forward Danny Ferry open for yet another three-pointer, his fourth of the half, which he promptly drained to put the final dagger in the hearts of Timberwolves fans everywhere. Wally Szczerbiak led the Wolves with 20 points and played inspired basketball, but it wasn't enough. "Each time we walk away from the first round, it burns inside me," said Garnett, who added 19 points and 15 rebounds in the loss.

Following the season the Wolves were able to make a few key deals, with the biggest being the re-signing of Joe Smith, who played for the Wolves from 1998-2000 before spending the 2000-01 season in Detroit. Smith, who later signed a six-year deal worth about $34 million under the team's mid-level salary-cap exception, was anxious to get back to Minnesota and play with his old pal, KG. But, because the team signed Smith, they were unable to afford Forward LaPhonso Ellis, who instead signed a three-year, $10 million contract with Miami.

The Franchise

They were also able to re-sign most of their top free-agents, including Sam Mitchell and Felipe Lopez, who, after averaging better than seven points per game and eventually worked his way into the starting lineup, took less money to remain with the team. In addition, the team inked Dallas free-agent, Gary Trent, the former "Shaq of the MAC" who played solid two-way ball in Big-D in 2001. Trent will fill in nicely down low in the paint, where the team is still trying to find that missing piece of the puzzle. Then, the team got a bargain in the draft with its only draft pick (the 46th selection of the 2nd round), when they snatched up seven-foot-one Center Loren Woods, who led the University of Arizona to the NCAA Final Four. A real steal, Woods, considered a potential lottery pick, fell in the draft after reports of an injured back.

Also re-upping was the all-time winningest coach in franchise history, Flip Saunders, who signed a five-year $20 million contract extension, ending any speculation that he was considering a move to Portland to take over the Blazers. Saunders (227-213) has led the Wolves to the playoffs in each of his five full seasons at the helm, and is widely considered as one of the league's premier young coaches. And, rejoining Flip on the bench is former T-Wolves assistant Randy Wittman, who had been recently fired as the head coach of the Cleveland Cavaliers.

All in all, the Wolves have come a long way since their inception back in 1988. They have made a great five-year post-season run and are very close to getting over the next big hurdle. Sure, the defection of Marbury and Googs hurt the team a few years ago, but with KG the franchise is in good hands. Players want to come to Minnesota to play with Da Kid, because of what he brings to the game. With Garnett, McHale and Saunders locked up for long-term deals, the future of pro hoops in the Gopher State is rock solid. It has been nearly a half century since the Minneapolis Lakers made us the champions of the NBA, but hey, who knows? Maybe this team can pull off a trade or two along the way to pick up a few more pieces of the puzzle that will ultimately get this franchise over the top. Stick around, it'll be worth the wait!

Catching Up With Wolves' G.M. Kevin McHale

Former Gopher and Boston Celtics Hall of Famer Kevin McHale proved that you can come home again when he was named as the Timberwolves' Vice President of Basketball Operations in 1995. The Hibbing native wasted little time in working to improve the team and after five straight post-season appearances, hasn't showed any signs of slowing down. Having achieved success at the high school, collegiate and professional ranks, McHale has an amazing passion for the game. In his current position he is responsible for the franchise's entire basketball operations department, including overseeing player personnel decisions, scouting and the coaching staff. Here is what he had to say about the current state of the state of his beloved hometown T-Wolves:

Kevin McHale

On being back in Basketball with the Wolves:

"The bottom line is that I still really love competing and to be involved with the Wolves gives me that opportunity. Overall, I am glad that I came back to Minnesota and came on board with the team. After retiring from the Celtics I knew that it was going to have to be a very special situation for me to be involved again and this was it. Plus, I was sort of able to ease into it, by first doing TV and radio and then getting involved in the front office. That transition really helped me to understand the business side of the organization."

What did your Experiences in Boston Teach You?

"I learned a lot from being around the Boston franchise for so many years too. Just to be around Red Auerbach (Boston's legendary coach and GM) was very special to me, and I learned a great deal from him about what kind of hard work and determination it takes to run a first class organization. He was a real mentor to me and I just learned a tremendous amount from him about what it takes to achieve success. He emphasized the team concept so much and just what kind of commitment it takes to be a champion.

On Running the Team:

"Overall, it's been a fun experience. I mean nothing can compare to playing, but this is another form of competition that is in some ways just as challenging. I do enjoy working with the guys and watching them improve. To teach them strategy is great and you do get a sense of accomplishment when the team gets better and grows collectively as well. It was never a dream of mine to manage a team, I was always a player, but it's very challenging and I do enjoy it. I also think we are really blessed here in Minnesota to have a guy like Kevin Garnett, who brings it every single night. He certainly makes my job a lot easier. And then, taking after what Red Auerbach did, we just got rid of the renegades and the guys who didn't fit in and tried to make a team that has chemistry. It's not what we accomplish individually in this game, it's about the teams' wins and losses, and that is the attitude and challenge we are trying to instill into this organization for the future. I think that is what we have done though, and now we just need to get better so we can take that next step into getting deep into the playoffs and beyond."

On How the Game Has Changed:

"Basketball is not about individuals, it's about the team, and sometimes through the media among other things we have somehow individualized our game a great deal. So, sometimes its hard to get guys to sacrifice for the good of the team. Nowadays kids are taught to score and make big dunks and just excel as individuals, so that's what you're up against with a lot of the new recruits. I mean the reason your top players score in key situations is because they are the team's best option to win the game at that point. They have proven over time that through hard work and practice that they can be the go-to guy in clutch situations when the game is on the line, but kids nowadays don't realize that those players have earned that right. They come in and expect the ball in certain spots on the floor in certain situations and it is sometimes frustrating as an executive to deal with that. They come in after being stars on their college teams or what have you, and they think they can score the same kinds of numbers at this level and it just doesn't work that way."

On Flip Saunders:

"We have a really special relationship. When I decided to come back here to take the job running the team, one of first guys I talked to was Flip. We have always been great friends, so to be able work together was just a wonderful opportunity. I had followed his success from way back to his days of coaching at Golden Valley Lutheran College to the CBA. I always knew he was going to be a great coach at the NBA level and it has all just worked out great. He came in as my assistant GM and then he quickly became the coach and has been a tremendous asset for the organization."

On the Future:

"The future looks good for the Wolves right now, but we do need to make some more moves to get to that next level. It is a slow process but one thing I definitely learned from Red Auerbach was patience. Chemistry and teamwork are so key at this level and we just need to do some tinkering to get better. I am not a believer in quick-fixes though, I just think we need to get better as a team over the long haul. Our ultimate goal is to win championships and that is something I think we are very capable of doing very soon."

Minnesota and the Continental Basketball Association (CBA)

The Rochester Flyers

Before disbanding midway through the 2000-01 season, the Continental Basketball Association had been the proving ground for the NBA. Originally created back in 1978, and later bought and sold by former Detroit Piston's All-Star Guard, Isiah Thomas, the CBA was an invaluable cog in the world of professional basketball. It served to fill a niche for those smaller cities throughout the country that were capable and willing to support minor-league basketball.

The league was full of talent, both with young players on their way up, and with the older veterans, still trying to hang on and get back into the "show" one last time. It gave countless young men the opportunity to move up the ranks and be seen. And it wasn't just a proving ground for players — as was the case for Timberwolves' television analyst Chad Hartman, who got his first break in the world of broadcast journalism by covering the Rochester Flyers as well.

Minnesota's first taste of the CBA came in 1987, when the Wisconsin Flyers moved to Rochester. They remained there for two seasons before moving on to become the Omaha Racers in 1989. The Flyers played in the CBA's Western Division along with the La Crosse Catbirds, Quad City Thunder, Rapid City Thrillers, Rockford Lightning and Wyoming Wildcatters. Rochester, which played its home games in the Mayo Civic Center, finished fifth in the Western Division of the 1987-88 season, with a 20-34 record. Then, in 1988-89, the team stunk it up by finishing in the Division cellar with a paltry 16-38 record.

The star of that team, however, was a kid with a pretty decent future ahead of him. His name was Tim Legler. Legler played with the Flyers in 1988-89, averaging 12.6 points per game while connecting on 34 of 91 three-point attempts. From there he went on to play on and off with the NBA's Phoenix Suns, Denver Nuggets, Utah Jazz, Minnesota Timberwolves and Dallas Mavericks. One of the highlights of the six-foot-four guard's career came in 1996, when, after averaging a career-high 9.4 points per game for the Washington Bullets, he won the "Three-Point Shoot-out" at the NBA's All-Star Weekend.

The Flyers were also very fortunate to land a real-life coaching legend in Bill Musselman, who had also led the Golden Gophers to a Big Ten title back in 1972 and later became the Timberwolves first-ever head coach in 1988 as well. Musselman, who coached in four pro leagues — the NBA, CBA, ABA and WBA, with a career record of 603-426, later went on to win four consecutive CBA championships. Ironically, in 2000, the 28-year coaching veteran, who was then serving as an assistant with the NBA's Portland Trail Blazers, died of bone marrow cancer at Rochester's famed Mayo Clinic. He was just 59 years old. Many of his players remembered him fondly.

"He remembered me," said Timberwolves' star Forward Sam Mitchell, who played for Musselman in the CBA and later in the NBA. "He didn't forget me and he signed me. He gave me my break. I mean, I love Muss. I'll always remember what he did for me."

"We had a very good relationship," added Sidney Lowe, who played for Musselman for three years in the CBA and also for the first year Musselman coached the Timberwolves. "Bill was one of those guys, one of those coaches that allowed you to go out and play. He allowed you to have the freedom to do what you were capable of doing if you showed it to him. … He was very demanding … but he was an excellent coach."

The Rochester Renegade

In 1992, the Rochester Renegade became that city's second CBA basketball franchise in six years. Formerly the Birmingham Bandits, the Renegade remained in Rochester for just two seasons before moving on to become the Harrisburg Hammerheads in 1994. The Renegade, which played its home games in the Mayo Civic Center, were, in a word, terrible. In 1992-93, they posted an unbelievably horrible 6-50 record, finishing no less than 26 losses behind the next worst team in the Mideast Division of the American Conference, the La Crosse Catbirds. They improved drastically that next year, however, finishing with a very respectable 31-25 record. Unfortunately though, La Crosse Rockford and Quad City all finished with better records, and the Renegade was relegated to the divisional basement yet again.

The Fargo-Moorhead Fever

The Fargo-Moorhead Fever became Minnesota's third CBA franchise, when the Tulsa Zone moved to the great northwoods in 1992. That first season the Fever, which played in the Fargodome, finished with an 18-38 record, good for last in the Midwest Division of the National Conference, behind the Sioux Falls Skyforce, Omaha Racers and Rapid City Thrillers. That next year, 1993-94, the Fever posted an improved 25-31 record, but still remained in the Midwest Division basement. Following that season the Fever moved to Mexico City, where they became the Aztecas.

Minnesota and the International Basketball Association (IBA)

The Fargo-Moorhead Beez and St. Cloud Rock'n Rollers were charter members of the International Basketball Association, which was founded in 1995. Other inaugural franchises included the Black Hills Posse, Dakota Wizards and Winnipeg Cyclones. That next year the Rock'n Rollers franchise was relocated to the Twin Cites, where it was renamed as the St. Paul Slam. The Magic City (Minot) Snowbears also joined that year, as did the Des Moines Dragons, Wisconsin (Appleton) Blast, Billings (Mont.) RimRockers and Mansfield (Ohio) Hawks.

In 1998 the St. Paul Slam franchise was moved to Rochester, where it was renamed as the Skeeters. Other teams to join the league that year included the Black Hills Gold, Rapid City Thrillers and Saskatchewan Hawks. In 1995-96 the Fargo-Moorhead Beez finished third in the IBA with a 10-14 record, while the St. Cloud Rock'n Rollers took fourth at 8-16. The Beez then eliminated Winnipeg, two games to one, in the first round of the play-offs. Then, in the semifinals, FM lost in two straight to the Black Hills Posse, 110-98 & 103-91.

That next season the Beez went into the tank, finishing with a miserable 6-24 record. The St. Paul Slam, which were the former Rock'n Rollers, finished just slightly better in fourth place, at 13-17. But they did make a post-season run, however, ultimately losing to Black Hills, 128-115 & 139-111, to end their season.

In 1997-98 the IBA expanded into two separate divisions, the East and the West. Minnesota's contingent, the Beez and Slam, wound up on opposite ends of the East, with the Beez finishing on top at 24-10 and the Slam winding up in the basement at 8-26. The Beez then beat Des Moines in the opening round of the playoffs in two straight, 117-16 & 114-107, to advance to the Finals. There, they lost Game One to Western champion Black Hills Posse, 118-103, but rebounded back to take Games Two and Three, 130-110 & 121-111, and win the IBA championship.

In 1989-99 the Slam moved to Rochester, where the newly renamed Skeeters finished third in the IBA's Eastern Division with a 17-17 record, while the Beez ended up at 14-20, good for fifth. Then, in the first round of the playoffs, the Skeeters were beaten two games to none by the Des Moines Dragons, 105-97 & 99-95, respectively.

In 1999-00 the Beez finished in second place in the Eastern Division with a 21-15 record, while the Skeeters finished in the cellar with a paltry 8-20 mark. Fargo then beat the Saskatchewan Hawks in the first round of the playoffs, two games to zero, but then lost in the championship game to Des Moines by the final scores of 99-96, 115-99 and 104-98.

Then, in 2001, the IBA caught a big break when the Continental Basketball Association (CBA) went belly-up. In an historic restructuring agreement, several of the CBA's former franchisees agreed to join forces with several of the IBA clubs to form a new league. The joint-venture then purchased the CBA's name, which it will now operate under. The only Minnesota team involved in the reaffiliation was Fargo-Moorhead, which, under owner Chris Holland, a Fargo trucking company executive, is excited about our state's triumphant return to big-time semi-pro basketball.

Joining the Beez over the two-year transition into the new CBA are Bismarck, Winnipeg, Saskatoon and Des Moines, while most of the old CBA clubs will join the new circuit in 2001 with two divisions playing a 16-week season. There will be no direct affiliation with the NBA, but there will be ties with regards to player development and a desire to work together in the future.

Leading the charge for the upstart CBA Beez is Head Coach Rory White, who has compiled a solid 52-44 (.542) record since the club's inception back in 1995. While the stars of the Beez have included former Gopher Townsend Orr in the past, it will be an entirely different ball-game in the future as this team steps it up a notch to playing with a new level of competition it has not seen before. The Fargodome will definitely be rocking in Fargo-Moorhead. Go Beez!

Homegrown Heroes

Hundreds of Minnesota natives, as well as those players who have played parts of their careers in Minnesota, have gone on to play at various levels of the professional ranks. Countless dozens more have gone on to play in the NBA and ABA. There are so many amazing Minnesotans who have made a difference in the world of basketball, and it is important to at least mention the accomplishments of many of them. So here are just a few (I apologize for those I did not mention!) of our local homegrown heroes who just simply need to be honored for their achievements in this book:

Askov's Vern Mikkelsen, who played with the Lakers; St. Paul's Howie Schultz, who played with the Lakers and Brooklyn Dodgers; Virginia's Johnny Norlander, who played with the Washington Capitals, St. Paul's Joe Hutton, Jr., who played with the Lakers; St. Paul's Jim Fritsche who played with the Baltimore Bullets and Fort Wayne Pistons; Minneapolis' Johnny Kundla, who coached the Lakers; Minneapolis' Tony Jaros, who played with the Lakers; Minneapolis' Don "Swede" Carlson, who played with the Lakers; New Ulm's Clarence "Kleggie" Hermsen, who played for nine professional teams over his career; Minneapolis' Don Smith, who played with the Lakers; Superior, Wis., native Harry "Bud" Grant, who played with the Lakers; Brainerd's Myer "Whitey" Skoog, who played with the Lakers; Duluth's John Clawson, who earned gold as a member of the 1968 U.S. basketball team in Mexico City and went on to play with the ABA's Oakland Oaks; Bemidji's Arnie Johnson, who played for the Rochester Royals; Hibbing's Dick Garmaker, who played with the Lakers; Rochester's John Green, who played with Los Angeles; Grand Rapids' Doug Bolstorff, who played with the Detroit Pistons; New Prague's Ron Johnson, who played with the Pistons and Lakers; Wayzata's Larry Mikan, who played with the Cleveland Cavaliers; Melrose's Mark Olberding, who played for Chicago and Los Angeles; Mounds View's Mark Landsberger, who played for the Los Angeles Lakers; Hibbing's Kevin McHale, who played with the Celtics; Bloomington's Steve Lingenfelter, who played briefly in the NBA; Fulda's Arvid Kramer, who played briefly with the Denver Nuggets; Stillwater's Chris Engler, who spent parts of five seasons with five NBA teams; Lake City's Randy Breuer, who played 11 years in the NBA with the Bucks and Timberwolves; St. Louis Park's Jim Petersen, who played for eight-years in the NBA; Coon Rapids' Tom Copa, who played with the San Antonio Spurs; Minneapolis' Ben Coleman, who played part of five seasons in the NBA; Duluth's Jay Guidinger. who played with Cleveland; Minneapolis' Jeff Lamp, who played with Portland and Los Angeles; St. Paul's Kevin McKenna, who played with Indiana, Washington and New Jersey; New Ulm's Brad Lohaus, who played with the Timberwolves; Edina's Mark Randall, who played for the Timberwolves; Bloomington's Kevin Lynch, who played with the Charlotte Hornets; Apple Valley's Bob Martin, who played with the Los Angeles Clippers; Minneapolis' John Thomas, who played for Boston and Toronto; Cottage Grove's Sam Jacobson, who played with Golden State and Minnesota; Slayton's Trevor Winter, who played with the Timberwolves; Minneapolis' Devean George, who currently plays with the Los Angeles Lakers; Monticello's Joel Pryzbilla, who plays for the Milwaukee Bucks; and Minneapolis' Khalid El-Amin, who plays for the Dallas Mavericks.

Not to mention the countless individuals who perhaps didn't play pro, but were stars in their own rights either as players or coaches: Grand Rapids' Frank McCabe, who was a member of the 1952 US Olympic basketball team; Austin's "Burdie" Haldorson, who was a member of the 1956 and 1960 US Olympic basketball teams; Austin's Vince Hanson, who was a three-time All-American at Washington State University from 1943-48, Winona's Ralph Crosthwaite, who scored 2,076 points at Western Kentucky University; St. Cloud's Alfred Robertson, who coached college basketball at Bradley from 1921-1943 and 1946-1948, recording a career mark of 316-186; Rochester's Fred Enke, who coached at the University of Arizona from 1926 to 1961, compiling an astounding career record of 525-340; and Duluth's Clarence "Nibs" Price, who coached at the University of California from 1925 to 1954 where he compiled a career record of 463-298. Or how about Ken Mauer Jr. from St. Paul, who has officiated in the NBA for 15 seasons; or even our very own Lute Olson who led the University of Arizona to a National Championship.

Hey, how about our Hall of Famers? In addition to Vern Mikkelsen and Kevin McHale, Mankato native Clifford Fagan was enshrined into the Hall in 1984, as a "Contributor," for his many contributions with regards to improving the games' officiating and administration. So was Detroit Lakes native George Keogan, who was enshrined in 1995. Keogan coached at Notre Dame, from 1927-43 and posted an amazing 327-96-1 record in South Bend without ever suffering a losing campaign.

This, is just a partial list folks. Minnesotans have truly made an impact at all levels of the game!

The Golden Gophers

*"Rah, Rah, Rah for Ski-U-Mah, Rah, Rah, Rah, Rah — Hat's off to the U of MMM...
M-I-N-N-E-S-O-T-A, MINNESOTA, MINNESOTA, HEEYYYYY GOPHERS... RAH!"*

Come on, is there anything better than the sound of that at the old Barn? Or how about when Ray Christensen used to scream: "This is Golden… Gopher… Basketball!" Hey, I know, how about Goldy spinning his big rodent head out at half-court during a time-out? OK, what about that fabulous raised floor in Williams Arena? Those are some awesome visuals, aren't they? And hey, those are just some of the wonderful memories that I think of when I ponder the thought of my beloved Gophers, a program who's wonderful history stretches back for more than a century.

To truly understand the myth and mystique of Gopher hoops, you have to go back, way back to the early 1890s — when the game of basketball was just in its infancy. It was a unique time in Minnesota sports history during this era. While the 20th century was looming just ahead, sports enthusiasts in the Land of 10,000 Lakes actually had quite a few options. Football was all the rage at the U of M, as well as at several of the MIAC schools — as were baseball and hockey. Throw in boxing, curling and golf — not to mention the great outdoors of hunting and fishing, and one could quickly see that there was indeed a lot to do to keep entertained up in the great north woods.

Now, enter the good doctor, James Naismith, who, in 1891, came up with a new game in his native Springfield (Mass.) involving a soccer ball and a peach basket, called "Basket Ball," which was suddenly all the rage out on the East Coast. That year, the Springfield Training School's newspaper, the Triangle, published Naismith's 13 rules and instructions for the new game. The paper was then circulated throughout many of the YMCAs throughout the nation. It just so happened that one of those young men's clubs was located in downtown Minneapolis, where, before long, the game quickly took off. The Y's gymnasium soon began to fill up on a regular basis with kids from throughout the Twin Cities all wanting to learn how to play the new sport.

George Tuck

Within a few years, many of Naismith's students from Springfield had gone on to help start college programs at places such as the University of Chicago, Vanderbilt, Yale and Stanford. Meanwhile, one of those kids, Raymond Kaighn, wound up at Hamline University, where he organized what is believed to be the first intercollegiate basketball game in Minnesota. The match between the Pipers and the University of Minnesota's School of Agriculture (what is now known simply as the St. Paul campus), took place on February 9, 1895, on Hamline's basement handball court — where the nine-foot-high ceilings made the game most interesting. The game, which featured nine players per side, and awarded three points for a field goal as well as three points for a free throw, was won by the farm-boys, 9-3.

By now the game had spread to other college campuses in Minnesota, including at Carleton, Macalester and St. Thomas, as well as in the private sector, where, in addition to the YMCA league games, the "Twin City Basket Ball League" had sprung up as well. That Fall, however, a significant event occurred that greatly helped to expand the development of Gopher basketball when a new Armory, complete with an all-purpose gymnasium, was constructed on campus. The enormous building would serve as the team's home court for more than three decades. In 1897, Dr. Louis Cooke, the director of the Minneapolis YMCA, and also an avid hoops fan, was then hired to manage the phy-ed department at the U of M. Dr. Cooke would later go on to become affectionately known as the "Father of Gopher Basketball."

Under Cooke's direction, the Gophers, who were uniformed in maroon sleeveless jerseys with maroon baseball pants, stockings and gold belt," went on to win their first ever game in the new Armory in the Fall of 1898, beating the YMCA Triangles, 11-5. That next season the Gophers emerged as a national power, and didn't slow down for nearly eight years. So good were the Gophers, in fact, that they went on to post an incredible 89-27-1 record from 1899-1907, even forging a 34-game winning streak from 1903-1904 along the way. Led by the team's first star player, Forward William Deering, of Fargo, the U of M squad quietly became the talk of college hoops.

Before long the team had established rivalries with Iowa, Wisconsin, Purdue, Ohio State, Nebraska, Cincinnati, North Dakota and even the University of Chicago, where they participated in a national tournament directed by legendary football coach, Amos Alonzo Stagg, who was also a former teammate of Cooke's back at Springfield. In 1902 the team went 15-0 and was named as the Helms Foundation's National Champions — then college's highest honor. The team posted another undefeated season that next year as well, thanks to the outstanding performance of Forward George Tuck, who, in 1905 was named by the Helms Foundation as Minnesota's first All-American.

Later that same year six schools: Minnesota, Wisconsin, Illinois Purdue, Chicago and Northwestern, got together to form the Western Intercollegiate Basketball Association — a new conference (later to become the Big Ten) which would determine the nation's champion of the West. Led by All-American Guard Garfield Brown, the Gophers, which posted an outstanding 13-2 record, went on to win the inaugural Western Conference crown — ultimately beating Wisconsin for the title. The team was named as co-champs that next year as well, but by the end of the decade had slipped into a slump.

By 1910, the Gophers, who were now led by All-American Forward Frank Lawler, were back on top of the Western Conference standings, where they finished tied with Purdue at 8-4. But over the next several years it would be all Wisconsin, who

The 1902 National Champion Gophers

ran off a streak of four straight titles. Minnesota got back on track in 1917 thanks to a pair of All-Americans in Harold Gillen and Francis Stadsvold, who led the team to another title.

Then, in 1919, the Gophers made history when they won their first Big Ten title (the conference name had changed now with the addition of a couple more Midwestern teams) as well as their second ever Helms Athletic Foundation National Championship. Led by All-American Guard Erling Platou, who, with his gaudy 11.8 points per game average, would be named as the College Player of the Year, along with Forward Arnold Oss (himself a future two-time All-American in both 1919 and 1921 and also pretty darn good football player to boot) and Center Norman Kingsley, Minnesota emerged as a force to be reckoned with that year. The team, which earned the nickname as the "1.000 Percent Team," because of its undefeated 13-0 overall record, trounced nearly every opponent along the way that season.

Erling Platou

In 1924 Dr. Cooke, after 28 years of loyal service, decided to step down as the head coach of the Gophers. Cooke, who had had guided Minnesota to two national championships and five conference titles, called it quits with an astonishing 245-137-2 (.641%) career record. His legacy would include taking a mere fad sport no more popular than a gym class activity and helping to turn it into one of our nation's greatest national pastimes.

Replacing a legend would be no easy job, but assistant coach Harold Taylor, who had been a high school coach in Aurora (Minn.), felt up to the task when he took over the reigns from Cooke that next season. The team was riding a wave of popularity by this time, and believe it or not, had simply outgrown the Armory's 2,000 seating capacity. (One of the reasons for this was due to the fact that the team oftentimes hosted dances following its home games, which got all the students to come out to enjoy an evening of fun for a mere 35¢.) So, Athletic Director Fred Luehring opted to have the team play its home games in the spacious, 6,000-seat Kenwood Armory (the site of the Guthrie Theater), in downtown Minneapolis.

Taylor, who did lead the Gophers to several impressive victories that year, including a win over Knute Rockne's Fighting Irish of Notre Dame, could muster no better than a sixth place finish. One of the highlights of the season though, occurred in a 36-16 shellacking of the Purdue Boilermakers, when Minnesota Guard Black Rasey, one of the premier dribblers of the era, scored a then-conference record of 20 points.

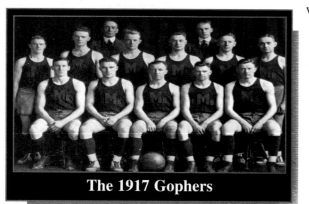

The 1917 Gophers

The team struggled through the rest of the 1920s, even finishing with one measly win in 1927. Taylor was fired as coach and New Yorker Dave McMillan was brought in to replace him. McMillan, who had played the game professionally, with the New York Celtics, and coached collegeiately, with the University of Idaho, had the dubious job of turning around a program that had fallen from its graces. There was one good thing though, and that was the fact that the construction of a huge new University Field House was underway, right across from Memorial Stadium on University Avenue — thus giving the program a campus arena its fans could be proud of once again.

The new coach was a task-master, and emphasized the fundamentals of the game. He demanded that his players exercise good ball-control, execute a lot of passing and that they play strong defense. It sounded good on paper, but the team struggled out of the gates — prompting some to question if he was indeed the right man for the job. They settled down as the season went on though, eventually gelling under Coach Mac's new coaching ideology.

The team, led by Molly Nydahl, George Otterness, Robert Tanner, George MacKinnon, Johnny Stark and Fred Hovde (who would go on to become the president of Purdue University), finally christened its new University Field House midway through that season against the Ohio State Buckeyes. The dedication game was quite a big deal as well. In addition to the more than 11,000 fans in attendance, several prominent dignitaries also came to see the Gophers play in their new state-of-the-art facility. Among the distinguished guests was the good doctor himself, Dr. James Naismith, who served as the game's honorary referee.

"It is no little satisfaction to me to see this vast assemblage out to witness a basketball game," said Naismith before the game, in Steve Pearlstein's 1995 book, "Gopher Glory." "It carries me back to the time when in a little gymnasium, 35-by-45, I stepped out on the floor to put the ball in play in what was the final test as to whether the game that we had prepared in the office would stand the test of practical experiment.

Bernie Bierman

It took only a few moments to convince me that the game would be a success. Within the life of a single individual it has spread into almost every nation and the rules have been translated into seven languages. I wish to congratulate the University of Minnesota as being one of the pioneers in the development of basketball under the direction of my lifelong friend, Dr. L.J. Cooke. I wish to express my appreciation of this visit and assure you that I shall follow the fortunes of your basketball team with more interest and enthusiasm for this personal contact with your institution."

The Gophers, who ultimately lost the big game, 40-38, in double overtime, finally got their first win in the "big barn" a few weeks later in a 30-18 victory over the University of Chicago Maroons. Overall though, it was a poor year for the Gophers, which finished ninth in the Big Ten for the second straight year. Things didn't get much better until the 1930-31 season, when McMillan's squad, which was led by all-conference Forwards Earl Loose and Harry Schoening, finished second in the circuit with a respectable 8-4 record. One of the highlights of the season came late in the year when Minnesota beat the Boilermakers, who were led by the National Player-of-the-Year, Guard Johnny Wooden. (Wooden, of course, would go on to become the greatest college basketball coach in NCAA history with the UCLA Bruins.)

The team would finish as the runner-up to Purdue that next season, but then hit the skids for the next four years — finishing with a pair of ninth and seventh place finishes. Finally, in 1936-37, Minnesota rebounded to share co-Big Ten title honors with Illinois. Led by sophomore Forward Johnny Kundla, who lit up the DePaul Blue Demons for 18 points in a 34-25 win at the Field House early in the season, the team went on to win nine of its last 10 games en route to a 10-2 conference tally. The other star of the team was All-American Guard Marty Rolek, who would go on to join Arnie Oss that next season as Minnesota's only other player to garner back-to-back All-American honors.

The Gophers, who were hitting on all cylinders thanks to the efforts of Kundla, Gordon Spear and Gordie Addington, came back to capture second place honors in 1937-38 with a 9-3 Big Ten finish. One of the highlights that season came over the Christmas break, when Coach McMillan took his boys on a train trip to New York and Washington D.C. to play in a tournament. In the Big Apple, where they played in the famed Madison Square Garden, Minnesota beat Long Island University, 56-41, followed by New York University, 36-31. From there, they headed to D.C., where they fell to future Celtics Head Coach Red Auerbech, who was the star of George Washington University, 35-27. After a trio of conference losses to Wisconsin, Indiana and Michigan, the Gophers came back strong to win their final nine games, including a thrilling 35-28 victory over the hated Wisconsin Badgers in front of 13,000 fans at the Field House.

The winning streak continued into the 1939 season as well, as the team rolled out of the gates to go 10-0 that year. But the wheels fell off after winning their first three Big Ten games against Chicago, Iowa and Michigan. From there they lost a close one at Northwestern, 32-31, followed by losses to Notre Dame, Ohio State, Purdue, Indiana and Wisconsin, to finish at 7-5 in conference play. When the season had ended John Kundla had emerged as the team's career leader in points scored — a feat which would forever make him one of the Minnesota's most celebrated athletes. (Kundla would later go on to lead the NBA's Minneapolis Lakers to six world titles, eventually becoming the Gophers head coach in 1959.)

Marty Rolek

Minnesota would play just marginally during the next couple of years which ensued. The team, which was led by Minneapolis Edison High School star, Don "Swede" Carlson, a star forward who would later play with the Minneapolis Lakers, managed to finish only in the middle of the pack during this era. World War II was going on and young men everywhere were being shipped off overseas. At the end of the 1942 season Dave McMillan decided to finally step down as Minnesota's Head Coach. The "Canny Scot" had posted a very respectable 159-133 record during his 15-year tenure behind the Gopher bench, highlighted by a co-Big Ten title in 1937, along with four conference runner-up finishes as well.

Replacing McMillan was Dr. Carl Nordly, a professor of physical education at the U of M who had received his Ph.D. from Columbia University. Nordly, who had been a football and basketball star at Carleton College, had a much different coaching philosophy than that of McMillan. Instead of focusing on the passing game, like McMillan had done, Nordly emphasized defense and also on his players being able to be creative out on the floor. He didn't want to hold them back, so he let them have the freedom to shoot the ball whenever they felt comfortable.

The good doctor led his new squad to a quick 4-0 start that Fall, only to lose to his former Carleton Coach, Ozzie Cowles', NCAA runner-up Dartmouth squad. The team would go on to finish just sixth that season, followed by a pair of disappointing seasons thereafter. Many of the players were being called upon to report to active military service and the team fell into disarray. After winning just two Big Ten games in 1944, Nordly stepped down as the team's head coach and was replaced by Wes Mitchell, who had coached at Minneapolis Central High School. Mitchell, who was inexperienced to say the least, put together a marginal 8-13 record that year. For his efforts, he was let go following the season, and was replaced by none other than Dave McMillan — who was convinced to come out of retirement and rescue a team which by now was playing to half-empty Field House crowds.

By now the War was over and McMillan could rebuild the program with a mix of veterans and young recruits. Joining Swede Carlson were veterans Tony Jaros (another future Minneapolis Laker), Louis Brewster, Max Mohr and Warren Ajax. Then, among the new recruits, was a six-foot-nine freshmen center from Patrick Henry High School by the name of Jim McIntyre, who would go down as one of the Maroon and Gold's best ever.

Johnny Kundla

The Gophers got off to a great start that next season, beating the heck out of South Dakota and South Dakota State by the combined score of 149-52, and then added a pair of wins over both Nebraska, 55-30, and Iowa State, 65-33, to go 4-0 out of the gates. After a pair of losses to Great Lakes and Michigan State, the team rebounded to beat North Dakota State, 69-46. From there Minnesota got one of its biggest wins in program history when, thanks to Two Harbors native Ed Kernan's 17-point performance, they beat the defending National Invitational Tournament (then considered the national championship) champions from DePaul University, 45-36, at the Field House. DePaul All-American George Mikan, who would go on to become a future Minneapolis Laker Hall of Famer, was held to just 11 points in the game by Gopher big-man Jim McIntyre. The huge win gave the kids a lot of confidence as they would ultimately go on to win their next five straight before finally losing a heart-breaker at Iowa, 63-61. The team, which went on to lose five of its next six games, did rebound to beat Iowa and Wisconsin in the final two games of the year. But, it was too little, too

Ozzie Cowles

Ozzie Cowles had been a star athlete at Carleton College, where he earned 11 letters in football, basketball, and baseball, and was an all-conference selection for three years in basketball before he graduated in 1922. He returned to Carleton as head basketball and baseball coach from 1924-1930. Later, after a stint at River Falls State Teachers College in Wisconsin, Cowles headed to Dartmouth, where he led the Big Green to seven Eastern Intercollegiate Conference (now Ivy League) championships and a trip to the 1942 NCAA Tournament finals against Stanford. He then spent two years in Ann Arbor, winning the conference championship for Michigan in 1947-48, before returning to Minnesota in the spring of 1948.

"The Old Barn"

Minnesota's version of Wrigley Field lies along University Avenue and Oak Street, in the heart of campus. Construction of the enormous nine-story structure began back in the spring of 1927 by local architect C.H. Johnston for the whopping cost of $650,000. At the time of its completion that next year, the Field House, as it was called, was the largest structure of its kind in the country at 446 feet long by 236 feet wide and 104 feet high. Originally outfitted with a 9,500-person capacity, the building also housed a pair of tennis courts, a 220-yard circular track, as well as big plot of dirt, which was used for football practices. (A tunnel was also added to connect the Field House with Memorial Stadium underneath University Avenue.) The basketball court, which was originally laid on a cinder foundation, was later reinforced and elevated three feet — to where it still stands proudly today. To increase attendance for basketball games, temporary bleachers were set up over the tennis courts (on either end of the baskets) to push the capacity to more than 15,000. However, before the fire-marshall came down, it wasn't uncommon to see well over 20,000 fans piled into the joint.

Dedicated in a game against Ohio State on February 4, 1928, the "Barn" as it has affectionately become known, is a Minnesota landmark and a real sacred cow. In 1950 the building was divided into two parts, with one end becoming the home of Gopher Hockey, and later being renamed as "Mariucci Arena." The other was renamed as "Williams Arena," in honor of former Gopher Football Coach Dr. Henry Williams, and has evolved into one of college basketballs best home-court advantages. In fact, it was even ranked by Inside Sports Magazine as the nation's third toughest venue for opposing teams to play in, behind only Duke's Cameron Indoor and UCLA's Pauley Pavillion.

Williams Arena

The first-ever game at the Barn

late though, as the Gophers wound up finishing 14-7 overall — good for just fifth in the very competitive Big Ten.

That next year a promising young freshman from Superior, Wisconsin by the name of Harry "Bud" Grant joined the team. Bud, who would go on to coaching success with the Minnesota Vikings, would emerge as a three-sport star at the U of M — also playing football and baseball as well. The team, which started out with six straight wins, posted an improved 7-5 conference record that year, good for fourth in the conference standings. In 1948 the team recorded a 16-10 overall record, but fell back to seventh place in the Big Ten with a less-than-average 5-7 mark. With that, McMillan, who was tired of the constant daily stress and concerned about his health, decided to once again step down as the team's head coach. After 18 seasons, the program's winningest all-time coach would retire with an impressive overall record of 197-157.

When the search for a new head coach commenced, one name quickly emerged as the leader — former three-time Purdue All-American, John Wooden, who, following the War, was interested in returning to the Big Ten as a coach. The Gophers immediately contacted Wooden, and, had it not been for a freak blizzard, maybe the "Wizard of Westwood," who went on to win 10 NCAA titles with UCLA, might have instead become the "Magician of Minneapolis." Here is how it went down:

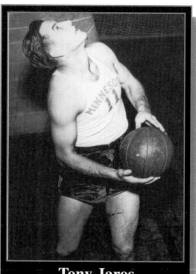

Tony Jaros

"It was early April of 1948 and I had already been offered the head coaching position by Frank McCormick, Minnesota's Athletic Director," said Wooden in Steve Pearlstein's 1995 book, 'Gopher Glory.' "He had offered me the position but he wanted me to keep Dave McMillan on as my assistant. Well, I liked Dave and I knew his record well but I felt that our coaching philosophies and techniques were so different that it would not have been in either of our best interests for him to be my assistant. I told Mr. McCormick that I wanted to bring my own assistant along. One day Minnesota was set to call me with their answer at 5:00 and UCLA, which had also been pursuing me, was to call at 6:00. They were willing to let me bring my own assistant and they wanted a definite answer when they called. Well, 5:00 came and went and I didn't hear from Mr. McCormick. When UCLA called at 6:00, I accepted the position. An hour later Frank McCormick called to let me know that he had arranged to let me bring my assistant but I told him that I had already given my answer to UCLA. Apparently a snow storm had knocked out phone service and that's why Minnesota couldn't reach me at 5:00."

With Wooden off to Los Angeles, the Gophers offered the position to Osborne Cowles, a Browns Valley (Minn.) native who, after earning 11 letters in football, basketball and baseball at Carleton College, went on to coach collegeiately at both Dartmouth and also the University of Michigan — where he led the Wolverines to the conference championship only a year earlier. Minnesota would jump out to an amazing start behind Cowles, winning its first 13 straight games. McIntyre, who averaged nearly 17 points per game that year, was joined by freshman Whitey Skoog, a speedy forward from Brainerd who would also go on to star for the Minneapolis Lakers.

The team gelled out of the gates and didn't slow down until suffering a dramatic 45-44 loss at Illinois — just one of three "L's" for Minnesota that season, with the other two coming at the hands of Ohio State and Wisconsin. The season-ending loss to the Badgers wound up costing the Gophers the Big Ten title though, as a pair of Whitey Skoog shots at the buzzer just couldn't find the net. With an 18-3 record, the Gophers would have to settle for second place in the conference to Illinois. Following the season, senior Jim McIntyre, who finished his collegiate career as the Western Conference's all-time leading scorer with 1,223 points, was awarded his second All-American selection.

Bud Grant

That next year the Field House got a much-needed makeover. The structure, which, in addition to getting a new roof, was then divided into two separate arenas — one for basketball and the other for hockey. (The basketball side would later be renamed as "Williams Arena" in honor of former Gopher Football Coach Dr. Henry L. Williams, while the hockey side would later be renamed "Mariucci Arena," in 1986, in honor of former Gopher Hockey player and coach, John Mariucci.)

The team missed McIntyre a great deal that following season, but his replacement, however, Plainview native Maynard Johnson, would fit in nicely by averaging 12.5 points per game. They would also miss Bud Grant, who decided to turn pro to play with the hometown Minneapolis Lakers. With that, junior Whitey Skoog, who was joined in the frontcourt by University of Nebraska transfer-student, Dick Means, emerged as the team's undisputed new leader. Minnesota once again came out of the blocks at full speed, going 8-1 to open the season. From there the team played inconsistently, ultimately going 1-5 down the stretch to finish 4-8 in the conference — good for just sixth place.

Minnesota, which, thanks to Maynard Johnson's 38-point performance in Game One, finished as the runner-up at the Big Seven Tournament to Kansas State in Kansas City, improved to finish with a 7-7 conference record in 1951. Skoog, who set a new school record for scoring with 374 points in 22 games, was once again named to the prestigious All-American team — putting the two-timer in a very elite fraternity.

The 1951-52 season would bring a new sense of optimism to Gold Country as a pair of freshman would invigorate a mostly veteran roster. The two, who would both go on to star with the Minneapolis Lakers, were Ed Kalafat, a six-foot-six widebody from Anaconda, Mont., and Chuck Mencel, a six-foot sharp-shooter from Eau Claire, Wis. The pair led the Gophers to a 15-7 overall record with a 10-4 tally in the Big Ten for a much-improved third place finish. Without question though, the crowning achievement of the season came on Dec. 13th, when Adolph Rupp's defending national champs from the University of Kentucky came to town. (It was also a homecoming of sorts for the Wildcats, who won the 1951 national title by beating Kansas State, 68-58, at Williams Arena — the first time an NCAA championship game was ever held in Minnesota.) There, with the eyes of the nation upon them, the Gophers went on to roll the top-ranked Cats, 61-57. Center Ed Kalafat, who tallied 30 points in the contest, was able to dominate the game due to the fact that Kentucky's All-American Center, Bill Spivey, was out with a knee injury.

Whitey Skoog

In addition to senior Bob Gelle's 12.8 points per game, the dynamic duo of Mencel, who averaged 18 points per game, and Kalafat, who added nearly 16 points and eight boards of his own, led Minnesota back to another respectable third place Big Ten finish in 1953 with an 11-7 mark in the conference's new 18-game expanded schedule. Another emerging star on the squad was Hibbing native Dick Garmaker, who seemingly did it all out on the court.

Behind Mencel, Kalafat and Garmaker, the Gophers once again placed third in the Big Ten in 1954, this time with a 10-4 record. One of the new faces on the roster that year was St. Paul Washington High School alum, Jerry Kindall, a two-sport star who would go on to later be enshrined into the College Baseball Coaches Hall of Fame after more than a quarter century of coaching at the University of Arizona.

That next season, with Kalafat off to the Lakers, Garmaker stepped it up big-time. Garmaker, who led Hibbing Junior College to the National Junior College Tournament in 1951, made his presence felt out on the court that year by averaging 24 points and seven rebounds per game en route to leading Minnesota to a second place Big Ten finish. The 15-7 Gophers also got a big scoring boost from both Chuck Mencel, and his 18.6 points per game, along with the Iron Ranger, Center Bill Simonovich, who added 15.3 points per contest as well. One of the highlights of the season came late in January, when the Gophers beat Purdue, 59-56, in a dramatic six-overtime thriller — then a college record. It was a part of a big seven game winning streak the team was on, as the club prepared to finish the season strong.

In the team's next game, against the Badgers, Mencel poured in 23, and Garmaker had 28 to lead the way. Wisconsin, led by Dick Miller, who scored 31 in the game, rallied to go up by seven at the half. In the second, Garmaker took over, scoring 12 points in first five minutes to get the score to 49-48. The Badgers held the lead until Garmaker's tip-in made it 63-63. It went back and forth with less then two minutes to go as Mencel stripped the ball from Miller. He passed it up to Garmaker, who put it in to make it 69-apiece. Now, with only 15 seconds on the clock, Mencel took the ball upcourt and got fouled. Then, with only six ticks left on the clock, Mencel nailed both free throws to ice the game, 71-69.

Jim McIntyre

The stage was now set for the Big Ten title game as hated Iowa came to town for the much-anticipated rematch of the titans. A record crowd of 20,176 squished into the Barn in anticipation of the dynamic duo of Mencel and Garmaker bringing down the vaunted Hawkeyes. (Williams Arena had never held so many spectators for a basketball game, and it will never again as fire codes now prevent such an occurrence.) The contest went back and forth as Minnesota shot 43 percent in the first half to take a 35-33 half-time lead. The Hawks were led by their big man, Bill Logan, who had 15 of his 25

Ed Kalafat

points in the first half. In the second half, the battle continued as both teams sparred like heavyweight champions. Then, with just over four minutes to play, Mencel scored six straight of his team-high 27 points to give the Gophers a 70-67 lead. But at 2:23, Iowa's guard play brought the Hawks back on top, 71-70. With two minutes to go, Mencel missed a key shot, as did Buck Lindsley, who had a chance to get the Gophers back into it, but missed a free-throw at the end of the game. It was Iowa's night, as they shot an incredible 67 percent in the second and held on to beat the Gophers, 72-70. It was a crushing loss for Minnesota, the league's best free-throw shooting team, and somewhat ironic in that Iowa was the league's worst from the charity stripe.

The season finale featured a rematch with the Badgers. The Gophers not only needed to win the game, but also had to have some help from Lady Luck to have any chance to win the conference title. It was the great Mencel's farewell to Williams Arena. Appropriately enough, his last game was against his home-state Badgers. Minnesota, its backs to the wall, hung it all out on the line that night. Coach Ozzie Cowles' boys held the lead at the half, 32-31, after Mencel popped a deuce from the post. Then, the Badgers went ahead, but the Gophers rallied with 12 minutes to go, narrowing the gap to 50-48 off a pair from Lindsley, who had 17 points. At the four-minute mark, the Gophers were still in it at 72-67, but that would be as close as they would come in the season finale. Cowles removed Mencel and Garmaker with a minute left and the crowd responded with a thunderous roar of appreciation for all their hard work over the years. Minnesota lost by the final of 78-72, thus sending Iowa to the NCAA Tournament. (How good was Iowa that year? Led by Logan, Carl Cain, and Sharm Scheuerman, the Hawkeyes waltzed past Penn State and Marquette before losing to All-American sensation Tom Gola and LaSalle in the Final Four, 76-73.)

"It was a letdown for me at the time, but also became the springboard to a much more expanded view of opportunity, both in an athletic and business sense," Mencel later recalled. "I'm not going to say we should have won the Iowa game, but we could have easily won it. I've got a video tape of the game and I still bring it out and watch it every now and then. It was a great, great game — a disappointment — but definitely my most memorable at Minnesota. The thing that stands out for me most, was that it was probably my best game as a Gopher, but we still lost. And then losing to Wisconsin in the next game was a tough way for me to bow out."

The Gophers led the conference in defense that season, and finished the year with a 10-4 record in the Big Ten, 15-7 overall. But because of the Wisconsin disappointment on the last day of the season, they wound up as the conference bridesmaids. Mencel, who passed Jim McIntyre on the career scoring list with 1,391 points, was named as the Big Ten's MVP, and was also named to the All-Big Ten and All-American squads. In addition, Dick Garmaker, who averaged 24.2 points per game, became just the second Gopher ever to be named as a consensus first-team All-American.

Bob McNamara

The team went through a rough stretch in 1956, finishing with a 6-8 conference record — good for just sixth in the Big Ten. They rebounded in 1957, however, as they came back behind Forward George Kline's 18.1 points per game to finish third in the circuit. Kline, who would be named to the All-Big Ten team, even broke Maynard Johnson's single-game scoring record when he lit up Iowa for 40 points in a 102-81 win at Williams Arena on February 25th.

That next season, 1957-58, the Gophers fell back into an ugly eighth-place finish in the conference. Kline, who averaged better than 20 points per game, was also joined by sophomore Ron Johnson, a center from New Prague who averaged 17.3 points per game as well. That next season didn't get much prettier either. The team, which was led by Johnson and Guard Roger "Whitey" Johnson, of Eau Claire, Wisc., both of whom combined to average 20 and 10 points per game respectively, struggled. Despite their efforts, the team could do no better than ninth place in the Big Ten, finishing just out of the conference cellar. With the poor finish, Ozzie Cowles resigned after the 1958-59 season. Cowles, who finished his 11-year career at Minnesota with a 147-93 record, would go down as one of the program's finest.

By this time the fans were tired of losing and anxious to get their program back on top. The administration knew that the team needed a spark, and that is exactly what it got when it was announced that former Gopher star Johnny Kundla, who had just led the Minneapolis Lakers to six world titles, had been named as the team's new head coach. In addition to senior Center Ron Johnson, Kundla would also have a pair of sophomores in forward Ray Cronk and Guard Paul Lehman to build around — something that made him very optimistic. Kundla, who would later be enshrined into the Basketball Hall of Fame, would bring an amazing sense of hope to the program. He had more credibility than arguably any coach in the world basketball at the time, and was excited about taking over at his alma mater. Cowles' conservative offense would now be shelved in favor of an up-tempo, fast-break game that only the NBA had seen the likes of.

Dick Garmaker

Hibbing native Dick Garmaker, a transfer student from Hibbing Junior College (where he led the team to the National Junior College Tournament in 1951), was one of the Gophers top players of the mid-1950s. The team's first consensus All-American, Garmaker, who scored 1,008 points and averaged better than seven rebounds per game in just 44 games, was a tremendous rebounder, defender, free-throw shooter and could do a lot of damage with his jump shot. Over his career at Minnesota, the speedy guard set eight scoring records. He went on to play in the NBA with the Minneapolis Lakers, and later finished his career with the New York Knicks, where he played from 1956 to 1961. He wound up averaging 13.3 points and 4.2 rebounds per game as a pro, playing in four all-star games along the way.

Ron Johnson averaged 21 points per game in 1959-60, as Kundla's Gophers went on to post a modest 8-6 record, good enough for a third-place in the Big Ten, while conference foe Ohio State, which whom the Gophers beat 70-61 that year, went on to win the national championship. Among the highlights that year was a win over nationally ranked Missouri, 80-62, as well as a controversial 73-72 loss to John Wooden's UCLA Bruins — in a game which saw Ron Johnson being called for a questionable foul with just seconds to go in the game, nearly causing a Williams Arena riot.

In 1961 Kundla lost not only Ron Johnson, to graduation, but also Ray Cronk, who was declared academically ineligible at the onset of the season. The loss of both stars would hurt the club, which finished the year with an 8-6 conference record, good for fourth place. In addition to Tom McGrann, who led the team with 14.2 ppg, as well as Dick Erickson and Bob Griggas, who added 10 points apiece, the team also welcomed its first African American player — All American Gopher Football Tackle Bobby Bell, who, after later starring for the Kansas City Chiefs, would go on to become enshrined into the Pro Football Hall of Fame.

After a pair of seventh and fourth place finishes in 1962 and 1963, respectively, Kundla's Gophers rebounded back to post a much-improved 17-7 overall record in 1964 — good for a third place Big Ten finish. They had taken their lumps during this era, especially from the two-time NCAA champion Ohio State Buckeyes, who were led by a couple of future NBA stars in Jerry Lucas and John Havilcek, as well as another kid by the name of Bobby Knight — who would later go on to torment the Gophers for years to come as the coach of the Indiana Hoosiers.

By now, former Minneapolis South High School star Eric Magdanz, who once lit up Michigan for a school-record 42 points and 18 rebounds, and his gaudy 25 ppg (conference) average were gone, and in were some new prospects who were ready to make a contribution. Among them were Minneapolis Patrick Henry High School Center Mel Northway, Duluth Central Guard Terry Kunze and a new kid who would go down as one of the program's all-time best. His name was Lou Hudson, and he wasted little time in making a name

Chuck Mencel

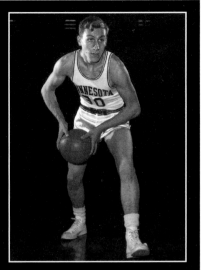

Chuck Mencel was born in Phillips, Wis., the oldest of three children. He grew up spending much of his time playing basketball at the local YMCA. "When my parents got divorced while I was in the seventh grade, the basketball gymnasium became my safe haven," said Mencel. He went on to play basketball at Eau Claire High School, becoming the only non-senior to make the squad. His team made it all the way to the Wisconsin State Basketball Tournament but lost in the championship game to St. Croix Falls. During that season, he broke his school's season scoring records. After his senior year he was selected to the national high school All-American team.

After a stellar prep career, Mencel accepted a scholarship to attend Bradley University in Peoria, Ill. But when allegations of a basketball betting scandal broke out that summer, Mencel elected to attend Minnesota. "The scandal was a big red flag for me, so I immediately decided to attend the U of M," said Mencel. Because of the Korean War, freshmen were allowed to participate in intercollegiate sports, and Mencel took every advantage of his playing time. While at the U, Chuck wound up living in possibly the most athletic dorm room of all time. That's because his roommate was Gopher hockey All-American John Mayasich.

On the hardwood, Chuck Mencel could flat-out shoot, and that's why he was one of the greatest guards ever to play for the Gophers. Mencel had poise, court-savvy, tremendous ball-handling skills, and was extremely accurate from the field as well as from the line. He worked hard at the fundamentals and optimized the cliché, "lead by example."

Chuck had the golden shooting touch and was acknowledged as one of Minnesota's greatest team players. He was widely regarded as the premier pure shooter of his day and, because of his quickness and shooting ability, revolutionized many aspects of the game. There's no telling just how good Mencel would have been if he had played in the NBA after the dawn of the three-point line.

Averaging 16 points per game, Mencel held five Gopher scoring records during his tenure at the U, still ranking ninth all-time in career scoring, with 1,391 points. (He held the school's scoring record for nearly a quarter of a century, until Mychal Thompson broke it in the late 1970s.) In 1955 Mencel was named to the All-Big Ten and All-American squads. For his efforts he was awarded with the Chicago Tribune's Silver Basketball Award, signifying the Big Ten's MVP.

An outstanding student, he graduated that same year with a Bachelor's Degree in Business Administration. What's even more impressive is that he did it all while taking care of his family. You see, Chuck married his high school sweet-heart when he was a sophomore at the U, and before he graduated, he had two children.

After his illustrious career at Minnesota, Mencel was drafted by the Lakers. But, that summer before his first season, he was invited to play on the traveling team that played the Harlem Globetrotters. It was a 24-city tour and he was paid $100 per game. This was a real team Mencel played for. They played to win and weren't stooges like the Trotter opponents are today.

Chuck then started as point guard for the Lakers and averaged seven points and led the team in assists, with three per game. His career was cut short after only two years in the NBA, due to the fact that he was required to fulfill his military obligation, which he had deferred out of college.

"Chuck was such a good, sound ballplayer," said Coach Johnny Kundla. "He was solid with the fundamentals and, not only that, he had such a great shot. He had his jumpshot of his down pat! He was a super guy and a great player. He had a great career at the University and he was a great addition to our Laker teams."

From there Mencel joined the Army as a second lieutenant in the Transportation Corps and was stationed in Fort Eustis, Va. After that, he decided to abandon the NBA and enter the world of business, where he applied that same zealous attitude of hard work and success that he had on the court. In fact, Mencel went on to become president and chief executive officer of Caterpillar Paving Products, based in Brooklyn Park, before finally retiring in 1994. The father of three, Chuck presently lives in the Twin Cities. He also remains active with his alma mater and was very involved in the capital campaign that helped finance the renovation and construction of various on-campus sports facilities.

"In hindsight, being a Gopher really set the table for a lifestyle that was unparalleled in my expectations as a young person," said Mencel. "To have played and been successful at a major institution like the U of M and in a conference such as the Big Ten was just incredible. As an athlete, it was wonderful stepping stone to the business world that gave me the ability to raise my family and live a standard of life that I never dreamed would be possible. If I had not come to Minnesota - who knows? I can't imagine that it would have been any better for me anywhere else. It was a wonderful experience."

Ron Johnson

New Prague's Ron Johnson averaged 21.1 points per game in 1960, finishing his Gopher career with a total of 1,335 career points. Johnson finished his collegiate career by being named first-team All-Big Ten and a UPI All-American honorable mention selection.

He was later drafted by the NBA's Detroit Pistons in the second round, where he played for one season before retiring. One of the best pure-shooters in Minnesota basketball history, Ron Johnson was simply awesome.

for himself — averaging 18.1 ppg in 1964, tops on the third place squad.

You see, it was the height of the Civil Rights Movement in America at this time and young African American men from the segregated South were being denied opportunities to play collegiate sports. Hudson, a three-sport prep star from Greensboro, North Carolina, actually wanted to attend neighboring Wake Forest University, but couldn't because of racial inequalities. But he caught a break when Wake Forest Coach Bones McKinney called his old friend from the Minneapolis Lakers, Johnny Kundla. McKinney encouraged Kundla to recruit the speedy forward, and that's exactly what he did — eventually convincing Hudson to head north, where he would have every opportunity to play ball in Minnesota.

Hudson agreed, and was also joined by two other young Black men on the team — Archie Clark, a quick guard from Detroit who had spent the previous three years in the Army, and Don Yates, from Uniontown, Pennsylvania (home of Gopher Football stars Sandy Stephens and Judge Dickson). They would all prove to be pioneers though, in helping to open the doors of integration for future generations of people of color in both the North and South.

(This was a controversial time in Gopher sports, and not all of the fans were supportive. Up until then, most of the Gophers' recruits were white, and from the Midwest. In fact, Gopher Football Coach Murray Warmath was also dealing with many of the same issues when he recruited several African American players from the South, including Bobby Bell and Carl Eller, from the Carolinas, as well as the aforementioned Sandy Stephens and Judge Dickson. Those young men, however, would go on to lead the Gophers to a National Championship and Rose Bowl in 1961 and 1962, respectively.)

By 1964-65, Hudson had emerged as one of the league's preeminent stars. He averaged a team high 23.3 points per game that season, en route to leading the Gophers to a 19-5 overall record (11-3 in the conference), and a second place finish in the Big Ten. "Sweet Lou" led the charge that season, but had a pretty decent supporting cast as well in Clark, Yates, Northway and Dennis Dvoracek, a six-foot-six junior forward from Eau Claire, who filled in nicely for Terry Kunze, was ruled academically ineligible early in the season. The team beat Wisconsin in the conference opener, and after falling to Illinois in Game Two, 75-72, went on a seven-game winning streak. Hudson was awesome over the stretch, scoring better than 30 points per game on several occasions. From there the team was beaten by the eventual national champion Michigan Wolverines, 91-78, at Williams Arena. They rebounded to beat Indiana and Iowa, but then lost to those same Wolverines once again, this time in Ann Arbor, 88-85, in a game which ultimately cost them the Big Ten title. They did manage to beat Iowa in a dramatic 85-84 overtime classic at the Barn though, to end their season ranked seventh in the nation.

In 1966, with both Northway and Kunze gone to the NBA (both were drafted by the St. Louis Hawks), the Gophers could only muster a fifth-place Big Ten finish. The big reason for the team's marginal 7-7 finish was due to the fact that early in the season, in a game against Creighton, Hudson, en route to tallying 32 points and 12 boards in a 89-77 win, was fouled hard while driving for a lay-up and broke his right wrist. Incredibly, with a cast on his hand, he still played in 17 of the team's remaining 24 games and even averaged 14 points per game during the stretch. (Even with the injury he was still named to the All-Big Ten second team!) Archie Clark picked up the slack though, averaging nearly 25 points per game in his absence, while Center Tom Kondla, who replaced Mel Northway in the pivot, Dennis Dvoracek, Paul Presthus and Wes Martins, all averaged in double figures that season as well.

(Clark, who was named to the All-Big Ten Team, would go on to be drafted by the NBA's Los Angeles Lakers, while Yates, who had left school early due to academic issues, was drafted by the St. Louis Hawks. For Hudson, who finished just six points shy of becoming the school's all-time leading scorer, he would go on to become a six-time NBA All-Star after the St. Louis Hawks selected him with the fourth overall pick of the first round. "Sweet Lou" would go on to score nearly 18,000 points in his illustrious 11-year NBA career.)

Bobby Bell

The next couple of seasons were pretty awful ones for Gopher fans. In fact, a pair of ninth place conference finishes were all it took for Coach Kundla to finally hang it up. He would go down as one of Minnesota's greatest ever coaches though, later being enshrined into the Pro Basketball Hall of Fame.

"Being a Gopher meant the world to me," Kundla would later say. "In those years, we weren't recruited to play basketball. I went out for the freshman team and made it. It was such a thrill just to play for the University of Minnesota. I was happy just to make the team and to be a Minnesota letter winner. Then, to be able to come back and coach my alma mater was something very special to me. It was a great honor to be a Gopher player and later their coach. I just wished that we could have won a championship for the U."

It was now 1968 and the U of M needed a new coach. They wanted to get someone who they felt could recruit, so they turned to Bill Fitch, who, in addition to having coached North Dakota for three seasons, had just led Bowling Green University to the Mid-American Conference title and a berth in the NCAA tournament. Fitch would do OK in Gold Country. His teams would ultimately show improvement, but, after posting a 25-23 record over two seasons, he too would call it quits. The team did manage to finish fifth in both 1969 and 1970, thanks in large part to the efforts of Forwards Larry Mikan (the son of Laker great, George Mikan) and Larry Overskei, as well as Guards Eric Hill and Ollie Shannon — a junior college transfer from New York City. While all four of the players averaged in double figures that season, it was Mikan who shined brightest — averaging 17.2 points and 14.5 rebounds per game, including a record 28-rebound performance in a home victory against Michigan.

One of the highlights of the 1969-70 campaign came on December 6th, when the Gophers lost in overtime to the three-time defending NCAA champs from UCLA, 72-71, at the Barn. "We were only one rebound, or one pass, or one basket away," said Fitch after the game. "But I don't want to say anything to discredit our kids. What they did was by guts, desire, and determination."

In 1971 both Mikan and Fitch headed to the NBA, Mikan to play with his old man's alma mater, the Lakers, and Fitch to take over the expansion Cleveland Cavaliers. (Fitch would go on to embark on an NBA coaching career which would last for more than a quarter century.) With Fitch's departure, the team was once again in the market for a new coach. This time, however, they stayed home, and hired longtime assistant and former Gopher Guard, George Hanson. In fact, a big part of the decision to hire Hanson was to ease the transition for several of the team's new players, including Jim Brewer and "Corky" Taylor, who were comfortable with Hanson. (Local businessman and best-selling author, Harvey Mackay, started getting involved in recruiting at that time, and was instrumental in the team landing Brewer — a top national recruit from Chicago.) As a result, the program passed on hiring an outsider to the program — namely Army Coach, Bobby Knight, who the program probably could've hired. (In fact, the search committee even brought in the hot young coaching prospect, who desperately wanted to coach in the Big Ten, for an interview, at the old Sheraton-Ritz Hotel in downtown Minneapolis — but they didn't hit it off, and Knight went on to become a legend at rival Indiana.)

Lou Hudson

A silky-smooth shooter who could score from anywhere on the court, Lou Hudson was a Gopher hoops legend. An All-American and first-team All-Big Ten selection in 1965, "Sweet Lou," averaged 24.8 points and 10.7 rebounds per game that year, leading led the Gophers to a second-place finish in the Big Ten.

Incredibly, that next year Hudson led the Gophers' charge for the Big Ten title with a cast on his shooting hand. He persevered though, played with the cast, and learned how to shoot with his left hand, averaging 19.0 points and 7.5 rebounds per game in his senior year.

Well liked by his teammates and adored by the fans, the Greensboro, N.C. native was the first African American star at Minnesota, overcoming adversity along the way to become a real hero. Hudson finished his illustrious career in Gold Country with 1,329 points, good enough for 12th-place on the all-time Golden Gopher scoring chart.

A 1966 NBA first round (fourth overall) draft pick of St. Louis, Hudson went on to star with the Hawks and the Lakers, becoming a six-time all-star in his eleven years in the league, amassing 17,980 points, and finishing 12th on the NBA's all-time scoring list upon retirement.

"It is a great honor for me to have the University think of me in this way, even now after all these years," said Hudson in 1994, when his No. 14 jersey was retired into the old Barn's rafters forever. "I have always had strong ties to Minnesota, and having my jersey retired is something very special, something not many athletes can say happened to them."

Little did they know, however, that the George Hanson experiment would last just one season. He did manage to produce a modest 11-13 overall record — good for the program's third straight fifth place finish, but that would be all. Following the season Hanson was asked to step down. What followed was the University's largest man-hunt in history. They needed a big-time coach to rescue the program from mediocrity. Attendance was way down and so was team morale. Sure, the club had some stars in Jim Brewer, Ollie Shannon and Eric Hill, who each averaged better than 16 points per game, but they needed a change of scenery, and they needed it fast.

Enter former Gopher Football legend Paul Giel, the University's new athletic director, who knew that he needed to turn the program around. With that, a search committee was established to hire a new coach. Their recommendation: Murray State University Head Coach, Cal Luther, who accepted the job, only to reconsider and turn it down just a few days later. So, the committee this time turned to a virtual unknown, Bill Musselman, a 30-year-old ball of fire from tiny Ashland College (Ohio), who, in six seasons had achieved an amazing 128-31 record. Musselman wowed the committee in his interview and let them know of his intentions to win immediately. With that, he was promptly hired.

The 1971-72 Gophers, under new Coach Bill Musselman, hit the court with one of the tallest and most talented lineups in the country. In addition to returning upperclassmen Center Jim Brewer, Forward "Corky" Taylor, and returning Guards Bob Murphy and Keith Young, Musselman added three junior college transfer players in six-foot-nine swingman Ron Behagen, who had been playing at Southern Idaho Junior College, six-foot-eight Forward Clyde Turner, who came over from Robert Morris Junior College (Illinois), and six-foot-three Guard Bob Nix, from Henderson County Junior College in Athens, Texas.

The JUCO transfers that Musselman brought in were not without controversy. He knew he needed to surround Jim Brewer, one of the best centers in the country, with some talented new players. So, he went outside the system and got some players who could help him right away. While today this is commonplace, back in the early 1970s it was extremely taboo. Back then, coaches recruited kids, redshirted them, and developed them into ball players. What Musselman did, in the eyes of many coaches, was to take a shortcut, and "cheat" the system. But Musselman didn't care. He had finally arrived to the big-time and simply didn't want to wait around to someday be a contender. He liked his players to execute a physical, tough rebounding, in-your-face style of basketball, and he now had the tools to do some immediate damage in the Big Ten.

He had the players, but he knew he still needed to fill Williams Arena with plenty of fans and excitement. So, Musselman, ever the consummate salesman and promoter, even took his players around the state for intra-squad games to sell tickets. In addition he instituted one of basketball's greatest pre-game warm-up shows, maybe even the best, with the possible exception of the one originated by the Harlem Globetrotters. The pre-game warm-up saw the players enter into a darkened arena, run through a giant spotlight, and form a circle. There, in addition to basketball finger-spinning, they would pass balls back and forth by zipping them through their legs, behind their backs and off their heads. The

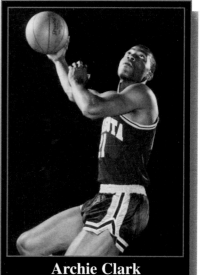

Archie Clark

Tom Kondla

opposing coaches and players hated it, but that didn't bother Musselman.

"It was the greatest exhibition of ball-handling that a lot of people had ever seen," said Musselman. "It was precision ball handling to music like 'Sweet Georgia Brown.' We used to fill up the arena an hour before game time so that people could watch our warm-up."

The Gophers went into their Big Ten Conference schedule with a modest non-conference record of 6-3. They even picked up a new walk-on player early in the season — a young man who would go on to become a pretty decent athlete in his day. Who was he? Well, in 1971, the University intramural basketball champs were a team called the "Soulful Strutters." The Strutters were led by a six-foot-six specimen from St. Paul Central High School with unbelievable athletic skills by the name of Dave Winfield, who was also a star pitcher on the Gopher baseball team at the time. Now, because the Strutters were the best intramural team on campus, they often-times scrimmaged against the Gopher Junior Varsity team — usually whipping them pretty good. When J.V. Coach Jimmy Williams saw Winfield play during one of those games, he couldn't believe his eyes. So, he told Musselman that he better give the kid a look. He did, and immediately asked him to join the team.

Their first Big Ten opponent that year was Indiana, at the old Barn, where the second-largest crowd in school history — 19,121, showed up to watch Musselman do battle with his old childhood pal from Ohio, Bobby Knight. Turner, Behagen, Nix, and Young all scored in double figures in this one as Minnesota went on to win the game 52-51, thanks to a blocked shot by Brewer and two last-second foul shots by Nix.

"I grew up just a few miles from Bobby, and as kids we used to shoot baskets by the hour together," said Musselman. "That game was one of the most competitive and intense games that I think I have ever been in, it was amazing!"

Minnesota added three more victories to make them 4-0 in conference play. Their next opponent was Ohio State. It was a big game, and everyone knew it. There were several sidebars going in as well — including how Buckeye Coach Fred Taylor didn't appreciate Musselman, a fellow Ohioan, recruiting JUCO kids. The media was all over it too. In fact, while the NHL All-Star Game was being played across town at the Met Center that same night, most of the media attention in the Twin Cities was focused on the basketball game. The Gophers had a chance to move into a first-place tie with a victory and the crowd was pumped. It would go down as one of the most significant games in Minnesota history. It was also the game that will forever be remembered as the beginning of the "Iron Five."

With the Buckeyes leading 50-44 and 36 seconds left in the game, Ohio State's star Center Luke Witte broke toward the basket. As Minnesota pressed, Witte outran the field and caught the inbound pass and, in the process, was fouled hard by both Clyde Turner and Corky Taylor. Turner was then called for a flagrant foul and was immediately ejected. Then, amazingly and nearly simultaneously, Taylor reached out to help Witte, who was on the court, to his feet, but instead of helping him up, proceeded to knee him in the groin. The crowd was stunned, and subsequent mayhem broke out. Ohio State's, Dave Merchant rushed over to help Witte, quickly pushing Taylor out of his way. Brewer and Taylor then ran down the court after Merchant, while Behagen, having already fouled out, came off the bench and attacked Witte.

Larry Mikan

For the next moments, complete pandemonium took over at Williams Arena. Some 18,000 fans went spontaneously crazy, and many started to pour on the court to partake in the festivities. Big Dave Winfield even got into the act and it got ugly in a hurry. Several Buckeye players were taken to the hospital, and a near riot ensued. Minnesota's Athletic Director, Paul Giel, then decided, after consulting with the game officials, to simply end the game and declare Ohio State as the winner. Outside, they started to throw rocks at the police cars as they took the players to the hospital. When it was all over, a huge black eye was left on the University of Minnesota basketball program.

The opposing players had much different stories as to what really happened though. "Witte was gong up to take the shot, and Clyde Turner and myself fouled him," said Taylor. "It was really how hard I fouled him that precipitated my helping him up. Basically, it was a situation where he had an easy two points, and we were trying to make sure he didn't score. When I went to help Luke up, he spit at me and I got pissed! It was a very tough game, and I kicked him. When I turned around, the entire floor had erupted. It was a scary situation."

Ron Behagen

To better understand the entire "situation," you have to go back to the end of the first half where an incident took place that may have instigated the ensuing event. As the players ran off the court and into the locker rooms, Bobby Nix waved to the pumped-up crowd by raising his fists in the air towards the scoreboard. "Luke Witte, (who had been described as a rough, 'Bill Laimbeer-type' player) crossed in front of me," said Nix. "There's no question in my mind or anybody's that saw it. It was a deliberate elbow to my face. He just threw it, and he damn near decked me. It was seen by a lot of people, except the officials."

That night, following the incident, replays of the fight were played on virtually every newscast in the country. Every paper ran a story about it, and the next week, Sports Illustrated featured the brawl as their cover story. All fingers pointed at Musselman as the instigator. They tried to paint a picture that Musselman's "win at any cost" attitude had animalized his players into a fit of rage. National media had concentrated only on the game-ending fight, and they never mentioned the half-time incident that precluded the retaliation. Attempts were made to dramatize and polarize Musselman and the Buckeyes' Fred Taylor, the two coaches (both with roots to Ohio). Taylor was a Big Ten coaching legend who built programs traditionally. Musselman, on the other hand, was a rookie who they said took short-cuts to success by obtaining junior college players. Racism and even the Vietnam War were thrown into the stew. People were searching for a scapegoat, and the media had found one in Musselman.

"A lot of things were said in print that were wrong," said Musselman in Bill Heller's 1989 book entitled: "Obsession: Timberwolves Stalk the NBA." "I was blamed for the fight or for not stopping the fight, yet the fight was the last thing I wanted. My insides were torn up. My hopes and dreams were shattered that night. I couldn't believe life was like that. I believed if you were dedicated and outworked everyone, you'd be successful. That night it seemed like everything I believed in was wrong. I went home and got down on my knees and prayed. And I thought then, 'Well, you asked for this; you wanted to coach in the big time.' Since then, my beliefs have been reaffirmed. But it was my background that got me through that situation. If I hadn't been mentally tough, I wouldn't have survived that incident."

"Obviously the fight was wrong, but I always felt that it was racially motivated," added Musselman (25 years later). "It was during the early 1970s, and there were a lot of racial overtones. The game got out of hand, and the officials let too much loose play go on. I took a lot of heat for it. It was ridiculous that people would insinuate that I wanted to have a fight. They tried to blame it on my pre-game warm-up routine, saying that it hyped the fans into a frenzy. It was too bad that it happened, but it was an intense heat of the battle thing. The sad part about it was the fact that all the players were good people. Back then our kids never got into any trouble, and they got their degrees. They all made a contribution to society and were all great kids."

Following the game, Behagen and Taylor were suspended for the remainder of the season. (Ohio's governor even suggested publicly that the two ought to be thrown in jail.) The new squad stayed focused though, and even used the suspensions as a personal vendetta to salvage the season. So

Corky Taylor

Musselman went almost exclusively with a five-man lineup: Turner and Winfield at the forwards, Brewer at center, and Nix and Young as the guards.

The next game was at Iowa. There were plain-clothed police officers everywhere and the fans were skeptical. "The fans there were vicious," said Winfield, who, after accidentally knocking a Hawkeye player to the ground at one point during the game, even drawing blood, thought he might get attacked right there on the court. "One of them grabbed me. One of them threw beer on me. It was tense. That's the way it was after that, every game, every week, always with the sense that a fight might break out."

The Gophers won the Iowa game 61-50, and just kept on winning. Then, with Ohio State reeling in a tail-spin, Minnesota put it all on the line at Purdue, with a chance to win the Big Ten title.

Minnesota then headed to West Lafayette, for the year's final regular-season game against Purdue. There, behind Jim Brewer and Clyde Turner's 12-point performances, the Gophers hung on to beat the Boilers, 49-48. With the victory, they became the first Gopher team in 53 years to win an undisputed Big Ten title.

Clyde Turner

"We had a one point lead and held them scoreless for the last 20-some seconds to win," said Musselman. "Our defensive effort was incredible because they didn't get a good shot off at all when they could've won it. Winfield grabbed the last rebound to seal it."

Then, in their first-ever NCAA Tournament appearance, the Gophers were upset by Florida State, 70-56, in the NCAA Mideast Regional game in Dayton, Ohio. From there they did manage to come back to beat Marquette, 77-72, in the Mideast Regional consolation game. With the top defense in the nation, the 10th ranked Gophers allowed just 58 points per game that season, finishing with an impressive 18-7 record. Brewer was named as the Big Ten's MVP, and both he and Behagen were named to the All-American team as well. Musselman, who said going in that he did not believe in "rebuilding years," kept his word and made his first year in Gold Country one of the program's most exciting, and dare we say "eventful" in history.

With all of the "Iron Five," along with Corky Taylor and Ron Behagen, returning that next season, Minnesota opened the season by going 9-0, and emerging once again as a national power. Then, after losing the conference opener in Iowa City, to the Hawkeyes, 65-62, in overtime, they won back-to-back contests over Wisconsin as well as the No. 2-ranked Marquette Warriors. Some 18,000 Gopher fans jammed into the Barn to see the Gophers win this classic, 64-53, with another 4,000 watching the game next door in the hockey arena on closed-circuit TV.

At 11-1 Minnesota looked like they were in cruise control, but that's when Bobby Knight's Indiana Hoosiers brought them back to earth, beating the Gophers, 83-71. Musselman got his boys back on track after that though, as the team went on to win its next nine straight Big Ten games. Then, at 10-2, and their second straight conference title within their grasp, Iowa came to town. It was a huge game, complete with all the fan-fare of having Jim Brewer's No. 52 retired in a pre-game ceremony. The Gophers, who led by 13 at the half, stunk it up in the second period though, and got upset, 79-77, thanks to Hawkeye Center Kevin Kunnert's last second lay-up and free-throw to ice the game. Now, with their backs against the wall, the Gophers headed to Evanston, to play Northwestern. There, with their title hopes

Jim Brewer

Center Jim Brewer was an All-American for the University of Minnesota in 1973, and also served as a member of the 1972 US Olympic basketball team as well. During his career in Gold Country the three-time team MVP scored 1,009 points and 436 rebounds while averaging 13.5 points per game. In 1973 his No. 52 jersey was retired into the old Barn's rafters forever. From there the Illinois native was drafted by the NBA's Cleveland Cavaliers. The big center went on to play for nine seasons in the NBA, later with Detroit, Portland and LA, and averaged nearly six points and six rebounds per game over his pro career. He later began a successful coaching career, most recently serving as an assistant with the LA Clippers.

Dave Winfield

Winnie

Dave Winfield is arguably the greatest athlete ever to hail from the great state of Minnesota. Dave grew up in St. Paul loving sports. After a phenomenal prep career at St. Paul Central High School, Winfield opted to stay close to home and attend the University of Minnesota to pitch for legendary Coach Dick Siebert on a baseball scholarship. He was eventually "discovered" by Gopher basketball Coach Bill Musselman while playing in an intramural basketball league on campus. The Gopher junior varsity basketball team needed some tough competition to practice against, and since Winfield's intramural team, the "Soulful Strutters" were campus champs, a scrimmage was arranged. There, upon seeing Winfield's incredible athleticism, Musselman immediately made the six-foot-six forward a two-sport star at the U of M.

"I switched from a baseball scholarship to a basketball scholarship," said Winfield. "Baseball was only partial, so I needed a full ride. A poor kid from St. Paul… so I switched, and the rest is history."

Making the jump to the hardcourt, Winfield played two seasons with the Gopher basketball team, becoming a starter on the 1971-72 team that went 18-7 and won the Big Ten championship — the school's first in 53 years. His big break though, ironically enough, came on the heels of the now infamous "Ohio State Brawl," in which several players were suspended from the team. Thrust into the starting lineup as a member of the notorious "Iron-Five" squad, Winnie went on to average 6.9 points per game that season. Then, in 1972-73, he averaged 10.5 points per game en route to leading the Gophers to a 21-5 record — good for second in the Big Ten.

"Dave is one of the most extraordinary athletes that I have ever been around in my life," Coach Musselman later recalled. "He is one of the hardest working people, and one of the most sincere athletes that I have ever seen. For 20 years, the first thing that I checked every day during baseball season was Dave's box score wherever he was playing. We are good friends, and I think the world of Dave. I have so much respect for him, because he was on a Gopher baseball scholarship and didn't have to play basketball. What he sacrificed knowing that he had a career in baseball was incredible. I mean that he could have gotten injured. I have never seen anybody play harder than Dave Winfield. He had the most incredible endurance and was the best rebounder I have ever seen. When he was 28, he told me he was going to play baseball until he was 45, and I think he finally retired at 44. He took great care of himself, and his combination of speed and strength was just awesome."

His Gopher sports career was nothing short of incredible. On the diamond Winfield was a three-time All-Big Ten pitcher and was a career .353 hitter. In 1973, he led the Gophers to the Big Ten title, and was selected as an All-American as well as the MVP of the College World Series. As a pitcher, his 19-4 career record afforded him an amazing winning percentage .826. He finished with 229 career strikeouts, second only to Paul Giel's 243, and his single season record of 109 strikeout's stood for nearly 25 years.

"For me, I was a baseball player first," he said. "But I loved playing basketball for the Gophers as well, and I was lucky enough to play both sports. I really liked all the guys on the basketball squad, and we had a lot of good competitors on that team. Mentally and physically I thought I was ready, and each game I thought I got better. It was here and now, and we just had a good time. That's why we were successful."

"He is truly an amazing athlete and, as our captain, he was a strong team leader," recalled Dick Siebert. "I don't know of any sport he can't excel at. I remember when David asked for a half-hour off from baseball practice to compete with his buddies in an intramural track meet. He had never before high jumped, and all he did was place first, going 6-foot 6-inches while still in his baseball uniform. He may be the finest all-around athlete I have coached, or for that matter to ever compete for Minnesota. To top it all off he was also a fine student."

Upon graduating from the U of M in 1973, Winfield found himself with several post-graduate options. In fact, so gifted an athlete was Winnie that he became the first man ever to be drafted by four professional sports teams. He was taken in baseball by the San Diego Padres, in basketball by the NBA's Atlanta Hawks as well as the ABA's Utah Stars, and in football by the Minnesota Vikings.

"In football, they drafted me strictly as an athlete," said Winfield. "I was six-foot-six and 230 with good hands, speed, and strength. The Vikings officials figured they could make me into a tight end. Who knows? It would have been great to have caught some of those Fran Tarkenton passes! There's no question that I made the right choice though, and I would have had a short career playing football."

Not surprisingly, Winfield chose baseball, going directly to the big-leagues to join the Padres, where he batted .277 his first year. (Not bad for a guy drafted as a pitcher!) In 1980 he signed with the New York Yankees and became the richest man in sports. He stayed with the Bronx Bombers until being traded to the California Angels in 1990. He signed with the Toronto Blue Jays in 1991 and won a World Series with that club in 1992. Then, in 1993, he came home to join the Twins, where, on September 16th, Dave got his 3,000 hit off of Oakland's vaunted relief pitcher, Dennis Eckersley, becoming only the 19th player in major league history to achieve that mark.

"It was great," he said. "I was so glad to come home and to have been able to accomplish such a major milestone in front of my home crowd in the Metrodome. That was definitely a special event for me in my career, and it's something that I will always remember."

And, while he finished his illustrious career with the Cleveland Indians, he certainly made Minnesota proud. Spanning nearly a quarter of a century, two countries, two leagues, and six cities, Winfield has done it all. The 12-time all-star won seven Gold Gloves and six Silver Bat awards. He amassed more hits than Babe Ruth, more home runs than Joe DiMaggio, and more RBIs than both Mickey Mantle or Reggie Jackson. He is one of only five players with over 3,000 hits, 450 homers, and 200 stolen bases. In the summer of 2001, Winnie was finally given his due when he was inducted into the Baseball Hall of Fame, alongside fellow Minnesota sports icon Kirby Puckett. An all-star and fan-favorite who played hard well into his forties, Winnie will always be remembered as one of the game's great ones.

"I always looked at baseball three ways," said Winfield. "It was a game, a science, and a business. I used it as a springboard to do the other things that I am doing in life such as the Dave Winfield Foundation. I met a lot of people, traveled the world, and have done a lot of great things. I have become a role model, if you will, for a lot of young people. I think I have become someone that people listen to and they respected the way I went about my work, and I am proud of that. It seemed that the better I played, the more I was able to accomplish."

Off the field, his accomplishments are equally impressive: He served on the board of President Bill Clinton's National Service Program. He was a Williams Scholar at the U of M. He received the first Branch Rickey Community Service Award, and he was given baseball's coveted Roberto Clemente Award. Now Dave devotes much of his time to what might be considered to be his crown jewel of achievements, the Winfield Foundation — a non-profit foundation, which for more than a quarter century has been a reflection of his commitment to children. Winnie has always been a very popular athlete and role model and has given of himself long before it became fashionable. His foundation's message to kids isn't "be a superstar" but rather "be the best that you can be." His generous monetary gifts, contributions of time, creativity, and commitment are immeasurable. He has traveled coast to coast to conduct drug-prevention assemblies and seminars. His organization has generated and distributed millions of dollars, and worked with four presidential administrations, government, organizations, corporations, media, celebrities, and every-day people to bring forth grassroots programs that have touched countless thousands on a one-to-one basis.

One of our most precious of native sons, Dave Winfield is without question one of the greatest all-around athletes in the history of modern sports.

laying in the balance, Minnesota, despite outstanding performances from Behagen, Brewer, Young and Turner, got upset 79-74, to finish second in the Big Ten.

They did receive an NIT (National Invitational Tournament) bid though, where, thanks to Ron Behagen's 18 points, they beat Rutgers, 68-59, in Madison Square Garden. Next up was Alabama in the semifinals, where, despite Clyde Turner's 21 points, the Gophers gave up a last-minute Crimson Tide run and got beat, 69-65, to end their season. At 21-5, it was the program's first-ever 20-win season though, an amazing accomplishment for Musselman in just his second season of coaching the club.

After the season no less than five Gophers were selected in the NBA draft: Jim Brewer was taken second overall by the Cleveland Cavaliers, Ron Behagen was chosen seventh overall by the Kansas City Kings, Clyde Turner went to the Milwaukee Bucks, and Corky Taylor wound up going to the Boston Celtics. And, if that weren't enough, Dave Winfield made history when he became the first and only athlete, ever, to be drafted by four professional teams: The NBA's Atlanta Hawks, the ABA's Utah Stars, MLB's San Diego Padres, and the NFL's Minnesota Vikings — who drafted him based on "pure raw talent." ("Winnie" ultimately decided to play pro baseball, where, after playing more than 20 seasons of big-league ball with the Padres, Yankees, Angels, Blue Jays, Indians and hometown Twins, was enshrined into the Baseball Hall of Fame in the summer of 2001.)

Tony Dungy

That next year the Gophers had to completely rebuild. Musselman was able to bring in some more JUCO's, as well as a kid from Ohio named Philip "Flip" Saunders, who would, of course, go on to become the Minnesota Timberwolves' all-time winningest coach. The team struggled and ultimately wound up finishing with a less-than-average 6-8 conference record — good for just sixth place. It was tough. After all, the team's Center, Pete Gilcud, was only six-foot-six, and the club simply had no depth. Dennis Shaffer did manage to lead the team in scoring with 17.3 points per game, while the gutty guard, Saunders, added 10 points as well.

Ollie Shannon

The 1974-75 Gophers played inspired basketball under Coach Musselman. He was also able to bring in a pair of Minnesotans in Mark Olberding and Mark Landsberger, both forwards, as well as to recruit a pair of freshman studs by the names of Mychal Thompson and Osborne Lockhart — both of whom would prove to be outstanding players. The team jumped out to a quick 7-1 non-conference record, and then went 3-0 in Big Ten play thanks in large part to the efforts of Mark Olberding, who had emerged as the team's go-to guy. From there though, the team got streaky. After losing a pair to Ohio State and Indiana, they rebounded to beat Michigan and Michigan State. Then, after falling to Iowa, 53-44, they rattled off three straight wins over Northwestern, Illinois and Ohio State. Minnesota wound up going 3-4 down the stretch, which included a couple of heart-breaking overtime losses at both Michigan and Michigan State, to finish the season with a very respectable third place record of 11-6.

Following the season things began to fall apart for Musselman. His intensity and demanding style of coaching finally caught up with him when the team's second leading scorer, Mark Landsberger, transferred to Arizona State. (Incredibly, Landsberger was one of nearly a dozen players who opted to transfer out of Minnesota during Musselman's tenure behind the Gopher bench.) And, if that weren't enough, the NCAA was investigating his program for alleged rules violations including, recruiting infractions, allegations of players receiving money from boosters, and even of players scalping their complimentary tickets for cash. When it was all said and done, the specter of both the University's and NCAA's investigations would prove to be too much of a distraction for the Coach, who finally opted to part ways with Minnesota and become the Head Coach of the ABA's San Diego Sails. There, he signed a three-year contract worth more than $135,000 — not bad for a guy who made a mere $23,000 at Minnesota.

(The NCAA would, in fact, later determine that the Gophers had committed some 128 rule violations, and as a result, would ultimately give the school a two-year penalty, which included reducing the number of available scholarships from six to three, canceling any national television appearances and putting a ban on post-season play.)

"When I looked at my situation in 1975, the University did not pay me a lot of money and the pressure of that job, with the football program being down, was tremendous," said Musselman in Steve Pearlstein's 1995 book, "Gopher Glory." "I was told I had to fill the arena because the program needed money and we not only filled the arena, but we also filled the hockey arena. If it wasn't for the basketball camp I ran during the summer, I would hardly have made any money. I love the University of Minnesota, it's a great school, and I have great memories there. But for the pressure that I was under, I just couldn't do it forever."

Musselman left Gold Country with a 69-32 record, good for a .683 winning percentage, the best in school history, and attendance nearly doubled at Williams Arena in his four-year tenure as well. He ultimately rescued the program, and for better or for worse, he got people excited about basketball again. And, despite his leaving under the shadow of allegations and investigations, Bill Musselman should be remembered as one of the program's greatest all-time coaches.

Bob Nix

Once again, the University's search committee was asked to sharpen their pencils and prepare to select its fifth coach in just eight years. This time, they needed to find someone who was squeaky clean, and could bring the program back into the good graces of the community. It was not going to be an easy task. Sure, the fans and boosters wanted a clean program, but they also wanted a winning team. With that, the committee decided to offer the position to University of Michigan Assistant Coach, Jim Dutcher. Dutcher, who had also served a six-year stint as the Head Coach of Eastern Michigan, would now have to try and resurrect a program that was under a very dark cloud of controversy.

The new coach's first task as Minnesota's head coach was to try and retain the team's recent defectors, including Mark Olberding, who left school early to sign with Musselman in San Diego, and Mark Landsberger, who had transferred to Arizona State. He first flew to Arizona, where Landsberger

Bill Musselman

A native of Wooster Ohio, Bill Musselman went on to Wooster High School where he was the captain of the basketball, football, and baseball teams. He also lettered in those same three sports at Wittenberg University in Ohio, and later earned his Master's Degree from Kent State.

In 1971, at a ripe old age of 32, Musselman became the youngest head basketball coach in Minnesota's modern history. He would be the architect of a re-building program that would be both exciting and memorable — for many different reasons.

Attendance nearly doubled at Williams Arena in his four-year career in Gold Country, and Musselman was the impetus, compiling a 69-32 record, for a .683 winning percentage, the best in school history. He rescued the program and for better or for worse got people excited about basketball again. Not afraid to go outside the system and bring in junior college transfers, Musselman left in 1975 under the shadow of allegations and investigations by the NCAA. Bill Musselman will always be remembered in Minnesota for a lot of reasons. Most importantly he will be remembered as a great coach.

"I was always impressed with the University of Minnesota," Musselman would later recall. "The thing that impressed me the most about coaching there was how loyal the fans are. I think they are the best basketball fans in the country. They were the most enthusiastic too, the noise in Williams Arena was unbelievable. Every time I run into someone from Minnesota, they always make outstanding compliments about the time that I was there, and how much they appreciated the good basketball."

After starting out coaching at Kent State High School, Musselman went on to coaching stardom. His amazing coaching career included posting a record of 233-84 as a college coach at Ashland, Minnesota and South Alabama. He had been a head coach in four pro leagues — the NBA (with the Cleveland Cavaliers and the Minnesota Timberwolves), CBA, ABA and WBA. His overall career record in the pros was 603-426, and he was named CBA Coach of the Year in 1987 and 1988, winning four consecutive championships along the way.

"When I coached the Timberwolves they broke every NBA attendance record," said Musselman, who served as the franchise's first-ever coach. "There aren't many places where you are going to get 40,000 people to come to a basketball game! The fans there were just incredible, where else can you find fans like that?"

He later served as an assistant with the NBA's Portland Trailblazers until his tragic and untimely death in 2000, from cancer, at the age of 59.

"I think my teams always played hard and played together," added Musselman. "I think that I have always had the ability as a coach to get the most out of players, and my teams have always played as hard as they could. I always taught my players to get out of life what they put into it. I think it is important to teach an athlete to be able to face and handle adversity. Mental toughness is important to me, and I always wanted my players to be able to be prepared to handle the good times along with the bad."

"He was tough," said Dave Winfield. "He was a competitive guy and he loved coaching. People may question his style, but he was a very knowledgeable coach and he made us work very hard. I kind of likened the practices and games to boot-camp in the service. It was tough, we wore weighted jackets and competed hard. I don't think I have ever been in that good of shape. I think that he liked me because I gave it my all, and I was a very aggressive rebounder. I really enjoyed playing for him. He's something else. And he's all-right with me!"

said "thanks, but no thanks," and then caught a flight to Miami, where he met with both Mychal Thompson and Osborne Lockhart (both of whom were natives of the Bahamas), and this time was able to work his magic and convince the two to stay put in Minneapolis. By the time the smoke had cleared, Dutcher was left with six scholarshiped players and six walk-ons.

The Jim Dutcher era opened on November 29th at the Barn when the Gophers pummeled South Dakota State, 96-74, with Mychal Thompson scoring 31 points and adding 15 rebounds. From there the team would go on to win its first nine non-conference games before finally losing to Purdue, 111-110, in overtime. The season was, at times, bizarre. At one point, Mychal Thompson even missed a game, against Northwestern, because he was testifying before the NCAA Rules Committee over admittedly selling his complimentary game tickets — a blatant NCAA rules violation And, although he was declared ineligible over the incident, his attorneys fought for a court order which allowed him to play until the issue was resolved.

With that, Thompson rejoined the team in Wisconsin to take part in a wild, technical foul-filled, 96-84, victory over the Badgers, which saw the six-foot-ten center score 29 points and 17 rebounds. The team had its shares of ups and downs though, including a nationally televised win over Michigan State, 71-61, as well as an 81-79 victory over nationally ranked Michigan, thanks to Thompson's 32 points and 10 rebounds. The team lost its final game on the road to Purdue to ultimately finish with a 16-10 overall record — good for sixth in the Big Ten. Thompson wound up leading the Big Ten in rebounding with 12.3 boards per contest, en route to finishing second in scoring, with 26.4 ppg, while Williams was fourth in the conference with 22.1 ppg as well.

The 1977 season is one that will have a lasting legacy in Gold Country. It was historic for many reasons. First, there was the addition of a six-foot-ten freshman power forward from Hibbing by the name of Kevin McHale, and the other was the fact that, technically, the season never happened. That's right. You see, after the season, Thompson lost his battle with the NCAA and, as a result, he was thereby ruled "retroactively ineligible" for the year. But, because the season was over by then, the Gophers, who wound up finishing the year with an amazing 24-3 overall record (second in the Big Ten with a 15-3 conference record), were forced to officially forfeit all of the games which Thompson, an "ineligible" player, took part in. So, the official box-score for the 1976-77 season read simply: 0-27.

The reaction was swift in Gold Country. Fans everywhere were upset and rightly so. The team, which was nationally ranked in the Top 10 in many polls, had produced magnificently, but was being punished after the fact. Among the highlights of the "phantom" season were big wins over the eventual national champs from Marquette, 66-59, a 91-65 win over the Buckeyes — thanks to Kevin McHale's 23 points and 15 rebounds, and also an 84-78 victory over Purdue at Williams Arena, thanks to Ray Williams' 29 points, 16 rebounds and seven assists.

One thing the NCAA couldn't take away though, was the fact that Mychal Thompson, who averaged 22.0 points and 8.9 rebounds per game, and Ray Williams, who added 18.0 points, 7.5 rebounds and 6.1 assists ppg, became the Gopher's first All-Americans since Ron Behagen and Jim Brewer, back in 1973. Who knows, it might just have been the best Gopher squad ever.

In 1978 Ray Williams was selected by the NBA's New York Knicks with the 10th overall pick in the draft, but Mychal Thompson, who turned down what surely would've been millions, opted to return for his senior year. The non-conference schedule got off to a shaky start when it was learned that Thompson had to sit out a seven-game NCAA suspension. McHale, Lockhart, Dave Winey, Steve Lingenfelter and James Jackson, a transfer from Boston College, picked up the slack though, as the team went on to post an impressive 17-11 overall record.

The team opened its conference schedule against Michigan State, which was led by freshman-extraordinaire Earvin "Magic" Johnson, who tallied 31 points in an 87-83 Spartan victory. After losing to Michigan, the team rebounded to win four straight over Indiana, Ohio State, Illinois and Wisconsin. Then, after a 72-64 loss to Purdue, which was led by Center Joe Barry Carroll, the Gophers rallied to go on an eight-game winning streak before finally losing to the Buckeyes, 94-87, in overtime. They split their final two against Michigan and Michigan State to finish the season with a remarkable 12-6 Big Ten record — good for second place in the conference.

When it was all said and done, Thompson, who had led the conference with a 22.7 scoring average and he was second in rebounds with 11.6, was again named as an All-American, this time a consensus pick. He went on to be drafted by the Portland Trailblazers with the first overall pick of the 1978 draft — the only Gopher ever to hold that prestigous honor. Winey and Lockhart were drafted by Boston and Philly, respectively, but Lockhart wound up as a mainstay with the famed Harlem Globetrotters instead.

The 1979 season was a rebuilding one in Gold Country. Kevin McHale would emerge as the team leader that season, averaging nearly 18 points and 10 rebounds per contest, but the team was young and inexperienced, ultimately finishing eighth in the Big Ten with an 6-12 conference record. With the exception of James Jackson, the team was comprised mostly of youngsters, including a freshman forward named Trent Tucker, who would go down as one of the program's all-time greats. Among the other new recruits were Darryl Mitchell, Mark Hall and Gary Holmes — all of whom would make contributions that year. In addition, Dutcher had also signed a

Flip Saunders

seven-foot-two center from Lake City, Minn., by the name of Randy Breuer — another player who would go on to play for many years in the NBA.

Mark Olberding

"Kevin is one of the premier big men in the nation," said coach Jim Dutcher of Mr. McHale at the beginning of the 1980 season. "He has the ability to score inside or outside. We feel he is one of the most complete players in the country. He can rebound, score, block shots, and run well."

McHale, the team captain, had taken the young group under his wing the year before when he found himself starting alongside of four freshmen — Forward Trent Tucker, Center Gary Holmes, and Guards Mark Hall and Darryl Mitchell. The Gophers opened their non-conference schedule by reeling off four straight wins before losing to both Tennessee and Florida State. After beating Kansas State, Minnesota won the Pillsbury Classic tournament. Then, they dropped their conference opener, 71-67, at Michigan, but rebounded two nights later with an impressive 93-80 win over the defending Big Ten and NCAA champs from Michigan State. It was up and down for the young Gophers though, as they lost several close games on the road after that. Included were three tough overtime defeats against the Illini, Buckeyes, and Boilermakers, as well as a 73-63 set-back at the hands of Iowa for their only home loss. Minnesota did, however, go on to beat Indiana, 55-47, as well as Ohio State, 74-70, Purdue, 67-61, Illinois, 79-75, and Michigan, 68-67.

All in all, it was a good season for the Gophers and a great senior season for McHale. Minnesota finished the regular season with a 17-10 record, tied for fourth place in the Big Ten with Iowa at 10-8. Although they didn't make the NCAA Tournament, the Gophers did get an invitation to the 43rd annual post-season NIT tourney. There, in the first round, at Williams Arena, the Gophers rolled over Bowling Green, 64-50, and followed that up with wins over Mississippi, 58-56, and Southwestern Louisiana, 94-73, thanks to Tucker and Breuer, who had 18 points apiece, while Hall and McHale added 16 and 15, respectively. Next, it was off to the NIT's version of the Final Four at New York City's famed Madison Square Garden.

In the semifinals, the Gophers, thanks to Breuer's 24 points, avenged their overtime loss to fellow Big Ten rival Illinois in a nail-biter, 65-63, and, in so doing, set the stage for the championship game against seven-footer Ralph Sampson and the Virginia Cavaliers. The Gophers jumped out to a 21-12 lead in the first 10 minutes of the game behind the strong play of McHale, Tucker and Randy Breuer. But, behind Sampson, who had 15 points and 15 rebounds, the Cavs took the lead into halftime.

It was a back and forth affair for both squads throughout the second half. Then with 1:31 to play, Sampson sank two free throws to put Virginia ahead, 54-53. Now with 1:06 remaining in the game, McHale's pass to Breuer was intercepted. With only 33 seconds on the clock, Minnesota fouled Virginia's Terry Gates. Gates missed the one-on-one, but the Cavaliers came up with the rebound. Jeff Lamp, a Cavalier guard, was then fouled and proceeded to sink both shots and go up by three. With 11 seconds left, McHale, in desperation, drove for a dunk on Sampson and was fouled. He made both shots to get the Gophers within one point. But, Minnesota was forced to foul immediately, and unfortunately for the Gophers, it was Lamp again who would go to the line. He then calmly stepped up to the line and sank both free throws to ice the 58-55 win for Virginia.

"We just got too cautious," said Dutcher, whose squad finished the year with an impressive 21-11 record. "We didn't push the ball down the floor and look for any fast breaks. And we got so conscious of getting the ball inside that we didn't take the outside shots we had." Mitchell, who had a game-high 18 points, along with Breuer, were both named to the all-tournament team.

"I remember the game very well," added McHale who scored eight points in the game. "We got

Ray Williams

Mychal Thompson

Born on January 30th, 1955, in Nassau, Bahamas, Mychal Thompson should be remembered as one of Minnesota's greatest ever. Thompson, who grew up in the Bahamas, later moved in the 10th grade to Miami, where he later led Jackson High School to the State's AAAA title. From there the prep All-American decided to head north, to Minnesota, where he became an instant star.

A deeply religious individual, Thompson adapted to the new lifestyle and excelled both on and off the court. Mychal finished his tenure in Gold Country as the team's all-time leading scorer with 1,992 points, good for an impressive 20.8 points per game average, as well as the team's all-time leading rebounder, with 956 — good for 10.0 rebounds per game. A two-time All-American, Thompson was also a three-time All-Big Ten selection. So well respected was the big man that in 1978 his No. 43 jersey was retired into the old Barn's rafters forever.

From there the six-foot-ten center went on to become the school's only No. 1 overall pick in the NBA draft, when he was selected by the Portland Trailblazers in 1978. He then went on to play in the NBA for 12 seasons, both with Portland and Los Angeles, where he won a pair of world championships with the Lakers. Overall the forward wound up finishing with 12,810 total points, averaging 13.7 points, 7.4 rebounds and 2.3 assists per game over his career.

all the way to the Finals and, unfortunately, we didn't play particularly well that night. I was sad on a lot of levels, besides losing the game, it was my last game as a Gopher. I felt a lot of anxiety at that moment because there were some big, big changes coming my way in a hurry."

McHale, who averaged 17.4 points and 8.8 rebounds per game, was named to the All-Big Ten team that season,. He would finish his illustrious career in Gold Country by averaging 16.7 points and 10 rebounds per game — good for 1,704 points, 950 rebounds and a record 235 blocked shots. He would, of course, go on to become a Hall of Famer as a member of the famed Boston Celtics.

The 1980-81 Gophers featured several local boys, including Lake City Center Randy Breuer, Prior Lake Center Brian Pederson and Woodbury Guard Bruce Kaupa, as well as freshman Forward Jim Petersen, from St. Louis Park and Duluth Guard Brian Hansen. Tucker, Hall, Holmes, Mitchell and Breuer would prove to be the main-stays though, as they led the team to a solid 19-11 overall record. One of the highlights of the season came early, when the club beat the defending national champions from Louisville, 62-56, to kick off an impressive 9-1 start to the season before finally losing to Michigan at home, 68-67, in double overtime. From there it was up and down, with the team eventually cracking the top 20 in the national rankings.

The club managed to go 4-3 down the homestretch that year, accented by a big double overtime victory over Michigan State, 92-89, thanks to Breuer's 25 points and nine rebounds. They rounded out the season with a heart-breaking, 60-58, overtime loss to Wisconsin to finish at 9-9, good for fifth in the conference. It was good, but not good enough for a coveted NCAA bid, so the team once again headed back to the NIT. There, behind 21 points each from Breuer and Holmes, Minnesota dumped Drake, 90-77, to open the tournament at the Barn. From there they headed to Hartford to take on Connecticut, and thanks to Tucker's amazing 35-point outing, the Gophers crushed the Huskies, 84-66. But, from there it got ugly, as the Gophers came home to get upset by West Virginia, 80-69, to end their season. It was a sad ending to a campaign that came up short of expectations.

The Minnesota faithful had good reason to be optimistic for the upcoming 1981-82 season. After all, the team was returning all of its starters and even opened the season ranked in the top-10 in the nation. Led by Tucker, Breuer, Mitchell, Hall, Holmes, Petersen, and Tommy Davis, the Gophers won their first five non-conference games that year, including victories over San Francisco State, Dayton, Loyola, Drake, and an impressive 76-54 win at Marquette. After losing to Kansas State, they returned home to the friendly confines of Williams Arena where they first crushed Army, 79-37, and then the Arizona Wildcats, 91-62, en route to capturing their eighth consecutive Pillsbury Classic holiday basketball title.

In their final non-conference game, the brilliant Tucker led the way with 22 points, as Dutcher's contingent easily handled Cal State Long Beach, 75-67. With an impressive 8-1 record, the stage was now set for the start of the 1982 Big Ten Conference race. Unfortunately though, the Gophers lost the opener to a very tough Ohio State team, 49-47, in Columbus. Minnesota bounced back two nights later, however, with a 64-58 victory against Michigan State at East Lansing. The next stop was Williams Arena and the hated rivals to the south, the Iowa

Kevin McHale

Hawkeyes. There, more than 17,000 zealous fans jammed the barn that Thursday night to watch the Gophers upend the Hawkeyes. Behind Randy Breuer's 22 points, Minnesota did just that, winning the game, 61-56. Two nights later, Tucker stepped up to pour in 21 points as his team triumphed, 67-58, over the Michigan Wolverines.

Minnesota continued to build its confidence throughout the season, with Tucker and Breuer shouldering much of the load. The fans were turning rabid as the Gophers started to show signs that they were for real. That next week, the now 5th ranked Gophers simply outplayed the Badgers in Madison, winning in a blowout, 78-57. Their next opponent, Illinois, would give them trouble all season. The Illini came to town on January 23rd and knocked off Minnesota, 64-57. The loss could have been a turning point for the team, but they would have little time to dwell on it as they traveled to Evanston, Ill., and Bloomington, Ind., the following week. But, in what was starting to become a trend for the squad, they rebounded from the Illinois loss by beating the Northwestern Wildcats, 61-53, and Bobby Knight's Indiana Hoosiers, 69-62, in a game where all five Minnesota starters scored in double figures

They followed this up with a 73-50 drubbing of the Purdue Boilermakers at home, but stumbled against the Hoosiers at Williams Arena, losing a squeaker, 58-55. Unfazed and determined, the Gophers sucked it in and won three in a row against the Badgers, Boilermakers, and Wildcats to set up the much anticipated rematch with the Illini in Champaign. There, in a game that was closer than the final score would reflect, the maroon and gold once again fell to Illinois, 77-65.

It was crunch time for the Gophers as they headed into the final two-week stretch of the season.

The Gophers, of course, were still very much in contention for the coveted Big Ten title. First, they invaded Michigan, where they hadn't beaten the Wolverines since 1963. That 0-16 record fell in a big way on that day though, as Minnesota prevailed, 60-51. With their confidence higher than ever, the Gophers then traveled to Iowa City to do battle with the Big Ten front-runners, in the biggest Big Ten game of the year. The implications were enormous as Iowa led Minnesota in the conference standings.

This one was back and forth throughout the entire contest. It seemed that every time Minnesota struggled to gain the lead, the Hawkeyes found a way to pull ahead. It was a thriller that went down to the wire, and the two teams ultimately wound up going into overtime. Then another overtime and amazingly, one more. Finally, in the third exhausting extra session, Darryl Mitchell, who led the Gophers with 21 points, sank two huge free throws with no time showing on the clock to clinch a stunning 57-55 Minnesota triumph.

"That triple overtime game against Iowa was probably the most memorable game I ever played in — it was just unbelievable," said team captain Trent Tucker. "It was a really tough situation in a very hostile environment, but we got a total team effort to win it. I'll always remember Randy Breuer's big blocked shot to save us to get us back into it, and then Darryl Mitchell's two free throws to seal it. The whole thing was just incredible!"

The Gophers, now deadlocked with Iowa for the Big Ten lead, returned home to host Michigan State the following Thursday. In front of a packed mob of excited fans, the Gophers did not disappoint. Despite only shooting a paltry 35 percent from the floor, they upended the Spartans, 54-51, in another nail-biter, highlighted by a pair of Gary Holmes free throws with 11 seconds remaining to seal the deal. Mitchell led the way with 16, while Breuer added 14 and Tucker put in 13 as well. In an interesting side-bar, Illinois beat the Hawkeyes to put Minnesota in the driver's seat on the championship road. Then, in the final regular season game of the year, Breuer lit it up by scoring a career high 32 points and 12 rebounds while Tucker added 23, as the Gophers beat Ohio State, 87-75, to win the 1982 Big Ten championship.

Jim Dutcher

"For me, it was seeing all my expectations and goals come true," said Tucker. "I came to Minnesota in 1978 as a part of the biggest and most celebrated recruiting class in the history of the program. So the pressure was there from day one, and we were expected to someday win a championship. Now, it was year four, and we had matured to a level where we could win it all. To hear the final horn go off and to see the jubilation of the fans, the coaches, and the players was just great."

"It was a tight race all season long, but we held on to win it. It was amazing," added Breuer, who led the team in scoring, rebounding, and blocks. "It was tremendously gratifying because we were the team that was predicted to win it all from the beginning. We had a lot of seniors on the team, but it was a tough fought battle all season long. You couldn't relax for one game because the whole season was tight all the way."

Minnesota ultimately finished 14-4 in the conference, good enough to win their first Big Ten title in 10 years. For Dutcher, the 1981-82 team was his third team in seven years to win 20 or more games in a season. And for the first time, his squad earned an NCAA post season tournament bid.

After receiving a first-round bye, the team flew to Indianapolis to play the University of Tennessee-Chattanooga, in the Mideast Regional. There, the Gophers, who were led by 20 points from Tucker, 17 from Breuer, and 16 from Mitchell, squeaked by UTC, 62-61, in a thriller. Next it was off to Alabama, where they would have to take on Denny Crum's tough Louisville Cardinals. This time, despite 22 points apiece from Breuer and Tucker, the Gophers lost to Louisville down the stretch, 67-61. (Perhaps the team fell victim to the "Sheraton Jinx." You see, the Gopher basketball team was staying at the Sheraton Hotel in Birmingham, the same hotel that the Gopher Football team stayed at when they were beaten by Maryland in the Hall of Fame Bowl only five years earlier!) It was a disappointing loss and a sad ending for a fabulous season for the Gophers, who finished with an impressive 23-6 overall record. (They should also be given their props for being a "Sweet 16" team, because back then the "Tourney" was only comprised of 32 teams.)

Post-season honors were highlighted by the naming of Tucker to the All-American team. He would go on to be drafted in the first round by the New York Knicks, who took him sixth overall. Breuer and Mitchell were also named to the 1982 All-Big Ten team.

The 1982-83 Gophers would be led by returnees Randy Breuer, Jim Petersen, Tommy Davis, Zebedee Howell, as well as newcomers Marc Wilson, John Shasky and Roland Brooks. The team jumped out to a quick 8-1 non-conference record, highlighted by a 100-66 squashing of Marquette, and their All-American Guard "Doc" Rivers. From there they opened their Big Ten schedule with big wins over Illinois, thanks to 19 points each from Breuer and Davis, and Purdue, behind Wilson's 17 and Davis' 15, before finally losing at Michigan. They rebounded to beat Michigan State, 69-67, thanks to Barry Wohler's 15-footer at the buzzer. (It was his only shot of the day!) Wilson hurt his leg that game though, and the team got streaky. They did put together a nice winning streak over Wisconsin, Northwestern and Ohio State, but wound up losing three of their final four games to finish at 9-9 — good for sixth in the Big Ten. The big blow came at Illinois, where any hopes that the team had about going to the NCAA tournament were squashed after suffering a double-overtime loss, 70-67.

They were invited to play in the NIT though, where, despite 26 points from Breuer and 17 from Wilson, Minnesota wound up losing their opening round game to Ray Meyer's DePaul Blue Demons, 76-73, in Chicago, to end their season with an 18-11 overall record. It was tough loss which seemed to parody a tough season.

After averaging 20.4 points and 8.9 rebounds per game in 1982-83, Breuer was again named as a first-team All-Big Ten selection. He also wound up finishing as the Gophers' second all-time leading scorer with 1,755 points and third in all-time rebounds with 716. From there the lanky seven-footer went on to be selected in the first round of the NBA draft by the Milwaukee Bucks. (He would also later play for his hometown Minnesota Timberwolves as well.)

The 1984, 1985 and 1986 seasons would prove to be a rebuilding ones for the Gophers, which finished with a trio of eighth place finishes in the Big Ten. And, while there were several highlights over this three year stretch, including a dramatic win over Wisconsin in 1984 thanks to Roland Brooks' 18-

Jim Petersen

Steve Lingenfelter

foot hanging jumper with just two seconds left to seal a 68-67 come-from-behind win, as well as a couple of sweet upsets early in the '85 season campaign over the 6th ranked Illini and 19th ranked Hawkeyes, there was also a gigantic lowlight as well. It was something terrible enough to ultimately put a black eye on the program for many, many years to come. Here's how the whole saga went down.

Midway through the 1986 season, the Gophers, who, after knocking off No. 2 Michigan, 73-63, thanks to Marc Wilson's 24 points, as well as Michigan State, 76-71, behind 27 points from John Shasky and another 18 from Todd Alexander, were sitting pretty with a very solid 12-6 overall record. Then, on January 23rd, the team traveled to Madison, to play Wisconsin. There, after the Gophers beat the Badgers, 67-65, on an Alexander jumper at the buzzer, the team headed back to the hotel to celebrate. That night, three Minnesota players, Mitch Lee, George Williams and Kevin Smith, allegedly brought a local woman back to their hotel room. The next morning she reported to the authorities that she had been sexually assaulted.

Later that morning, as the players were preparing to fly back to Minneapolis on the team's charter plane, the local authorities pulled the players off one-by-one to question them. Shortly thereafter, it was announced that the three players would be arraigned, and all hell broke loose. At this point, University of Minnesota President, Kenneth Keller, announced that the team was not only going to forfeit its next game against Northwestern, but that he was also looking into the possibility of eliminating the basketball program at Minnesota altogether. The fans were shocked, and what heightened the scandal even more was the fact that sophomore Forward Mitch Lee, who was at the forefront of the investigation, had just been acquitted only a few weeks earlier of a criminal sexual conduct charge that had occurred during the 1985 season.

With the entire state of Minnesota reeling at the humiliating scandal, Dutcher, who was extremely upset with the administration's lack of support and refusal to give the situation more time to work itself out, decided to resign — effective immediately. With that, long-time assistant Jimmy Williams was named as the team's interim head coach. His dubious job: to somehow hold together a program on the verge of disaster, both on the hardcourt as well as in the even tougher court of public opinion — where the community was divided.

The three players, Lee, Williams and Smith, who, it is important to note, were later acquitted of the charges, were all kicked off the team. And, in addition, Todd Alexander and Terence Woods were also suspended for the rest of the year after the ensuing investigation found that they had violated various team rules. By the time the dust had settled, just John Shasky, Kevin Smith, Marc Wilson, Tim Hanson, Ray Gaffney and Dave Holmgren remained as the team's only scholarship players. So, Williams recruited several Gopher Football players to join the team to fill up the now-depleted bench. What was left was the program's second-coming of the "Iron Five."

After the Northwestern forfeit, the team came out and faced the Ohio State Buckeyes in what will go down as one of the team's greatest emotional wins of all time. Shasky, Gaffney, Hanson, Wilson and Smith came out and played inspired basketball, each scoring in double figures, to lead the Gophers past OSU, 70-65, in front of nearly 14,000 loyal fans. Then, after losing to Indiana, 62-54, on the road, the team came home to stun Iowa, 65-60, thanks to Wilson's 22 points and Shasky's 18. But from there, it was all bad news, as the team went 0-8 down the stretch to finish with a dismal 5-13 record — good for their third consecutive eighth place Big Ten finish.

The administration now needed to hire a new coach, and they needed to do it fast. They needed a miracle worker. Someone who they thought could come in and put together the pieces of a once proud program, now in shambles. Their choice: former NBA first-round draft pick Clem Haskins, who had served as the Head Coach of Western Kentucky University for the past six seasons. Clem was optimistic, and even though he would be given a ball club which featured no one taller than six-foot-seven, he had hope. He knew he had to win back the trust of the fans, and with that, he started a grassroots publicity program in which he and many of his players went to local dormitories, frat-houses and college organizations to recruit the students back to the old Barn. He knew it couldn't get worse, so he began to sell the fans on not what the team didn't have, but what it did have. And one of the things that team had was an incoming freshman by the name of Willie Burton, who he was able to convince to stick around through this entire mess. Burton, one of the most highly sought after prep players in the country, would ultimately prove to be the catalyst which turned an ailing program into a national power once again.

(In an interesting side-bar, there was talk at the time that perhaps what the program needed at the time was a change of venue. In fact, Men's Athletic Director Rick Bay thought it was crazy to keep dumping money into the old, run-down Williams Arena. There was even talk of building either a new multi-purpose arena for both basketball and hockey, or having the Gophers move down-town to play in

The National Invitation Tournament (NIT)

The National Invitation Tournament (NIT) has long been a part of college basketball. First started in 1938 by the Metropolitan Basketball Writers Association of New York City, primarily to pit New York's best college basketball teams against the best from the rest of the country, it has evolved into the nation's No. 2 post-season tourney, behind the NCAA's "Big Dance." In its early years, the NIT was easily as prestigious as the NCAA tournament, which began in 1939, and it offered smaller teams the chance to participate as well. At first, teams could even play in both, and in 1950 City College of New York became the first and only school to win each of them.

Originally, there were just six teams invited to the first tournament, but from there the field has expanded slowly but surely to 16, in 1968, and 32 in 1980, where it remains today. Since 1977, preliminary rounds have been played on the home courts of the top-seeded teams, and only the semi-finals and finals are staged at Madison Square Garden, in the Big Apple. The NIT, which is still the best option for "bubble" teams that did not get an invitation to the NCAA tournament's 64-team field, is still going strong after all these years.

Minnesota's NIT Championship Results:
1980   Virginia 58, Minnesota 55
1993   Minnesota 62, Georgetown 61
1998   Minnesota 79, Penn St. 72

Tournament MVP's:
1993   Voshon Lenard, Minnesota
1998   Kevin Clark, Minnesota

the Timberwolves' home, the Target Center. Luckily, nothing could be worked out and our beloved Barn is still going strong!)

In addition to returnees Gaffney, Hanson, Smith and Burton, Haskins also signed Center Richard Coffey, a 20-something who had served for several years in the military as a paratrooper prior to coming back to school. Needless to say, the expectations were quite low coming into the season. After beating North Dakota State, 70-53, in the opener, the team went on to post a modest 3-2 non-conference record. Then, after losing to tiny Austin Peay, 73-64, at Williams Arena, Clem lost it, and called his players back out onto the court after the game for a post-game practice that went well into the night. He wanted to send his players a message that he meant business, and, for a while, it worked. After winning their next five games, the team went on to win its first two Big Ten games, both over Wisconsin, 69-67, thanks to Kim Zurcher's 15-foot jumper with just a few ticks on the clock, and Northwestern, 60-53.

But from there, the honeymoon ended abruptly. That next week the Gophers got spanked by No. 2 Iowa, 78-57, followed by No. 6 Purdue, 86-59, and No. 8 Illinois, 80-58. In fact, Minnesota just kept on losing for the rest of the season. That's right, they went 0-16 down the stretch run, giving them their worst record in history with a 2-16 Big Ten tally. Ouch!

Clem was optimistic about his team's chances for the 1987-88 season though. After all, he had Forwards Willie Burton and Richard Coffey, Guards Kim Zurcher, Ray Gaffney and Melvin Newbern, as well as Center Jim Shikenjanski. In addition, he was able to land highly touted Bloomington Jefferson Forward Kevin Lynch, who had just been named as Minnesota's Mr. Basketball. Clem's hard work ethic was rubbing off on his players, and he knew that he could mold this bunch into winners. With that, the team went out and blew an 11-point second-half lead to lose its season opener to tiny Drake University of Iowa. It was safe to say that this was not the way Clem wanted to start out the season. After a thorough tongue-lashing, the Gophers came back and beat Western Illinois, ultimately running their non-conference schedule to 6-4.

Marc Wilson

Then, after losing to Kendall Gill and the Illini, 65-61, in overtime, in the conference opener, the team fell into a rut — losing five straight before finally ending their 21-game Big Ten losing streak to beat Michigan State, 59-56. With the win, Clem lit up a victory stogie — the dreaded streak, the longest in more than 40 years, was finally dead. Things didn't get much better though. After a pair of losses to the Hawkeyes and Hoosiers, they rebounded to beat Wisconsin at home, 71-62, but then lost seven of their final nine games (they beat lowly Northwestern, 82-67, and Michigan State, 62-61) to finish with a 4-14 conference record — good for ninth in the Big Ten. Burton and Newbern led the team with 13.7 and 10.6 points per game, respectively.

As the 1988-89 season was approaching, the team once again got dealt some bad news. As it turned out, the NCAA decided to issue a violation to the program for recruiting infractions that it determined had occurred back on Jim Dutcher's clock. The result: the team was placed on a two-year probationary period.

Down but not out, Clem's Gophers came out and played basketball that season. And, despite dropping their opener to tiny Ball State, 63-57, in overtime, the team did manage to put together a respectable 8-2 non-conference record. The Gophers then dropped their first two Big Ten games to the Badgers, 75-67, and the No. 7 ranked Wolverines, 98-83, before coming home to beat the 5th ranked Hawkeyes, 80-78, on Shikenjanski's dramatic tip-in with just seconds remaining on the clock. From there the squad was up and down, posting wins over Purdue, the No. 1 ranked Illini, Ohio State, Wisconsin, on a last-second Hail-Mary, and Michigan, before reeling off an impressive three-game winning streak over Northwestern, Michigan State and Ohio State to finish the season with a much-improved 9-9, fifth place conference record. With that, the Cinderella Gophers were given an invitation to the coveted NCAA Tournament. It was the story of the year in Minnesota sports, and it was just getting good!

The bubble team then headed south, to Greensboro, North Carolina, to play Kansas State — a team they had beaten, 72-67, earlier in the season. This time it would be even sweeter though, as the Gophers hung on to advance to the second round with an impressive 86-75 win. Next up was tiny Siena, a team which had upset a highly ranked Stanford squad in the first round, and had a lot of momentum. Minnesota did what it needed to do however, and, despite playing some pretty sloppy basketball, held on to take a 80-67 victory. With that, the improbable Gophers had advanced to the NCAA's "Sweet 16" for the second time in school history. By now Minnesota fans everywhere were going crazy. T-shirts were flying off the racks as "March Madness" was sweeping across the Land of 10,000 Lakes. Willie Burton, who, with his gaudy 18.6 points per game, had emerged as a big-time fan-favorite, becoming the team's poster-boy with his now infamous "Friday the 13th hockey goalie mask" that he had to wear in order to protect a broken nose he suffered in an earlier game.

Next stop: East Rutherford, New Jersey, where Minnesota was set to do battle with national powerhouse Duke — regulars of the Final Four. Droves of loyal Gopher fans made the trip to see the historic game, which, turned out to be a big disappointment. The team played hard, but in the end, came up short, 87-70. It was a sad ending to an otherwise amazing season which had truly put the Gophers back on the basketball map.

Minnesota & "The Big Dance"

While the old barn was the site of the NCAA Men's Basketball Championship Finals in 1951, the Hubert H. Humphrey Metrodome played host to the Final Four in 1992 and 2001. In 1951, Kentucky, led by legendary Coach Adolph Rupp, beat Kansas State, while in 1992 Duke beat Michigan, and in 2001 Duke beat Arizona to take the collegiate crown. The Metrodome was also awarded the 2008 Big Dance as well.

The Dome has hosted a pair of Final Fours

Clem Haskins

The expectations were at an all-time high for the 1989-90 Gophers, a team which entered the season ranked 20th in the nation — the program's first national ranking since finishing seventh back in 1982. After a summer exhibition tour of Australia, the team, which was pretty banged up, returned home to begin its non-conference schedule. They also returned home to face another distraction — this one from the ever-probing NCAA, which this time alleged that former University administrator Luther Darville had misappropriated University funds by issuing payments to both football and basketball players. The case lingered on and proved to be a real distraction.

Moving on, the team went out and posted a 9-1 non-conference record that year — losing just their season opener on a buzzer-beater, 66-64, to the Bearcats of Cincinnati. From there the Gophers, led by Melvin Newbern's 27 points, went out and crushed the No. 4-ranked Illini, 91-74, in the Big Ten opener. They dropped two straight after that to both Purdue, 86-78, and Michigan, 87-83, but rebounded to spank Northwestern, 97-75, and Ohio State, 83-78. Their momentum was short-lived though, as the team got upset that next week in Madison, 77-75, on a last-second Badger dunk. Back at the Barn three nights later, Minnesota upended Iowa, 84-72, thanks to Willie Burton's 21 points and 10 rebounds, and Richard Coffey's 14 points and 13 rebounds. They followed that up with a huge 108-89 home win over the Hoosiers on Super Bowl Sunday, with Burton, Coffey, Lynch, Newbern, Shikenjanski and Walter Bond, all scoring in double figures. It was the most points ever scored against a Bobby Knight-coached team.

After losing to Illinois, Minnesota came home to the old Barn where they knocked off Purdue in one of the season's best games. Newbern was the hero du jour, nailing a turn-around jumper in the final seconds to seal a 73-72 victory for the nearly 17,000 Gopher faithful in attendance. The Gophers then climbed up to the No. 17 spot in the AP poll after beating Michigan State, 79-74, but once again fell to earth after a 99-72 spanking by the Illini. After edging Purdue, 73-72, on yet another Newbern jumper in the game's final seconds, Minnesota was beaten by Michigan, 77-73, to abruptly end their impressive 12-game home winning-streak. They rebounded to beat Northwestern, 90-72, followed by Iowa, 102-80, and Indiana, 75-70, to make it 20 wins for the season. But, they wound up losing their final two conference games of the year to eventual Big Ten champion Michigan State, on Senior Night, in an overtime heartbreaker, 75-73, and also to Ohio State, 93-83, despite a career-high 31 points from Willie Burton. (The five Gopher seniors — Burton, Richard Coffey, Connell Lewis, Newbern, and Jim Shikenjanski took a farewell lap around Williams Arena on Senior Night, and Willie whooped it up big-time by getting up on a chair and waving a towel to all the fans for his final curtain call.)

With that, the No. 6 seeded Gophers received another NCAA bid for the Big Dance. Their first opponent: the University of Texas-El Paso, at the Southeast Regional in Richmond, Virginia. There, behind Kevin Lynch's 18 points and Coffey's 11 rebounds, the Gophs hung on to win ugly, in overtime, 64-61.

"It was awesome because everything that coach Haskins had said and told us began to really come true," said Burton. "The hard work, running in the mornings, being put down all the time by the fans at the other schools, it was tough, but it all came together, and we were a force to be reckoned with."

Two nights later the team faced the Northern Iowa Panthers in the round of 32. There, behind Burton's 36 points and 12 rebounds, Minnesota rolled to an 81-78 victory — earning their second trip to the "Sweet 16" in as many years. With the loss of Duke still fresh in their minds from the year before, the Gophers then headed to the New Orleans Super Dome, to take on the mighty Syracuse Orangemen. Led by future NBA stars Billy Owens and Derrick Coleman, the Gophers knew they would have their hands full.

"My club has come a long way," Haskins said before the game. "They have shown great improvement and they remember getting to the 'Sweet 16' a year ago only to get whipped by Duke. They haven't forgotten that. And they'll carry that memory into the Syracuse game."

What happened next though, was pure magic. Down by four at half-time, the team came back and shot nearly 80% from the field in the second half, en route to an impressive 82-75 victory. Fully five players scored in double figures, including 20 from Newbern, 18 from Lynch, and 10 from seven-foot Center Bob Martin of Apple Valley — one of the team's most beloved players. Even the ex-paratrooper, Richard Coffey, got into the act, snatching a much-needed 12 boards as well.

The next step for the Cinderella Gophers was their first-ever appearance in the Tourney's "Great Eight," where they would face off against the Georgia Tech Yellow Jackets, and their "Lethal Weapon Three" trio of sharpshooters: Kenny

Randy Breuer

Seven-foot-three Center Randy Breuer grew up playing basketball in Lake City, Minn., and dreamt of one day wearing the Maroon and Gold. His wish came true in 1980, when, as a freshman, he teamed up with Kevin McHale to lead the Gophers to the NIT Finals against Virginia. As a sophomore, Breuer helped to lead Minnesota to the Big Ten Championship and a post-season NCAA tournament berth. From there he just kept plugging along until he had become one of the best in Gopher history. A two-time first team All-Big Ten selection, Breuer was also honored by being awarded the coveted Big Ten Conference Medal of Honor as well. In his senior year, of 1983, Breuer finished as the Big Ten's leading scorer with 377 points, good for a 21 points per game average. He also led the league in blocked shots with 54, was second in rebounds with 167 and third in field goal percentage with a .586 mark. For his efforts he was named as the team's MVP, and conference co-MVP.

Breuer finished his career by scoring an impressive 1,755 points in 118 games — then the second highest total ever at Minnesota behind only Mychal Thompson's 1,992. He also wound up with 716 career rebounds — then ranking seventh on the all-time list. In addition, he set a Minnesota career record for field goal accuracy with a .570 mark, for the number of free throws attempted, with 563, and for free throws made, with 411. From there Randy went on to play 11 seasons in the NBA, with Milwaukee, Minnesota, Atlanta and Sacramento, averaging 6.8 points and 4.4 rebounds per game.

Anderson, Dennis Scott and Brian Oliver. In what would go down as one of the greatest games in Gopher history, Minnesota came out and played valiantly.

"I finally realized, in my heart, that if we lost, we would never play together again as a team," said Burton. "We didn't want it to be over, so we went out there with destruction on our minds. We just didn't want the ride to end."

It was a back and forth contest all day, but in the end, the Jackets came out on top — thanks in large part to the fact that the referees wound up issuing an unbelievable 35 free throws to Georgia Tech, compared to just 11 for the Gophers. That disparity would ultimately cost the Maroon and Gold the game. Despite that fact though, the team battled down to the wire, and they refused to roll over.

Willie led the Minnesota attack, and the Gophers jumped out to a 12-point lead, but the Yellow Jackets closed the gap and trailed by only two, 49-47, at halftime. Later in the fourth, now down 93-88 with just seven seconds left on the clock, Burton dribbled down and pulled up from the top of the circle to nail a dramatic three-pointer to make it 93-91. Then, when Tech got the ball in-bounds, the Gophers quickly fouled Guard Kenny Anderson. Anderson, who would go on to NBA stardom, stepped up and nervously missed the front end of the one-and-one free-throw.

With that, Richard Coffey, the rebounding machine, grabbed the ball and heaved it to an awaiting Mario Green, who in turn, tossed it to a streaking Kevin Lynch at mid-court. Lynch then dribbled down to the right corner of the court, and with time running out, stopped and fired an off-balanced three-pointer over the top of the outstretched Forward Johnny McNeil's fingertips. At that moment, it was like slow-motion. The ball just hung in the air for what seemed like an eternity. Then, as the buzzer sounded, the ball bounced harmlessly off the front of the rim — putting the final dagger into the collective hearts of the millions of Gopher fans who were tuned in. Minnesota's "Final Four" dreams were over, as the team watched in disbelief.

It was a sad ending for an otherwise brilliant season. The improbable 23-9 Gophers had shocked the world and emerged as a real contender. And, for seniors Willie Burton, Melvin Newbern, Jim Shikenjanski, Richard Coffey, Connell Lewis, as well as Coach Haskins, the collective group of newcomers who came into a program in shambles back in 1986, it was the end of an amazing ride. Their legacy will live on at the

Trent Tucker

Trent Tucker grew up in Flint, Mich., absorbing everything he could about sports. He played basketball and baseball at Flint Northwestern High School, just north of Detroit. There, the six-foot-five guard averaged 29 points and 12 rebounds per game, good enough to be named a high school All-American. Out of high school he was heavily recruited throughout the Big Ten, especially by the home state Wolverines at the University of Michigan.

Tucker had always been a big-time Michigan Football fan. But, luckily for Gold Country, he was recruited by Jesse Evans, an assistant coach with the Gophers who was his junior high school basketball coach. And, as luck would have it, when Trent came to Minnesota on a recruiting trip, he watched the Gophers upset his Wolverines at Memorial Stadium, and from that point on he knew that he wanted to be a Gopher.

Tucker wore the maroon and gold from 1978-1982. He went through a lot during his tenure in Gold Country, including learning the game from a couple of pretty fair teammates, Mychal Thompson and Kevin McHale. For his career, he finished seventh all-time in scoring with 1,445 points, 12th all-time in assists with 219 and fifth all-time in steals with 153. He averaged 12.5 points and 3.4 rebounds per game over his four-year career, while shooting 50 percent from the field and nearly 80 percent from the charity stripe. For his efforts he was named as an All-American, after leading the Gophers to the Big Ten title in 1982.

After his brilliant career at the U, Tucker went on to play 11 seasons in the NBA, nine of them with the New York Knicks, who drafted him sixth overall in 1982, but also with Michael Jordan and the Chicago Bulls, where he won a championship ring in 1993. He retired from active competition after that season. For his career in the NBA, Tucker averaged 8.2 points, 2 assists and 2 rebounds per game. He tallied 6,236 career points, of which 1,725 were three-pointers. He later became a TV analyst for the Minnesota Timberwolves as well.

Tucker was one of the greatest pure shooters ever to have come out of Minnesota. His jump shot was legendary, and one could only imagine what he would have done if they had a three-point shot back then. He will always be remembered not only for being an incredible basketball player who led the school to a Big Ten title, but also because he is a genuinely nice person who always played team basketball. The common denominator found most often when describing "Tuck," was that everyone thought he was just a great guy.

"As a freshman, I didn't understand what it really meant to be a Gopher because I was too young to understand," said Tucker. "But as I progressed and got older, the significance of being a Gopher and what it meant to the community became apparent to me. It was an unbelievable experience and something I will always treasure. I looked upon my teammates just like we were a family. You'd go through the ups and downs with your teammates and when the last game was played, all you have is memories. I miss those moments of guys pulling together, trying to overcome all the adversity, and then finding a way to win as a team. Aside from furthering my education, the University of Minnesota also afforded me the opportunity to fulfill my lifelong childhood dream of playing in the NBA. Knowing that all that hard work had paid off was very gratifying to me."

U as the team that completed one of the greatest turnarounds in Minnesota sports history. When they were freshmen and sophomores, the group was a part of teams that lost 21 straight Big Ten games. They had joined a ravaged and ragged Gopher program, and, as seniors, stepped down from active intercollegiate play as saviors, giving Gold Country fans two magical back-to-back trips to the Big Dance.

For Burton, who emerged as one of the program's most beloved all-time players, it was a very sad and emotional ending to an incredible career in Gold Country. "It almost went in. It really bothers me because it was a good shot, and he barely missed it," said Willie B., who, after averaging 24.4 points per game, was named to the All-Big Ten Team and received honorable mention All-American honors. "Personally, I think that the last shot was just too much pressure for him (Lynch) to take. I mean at the time he was open, going top speed and he had a look at the hoop, but it was a lot of pressure to deal with. When Kevin missed, I was so bummed out because I didn't want it all to end like that. I remember that, after the game, I stopped and looked hard at everyone. I took a picture of everybody together in my mind for one last time."

"They shot 25 more foul shots than we did, and they won by two," added Burton, when asked about the blatantly lopsided refereeing during that game. "I had 35 points and never took a foul shot the entire game. Maybe it was because those refs were from the ACC, Georgia

Willie Burton

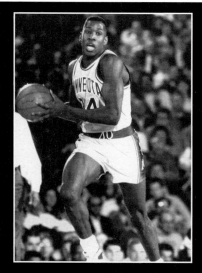

Born on May 26, 1968, Willie Burton grew up in inner city Detroit playing baseball, basketball, football, and track. He was proficient in both athletics and academics in high school where he graduated with a 3.6 GPA. His prep athletic credentials also were impressive. As a senior, he averaged 22 points and 12 rebounds per game. He earned three letters in basketball and two in baseball. In basketball, he was a two-year All-State selection as well as an All- Detroit honoree.

From there Willie decided to attend the U of M, where, after four glorious years, he was named to the All-Big Ten Team, received honorable mention All-American honors, and for three straight years was voted as the team MVP. Willie finished his Gopher career averaging 19.3 points and 6.4 rebounds per game. Upon graduation, he ranked ninth in career rebounding (705), sixth in career blocks, (79) and was third on the all-time scoring list, with 1,800 points, behind only Mychal Thompson and Voshon Lenard.

"The reason I went to the University of Minnesota was because it had more to offer after basketball," said Burton. "I took a recruiting visit to the Twin Cities and just fell in love with the region. I thought it was a beautiful place, the people got along, I loved the mix of the cultures that were there, and it was just a dream place as far as where I would like to live once my basketball days were over. I knew in my heart that it was the place that I wanted to be. I signed a letter of intent for coach Jim Dutcher one month before the program's troubles in Madison. But, through it all, I never said I would leave because my goal was to be a Gopher and to live in Minnesota. Coach Haskins and I started out together and we just started the basketball program over. All of us seniors came in together when Clem took it over, and that's why we were so close to each other. We went through a lot of scrutiny after all that happened, but when it was all over we showed the world we could go a long way."

After his memorable career with Minnesota he went on to become a first-round NBA pick, where he was selected ninth overall by the Miami Heat. He would later find himself playing for the Philadelphia 76'ers, where he scored a career high 50 points in 1995. He bounced around with several teams after that, including Atlanta, San Antonio and Charlotte, and has been a steady pro player ever since, averaging better than 10 points and three rebounds per game over his career. His quick first step and fine post-up ability made him one of the best-ever to hail from Minnesota.

"Playing at the University of Minnesota was the most meaningful thing in my life," said Burton. "The time I spent on campus was the best four years of my life. My teammates and I were like brothers who all genuinely cared about each other. I loved it there. I lived in Centennial Hall for all four years that I was there, and it was great. I still proudly wear a University of Minnesota baseball cap because I've earned the right to wear it always. I can't put into words what the University of Minnesota meant to me. The experience was just awesome."

Tech's home conference. We just couldn't get a break that night, and it was frustrating because the referees just wouldn't blow their whistles for us."

Several thousand fans showed up at the Twin Cities International Airport following the Georgia Tech loss to show their appreciation for an unbelievably entertaining and exciting season. The Gophers had captured the hearts and imaginations of the state of Minnesota that season, finally putting the program back on track and into the national spotlight.

The 1990-91 season would prove to be another rebuilding year for the Gophers though. Willie Burton, and his 19.3 points and 6.4 rebounds per game, was off to the NBA, playing with the Miami Heat, while Newbern, Coffey and Shikenjanski had all graduated as well. Kevin Lynch, who averaged 13.4 points per game, and Walter Bond, who added 10.5 of his own, were back though, and it would be their team to lead.

Minnesota opened its season by beating up on Robert Morris College, 74-61, thanks to 19 points from Lynch and 12 from freshman Center Randy Carter, but lost Walter Bond in the process, when he broke his foot while chasing a loose ball in the game. The Gophers went on to win the next five games before losing to Cincinnati, and finally finishing their non-conference schedule with a 7-3 record. The team opened its Big Ten schedule in Madison, where, despite Kevin Lynch's 17, Minnesota lost, 72-62. After losing three nights later in Illinois, on a last-second free-throw, 67-66, the Gophers rebounded to beat Iowa, 79-77, behind 26 points from Lynch, and then Purdue, 59-56, at home.

Then, after dumping a pair of games to the defending Big Ten champions from Michigan State, 73-64, followed by an 80-70 loss to the No. 4 Ohio State Buckeyes, Minnesota came back behind Randy Carter's 29 points and 15 rebounds to beat Northwestern, 85-68. From there it got ugly in a hurry. Following a heartbreaking 66-62 loss at the hands of Michigan, the Gophers went on to lose nine of their next 11 games. They did finish the season on a high note by beating the cheese-heads from Wisconsin, 80-70, thanks to 18 points from Lynch as well as 11 apiece from seniors Mario Green and Rob Metcalf. The team would end the season at 12-16 overall, and 5-13 in

the Big Ten — good for a miserable ninth-place finish in the Big Ten.

The 1991-92 Gophers were led by a freshman phenom guard from Detroit by the name of Voshon Lenard, who would average nearly 13 points per game during that season. The team kicked off the year by losing to the No. 2-ranked Arkansas Razorbacks, 92-83, at the Maui Invitational in Hawaii. They did rebound to beat Providence, 89-82, behind Lenard's 20 points, followed by Arizona State, 69-37, to finish third in the tourney. After finishing their non-conference season with an 8-5 record, the Gophers began the Big Ten season on the road in Indiana, where they were crushed by No. 10-ranked Hoosiers, 96-50. They rebounded to post a trio of victories, first over the No. 11-ranked Wolverines at Williams Arena, 73-64, behind Lenard's 25 points, then at Wisconsin, 49-48, followed by Michigan State at home, 70-66, on Townsend Orr's 20 points.

After losing to Ohio State on the road, the Gophers went on to eke out Illinois, 54-53, on Dana Jackson's last-second free throw. From there, behind Bob Martin's 17 points, they cruised by Northwestern, 92-50 to get their conference record to an impressive 5-2 mark. They got streaky from there though, losing a pair at both Iowa and Purdue, before beating Northwestern, 57-55, on Arriel McDonald's last-second shot, and the No. 4-ranked Indiana Hoosiers, 71-67. The team then lost six of seven, to finish the season at 15-11, and 7-6 in the Big Ten.

With that they received an NIT Tournament bid to play Washington State, on the road. There, despite 20 points by McDonald, 16 from Lenard and 12 from Forward Jayson Walton, Minnesota came up on the short end of a 72-70 nail-biter. So distraught was Haskins over the officiating, that he was even ejected for arguing with the refs late in the first half.

It is important to note that in 1992 the NCAA's Final Four was held for the second time ever in Minnesota, this time at the Metrodome, with Duke beating Michigan's "Fab-Five" for the national championship. The city came alive for the gala event, showing the world that hoops is big-time in the Gophers State. Oh, how sweet it would've been had our Gophers been at that Big Dance!

Optimism was running high that next year. After all, only one senior, Bob Martin, would not be back for the 1992-93 campaign. Minnesota jumped out to a quick start that season, winning its first six games before finally being upended by Iowa State in Week Seven. They came back to take their next four though, including a pair of Big Ten wins over Michigan State, 64-57, behind Owatonna Center Chad Kolander's 13 points, and Purdue, 81-60, thanks to Forward Nate Tubbs' 16 points. With the win, the top-20-ranked Gophers headed to Iowa City, where the Hawks prevailed, 84-77. Losses to Wisconsin and the "Fab-Five" of Michigan followed, until the Gophers got back on track against Northwestern, where, behind Forward Jayson Walton's 21 points and 10 rebounds, the Gophers prevailed, 70-55.

After falling to Indiana, 57-61, Minnesota came back to beat Penn State, 95-67, on Forward Randy Carter's 16 points and 10 rebounds. From there they lost a pair to Michigan State and Purdue, followed by a pair of wins over Iowa, 91-85, and Wisconsin, 85-71. (Lenard scored a career-high 32 points against the 13th-ranked Hawkeyes and another 23 points against the Badgers.) Minnesota went 3-3 over its next six game, losing to Michigan, Indiana and Ohio State, while beating the likes of Northwestern, 79-60, Illinois, 67-65, on Senior Night, and Penn State, 67-41, to finish up their season at 9-9 in the Big Ten — good for fifth place.

Melvin Newbern

With 17 wins, the Gophers were expecting an invitation to the Big Dance, but when the tournament selection committee factored in the cream-puff teams that Haskins had played during the non-conference schedule, all the club could get was an NIT invite. Minnesota, just happy to be playing ball in late March, gladly accepted the bid though, and kicked off the tourney by hosting Florida at the Target Center. There, behind McDonald's 17 points, Minnesota out-muscled the Gators, 74-66. They then hosted Oklahoma five nights later before a near sellout crowd of 18,254 at the Target Center. This one wasn't even close though, as the Gophers smothered the Sooners with their defense and rolled to an 86-72 victory. From there the team packed up and headed to a sold-out Met Center in Bloomington, where nearly 16,000 fans showed up to watch Minnesota's stifling defense shut down USC in the NIT quarterfinals, 76-58, thanks to Lenard's 25 points.

Walter Bond

After a victory lap around the court, the Gophers got ready to head to the Big Apple, where they would make a Final Four appearance at Madison Square Garden, against the Providence Friars. The hero in this one was once again Voshon Lenard, who's 25 points (17 came in the second half) proved to be the difference in a 76-70 win. Next up: the Georgetown Hoyas in the NIT Finals. Aiming to prove the NCAA selection committee wrong, Minnesota came out and played hard in this one, forcing the Hoyas to take bad shots with their pressing defense. The game was a back and forth affair all night, with the Gophers taking an 11-point lead with just under five minutes to go. Arriel McDonald, who led the team with 20 points, was all over the floor, while Lenard, who added 17 in the game, played amazing defense as well.

From there Georgetown put the hammer down though, and came out with a 10-0 run to close the gap to just one point with under 10 seconds to go in the game. That's when Randy Carter came up with a huge blocked shot, followed by Lenard, who would be named as the tournament's MVP, hustling to grab an incoming Hoya lob pass down low in the paint to secure a 62-61 Gopher victory. Incredibly, it was the program's first ever postseason championship, and more importantly, it was sweet vindication for being snubbed by the NCAA.

The 1992-93 NIT champion Gophers, complete with all five of their returning starters, opened the 1993-94 season in the newly renovated Williams Arena. (A new Mariucci Arena was constructed across the street and the old arena was then converted into the Gopher Women's Sports Pavilion.) In addition to new entrance lobbies the Barn also got rid of its old wooden benches and replaced them with some new fancy contoured plastic seats. As a result, the capacity of the venue was reduced from 16,549 to 14,321.

The team, which was ranked 10th in the nation in the pre-season AP Poll, jumped out to a quick 2-0 start that year by winning its first two games against Rice and Georgia at the pre-season NIT tournament. They came back to earth though, when they lost their next two to powerhouses Kansas and North Carolina. They went 7-1 over the remainder of their non-conference schedule before kicking off their Big Ten season with a pair of wins over Northwestern, 73-65, thanks to 23 points from Voshon Lenard, and No. 12-ranked Wisconsin, 90-53, behind yet another 23 from Lenard.

From there the team headed out to Happy Valley, where they were upset by lowly Penn State, despite Chad Kolander's 15 points. They rebounded though, to beat both Michigan (Wolverines Juwan Howard and Jimmy King were both out with chicken pox), 63-58, followed by Michigan State, at the Barn, 68-66, on the strength of Ariel McDonald's clutch 16-point effort. Then, after dropping a pair to the Hoosiers, 78-66, and Glenn "Big Dog" Robinson's Purdue Boilermakers, 75-72, at the Barn. They came back to beat St. John's, 92-64, behind 27 points from Lenard, but then came up short in a 92-88 loss at Iowa three nights later.

The team's next game against Northwestern at the Barn was a bizarre one to say the least. In it, Wildcat Coach Ricky Byrdsong had an emotional breakdown of sorts, spending much of the game bouncing around the Williams Arena stands, making conversation with the Gopher fans and seemingly not caring about what his team was doing on the court. The clincher came near the end of the 79-65 Northwestern loss when an usher actually kicked the disturbed coach out of a Gopher season-ticket holder's seat.

Kevin Lynch

Following that debacle, Minnesota rattled off three big wins over Ohio State, 79-73, behind

Bob Martin

Lenard and Carter's combined 46 points, Wisconsin, 109-78, followed by Penn State, 94-66, thanks to Lenard's 30 points. Even Hosea Crittenden, a "Rudy-like" guard who became a cult-like icon on campus, got into the action against the Lions, nailing a three-pointer with under a minute to go to put the crowd into a frenzy.

The Gophers then lost a pair to both Michigan and Michigan State after that, but rebounded behind Lenard's 35 points to spank the 12th-ranked Indiana Hoosiers at the Barn, 106-56. Then, after falling to Purdue, 86-70, Minnesota came back to beat Iowa in a classic triple-overtime thriller, 107-96, at home. It was an extra special Senior Night for Arriel McDonald, Randy Carter and Ernest Nzigamasabo, a popular center from Mound High School, as the team won this one down the wire. Lenard was elevated to God-like status in this one as he finished with a career-high 38 points and single-handedly kept the Gophers in this one down the stretch — nailing a desperation three-pointer to send the game into a second overtime, and then hitting a clutch free-throw to send it to a third.

The team lost its final game, on the road against the Illini, 90-75, but didn't care — after all, they were going to the NCAA Tournament. That's right, with 20 wins, the team was off the Big Dance yet again, this time earning a sixth seed in the West Regional in Sacramento, where they would take on the Southern Illinois Salukis in the opening round. There, behind 18 points from Lenard, 15 from McDonald, 12 from Kolander and nine from Big Ernie, the Gophers cruised to a 74-60 victory.

From there the team prepared to face a very tough Louisville team, which, behind legendary coach Denny Crum, had been there before. The Gophers played tough in this one, even jumping out to a 12-point lead at the half, but were hurting without the injured Jayson Walton. Lenard did manage to shutdown the Cardinals' leading scorer, Clifford Rozier, holding him to just two points, but in the end Louisville was just too much. Minnesota committed 17 fouls down the stretch and Crum's Cards took advantage, advancing to the "Sweet 16" by the final score of 60-55.

That next year the Gophers were blessed with the news that Voshon Lenard had decided to return to Gold Country for his senior season. He did, however, test the NBA waters so to speak though, taking advantage of a new NCAA rule, that allowed a player to declare himself eligible for the draft, but return to college if he didn't go as high as he would've hoped. Well, Lenard was drafted by the Milwaukee Bucks, but not until the second round, so he decided to come back to Minnie for the 1994-95 campaign. The preseason all-Big Ten guard would be joined by another outstanding player that year as well when Park-Cottage Grove High School Guard Sam Jacobson, one of the state's most highly touted recruits ever, signed on to wear the Maroon and Gold. In addition, Center Trevor Winter from Slayton, and John Thomas, from Minneapolis Roosevelt, also joined the team. It was one of the best recruiting classes in Gopher history.

With that, Minnesota began their centennial season by winning the Great Alaska Shootout, upsetting the fifth-ranked Arizona Wildcats, Villanova and BYU along the way. Townsend Orr, who had 15 points in the Finals despite playing with a bum ankle, was named as the tournament's MVP. From there the 15th-ranked Gophers went on to post a 10-2 overall non-conference record, losing to both Cincinnati, 91-88, in overtime, and Texas Southern, 71-50, in an inexplicable aberration.

The team then rallied to win its Big Ten opener over Penn State, 69-67, behind David Grim's last-second three-pointer. Purdue was up next, as the Boilers continued their domination over the Gophers by winning their 14th straight over the club, 68-60, a sick stat dating back to the early 1970s. The team went up and down from that point on, beating Northwestern later that week, 105-74, behind Lenard's 27 points — which included a school-record seven three-pointers. Then, after losing at Wisconsin, 74-67, Minnesota rebounded to win a pair over Ohio State, 81-61, and Illinois, 77-66, behind Orr's 18 points and Kolander's 14. They followed that up with a tough 54-53 loss to Michigan State; but came back to beat Iowa, 55-54, on Thomas' last-second dunk; Michigan, 80-58, on 20 points from Orr and another 19 from Lenard; and Indiana, 64-54, at Assembly Hall, thanks to Lenard's 21 points.

Looking good, the Gophers came out and fell flat against Iowa at home, losing an ugly one, 74-70. Once again, they rebounded though, this time beating the top-10-ranked Michigan State Spartans, 66-57, behind Lenard's 17, Walton's 14, Thomas' 12 and Jacobson's 10. Next up were the Illini, and, despite losing, 94-88, in overtime, Voshon Lenard rewrote the record books by scoring his 1,993rd career point, thus passing Mychal Thompson as the program's all-time leading scorer.

They continued their slide, losing to lowly Ohio State, 73-65, but came back to beat both Wisconsin, 78-70, behind Jayson Walton's 19 points, and Northwestern, 82-70, on Lenard's 30 points. They then rolled over and played dead, losing to both Purdue, 72-59, and Penn State, 69-60, in their final two games of the season to finish at 20-10 — good for the team's third consecutive 20-win season.

Arriel McDonald

With that, the team got yet another coveted NCAA bid, this time to the East Regional in Baltimore to take on St. Louis University. There, the Billikens, with no starter taller than six-foot-six, pulled off an upset for the ages, beating the Gophers in overtime, 64-61. Minnesota came out and stunk up the joint, missing its first 10 shots to fall behind, 19-3. From there St. Louis bombed away with three-pointers, demoralizing the Gophers with every shot sank. The Maroon and Gold did rally though, behind Chad Kolander's dramatic lay-up to tie the game with just 10 seconds to go to send it into over-time. That was as far as they would get though, as the Billikens controlled the extra session and came away with the "W."

Lenard, who averaged 17.3 points per game that year, went off to the NBA's Miami Heat that next season, leaving swing-man Sam Jacobson and six-foot-nine Center John Thomas to steer the ship. The Gophers opened their 1995-96 season at the "Big Island Invitational" in Hawaii. There, the team cruised to a pair of wins over Valparaiso, 70-66, and Wichita State, 64-55, before losing to Nebraska, 85-96, despite freshman Quincy Lewis' 26-point effort. From there they rattled off an impressive 7-2 non-conference record before going on to upset the 13th-ranked Illini, 69-64, in the Big Ten opener — thanks in large part to the efforts of freshman Forward Courtney James, who scored 13 points and grabbed 16 rebounds.

It was tough from there on out though, as the team struggled and lost three straight to Iowa, 92-63, Penn State, 76-61, and Purdue, 76-62. They rebounded to beat Ohio State, 60-56, behind Jacobson's 15 points, but then were defeated at Wisconsin, 73-65, in overtime. Minnesota lost two of its next three games as well to both Michigan State, 68-54, and Indiana, 81-66, while beating Northwestern, 77-68, thanks to Sam Jacobson, John Thomas, Bobby Jackson and Eric Harris, who all scored in double figures. They heated up from there, running a four-game winning streak over the likes of Northwestern, in Evanston, 66-47, on Jackson's 18 points, followed by a 64-63 double-overtime win at Michigan State behind James' 18 points and 12 boards. They also knocked off Wisconsin, 70-66, and Ohio State, 60-57, as well, thanks to Bobby Jackson's 17 points 11 rebounds. In addition, Courtney James' pair of double-doubles vs. Wisconsin and Michigan State were enough to garner him Big Ten Player of the Week honors as well.

Minnesota's streak came to an end as they suffered a pair of tough road losses to Michigan, 65-62, and Purdue, 67-61, but they bounced back to upset 12th-ranked Penn State, 62-60, thanks to senior David Grim's 16 points off the bench. Next up were the 19th-ranked Hawkeyes, which, thanks to Jackson's 21 points, were beaten, 72-64, as were the Illini, who went down, 67-66, in one of the best games of the year. Minnesota, which had not won in Illinois' Assembly Hall since 1978, spoiled Illinois Coach Lou Henson's final home game thanks to Jacobson's game-winning jumper with 15 seconds to go.

Chad Kolander

With that, the Golden Gophers had gone from 3-6 in the Big Ten to 10-8, earning a fifth-place finish – good enough for an invitation to the NIT. It was the fifth consecutive year, and the seventh time in the last eight seasons that the Gophers had made it to post-season play. There, the team played host to St. Louis in the first round at home, and thanks to Bobby Jackson's 17 points and Grim's 15, Minnesota made quick work of the Billikens, winning 68-52. With that, the Tulane Green Wave came to town, hoping to stop the streaking Gophers. But, the Wave held the golden ones to a paltry 34% shooting, including 3-17 from beyond the arc, to end their season by the final score of 84-65. Sam Jacobson did score 19 points, while John Thomas added 17 points and 17 rebounds in the losing effort.

The 1996-97 Gophers, behind Bobby Jackson, the improbable transfer-student from Western Nebraska Community College, Sam Jacobson, Courtney James and John Thomas, who all received honorable mention All-Big Ten honors the year prior, came into the season with high expectations of making a serious run at winning the Big Ten title. They had their nucleus back and were the buzz of the Twin Cities. Clem had instilled in the kids that they had been jobbed that last season by not getting an NCAA tourney bid, and the kids responded by working hard that summer in the off-season. They played basketball every day, lifted weights, got into shape, and hung around each other — building the chemistry that would take them farther than any Gopher team in history.

Eric Harris

The team opened its season by winning its first five non-conference games before getting bumped off by a pesky Alabama team, which hit a three-pointer with just seconds remaining to win, 70-67, in early December. They rebounded to post an impressive 11-1 non-conference record, even crushing lowly Alabama State, 114-34 (the program's largest all-time margin of victory), along the way.

Minnesota's Big Ten opener against Wisconsin turned into a 68-43 victory as the backcourt duo of Jackson, who exploded for 20 points and 10 rebounds, and Harris, who added 16 points, manhandled the Badgers from the opening tip. From there the Maroon and Gold headed to East Lansing, where they spanked the Spartans thanks to a 53% shooting percentage in a 68-43 victory. The team's next game, at Indiana, would prove to be a pivotal one, as the Gophers somehow pulled off an amazing come-from-behind overtime victory over the Hoosiers. Down by seven points with just under a minute to go, Harris, Jacobson and Jackson all came up with clutch three-pointers to force overtime. There, Jacobson hit the first six points of the extra session, and the Gophers never looked back. Jackson led the squad with 26 points, while sophomore Guard Quincy Lewis added 20 points as well.

It was all Jackson again later that week as he posted 20 points and 11 rebounds in a 70-64 win over Michigan. For his efforts, he was named as the Big Ten Player of the Week. The team's incredible 10-game winning streak came to a halt that next week at Illinois though, as the Illini shot 11 three-pointers in a 96-90 defeat. After dumping Ohio State, 73-67, behind Harris' 16 points, the 15th-ranked Gophers hosted the 23rd-ranked Iowa Hawkeyes at Williams Arena.

There, in front of a national television audience on ESPN, Sam Jacobson poured in a career-high 29 points, including five three-pointers and an electrifying dunk in the first half, en route to leading Minnesota to a 66-51 victory.

The group gelled early under Coach Haskins' system, but were often substituted for. Guys like Quincy Lewis, Charles Thomas, Trevor Winter and Miles Tarver were routinely called upon to play big minutes, and they performed masterfully. Throughout the season, nine Gophers averaged double-figure minutes. "The only reason we have five starters is because five players have to start," said Guard Eric Harris of his team's stellar bench play.

From there they cruised past Purdue, 91-68, Northwestern, 75-56, and then returned home to beat Penn State, 85-70. They then went back to Purdue to beat the Boilers, 70-67, on Jacobson and Jackson's 13-point efforts. At Iowa, Eric Harris and John Thomas each hit key free throws down the stretch to lead the team to a 68-66 victory. Then, against Ohio State, back at the Barn, the Gophers held the Buckeyes to just 34% shooting in a 60-48 win. By now the team was on cruise-control and had a chance to clinch at least a share of the Big Ten crown by avenging their earlier loss to the Illini, this time at home. There, behind Thomas' two free throws with just four seconds remaining, the Gophers sealed a 67-66 victory to clinch the title.

Jackson again led all Minnesota scorers, this time with 18 points, in a big 55-54 win over Michigan at Crisler Arena — a building that had not surrendered a victory to the Gophers since 1982. This one was all about the Gophers' stifling defense, which held the Wolverines to 38% shooting. The

Quincy Lewis

Bobby Jackson

Bobby Jackson was born on March 13, 1973, in Salisbury, N.C. He grew up in basketball country, playing and dreaming of playing college ball. Jackson went on to average 22 points per game over his junior and senior seasons at Salisbury High School, earning all-conference and all-state honors in those same two seasons. From there, the speedy guard went to Western Nebraska Junior College in Scottsbluff, Neb., where he garnered second team All-American honors in 1995.

Jackson then transferred to Minnesota for the 1996 season, and although he was only in Gold Country for two seasons, he made the most of his time here. With his patented long white socks, he finished his illustrious tenure in Gold Country with a career scoring average of 14.4 points, 5.5 rebounds, and 3.5 assists per game. Not only was Jackson named the Big Ten MVP, he was also the conference's Defensive Player of the Year. He also earned second team All-America honors.

"Coming out of junior college, I could've gone to Wake Forest, Cincinnati, or Minnesota," recalled Jackson. "I chose Minnesota because of their team concept. I was looking for an opportunity to come in and help my team out right away and make an impact. I wanted to come in and win a conference championship, and that's exactly what we did during my last year. Being a Gopher really means a lot to me. There are only a certain amount of people that get to wear the maroon and gold, and I am just happy that Coach Haskins let me be a part of it all."

After receiving his degree in sports management, Bobby was selected by the Seattle SuperSonics in the first round (23rd pick overall) of the 1997 NBA Draft. Jackson was then immediately traded to the Denver Nuggets, where he emerged as one of the league's top young players. Two years later he was dealt to his hometown Minnesota Timberwolves, where he rekindled his relationship with the fans. In 2000 he was sent to Sacramento, where, in his fifth year in the league, he has surpassed the coveted 2,000-point plateau.

Bobby Jackson could just flat out play. He is an amazing scorer, who can light it up at any time during the course of a game. He possesses unbelievable speed, quickness, and an explosive first step. With his fantastic court vision and unselfish passing abilities, he has become a tremendous NBA player.

finale came down to Harris' dramatic steal and desperation pass to a streaking Bobby Jackson to set up the game-winning free throws in the final seconds. The next game, a 75-72 win over the Indiana Hoosiers, at the Barn, was a classic. Nearly 15,000 Gopher fans showed up to cheer on the Maroon and Gold in this one as Courtney James dished in 14 points, Charles Thomas added 13 and Trevor Winter grabbed a career-high 10 rebounds. The team's home season concluded with an 81-74 victory over Michigan State on Senior Night to round out an amazing 15-0 home record. Before the game, the senior foursome of Bobby Jackson, John Thomas, Trevor Winter and Aaron Stauber, hoisted the 1997 Big Ten championship banner up to the old Barn's raftors for all to see.

They wound up losing their final game of the year in Wisconsin, 66-65, as Sam Jacobson was stripped of the ball while he was attempting a last-second shot which could've won the game. With it, the team's 12-game winning streak was snapped, but they still managed to finish the regular season with the best record in school history at 27-3. And, believe it or not, that was just the beginning of one of the greatest rides in Minnesota sports history.

A March to Madness... The Big Ten champion Gophers were then rewarded with a coveted No. 1 seed in the NCAA's Midwest Region, in Kansas City. Thousands of Gopher fans made the trip to KC to watch the Gophers open the 64-team tourney against Southwest Texas State, and thanks to Charles Thomas' 14 points off the bench, Minnesota cruised to a 78-46 victory. Next up was legendary Coach John Chaney's talented Temple squad, known for its trapping defense. But, thanks to double-figure scoring from Harris, Jacobson, Jackson and Thomas, the Gophers cruised to a 76-57 victory, and a trip back to the "Sweet 16," this time in San Antonio.

Next up for the Gophers was Clemson, a team that would test the very moral fiber of their being. This one came down to a dramatic double-overtime thriller with Minnesota somehow emerging victorious on a 90-84 win. Jacobson and Jackson combined for 65 points, posting career highs of 29 and 36 points, respectively, as the team rallied for its biggest win of the season. The good news was that the team was headed to the "Elite Eight" to face the mighty UCLA Bruins in the regional final.

Trevor Winter

With a Final Four berth on the line, Guard Eric Harris, who had gone down with a shoulder injury in the Clemson game, stepped it up and decided to play with pain. The Gophers would need him in this one, the biggest game in the history of the program. The game was a back and forth affair, with Minnesota finding itself down 33-28 at halftime. But, behind a 52-point barrage in the second half, highlighted by Midwest Regional MVP Bobby Jackson's 18 points, the Gophers hung tough and pulled off an amazing 80-72 victory, to earn the school's first-ever Final Four appearance. After the game the players climbed a ladder to proudly cut down the net, a truly amazing site for everyone to see back in Minnesota.

Next stop was the Final Four at Indianapolis' RCA Dome to take on defending national champions from Kentucky. No other Gopher hoop squad had ever made it as far in the NCAA tournament, but in reality, there was nothing Cinderella about this team. The Gophers had won the Big Ten outright and had deservedly earned a No. 1 seed in the tournament. No. 1 seeds are given that designation for a reason. What was unexpected was the active support of all the Minnesota fans. When the team came back to Minneapolis, they arrived to a homecoming celebration at the Barn, which was filled well beyond its seating capacity.

Now, there was all kinds of drama leading up the game against Kentucky, especially with Clem Haskins, who grew up in Campbellsville, Kentucky, and was a big prep star there. But because of segregation issues back in the early 1960s, Haskins who wanted to attend at KU to play for legendary Coach Adolph Rupp, opted to instead attend Western Kentucky University, where he became the program's first black player.

Finally, in Indy, as the team made its way to the dome, nearly 10,000 Gopher fans turned out for a rally before the big game to support their team. It was going to be a battle. Things didn't start out so hot for the Gophers though against Kentucky's Wildcats in the opening game of the semifinals. In fact, it would be safe to say that it would be a tale of two halves. In the first 20 minutes, a tense squad in maroon and gold turned the ball over 15 times, and the stalwart bench that usually delivered the goods was nowhere to be found. Further, Kentucky's relentless defense was clearly presenting problems for Minnesota.

Then with 14:31 remaining in the second half and Kentucky leading 47-43, James went down the lane and scored on a monster dunk. Everybody in the dome, including droves of North Carolina and Arizona fans, who by now were rooting for the underdog Gophers, went berserk. The deafening roar of the crowd was drowned out, however, by the sound of the referee's whistle, as he negated the basket and called a charging foul on James. Coach Clem was apoplectic and his suit coat went flying. Then, before the Armani jacket could hit the floor, the referee slapped Clem with a "T." It was just one turning point in a game that had many. The resultant six-point swing put the Wildcats up by 51-43.

Sam Jacobson

Sam Jacobson will go down as one of Minnesota's greatest ever basketball players. Heavily recruited out of Park-Cottage Grove High School, the six-foot-four guard went on to stardom at the University of Minnesota. There, "Slammin Sam" scored 1,709 points, ranking him fifth on the all-time scoring list. He also averaged 13.1 points, 4.8 rebounds and 1.7 assists as well. After his senior year, averaging better than 18 points per game, Sam was named as an Honorable Mention All-American.

After school, Sam was drafted in the first round (26th overall) of the 1998 NBA Draft by the Los Angeles Lakers. He was later dealt to the Golden State Warriors, where he averaged 4.9 points and 1.4 rebounds per game. From there he signed on as a free-agent with his hometown Minnesota Timberwolves. He played sparingly during the 2000-2001 season, overcoming injuries along the way.

The Gophers came back as they had done all season long though. First, Jacobson floated in mid-air to hit a jumper. Then, Jackson proceeded to hit a leaning double-pump lay-up, and then popped in a three-pointer. The RCA Dome exploded in noise as the Gophers were finally fighting their way back from pesky turnovers and fouls to take the lead, 52-51, with 10:45 to play. Now, with nine minutes left, the game was tied at 54.

Then it got ugly for the Maroon and Gold. The Wildcats, led by All-American Ron Mercer, reeled off 14 of the next 17 points. The fat lady was, regrettably, warming up her vocal chords. Unable to play at Kentucky Coach Rick Pitino's torrid pace, the Gophers ran out of gas down the stretch and lost the game, 78-69. In the end, Minnesota, the escape artists of college hoops, had succumbed to great coaching, a blown

John Thomas

charge call, and a terrific Kentucky defense. Throw in the fact that Sam Jacobson, Charles Thomas and Eric Harris were all playing hurt, and it gets even worse. The previously mistake-free Gophers had yielded to the relentless Kentucky press that caused them to turn over the ball to the Wildcats a sick 26 times. (Incidentally, the University of Arizona, led by Coach Lute Olson, a former standout basketball and football player at Augsburg College, wound up winning its first national championship that year by beating that Kentucky squad in overtime two days later in the NCAA title game.)

The Golden Gophers gave us all some great memories during the 1997 season though, and renewed our pride in Minnesota basketball. Jackson, who finished the game with 23 points, had a once-in-a-life-time season. For his efforts in the tournament, he was named to the All-Final-Four team

"Words can't describe how great that season was for me," said Bobby. "We worked really hard to get where we went, even when it seemed everybody doubted us. We just wanted to play hard and show everybody what we were about. I had never been in a Final Four situation, and it felt so good to accomplish that much. The Gopher fans played a major part in our success, and I would like to thank them for being there for us."

Kentucky played a lot of great teams that season, but nobody pounded them like the Gophers did at the RCA Dome. "We beat a team that was as physically and mentally tough as any I've coached against since I've been at Kentucky," Coach Pitino said after the game. "They got up in our pants, they took us out of our offense, and they were very tough-minded. I have tremendous admiration for Minnesota."

Joel Przybilla

All in all, it was a storybook season that Gopher fans will never forget. The basketball team finished with an amazing 31-4 record en route to winning its first Big Ten title in 15 years. Led by the NCAA Coach of the Year, Clem Haskins, the Gophers made it all the way to their first-ever Final Four and were ranked as high as No. 2 in the nation for much of the season.

After the season, the awards started to roll in. Bobby Jackson, a consensus second team All-America selection, was named as both the Big Ten Player of the Year and Big Ten Defensive Player of the Year. John Thomas was a second team All-Big Ten selection, Harris was third teamer and James earned honorable mention honors. Jackson and Thomas were also both chosen in the first round of the NBA draft that June, while several of the other players went on to play pro ball as well.

The 1997-98 Gophers had some big shoes to fill. Gone were stars Bobby Jackson and John Thomas, as was Courtney James. Not only had the team lost their star shooting guard, they lost an experienced big man and a wide body. They would be thin everywhere, but especially down in the post area. It would be a rebuilding year in Gold Country, and everyone knew it. Everyone except the players that was. They didn't care about who was gone, they cared only about who was there. Joining redshirt freshman Center Kyle Sanden and top recruit Kevin Clark, were seniors Sam Jacobson and Eric Harris, as

Gopher All-Americans

Year	Name	Position
1905	George Tuck	Center
1906	Garfield Brown	Guard
1911	Frank Lawler	Forward
1917	Francis Stadsvold	Forward
1918	Harold Gillen	Forward
1919	Erling Platou	Guard
1919	Arnold Oss	Forward
1921	Arnold Oss	Forward
1937	Martin Rolek	Guard
1938	Martin Rolek	Guard
1948*	Jim McIntyre	Center
1949	Jim McIntyre	Center
1950	Whitey Skoog	Guard
1951	Whitey Skoog	Guard
1955	Dick Garmaker	Forward
1955	Chuck Mencel	Guard
1960	Ron Johnson	Center
1965	Lou Hudson	Forward
1967	Tom Kondla	Center
1973	Jim Brewer	Center
1973	Ron Behagen	Forward
1977	Ray Williams	Guard
1977	Mychal Thompson	Center
1978*	Mychal Thompson	Center
1982	Trent Tucker	Guard

Consensus Selection

well as forward Miles Tarver and junior Guard Quincy Lewis — a player who would develop into one of the program's best.

With that, the Gophers went out and posted a 7-4 non-conference schedule record, starting with a strong with a 68-55 victory over Villanova in the BCA Classic at the Target Center. One of the highlights came in Game Nine, when the Maroon and Gold upset 15th-ranked Fresno State, complete with six McDonald's All-Americans, and coached by the legendary towel chewer himself, Jerry Tarkanian. The nationally televised game saw Jacobson tally 22 points, while Kevin Clark added 21 in the 92-72 win.

What happened next, however, was just plain ugly. What started with an 87-83 loss to Purdue in the Big Ten opener, turned into a six-game losing streak, followed by Northwestern, 66-59, at Penn State, 75-68, Michigan State, 74-60, Iowa, 82-69, and at Michigan, 65-57. At 0-6 in the conference, the defending Big Ten champions were looking pretty bad. They put it together though, in a pair of wins over Ohio State, 76-53, behind Jacobson's eighth consecutive 20-plus point outing, followed by Wisconsin, 58-48, on Lewis' 20-point effort.

A pair of road losses at Indiana, 82-95, and Illinois, 68-56, followed, but the team stayed strong and rallied to beat Michigan, 88-78, at home on national TV thanks to Eric Harris' 24 points. They followed that up with a big upset win at Iowa later that week, 73-71, as Clark drained 21 points in the assault. Then, after dropping the next game at Michigan State, 71-59, the Golden Gophers rallied to beat Penn State, 82-77, at the Barn, on Jacobson's 23 points and Harris' 20. They lost at Purdue, 87-83, that next week, but responded on Senior Day to beat Northwestern, 59-54, thanks to Harris' 20 points and Jacobson's 14.

From there the team headed into the inaugural Big Ten Tournament at Chicago's United Center. At 12-14 the Gophers needed to finish the season strong and gain at least two wins in order to reach the .500 mark, and have any shot at a post-season tourney invite. Luckily, their first opponent would be Northwestern, a team they had just beaten. So, they responded by dumping the Cats yet again, this time, 64-56, in the opening round, thanks to Quincy Lewis' 25 points and "Slammin Sam's" 23. Next up were the Michigan State Spartans and Big Ten MVP Mateen Cleaves. But, thanks to Eric Harris' amazing 29-point effort, the Gophers upset the No. 12-ranked Spartans, 76-73. That next night though, they were pummeled by Michigan, and their 13 three-pointers, 85-69, despite Lewis' 25 points.

But, with their record now at .500, the Gophers were rewarded with an NIT bid — marking the seventh consecutive year the program had advanced to postseason play. They gladly accepted and immediately went to work by beating 20-game winner, Colorado State, at home, 77-65, on the strength of Jacobson's 20 points and Harris' 19. The Gophers were then awarded yet another home game in the second round of the tournament, this time against the University of Alabama at Birmingham, where, thanks to Quincy Lewis' 21 points and Clark's 17, Minnesota cruised to a 79-66 victory.

With that, the team was awarded another home game, with the opponent this time being Marquette. This one would turn into a classic, as Jacobson took over and broke a 71-71 tie with an amazing reverse lay-up with just 25 seconds on the clock to lead Minnesota to dramatic 73-71 win. The defense then came through huge, as the Golden Eagles tried in vain to win it in the game's final moments. When the time ran off the clock, the student section swarmed the Barn's raised floor to join in on the festivities. It was now off to New York's Madison Square Garden for the NIT's Final Four. No one was happier than New York City native, Eric Harris, who was going home.

There, they would meet their old nemesis' from Fresno State — a team they had beaten up on in the preseason. This one was a back and forth affair, with Minnesota leading by four points at halftime. Throughout the game there would be seven lead changes, complete with five ties as well. Then, with 35 seconds left on the clock, Fresno State nailed a three-pointer, followed by an easy lay-up just 10 seconds later to take a three-point lead. Down, but not out, the Gophers rallied behind Quincy Lewis, who grabbed Clark's missed rebound and calmly hit the

J.B. Bickerstaff

tying three-pointer with five seconds to go to force overtime. There, a stifling defense, combined with an impressive 10-for-10 shooting effort from the free-throw line, won the game in the extra session, 91-89, for the Gophers. Kevin Clark would finish the contest with a career-high 30 points, followed by Jacobson's 24 and Lewis' double-double of 19 points and 10 rebounds. The improbable Gophers were now headed back to the NIT Finals, this time to take on their Big Ten rivals from Penn State.

The NIT Finals would become the "Lewis and Clark Expedition" for the media, which fell in love with the young Gophers from the get-go. This game was all about defense for Minnesota as Harris and Clark led the way, shutting down Penn State sniper Pete Lisicky, by holding him to just 11 points, as well as Center Calvin Booth, holding him to a mere 14. On offense, meanwhile, Clark scored 28 points, while Jacobson and Lewis added 23 and 15 points, respectively, as Minnesota played great all-around basketball and cruised to a 79-72 victory. After the game the team celebrated and proudly cut down the nets for all to see back in the Land of 10,000 Lakes.

Kevin Clark, who scored 30 and 28 points in Madison Square Garden, was named as its MVP, while Lewis and Jacobson, who each averaged nearly 20 points over that same stretch, were also named to the all-tournament team. For Minnesota, which came from nowhere to notch its sixth consecutive 20-win season and its second NIT title in six years, it was yet another storybook ending to a truly remarkable season. The team never gave up, and for that, they should be remembered as one of the program's best-ever.

The men of Maroon and Gold had some big shoes to fill in 1998-99. Coming off of a Final Four appearance and an NIT title in consecutive seasons, the expectations were set high for this bunch of underachievers. And, with Sam Jacobson and Eric Harris gone, the team's new dynamic duo of "Lewis and Clark" would be left to shoulder the load. They had a new weapon, however, in Monticello freshman Center, Joel Pryzbilla — one of the most highly recruited players in Minnesota history.

The Gophers jumped out to yet another quick start that year, winning their first six games before losing to No. 4-ranked Cincinnati, 62-61, in overtime. They came back to with their next three, to improve their non-conference record to an impressive 9-1. From there, the team went up and down, losing their Big Ten opener, 58-55, to Northwestern — a team that owed them big-time for knocking them out of the conference tourney the year before. They came back to beat Penn State, 75-60, in a rematch of the NIT Finals, thanks to Lewis' 24 points and Pryzbilla's 17 points, 13 rebounds and six blocks.

From there the team got routed by Michigan State, 71-55, but rebounded to beat both Iowa, 75-70, and Michigan, 76-70, on Quincy Lewis' 29 and 30-point efforts. After falling to Ohio State, 89-60, the Gophers went on to beat Indiana at the Barn, 90-83, in overtime, thanks to Lewis' 35 points and Clarks' 17. Miles Tarver also came up huge with 17 boards as well. But the Gophers were streaky, and unable to put together a nice run. That next week they lost to Wisconsin, 61-50, only to rebound and beat the Illini, 75-63, four nights later behind Lewis' 28 points. From there Minnesota, which was having all kinds of trouble winning on the road, lost three close ones to Michigan, 75-65, Iowa, 76-73, and Michigan State, 84-82. Lewis and Pryzbilla led the charge in a win over Penn State, 69-63, only to see their squad fall flat the next week to Purdue, 54-42. They did manage to put together a nice run at the finish though, beating both Purdue, 62-48, and Northwestern, on the road, 58-51, as Lewis once again proved to be the savior, scoring 27 and 31 points, respectively.

The Maroon and Gold had once again come through in the clutch, giving themselves a good shot at earning an NCAA Tournament bid. And, even though the Gophers were downed by Illinois, 67-64, in the Big Ten tournament, they still managed to eke out a tourney bid during that nerve-racking "Selection Sunday" when they were awarded a seventh seed in the first round of the NCAA's West Regional in Seattle. There, they would play tenth-seeded Gonzaga, a giant-killer which had become famous for its ability to knock-off highly seeded teams in the Big Dance. Led by their fiery young coach, Dan Monson, the Bulldogs were not to be taken lightly.

Then, in one of the biggest sports stories of the year, controversy hit the Gopher program like a ton of bricks. Just before the opening tip-off of the game, it was announced that four Gopher players, including three seniors, were not allowed to play on account of several alleged academic wrong-doings. It would be the beginning of what would become known as the "Gopher Cheating Scandal," a mess that would last for several years, ultimately casting an extremely dark shadow over the program and its players.

Meanwhile, there was a game to be played, and the remaining Gophers had to try and focus on winning. Gonzaga came out of the gates smoking in this one though, raining down three-pointers left and right. Minnesota, already shell-shocked over the ensuing scandal, simply tried to keep pace with the speedy Dogs. They did manage to put together a nice run to cut the lead to four late in the second half, but it was too little, too late. Lewis and Clark played solid, as did freshman Forward Dusty Rychart, from Grand Rapids, who kept Minnesota in the game by scoring a career-high 23 points and hauling in 17 rebounds. But in the end, the specter of another NCAA investigation was simply too much of a distraction. The Bulldogs blew it wide open in the end, winning easily, 75-63, to end Minnesota's season. Lost in the mess was the outstanding play of Quincy Lewis, who won the Big Ten scoring title with 25.5 points per game, ranking him third nationally.

When the team came home to face the music, the media was swarming like buzzards. That off-season was the most turbulent in Gopher history. As the story grew, so did the allegations about who was involved in what. After a lengthy internal investigation by both the University of Minnesota and NCAA, it was discovered that systematic, widespread aca-

Minnesota and the Draft

The University of Minnesota is fifth overall in the number of NBA first-round draft picks since 1972 with 14, and is tied for seventh all-time with 15 first rounders. The U of M has always had an impact on draft day. In fact, since 1949, the first year NBA draft records were kept, 48 Gophers have been selected — 15 of which have been first-round picks. (Incidentally, Minnesota's first player ever drafted was Pro Football Hall of Famer Bud Grant, when the Minneapolis Lakers took him in 1950. Oh yeah, Bud won a world championship that year as well!)

Total number of NBA first-round draft picks since 1972:

1. North Carolina	26
2. UCLA	20
3. Michigan	17
Kentucky	17
5. Minnesota	**14**

Minnesota's All-Time First Round Draft Picks:

1966	Lou Hudson	St. Louis (4th)	
1973	Jim Brewer	Cleveland (2nd)	
	Ron Behagen	Kansas City-Omaha (7th)	
1975	Mark Olberding	San Antonio (7th ABA)	
1977	Ray Williams	New York (10th)	
1978	Mychal Thompson	Portland (1st)	
1980	Kevin McHale	Boston (3rd)	
1982	Trent Tucker	New York (6th)	
1983	Randy Breuer	Milwaukee (18th)	
1990	Willie Burton	Miami (9th)	
1997	Bobby Jackson	Seattle (23rd)	
	John Thomas	New York (25th)	
1998	Sam Jacobson	Los Angeles Lakers (26th)	
1999	Quincy Lewis	Utah Jazz (19th)	
2000	Joel Przybilla	Houston Rockets (9th)	

(The NBA draft wasn't tabulated on a per-round basis until 1957, so records prior to that are incomplete.)

The All-Century Team

In 1995, as part of the celebration of the University's 100th season of basketball, the Department of Men's Athletics sponsored a fan vote to choose the best player of each decade as well as the Player of the Century. More than 80,000 fans cast their ballots, and here are the results:

1900s: George Tuck (All-American in 1905)
1910s: Erling Platou (All-American in 1919)
1920s: Arnold Oss (All-American in 1919 & 1921)
1930s: John Kundla (Team MVP in 1939 and Coach from 1959-68)
1940s: Tony Jaros (Team MVP in 1946)
1950s: Whitey Skoog (All-American in 1950 & 1951)
1960s: Lou Hudson (All-American in 1965)
1970s: Mychal Thompson (All-American in 1977 & 1978)
1980s: Kevin McHale (All-Big Ten in 1979 & 1980)
1990s: Voshon Lenard (Only Gopher to score more than 2,000 points)
Player of the Century: Kevin McHale

Dan Monson

Born on October 6, 1961, Dan Monson attended Idaho's Moscow High School, where he emerged as a prep star in several sports. He went on to graduate from the University of Idaho in 1985 with a bachelor's degree in mathematics, and later obtained his master's degree in athletic administration from the University of Alabama-Birmingham in 1988. A football player for the Vandals, Monson turned his attention to coaching when a knee injury cut short his gridiron career. He coached the boys' basketball team at Oregon City High School in Oregon City, Ore., for one season (1985-86) prior to taking the UAB graduate assistant post.

From there Monson became an Assistant Coach at Gonzaga University, where, in 1997, he was hired as the program's Head Coach. Monson invested nine years in helping build the Gonzaga program into a perennial post-season team. A former Coach of the Year, Monson led the Bulldogs to a record of 52-17, and became known for his ability to recruit quality student-athletes to the private Spokane, Wash., institution.

Then, after leading the Bulldogs to within a breath of the 1999 NCAA Final Four, Monson was hired as the University of Minnesota's newest coach. He came in under some pretty extraordinary circumstances, but has done an amazing job. He has already instilled a very positive and winning attitude during his short tenure in Minnesota, and has already begun to turn around a program in shambles.

Monson is the son of former Idaho and Oregon Head Coach Don Monson, a native of Menahga, Minn. The elder Monson was an assistant coach under Jud Heathcote at Michigan State University (1976-78). Together, the Monsons' have 298 wins and a .561 winning percentage, putting them ninth all-time on the NCAA's all-time winningest father-son coaching list.

"The tradition here is outstanding," said Monson of Minnesota. "Just a few short years ago, the Gophers were at the pinnacle of college basketball and in the Final Four. The program has averaged 20-plus wins per season for the last decade. It has ranked in the top 20 in attendance for over 25 years. The numbers and statistics to prove how successful this program has been are endless. When you walk into Williams Arena, you feel the tradition and the history. I know from my relationships with other coaches that this place (Williams Arena) is one of the more dreaded places to play as a visiting team. My goal is to use the existing advantages we have, build on those and add the next chapter of success in the storied Golden Gopher basketball tradition."

demic fraud and other rule violations had been committed throughout the men's basketball program. As a result of the probe, University President Mark Yudof announced that several top administrators in the men's athletics department, including McKinley Boston, the vice-president of student development and athletics, and Mark Dienhart, the men's athletic director, would not have their contracts renewed. — despite the fact that they knew nothing of the widespread academic misconduct which dated back to 1993.

The biggest blow, however, came when the University bought-out Coach Clem Haskins' contract for $1.5 million, shortly after the scandal was reported. (The school later sued to get the money back.) The investigation alleged that Haskins, who coached the basketball team during that time, knew that several members of the academic counseling staff (highlighted by the testimony of former tutor Jan Gangelhoff) had, on occasion, prepared various coursework that was turned in by at least 18 players. In addition, the investigation turned up evidence of mail fraud, wire fraud and even the misappropriation of federal funds (in the form of Pell Grants), as well. The report also alleged that Haskins broke rules by making cash payments to players and by telling players to mislead attorneys looking into academic fraud.

After 13 seasons behind the Gopher bench, which included an impressive 240-165 record, as well as nine trips to the post-season, the Haskins era came to a screeching halt. Haskins, who was one of Minnesota's most beloved sports figures, was allowed to operate his program in "an isolated fiefdom, virtually unchecked," thus making it possible for all of these allegations to occur. The coach has insisted he was unaware of any cheating and has remained silent throughout the ongoing saga. The ultimate fall-out, however, was this: the NCAA Final Four run of 1997 was stricken from the books. That's right. Along with expense payments and prize money that was returned, some-

how, the University and all of its fans are supposed to pretend that it all was just a dream. Well, it was a huge mess all right, but that Final Four run was something special that Minnesotans will never forget — regardless of what went down behind the scenes. The NCAA came down hard on the program, imposing future sanctions regarding scholarships and post-season play. The record books were also changed, taking stats away from players and reducing all-time records — but those are just numbers, the fans know better, and are still proud of the players that did play by the rules and made Minnesota proud.

Michael Bauer

Somehow the Gophers got through it, and started the road to healing and closure on July 24, 1999, when, after an exhausting national search, it was announced that Gonzaga Head Coach Dan Monson, yeah, the guy who had just beat the Gophers in the NCAA tourney in March, had been hired as the team's new coach. Monson, in the understatement of the century, would inherit some serious baggage.

"I think that the student-athlete must be a student first," said Monson. "For the majority of these young men, basketball will fill a small window of their lives. Their degree and their chosen path of employment will be with them forever. My job as the leader of this program is to ensure that the student-athletes get their degree, but that along the way, they enjoy a rich collegiate experience. I want them to leave the University of Minnesota as educated, mature men who can go out and be productive members of society and make the school and the entire state proud. In my mind, even the most successful players who may get a chance to play professionally will be much more rounded people by getting their education and obtaining a degree."

"My immediate priority is to re-establish this program as one of the best in the country," added Monson. "The school, fans, alumni and citizens of the state of Minnesota deserve a program that consistently competes for the Big Ten title and competes at an elite level nationally. In addition, we must rebuild the people's trust and belief in what Minnesota basketball stands for on the court, in the classroom and in the community. And included in that philosophy is encouraging the student-athletes who come through this program that getting your degree should be their number one priority while they are Golden Gophers."

The young Monson was ready for the challenge though. He was squeaky clean, put a strong emphasis on academics and knew how to win. He was also a solid recruiter who had always dreamt of one day coaching in the Big Ten. With that, the rebuilding process for the 1999-2000 season began. Monson did have the nation's top big-man in Joel Przybilla, Guards Kevin Burleson and Terrance Simmons, as well as Forwards Dusty Rychart, Michael Bauer and J.B. Bickerstaff — a transfer student from Oregon who instantly became one of the team's biggest fan-favorites.

Dusty Rychart

The team opened its schedule by beating Texas-Arlington, 90-62, behind Dusty Rychart, who, following his 22-point, 13-rebound performance, was named as the Big Ten Player of the Week. From there they took six straight wins en route to posting a very optimistic 8-2 non-conference record. Offensively, things were starting to gel. It took the players a while, but eventually they adjusted to Monson's "motion offense" system, which required patience and timing. The club opened its Big Ten schedule by surprising everyone to beat Michigan, 85-68, thanks to Przybilla's 16 points and 11 rebounds. Then, after losing to Ohio State, 71-63, the Gophers rebounded to beat a very good Iowa team, 85-82, at the Barn, on Przybilla's 28-point, 18-rebound monster-outing.

The team lost four straight after that though, before finally getting back on track against Northwestern, a team the Gophers were able to hold off, 69-60, behind Mitch Ohnstad's 18 points off the bench. The club's next game against Indiana would prove to be its most significant of the season for several reasons. First, the Gophers were able to upset the Hoosiers, 77-75, thanks to Przybilla's 33-point, 14-rebound effort. But, midway through the game, the team's on and off the court leader, J.B. Bickerstaff, suffered a season-ending broken leg. Then, if that weren't enough, Joel Przybilla got into some hot water with Coach Monson over some academic issues. Przybilla, who decided that focusing on his ensuing professional career in the NBA was more important than his time with the Gophers, decided to quit the team in mid-season. And, while Shane Schilling and freshman Center Ryan Wildenborg would be called upon to step it up — there was simply no way the team could replace the seven-foot-two freak-of-nature. The team's top scorer, rebounder and shot blocker was simply awesome, and the team was going to dearly miss him. Monson quickly squashed the scandal-to-be though, and gained the respect of everyone for his firm stance on the importance of academics.

For the players, the news was devastating. Sure, Przybilla was going to be a lock lottery pick in that upcoming NBA draft, but to leave the team midway through the season, under those circumstances, was shocking. So, with Bickerstaff and Przybilla gone for the season, the young Gophers tried to overcome the odds and finish strong. The result: a seven game losing streak culminated by a 81-78 Iowa defeat to end the season in the Big Ten Tournament. The 12-16 Gophers had to overcome a great deal of adversity that year, playing with an already short bench and very little depth due to departures and injuries. It was not the way Coach Monson wanted to start out his tenure at Minnesota.

The nucleus of the team was back in 2000-2001 though. Sure, their mark of seven consecutive winning seasons had been broken, but the team, as well as the fans, were optimistic that brighter days lied ahead for the Golden

Gopher All-Time Records

Gophers All-Time Career Scoring Leaders

Player	(Years)	Points
1. Voshon Lenard	('92-95)	2,103
2. Mychal Thompson	('75-78)	1,992
3. Willie Burton	('87-90)	1,800
4. Randy Breuer	('80-83)	1,777
5. Sam Jacobson	('95-98)	1,709
6. Kevin McHale	('77-80)	1,704
7. Quincy Lewis	('95-99)	1,614
8. Tommy Davis	('82-85)	1,481
9. Trent Tucker	('79-82)	1,445
10. Chuck Mencel	('52-55)	1,391
11. Marc Wilson	('83-86)	1,386
12. Kevin Lynch	('88-91)	1,355
13. Tom Kondla	('66-68)	1,350
14. Ron Johnson	('58-60)	1,335
15. Lou Hudson	('64-66)	1,329
16. Arriel McDonald	('91-94)	1,273
17. Melvin Newbern	('88-90)	1,224
18. Jim McIntyre	('46-49)	1,223
19. Archie Clark	('64-66)	1,199
20. Randy Carter	('91-94)	1,186

Gophers All-Time Career Rebounding Leaders

Player	(Years)	Rebounds
1. Mychal Thompson	('75-78)	956
2. Kevin McHale	('77-80)	950
3. Jim Brewer	('71-73)	907
4. Richard Coffey	('87-90)	904
5. Mel Northway	('63-65)	841
6. Ron Johnson	('58-60)	820
7. Randy Carter	('91-94)	736
8. Larry Mikan	('68-70)	735
9. Randy Breuer	('80-83)	730
10. Willie Burton	('87-90)	705

Gophers All-Time Career Assists Leaders

Player	(Years)	Assists
1. Arriel McDonald	('91-94)	547
2. Eric Harris	('95-98)	433
3. Townsend Orr	('92-95)	401
4. Marc Wilson	('83-86)	375
5. Melvin Newbern	('88-90)	369
6. Voshon Lenard	('92-95)	322
7. Kevin Lynch	('88-90)	301
8. Ray Williams	('76-77)	296
9. Phil "Flip" Saunders	('74-77)	295
10. Osborne Lockhart	('75-78)	268

Gophers All-Time Career Blocks Leaders

Player	(Years)	Blocks
1. Kevin McHale	('77-80)	235
2. Randy Breuer	('80-83)	229
3. Bob Martin	('89-92)	146
4. Mychal Thompson	('75-78)	113
5. John Shasky	('83-86)	111
6. Quincy Lewis	('95-99)	93
7. Joel Przybilla	('98-00)	84
8. Willie Burton	('87-90)	79
9. Chad Kolander	('92-95)	75
10. Jim Petersen	('81-84)	70

Gophers All-Time Career Steals Leaders

Player	(Years)	Steals
1. Melvin Newbern	('87-90)	215
2. Eric Harris	('95-98)	194
3. Quincy Lewis	('96-99)	179
4. Townsend Orr	('92-95)	173
Voshon Lenard	('92-95)	173
6. Arriel McDonald	('91-94)	163
7. Trent Tucker	('79-82)	153
Darryl Mitchell	('79-82)	153
9. Marc Wilson	('83-86)	138
10. Kevin Lynch	('88-91)	127

Rick Rickert

Gophers. The club opened with a quick 6-0 record, finally losing to Georgetown, 76-60, in the Finals of the Hawaii Pacific Tournament. From there they went on to beat Florida State, Marquette and Nebraska, among others, to post an amazing 14-1 non-conference record — the school's best ever.

The Big Ten campaign opened on a sour note though, as the Illini upended the Gophers 80-64. They rebounded to beat Wisconsin at home, 54-49, only to drop their next game to Ohio State, 75-72, despite Terrence Simmons' 27-point effort which helped to rally the team back from a 23-point deficit. The team then rattled off a pair of big wins over both Purdue, 70-67, on Rychart's 23 points, and Indiana, 78-74, thanks to Rychart's six straight free-throws in overtime to seal the deal. Four straight losses ensued though, to Iowa (twice), Purdue and Ohio State. Minnesota then got back on track by beating Northwestern, 66-59, as reserve Forward Travarus Bennett led the way with 16 points and 11 rebounds. But, the big loss in the game came when J. B. Bickerstaff, who missed the final seven games of the 2000 season, suffered yet another season-ending broken leg. The news was devastating.

Minnesota reeled into a three-game losing streak after that, falling to Michigan State, 94-83, Penn State, 82-62, and Wisconsin, 64-54, before finally beating Michigan, at Crisler Arena, 93-75, Behind Simmons' 30-point effort. That next week, however, they were pounded by Indiana, 89-53, who out-rebounded the Gophers, 48-24. From there the team went on to get dumped by the No. 5-ranked Illini, 89-53, followed by Purdue, 91-77, in the Big Ten Tournament. But, with 17 wins, the team kept its fingers crossed and was able to get an NIT invitation — a remarkable feat considering what had happened the year before.

The Gophers were able to host the first-round NIT game, which saw Villanova come to town. And, thanks to Kevin Burleson's 21 points and Travarus Bennett's 12 rebounds, Minnesota was able to sneak past 'Nova, 87-78. The Cats made a serious run late in the game to take the lead, but with five minutes to go, Monson's men hung tough and cruised to a 10-point victory. All of the Gopher starters scored in double figures in this one, as the team shot an impressive 52% from the field as well.

Next up was Tulsa, a team that should've been in the NCAA tournament. This one was a different story, as the Gophers found themselves down early. Minnesota then rallied back from a 17-point second-half deficit to force overtime, behind Terrance Simmons' driving lay-up with just 14 seconds to go in the game. Tied at 65-65, both teams played hard in the extra session, but the Gophers, who were led by Terrence Simmons, who tallied 28 points, and Dusty Rychart, who added 23 points and 15 rebounds, couldn't get over the hump and lost in the final seconds, 76-73. It was a sad ending to a season which started out with so much promise. Sure, when the Gophers were at 15-3, things were looking great, but the team ran out of gas down the stretch due to the untimely and unfortunate injury of Bickerstaff. But, the Monson era was just getting started in Minnesota, and the fans were behind him in a big way.

"If you are a competitor, you want to win every game you play," said Monson. "Even though we've played shorthanded the past two years, our goal was to play in the NCAA Tournament. We've fallen short, but hopefully we can get over that next hump this season. Our players learned last season that ability only goes so far. A team's success hinges on effort, leadership and mental roughness as much as talent. We feel our talent level is higher than it's been, but the question is which players on this year's team will step up and provide the intangibles that leaders give you."

Several new recruits highlighted the 2001-02 season under third-year Coach Dan Monson, including six-foot-ten Forward Rick Rickert, a McDonald's All-American top-10 national recruit who averaged 29 points per game for the Duluth East Greyhounds. In addition, the team landed Maurice Hargrow, a six-foot-four shooting guard who averaged 18 points, six assists and six rebounds per game for St. Paul's Highland Park High School, as well as Jerry Holman, a six-foot-eleven center who averaged 13 points, seven rebounds and three blocks per game for Minneapolis Community and Technical College. Overall, Monson was able to land what many national recruiting services have referred to as a "top-10" national recruiting class. In addition, the team will also benefit greatly from the addition of former DeLaSalle High School Guard Ben Johnson's transfer from Northwestern to the Gophers. Johnson, who averaged 10.7 points as a sophomore, passed on going to Michigan State and instead opted to come home — where he will make a wonderful addition to what is shaping up to be the "Class" of the Big Ten.

"The tradition here is outstanding," said Monson. "Just a few short years ago, the Golden Gophers were at the pinnacle of college basketball and in the Final Four. The program has averaged 20-plus wins per season for the last decade. It has ranked in the top 20 in attendance for over 25 years. The numbers and statistics to prove how successful this program has been are endless. When you walk into Williams Arena, you feel the tradition and the history. I know from my relationships with other coaches that this place (Williams Arena) is one of the more dreaded places to play as a visiting team. My goal is to use the existing advantages we have, build on those and add the next chapter of success in the storied Golden Gopher basketball tradition."

Ray Christensen

One name that has become synonymous with Gopher sports is broad-caster Ray Christensen, who, after more than 50 years behind the microphone, decided to finally hang it up in 2001. Christensen's signature voice is synonymous with Golden Gopher basketball and football broadcasts and he is a truly a part of the fabric of the state of Minnesota. He has called more than 1,300 basketball games and 510 football games for the Maroon and Gold, entertaining and informing us all along the way. With his wonderful play-by-play and color-commentary, Ray became an icon both with WCCO-Radio, as well as with the thousands of adoring fans who listened to his broadcasts for more than a half-century.

All in all, things are looking great in Gold Country under Coach Monson. His players and philosophies have matured in each of his first two seasons in Minnesota, leading to even higher expectations for the future. The state of the state of college hoops in general also looks good. The NCAA recently signed an 11-year, $6 billion deal with CBS that begins in 2003, thus insuring big-time sponsorship and plenty of television viewing during the long, cold Minnesota winters for our beloved Gophers. Stay tuned, because this Gopher program is on the way back up, and it won't stop until it gets back to the Final Four — and beyond. ***RAH!***

In the early 1900's the organization and control of basketball was for the most part student-centered. Issues such as eligibility restrictions, scheduling procedures, awarding championships, and the establishment of consistent rules and regulations were sporadic at best. As a result, conferences and associations began to appear in an attempt to formalize athletic competition.

One such organization was the Tri-State Conference, which was made up of colleges from both Minnesota and the Dakotas. In 1919, after a heated debate between the two state factions regarding rule changes and eligibility, the Minnesota contingent broke away and formed its own conference called the Minnesota Intercollegiate Athletic Conference. The MIAC's first charter members included: Carleton College, Gustavus Adolphus College, Hamline University, Macalester College, St. John's University, St. Olaf College and the University of St. Thomas. (Concordia College-Moorhead joined the conference in 1921, Augsburg College in 1924 and St. Mary's University in 1926. Bethel College later joined in 1977.) In addition, UM-Duluth, which had joined the MIAC in 1950, later made the jump to the Northern Sun Intercollegiate Conference in 1976. Also, an annual four-team MIAC Tournament was later initiated in 1985, making it one of the most entertaining and intense Division III post-season tournaments in the country.

Recognized as one of the toughest and most prestigious NCAA Division III intercollegiate athletic conferences in the country, today, the MIAC sponsors championships in 23 sports — 12 for men and 11 for women. And, because its members are all private undergraduate colleges, none of them can offer athletic scholarships to its student athletes. So it really is about the kids, good sportsmanship, fun and plain ol' basketball.

Hamline University

Founded back in 1854, when Minnesota was still a territory, Hamline was the state's first university. Fittingly, it was also the first school in the entire nation to play a formal intercollegiate basketball game. That's right, the Pipers, right here in St. Paul, were the first to get it all started. According to Basketball Hall of Fame records the momentous game happened on February 9, 1895, when Hamline College, as it was then known, played the Minnesota School of Agriculture (now the Ag School on the U of M's St. Paul campus) on Hamline's campus in the Old Science Building. Hamline, which was guided by fellow-student and physical education director Ray Kaighn, was defeated by the Aggies by the score of 9-3, but it was a big deal in the world of sports nonetheless. (Kaighn was a former student of Dr. James Naismith, back East.)

By the end of that year a local basketball league had been created consisting of several teams. Several teams, in

Vern Mikkelsen

The 1947 Champs from Hamline

addition to Hamline and the Ag School had joined including: the Minneapolis YMCA, Macalester College and Military Company A of Minneapolis. This was nine-man basketball, played in small rooms with low ceilings, complete with goalies and peach baskets for hoops. (Kaighn, along with his teammates from that original 1891 team, were all inducted into the Basketball Hall of Fame in Springfield, Mass., in 1959.) One month later the University of Chicago, led by future coaching legend Alonzo Stagg, played the University of Iowa. College basketball in America had officially arrived, with Hamline being given credit as its official birthplace.

The Pipers went on to become Minnesota's first national powerhouse thanks to the leadership of coaching legend Joe Hutton. Hutton, who took over at Hamline in 1930, following his stellar playing career at Carleton College, guided the Pipers to three National Association of Intercollegiate Athletics (NAIB) championships, which were held annually in Kansas City, in 1942, 1949 and 1951. Over the next 35 years Hutton racked up an incredible record of 588-186 (.760) en route to winning 19 MIAC titles and qualifying for 12 NAIA post-season tournaments. At the time of his retirement, Hutton was sixth all-time among the nation's top basketball coaches (from both large and small colleges and universities) in total wins. He was, in a word, awesome.

When the Lakers came to town in 1947 they begged him to be their coach, but he said no thanks. He was a Piper, and was going to stay a Piper. His two sons, Joe Jr. and Tom also played for him as well — Joe in the late 1940s and Tom in the late 1950s. In 1937 historic Norton Fieldhouse was christened with an exhibition game between mighty Stanford University and Hamline. That arena would later be renamed as Hutton Arena in his honor in 1986.

So good was Hamline back then, that they could've and should've represented the United States in the 1948 Summer Olympics in London. You see, back then the NCAA tournament champion was designated as Team USA. But Hutton, who was the Chairman of the NAIA, a rival tournament at the time, felt that he had to be loyal to his organization. So, Adolph Rupp's Kentucky Wildcats went instead and won the gold medal. Who knows what might have been?

The 1948 Champs from Hamline

Incredibly, eight of Hutton's former players went on to play pro basketball in an era when there just weren't that many pro jobs available. The most famous, of course, was Vern Mikkelsen, who, after starring for the Minneapolis Lakers, was inducted into the Hall of Fame. Other players included: Don Eliason (Class of '42), who played briefly with the Boston Celtics; St. Paul native Howie "Stretch" Schultz (Class of '45), who not only played with the Anderson Packers, Fort Wayne Pistons and Minneapolis Lakers, but also played pro baseball with the Brooklyn Dodgers from 1943-47 as well; Virginia, Minn., native Johnny Norlander (Class of '43), who played with the Washington Capitals from 1946-1951; Rollie Seltz (Class of '46), who played with the Anderson Packers and Waterloo Hawks from 1946-50; Joe Hutton, Jr. (Class of '50), who played for the Lakers from 1950-52; Hal Haskins (Class of '50), who played for the Saint Paul Lights and the Waterloo Hawks; Humboldt High School's Jim Fritsche (Class of '53), who played for the Lakers, Baltimore Bullets and Fort Wayne Pistons from 1952-55.

Joe Hutton & Howie Schultz

The first coach ever selected to the Helms Foundation Hall of Basketball Immortals, in 1949 Hutton was named as the president of the National Association of Intercollegiate Athletics, and during the summer of 1945, he was one of four coaches selected by the Special Services Division of the Armed Forces to conduct basketball clinics for American occupation forces in Europe. Widely known as a modest, mild-mannered gentleman who was extremely popular with his players and students alike, Joe Hutton died in 1988.

In 1995 Hamline recognized the 100th anniversary of the first inter-collegiate basketball game with a reenactment game and banquet held in Hutton Arena on February 4, 1995. Legendary UCLA coach John Wooden, whose teams won 10 NCAA championships, was the keynote speaker at the event as then-Governor Arne Carlson made a presentation declaring that day to be "Basketball Heritage Day in Minnesota." President Clinton even sent a note of congratulations, truly giving the Pipers the props they deserve.

Meanwhile, despite the fact that the team's last MIAC title came more than 40 years ago, in 1960, the program has, and continues to be one of the best in the conference. In addition to all of those MIAC titles throughout the 1930s, 40's and 50s, the team also made an appearance in the Division II national tournament in 1962, as well as a trio of appearances in the Division III nationally tourney from 1975-77. Today the Pipers are going strong and will only get better under Head Coach Tom Gilles.

University of St. Thomas

Founded in 1885, in what was once a farmers field, the University of St. Thomas originally began as St. Thomas Aquinas Seminary. From those original 62 students, the school has evolved into Minnesota's largest independent university with more than 11,000 students. With a rich basketball tradition that goes all the way back to the turn of the century, St. Thomas has been a small college power in Minnesota for nearly 100 years.

St. Thomas' program began in 1904 under Coach C.L. Sheeran. The team posted a 10-4 record that year that year and so began one of the state's best basketball traditions. Incredibly, no less than two Hall of Fame coaches have guided the Toms through the years. The first was George Keogan, a Detroit Lakes native, who coached St. Thomas

St. Thomas' Career Points Leaders

1. Bob Rosier	1970-74	2,133
2. Steve Fritz	1967-71	1,944
3. Karnell James	1993-97	1,854
4. Ted Hall	1952-56	1,688
5. Dennis Fitzpatrick	1969-73	1,486

College in 1915-16, and led the Tommies to a 13-2 record. Keogan later went on to post an amazing 327-96-1 record as the head coach of the Fighting Irish of Notre Dame without ever suffering a losing campaign. One of the college game's more notable innovators of strategy and technique, Keogan's legacy might have been much greater than it was, but he tragically died during the middle of the 1943 season.

Bob Rosier

The second Tom's skipper to enter the Hall of Fame was Johnny Kundla. Kundla guided St. Thomas to a modest 11-11 record in 1947 before going on to lead the Minneapolis Lakers to six world championships.

Through the years St. Thomas has won 19 MIAC titles: (1924, 1944, 1946, 1949, 1966-67, 1970-74, 1981, 1989, 1990-92, 1994-95 and 2000) (Prior to joining the MIAC, St. Thomas was a charter member of the North Central Conference, along with South Dakota State College, Des Moines College, Creighton University, North Dakota Agricultural College, University of North Dakota, and Morningside.) In addition, they have also appeared in the annual MIAC Tourney a record 13 times, bringing home the gold on four occasions since its inception back in 1985.

Greg Hendricks

Head Coach Tom Feely was the patriarch of the Tommy program, leading his Toms to an amazing record of 417-269 from 1954-80. He was replaced by Steve Fritz, who has been at the wheel ever since.

The program has also enjoyed a great deal of post-season success as well. In fact, St. Thomas made a total of eight appearances in the NAIA Tourney, then held annually in Kansas City. Their first trip to the post-season saw them beating Peru State, Neb., 74-44, in round one, before losing to Regis (Colo.), 53-52, in the second game. That next season the Toms lost in the opening round to Davis & Elkins (WV), 79-53.

In 1966 UST lost its opening round match to Central State (Ohio) 92-69. They fared better that following season, beating Claremont-Mudd, 72-63, in round one, only to get upset by Eastern New Mexico, 69-67, in round two. In 1970 and 1971 the Toms made a pair of first-round exits to Central State and Kentucky State, 69-60 & 100-65, respectively. They made a decent run in 1972, beating Fairmont State in round one, 78-61, Ouachita Baptist, 93-87, in round two, followed by a 66-57 loss to Kentucky State in round three.

Their final NAIA tourney appearance came in 1974 when the Toms pounded Grand Valley State in round one, 95-71, only to lose to Midwestern in round two, 92-78, to round out the season.

St. Thomas has also made five appearances in the Division III National Tournament. In 1989 the Tommies beat Dubuque, Iowa, 65-55, followed by a 75-69 double-overtime thriller over DePaw, Ind., before downing Nebraska Wesleyan 77-71 in the Finals.

In 1993 St. Thomas beat St. John's, 75-61, in the opening round of the tourney before losing in round two to UW-Platteville, 70-60. The 1994 Tommies made it all the way to the Final Four before finally succumbing to New York University, 75-68, and then Wittenberg, 73-62. Along the way the Toms beat Central Iowa, 73-62, Hampden-Sydney, 80-66, and Greensboro, 84-74. That next year St. Thomas beat Central, 62-58, before getting spanked by Nebraska Wesleyan, 94-74, in round two. Then, in 2000, STU won its first round tourney game against Nebraska Wesleyan, 80-58, only to get upset by Buena Vista in round two, 69-66.

Steve Fritz

Currently the Toms are led by Head Coach Steve Fritz, himself a former player who has since become a coaching legend in his own right. Since 1904, the first year St. Thomas records were kept, the Tommies have won a total of 1,273 basketball games. As a three-time all-MIAC player (1967-71), assistant coach (1971-80) and head coach (1981-present), Steve Fritz has been associated with 515 of those victories. In those 32 seasons, STU went 570-295 (.659) with 13 MIAC titles and 20 top-three MIAC finishes. UST has never had a losing season in his 20-years as head coach. Fritz is a nine-time MIAC Coach of the Year, and his teams have won eight conference championships while advancing to the conference playoffs 12 of the last 13 seasons.

Mark Buri

Fritz's Toms also have earned five berths in the NCAA Tournament in the last 11 seasons, reaching the round of 16 in 1990 and 1993, and playing in the 1994 Final Four. His career record is 350-182, including a 286-112 mark in MIAC regular-season games. His career winning percentage of .658 ranks him among the top 50 collegiate coaches in the country. Fritz, who also serves as the school's director of athletics, took part in his 500th game as head coach in February of 1999.

Lute Olson

Coaching legend Lute Olson got his start in Minnesota, when he was a three-sport athlete at Augsburg College from 1953-56. Olson was a six-foot-four forward in basketball, a tight end & defensive tackle in football and a first baseman in baseball. He played under Auggie coaching legends Edor Nelson and Ernie Anderson, and knew early on that this was his life's calling. Olson grew up in tiny Mayville, N.D., and chose Augsburg and its coaches because he wanted to go to school in a similar small-town atmosphere. While at college his life was anything but traditional. He married his high school sweetheart, Bobbi, during his sophomore year, and as a result, had to work the night shift at a local soft drink plant to support his family. He received no athletic financial aid, but worked hard both on the athletic field, in the classroom and at his job.

After college, Olson's first coaching job was at Mahnomen High School, where he spent one season before moving on to teach and coach at Two Harbors High School. His first big coaching gig was at the University of Iowa, where he led the Hawkeyes to six 20-victory campaigns, a league title, and a trip to the NCAA Final Four in 1980. From there he took over as the head coach of the Arizona Wildcats, where his record has been close to phenomenal with 11-straight 20-win campaigns. He went through a lot at Arizona, losing several times in the early rounds of the NCAA's Big Dance. In 1997, however, he finally got the monkey off his back when his Cinderella Wildcats upset the University of Kentucky to win the National Championship. He made a return home in 2001 when he led his Cats back to the Final Four, this time at the Metrodome, just a stone's throw away from his old stomping grounds at Augsburg. A true coaching legend, Olson has amassed more than 600 career victories and has truly made Minnesota proud.

Augsburg University

Founded in 1872, in Minneapolis, Augsburg University has had a long basketball tradition. The Auggies won their first MIAC title in 1927 under Head Coach Si Melby, but wouldn't get their second until 1963. Augsburg, behind Head Coach Ernie Anderson and their star player, Dan Anderson, went on a three-year title run from there, taking a trio of conference crowns in 1963, 1964 and 1965. They would add several of more through the years as well, including: 1975-77, 1980, 1984-85 and 1988-89.

Their first taste of the post-season came in 1946, when the 19-2 Auggies finished in the top-16 nationally by defeating Washburn University (Kansas), 64-36, at the 32-team NAIA National Tournament in Kansas City, before losing to Drury College (Mo.), 55-47.

The 1926 Auggies coached by Si Melby, the "Father of Augsburg Athletics"

In 1963 Augsburg edged St. Cloud State, 56-55, to advance to the NAIA National Tournament in Kansas City. There, the 25-3 Auggies topped West Virginia State, 67-57, only to fall to Fort Hays State, 82-71, in round two. That next year Augsburg once again defeated St. Cloud State, 65-60, en route to the national finals. This time, however, they made it to the Great Eight by first pounding Central Connecticut, 107-87, followed by a nail-biter over Hastings (Neb.), 66-65, only to fall to Central (Ohio), 66-57, in Game Three.

Si Melby

The program went on a NAIA post-season play-off binge throughout the decade of the 1970s. In 1977 they emerged once again to reach the NAIA National Tournament in Kansas City, this time losing a heart-breaker to Clarion (Pa.) State, 88-84, in overtime, to spoil an otherwise amazing 23-7 overall record. Then, in 1980, the Auggies earned a No. 4 national ranking by advancing to the NAIA Tourney, this time beating

Devean George

Devean George, who starred for Benilde-St. Margaret's High School, went on to become a superstar at Augsburg in the late 1990s, rewriting the record books along the way. In 1999, his senior year, George averaged nearly 30 points per game while adding better than 11 rebounds as well. For his efforts he became the first Division III player ever selected in the first round of the NBA Draft when he was chosen by the Los Angeles Lakers. George has since gone on to win a pair of world championships with the Lakers, getting more and more minutes of playing time as time goes by. One highlight came on April 9, 2001, when George scored 10 points for his Lakers in a 104-99 win over the Timberwolves, in front of his hometown fans.

Dan Anderson went on to play in the NBA with Philly in the 1960s

Mankato State, 59-58, in overtime, before losing to the University of Central Arkansas, 67-61, to end their season.

In 1981 the No. 2 Auggies made it back to the Big Dance, this time beating both Drury (Mo.), 56-54, and Kearney (Neb.) State, 81-77, before falling to Bethany Nazarene (Okla.), 84-69, to end their outstanding 29-2 season.

In 1985 the format was changed, and the Auggies lost to Lemoyne-Owen, 75-55, in the South Regional (at Greensboro, N.C.) of the NCAA Division III Tournament. They made it back to the NCAA Division III Tournament in 1998, behind their star, Devean George, this time losing to rival Gustavus in the first round.

Overall, the Auggies have been solid, competing in eight national postseason tournaments (2 NCAA, 6 NAIA). In NAIA national tournament play, Augsburg was 6-6 in its six appearances and finished in the final eight twice (1965 and 1981). The 2001 season marks the 16th time in school history that the team has advanced to postseason competition of any kind in men's basketball.

Ernie Anderson

Concordia College

Concordia College was founded in 1891 in Moorhead as a mostly Norwegian Lutheran school. The Cobbers have featured one of the MIAC's strongest programs, consistently fielding tough, competitive teams. Concordia won its first MIAC title back in 1931, but wouldn't win another for more than 50 years. Then, in 1982, the team went on a tear, winning back-to-back conference crowns in both 1982 and 1983.

One of the early stars of the program was Edwin "Sonny" Gulsvig, who arrived on campus in 1946 as a freshman from Elbow Lake High School. His commanding presence, booming friendly voice and warm humor made him virtually synonymous with Cobber sports both as a teacher and coach until he retired in 1991. As a football, basketball and baseball athlete, Sonny earned nine varsity letters before graduating in 1950 with a degree in Economics, Physical Education and Health. In 1955 he took over as the team's basketball coach, and over the next 23 seasons he racked up 237 career wins. The 1976 NAIA District 13 Basketball Coach of the Year also served as an assistant football coach for 36 years and his duties as both a head and assistant baseball coach spanned 20 years as well. A real coaching legend, he was also one of Concordia's most well-liked and respected teachers.

Today Concordia is led by Head Coach Duane Siverson, who has been running Cobber men's basketball since 1991. He has amassed a 263-160 career coaching record and in his 10 years as the Cobber's head coach and has already put together two of the three winningest seasons in Cobber history. His 1994-95 team went 18-7 and his 1995-96 squad went 16-4 in the MIAC, captured the MIAC playoff championship and was 21-6 overall. The 1995-96 Cobbers earned a first-ever NCAA men's basketball tournament bid. Siverson ended the 1996-97 season as the school's all-time winningest basketball coach.

Concordia's Career Points Leaders		
1. Bob Laney	1964-68	1,847
2. Dick Peterson	1966-70	1,469
3. Bob Peterson	1966-70	1,373
4. Dave Reiten	1970-73	1,101
5. Jim Bjorklund	1971-74	1,098

That team won 10 of its final 12 games and put the Cobbers in the MIAC's top four for the third consecutive year. He served as an assistant coach for the Running Cobbers from 1978-1984, during which time the Cobbers captured two MIAC titles as well. In 1984 Siverson took over as head coach of the Cobber women's program and guided them to four MIAC titles, the 1988 NCAA Division III National Championship and seven NCAA tournament appearances. He was NCAA Division III National Coach of the Year in 1988. With Siverson steering the ship, the Cobbers are poised to do well in the years to come.

Carleton College

Founded in 1866, Carleton College is one of Minnesota's finest higher institutes for learning. Although the program became a charter member of the MIAC in 1921, Carleton's basketball history goes back much, much further. In fact, there is evidence in The Algol, Carleton's yearbook, that the game was played there on an informal basis as far back as 1892 when Max Exner, who was hired as the College's Director of Physical Culture, introduced it on campus. Exner was a roommate of James Naismith back in Springfield, Mass., where Naismith invented the game just a year earlier.

The game was played on an informal basis for the next decade or so before the first official team took the floor in 1910. Since no on-campus facility existed, the team played in the Northfield YMCA against teams such as St. Thomas, Hamline, Shattuck St. Mary's and St. Olaf. It soon became apparent that a larger facility was needed to accommodate the popular new sport. So, in 1910, Sayles-Hill Gymnasium was completed. It was such a first-rate facility that it would become the first venue to host the Minnesota State High School tournament, which it proudly did from 1913-1923.

Carleton was the early power of the MIAC, however, winning the conference's first three titles from 1921-23 under Coach Everett Dean. Ironically, those would be the last conference crowns the program would win. During this era Carleton was blessed with three individuals who would all go on to become coaching legends in the world of basketball. First, was Everett Dean, who guided the Knights to an amazing 40-4 record from 1921-24, before going on to

Joe Hutton

coach at his alma mater, Indiana University. An All-American at IU back in 1920, Dean led the Hoosiers to their first Big Ten Championship in school history in 1926. He coached Indiana to three Big 10 titles over his 14 seasons in Bloomington and finished with a record of 163-93. He also guided the Hoosier baseball team to three Big 10 baseball crowns as well. Then, in 1938, he decided to head west, and take over at Stanford, where he led the Cardinal for 11 seasons en route to a 167-120 career record. The highlight, however, came in 1942, when Dean led Stanford to its only National Championship when they beat Dartmouth, 53-38, in the Finals. The star of that team was none other than Jim Pollard, a future Laker Hall of Famer with our very own Minneapolis Lakers. Dean was later enshrined into the Basketball Hall of Fame in 1966.

Carleton's 1921 MIAC Title Team

The other coaching prodigys to come out of this era were a pair of teammates in Joe Hutton and Ozzie Cowles. Hutton, of course, would go on to lead rival Hamline from 1930-65, winning three National championships en route to compiling an astounding 591-208 record along the way. Cowles, meanwhile, would also go on to coaching greatness, first at Carleton, where from 1924-30 he led the Knights to an impressive 65-26 record. From there he headed east, to Dartmouth, where he led the Ivy Leaguers to seven league titles, as well as an NCAA runner-up in 1942, when he lost to Everett Dean's Stanford team. From there he he guided the the University of Michigan Wolverines, leading them to the Big Ten title in 1948. Finally, it was back to the University of Minnesota, where he served as the team's head coach for 11 years — leading the Gophers to a pair of Big Ten runner-up finishes en route to a career record of 147-93.

The team fared well in the late 1920s and early 1930s. Carleton was a perfect 14-0 under legendary coach Everett Dean in 1924 and between 1928 and 1933, the Knights went 82-11 and even beat Iowa twice and Minnesota twice. They even went on a 64-game home winning streak between 1926 and 1935 in Sayles-Hill Gymnasium (the longest such streak in state collegiate history), which was finally broken by Cornell College on January 11, 1935. Perhaps the best team ever was the 1933 squad which was dubbed as the "Victory Five." Led by All-American Forward Dick Arney, who later coached Austin High School to the state title in 1935, the team blew out most schools in their path. They either won or shared seven consecutive Midwest Conference championships from 1926-34, and became quite a basketball power.

Carleton's Career Leaders:

Points Leader: 1,967, Josh Wilhelm, 1995-99
Rebounds Leader: 838, Mark Wandmacher, 1980-84
Assists Leader: 479, Chad Boger, 1993-97

A couple of key members of this era include: Oliver "Hon" Nordly '27, a two-time all-conference player who went on to coach at Rochester High School and the University of Northern Iowa, and also Gus Young '32, who, after playing on the fabled "Victory Five," went on to lead Gustavus to three straight MIAC titles from 1963-56. (The basketball court there is even named for him.)

The coach of this era was Marshall Diebold, who headed up the golden age of Carleton basketball until World War II. Hoops continued through the war, as the team included three Japanese-American players during this difficult period. One star, however, was Sonny Olson, who was named as a Converse All-American in 1939.

In the early 1950s the team twice posted a 18-win seasons, and posted some decent teams. Former Purdue Coach Mel Taube led the Knights from 1950-60, compiling a 133-83 mark, and then passed the torch to Jack Thurnblad, who coached the Knights from 1960-83, posting a 244-273 record and leading them to the 1966 Midwest Conference title. Also during this time, Carleton opened West Gymnasium, which was dedicated on May 20, 1964. One player of note during this era was two-time all-Midwest Conference Forward Michael Armacost '58, who went on to become the ambassador to Japan.

With an all-time record of 1,001-787-2, Carleton has qualified for MIAC Tournament eight times in its last 11 seasons, including a trip to the title game in 1997, where the Knights won their first playoff game in school history. Today the team is led by Guy Kalland, who has led the Knights to a 212-193 record over the past 17 seasons. A 1974 graduate of Concordia College, Kalland led his team to the MIAC playoffs in 1998-99, marking the seventh time in nine years the team qualified for post-season play. Kalland, a

Carleton's 1923 MIAC Title Team

former assistant men's basketball coach at the University of Minnesota from 1979-80, spent four years at Inver Hills (Minn.) Community College, leading the team to a 1982 state championship as well. Kalland is also a professor of physical education, athletics and recreation at Carleton.

Two players of note in recent times are Gerrick Monroe and Josh Wilhelm. Monroe was Carleton's first All-America since 1939, earning NABC All-America honors in 1993. From 1989-93 Monroe scored 1,903 points. Wilhelm bested Monroe's career scoring total, holds the single-season record of 588 points in 1999 and the career record of 1,967 from 1995-99. He played in the MIAC with a class that included Devean George of Augsburg, Luke Schmidt of Gustavus and Eric Joldersma of Bethel — a group of talent capable of playing in nearly any conference in America. In 2000-01 the Knights posted a record of 9-15, but are poised to improve in the years to come.

Coach Everett Dean

Gustavus Adolphus College

Founded in St. Peter in 1862 by Swedish immigrants, Gustavus Adolphus College bears the name of the famous 15th century Swedish monarch, Gustav II Adolph, better known as the "Warrior King." Fittingly, today's Gusties boast one of the premier Division III basketball program's in the state. The Gusties first hit the hardcourt back in 1904 under Coach E.S. Youngdahl. They went 0-1 that year, but came back to post their first winning season in 1913, when they went 12-1. Gustavus won its first MIAC title in 1925, and kept on going from there, winning it again in 1926 and 1928 as well. The coach of that era was Teddie Lindenberg, who from 1926-33 posted an impressive record of 167-83.

Coach George Myrum led the squad to its next conference title in 1939 and then tragically died later that fall in a bus crash coming home from a Gustavus football game. The team got back on its feet under Coach Gus Young, who thrust the basketball program into the national limelight. Gus had a flair for showmanship and drew huge crowds to Myrum Fieldhouse. Gustavus had many famed battles with Hamline during this era, as the two schools finished first and second eight times during the 1950s.

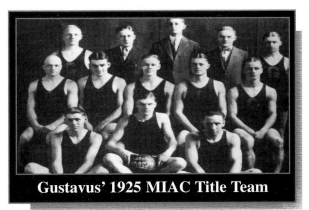

Gustavus' 1925 MIAC Title Team

It wouldn't be until after the war when the Gusties took their next crown, but they came back with a vengeance, winning three straight titles from 1954-56 under Coach Whitey Skoog. Those Gustie championship teams included some of the programs biggest and most talented players: Jim Springer, Bill Patterson, Dick Kumlin, Duane Mullin, Cliff Straka, Jack Colvard, Johnny Patzwald and Bob Erdmann. (Erdmann would return to guide the program in the 1980s.) Skoog, a Brainerd native, starred for the Gophers before going on to become a Minneapolis Lakers legend. Skoog would add two more titles, in 1968 and 1975, before retiring in 1981 with a record of 292-301. That 1975 squad also made it to the NAIA national tournament in Kansas City. Standouts of this era included: Bill Laumaun, Carl Johnson, Dennis Wentworth, Jim Ellingson, Dan Hauck, Tom Carlson, Jim Chalin and Ron White. Of that group, Wentworth and Laumann were three-time all-MIAC players and both had professional tryouts.

When Whitey Skoog stepped down in 1981, the college brought back one of its standouts from the Golden Fifties, naming Bob Erdmann as the 20th mentor of the Gustavus basketball program. Erdmann would build his team around all-American Mark Hanson, a six-foot-six center who would become the all-time scoring leader and a rare four-time all conference player. Erdmann left the program after five years, leaving a solid foundation that would lead to four first division finishes to close out the 1980s.

Whitey Skoog

The team got another couple of titles in 1988 and 1990 earning NCAA tournament bids each of those seasons during Brock's three-year tenure. Leading the way for the Gusties were Jay Coatta, MIAC MVP in 1987, as well as Mike Haldorson and Steve McDermott. From there the Gusties then went on to become one of the MIAC's most dominant teams in the decade of the '90s. Hanson, the former Gustie standout, took over behind the bench in 1990. The Dodge Center native graduated in 1983 as the program's all-time leading scorer with 1,774 points. He was also a two-time NAIA All-America selection, an Academic All-America selection, a three-time Gustavus Adolphus MVP and a four-time All-MIAC selection.

Since then he has gone on to win some 200 games en route to posting four MIAC titles along the way: 1991, 1992, 1996 and 1997.

Gustavus' Career Scoring Leaders

1.	2,011	Luke Schmidt	(1996-99)
2.	1,774	Mark Hanson	(1979-83)
3.	1,768	Carl Johnson	(1966-70)
4.	1,662	Jim Springer	(1952-56)
5.	1,615	D.L. Smith	(1955-59)

Then, in 1999 the Gusties had a dream season. Led by 2,000-point scorer Luke Schmidt, Gustavus beat Augsburg in the MIAC tourney to advance to the NCAA D-III Playoffs. There they went on an amazing run, beating Pomona-Pitzer in round one, 67-37, Upper Iowa University in game two, 58-55, Franklin College in Game Three, 66-65, and then lost to UW-Platteville in the Final Four, 61-47. In 2001 the No. 14-ranked Gusties, led by Bobby Johnson's 21 points, lost to St. John's, 84-75, in the second round of the NCAA tournament. It was a sad end to an otherwise outstanding season. Regardless, the Gusties seem poised for greatness under Coach Hanson, who has already been named MIAC Coach of the Year on three occasions.

St. Olaf College

St. Olaf was founded in 1874 as a coed, residential, four-year private liberal arts college. The school's basketball program was begun in the early 1900s, and has since been strong. The Oles won their first MIAC title back in 1929, and followed that up with an other one the next year to make it two in a row. It would be another 60 years until the Oles would win another one, however, when in 1989, led by All-American Mike Moes, they shared the conference crown with St. Thomas.

The program has had its share of tremendous players, including the all-time leading scorer, Bruce Govig, who from 1976-80, tallied an amazing 1,813 points. Today the Oles are led by Head Coach Dan Kosmoski, who has guided the team for the past seven seasons. Prior to coming to Northfield, he served an assistant coach at the University of Minnesota under Jim Dutcher, Jimmy Williams and Clem Haskins. Kosmoski, a three-sport stand-out at Owatonna High School, went on to play for the Gophers under Dutcher. From there he served an assistant coach at Golden Valley Lutheran Junior College before returning to become an assistant with the Gophers.

St. Olaf's Career Scoring Leaders

1. Bruce Govig	1976-80	1,813
2. Dan Halvorsen	1970-73	1,388
3. Mike Moes	1988-92	1,332
4. Tim Schilling	1993-97	1,251
5. Rahn Hagberg	1981-84	1,146

In addition, the St. Olaf basketball program got an indirect boost in February of 2001 when Chris Thomforde was hired as the school's new president. Thomforde, a six-foot-nine former all-Ivy League Center from Princeton, led his Tigers to two NCAA tournaments en route to becoming the program's 14th all-time leading scorer. He went on to become a draft choice of the New York Knicks in 1969, but had a change of heart soon after training camp. He ultimately decided to skip the NBA and instead went to Yale Divinity School, became a Lutheran pastor and moved on to educational administration. Today he is in Northfield, serving as St. Olaf's new CEO.

Bethel College

Bethel College, in Arden Hills, began its four-year Christian liberal arts instruction in 1947, but can trace its roots all the way back to Bethel Seminary, with was founded in 1871.

Paul Edwards was the team's first coach, racking up a 36-29 record from 1946-50. He was replaced by Del Ray Peterson, who posted a very respectable 85-74 tally over the next eight years. Jerry Healy took over in 1958, guiding Bethel to a 87-76 mark over eight seasons, only to see Jack Treager come in for the 1968 season and guide the club to a 81-135 record.

In 1977, Roger Davis took over as the head coach of Bethel, and led the club to its first season of MIAC play by posting an 8-17 record that year. After a couple of up and down seasons, George Palke took over in 1980, and for the next 17 seasons led Bethel to a modest 226-239 overall record. Several of the program's alumni have also gone on to play in various levels of the pro ranks. Among those who played briefly in the NBA include: Ron Pederson, who tried out with the New Jersey Nets in 1969; Steve Scroggins, who tried out with San Antonio Spurs in 1974; Jason Velgersdyke, who tried out with Detroit Pistons in 1984; and Dale Turnquist, who tried out with the Cleveland Cavaliers in 1992.

Bethel's Career Scoring Leaders

1. Steve Scroggins	1970-73	2,291
2. Ron Pederson	1966-69	2,035
3. Dale Turnquist	1989-91	1,746
4. Eric Joldersma	1995-99	1,706
5. Dave Blanchard	1977-80	1,506

Today Bethel is led by Head Coach Bob Bjorklund, who is entering his fifth season at the helm of the men's basketball program. His first four years at Bethel have resulted in a vast improvement for the program. In 2001, he led the Royals to a 17-9 record and their second consecutive post-season appearance in the conference playoffs and fourth place in the MIAC. Bethel first beat Augsburg, 72-59, but then lost to Gustavus, 47-63, to finish out their season.

Before beginning his career at Bethel, Bjorklund spent 22 years coaching high school basketball in Minnesota, most recently as the head coach at Fergus Falls High School. During that time, he posted a record of 330-165, including state tournament berths in 1984, 1986, and 1990. With Bjorklund leading the way, Bethel is a program on its way up.

St. John's University

Founded in 1857, St. John's University has a long tradition of basketball success. The program first began back in 1902 and has been a Minnesota power now for more than a century. In fact, St. John's has won no less than seven MIAC titles through the years: 1969, 1978, 1979, 1986, 1987, 1993 and 2001. The Johnnies also won MIAC playoff titles in 1985, 1986, 1988, 2000 and 2001.

Now, talking about basketball at St. John's can mean only one thing. As is Coach John Gagliardi to the Johnny Football team, so too is Coach Jim Smith to the Johnny hoops program. A living legend, Smith is the winningest collegiate coach on any level in Minnesota, having amassed an astounding 589-387 career record in 37 seasons as a collegiate head coach. He took over the Johnny program in 1964 and hasn't looked back. But prior to Coach Smith, there were some pretty good teams led by some pretty good players up in Collegeville.

From Coach Flynn in the 1910s, to coach Johnny Benda in the 1930s and 40s, and even coaches Hiller, Osborne and Hasbrouck of the 1950s and early '60s, St. John's has always fielded some great teams. One of the program's best eras, however, was in the late 1950s. Several players emerged as big-time stars from this period including three of the program's top-five all-time scorers: Bill Sexton, who tallied 1,480 career points; Dick Matchinsky, who scored 1,581 and Norb Kowalkowski, who added 1,406 as well. In the late 1960s it was Paul Bernabei, who scored 1,413 career points, and in the late 1970s it was the best yet, Frank Wachlarowicz. Big Frank, who played from 1975-79, remains as the all-time leading scorer for all divisions of Minnesota collegiate

Bernie Kukar (1959-62) ranks sixth among the top scorers at SJU with 1,389 career points. Kukar currently works as a referee with the National Football League and was selected to work Super Bowl XXXIII in January 1999.

Bernie Kukar

Frank Wachlarowicz, who played from 1975-79, is the Johnnies' all-time leading scorer (as well as for all-divisions of Minnesota statewide collegiate basketball) with 2,357 points. He is also the program's all-time career leader in rebounds with 1,093.

Travis Weiss (1991-94) holds the single-season all collegiate (Divisions I, II and III) field goal percentage record, which he set by shooting 76.6% from the field during the 1993-94 season.

Travis Weiss

Dave Landsberger

St. John's Career Points Leaders

1. Frank Wachlarowicz	(1979)	2,357
2. Dick Matchinsky	(1957)	1,581
3. Bill Sexton	(1955)	1,480
4. Paul Bernabei	(1969)	1,413
5. Norb Kowalkowski	(1959)	1,406

basketball with 2,357 points. And, in addition to being the Johnnies' all-time leading scorer, he is also the program's all-time career leader in rebounds, with 1,093.

But it has been the Smith era that has put the Johnnies on the map. Smith gained his 500th win on Dec. 9, 1995, with a win over Macalester, becoming only the second coach in the history of Minnesota collegiate basketball to win over 500 games. Smith became the winningest coach in Minnesota collegiate basketball history on March 3, 2001, when SJU defeated Gustavus Adolphus in the second round of the NCAA Division III basketball championship tournament, 84-75, passing legendary Hamline Head Coach Joe Hutton. (The Johnnies ultimately lost to Christopher Newport, 71-65, in the "Sweet-16.")

Smith has led his teams to seven MIAC titles, five MIAC playoff titles, nine trips to the NAIA tournament and seven trips to the NCAA Division III playoffs, including an appearance by the Johnnies in the 2000 and 2001 NCAA tournaments. Since 1964, SJU has enjoyed 26 winning seasons under Smith's direction. In 2001, SJU qualified for the sectional round of the NCAA Division III tournament. A three-time NAIA District Coach-of-the-Year, Smith is a past president of the National Association of Basketball Coaches. In 1992-93 and 2000-01, Smith was named the NCAA Division III West Region Coach-of-the-Year. Smith also was named MIAC coach of the year in 2000-01, which is the sixth time in his career he has received that prestigious honor. Besides ranking first among college coaches in Minnesota, Smith is also second among active NCAA Division III coaches for most victories and fourth all-time in Division III basketball history.

A 1956 graduate of Marquette University with a bachelor's degree in English and history, Smith was a four-year letter winner on the Warriors' basketball team. In addition to his duties as basketball coach, Smith serves as athletic director at SJU. The Elgin, Ill., native is also an associate professor of physical education and has also coached golf, cross country and track during his tenure on campus.

In addition, in 2002 Coach Jim Smith will have the honor of coaching his grandson, Brandon, marking the first time in NCAA basketball history for a grandfather-grandson connection on the court. Things are good in Johnny-ville these days. The 22-6 Johnnies, led by MIAC Player of the Year, Troy Bigalke, won their seventh MIAC title in 2001 and are poised to keep it rolling in Sexton Arena. Oh yeah, Coach Smith also won yet another Coach of the Year award as well. It's just business as usual in Collegeville.

Coach Jim Smith

Troy Bigalke

Macalester College

Founded in 1874, Macalester College has long been one of Minnesota's premier higher learning institutions. Macalester was a charter member of the MIAC, joining in 1919, and going on to win its first conference crown in 1937. It would be another 44 years, however, before the Scots could celebrate another title, which they did in 1981.

The program has seen its shares of highs and lows through the years but seems to be poised to improve under fifth-year Coach Curt Kietzer. In 2001 Macalester finished with an overall record of 10-13, its first double-digit win season since 1988 when it finished at 10-13. The team ended its campaign with eight conference wins, just missing the six-team conference playoffs. Back-to-back defeats in Northfield in early February to Carleton and St. Olaf, followed by a one-point loss at Gustavus, took the Scots out of the hunt for a playoff bid. Leading the charge for the Scots are Ryan Gerry, who, in addition to averaging 14.2 points per game, was seventh in the nation in three-pointers with 3.3 per game. In addition, Doug Benson emerged as one of the MIAC's top centers, averaging 13.0 points and 7.8 rebounds per game, and Ben Van Thorre was named to the MIAC's all-newcomer team after tallying 13.3 points per game as well.

Former NFL star, Irv Cross, is now Macalester's Athletic Director

St. Mary's University

Founded in 1912 in Winona, St. Mary's has had a long and storied athletic tradition. Their basketball program has seen its share of ups and downs over the years, but has seen its share of highlights. The Cardinals won a pair of MIAC titles in 1939 and 1940 and in 1945 had their most wins ever when they garnered 21 victories. One of the early stars of that era was Clint Wager, who after attending St. Mary's, went on to play professionally in the NBA from 1943-50 with Oshkosh, Hammond Calumet Buccaneers and Fort Wayne.

Dave Theis was one of the stars of the 1950s, emerging as the program's all-time leading rebounder with 1,063 boards. In the '60s it was Joe Keenan, who still holds the team's career scoring average with 19.1 points per game from 1967-71. And then there was Marvin Tunstall, who remains the program's all-time leading scorer after tallying 1,911 points from 1975-79.

Today St. Mary's is led by former player-turned coach, Bob Biebel, who is entering his sixth season behind the Cardinal bench. Over that span he has produced a 30-66 record. In 2000, however, Biebel's Cardinals enjoyed their highest win total since the 1987 season when they went 11-13. In 2001 the Card's went 5-19 and are looking to get back in the groove.

The Northern Sun Athletic Conference

In 1923 a junior college sports conference was organized in Minnesota, consisting of the state's teacher colleges (Winona, Mankato, St. Cloud, Moorhead, Bemidji and Duluth), as well as its junior colleges (Duluth, Virginia, Hibbing, Itasca and Rochester), with the purpose of placing the two on an equal basis regarding eligibility of athletes, scholastic requirements, length of participation of athletes, and regulation of transfer students. It was called the Northern Intercollegiate Conference (NIC). Then, in 1932, the league changed its name to the Northern Teacher's Athletic Conference (NTAC). Charter members of the new circuit included Bemidji State University, Mankato State University, Moorhead State University, St. Cloud State University and Winona State University.

Mankato State Teacher's College won the first NTAC title in 1932, with a 6-2 record, but Duluth State Teacher's College (UM-Duluth) pushed the Indians aside the next winter, winning the first of four straight titles. The Peds (short for Pedagogues, or teachers), as the Bulldogs were originally known, had their mini-dynasty overthrown following the 1937 season by Winona State Teacher's College, whose Warriors went on to claim back-to-back titles.

Bemidji State won three straight crowns from 1940-43 before St. Cloud State came in to win its first title in the newly-named Northern Intercollegiate Conference (NIC). After a two-year pause for World War II, NIC hoops got a big boost thanks to a big batch of crusty service veterans who came home from overseas and wanted to play some ball. St. Cloud State captured that first post-war title before Mankato State reeled off the first of five state crowns. It was indeed a golden decade for the Indians, an era that produced nine titles in 10 years and a runner-up finish at the 1947 NAIA National Championship.

St. Cloud State then emerged as a real power under Coach Red Severson, who came in as the Huskies' new skipper in 1958, and led his boys to nine league titles in 11 years, and a pair of trips to the NAIA National Tournament. By the early 1960s, the Huskies had settled down, and no less than five different teams would rise to the top of the NIC in the next six years. Michigan Tech, featuring future Vikings legend "Bench-Warmer" Bob Lurtsema, grabbed a share of its first title in 1963, and two years later Moorhead State followed suit.

In 1968, Bemidji State became the first league team to reach the coveted 12-win plateau. St. Cloud State knocked off the Beavers that next year though, en route to adding three more crowns to its already crowded trophy case. Following that, Moorhead State got hot in 1971 when they finished with an impressive 24-1 regular season record — good for a No. 4 national ranking by the National Association of Intercollegiate Athletics (NAIA). That next season Winona State took over as the conference's new power, cruising to four consecutive league titles along with a pair of invitations to the NAIA nationals. Winona State's dynasty would fall in 1976, though, as St. Cloud State, Minnesota-Morris, Mankato State and Michigan Tech would each gain at least a share of one NIC title to round out the 1970s.

The Minnesota-Duluth Bulldogs simply dominated the better part of the 1980s and 1990s, as they either won or shared no less than 11 league titles during that span (1981-84, 1985-92 and 1997). In 1992 the NIC and the all-women's Northern Sun Conference merged, with the conference yet again changing its name to the Northern Sun Intercollegiate Conference (NSIC). The University of Minnesota-Morris, which joined the conference in 1966, followed by Southwest State in 1969, were both joined by the University of Minnesota-Duluth in 1975. (Mankato State and St. Cloud State, which had both been long-time members of the NSIC, withdrew in the 1975 and 1983, respectively, to join the North Central Conference.)

Northern State, which joined the league in 1980, has won eight titles of its own (1983-84, 1984-85 and 1992-93 and 1994-99). The University of Minnesota-Crookston and Concordia-St. Paul were also both added to the league in 1999. The league's newest members, Wayne State (Neb.), went on to win both the 2000 regular season and tournament titles in its first season, while Southwest State took the crown in 2001.

All-Time NSIC Titles:

Team	Titles	Last Title
St. Cloud State	17	1976
Minnesota-Duluth	15	1997
Mankato State	13	1979
Northern State (SD)	8	1999
Winona State	8	1975
Bemidji State	8	1967
Moorhead State	4	1982
Minnesota-Morris	3	1994
Michigan Tech.	2	1980
Wayne State (NE)	1	2000
Southwest State	1	2001

NSIC Member Schools:

Team	Nickname	Joined NSIC
Bemidji State	Beavers	1932
Moorhead State	Dragons	1932
Northern State, SD	Wolves	1978
Southwest State	Mustangs	1969
Minn.-Duluth	Bulldogs	1932 & 1975
Minn.-Morris	Cougars	1966
Winona State	Warriors	1932
Wayne State, NE	Wildcats	1998
Minn.-Crookston	Golden Eagles	1999
Concordia-St. Paul	Golden Bears	1999

The University of Minnesota-Duluth

The history of the University of Minnesota-Duluth dates back to 1895, when it was founded as the Duluth State Teachers College. The Peds (short for Pedagogues, or teachers), as the Bulldogs were originally known, first began to play basketball on an informal basis shortly after the turn of the century. They played mostly northern schools, but also traveled to the Twin Cities to play the local college and university teams there as well.

UMD's 1965 NCAA Playoff Team

In 1931 the Duluth State Teachers College fielded its first "official" varsity men's basketball team. Led by head coach Frank Kovach, who also headed the DSTC men's hockey and football programs, the "Peds' went 6-9 in their initial season with wins over teams such as Duluth Junior College., Eveleth Junior College. and Hibbing Junior College. Legendary coach Lloyd Peterson took over in 1932 and enrolled his team into what was then known as the Northern Teacher's Athletic Conference. Peterson dominated the early part of the league, leading his club to 15 NSIC championships along the way.

One of Duluth's biggest games of this era came in 1935, when the famed Harlem Globetrotters came to the port city to play. The Trotters, which played it straight back then, were famous for their incredible players and for their ability to seemingly never lose. But on this night, it was all Duluth. That's right, Duluth Teachers College, behind John Boucinovich, who later coached at both Cathedral and Central High Schools for some 35 years, hung on to upset the legendary club. Boucinovich held Inman Jackson, who was the star of the Trotters team, in check and the team hung on to take the victory in front of a packed Duluth Amphitheater crowd.

In 1950 Duluth left the conference to join the Minnesota Intercollegiate Athletic Conference. They quickly became a power in the MIAC, as one team after another came to Romano Gymnasium to find out that these Bulldogs, as they were now known, were for real. UMD christened their new arena on December 12, 1953, with a 73-72 triumph against Gustavus Adolphus College and have since managed to amass a 471-133 record there for an amazing .781 winning percentage.

In 1954, Norm Olson took over as the team's new head coach. He would remain behind the Bulldog bench for the next 15 years, bringing Duluth a total of four MIAC titles, in 1958, 1959, 1961 and 1962. Then, after nearly a 30-year absence, UMD dropped out of the MIAC and rejoined the Northern (Sun) Intercollegiate Conference in 1976, where they have been ever since.

Josh Quigley

George Fisher replaced Dave Hopkins in 1978 as the Dogs' new skipper and wasted little time in making his mark. He took the fifth place club and turned them into what would become a power — winning a trio of titles from 1982-84. Dale Race took over that next year and picked up right where Fisher left off. Race led the Dogs to seven straight conference crowns from 1986-92, finishing with no worse than 23 wins per season along the way. It was one of Minnesota basketball's greatest dynasties. Race's squads cooled down in the 1993 & 1994, but rebounded to take a pair of runner-up spots as well as one more title in 1997.

Dale Race

In 1998 long-time Bulldog assistant Gary Holquist took over as the team's new head coach, replacing Race, who stepped down after 14 seasons to become the school's first Bulldog Club/athletic marketing coordinator. Race ended his career as the winningest head coach in UMD history with a record of 293-120. Holquist inherited a sub-.500 basketball team that year and molded them in to a conference title contender in just two seasons. Holquist led the Bulldogs to an 18-14 record in 1999-00, however, and a third-place regular season finish in the Northern Sun Intercollegiate Conference at 13-5. UMD won 12 of its last 15 games that year and made it to the finals of the inaugural NSIC tournament. Overall Holquist is 47-40 in his three years as the Bulldogs' head coach.

Despite the fact that it is in the heart of hockey-country, UMD has proven to be one of Minnesota's premier basketball programs. The UMD men's basketball program, which has won more NSIC titles than any current league member, is now in its 70th year of existence. And, contrary to what the puck-heads might think, the men's basketball program has the distinction of being the school's longest running program. In fact, they have endured just three losing seasons at home through the years: (1966, 1969 and 1970). The Bulldogs are 93-51 (.646) in NSIC play

UM-Duluth's All-Americans

1999-00	Josh Quigley	C
1993-94	Jerry Meyer	G
1990-91	Jay Guidinger	C
1989-90	Jay Guidinger	C
1988-89	Jay Guidinger	C
1987-88	David Thompson	F
1986-87	Jeff Guidinger	F
1982-83	Nicky Johnson	G

Dave Baker

Jay Guidinger

since the beginning of the 1991 season and were 117-32 at Romano Gymnasium in the 1990's, which included a school-record 41-game home winning streak to boot from January of 1989 to November of 1991.

Today the Dogs are looking solid from top to bottom. They play in the 2,759-seat Romano Gymnasium, a facility which underwent an extensive $2 million facelift following the 1987 season when it was renamed in honor of the late Ralph Romano, UMD's Director of Athletics from 1969-83. In addition, several new stars are leading the way for the club into the future.

Chris Stanley and Jake Nettleton are each members of the coveted 1,000-point club, and helped lead the Dogs to a 16-12 record in 2001 — good for a third place finish in the Northern Sun Intercollegiate Conference. They advanced to the semifinals of the NSIC Tournament that year though, ultimately falling to NCAA Elite 8 participant Southwest State University. The team came on strong for the stretch run though, winning eight of its last 11 games – with the three losses all coming from teams that advanced on to the NCAA Division II playoffs. With Coach Holquist steering the ship, these Bulldogs are poised for another big run. Stay tuned!

UMD's All-Time Scoring Leaders		
1. Dave Baker	(1957-61)	18.0
2. Charles Hiti	(1952-54)	17.8
3. Mike Patterson	(1961 -65)	17.1
3. Rudy Monson	(1947-50)	17.1
5. Bill Mattson	(1958-62)	16.8

Dave Thompson

UM-Crookston

While Crookston was founded in 1966 as a two-year school, and later became a four-year institution in 1993, the school's roots go back to the 1920s, when it was known as the Northwest School of Agriculture. It soon began an affiliation with of the University of Minnesota, and started playing solid basketball in the junior college ranks.

Former Underwood and Eveleth High School Coach Gary Senkse took over as the head basketball coach at Crookston in 1981 and has been at the helm ever since. His NJCAA teams at UMC compiled 176 wins against 117 losses for a 61% win-loss record that included 12 consecutive winning seasons, a division championship, four division runners-up, a State Championship, and a Region XIII runners-up title. The 1986 team recorded the most wins in a season with 21, and the 1992 squad recorded the fewest losses with six; both are school records. Over the past 29 years as a head coach Gary Senske has achieved a career record of 362 wins and 290 losses.

Birman Jenkins & Jason Marshall

In the late 1990s UMC was led by a pair of NAIA Division II All-Americans in Malcolm White, who, in 1997 led the conference in rebounding with an average of 11.4 rpg and was second in the conference in scoring with an average of 18.0 ppg. That next year Guard Tom Andrades also received All-American honors as well. That 1998 season saw U of M-Crookston advance to the NDCAC playoffs, where they beat Dickinson State, 64-57, in the quarterfinals, and then lost to Mayville State University, 85-56, in the semi's.

In 1999 the Golden Eagles joined the NSIC, which expanded to become a 10-member league, and are hoping to take that next step in eventually becoming a title contender.

Minnesota State-Moorhead

The Dragons have a long hoops history in Minnesota dating all the way back to the early 1900s. Moorhead State began playing in 1923 in the state's teacher college circuit and later became charter members of the Northern Teacher's Athletic Conference in 1932. They won their first conference crown in 1965 and added another in 1971, behind All-Americans Mike Berg and Charlie Williams, when they finished with an impressive 24-1 regular season record — good for a No. 4 national ranking by the National Association of Intercollegiate Athletics (NAIA).

Coach Larry MacLeod had a special squad in 1965. After falling to St. Cloud late in the season, the Dragons rallied back behind a late seven-game winning streak to beat Mankato State, 86-79, to give them a piece of the league title. With that, the team was extended an invitation to the NCAA Division II Midwest Regional Championships at Grand Forks, N.D. It marked the Dragons' first post-season appearance, and MSC seized the moment with a 75-73 upset of Colorado State on the opening round.

Cactus Warner

The triumph then brought a rematch with Phil Jackson (the future Knicks star and eight time world champion coach of the Chicago Bulls and L.A. Lakers) and the mighty North Dakota Sioux. UND was tough, and sealed the deal in the second half of this one with a 83-57 victory that sent the Sioux to the national tournament, and ended a remarkable 21-4 finish for the Dragons. Pete Lysaker, a sharp-shooter from Detroit Lakes, led the Dragons in scoring with 19.2 ppg, and joined Wally Halbakken, Jim Jahr and Erwin "Cactus" Warner on the All-NIC squad.

The marvelous winter of 1971 was the year of the Dragon in small college basketball. Moorhead State roared to an impressive 24-2 finish which included a 15-game winning streak — the longest in MSC history. With that, the Dragons collected the NIC title with a 11-1 record, placed fourth on the final NCAA small college poll, and 12th on the Associated Press College Division poll.

From there MSC advanced to the post-season playoffs as well, but suddenly the story took a turn to the dark side. The Dragons secured homecourt for the opening round of the NAIA District 13 playoffs, and a first trip to the 32-team NAIA National Championships at Kansas City, MO appeared with their grasp.

But just as quickly as the magic appeared, it all evaporated in a loss to Augsburg College in the opening round of the NAIA District 13 playoffs. Riddled by injuries but unfazed by the high drama that had unfolded at MSC, Augsburg stunned the Dragons with a 85-84 knockout that silenced the dream, creating an emotional void that many players refused to discuss for many years.

In 1975 Dave Schellhase, a two-time All-American at Purdue and a national scoring champion, was brought in to serves as the Dragons new head coach. He wasted little time in making a name for him-

Brett Beeson

self as well, leading the team to a pair of NIC titles and trips to the NAIA National Championships in 1980 and 1982 before departing for the head coaching post at Indiana State University.

Schellhase's ties to his native Indiana opened up a fertile recruiting lode, and Jim Kapitan, Matt Brundige, Walt Whitaker and a batch of other Hoosiers soon made a huge imprint at State. Meanwhile, Minnesotans provided some marvelous support as well, especially All-American Kevin Mulder of Renville. With Whitaker collecting a national rebounding title and earning NAIA honorable mention All-American laurels, the Dragons claimed the NIC title, toppled Concordia College 82-76 in a memorable district playoff showdown, advanced to Kansas City, MO and the big dance, and exited 24-7.

Today the Dragons are "Rebuilding the Tradition" In the late 1990s the program was blessed with a pair of All-Americans in Brett Beeson and Dave Mantel, both of whom have done the Dragons proud. Brett Beeson, an Eden Prairie product, collected a batch of honors during a remarkable collegiate career at MSUM in the 1990s. He was saluted as the NCAA Division II Player of the Year in 1996 after lead-

Walt Whitaker

ing the nation in scoring at 33.3 ppg. Beeson also set a MSUM single game scoring record of 54 points as a senior, the highest single game mark in the NCAA II in 1996. A first team GTE Academic All-American, he was also named the NCAA Division II Academic Player of the Year, and earned an NCAA Post-Graduate Scholarship. Following his graduation from State, Beeson played professionally in Europe.

Moorhead's All-Time Scoring Leaders		
1. Ralph Western	(1988-92)	2,015
2. Mike Polomny	(1988-93)	1,946
3. Brett Beeson	(1991-96)	1,825
4. Kevin Mulder	(1976-80)	1,797
5. Greg Duke	(1994-98)	1,679

In addition to a new coaching staff and increase in scholarship funds, Alex Nemzek Hall, the home of the Dragons, has undergone a complete make-over; including a new weight room, team locker-rooms, and $7 million worth of changes to the arena and overall facility. The changes have given the basketball program at MSU Moorhead a great shot at big-time improvement in the years to come.

Today Mike Olson is steering the ship, having replaced Coach Schellhase, who served as the Dragons mentor for 18 years. Olson led the much improved Minnesota-State Moorhead Dragons to a 10-win season in 2001 and will certainly continue to grow and build the program from there.

Southwest State University

Marshall's Southwest State University first joined the NSIC in 1968-69 and has since come a long way. Fully 32 years after being admitted into the Northern Sun, the Mustangs finally won their first conference title in 2001.

It all began for SWSU on December 2, 1967, when the Mustangs opened their inaugural campaign. The Physical Education Gym was in the construction stage, so the team played at Marshall High School. They moved into the PEG that following season though, and called it home for the next 28 seasons before moving into the R/A Facility in 1996.

The program has seen its share of decent teams, including a nice stretch from 1974-77, when the club went 25-7 in the conference, and then again from 1983-87, when the team posted a 32-8 record. Then, after some up and down seasons, the club got hot in the late 1990s, going 10-3 in 1999, and then winning its first conference title in 2001.

That was a magical year for SWSU. Led by All-American Scott Koenen, and NSIC Coach of the Year,

SW State's All-Time Scoring Leaders		
1. Mike Tobin	(1982-86)	1,600
2. Andre Beasley	(1990-93)	1,494
3. Sam Leggett	(1974-76)	1,244
4. Charlie Taylor	(1981-83)	1,226
5. Frank Belmont	(1971-75)	1,103

Southwest State University

Bobby Johnson and David Heiss, both of whom earned NSIC scoring titles. He was finally replaced in 1995 with former North Dakota Head Coach, Dave Gunther.

Following the 2000 season, legendary Coach Dave Gunther decided to step down after 28 years behind the bench. He spent five years at BSU, compiling a 39-96 record, but had racked up a career mark of 466-311.

With that, in 2001, former Southern Utah assistant coach Jeff Guiot was named as the head coach at Bemidji State University. "The University wants to get the basketball program to where it needs to be," said Guiot, himself a former McDonald's High School All-American from Kansas. "There is a big challenge ahead, but I've faced them before. I'm excited about doing this on the NCAA Division II level."

Concordia University, St. Paul

The Concordia-St. Paul Golden Bears joined the NSIC in 1999 and have since become one of the conference's top up-and-coming programs. Established in 1893 in St. Paul, Concordia University is a private, four-year liberal arts school of the Lutheran Church. True to its vision to be an exemplary Christian university in athletics as well as academics, in 1993 Concordia built Ganglehoff Center, a state-of-the-art athletic facility that quickly became the hub of its sports program.

The school's basketball program has made steady progress and in 2002 the Golden Bears will make a big jump by playing a couple of Division I teams, including the University of Wisconsin-Milwaukee. Prior to joining the NSIC, the Golden Bears, or Comets as they were known as back then, played in the Tri-Lakes, Twin River and Upper Midwest Conferences. In 1993 the school made the leap to go Division II and at that point changed their name to the Bears. Since then, they have gone on to beat many of the conference's top team, and continue to only get better. The school has had a host of outstanding coaches along the way, including Dennis Getzlaff, who went on to spend nine years coaching at Kansas University.

The school also got a big boost in 2001 when it hosted the nationally televised annual "Slam Dunk & Three Point Competition" as part of the NCAA National Championship March Madness Week, which was held in the Twin Cities that year. Horace Jenkins of William Patterson won the Slam Dunk contest, while Joe Crispin of Penn State and Holli Tapley of Kansas State shared the "Three-Point Shoot-Out" crown. Vikings All-Pro Receiver Randy Moss was one of the judges for the event, which received a great deal of media attention for the university.

The North Central Conference

Widely acclaimed as one of the top NCAA Division II athletic conferences in the nation, the North Central Conference has a strong tradition which dates back to the Fall of 1921 when the groundwork was laid to create the new circuit. Originally called the North Central Intercollegiate Conference, the league featured seven original members including: The College of St. Thomas, South Dakota State College, Des Moines College, Creighton University, North Dakota Agricultural College, University of North Dakota, and Morningside. In 1932 the circuit was renamed as the Northern Teacher's Athletic Conference and a decade later it would become known as the State Teacher's College Conference of Minnesota. In 1962 it switched its name to the Northern Intercollegiate Conference and it later became known as the North Central Conference.

The league has since seen its share of highlights over the years, as well as a good bit of expansion from other schools along the way. Minnesota's current contingent, Minnesota State, Mankato and St. Cloud State University, both left the NSIC to join the NCC in 1975 and 1982, respectively. Since their arrival, Mankato has won one title, in 1976, while St. Cloud won three straight crowns from 1986-88.

NCC Member Schools
St. Cloud State
Minnesota State, Mankato
Augustana
Morningside
Nebraska-Omaha
North Dakota
North Dakota State
Northern Colorado
South Dakota
South Dakota State

Minnesota State University, Mankato

In 1868 Mankato Normal School first opened its doors in the picturesque river valley town of Mankato, with its primary role being to train teachers for work in rural schools throughout Southern Minnesota. In 1921 the school became Mankato State Teachers College and was authorized by the State to offer a four-year curriculum.

The school began playing basketball on an informal basis from around the turn of the century, primarily against local high school teams, and later against regional college teams from around the state. In 1921 the program hit the hardcourt on a formal basis under the tutelage of Coach C.P. Blakeslee. Blakeslee, who led the Mavericks until

Dan McCarrell

1939, had an 18-year career that saw him build a 121-87 career record. He was replaced by Jim Clark, who posted some decent records throughout the early 1940s. Then, in 1945, Jim Witham took over behind the Maverick bench and led his club to a second-place finish at the 1947 National Association of Intercollegiate Basketball tournament (the precursor to NAIA). Mankato State Teachers College, which finished with a 17-11 record that year, was led by All-American Hank Epp. The Mavs won four straight post-season games before falling to Marshall, 73-59, in the NAIB national championship game. Witham would stay on until 1956, en route to posting an outstanding 161-72 career record.

Bill Morris took over in 1956 and over the next 11 seasons led Mankato to a 134-112 record. A couple of the stars of that era included Mountain Lake native John Schultz, who, from 1958-61, scored 1,720 points, a stat which still ranks second on MSU's all-time scoring list. One of five MSU players to have multiple 500-point seasons, a feat he accomplished twice, Schultz was the NIC MVP in 1961. Another star was Jon Hagen, who, from 1963-65, led the Mavericks to 48-25 record. Along the way Hagen racked up a single-game scoring record of 50 points against Northern Illinois in 1965. The program's record-holder for career free-throw percentage, at 90%, the 1964 NIC MVP still ranks third all-time in the NCAA in that category.

MSU's All-Time Scoring Leaders

1. Brian Koepnick	(1985-89)	1,754
2. John Schultz	(1957-61)	1,720
3. Curt Clark	(1976-79)	1,657
4. Pat Coleman	(1995-96)	1,623
5. Tim Wahi	(1977-81)	1,529

From 1972-84 Butch Raymond served as the team's head coach, and he led the Mavs to their first and only North Central Conference title and a NCAA regional tournament appearance in 1976. That year the school went through some major changes, going from College status to an official University. They also joined the Northern Intercollegiate Conference, and even decided to get politically correct by changing their mascot from the "Indians" to the "Mavericks." It was a special year on the court though. Led by All-American Elisha McSweeny, a two-time All-North Central Conference selection who led the league in scoring with 22.9 ppg. that season, MSU captured the NCC crown en route to a berth in the NCAA post-season tournament. There, the Mavs dropped a 72-67 double-over-time thriller to UW-Green Bay in first-round action before claiming third place with a 95-73 win over Nebraska-Omaha.

Raymond led the Mavericks to a 163-133 record during this period. One of the early stars of this era was Waseca native Gene Glynn, who holds most of the school's single-game, single-season and career records for assists and steals. Glynn, who played in Mankato from 1975-79, went on to become a coach with the Chicago Cubs. Raymond, who left Mankato to take over at rival St. Cloud in 1984, was then replaced by

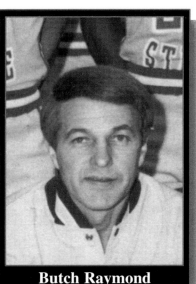

Butch Raymond

Career scoring leader Brian Koepnick tallied 1,754 points from 1985-89. Koepnick also owns the MSU single-season free throw percentage record with 92.9 in 1987-88, a mark that ranks as the 11th best in NCAA Division II history.

For 28 seasons, John Schultz held the title of MSU's career scoring leader with 1,720 that he racked up from 1957-61, and remains in second place in that category to this day. He one of only five Mavericks to have multiple 500 point scoring seasons, a feat he accomplished twice.

MSU single-season scoring leader Dave Gilreath had 716 points in 1984-85. Gilreath owns the North Central Conference record for field goals in a season when he connected on 210 shots in the 1984-85 campaign. He is second in MSU career points per game (20.55)

Single-game scoring record holder Jon Hagen had 50 vs. No. Illinois in 1965. Hagen is MSU's all-time leader in career free-throw percentage (90.0), a mark that stands third on the NCAA Division II all-time list. Hagen led the nation twice in free throw shooting percentage.

Elisha McSweeny averaged 26.1 ppg in North Central Conference in 1975-76, and still holds the North Central Conference record for career scoring average. McSweeney is the MSU career leader in points per game (25.22) and rebounds per game (12.26).

Gene Glynn (1975-79) holds most of MSU's single-game, single-season, and career records for assists and steals. Glynn, who is now the third base coach for the Chicago Cubs, also holds North Central Conference records in Assists Per Game in a season and in a career.

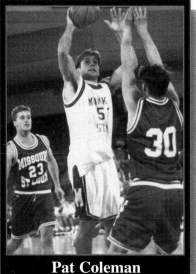

Pat Coleman

Dan McCarrell. He would go on to become an MSU coaching legend. In 2000-01, after 17 years, he retired as the program's all-time winningest coach with a career record of 284-189.

McCarrell's 1989-90 squad went 20-10, marking only the fourth time in the program's 65 years that a Maverick team has achieved 20 wins in a season. In 1997, McCarrell became the 21st active coach in NCAA Division II to pass the 500-career win plateau, and in the last game of the 1999-2000 season, the former North Park College skipper coached his 900th career game. He currently ranks in the top-10 for all-time victories in NCAA Division II Basketball, just 11 wins behind another Minnesota coaching legend, Hamline's Joe Hutton. (McCarell is also just ahead of Billy Tubbs of Texas Christian University for 45th on the NCAA all-time all-division coaching victory list, and just 16 wins behind such D-I college coaching legends as Duke's Mike Krzyzewski and Syracuse's Jim Boeheim.)

A noted teacher and strong strategist, McCarrell has coached several outstanding Maverick players. Among them include a trio who have led the conference in scoring: Dave Gilreath, who finished third in NCAA Division II in 1984-85 with 25.6 ppg; Brian Koepnick, who holds several MSU records and is the school's all-time leading scorer with 1,754 points; and Mankato native Pat Coleman, who earned All-America honors and was the NCC's MVP his senior season in 1996.

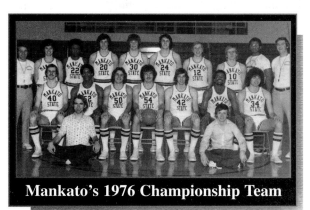

Mankato's 1976 Championship Team

Coleman, who averaged 23.4 points and 10.5 rebounds per game in his final season, ranks fourth on MSU's all-time scoring list with 1,623 points. (In the late 1990s the school, in an effort to bolster its image, also changed its name from Mankato State University to Minnesota State University.)

In 2000-01 MSU named former South Dakota State assistant Matt Margenthaler as its 10th coach. Margenthaler led the Mavs to an impressive 17-11 record during his inaugural campaign behind the Mankato bench. The future looks bright for these Mavs, who today play in one of the state's finest facilities, Bresnan Arena in Taylor Center. A state-of-the-art, 5,000-seat, multi-purpose facility which opened in the fall of 2000. The Taylor Center was a result of Minnesota State University, Mankato alum Glen Taylor's generous $8 million donation. The Timberwolves owner has given a lot to his alma mater, and they have responded by fielding some great teams.

The Taylor Center

St. Cloud State University

Founded in 1896, St. Cloud State University was once known primarily as a teacher's college. The school, which has been playing basketball for more than a century, has a long and storied hoops tradition. The first recorded game under inaugural coach Warren Hull, took place with the St. Cloud Normal School losing to Minneapolis Central High School, 13-10. From there they beat Park Rapids and Brainerd High Schools to round out that 1901 season. Then, in 1903, St. Cloud went undefeated and claimed the state's "Mythical" championship. Big wins that year came against Brainerd, Sauk Centre, and Minneapolis Central High Schools, as well as the Minneapolis Ag School. They also pounded on Anoka, 53-0, and Park Rapids, 52-1, too.

Legendary SCSD Coach Red Lynch took over from there and guided the program through 1929. One of his players, Sig Williams, is even given credit for inventing the one-handed pivot-shot before the rest of the country had even heard of it. SCSU brought home conference titles in 1909, 1910, 1913 and 1920. (Conference affiliations at that time were loosely based.) St. Cloud won its first official league title in 1923, as members of the Minnesota State College Conference. They added another one in 1930, under the tutelage of Coach John Weisman, before joining the Northern Teacher's Athletic Conference in 1932. (The team also opened Eastman Hall that year, which would serve as the home of Husky basketball until the opening of Halenbeck Hall in the 1960s.)

In 1936 Warren Kasch was named as the

Butch Raymond

Championship Seasons at SCSU

North Central Conference
1986, 1987, 1988

Northern Intercollegiate Conference
1941, 1943, 1946, 1956, 1957, 1958, 1959, 1960, 1962, 1963, 1964, 1965, 1966, 1968, 1969, 1970, 1976

Minnesota State College Conference
1930, 1923

SCSU's All-Americans

1998	Jon Hinzman
1988	Reggie Perkins
1986	Kevin Catron
1985	Kevin Catron
1966	Izzy Schmeising
1957	Vern Baggenstoss

Orieon Thurston

school's head coach. He went on to coach the Huskies for 11 seasons, while posting a 119-73 record. In 1941 Coach Kasch led SCSC to its first NIC title with a 13-3 record, and brought home another title in 1943, before taking off two seasons due to World War II.

Then, in 1946, George Lynch returned to coach for one season and led his Huskies to a 12-2 record and another NIC title. Les Luymes took over as the head coach in 1951 and went on to post a four-year record of 50-36. Ken Novak and Roger Westlund were a couple of the early stars of this era, each becoming members of the 1,000-point club.

The 1964 NIC Championship Team

In 1956 Paul Meadows was named as the head coach, immediately turning SCSU into an NIC power. The Huskies went on to win NIC titles in 1956, 1957 and 1958 under his leadership. One of the program's brightest eras, from 1956-70, the Huskies won no less than 13 Northern Intercollegiate Conference championships. Under the leadership of Coach Red Severson, the Huskies won nine NIC crowns from 1959-69 alone. Severson guided the Huskies to the NAIA playoffs six times, including trips to the national Finals in 1962, 1964 and 1968. In his 11 seasons, Severson posted an outstanding 207-66 record.

Brothers Roger and Dave Westlund were the next stars for the program, leading the Huskies into the early 1950s. Vern "Moose" Baggenstoss was the program's first All-American in 1958, as he led the club to three straight NIC crowns in his tenure on the court. Izzy Schmeising was the next NAIA All-American, in 1966, and still ranks on many of the school's all-time record books. (He once lit up Michigan Tech for 56 points in a game in 1966!)

All in all the Huskies were dominant from 1941-1976, when they won 17 conference titles and produced many of the state's top players. In 1965 Halenbeck Hall opened and in 1968 the Huskies, led by Coach Noel Olson and his star players: Terry Porter, Mike Trewick and Tom Ditty, made a trip to the NAIA finals. Olson would remain as the team's head coach until 1981, ultimately finishing with a modest 155-162 record.

Jason Kron

In 1974 the Huskies gained their first ticket to the NCAA Division II playoffs, where they defeated North Dakota State in the first round before suffering losses to Kentucky Wesleyan and North Dakota. They captured another NIC title in 1976 thanks to the efforts of team stars Al Anderstrom and Bryan Robs. In the early 1980s the big story was the amazing play of Dan Hagen, who became the program's all-time scoring leader in 1981 with 2,136 points.

That next year the Huskies left the NSIC to open play in the North Central Conference. Shortly thereafter former Mankato State Coach Butch Raymond began what would amount to a 13-year run as SCSU's head coach. Raymond would go on to post a 231-142 record with the Huskies. In 1986, behind the power of All-America selection Kevin Catron and All-NCC choice John Anderson, SCSU won its first NCC title with a 26-4 overall record. The team also advanced to the NCAA playoffs for the first time since 1974, ultimately losing in the first round.

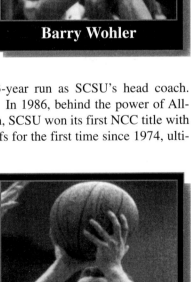
Barry Wohler

In 1987 the Huskies, led by All-American Reggie Perkins, won another NCC title and also advanced to NCAA "Elite Eight" quarterfinals — this time losing a heart-breaker to Delta State, 78-73, in overtime. (Perkins would go on to play with the famed Harlem Globetrotters!) They won another crown in 1988 and in 1992 the team posted a 20-12 record and made it back yet again to the NCAA playoffs.

In 1995 Chisholm standout Joel McDonald ended his brilliant career with 1,565 points — good for third in SCSU's records. Two years later long-time assistant and former player Kevin Schlagel was named as the new head coach at SCSU. In 1998 the Huskies finished in second place in the NCC as Jon Hinzman earned NCC MVP and All-America honors. He would finish his illustrious career in St. Cloud with 1,343 points and 804 rebounds.

The 2000 season saw SCSU reach the playoffs for the first time in seven seasons with an 18-10 record. The Huskies advanced to the

The 1986 NCC Championship Team

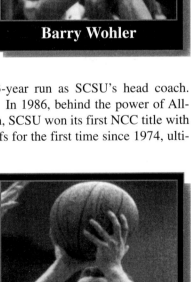
Dan Ward

NCAA Division II North Central Region Tournament in Denver, where the season ended with a 90-80 loss to Wayne State. Rado Rancik was named to the AII-NCC squad, while Jason Kron was the NCC Freshman and Defensive Player of the Year. Then, in 2001, the Huskies, led by All-Conference stars Rado Rancik, Forrest Witt and Jason Kron, posted a 25-6 record, the third best in school history. With that they made their seventh ever NCAA Playoff appearance, their second straight. In addition, they won the NCC Conference Tournament.

For the past century St. Cloud State has continued to build on its rich tradition of hardwood success, and has its sights set on only get better in the years to come. In fact, St. Cloud State University currently has a 1,023-673 overall record, which ranks them 29th in NCAA Division II victories.

Today Coach Schlagel's Huskies are looking great. The Rush City native has taken over a tremendous program and continues to produce great players and solid teams which are always competitive.

Todd Bouman was a two-sport star at St. Cloud State before going on to become the Minnesota Vikings' back-up quarterback

SCSU's All-Time Scoring Leaders

1. Dan Hagen	(1977-81)	2,136	19.8
2. Terry Porter	(1964-68)	1,694	16.6
3. Joel McDonald	(1991-93)	1,583	13.8
4. Reggie Perkins	(1984-88)	1,582	14.2
5. Jon Hinzman	(1994-98)	1,543	14.3

Joel McDonald

The History of the NAIA

In 1937 a group of Kansas City businessmen got together to organize a college basketball tournament to replace the Amateur Athletic Union tournament, which had moved to Denver. The result was the formation of the National Small College Basketball Tournament, which featured the champions of eight Midwestern conferences. The field expanded to 32 teams in 1938 and in 1940 the National Association of Intercollegiate Basketball (NAIB) was created with the purposes of operating the tournament and to establish standards of eligibility for member schools and conferences. The NAIB was renamed the National Association of Intercollegiate Athletics (NAIA) in 1952, and has been going strong ever since. In 1992 the NAIA reorganized into two divisions (D-II and D-III) and began facilitating national tournaments for each.

The Upper Midwest Athletic Conference

An affiliate of the National Association of Intercollegiate Athletics (NAIA), the Upper Midwest Athletic Conference (UMAC) is also affiliated with the National Christian College Athletic Association (NCCAA). Several of the schools located in Minnesota play various MIAC schools, and provide countless kids the opportunity to play ball at the next level.

School	Nickname	Location
Martin Luther	Knights	New Ulm
Crown College	Crusaders	St. Bonifacius
Northwestern	Eagles	St. Paul
St. Scholastica	Saints	Duluth
Mount Senario	Saints	Ladysmith, (Wis.)
Northland	Lumberjacks	Ashland, (Wis.)

Tourney Time!

March Madness in the Land of 10,000 Lakes can only mean one thing — the ushering in of the annual State High School Basketball Tournament. One of the largest tournaments in the entire United States, the "tourney" has become an institution in Minnesota. And, while today there are several classes of tournament play for different sized schools, back in the day, there was just one — which made for some awesome match-ups between tiny rural towns and major suburban power-houses. Like it was so brilliantly portrayed in the movie "Hoosiers," Minnesota has also had its share of amazing David vs. Goliath stories.

The "Big Dance" has also seen quite a bit of real-estate through the years as well. From what started at the Sayles-Hill Gymnasium at Carleton College in Northfield back in 1913, has moved to the Kenwood Armory in Minneapolis, to the University of Minnesota's Fieldhouse (later renamed as Williams Arena), to the Minneapolis and St. Paul Auditoriums, to Bloomington's Met Center, to St. Paul's Civic Center, to the Metrodome, to St. Thomas, to the Roy Wilkins Auditorium in St. Paul, to the University of Minnesota's Women's Sports Pavillion, and finally to the Xcel Energy Center in St. Paul — where it will hopefully get comfortable and stay a while!

It has been a wild ride to say the least. But to fully understand just how special this wonderful event really is, you have to go back — all the way back to the beginning, when, in 1913, a man by the name of Claude J. Hunt, long considered to be the "Father of the Minnesota State Basketball Tournament," had a vision. This is the story of our beloved "State Tourney."

By the turn of the century high schools throughout the country, including in Minnesota, were offering the new sport of basketball. What was started by Dr. James Naismith as a fad exercise for students in physical education classes at Massachusetts' Springfield College, had quietly turned into a national phenomenon. Gone were the peach baskets and soccer balls, and in were hardwood floors and rubber-bumper sneakers. In Minnesota, where the winters were brutal, it was shaping up to be the ultimate compliment to hockey, only this was much warmer!

So, in 1913, shortly after the new Sayles-Hill Gymnasium was completed at Northfield's Carleton College, the school's Athletic Director, Claude J. Hunt, decided that it would be the perfect venue to host what he envisioned to be the first-ever State High School Basketball Tournament. The fan interest was there, and so was the talent — as evidenced by the fact that many of the state's kids were going on to fill up the rosters of college teams around the country at that time. Sure, there had been "mythical" state champion basketball teams in the past (Madison was named as the champion in 1910 for instance), but they were mythical in the sense that they were merely chosen as the titleist by various newspaper reporters — many of whom would pick certain teams in their areas, and even the ones that fed them the best when they came to visit! It was unscientific to say the least, and the fans wanted there to be a system in which the teams themselves could finally play against one another at the end of the season to determine a "true" state champ. With that, Mr. Hunt went ahead and began organizing the logistics for what would become the inaugural state high school tournament.

1913: Fosston vs. Mountain Lake

Hunt immediately started corresponding with nearly every school throughout the state, requesting them to submit their team's season records. Some 20 schools responded, and with that, Hunt, along with a group of faculty members, invited what turned out to be 13 teams to participate in the first state high school tournament. They were: Austin, Blue Earth, Faribault, Fosston, Grand Rapids, Luverne, Madison, Mankato, Mountain Lake, Plainview, Red Wing, Stillwater and Willmar. (There was originally supposed to be 12 teams in the tourney, but Blue Earth, which first declined because of too many sick kids on the squad, got healthy, and was allowed back in.)

"Most of the schools that year were from the southern Minnesota area, but you could easily tell from the beginning that the meet would soon have state-wide appeal," Hunt would later recall.

The teams then gathered in Northfield that first weekend of April to play for the so-called "Mythical" state championship. (The first tourney was mythical because not all of the teams in the state were entered.) There, teams of all skill levels came to compete against one another. Rules had to be laid out, as per the fact that many of the schools were playing under "house rules," with their own interpretations of Dr. Naismith's original guidelines. Some teams were better than others, but all "fared well and had fun".

Mountain Lake beat Blue Earth in the tourney's first game, 40-9, followed by Fosston, which beat Willmar, 27-17 and Plainview edging Austin in a close one. Then, in the evening games, Mankato topped Faribault, 27-22, Luverne defeated Grand Rapids, 32-17, and Stillwater crushed poor Madison, 32-4, in a game in which Madison did not even score a field goal. In Day Two, Mountain Lake edged Red Wing 49-28, Luverne upset Mankato, and Fosston knocked off Plainview, 38-27. From there Mountain Lake beat Stillwater, 31-24, and Fosston upset Luverne, 36-26, in the semifinals.

Then, in the championship game, witnessed by some 2,000 enthusiastic fans, tiny Fosston, from northwestern Minnesota, defeated Mountain Lake by the final score of 29-27, and thus became the inaugural state champs. Fosston, who's starting line-up averaged a whopping 130 pounds, rallied from a 16-16 half-time stalemate behind the stellar play of Ralph Movold, and simply held on down the stretch.

News quickly spread that the tournament was a big success, and before long dozens of other schools were writing to Hunt to tell him that they too wanted to participate. At that point Hunt knew that he had created a monster, and was going to need some serious help. He consulted with some other coaches from around the Midwest and then came up with a plan to accommodate all of the new entries.

"It wasn't long before we felt that running an invitational tournament was not fair, since too many schools with good teams were being left out," said Hunt. "It was then that we figured that we would have to hold

THE 1913 STATE TOURNAMENT CHAMPIONS

This was the first State High School Championship basketball team, Fosston in 1913. Left to right, Ralph (Curly) Movold, Larry Rue, Al Hanson, Charles Quarness and Carl (Cully) Fogelberg with Leo Movold holding the basketball.

FIRST STATE TOURNAMENT EVER

The Inaugural 1913 State Champs from Fosston

Carleton's Sayles-Hill Gymnasium

elimination tournaments, and breaking down the state in districts followed with those winners advancing into the state meet at Carleton."

So, that next year a committee of high school officials got together to devise a method for selecting the teams and establishing the initial eligibility rules for inter-scholastic play. Ten "congressional districts" were then formed to comprise the basis of qualification. (Although in the beginning, nine finalists competed in the tournament, with the exception the fifth district, in the Minneapolis area, which wasn't represented.) However, since all congressional districts did not have teams, the number of tournament participants varied from year to year. (This number grew as the tournament grew in years to come.)

1914: Stillwater vs. Winona

The second annual Minnesota High School Basketball Tournament was once again held at Carleton College with nine district champion teams this time filling out the field. (There was supposed to be 10, but District Five didn't send a representative.) They included: Winona (1st), Mountain Lake (2nd), Stillwater (3rd), St. Paul Humboldt (4th), Aitkin (6th), Madison (7th), Hibbing (8th), Fosston (9th) and Howard Lake (10th).

The tourney opened with the defending champs from Fosston sweeping a pair of games over St. Paul Humboldt, 23-21, and Mountain Lake, 19-18, to advance to the quarterfinals. Stillwater then spanked Aitkin, 57-11, while Winona and Hibbing beat Howard Lake and Madison, respectively. In the semi's. Winona defeated Hibbing, 25-20, while Stillwater upset mighty Fosston, 32-19, to make it to the Finals. There, in the championship game, Stillwater jumped out to a 12-1 first half lead over Winona and then cruised to a 30-4 victory. Ronald Parkhurst led the way for the Ponies by scoring a game-high 18 points. Oh, and just how tough was Stillwater's defense? Winona didn't make a field goal throughout the entire game!

1915: Red Wing vs. Mountain Lake

The 1915 tourney featured eight new teams, with only Fosston and Mountain Lake returning from the previous year. St. Paul Mechanic Arts beat Breckenridge, 31-22, in the opener, while Mountain Lake edged Willmar, 29-22, in Game Two. In the afternoon games Red Wing defeated Fosston, 27-21, while Virginia narrowly got past Lake City, 27-26. Then, in the night games, Bemidji beat Rush City, 32-14, while Mountain Lake won its second contest of the day, this time defeating Mechanic Arts, 30-20.

Mountain Lake beat Bemidji, 35-28, and Red Wing eliminated Virginia, 28-11, in the semifinals, to set up an all-southern Minnesota final. There, some 1,200 fans showed up to watch Red Wing, which had somehow miraculously played the entire season without a coach, jump out to a commanding 18-3 half-time lead. Mountain Lake rallied back in the second half, but came up short though, losing down the stretch, 30-18. Incredibly, Heibert scored all 18 points for Mountain Lake!

1916: Virginia vs. Mechanic Arts

By 1916 the tournament had grown into quite the event. Carleton was doing a great job in hosting the gala, but knew that it needed some big-time help to get it to the next level. With that, the Minnesota State High School League (MSHSL) was officially formed, assuming full responsibility for the tournament thereafter. With the formation of the new organization, a constitution was adopted and by-laws providing uniform eligibility rules for interscholastic play were established.

The tourney, which was still being held at Carleton, kicked off with Rush City upsetting Little Falls, 32-23, followed by Mechanic Arts beating the local favorites from Northfield High in a real barn-burner, 15-7. From there Austin eliminated Willmar, Virginia beat Slayton, 39-10, Fergus Falls edged Thief River Falls, 27-24, and in the final game of the day Mechanic Arts defeated Rush City, 27-16.

In the first semifinal, Virginia, led by the Rooney brothers, held off Austin, 33-30, in the tourney's first-ever (five minute) overtime game. Mechanic Arts then got by Fergus Falls, 12-7, to advance to the championship game where they would face Virginia. There, Virginia's stiffling defense held Mechanic Arts to a paltry pair of free throws in the second half, as they went on to take the title, 20-9.

1917: Rochester vs. Mountain Lake

Due to a change in districting, 12 teams competed in the fifth annual tourney. In the opening round games New Ulm, Albert Lea, Rochester, Sandstone, Mountain Lake and Fosston all got wins, while in the evening Rochester pounded Sandstone, 42-15, and Albert Lea beat New Ulm, 25-11.

In the semifinals Rochester was all over Fosston, 28-7, and Mountain Lake escaped past Albert Lea, 19-17. Then, in the Finals, Rochester, behind the scoring of Bay and Mattson, jumped out to an 11-2 half-time lead over Mountain Lake and never looked back. With their superior size and great teamwork, they went on to win their first title, 19-8.

1918: Waseca vs. Duluth Central

Fully 164 teams throughout the state of Minnesota, representing 14 districts, battled for the right to travel down to Northfield this year. The contrasting styles were evident, as Waseca beat New Ulm in the opening round, 44-12, while Foston edged Buffalo by the final score of just 13-9. Other first round scores included: Albert Lea over Ortonville, 40-14, Detroit Lakes over Litchfield, 23-19, Duluth Central barely edging Little Falls, 25-24 and St. Paul Humboldt all over Pine City, 37-6.

The quarterfinals featured contrasting team strategies as Albert Lea edged Lake City, 14-9, Waseca beat Detroit Lakes, 35-11, Duluth Central escaped past Humboldt, 32-31 and Fosston crushed Windom, 30-13. Then, in the first semifinal game Waseca rallied back to beat Albert Lea, 18-14, while Duluth

Stillwater's Frank "Flash" Gordon was the undisputed Michael Jordan of the 1800s, having (unofficially) averaged nearly 100 points per game in the 1849 season alone!

Central cruised past Fosston, 34-19.

The Finals saw Duluth Central jump out to an early 7-2 lead, with O'Neil, Ritchie and Shaw finding the basket. L. Juhnke and Jacobson then tied the score at 7-7, followed by Wyman's basket to give Waseca a 10-7 lead at the half. But the second period was all Waseca though, as they came out and outscored Duluth 14-3 and cruised to a 24-10 victory.

(Incidentally, Duluth Central would go on to represent Minnesota by playing in a national tournament in Chicago that year, beating teams from Ohio and Indiana before losing to an Illinois club in the Finals.)

1919: Albert Lea vs. New Ulm

The 1919 tourney opened with the following scores: Albert Lea over Red Wing, 27-18, Little Falls over Buffalo, 33-6, Barnesville over Pipestone, 22-16, Chisholm over St. Paul Humboldt, 23-15, Olivia over Wheaton, 18-14 and New Ulm over Sandstone, 42-22. Albert Lea then beat Fosston, 32-13, in the first round of the quarterfinals, followed by Little Falls blowing out

The 1920 State Champs from Red Wing

Barnesville, 39-6, Chisholm beating Olivia, 29-14, and New Ulm narrowly getting by Waseca, 13-12. How exciting was this one? While neither team could score for the first five minutes of the game, the contest was won on a thrilling last-second jumper, by Schulke, with just six seconds left to play in the game.

The semifinals were equally as exciting, as Albert Lea beat Little Falls, 22-18, in a rough and tumble game which saw several players get kicked out. Then, in the other game, New Ulm hung on to beat Chisholm, 26-21, to advance to the championship game. There, Albert Lea absolutely dominated, racing to an impressive 18-1 half-time lead and cruising to a 37-8 blow-out.

1920: Red Wing vs. Mankato

In 1920 the MSHSL divided the state into 16 geographical districts, with one team from each qualifying for tournament play. That year the opening round saw the following: Red Wing beat Little Falls, 22-10, Stillwater got past Morton, 18-14, New Ulm beat Kasota, 23-11, Faribault pounced on Fergus Falls, 32-9, Mankato edged Buffalo, 13-9, Fulda beat Stephen in a real scoring fest, 11-6, Virginia topped Wheaton, 17-9, Minneapolis South got by Sandstone, 16-14, and Red Wing had just enough to beat Stillwater, 20-18.

The second round games saw Faribault knock off New Ulm, 21-16, Mankato edged Fulda, 14-10, and Virginia topped South, 19-15. There were then two semifinal games played and both were upsets. The first was Red Wing, which defeated Faribault, 24-14, followed by Mankato, which terminated Virginia by the final score of 23-14. Then, in the Finals, more than 2,000 people crammed into Sayles-Hill Gymnasium that night, with several hundred more being turned away at the door, to watch Red Wing do battle with Mankato. Red Wing rallied back from an early deficit in this one to take a 9-6 half-time lead. From there Mankato pulled ahead by one, 9-8, only to

The 1921 State Champs from Mpls. Central

see Red Wing once again rally back behind Lidberg's 13 points, this time for good to win the state championship, 21-10.

1921: Minneapolis Central vs. New Ulm

The 1921 state tournament's opening round saw plenty of good action: Worthington beat Wheaton, 20-15, Mankato upended Morton, 26-15, Hibbing topped the defending champs from Red Wing, which was without their two biggest stars, C. Hartupee & K. Brown, who were sick, 27-20, New Ulm edged Fosston, 30-25, Minneapolis Central escaped Faribault, 24-20, Sandstone eliminated Arlington, 28-21, Alexandria got by White Bear, 23-19, and St Cloud breezed by Buffalo, 27-20.

Second round action saw Mankato pounding Worthington, 20-6, New Ulm getting by Hibbing in a thriller, 23-21, Minneapolis Central having no trouble with Sandstone, 31-22, and St. Cloud topping Alexandria, 39-23. Then, in the semi's, Minneapolis Central blew out St. Cloud, 33-14, while New Ulm eliminated Mankato, 21-11, to set the stage for a much-anticipated Finals. In the big game

Minneapolis Central jumped out to a quick 7-4 lead over New Ulm in the first quarter and increased it to 12-7 at the half. From there the Mill City boys got soft, letting New Ulm creep back into the game to get to within one point in the third. But, in the final period, Central limited New Ulm to just one measly free-throw and hung on to win the tilt by the final score of 19-15. Incredibly, Central's team captain, Martin Norton, scored 17 of his team's 19 points.

1922: Red Wing vs. Madison

First round action of the 1922 big dance saw Wadena beat New Ulm, 27-17, Stillwater get by St. Peter, 30-23, Mankato outscore St. Paul Johnson, 23-15, Madison eliminate Little Falls, 28-15, Sandstone upend Mountain Lake, 27-17, Red Wing top Crookston, 33-27, Austin trounce Hancock, 31-17, and Duluth Central narrowly get by Buffalo, 19-18.

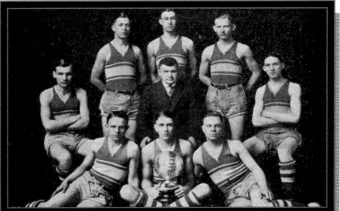

The 1922 State Champs from Red Wing

The 1923 State Champs from Aurora

In round two Wadena had no trouble with Stillwater, 25-15, Madison barely got past Mankato in a defensive slug-fest, 13-12, Red Wing pummel Sandstone, 46-14, and Duluth Central edge Austin by the final score of 36-25. From there Red Wing got past Duluth Central, 30-25, and Madison squeezed by Wadena 36-34, in the semifinals.

More than 1,000 fans came by train from Red Wing to watch their team match up against Madison in the Finals, and they would not be disappointed. Red Wing came out of the gates swinging and led from start to finish to win the title, 34-27, thus continuing their amazing 24-game winning streak.

1923: Aurora vs. Austin

By 1923 the 16-team tournament had gotten so big that it finally had to be moved from Northfield and into Minneapolis, where it was relocated into the Kenwood Armory — a venue which had much more seating and was more centrally located. In opening round play Rochester dumped Madison, 34-10, St. Peter defeated St. Paul Johnson, 26-23, Austin was all over South St. Paul, 28-8, Blue Earth barely eked out a 18-15 win over Crookston, Aurora punished Marshall, 38-16, St. Cloud edged Minneapolis Central, 18-16, Hopkins got by Wadena in a thriller, 17-16, and Hancock topped St. James, 29-13.

Quarterfinal action then saw Rochester beating St. Peter, 16-11, Austin edging Blue Earth, 14-13, Aurora whipping St. Cloud, 23-9, and tiny Hancock upending Hopkins, 19-8. In the semifinals Rochester jumped out to a quick 11-8 lead over Austin by half-time, only to see the Packers mount a serious comeback in the second and take the game by the final of 22-16. Then, in the other semifinal contest, Aurora eliminated Hancock 20-7.

Some 3,500 fans showed up in the championship game to watch tiny Aurora battle Austin. There, Aurora, led by Pete Dan Colovic, took control of the game with a 10-1 lead in the first. By half-time it was 12-5, and by the time the final whistle blew, Aurora was on top, 24-14, to win its first-ever title. (From there Aurora went on to represent Minnesota in the National High School Basketball Tournament in Chicago, where they were upended in the opening round by Lorain High School, of Ohio, 28-24.)

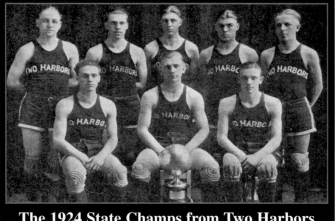

The 1924 State Champs from Two Harbors

1924: Two Harbors vs. Minneapolis South

The 1924 tourney opened with McIntosh topping Morton, 19-16, Two Harbors eliminating Princeton, 17-7, St. Cloud beating a very tough Fairmont squad, 29-7, St. Paul Johnson spanking Winona, 28-17, Tyler doubling Montevideo, 22-11, Owatonna pounding Pipestone, 26-15, Moorhead edging Willmar, 22-19, and Minneapolis South having no problem with Kasota, 22-14.

In the quarters, Two Harbors defeated McIntosh, 31-18, St. Cloud jumped all over St Paul Johnson, 28-8, Moorhead handled Tyler 25-18, and Minneapolis South eliminated Owatonna, 19-14. In the semifinal games played that night, Two Harbors came up with the upset of the tournament when they defeated the odds-on favorites from St Cloud, 23-14, while Minneapolis South beat Moorhead, 25-14, to reach the Finals.

Two Harbors, the Cinderella story of the tourney, jumped out to an early lead over Minneapolis South in the championship game. But South, to the delight of the 8,000 fans in attendance, rallied back time and again to make it interesting. South threatened late in the third, but Two Harbors pulled away in the fourth. Led by Center Howard Johnson and Guard Herman Anderson, Two Harbors went on to win it by the final of 21-12.

(Two Harbors then defeated Jackson High, in Michigan, 25-24, in the first round of the National Scholastic High School Basketball Tournament in Chicago, only to lose to Emporia of Kansas, 39-9, in round two.)

1925: Mechanic Arts vs. Buffalo

The 1925 State Champs from Mechanic Arts

By 1925 there were 32 districts in the state which were then divided into eight regions. As a result, just eight teams would qualify for post-season play from that point forward. In addition, the Minneapolis High Schools decided not to be represented in the tournament, choosing instead to participate in a play-off event of their own.

The tourney got under way with New Prague, which was led by John Matyas and Jerry Vanek, cruising to a 23-12 victory over Austin. Game two saw Buffalo beat up on Moorhead, 21-13, while Game Three featured Faribault, and their high-flyer, Fred Krampf, eliminating Grand Rapids, 25-11. Then, in the last quarterfinal, a highly favored Mechanic Arts team hung on to beat Wayzata in a defensive battle, 12-9.

In semifinal action Buffalo beat New Prague, 28-18, while the powerful Mechanic Arts team knocked off Faribault, 21-11, even shutting them out in the fourth quarter. Now, in the Finals, Mechanic Arts' defense was awesome, allowing just six Buffalo points in the first half followed by just two throughout the entire second half. Mechanic Arts, behind Nelson and Jung, cruised from there and went on to take the crown, 20-8.

(Mechanic Arts then went on to beat Hume Fogy High School, of Nashville, 22-19, on Jimmy Dunn's last-minute shot, in the opening round of the National Scholastic High School Basketball Tournament held in Chicago. The Toilers then beat Clarkston, of Washington, 25-19, in the second round, before finally losing a heart-breaker in Round Three to Westport, of Kansas City, 29-28. The annual tournament would be abandoned shortly thereafter.)

1926: Gaylord vs. Gilbert

Gaylord, behind Lichttenegger's 13-point effort, opened tournament play by bumping off a favored Moorhead team, 18-14. In the second game a pair of veteran tourney teams, Austin and Wayzata, hooked up. Tied at 8-8 at the half, the Packers simply hung on to beat Wayzata, 14-12. In the evening games Buffalo scored 17 fourth quarter points en route to rallying past Winona, 22-18, while tiny Gilbert defeated Minneapolis Edison in the final game of the day, 29-11

The 1926 State Champs from Gaylord

The first semifinal had Gaylord jumping out to a 11-4 half-time lead over Austin, and then cruising, behind Lichttenegger's 16 points, to a 22-12 win. Game Two then saw Gilbert double Buffalo, 22-11, in a game where the speedy Gilbert team held Buffalo to just two points throughout the entire second half.

Two small schools, Gilbert and Gaylord, then hooked up in the title tilt, with both defenses playing great. Gilbert quickly grabbed the early lead over Gaylord thanks to the stellar play of Mestnick, who wound up scoring all of the points for his Gilbert team. Then, with the score tied 5-5 at the half, Gaylord hung on down the stretch to upset Gilbert by the final score of 13-9. For Gaylord, which had a population of only 800 souls and just 27 boys in the entire high school, it was an amazing accomplishment.

(With the win Gaylord would now represent Minnesota in the National High School Basketball Tournament held at the University of Chicago. Incredibly, just hours after the team had won the state title, more than $500 was raised by passing a hat to finance the trip to the Windy City. And, if that weren't enough, about 300 fans from Gaylord made the trek to watch their team do battle. The 40-team tourney, which featured all but eight state champions from around the country, got underway with Gaylord beating Memphis, 25-24, in a thriller. While the game was being played the telegraph depot back at Gaylord was overrun with local townspeople who couldn't make the trip, but wanted to find out the score. Gaylord then went on to beat Technical High School of Atlanta, 23-7, in the second round, but then got knocked off by Fargo, in Round Three, 25-20. Down, but not out, tiny Gaylord had certainly made their hometown, as well as the state of Minnesota, very proud.)

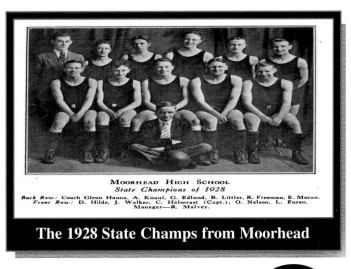

The 1927 State Champs from Mpls. South

1927: Minneapolis South vs. Excelsior

Wanting to put more of an emphasis on the consolation title, the league decided to mandate that every team in the tournament would now play in at least two games. (Previously the losers of the semifinal game met for the consolation title.)

The 1927 tourney got underway with Faribault, led by Captain Hildebrandt and Fay Butterwick, who each tallied 14 and 12 points, respectively, beating up on Moorhead, 30-16. Excelsior had little trouble in eliminating the kids from Bagley. Excelsior's Steve Eddy led all scorers with 9 points, as his squad cruised to a 27-10 victory. Minneapolis South then ended New Ulm's 21-game winning streak with a 23-13 triumph in Game Three, while Appleton disposed of Albert Lea, 33-17, on H. Schoening's 16-point effort.

In the semis it was Excelsior's Steve Eddy, who tallied 13 points, who paced his club to a 16-14 victory over Appleton. Then, in the other semifinal, South outlasted Faribault, 23-17, on Tverra's 8 points. South continued to roll through the Finals by next beating Excelsior, 32-13. South led 10-7 at half-time and held Excelsior scoreless in the fourth quarter to cruise to an easy victory. Tverra, was again the leading scorer with 13 points, while his teammate, Westman, added eight as well.

1928: Moorhead vs. Edison

In 1928 the tournament was moved to the spacious University of Minnesota Field House, later known as Williams Arena, and it got off to a thrilling start when New Prague's Vanek scored the game-winning overtime basket to beat Excelsior, 15-13. Moorhead then scored a close 13-12 victory over Virginia, while Northfield, behind the scoring of Reber and Newly, ripped Austin, 30-22. In the final quarterfinal contest, a very speedy Minneapolis Edison squad knocked off Appleton, 19-16, thanks to Petroske's nine-point effort.

Edison then held off Northfield, 28-22, in the first semifinal game, while a sharp shooting Moorhead club, paced by Cliff Halmrast's 22-point outing, scored 25 second half points and went on to crush New Prague, 37-17. The championship game turned out to be a classic, as a sensational sec-

MOORHEAD HIGH SCHOOL
State Champions of 1928
Back Row: Coach Glenn Hanna, A. Knauf, G. Edlund, B. Littler, R. Freeman, E. Moran.
Front Row: D. Hilde, J. Walker, C. Halmrast (Capt.), O. Nelson, L. Euren.
Manager—R. Malvey.

The 1928 State Champs from Moorhead

The 1929 State Champs from Moorhead

Back Row (Left to Right): G. A. Hanna (Coach), Marquardt, Littler, Fridlund, Nelson (Mascot)
Front Row (Left to Right): Malvey, Moran (Capt.), Euren, Hilde, Knauf.

ond quarter rally by Moorhead lifted the Spuds to a 29-16 win over Minneapolis Edison. Down 8-1 at the end of the first quarter, Moorhead rallied to score 10 points to make it 12-11 at half time. Moorhead then pushed ahead in the third quarter and by the fourth was up, 20-15. Freeman and Petroske then led the charge down the stretch as they cruised to a commanding 13-point victory.

1929: Moorhead vs. Red Wing

St. Cloud Tech recorded the first win of the 1929 tournament by edging Preston, 18-14. Moorhead topped Ely in Game Two, 25-22, thanks to Malvey's last-second game-winner. Game Three then saw Red Wing, which was led by six-foot-two Center Wilburn Olson, the tournament's tallest player, upend Willmar, 24-18. In the final game of the day Mechanic Arts beat Hendricks, 23-18, behind the solid play of Forward Welsey Anderson.

Moorhead pounded St. Cloud Tech, 31-18, in the first semifinal, while Red Wing Guard Lawrence Santleman nailed what proved to be the game-winning free-throws in an 18-16 victory Mechanic Arts in the other. A crowd of over 10,000 fans then showed up to watch the defending champs from Moorhead battle Red Wing in the championship game. They would not be disappointed either, as this one came down to the wire. With the Spuds ahead 14-5 in the third period, the Wingers mounted a comeback. They got it to within two points with just a few seconds left and were thrust into overtime when Winger Guard Kenneth Kerman intercepted a Moorhead pass to tie the game 14-14. Nordly scored a field goal to send Red Wing ahead 16-14 but Malvey's basket tied the game for the Spuds. That's when Moorhead Center Bliss Littler took over and nailed a pair of game-winning field goals to give Moorhead a 20-16 victory and their second straight title.

The 1930 State Champs from Mechanic Arts

1930: Mechanic Arts vs. Moorhead

Moorhead opened the tourney by showing its power in a stunning 27-10 defeat over Wells, which had allowed its opposition an average of just eight points throughout the sub-district and regional games. Redwood Falls almost pulled off the upset of the day when it jumped out to a 9-3 half-time lead over Chisholm, but Chisholm exploded in the second half for 23 big points to smother the Falls, 26-13. Red Wing then downed Appleton, 34-21, in Game Three, while Mechanic Arts beat up on Columbia Heights, 31-15, in the finale.

Moorhead and Chisholm then met head-on in the opening round of the semifinals. Chisholm got off to an 11-8 lead by the half only to see Moorhead, behind the scoring of Moran, Marquardt and Knauf, rally back to take a 19-12 victory. Then, in the second game of the day, Mechanic Arts tipped Red Wing, 19-15, to advance to the Finals. There, they just kept on rolling, and beat up on favored Moorhead, 23-13, for the state crown. Delmont led the way for Mechanic Arts, by scoring 10 points in the big win.

The 1931 State Champs from Glencoe

Back Row, Left to Right: Coach Jack Sterrett, Waldron Rogers, Glen Barnum, Bud Thoeny and Werner Michaelson, Faculty Manager.
Middle Row, Left to Right: Shamla, Trainer; Bob Lindner, Captain Walter Kruger and LeRoy Karstens.
Front Row: Arvid Brinkman, Milo Levins, Jimmy Baker.

1931: Glencoe vs. Buffalo

Glencoe kicked off the 1931 tournament by hammering Rochester, 16-7, showing why the Rockets' defense was one of the top in the state. Chisholm then rolled Bemidji, 23-14, while Buffalo, thanks to Thompson and Bauer's late buckets, narrowly got past Moorhead, 22-20, despite the fact that the Bison's tallest player was just five-foot-nine. Mankato then beat St. Paul Central, 22-18, in the final quarterfinal contest.

Buffalo, led by Gordon Mills and Chester Thompson, routed Mankato in the opening semifinal contest, 28-11, outscoring Kato 19-5 in the third period alone, while Glencoe squeaked by Chisholm in the other semi, 15-14, on LeRoy Karsten's last-second game-winning jumper. With that, it was Glencoe vs. Buffalo in the Finals, with Glencoe rallying back from an early 7-4 deficit to cruise to a 22-14 victory. Karsten, Baker and Rogers all played well for Glencoe, as the team celebrated its first ever title.

The 1932 State Champs from Thief River Falls

Left to Right: Lloyd Aanstad, John Langseth, Wendell Kielty, Arnold Stadum, Paul Dahl, Arthur Myrom, Ingvold Hendrickson, Lester Ihle, Captain John Chommie, Lawrence Nicholson, Coach Roger W. Dooley.

1932: Thief River Falls vs. Chisholm

Thief River Falls ousted Balaton in the opening round of the 1932 quarterfinals, thanks to the outstanding play of Center Lloyd Aanstad, who had 10 points in the 31-17 victory. Winona then beat Crosby-Ironton by the 27-15 score, due in large part to the efforts of George Davis, who scored 10 points in the game. Game Three saw Chisholm outscore Princeton, 20-16, while the finale featured Mankato narrowly beating Northfield, 17-15, thanks to Earl Pennington jumper with just under a minute to go.

In the first semifinal game Thief River Falls stormed back from a 10-7 half-time deficit to overtake a very tough Winona team, 17-12, while Chisholm spanked Mankato, 22-8 in the other semi to advance to the title game. There, with a crowd of 7,500 looking on, Thief River Falls started out strong and hung on to beat Chisholm, 21-15. Arnold Sladum came up with a clutch defensive play late in the game to preserve the big win, while Chommie and Kietly provided the scoring punch.

Left to Right: Coach Ray C. Johnson, Captain A. Lillyblad, L. Fridell, R. Seebach, L. Frick, V. Skogan, W. Hultquist, E. Gisslen, Student Manager V. Olson and R. Perrot.

The 1933 State Champs from Red Wing

1933 Red Wing vs. Minneapolis North

The 21st annual Minnesota State High School Basketball Tournament was moved from the University of Minnesota's Field House to the Minneapolis Auditorium. First round action of the big event saw Chisholm whip tiny Ada, 34-12, on Pete Burich's 12 points. Game Two had Red Wing edging Brainerd, 21-19, as Guard Bill Holtquist nailed the game-winner with just 45 seconds remaining on the clock. Montevideo then beat Rochester, 23-19, in the first evening quarterfinal, behind Tuffy Thompson's game-high 10 points. The last game of the day saw Minneapolis North eliminate Mountain Lake, 28-15, behind Griffin's 14-point effort.

Chisholm jumped out to a 14-10 lead at the half only to see the Red Wing Wingers rally behind Dick Seeback's three straight field goals late in the game to take a 29-23 semifinal victory. Minneapolis North then beat Montevideo, 29-22, in the other game, as Griffin was once again the hero by pouring in five straight baskets to ice it for the Polars. More than 10,000 fans came out to watch the championship game between Red Wing and Minneapolis North. Red Wing emerged with an early lead in this one and made it 11-4 at the half. From there Shogan and Seeback each tallied for the Wingers as they withstood a late-game rally, 16-13.

Back Row, Left to Right: Lamuth, Manson, Trainer; Kotchevar, Asst. Coach; H. J. Roels, Coach; Margo, Trainer; Rogge.
Front Row: Hydukovich, Gostovic, P. Burich, Tramontin, G. Burich, Captain; Turk, Kuzmanoff, Gornick.

The 1934 State Champs from Chisholm

1934: Chisholm vs. Mechanic Arts

Wesley Phillip's 14 points led Moorhead past Winona in the opener 32-25, while the Burich brothers, Gordon and Pete, led Chisholm over Cass Lake, 33-12, in Game Two. The evening games then saw Redwood Falls upset Minneapolis South, 24-16, and St. Paul Mechanic Arts beat Mankato in a wild one, 29-28, thanks to Don Pivec's basket with just 22 seconds left in the game.

Chisholm then routed Moorhead in the first semifinal contest, 50-17, on Turk's 16 points, while Mechanic Arts got by Redwood Falls, 21-17 in the night-cap. The big Center, Sullivan, led Mechanic Arts with seven points. The title tilt between Chisholm and Mechanic Arts was a dandy. With the score tied, Pete Burich's free throws put Chisholm ahead at the half, 14-12. Then, late in the game, Mechanic Arts rallied to cut the score to 27-26, but when Burich nailed a 20-footer from the top of the key, it was all over. Chisholm hung on to win, 29-27.

1935: Austin vs. Glencoe

Bemidji got by St. Paul Humboldt, 26-18, in the opening quarterfinal game, while Buhl, which at one point had a commanding 12-4 lead over Glencoe, was overtaken, 22-12, in Game Two. Then, Austin, behind the sharp-shooting of Kennard Skyberg and A. Hanson, beat Luverne 37-30, in the first evening game, while Minneapolis Edison barely eked out a win over Crosby-Ironton, 37-35. Crosby-Ironton jumped out to a quick 21-2 lead in this one, only to see Edison, behind Bill Warhol and Frank Marmeczak, mount an amazing come-back.

The Lumberjacks of Bemidji jumped out to a quick 16-9 lead over Glencoe in the first semi, only to see Glencoe rally back to win a thriller, 23-22. The second game of the night featured the tallest team of the tournament, Austin, against the smallest, Minneapolis Edison. Late in the second quarter with Edison leading, 17-14, the Packers got some bad news when their star, Art Hanson, fouled out after he had scored 11 points. They rallied behind their fallen leader though, and thanks to Don Hemer's 12 points, Austin hung on to beat Edison 36-27.

Austin kept it rolling in the championship game, beating Glencoe in a thriller, 26-24. The Packers led 13-10 at the half, but just before the third quarter ended Don Bongard nailed a jumper goal to give Glencoe a 15-14 lead. They expanded their lead to 22-18 with two minutes remaining in the game, but Ray Stromer and Art Hanson's field goals tied the score at 22-22. From there, Austin's Oscar Anderson hit what he though was the game-win-

Back Row, Left to Right: Assistant Coach Hainer, Braun, Hartman, Rector, Rahilly, J. Farnsworth, Veverlsa, Ekedal, Evenson, Lowe, Lane, Gunderson, Coach Arney.
Front Row: Manager Vogel, G. Farnsworth, Stromer, S. Hanson, Anderson, A. Hanson, Hemmer, Twedell, Atwood, Holleque, Dugan.

The 1935 State Champs from Austin

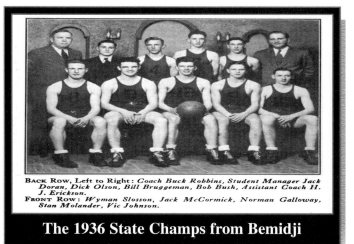

BACK ROW, Left to Right: *Coach Buck Robbins, Student Manager Jack Doran, Dick Olson, Bill Bruggeman, Bob Bush, Assistant Coach H. J. Erickson.*
FRONT ROW: *Wyman Slosson, Jack McCormick, Norman Galloway, Stan Molander, Vic Johnson.*

The 1936 State Champs from Bemidji

ner with just 15 seconds to go, only to see Glencoe's Omer Huntington tie it up with only two ticks on the clock. Finally, in overtime, Art Hanson scored what proved to be the game-winning shot, as the Pack came away with one truly amazing victory.

1936: Bemidji vs. Wadena

In the opening game of the 1936 tournament Bemidji rallied back to defeat Albert Lea, 36-32. That's when Vic Johnson and Norm Galloway, who had 16 and 11 points respectively, took over and led their squad into the semifinals. Game Two saw Red Wing top Luverne, 29-27, behind Myrvin DeLapp's 13 points. Then, in Game Three, Wadena mounted a late 8-0 run, capped by Bill Brown's buzzer-beater, to edge an undefeated Sleepy Eye club, 20-18, while the final game of the day saw tiny Buhl, behind the 12-point efforts of John Dicks and Mike Pineovich, upset Minneapolis Edison, 41-32.

In the opening semifinal games Red Wing was defeated by Coach Buck Robbin's Bemidji squad, 34-23. Bemidji's Norman Galloway and Vic Johnson each tallied 11 and 10 points, respectively, in leading their club to its first-ever Finals. The other semi saw Wadena barely escape the men of Buhl, 28-27, in one of the tournament's best games. Wadena led by one at the half, 15-14, but Buhl, behind John Dicks' 15 points, mounted a rally that just barely came up short.

More than 9,500 fans were on hand to watch Bemidji and Wadena square off in the championship game. Bemidji jumped out to a 13-6 half-time lead behind Victor Johnson and Norman Galloway's early points, only to see Wadena narrow the gap in the second half. Galloway took over down the stretch though, scoring six of his game-high 16 points in the fourth as his club went on to win, 26-20.

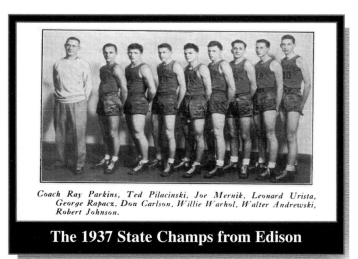

Coach Ray Parkins, Ted Pilacinski, Joe Mernik, Leonard Urista, George Rapacz, Don Carlson, Willie Warhol, Walter Andrewski, Robert Johnson.

The 1937 State Champs from Edison

1937: Minneapolis Edison vs. Virginia

The first game of the tourney got underway with a big upset as underdog Thief River Falls bumped off Farmington, and their one-two scoring punch of John Barger nor Tom Feely, 26-17. Virginia, behind Walt Salmi's final two buckets, then rallied back from an 11-0 deficit to beat Rochester, 28-26, in a thrilling Game Two. Game Three saw New Ulm top tiny Triumph-Monterey (Population of 485) in the second upset of the day. With New Ulm up 17-13 at the half, Trimont, behind Wes Smock and John Frahm, mounted a rally. But the Eagles, who were led by Aufderheide and Kusske, hung in there and came out with a dramatic 29-26 win. The last quarterfinal saw Minneapolis Edison cruise to a 38-27 victory over Crosby-Ironton, thanks to the play of their big-three: Center Walt Andruski, and Guards Willie Warhol and Guard Joe Mernik.

The semifinals then saw Virginia trample Thief River Falls, 37-17, behind the amazing play of Nick Pepelnjak, who tallied 14 points in the big win. The real story though was the awful shooting of Thief River Falls, which was just six of 51 shooting on the day! The other semifinal was the biggest blowout in state tournament history as Edison pulverized New Ulm, 62-23. Mernik tallied 18 points in the win..

The Finals then saw high scoring Edison taking on the Iron Rangers from Virginia for the right to be called champion. This one was a rough one as Virginia's star Center, Howard Hedenstad, fouled out early — leaving a big void for the squad. Virginia Forwards Koski and Pepelnjak picked up the slack, but in the end, Edison was too tall, and too powerful. Virginia mounted a late rally, but Edison's defense stopped them on nearly every trip down the court. It was once again the trio of Edison's All-Stater's: Andruski, Warhol and Mernik who did the damage, with Andrewski leading the way with 12 points in the 37-24 victory.

1938: Thief River Falls vs. Minneapolis North

The opening quarterfinal game of the 1938 tournament saw Crosby-Ironton eliminating a Virginia team which was with out two of its best players,

who were sick. Down at the half, Virginia did rally fourth quarter comeback, spearheaded by Nick Pepelnjak, who had 10 points. But Crosby-Ironton's Glenn Gunlin then scored five straight to cap a 37-27 final score. Thief River Falls, led by Roy Lee's 10 points, then beat Faribault, 37-29, in Game Two, while St. Paul Central tipped Luverne, 40-35, in Game Three. Minneapolis North, behind Dick Burk's 15 points, then beat Appleton, 43-28, to round out the quarters.

A capacity crowd of 10,000 watched Thief River Falls edge Crosby-Ironton, 30-28, in the opening semifinal game. Crosby-Ironton controlled most of the rebounding throughout the game but was unable to score when it really mattered. Crosby-Ironton was up with five seconds left in the game, only to see the Falls' Roy Lee nail a jumper to tie it up to send it to overtime. (The rules of sudden death overtime back then had the first team to score two points as the winner.) There, Mickelson took a pass from Lee and scored the winning basket giving Thief River Falls the thrilling victory. The second semifinal then saw Minneapolis North, which was led by the two Dicks:

Earl Nicholson, Loren Stadum, Coach George E. Lee, Clark Mickelson, Donald Lorentson, Roy Lee, Reuben Mickelson, Gordon Caldis, Melford Haughom.

The 1938 State Champs from Thief River Falls

Hallman and Burk, tip St. Paul Central, 34-27. North was ahead 16-11 at the half, thanks to Jerry Goodman's 10 points, and the Polars never looked back from there.

Thief River Falls then capped a 27-0 season — the best in Minnesota prep history at that time — by scoring a 31-29 comeback victory over a very tough Minneapolis North squad. Trailing most of the game, the Prowlers, behind Center Loren Stadum, came back to get to within one in the fourth. There, Roy Lee nailed the go-ahead jumper, and from there the team resorted to a stalling tactic to keep the Polars at bay.

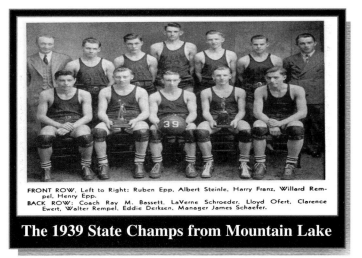

FRONT ROW, Left to Right: Ruben Epp, Albert Steinle, Harry Franz, Willard Rempel, Henry Epp.
BACK ROW: Coach Ray M. Bassett, LaVerne Schroeder, Lloyd Ofert, Clarence Ewert, Walter Rempel, Eddie Derksen, Manager James Schaefer.

The 1939 State Champs from Mountain Lake

1939: Mountain Lake vs. Minneapolis Marshall

The 27th Minnesota High School Championship opened up at the St. Paul Auditorium. There, Breckenridge, led by Raymond Cumbura, pulled away from Hutchinson and coasted to a 34-21 victory. Minneapolis Marshall, led by Forward Don Mattson's 15 points, then downed Gilbert, 33-25, in the second game of the first round. In the first evening game Mountain Lake edged Austin, 29-28, while South St. Paul, behind Guard Nick Vujovick's 11 points, beat Thief River Falls, 33-26, in the finale.

Marshall then trampled Breckenridge, 38-22, in the first semifinal game. Marshall Center John Moir took the scoring honors, with 20 points, while Melvin Ruud had nine for Breckenridge. Then, in the second semi, Mountain Lake, behind the stellar guard play of Ruben Epp, eliminated South St. Paul, 41-21.

The Finals then saw tiny Mountain Lake down a tough Minneapolis Marshall squad, 37-31, to be crowned as the 1939 state champs. Marshall, led by Don Mattson's 18 points, quickly jumped out to an early 6-0 lead. Marshall was up 16-12 in third quarter when the Lakers started fighting back. Behind the two Epp boys, Ruben and Henry, Mountain Lake tied it up 16-16. From there it was all Lakers, as they pulled away by scoring 10 points down the stretch to take the emotional victory.

1940: Breckenridge vs. Red Wing

An afternoon crowd of 6,000 was on hand to watch Mountain Lake, which was led by Henry Epp's 12 points, eliminate Tracy, 29-23, in the opener. Red Wing led by Preston Daniels, Vic Kulbitski, Jim Maetzold and their big center, Neal Strom, then exacted a little revenge by edging out a very tough Rochester squad, 33-30, in Game Two. On tap next was Breckenridge, which upset the heavily favored Bemidji Lumberjacks, 38-24, on the fine play of Ray Cumbura, who led all scorers with 12 points, followed by Mel Rund and Gene Stanbra, who added 11 and 9, respectively. The final game also proved to be a cliff-hanger as Marshall beat Chisholm, 31-29, in what turned out to be a classic. The game turned out to be a scoring battle between Marshall Center Red Mattson, who tallied 21 points and Chisholm Guard Orlando Bonicelli, who tallied 19 of his own. With the score tied at 25-25 late in the game, Bonicelli stole the ball and scored to put Chisholm ahead 27-25. Bill Ekberg followed that with a tip in, only to see Mattson nail a jumper down the stretch which turned out to be the game-winner.

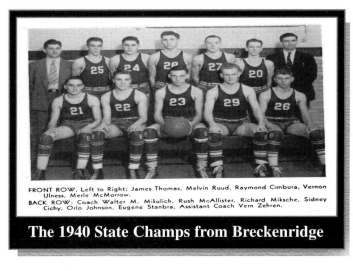

FRONT ROW, Left to Right: James Thomas, Melvin Ruud, Raymond Cimbura, Vernon Ulness, Merle McMorrow.
BACK ROW: Coach Walter M. Mikulich, Rush McAllister, Richard Miksche, Sidney Cichy, Orlo Johnson, Eugene Stanbra, Assistant Coach Vern Zehren.

The 1940 State Champs from Breckenridge

Red Wing dumped Mountain Lake, 30-26, in the first semifinal, due in large part to the great defensive job Billy Peterson did on Mountain Lake's high scoring center, Henry Epp. Red Wing capped the victory when Vic Kulbitski and Bill Peterson each nailed some clutch on free throws in the last few minutes of the game. Then, Breckenridge, led by Forward Melvin Ruud's 18 points, pulled out a narrow 32-30 victory over Minneapolis Marshall in the other semifinal game. Cumbura was the hero when he stole the ball and on a fast break and then promptly scored what proved to be the game-winning basket.

The Finals were also tight, with Breckenridge holding off Red Wing, 43-40, to take the championship . Red Wing got off to an early lead only to see Breckenridge pull ahead to take a six-point, 20-14, half-time edge. From there Red Wing's Vic Kulbitski and Bill Peterson lit it up. They pressed and came on strong, but Breckenridge, behind Melvin Ruud, Vern Ulness and Cumbura, held off the late rally and pulled away for the big win.

1941: Buhl vs. Red Wing

The 29th annual Minnesota High School Tournament moved back to the Minneapolis Auditorium this year after a two-year hiatus at the St. Paul Auditorium. Things were going well for the tourney, which drew nearly 36,000 fans this year. The opening quarterfinal game saw Bemidji rip Moorhead, 42-23, as Jack Johnson and Hector Brown had 10 and 9 points, respectively for the victors. Red Wing led by Dick McWaters and Jim Maetzold, trounced Austin, 45-29, in the second game of the afternoon. In Game Three, more than 12,000 fans showed up to watch tiny Buhl, which was led by Ed Nylund's 14-point effort, upset Mankato, 37-35. Minneapolis Washburn, led by its star Forward, Dave Ruliffson, who tallied 17 points in the game, then overpowered Lester Prairie in the finale by a margin of 30-19.

Red Wing rolled over Bemidji in the first semifinal, 37-24, on

FRONT ROW: R. Mallaro, G. Smilanich, Capt. John Klarich, N. Lubotina, R. Delich, L. Sartori.
BACK ROW: Assistant Coach Gordon LeBeau, G. Klasna, G. Krynovich, Dan Knezovich, Edward Nylund, William Kochevar, Russell Willberg, Coach M. G. Anderson.

The 1941 State Champs from Buhl

BACK ROW, Left to Right: Coach Mario Retica, William Kochevar, James Ozanich, George Klasna, Dan Knezovich, Edward Nylund, Assistant Coach Gordon Le Beau.
FRONT ROW: Mike Galovich, George Smilanich, John Klarich, Russell Willberg, Robert Delich, Lawrence Pervenanze, Jr.

The 1942 State Champs from Buhl

McWaters' 13 points while teammate Jim Maetzold added 11 of his own in the win. Game Two then saw the speedsters from Buhl upset Washburn in a close one, as Ed Nylund scored 14 while Dave Ruliffson and Matt Sutton had 13 and 10 respectively.

Then, in the Finals, the underdog sentimental favorites from Buhl did the impossible when they knocked off Red Wing by the final score of 31-29. The game started out slowly, and by half-time it was just 8-8. Both teams opened it up in the second though, and the score was tied at 21-21 with only three minutes to go. But Russ Willberg, John Klarich and Ed Nylund took over down the stretch and led the Bulldogs to a dramatic victory.

1942: Buhl vs. Marshall

The 1942 tourney moved from the Minneapolis Auditorium back to the University of Minnesota's Field House. There, the defending state champs from Buhl, riding an amazing 33-game winning streak, met up with the mighty Fairmont Cardinals. Buhl's all-state Guard Russ Willberg opened the scoring in this one as the Bulldogs jumped out to a 30-15 lead at the intermission. From there it was all Bulldogs, as they cruised to a 52-38 victory. John Klarich paced Buhl with 16 points while Cady and Gould led Fairmont with 11 points apiece.

Moorhead, led by Dick Hidlen and Wally Solien, beat Austin in the second game, 47-39, while Marshall, which got 14 points from Jack Hiller and another 11 from Bernie Gervais, trounced St. Paul Washington, 37-21, in Game Three. The last quarterfinal then saw Hopkins dominate tiny Bagley, 27-13, on Steve Skoglund's 8-point effort.

In the opening semifinal games Buhl beat up on Moorhead, 53-29, thanks to the fine play of Russ Willberg, George Klasna, Ed Nylund and John Klarich. Marshall then knocked off Hopkins in Game Two, 38-23, on Jack Hiller's 10 points. Incidentally, the Marshall squad was made up almost entirely of players from their football team, which was riding an impressive 38-game winning streak.

The championship game was now set: Buhl vs. Marshall. This one was tight from the get go as Buhl led 14-12 at half time and 25-24 at the third quarter mark. Then, early in the fourth, Buhl got some bad news when their star John Klarich, had fouled out. They hung in there though, and kept battling. Now, late in the game, with the score tied at 27-27, Buhl got its second bad break of the game when its little forward, Klasna, was knocked out in a scramble under the basket. They still managed to rally though, and thanks to Klasna's clutch free-throws with under a minute to go, Buhl hung on for a thrilling 30-29 victory. Leading the charge for the back-to-back state champs from Buhl was Forward John Klarich, who led the Bulldogs with 15 points.

1943: St. Paul Washington vs. Alexandria

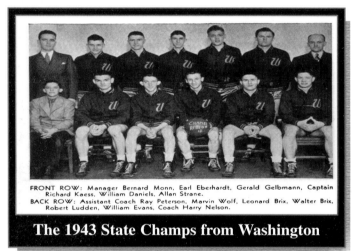

FRONT ROW: Manager Bernard Monn, Earl Eberhardt, Gerald Gelbmann, Captain Richard Kaess, William Daniels, Allan Strane.
BACK ROW: Assistant Coach Ray Peterson, Marvin Wolf, Leonard Brix, Walter Brix, Robert Ludden, William Evans, Coach Harry Nelson.

The 1943 State Champs from Washington

Alexandria, which was led by their great center, Hal Haskins, who had scored 45 of Alexandria's 79 points in their two regional contests, opened the quarters by knocking off Mankato, 28-26. In the second match, Virginia, led by Bill Connor's last-second game-winning jumper, upended Bemidji in Game Two, 43-39, as this one saw several lead changes right up until the end. St. Paul Washington rolled Hutchinson, 41-25, in Game Three, thanks to Dick Kaess' 12-point effort. The last game of the evening then saw Austin edging Minneapolis Edison in a thriller as this one came down to Dick Nelson's game-winning free throws in the final seconds to make the score, 39-36.

Alexandria knocked off Virginia in the opening semifinal contest, 38-32, thanks to Walt Grodahl's pair of last-second baskets to give his club the "W." St. Paul Washington then beat Austin in a defensive gem, 21-18. In fact, Washington held Austin scoreless in the second quarter and led 9-6 at the half. From there Walt Brix, Jerry Geibman and Dick Kaess took over, as they led their club into the Finals.

St. Paul Washington had a simple game plan for Alexandria: triple-team Hal Haskins! Washington took a 15-7 lead at the end of the first quarter and had a 28-19 edge at the half but, with Haskins leading the attack, Alexandria made it 33-27 by the third. But, when Haskins fouled out of the game with five minutes left in the game, it was all but over. Washington, which shot an an amazing 48 percent in the game, and was led by Geibman and Kaess' veteran leadership, coasted from there to post a 55-33 victory.

1944: Patrick Henry vs. Crosby-Ironton

Back once again at the St Paul Auditorium, the 1944 state tourney kicked off with Crosby-Ironton surprising Virginia, 46-45, thanks to Frank Formanek's two clutch free-throws late in the game to ice the victory. Bemidji then bested Brownton in the second game, 61-55, on Phil Feir's 19 points; while Rochester's Joe Daly scored the dramatic game-winning basket in the final seconds to beat Stillwater, 37-36. Patrick Henry, led by Center Jim McIntyre's 29 points, then demoralized Mankato, 48-18, in Game Four.

The semifinals opened with powerful Patrick Henry overwhelming the

FRONT ROW: R. Greene, F. Sanders, J. McIntyre, R. Mealey, D. Bailey, C. Kermeen.
BACK ROW: V. Wobig (Faculty Mgr.), W. Joyce, R. Gardner, A. Mickelson (Student Mgr.), R. Brimi, W. Weller, F. Cleve (Coach).

The 1944 State Champs from Patrick Henry

Rochester Rockets, 40-23, as Jim McIntyre pumped in 21 points to lead his team to victory. The other game then saw Crosby--Ironton eking out a narrow 38-36 victory over Bemidji, thanks to Gordy Hawks and Lou Petrich's pair of late field goals — followed by a couple of Petrich free-throws — to put Crosby-Ironton ahead for good.

It was all Patrick Henry in the Finals, as the Patriots went on to beat Crosby-Ironton, 51-42, for their first state championship. Guard Bob Mealey kept dishing the ball to Jim McIntyre who did the rest. McIntyre scored 36 points for the champs, as they held off a late Ed Jacobson-led Crosby-Ironton comeback to preserve the win.

1945: Patrick Henry vs. Ely

Back at the U of M's Field House, the 1945 tourney opened with the Iron Rangers from Ely knocking off the runner-ups from last year's tourney, Crosby-Ironton, by the final of 43-33. Dick Buckley tallied 15 points while Dick Banks added 13 in the win. Game Two then saw Hutchinson overtake

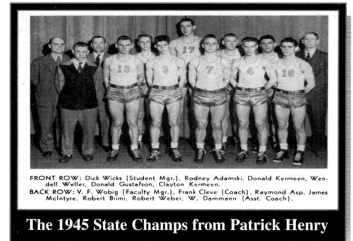

FRONT ROW: Dick Wicks (Student Mgr.), Rodney Adamski, Donald Kermeen, Wendell Weller, Donald Gustafson, Clayton Kermeen.
BACK ROW: V. F. Wobig (Faculty Mgr.), Frank Cleve (Coach), Raymond Asp, James McIntyre, Robert Brimi, Robert Weber, W. Dammann (Asst. Coach).

The 1945 State Champs from Patrick Henry

Red Wing, 47-35, on Bill Van Lanen's 16 points; while Mankato edged Faribault, 37-33, in overtime, in the third contest. With Faribault leading 31-29, and only 12 seconds left to play, Mankato's Don Olson, hit a huge bucket to tie it up 31-31 and send the game into sudden death. There, Olson, who posted a game-high 18 points, scored three more points to pace his team a thrilling victory. The finale then saw the defending champs from Patrick Henry roll over Bemidji, 59-49, as Center Jim McIntyre hit for 35 points.

The first semifinal saw Ely barely top Hutchinson, 43-41, thanks to the coach's son, Dick Buckley, and Forward James Rolando, who each scored 17 points in the victory. Patrick Henry continued to cruise in the other semi, this time spanking Mankato, 37-25, on big Jim McIntyre's solid 22-point effort.

In the Finals it was all Patrick Henry though, as they crushed Ely, 66-35, to win their second straight state championship. Henry built up a 32-16 half-time lead and went on to score 34 more points in the second. Jim McIntyre was once again huge, this time scoring an amazing 43 points. He set several records that year, not to mention scoring at least 100 points on at least three occasions.

1946: Austin vs. Lynd

Austin, led by All-State Center Dick Ravenhorst, jumped out to a 32-11 half-time lead over Roseau in the opener and never looked back as they crushed the Rams, 66-39. Mountain Lake then upset Tower-Soudan in Game Two, 59-46, on Center Ray Wall's 18-point effort. The first evening game then saw tiny Lynd beat Crosby-Ironton, 58-47, thanks in large part to the efforts of Duane Londgren and Jim Malosky (the future UMD Football coaching legend), who scored 20 and 19 points, respectively. Stillwater then narrowly

FRONT ROW: James Vest, Harold Ball, Dick Brown, Coach Berven, George Vest, Lloyd Hammer, Robert Morem.
BACK ROW: Don Freeberg, Asst. Mgr., Harper Richardson, Dick Ravenhorst, Robert Roach, James McGuire, Arnold Carlson, Mgr.

The 1946 State Champs from Austin

edged Washburn in the finale, 37-36, as the Ponies worked for a 25-17 lead at the half and then held off a late rally to win the game.

Austin then took care of Mountain Lake, 38-31, in the first semifinal contest. The Packers, behind Harper Richardson's 12 points, jumped out to a 20-11 half-time lead, and kept it going until the final whistle. Complicating things for Mountain Lake was the fact that their star Center, Ray Wall, fouled out with just three minutes left in the game. The second semi then saw Lynd upset Stillwater, 46-39, in a close one. After battling to a 22-22 tie at the half, Lynd pulled ahead for good in the fourth when their star Forward, Duane Londgren, scored eight straight points down the stretch to ice the game.

Austin and Lynd then met on Saturday for all the marbles, and joining them were 16,091 fans — the largest crowd ever to watch a high school game in Minnesota. But this one wasn't even close as Austin erupted for a 30-15 half-time lead and never looked back, winning easily, 63-31. Dick Ravenhorst led the Packers with 24 points while Casper, Fisher and Pat Clark scored 10 points apiece for Lynd.

1947: Duluth Denfeld vs. Crosby Ironton

Crosby-Ironton, led by its pair of All-Staters, Ken Novak and John Widmar, beat St. Paul Marshall by the final score of 36-31 in Game One. In the next contest it was Minneapolis Marshall beating Austin, 51-43, while Mountain Lake, riding a string of 23 straight victories, then took care of Bemidji in Game Three, 51-39, on All-State Center Ray Wall's 27 points. Game Four then saw Duluth Denfeld eliminate Granite Falls, 44-37, thanks to Paul Nace's 12 points and solid defense.

In the first semi, Minneapolis Marshall jumped out to a quick 13-9 first quarter lead only to see Crosby-Ironton hold them scoreless in the second. Crosby-Ironton rallied to take a 33-29 advantage at the end of the third quarter, only to see Jerry Exberg score a pair of his game-high 18 points which gave Marshall a 39-38 lead with just 90 seconds to go in the game. From there Crosby-Ironton Guard Don Jacobson emerged as the hero when he grabbed the ball and raced the length of the floor to score what turned out to be the game-winning basket with just 30 seconds on the clock. Marshall

FRONT ROW: Eugene Norlander, Laurence Tessier, Rudolph Monson, Kenneth Sunnarborg, Paul Nace, Keith Stolen.
BACK ROW: Coach Lloyd Holm, Gerald Walzak, Bruce Budge, Howard Tucker, Anthony Skull, William McNelis.

The 1947 State Champs from Duluth Denfeld

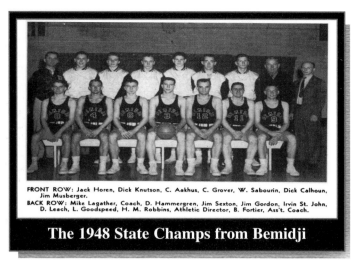

FRONT ROW: Jack Horen, Dick Knutson, C. Aakhus, C. Grover, W. Sabourin, Dick Calhoun, Jim Musberger.
BACK ROW: Mike Lagather, Coach, D. Hammergren, Jim Sexton, Jim Gordon, Irvin St. John, D. Leach, L. Goodspeed, H. M. Robbins, Athletic Director, B. Fortier, Ass't. Coach.

The 1948 State Champs from Bemidji

tried to rally but Crosby-Ironton shut them out to preserve a 40-39 victory.

Duluth Denfeld barely escaped a late Mountain Lake rally to emerge victorious in the other semifinal contest, 30-29. The game started out pretty even, with both teams heading to the lockerroom at half-time tied at 15 apiece. Then, midway through the fourth quarter, Mountain Lake's All-State Center, Ray Wall, fouled out, giving Denfeld the green light to attack down in the paint. Both teams exchanged the lead in the final minutes, only to see Bob Guertzen's free throw give Mountain Lake a 29-28 lead with under :30 seconds to go. That's when Denfeld's Paul Nace scored his dramatic game-winning jump-shot to give his club a 30-29 victory.

Duluth then met Crosby-Ironton in the Finals, where the packed Fieldhouse crowd was treated to yet another exciting finale. Crosby-Ironton opened the scoring and led 23-19 at halftime, only to see Denfeld, behind Rudy Monson, rally to take a 34-32 lead at the third quarter mark. Then, with three minutes to go, Widmar and Valentino each tallied to give Crosby-Ironton a 42-40 lead. But Duluth, behind Gene Norlander's field goal and free throw, regained the lead, while Paul Nace1s free throw and Ken Sonnarborg's field goal added some much-needed insurance. Duluth Denfeld then simply held on down the stretch to preserve their dramatic 46-44 victory.

1948: Bemidji vs. Hopkins

Hopkins, behind Ed Korsmo's dozen points, opened the 1948 state tourney by rolling over Crosby-Ironton, 51-37. Anoka's Pete Castle also had a dozen points in his team's dramatic 37-35 win over Hibbing in Game Two. Milan Knezovich's 20 points kept Hibbing close, but Anoka hung on to take the narrow victory. The third game of the tournament then saw Mountain Lake edging Waseca, 40-38, on Don Reimer's dramatic game-winning basket in the game's final seconds. The last quarterfinal of the day saw Bemidji beating Hutchinson, 43-30, as Chuck Aakhis and Charles Grover provided the early offense with Dick Knutson, and his 13 points, sealing the deal late.

Hopkins, behind Virgil Miller's game-high 18 points, pounded on Hibbing, 42-30, in the first semifinal. Hopkins led 22-15 at the half and shut down Milan Knezovich in the third and fourth quarters to preserve the win. Bemidji, behind Charles Grover's game-high 17 points, then topped Mountain Lake by the final score of 40-37 in Game Two. The Lumberjacks had a 34-25 lead going into the fourth quarter, only to see Mountain Lake score seven unanswered points to go ahead. The game then went back and forth in the final minutes with Mountain Lake's Don Reimer and Bob Reiger each scoring to get the score to within one. But that was as far as they got as Lumberjacks' Forward Dick Knutson iced the game on a clutch lay-up in the game's final moments.

Bemidji and Hopkins hooked up for the title match, with Bemidji coming out on top. Chuck Jerisek's basket gave Hopkins an 18-16 halftime lead, but the Lumberjacks rallied back to take a 28-22 advantage by the end of the third period. Then, with Wes Sabourin leading the charge, Bemidji broke the game wide open and cruised to a 38-29 victory.

1949: St. Paul Humboldt vs. Mankato

Mankato opened the first quarterfinal game by rolling over Brainerd, 52-34. Brainerd's Smith boys, Don and Jim, rallied the Warriors' come-back but the Scarlets, behind Griffen's 18 points, were too much down the stretch. Game Two action saw Rochester downing Dawson, 54-46, thanks in large part to the solid two-way playing of Carl Brunstring, Shorty Cochran and Jim Larson, who tallied a game-high 22 points for the Rockets. Minneapolis Central then knocked off Hibbing in Game Three as Center Milan Knezovich, arguably the best big-man in the state, fouled out late in the game after scoring 18 points for the Blue Jackets. From there it was all Central, as Carl Thomas, who tallied 16 points in the game, paced his club to a 37-34 victory. St. Paul Humboldt then eliminated Bemidji in the final quarterfinal of the day, 48-39, on Center Jim Fritsche's amazing 26-point effort.

Mankato rolled Rochester, 42-34, in the first semifinal. The Scarlets, behind Norman Ness's 12 points, took a 27-19 at half-time and never looked back in this one. The other semi then saw St. Paul Humboldt eliminate Minneapolis Central, 53-47. Humboldt cruised to a 24-18 lead at the intermission on Jim Fritsche's 15 first half points, and rolled to victory behind Finn's 10 points in the second.

In the Finals, St. Paul Humboldt was able to use its superior size and speed to beat Mankato, 47-35. With Fritsche and Finn controlling the boards, Humboldt took a 13-4 first quarter lead and expanded it to 20-10 at the half. Mankato mounted a late rally, but when Fritsche scored eight of his game-high 21 points in the third, it was all but over. Humboldt stalled in the final period to squash the Scarlets late comeback attempt, and cruised to their first state championship victory.

1950: Duluth Central vs. Robbinsdale

A pair of last-minute field goals by Jim Larson gave Rochester a 44-38 victory over South St. Paul in the opening quarterfinal game of the 1950 tourney. Bruce Bauman's jumper with just over a minute to go gave the Packers a 36-32 lead, but the Rockets rallied back and cruised to the big win. Robbinsdale beat up on Bemidji in Game Two, 48-34, on Center Don Dale's 21 points; while Duluth Central eliminated Alexandria, 52-47, in Game Three thanks to Center John Stephan and Forward Charles Bennett's 22 and 12-point outings. Tiny Canby then ousted Mankato, 42-32, in the finale. After jumping out to a 21-5 lead, Canby, led by Ron Smith's 13 points, held off a late Mankato rally to take the big win.

Robbinsdale then eliminated Rochester in the first semifinal by the nar-

FRONT ROW: George Bohrer, Richard Lee, Charles Petrowske, James Fritsche, Myron Finn, Melvin Koppen, Ray Kempe.
BACK ROW: Coach Arthur Peterson, Richard Amer (Mgr.), John Bohrer, Richard Gieske, Ronald Adams, Arnold Rehmann, Michael McDonough (Athletic Director).

The 1949 State Champs from St. Paul Humboldt

row margin of just 56-55. Robbinsdale leaped out to a 15-2 lead, only to see Rochester score eight straight points to take a 40-38 lead at the end of the third quarter. Pete Hayek's free throw gave Robbinsdale a 50-49 lead, but Don Dale, who bagged 37 points in the game, answered by hitting three straight buckets to make it 56-49. Lee, Larson and Harman each tallied for Rochester down the stretch, but Owen Thompson's free throw proved to be the game-winner as the Robins hung on for the huge win.

Duluth Central then made easy work of Canby in the other semi, winning 38-25. Down in the first, Canby actually came back and scored six straight points to take a 15-14 advantage at the inter-mission. But Duluth was too strong in the second, as they poured it on behind the shooting of Charles Bennett and John Stephan, each of whom tallied 10 points in the game, to cruise into the Finals.

From there Duluth Central met up with Robbinsdale, in a match-up featuring a pair of former Two Harbors prep stars-turned-coaches: Ed Kernan of Robbinsdale and Ray Moren of Duluth Central. Duluth led 23-19 at half-time, only to see the Robbins rally behind Pete Hayek's rebound and tip-in to get his Central squad back to within two points at 40-38. Then, with just 33 seconds remaining, Duluth's John Stephan nailed a free throw and Owenn Thompson followed with a clutch jumper from the top of the circle to give their club a one point lead. Now, with 10 seconds left on the clock, the Robins were forced to foul. That's when Duluth's Chuck Hill stepped up and added a one-point insurance policy as his club held on to take a dramatic 42-40 victory. Duluth Central's Center, John Stephan, paced his club with 15 points while Don Dale added 22 for the Robins.

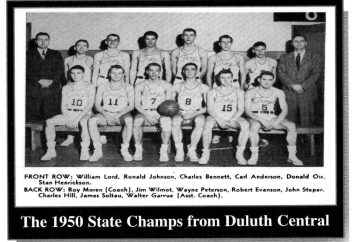

The 1950 State Champs from Duluth Central

FRONT ROW: William Lord, Ronald Johnson, Charles Bennett, Carl Anderson, Donald Oie, Stan Henrickson.
BACK ROW: Roy Moren (Coach), Jim Wilmot, Wayne Peterson, Robert Evanson, John Stepan, Charles Hill, James Soltau, Walter Garvue (Asst. Coach).

1951: Gilbert vs. Canby

Brainerd beat East Grand Forks, 66-54, in the tourney opener, despite the outstanding effort of John Haaven, who led East Grand Forks with 33 points. Game Two then saw Canby upset Hopkins, and their amazing broth-er-duo of Dan and Dave Tschimperle, by the final score of 45-43. The first evening quarterfinal saw the introduction of Gilbert's star six-foot-nine Center, Bill Simonovich, who, in addition to out-playing Austin's six-foot-eight Center, Burdett Haldorson, scored 39 points in a 67-56 victory over the previously undefeated Packers. Mountain Lake then edged St. Paul Monroe in the last quarterfinal, 47-46, on Leroy Loewen's last-second game-winning free-throw which nearly brought the house down.

The first semifinal game saw Canby crush Brainerd, 63-34, behind the fine play of Ron Smith, Mike Dunphy, Ervin Mikkelson and Wendell Miller, who all played solidly on both ends of the court. The other semi then featured Gilbert topping Mountain Lake in overtime. The Lakers did a great job in defending Bill Simonovich, who didn't score a single point in the first half, but couldn't contain the big man in the second. Simonovich's free throw gave Gilbert a 43-42 edge with 3:20 remaining but Meyer's free-throw tied it at 43-43 and sent it into overtime. There, Leroy Loewen's free throw gave Mountain Lake a 44-43 lead, but Andy Snyder's jump shot just a few seconds later gave Gilbert what proved to be the game-winner. Jim Gentile added a free throw and with that the final score was 46-44, in favor of tiny Gilbert.

The 1951 State Champs from Gilbert

FRONT ROW: Wayne Keto, Coach; Bill Erchul, Andy Snyder, Bill Simonovich, Tom Richardson, John Ferkul, Don Sandstrom, Student Manager.
BACK ROW: Hjalmer Anderson, Asst. Coach; Jack Erchul, Ronnie Debeltz, Ben Verbick, Jim Gentile, Dick Champa, Steve Kerzie, Athletic Director.

Gilbert just kept it going in the Finals, easily beating Canby, 69-52, for their first title. With Canby focusing on stopping Simonovich, Gilbert's other players stepped it up. Tom Richardson opened the scoring for Gilbert by scoring the game's first six points, and Andy Synder gave Gilbert a 54-38 lead going into the fourth when he made a desperation heave from half-court which found the back of the net. From there Gilbert cruised to the championship as the nearly 15,000 fans stood in appreciation. Richardson led Gilbert with 26 points, followed by Synder and Simonovich, who had 18 and 17, respectively. Canby, on the other hand, was led by Miller, Mikkelson and Dunphy, who each had 10 points apiece.

1952: Hopkins vs. South St. Paul

South St. Paul began the 1952 state tournament by topping Appleton, 60-56, on Tom Hammond's 21-point effort, while little Halstad, led by Jim Akason's 14 points, upset Virginia in Game Two, 56-55. Virginia lost the game on a controversial call by the officials, who declared that Jack Stromberg's would-be game-winning shot at the buzzer came too late. The first evening game saw Hopkins narrowly edging Mountain Lake, 46-45, on Daryle Jersak and Dave Tschimperle's 14 and 13-point efforts. Down late, Mountain Lake rallied behind scores from Maynard Meyer, Leroy Loewen, Pete Tranz and Gaylord Hubert, but Hopkins held on down the stretch for the win. Then, in the final quarterfinal game, Austin, led by its identical twin guards: Doyle and Don Rasmussen, who scored 19 and 12 points, respectively, rolled Crosby-Ironton, 70-50.

The opening semifinal game pitted South St. Paul vs. Halstad, with

The 1952 State Champs from Hopkins

FRONT ROW: Dan Tschimperle, Dick Smith, Dave Tschimperle, Bob Wagner, Jerry Porter, Daryl Jersak, Ted Dvorak.
BACK ROW: Bob Kurvers, Charles Carlson, Mickey Moore, Don Pagelkopf, Dick LaRue.

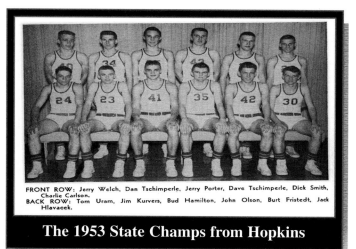

FRONT ROW: Jerry Welch, Dan Tschimperle, Jerry Porter, Dave Tschimperle, Dick Smith, Charlie Carlson.
BACK ROW: Tom Uram, Jim Kurvers, Bud Hamilton, John Olson, Burt Fristedt, Jack Hlavacek.

The 1953 State Champs from Hopkins

South St. Paul emerging victoriously, 61-48. Hammond and Kimball paced the Packers with 16 points apiece while Akason added 16 points for Halstad. The other semi then saw Hopkins having no problem with Austin, winning 45-34. Hopkins led 30-25 at the half, and expanded their lead to 10 when Terry Porter nailed three straight free throws followed by Dave Tschimperle's hanging jumper. From there the Royals cruised, giving Head Coach Butsie Maetzold yet another shot at a state title.

Hopkins jumped out to a quick 20-9 lead over the Packers in the championship game, only to see South St. Paul rally behind field goals from Hammond, McKay and Kimball to make it 32-28. Hopkins answered though, as Dave Tschimperle and Bob Wagner both scored on a pair of rebound tip-in's to get the lead back to 10. The Pack tried to rally late in the game, on All-Stater Jack Wade's solid play, but Hopkins' defense was smothering. The Royals, on Jerry Porter's game-high 16 points, hung on and cruised to a 42-29 victory.

1953: Hopkins vs. Hibbing

Granite Falls, behind Rod Westrum's 14 points, won 72-53 over Moorhead in the first quarterfinal game, while Hibbing made quick work of Madelia in Game Two, 64-45, on A. Rice's 20 points. The first evening quarterfinal turned out to be a dandy between Hopkins, which was riding a 44-game winning streak, and Red Wing, which had won 22 in a row of its own. Hopkins, behind two time all-stater, Dave Tschimperle's 26 points, was just too tough though, as they went on to beat the Wingers, 59-47. The final game of the day turned out to be the best as Austin outlasted Bemidji, 75-73, in a game which saw the lead change hands some 40 times! Fast-forward now to the fourth quarter with everything all tied up. That's when 15-year-old Center, Jack Whiting, took a pass and popped in the game-winning jumper to give Bemidji one of the tournament's greatest all-time victories.

Hibbing eliminated Granite Falls in the first semifinal game, 55-47. It was a see-saw affair throughout the game until the fourth quarter, when the Blue Jackets took the lead for good on the merits of Rice and Kepler, who led the team on both ends of the floor to preserve the big win. Game Two then saw Hopkins eliminate Bemidji, 69-56, on some spectacular shooting. Hopkins, led by J. Porter and Dave Tschimperle's 20 and 18-point performances, made 21 out of 22 free-throws and nailed 24 out of 40 field goals in the win.

The defending champs from Hopkins just kept it going in the Finals, beating Hibbing by the final score of 58-49. The Royals went into the intermission up by one at 23-22, only to see the Blue Jackets, behind M. Marion, who had 15 points in the game, rally in the third. But Dave Tschimperle, who tallied 26 points of his own in the contest, broke a 32-32 tie by nailing a jumper, as well as the ensuing free-throw, to lead his team back to the promised land. The Royals then held firm in the fourth and cruised to the easy victory.

1954: Brainerd vs. Bemidji

Renville iced Hibbing in Game One, 49-47, on W. Brandt's last second shot followed by Charlie Huselid's free-throw, while Bemidji dumped St. James in the second quarterfinal, 60-54, on Forward Jack Whiting's 19 points. Austin won the first evening game, 43-40, over a very tough Willmar team that, behind Center Bob Anderstrom's 20 point game, rallied back from a 10-point half-time deficit to make it close in the fourth. The mighty Packers, however, led by six-foot-five Hugh Hall, six-foot-five Jerry Olson and six-foot-six John Lightly, were too tough though and hung on to advance into the semi's. Brainerd then edged Red Wing in a real barn-burner, 56-55. Brainerd jumped out to a 32-27 lead at the half, only to see the Wingers tie it up at 52-52 late in the game. From there, they went up by four on a pair of free-throws from both Johnson and Jelacic. Red Wing then rallied behind Willie Fjerstad's basket and ensuing free-throw, but with three seconds to go Brainerd stalled and won the game in dramatic fashion.

The opening semifinal was an exciting one as Bemidji topped Renville, 46-44, on Johnson's 13 points. Renville jumped out to an early lead in this one, but Brainerd came back to tie it at 44-44 late in the fourth. Now, with just two minutes to go, Renville got the ball and stalled for a last-second shot. Then, with 15 seconds on the clock, they drove but missed — sending the game into overtime. There, both teams shut each other out, and it went into double overtime. Finally, Bemidji controlled the opening tip-off in the second OT and Jack Whiting nailed what proved to be the game-winning shot.

Brainerd kept it going in their semifinal by knocking off Austin, 57-56. Austin led 31-27 at halftime and 41-39 as the fourth quarter began, only to see Brainerd, behind their star, Rod Skoog (the brother of Laker great Whitey), tie the score at 44-44. But then Skoog fouled out and Austin pulled ahead 48-46. That's when Roger Adair, who tallied 16 points in the game, came up big and led Brainerd to a 56-50 lead. Austin cut the margin to one and had a chance to win it in the final seconds, but just came up short in the end.

It was an all Northern Finale when Brainerd and Bemidji hooked up in the Finals. Brainerd quickly jumped out to a 13-2 lead on Rodney Skoog, and Roger Adair's sharp-shooting, only to see Bemidji rally to get it to 44-41 at the end of the third quarter. From there Brainerd, behind Adair and Jelacic's jumpers got the lead, but Jack Whiting's free throw and Don Hoffman's long-range shot with 4:27 remaining made the score 49-46. Bemidji Guard Bob Parker then added a free throw to make it 49-47, but that was as close as the Lumberjacks would get. They had three possessions in the final moments, but clanged each one off the rim to end the game. Skoog led Brainerd with 19 points while Whiting paced Bemidji with 14 points of his own.

Front Row: Rodney Skoog, Darien DeRocher, Tom Jacobson, Roger Adair, Gene Loya, Leonard Hildebrandt.
Back Row: William Miller, John Jelacic, Kenneth Wasnie, Merle Speed, James Guin, James Johnson, Coach Fred Kellett.

The 1954 State Champs from Brainerd

1955: Minneapolis Washburn vs. Austin

By 1955 attendance at the tournament had soared to 84,000 fans, and one of the reasons for this was the fact that seemingly everyone wanted to come out and see the darling of this year's classic, tiny Esko (population: 130). Esko would not have an easy first-round opponent, however, as they were forced to play New Prague, and their six-foot-six junior swing-man, Ron Johnson, who would go down as one of the state's greatest ever. He single-handidily took over the game and dumped in 32 points en route to leading the Trojans to a 56-38 win.

Minneapolis Washburn coasted past Morris, 71-50, in the other quarterfinal, while Bemidji, behind Darrell Erickson and Jack Whitney's 18-point efforts, had little trouble with Ortonville, winning easily, 74-59. The final quarterfinal of the evening then pitted mighty Fairmont against the unbeaten Austin Packers. The Cardinals jumped out to a 35-30 halftime lead on the solid shooting of Roger Smed and Tom Idstrom. Then, with Fairmont ahead late in the game, Austin's John Lightly hit an off-balance jumper to send the game into overtime. There, Austin's experienced players took over and went on a 6-0 run, beating the Cards by the final score of 76-69.

Front Row: Mike Murphy, Bob Farrington, Neil Feinberg, Pat Sweeney, Dave Wiggins, Tom McBurney.
Second Row: Student Manager Mike Olson, Asst. Student Manager Dick Lindholm, Bruce Sachs, Jack Medcalf, 2nd Asst. Coach Chuck Hoffman, Coach Ray Ross.
Back Row: John Knudtson, Tal Tischer, Gordie Sundin, Stu Hanson, Dave Michaelson, Lee Chapman, Jerry Hedin.

The 1955 State Champs from Washburn

Washburn then upset New Prague in the opening semifinal, 65-48, as Stuart Hanson, who tallied 27 points in the game, out-dueled Ron Johnson. Washburn rallied for a 29-25 lead at the half, but New Prague used a zone defense to rally back. It was too little, too late though, as Washburn stalled during the game's final minutes to advance into the semifinals.

Bun Fortier's Bemidji Lumberjacks came up one point short in their 56-55 loss to Austin in the other semifinal. Bemidji came out smoking in this foul-fest and led 11-10 at the end of the first quarter. Austin's Jerry Olson then scored eight straight points to make it a 28-27 halftime score. Jack Whitney led Bemidji to a 37-30 lead in the third quarter but with 48 seconds remaining in the game, Austin's Terry Meyer broke a 55-55 tie when he nailed a clutch free throw to give the Packers a 56-55 victory.

Washburn then cruised past Austin in the Finals, 67-58, to take their first title. Washburn trailed in the opening stanza by as much as 17-11 before closing the gap to 19-17 going into the second. Then, thanks to scores from Gordie Sundin, Dave Michaelan and Pat Sweeney, they moved ahead, 34-27 at the half. Washburn opened up a 42-33 margin in the third, only to see John Lightly and Jerry Olson bring Austin back to within five. It as as close as they could get though, as Washburn cruised down the stretch to take the big win.

1956: Minneapolis Roosevelt vs. Blue Earth

Blue Earth opened the '56 tourney by dumping Glenwood, 53-43, on George Dean's 14 points and 22 rebounds. Game Two then saw Winona beat Montevideo in a phenomenal comeback victory. With just two minutes remaining in the game and trailing by 10 points, Winona rallied, and on Chuck Wally's field goal, went ahead for the improbable 70-66 win. New Prague, behind Ron Johnson's 34 points, beat a determined Bemidji squad in the first evening game by the score of 75-71. Big Ray Cronk scored 20 points and 14 rebounds in the loss. Roosevelt, behind the solid play of Bob Freund and Tom Nordland, then rolled Aurora in the other quarterfinal to advance into the semi's.

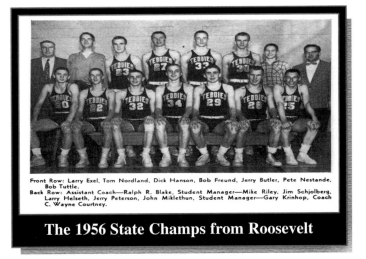

Front Row: Larry Exel, Tom Nordland, Dick Hanson, Bob Freund, Jerry Butler, Pete Nestande, Bob Tuttle.
Back Row: Assistant Coach—Ralph R. Blake, Student Manager—Mike Riley, Jim Schjolberg, Larry Helseth, Jerry Peterson, John Miklethun, Student Manager—Gary Krinhop, Coach C. Wayne Courtney.

The 1956 State Champs from Roosevelt

Blue Earth then took care of Winona in the first semifinal, 62-57. Blue Earth played well early and went up by four at halftime, 27-33. From there Winona kept it tight, but couldn't close the gap. Darryl German and Al Henke scored late while George Dean and David Abel played tough defense for the Bucs as they cruised to the big victory and their first-ever appearance in the state finals.

Game Two was a blow-out as Roosevelt upended New Prague, 70-53. Ron Johnson again played a brilliant game, scoring 27 points, but the bigger, stronger Teddies held him in check down the stretch to pull out the big win. Jerry Butler scored 18 points while Pete Nestande added 16 for the Teddies.

Roosevelt then absolutely demoralized the Bucs in the Finals, establishing a new all-time championship game record by scoring an amazing 101 points. The Teddies jumped out to a 26-12 lead after the first quarter and made it 47-30 at the half. From there they just put it in cruise control. Roosevelt, which was led by All-Staters Pete Nestande, Jerry Butler and Larry Exel, shot 52% in the monsterous victory.

1957: Minneapolis Roosevelt vs. Red Wing

The defending champs from Minneapolis Roosevelt kicked off the 1957 tournament by picking up right where they left off. Bemidji, on Ray Cronk's solid play, had the early lead in this one, but Roosevelt came back to tie it up at 66-66 on Darrell Miller's jumper and forced the game into overtime. There, with the score knotted at 70-70, Jerry Butler's field goal and Greg Larson's ensuing free throw iced the victory for the Teddies, 73-70.

Fergus Falls edged out a very tough Hibbing club, 57-55, in Game

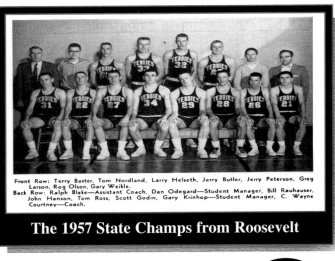

Front Row: Terry Baxter, Tom Nordland, Larry Helseth, Jerry Butler, Jerry Peterson, Greg Larson, Rog Olson, Gary Weikle.
Back Row: Ralph Blake—Assistant Coach, Dan Odegard—Student Manager, Bill Rauhauser, John Hanson, Tom Ross, Scott Godin, Gary Krinhop—Student Manager, C. Wayne Courtney—Coach.

The 1957 State Champs from Roosevelt

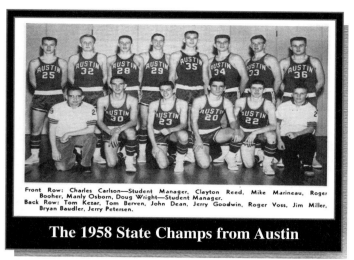

The 1958 State Champs from Austin

Front Row: Charles Carlson—Student Manager, Clayton Reed, Mike Marineau, Roger Booher, Manly Osborn, Doug Wright—Student Manager.
Back Row: Tom Kezar, Tom Berven, John Dean, Jerry Goodwin, Roger Voss, Jim Miller, Bryan Baudler, Jerry Petersen.

Two. Eddie Ohman, who scored 19 for the Otters, pushed Fergus to a 56-51 lead late in the game. But the Jackets rallied back in the final moments on Jack Kupla's bucket and ensuing free-throws, only to come up short. Red Wing got nine fourth quarter points from Dick Johnson to ensure their 54-46 victory over Rochester, while tiny Walnut Grove, behind Dale Anderson's 16 first half points, topped Pemberton in the final quarterfinal of the day, 70-65.

Roosevelt pounded Fergus Falls in the opening semifinal, 83-59, thanks to a tremendous fourth quarter surge. Tom Nordlund led the way for the Teddies by scoring 31 points, while his teammate, Jerry Butler, also played outstanding in added 24 of his own. The other semi then saw Red Wing outlast Walnut Grove, 88-74. The Wingers took a commanding 21-3 lead early in the first quarter largely due to the efforts of Steve Malmar and Curt Thalberg. From there they upped their lead to 43-22 at the intermission, and then 61-37 into the fourth quarter. Steve Malmar scored 25 points for the Teddies while Tom Nordlund scored 24 points for Walnut Grove.

Roosevelt just kept on cruising into the Finals, where they beat Red Wing, 59-51, to take their second straight state title. The Wingers led 12-10 at the first quarter, only to see Roosevelt rally back to take a 27-23 half-time lead. It was back and forth from there until Red Wing's star Jim Hayes fouled out late in the game. From that point Roosevelt, behind the solid play of Tom Nordlund, Greg Larson and Jerry Butler, took a commanding lead and never looked back. The Teddies were two-time champs.

1958: Austin vs. Brainerd

Austin surprised everybody by going into a zone defense in their opening quarterfinal game against Cloquet, but the strategy paid off as the Packers came out with a 53-51 win over a tough Lumberjack club which was led by All-Stater Dick Millen, who posted 22 points and 21 rebounds in the loss. Willmar topped Brownton, 66-55, in Game Two thanks to Dean Anderson's 26 points, while Brainerd, on Guard Jim Brown's 31 points, edged Bemidji in the first evening game, despite Center Ray Cronk's amazing 26-point effort. Then, Mankato edged a scrappy Mora squad in the finale by the final score of 71-69, on Herb Stanglund's thrilling last-second jumper to ice the game.

Nearly 19,000 fans showed up to watch Austin defeat Willmar, 59-56, in the first semifinal game. As the first half came to a close, Dean Anderson and Red Harvey gave Willmar a 33-28 lead. But Austin came back in the second behind Tom Kezar's 28 points to tie it up. That's when Manly Osborne nailed what proved to be the game-winner with 12 just seconds remaining on the clock to sew it up for Austin. Brainerd then edged Mankato in the other semi, 59-56. Jimmy Brown led the early charge for Brainerd, leading them to an early 10-8 lead. Herb Stanglund led the Scarlets in their second half comeback though, scoring 20 of his game-high 25 points in the final period to get his club back in the ball game. It was too little too late, however, as Brainerd's John Emerson scored 14 points down the stretch to preserve the big win for the boys from the north.

In the Finals it was Austin beating Brainerd, 68-63, thanks to the efforts of their star, Roger Voss, who, after sitting out the second quarter because of early foul troubles, came back to lead his Packers to victory. Brainerd had the early lead in this one, but Austin, behind the stellar play of All-Stater's Manly Osborne and Tom Kezar, rallied back to tie it at 53-53 early in the fourth. From there the Packers opened it up and never looked back, winning their first-ever title in style.

1959: Wayzata vs. Carlton

In the opening round of the 1959 State Tournament Wayzata leaped out to a 22-8 lead and just kept on cruising, beating Mankato, 57-51. Austin beat tiny Hawley in Game Two, 62-57, thanks to All-Stater Tom Kezar's basket and two free-throws to ice it in the contest's final moments. Then, in the first evening quarterfinal, Carlton upset Bemidji, 65-58, on Ron North's hot hand. Carleton, also led by John Pierson's stellar two-way play, continuously rallied back from no less than four 7-point deficits to rally back in this one. Vickey finished with 24 points for the Lumberjacks. North St. Paul, behind Don Arlich's 20 points, then defeated Granite Falls in the last game of the day, 60-52. Gerald Hegna had 15 points for the Kilowatts in their defeat.

With just a few ticks on the clock, Don Mueller stepped up to the charity stripe and calmly sank two free-throws to lead Wayzata past Austin in the first semi, 55-52. During the first half the lead exchanged hands 10 times before Wayzata pulled it out in the game's final moments. Mueller played a terrific fourth quarter, scoring 13 of his 17 points in the final frame, while Packers' star Tom Kezar played outstanding in the loss.

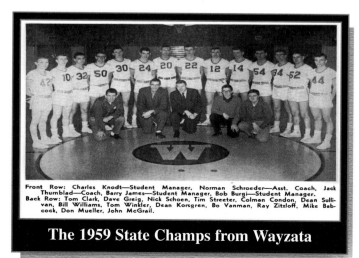

The 1959 State Champs from Wayzata

Front Row: Charles Knodt—Student Manager, Norman Schroeder—Asst. Coach, Jack Thumblad—Coach, Barry James—Student Manager, Bob Burgi—Student Manager.
Back Row: Tom Clark, Dave Greig, Nick Schoen, Tim Streeter, Colman Condon, Dean Sullivan, Bill Williams, Tom Winkler, Dean Korsgren, Bo Vanman, Ray Zitzloff, Mike Babcock, Don Mueller, John McGrail.

Carlton then narrowly beat North St. Paul in the other semi, 50-49, thanks to John Pierson's game-winning hoop with just 34 seconds remaining in the game. Fred North and Pierson led Carlton to a 19-10 second quarter lead before Polars swing-man Don Arlich finally got on the board. He led them back though, and made it one of the best games of the tourney.

With that, it was Wayzata and Carlton for all the marbles. This one got underway with the Bulldogs' two stars, John Pierson and Fred North, leading their club to an early 15-8 margin by scoring 10 unanswered points. Four quick points by the Trojans gave them a 23-19 lead early in the third period but a free throw by Pierson and a long jump shot by North tied it back up midway through the third period. From there Wayzata jumped out to an 11 point lead behind the balanced scoring of Vanman, Mueller, Zitzloff, Winkler and Sullivan, who each had 14, 12, 10, 10 and 7 points, respectively. By that point it was all over as Wayzata cruised to a 55-41 win, and their first state title.

1960: Edgerton vs. Austin

The 47th annual Minnesota High School Basketball Tournament kicked off with Granite Falls edging Melrose, 44-42. Granite Falls' star Gerald Hegna scored a free throw while his teammate, Dick Lundell, nailed a jumper to tie it up late at 42-42 tie. That's when Hemingson hit a pair of huge free throws as time was running out to ice the game for the Granites. In Game Two Austin spanked Thief River Falls, 55-41, on Clayton Reed's 20 points, while tiny Edgerton dumped Chisholm, 65-54 in Game Three on Dean Veenhof's 24 points. The final quarterfinal then saw Richfield eliminate North St. Paul, 60-51, as Bill Davis led Richfield with 20 points, and Larry Hansen guided the Polars with 25 in the loss.

Left to Right: Darrell Kreun, Larry Schoolmeester, Norm Muilenburg, Bob Wiarda, Dean Verdoes, Dean Veenhof, Robert Dykstra, Jim Roos, Daryl Stevens, Darwin Fey, LeRoy Graphenteen, Tom Warren.

The 1960 State Champs from Edgerton

While Austin upended Granite Falls in one semifinal, the big story was Edgerton, who, with their their 23-year-old coach, Richie Olson, quickly became the Cinderella-story of the tourney after they upset Richfield in the other semi, 63-60. Richfield jumped out to an early 10-3 lead in this one, only to see Edgerton come back to take a 30-28 lead at the half. The game remained close throughout the final period, but turned to Richfield's favor when Veenhof fouled out with 5:09 left and Edgerton leading. Now, with the score tied at 56-56, thanks to a pair of Bill Davis' game-high 26 points, and only six seconds to go in the game, Richfield went into a stall. Then, before they could set up their final shot, Edgerton stole the ball and forced it into overtime. There, with their top scorer, Dean Veenhof, and then star forward, Dean Verdoes, on the sidelines with five fouls, Darrel Kreun stepped it up and scored two of his 21 points with 1:28 remaining to put Edgerton on top, 58-56. Then, LeRoy Graphenteen took over, scoring a trio of free-throws in the game's final seconds to ice it for the Flying Dutchmen.

Now, in the championship game, it was tiny Edgerton, with a population of 961, taking on mighty Austin, whose population was nearly 30,000. It was David vs. Goliath, and the 19,018 fans, the largest to ever see a high school basketball game in Minnesota, loved every minute of it. They cheered every time a Dutchman player touched the ball, and clearly wanted the underdogs to win. Edgerton, the only undefeated team in the state, with 26 straight victories, jumped out to a quick 17-11 lead by the end of the first quarter and increased their margin to 36-24 at halftime. Austin, behind Clayton Reed's 21 points, tried to get back into it, but couldn't get anything started. From there Dean Veenhof took over, scoring 26 points down the stretch, while LeRoy Graphenteen added 15 and Dean Verdoes and Darrell Kreun, chipped in with 12 and 11 points, respectively. The crowd went nuts as Edgerton pulled away for the improbable 72-61 victory. Cinderella was alive and well, and living in Edgerton.

1961: Duluth Central vs. Bemidji

Duluth Central kicked off the quarters by defeating Danube, 74-52, largely in part to the efforts of freshman Forward Chet Anderson's 22 points. Sauk Centre ousted Mahtomedi in Game Two, 54-40, on Ed Pfepsin's 16 points, while Winona, behind Heise's 19 points, spanked Royalton, 71-51, in the

Front Row: Brian Cobb, Chester Anderson, Terry Kunze, Bill Lundston, Dan Howard, Charles Bradburn.
Back Row: Sherman Moe, Assistant Coach; Arden Staubs, Student Manager; Dan Cohen, Wallace Paschke, Roger Hanson, James Hastings, Coach; Larry Stevens, Neil Nordvall, Kris Johnson, Tom Brayden, Assistant Coach.

The 1961 State Champs from Duluth Central

first evening game. (Royalton replaced Minneapolis Roosevelt in the tourney because the Teddies had used two ineligible players in the section tournament.) Bemidji then upset the defending champs from Edgerton in the last game of the day, 76-67, as Larry Higgins scored 12 of his 26 points in the fourth quarter to lead Bemidji into the semi's.

Duluth Central kept it going in the semi's, spanking Sauk Centre, 75-53. Duluth led 36-25 at halftime, and thanks to the efforts of Chet Anderson, Terry Kunze and Roger Hanson, the Region Seven representatives made easy work of Sauk Centre and cruised into the Finals. Anderson led the way for Central with 26 points, while Hanson added 24 of his own in the big win.

Bemidji upended Winona, 57-51, in the other semifinal, thanks to Jack Phelps and Larry Higgins, who each tallied 20 had 18 points, respectively. The Lumberjacks jumped out to a big lead in this one, only to see Winona cut that margin to 27-26 at the half. Winona, behind Garrison's 14 points, then took a four-point lead midway through the third, but Bemidji rallied back to score 11 straight points for a 52-45 lead. From there the Lumberjacks pulled away and won it down the stretch.

In the championship game, Duluth Central jumped out to a 10-4 lead, only to see Bun Fortier's Bemidji Lumberjacks fight back to gain the nod at halftime, 26-24. Bemidji, behind buckets from Larry Higgins, Lee Faubush and Spencer Price, then took a 46-39 lead into the fourth. From there, Duluth's Dan Howard nailed a free throw, Roger Hanson hit back to back jumpers, and Chet Anderson scored on a tip-in to tie the score at 48-48. Then, with the score at 51-50, Bemidji stalled for the last final shot of the game, but Duluth's tough defense stymied them. The Lumberjacks couldn't find the back of the net and had come up short. For the second time in 11 years, Duluth Central was the champion of Minnesota basketball.

1962: St. Louis Park vs. South St Paul

Danube, with a population of 494, was the darling of the 1962 tourney.

Front Row: John Kappa, Bob Hill, Bruce Ackland, Mark Zanna, Gerry Brouwer, Gary Biewald.
Back Row: Bruce Fisher, John Zimmerman, Charles DeRemer, James Bloomquist, Jerry Orbeck, Larry Fundingsland, Gary McCulloch. (Larry Soper—missing from picture).

The 1962 State Champs from St. Louis Park

The Old Minneapolis Auditorium

They came out and beat Ada in their opening round match, 65-63, thanks to their star Guard, Bob Bruggers, who had 29 points in the big win. Ada, led by Herb Hasz's 31 points, rallied late, but came up one basket short. St. Louis Park then narrowly edged Crosby-Ironton in Game Two, 75-73, in overtime. Park's Charles Doumer scored with eight seconds left to send the game into overtime, and Bob Ackland's 15 footer with three seconds remaining in the extra session gave St. Louis Park the thrilling win. In Game Two South St Paul, led by John McLagen's 18 points, proved to be too much for Cloquet, and their star, Dave Meisner. The Packers jumped out to a 30-25 half-time lead and cruised to a 63-56 victory. Wells then beat tiny Lyle, 44-37, in the late game, thanks to the outstanding play of Ronald Meyer and Alan Redman, who tallied 14 points in the victory.

St. Louis Park ended Danube's wild ride in the first semifinal, 66-62, thanks to some timely shooting and solid defense. At the intermission Danube led 36-31 but St. Louis Park rallied to take a 42-39 lead in the third. Danube came back to take a two-point lead going into the fourth behind Bruggers, who scored 36 points on the day, but was just 10 of 23 from the free-throw line. But, with 2:14 remaining, Park's Larry Fundingsland nailed a jumper to make it 60-60. From there Bob Ackland and Fundingsland each scored a pair of free throws, while Mike Kurtz and Ackland, who led Park with 25 points, tallied late in the contest to seal the deal.

South St. Paul rolled Wells, 72-53, in the other semi, on John McLagen's 33-point outing. The Pack had a 35-27 lead at the half, and blew it open when McLagen scored five straight points to begin the third period. Alan Redman, who led Wells with 19 points, kept his Wildcats in it, but when George Feist, Wells' starting center, fouled out with 7:46 left, it was all over.

St. Louis Park then met South St. Paul in the Finals. Park had opened a 34-26 lead at the intermission and thanks to Ackland's three straight baskets in the early part of the third, the Orioles extended that to a commanding 50-41 margin at the beginning of the fourth. Dennis Pladon started the Packer rally though, hitting an off-balance jumper to cut Park's lead to 57-53 with 3:12 remaining in the game. The Packers kept it going on John McLagen's bucket, which made it 57-55, only to see Ackland's free throw give Park a three point lead. Now, with just over a minute to go, Dennis Pladson intercepted a pass took it to the hoop to cut Park's lead to 58-57. Bloomquist's rebound and ensuing tip-in moved Park ahead 60-57, and when Mark Zanna made a clutch steal, which led to a Fundingsland basket, it was all over. The final score was St. Louis Park 62, South St. Paul 57.

1963: Marshall vs. Cloquet

Marshall opened the festivities in the 1963 Big Dance when they beat Austin in a real thriller. Marshall led 42-29 at the half but the Pack, behind Bruce Miller's jump shot, pulled to within two points of Marshall at 57-55 midway through the fourth. John Nefstead's basket and Terry Porter's two free throws gave Marshall a 61-55 lead with 1:23 remaining. Then Austin's Harry Musser's two free throws followed by Dave Hartman's pair of buckets with just seven seconds remaining in the game, tied the score at 61-61 and sent the battle into overtime. There, Al Berg's basket was answered by Terry Porter's to keep it tied at 63-63. Then, with seven seconds remaining in the extra session, Porter was fouled and his ensuing two free throws gave Marshall a dramatic 65-63 victory.

Anoka eliminated Bemidji in Game Two, 54-48, when Bill Erickson scored six straight points down the stretch to seal the deal. The first evening quarterfinal then saw a battle between No. 1 Bloomington and No. 2 Cloquet. This one didn't live up to the hype though, as Cloquet upset the Bears, 87-67, thanks to the 30 and 29-point performances of Dave Meisner and Mike Forrest, whose clutch shooting down the stretch proved to be the difference. The final game of the day saw Sauk Centre top Wells, 64-58, as Alan Redman score 19 points and Don Schwanke scored a field goal and added a pair of free throws with just 24 seconds left to ice it.

It was Marshall crushing Anoka in the first semifinal contest, 61-35. Down in the first, Marshall scored 10 straight unanswered points to take a 33-15 lead at the intermission. Anoka's Dick Syring opened the second with a quick bucket, only to see Terry Porter and John Nefstead answer to make it 39-17. Marshall then led 54-26 into the third and put it in cruise control for the fourth, winning easily. Porter and Nefstead led Marshall with 17 and 15 points, respectively, while Hayes had 10 points for Anoka.

Cloquet then eliminated Sauk Centre by the final score of 87-81 in the other semi. The Mainstreeters led 22-18 at the end of the first quarter but Cloquet scored 20 points in the second period to take a 38-35 advantage into half-time. In the third period Sauk Centre struck back for a 42-40 lead but Cloquet rallied to take a three point lead into the third. Now, in the fourth, Sauk Centre's Joe Schmiesing and Allen Mickelson both fouled out and left a huge void out on the court. They hung tough though, and thanks to Dave Schwanke's two scores, pulled to within three points at 76-73. That was as far as they would get, however, as a trio of free throws by Welston, followed by Mike Forrest's jumper, gave Cloquet all the cushion they would need.

The championship game then featured a pair of old Morton High School grads in Cloquet's Bennett Trochil and Marshall's Glenn Mattke. There was no love loss in this one though, as the Lumberjacks jumped off to a 16-9 lead in the first quarter, behind Mike Forrest's 29 points, only to wind up tied at 43-43 at halftime. Opening the third period Cloquet's star, Dave Meisner, hit on a nice running jumper, but in so doing drew his fourth foul and was taken out of the game. With Meisner out, Porter, who tallied 22 points in the game, took over. He moved Marshall ahead, 66-59, only to see Cloquet strike back behind Boyer's field goal, which was then immediately followed by

Front Row: Dan Simpson, Glenn Mattke, Coach; Larry Drager, Jay Wiltrout.
Back Row: Brian Murphy, John Kirscht, Marion Paradis, John Nefstead, Dave Webb, Sandy MacDonald, Dennis Schroeder, Dick Larson, Terry Porter, Daryl Otten, Loren Johnson, Dave Markell.

The 1963 State Champs from Marshall

Meisner's quick steal and score. With Cloquet now up 66-65 with 3:34 left, Meisner took over. He scored a pair of buckets and dished out another to get the Jacks up by two. Then, after Marshall's Terry Porter and Cloquet's Mike Forrest exchanged baskets, Marshall's John Nefstead scored with under a minute to go to make it 74-73. Now, with just 15 seconds left, Marshall's Dennis Schroeder took a controversial foul, but stepped up and calmly hit a pair of free-throws to give his club the dramatic 75-74 victory and the State High School Basketball Championship. The 18,580 fans in attendance then promptly went nuts.

1964: Luverne vs. Rochester

Front Row: Curt Laudon, Brian Wells, Milo Herrmann, Rodger McKay, Robert Jessen, Greg Thone, Chuck Lippi.
Back Row: Ray Merry, Delbert Jessen, Tom Kozney, John Beyer, Bill Toms, Richard Iverson, Bob Lorentzen.

The 1964 State Champs from Luverne

Undefeated Proctor beat the Benson Braves in the opener, 64-63, in a real thriller. Proctor led 32-26 at the half and 52-41 going into the final period. But, with 1:42 remaining, Bob Laney, who scored 33 points and pulled in 32 rebounds in the game, scored two free throws to give Proctor a 63-56 lead. Benson then rallied behind Jim Hanson, Bill Brockmeyer and Dick Hawkins, all of whom scored, to slice Proctor's lead to 63-61 with just 18 seconds left. Hawkins then scored again, but when Ron Swenson nailed a clutch free-throw with just four seconds remaining, it was Proctor's ball game.

Luverne, led by Greg Thone's 20 points and John Beyer's 19, topped Hutchinson, 65-50, in Game Two, while Rochester got past Anoka, 61-54, in the other semi as Dave Nelson, an All-State quarterback in football, led Rochester with 21 points while Phil Johnson paced the Tornadoes with 16 of his own. Undefeated Edina-Morningside then spanked Bemidji, who was without their ill star center, Howard Hoganson, in the last quarterfinal, 44-28. Steve Kagol, Edina's speedy guard, scored 13 points for the region five champs, while Lumberjack Forward John Warford tallied 22 points in the losing effort.

With Del Jessen, John Beyer and Greg Thone, who scored 34, 15 and 14 points respectively, leading the way, Luverne crushed Proctor by the final score of 80-57. Proctor didn't score a field goal in the first five minutes and the Cards jumped out to a 15-2 lead. From there Jessen tossed in 11 points in the third and Luverne increased their lead to 59-45 going into the fourth. From there Luverne played great defense, holding the Rails to just 32% shooting. Bob Laney led Proctor with 19 points, while Don Hanson added 16 in what turned out to be Proctor's first loss in 25 starts.

Rochester then upset Edina-Morningside in the other semi, 76-61. Rochester led by their six-foot-seven Center, Dave Daugherty, took a 38-32 lead into half-time, and came out smoking in the third. Edina then tied the game at 42-42 on baskets by Steve Kargol and Dick Johnson and a free-throw by Tom Fiedler. From there it was back and forth, with both teams exchanging punches down the stretch. Finally, with Rochester leading, 63-57, with just over three minutes to go, Tom Aswumb, John Stably and Bryan Grohnke each nailed jumpers to tie it back up at 63-63. Dave Nelson then scored his first bucket of the game to fire the Rockets into the lead with 28 seconds remaining, only to see Edina's Bryan Grohnke hit two of his game-high 29 points to send the game into overtime at 65-65. There, Grohnke was awesome, but with 29 seconds left to go, Barley, who tallied 25 points in the game, made a pair of free-throws to put Rochester ahead, 74-71, followed by two more from Tony Christensen with just six seconds remaining. Edina pressed, but it was too little too late.

The title game between Luverne and Rochester was closer than the 72-66 final would appear. Luverne's John Beyer scored on a long shot with just four seconds remaining to give the Cardinals a 39-37 lead at the half, only to see Ron Cady open the third period by scoring a basket which ignited a Rochester rally. Rochester's Dave Daugherty then scored three of his 25 points while Dave Nelson added a bucket to knot the game at 55-55, with 6:34 remaining. Beyer kept Luverne in it though, hitting a clutch jumper to give his club a 61-55 lead with 2:08 to go. From there Greg Thone, who led all scorers with 26 points, and John Beyer, who added 20 of his own, played keep-away. The stall strategy would work like a charm, and the Cards came up victorious to win their first-ever state title.

1965: Minnetonka vs. Faribault

Minnetonka pounded Franklin, 76-54, on Bucky Ives' 23 points and Jerry Marquart's 18, in Thursday's first afternoon game. After jumping out to an 18-8 lead on five hoops by Paul Knight, the Skippers rallied from a two-point deficit in the second to pull away with the big win. Game Two saw Bemidji defeating Henning, 69-63, in overtime. Bemidji led 32-25 at half-time but Henning took a 58-54 lead with 2:54 to play. Howie Hoganson's field goal and two free throws then sent the game into an extra session, where, baskets by John Dow, who scored 26 in the game, and Duane Sheets, plus three foul shots by Bob Saeger, gave the Lumberjacks the "W." The first evening game had Faribault dishing Virginia, and its star, Jeff Ash, its first loss of the year, 60-55, on Tom Weaver's 30-point performance.

Then, in the final quarterfinal of the night, unbeaten Luverne and St. Paul Central hooked up. The lead see-sawed back and forth in this one with Central leading 33-25 at halftime, only to see the Cards, behind John Beyer's 23, score 11 unanswered points to pull ahead and win the game convincingly, 70-61. (This game was full of stars: Luverne's Del Jessen, who tallied 16 points in the game, went on to play football at the U of M, while Central's LeRoy Gardner, who tallied 21 points of his own, and John Beyer both went on to play Gopher hoops.)

Minnetonka opened the first period of its semifinal match against Bemidji by nailing 10 of its first 12 shots, but still found themselves behind, 22-21. Bemidji, on John Dow's six straight hoops, then took the lead in the second, only to see Paul Knight's tip-in at the 7:21 mark give Minnetonka a lead they wouldn't relinquish. The Jacks came back and made it close, but the Skippers, behind Knight, who scored 22 points, followed by Bucky Ives'

Front Row: Steve Meyers, Glen Thiessen, Jim Meyers, Ray Koupal, Tom Simon, Brian Mahin, Jerry Marquardt, Robert Carruth, Earl Christ, Coach.
Back Row: Art Ives, Doug Menke, Jon Hoffart, Paul Knight, Bob Abel, Trey Labatt, Dan Austin, Bob Berkey, Mgr.

The 1965 State Champs from Minnetonka

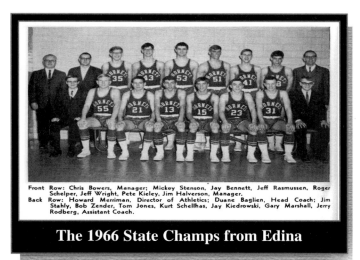

Front Row: Chris Bowers, Manager; Mickey Stenson, Jay Bennett, Jeff Rasmussen, Roger Schelper, Jeff Wright, Pete Kieley, Jim Halverson, Manager.
Back Row: Howard Merriman, Director of Athletics; Duane Baglien, Head Coach; Jim Stahly, Bob Zender, Tom Jones, Kurt Schellhas, Jay Kiedrowski, Gary Marshall, Jerry Rodberg, Assistant Coach.

The 1966 State Champs from Edina

18 and Jerry Marquart's 17, hung on for a 67-57 win. For Bemidji Head Coach Bun Fortier, who had brought 13 teams to the state tournament in 15 years, it was a tough loss.

Faribault knocked off the defending champs from Luverne in the other semi, thanks to Tom Weaver's tremendous individual performance of 26 points and 19 rebounds. Faribault led 27-23 at the half and kept it going for an impressive 57-50 win. Faribault 's Fred Zahn added 14 points in the win while Luverne was led by John Beyer's 18 points and Del Jessen's 10.

With the state crown on the line, Minnetonka stepped it up big-time to beat Faribault, 71-60. Neither team shot well in this one as Minnetonka hit for only 35% while Faribault was even chillier 28%. The Skippers were all about solid defense and fundamental rebounding in the game though, as they led 34-24 at the half and 51-39 after three. Dan Austin's 22 points led the way for Tonka, while Paul Knight, Skip Abel and Bucky Ives scored 16, 14 and 12, respectively. Faribault, on the other hand, was led by Tom Weaver's 23 points and Fred Zahn's 16. The win was big for Region Five, which had now won eight of the past 15 state titles.

1966: Edina vs. Duluth East

Duluth East dodged a huge bullet by the name of Ada in Game One of the 1966 state tourney. East won, 68-61, but got quite a scare from the very tough Vikings — who, behind Jim Stadum's 16 points took the Hounds down to the wire. In fact, Ada led by as many as nine in this one, only to see Duluth, on Dennis Falk's 17 points and 17 boards, rally back and take the victory.

The next game saw Hutchinson and Mounds View square off with Hutch battling back without their star center, Steve DeKoster, who was out with foul troubles, go on win by the final of 68-56. Ross Totushek and Tom Willard led Hutch with 18 and 17 points, while Tom Kunze scored 20 for Mounds View.

Game Three was all about tiny Henning, which flew by Blooming Prairie, 82-69, to become the darlings of the tourney. The Hornets jumped to a 34-28 half-time lead and never looked back. Leading the charge for Henning were Dick Peterson and Bob Peterson, who each scored 29 and 20, in the big win.

The last game of the day saw powerful Edina edging out a very tough Windom team, 60-59. Windom had a chance to win this one with under 30 seconds to go, but turned it over in the final moments to hand the Hornets the victory. Edina shot 50% from the field and was led by sophomore Bob Zender's 15 points, while Windom's Rich Frost led the way with 22 in the loss.

The first semi then saw Edina, with its more than 2,000 students, take on tiny Henning, which had far less inhabitants than that in its entire town. With that, Henning bolted to an early 21-16 advantage in the second, before Edina reeled off 12 unanswered points to take a 28-25 lead into the half. Henning hung around though, and thanks to Dick Peterson's basket followed by Bob Peterson's two more, they led mid-way through the fourth, 47-44. But Edina stayed calm, and when Kurt Schellhas tied the game at 49-49 to send it into over-time, you could feel the momentum swing for the Hornets. There, both teams played inspired defense, and matched each other tit for tat. Finally, in the third extra session, Edina's Tom Jones hit a running lay-up to give his squad the lead, and from there they cruised to a 62-55 victory.

Duluth East's journey to the title game was much easier than that of Edina's as East jumped all over Hutchinson, early and often. The Hounds led 43-28 at the intermission, 60-40, after three, and then 76-49 at the buzzer. East's relenting zone-press was rock-solid and confused Hutch, which was led by Steve DeKoster's 20 points, at every turn. Thanks to the scoring of Dennis Falk, who tallied 18 points, Chuck Baxter, who added 17, and Jeff Wells and Bruce Backberg, who each chipped in 15 apiece, East was on its way to the Finals.

The undefeated Edina Hornets matched up well with Coach Joe Mrkonich's Duluth East club on paper. But this one was played on the hard-court, with Edina pulling it out late, 82-75. East raced out of the blocks in this own, sinking their first seven shots to take a 21-14 lead in the first. Edina answered though, and rallied back to get to within one at the half. From there East tried to confuse the Hornets with their zone defense, but when Edina pulled out the old "1-3-1 half-court trap," in the fourth, it was a very different ball-game. The Greyhounds' smothering defense caused several turn-overs and ultimately gave the Hornets the ball-game. Now, down by four with just over a minute left, Edina got clutch baskets by Bob Zender and Jeff Wright to tie it up at 69-69. From there it went into overtime, and thanks to Jeff Wright's quick bucket off the tip, Edina gained the lead that they wouldn't relinquish. East came close, cutting the lead to one on two occasions, but the Hornets played keep-away and escaped with the 82-75 championship win. Jay Kiedrowski and Kurt Schellhas had 19 points apiece for Edina, while Jeff Wells and Dennis Falk scored 23 and 22 points, respectively, for Duluth East.

Front Row: Howard Merriman, Director of Athletics; Bob Downs, Doug MacLennan, Jeff Wright, Jay Bennett, Pete Kieley, Mike Burley, Duane Baglien, Coach.
Back Row: Jerry Rodberg, Asst. Coach; Rick Kitchen, Student Manager; John Tjaden, Bill Fiedler, Bob Zender, Kurt Schellhas, Jay Kiedrowski, Robb Jones.

The 1967 State Champs from Edina

1967: Edina vs. Moorhead

Hayfield's Gary Fritze caused nearly a half-hour delay for the opening of their game against Bemidji when his monster jam busted the Williams Arena back-board during the warm-ups. They got it fixed though, as Bemidji came out behind Jim Sutton's 14 points and edged Hayfied, 56-53. Mark Fredrickson connected on 18 for Hayfield, but came up just short in the end.

The second game of the day had the defending champs from Edina walloping St. Paul Central, 86-55. The Hornets, which graduated just one player from the year before, and were re-stocked by a group of sophomores which had just posted a three-year record of 56-0, were looking very good to go all the way in this tournament. They led 72-33 after three and thanks to Bob Zender's 25 points and Kurt Schellhas' 18, they outmatched Central, and their star, Jim Hill, who scored 21 points in the loss.

The first evening game had Duluth Central topping Luverne, 62-58, as

Mel Anderson scored two of his game-high 23 points with 5:33 to gave the Trojans a 49-48 advantage which they weren't about to lose.

Moorhead then rallied to defeat Walnut Grove, and their star, Tom Masterson, 72-68, in Thursday's final quarterfinal contest.

Edina played solid defense and got balanced scoring from Kurt Schellhas, Bob Zender and Jay Kiedrowski to beat Bemidji in the opening semifinal. The Hornets hung on to a 28-27 half-time lead and then came out and held the Jacks scoreless for nearly five minutes into the third quarter. From there they out-rebounded Bemidji, 29-18, and cruised to a 64-51 victory.

The Moorhead Spuds made their triumphant return to the Big Dance, having not played in the gala since 1930. Duluth Central leaped out to a 44-35 advantage in the third period, only to see the Spuds, behind Richard Isaman's 25 points, rally back to take the 73-69 semifinal win. Duluth, however, on Jim Hart's 28-point effort, got it to within three points, at 70-67, with three minutes to go, but scores by Pat Driscoll and Doug Hastad put it out of reach for Moorhead.

The Hornets rolled over Moorhead in the Finals though, spanking the Spuds, 72-55, to win their second straight title. Bob Zender led the Hornets with 23 points, while Jay Kiedrowski and Kurt Schellhas added 21 and 15, respectively, as their club cruised to a 21-9 lead after one and a 40-23 advantage at the half. Dick Isaman had 21 points and Pat Driscoll added 13 for Moorhead, but in the end Edina's defense was simply too much. Moorhead Coach Shocky Strand vowed to get back to the tourney that next year, and you know what? He was right.

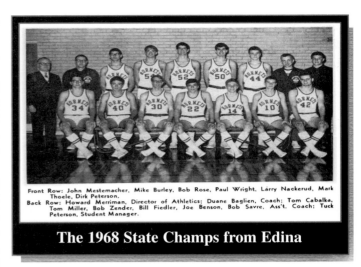

The 1968 State Champs from Edina

Front Row: John Mestemacher, Mike Burley, Bob Rose, Paul Wright, Larry Nackerud, Mark Thoele, Dirk Peterson.
Back Row: Howard Merriman, Director of Athletics; Duane Baglien, Coach; Tom Cabalka, Tom Miller, Bob Zender, Bill Fiedler, Joe Benson, Bob Savre, Ass't. Coach; Tuck Peterson, Student Manager.

1968: Edina vs. Moorhead

It was "David vs. Goliath" right out of the gates in the 1968 tourney as tiny Hayfield came up on the wrong end of a 63-49 ball-game against mighty Edina. Hayfield was down only 50-46 in the fourth quarter, but when Bob Zender and Bill Fiedler took over, each of whom scoring 19 and 15 points, respectively, the Hornets pulled away.

Duluth Central beat a tough Granite Falls team, 70-55, in Game Two, as Dick Pennington led the charge with 24 points while Richie Pearson added 20 of his own in the big win.

Game Three between Moorhead and St. Paul Highland Park was a real barn-burner. Offense was the word of the day in this one as both teams scorched the nets for a combined 196 points — a new MSHSL record. Moorhead led, 65-44, at the half, shooting 65% in the opening tile, while Highland shot an equally impressive 53% as well. The scoring was amazing: For Moorhead: Greg Troland—29, Gary Johnson—24, Tom Driscoll—21 and Paul Hanson—19; and for Highland Park: Rick Bulka—29, Jeff Ward—24 and Doug Eha—20.

Gary Hendrickson scored 18 points and Kevin Thom added 17 as Mankato rallied from a 33-30 half time deficit to spank East Grand Forks, 71-50, in the finale. Dale Skyberg had 18 points for East Grand Forks in the loss.

Edina faced its second straight unbeaten squad in as many days when they hit the floor against Coach Jim Hastings' Duluth Central Trojans in the first semifinal. Duluth emerged with the early lead in this one, but found itself at a big disadvantage when Dick Pennington got into early foul trouble. Edina roared back to take a 39-28 lead at the half thanks to Bob Zender's 35 points and Bill Fiedler's 27. The Hornets cruised down the stretch, dishing Central its only loss of the year, 91-61.

Moorhead started out slowly but turned it on late to blow-out Mankato in the other semi, 77-57. After leading by one at the half, the Spuds, behind Greg Troland's 25 points, Paul Hanson's 21 and Gary Johnson's 18, won it easily down the stretch. With the win, Moorhead had made it back to the Finals, where they would once again face their old nemesis, the Edina Hornets, for all the marbles.

Edina led 14-9 early, and thanks to some clutch shooting by Bill Fiedler, Bob Zender, and Tom Cabalka, the Hornet opened up a commanding 36-18 lead at the half. Moorhead rallied in the third behind Paul Hanson and Gary Johnson, and got their zone press working. They closed the gap to 37-28 in the third, but when Moorhead's star Greg Troland had to sit with foul trouble, Edina pulled away, taking a 50-35 lead after three. In the fourth quarter, the Hornets, behind Zender's 19 points, outscored the Spuds, 20-10, and hung on down the stretch to win it easily, 70-45. With that, Edina made history by becoming the first team in state history to win three straight state titles. Just how good was Edina? Their overall record in the just-completed five-year span, which included three straight titles, was 123-5. It was an official "Edinasty."

1969: Rochester John Marshall vs. Duluth Central

Richie Pearson's 19 points led Duluth Central past Alexander Ramsey in the opening round, 52-40, while Crosby-Ironton upset Minneapolis South, 75-69, in Game Two. Bob Taylor and Paul Heglund led Crosby-Ironton with 21 and 18 points, respectively, while Sheldon Anderson had 25 points for South. Dave Hollander's 26 points were more than enough to lead Rochester John Marshall past Wells, 75-62, in the first evening game. Wells, which was led by Steve Schultz's 19 points and Steve Feist's 18, simply couldn't keep up with the Rockets, who exhibited amazing all-around play at both ends of the court. Then, in the last quarterfinal of the day, Bemidji beat Gaylord, 63-48, as Tony Burke led the way with 21 points.

Duluth Central eliminated Crosby-Ironton in the opening round of semifinal action that Friday. Their size and depth were too much for tiny Crosby-Ironton, especially six-foot-eight Bill Haddon, who was dominant down in the paint. Bob Kunze led Central with 18 points while Bob Taylor led Crosby-Ironton with 13 of his own.

Bemidji's pressing defense was not good enough in the end to up-

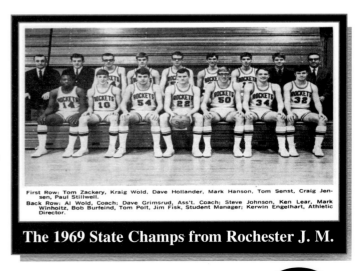

The 1969 State Champs from Rochester J. M.

First Row: Tom Zackery, Kraig Wold, Dave Hollander, Mark Hanson, Tom Senst, Craig Jensen, Paul Stillwell.
Back Row: Al Wold, Coach; Dave Grimsrud, Ass't. Coach; Steve Johnson, Ken Lear, Mark Winholtz, Bob Burfeind, Tom Polt, Jim Fisk, Student Manager; Kerwin Engelhart, Athletic Director.

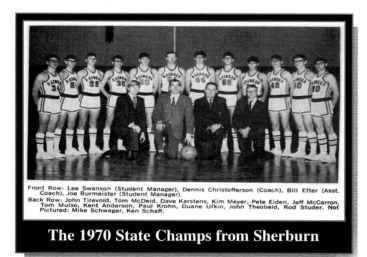

Front Row: Lee Swanson (Student Manager), Dennis Christofferson (Coach), Bill Etter (Asst. Coach), Joe Burmeister (Student Manager).
Back Row: John Tirevold, Tom McDeid, Dave Karstens, Kim Meyer, Pete Eiden, Jeff McCarron, Tom Mulso, Kent Anderson, Paul Krohn, Duane Ufkin, John Theobald, Rod Studer. Not Pictured: Mike Schwager, Ken Schaff.

The 1970 State Champs from Sherburn

root a very powerful Rochester John Marshall ball club, which wore down the Lumberjacks, 65-55. Size was again a big factor in this one, as evidenced by the fact that Bemidji's tallest regular was only as big as John Marshall's shortest starter. Craig Jensen led the Rockets with 21 points, while his teammates: Tom Senst, Mark Hanson and Dave Hollander each tallied 16, 13 and 12 points, respectively.

The Finals were now set, with Rochester John Marshall vs. Duluth Central for the state championship. This one was tight from the get-go, as both teams exchanged leads early on. Fast-forward to the fourth quarter, where the Trojans, on a pair of Richie Pearson's 19 points, held a delicate 34-32 lead. That's when John Marshall got hot thanks to Kraig Wold's long jumper, followed by clutch buckets from Mark Hanson and Craig Jensen, to give the Rockets a 38-34 advantage. From there JM, behind Craig Jensen's 25 points, was money, hitting 10 field goals down the stretch, while Duluth could manage only three. When the clock struck zero, it was John Marshall winning easily, 58-42.

1970: Sherburn vs. South St. Paul

The 1970 state tourney kicked off with the tiny Sherburn Raiders, who were averaging 81 points per game that year, while giving up just 49, eliminating Melrose, 65-54. Tom Mulso led the charge for the Raiders, scoring a game-high 29 points in the big win.

Game Two then saw Marshall spank Kenyon by the final score of 74-63. The Tigers bench was the key in this one as five-foot-six spark-plug Rick Manke came off the bench to ignite a fire storm. His hustle and drive got the crowd going, especially when he dove off of the raised Williams Arena floor to save a loose ball. His 13 points along with fellow reserve Rick Wollin's 17 were the big difference in this contest.

Robbinsdale had little problem with Eveleth in the first evening game, winning easily, 51-35. The Robins simply double-teamed Eveleth's big-man, Dennis Riley, and forced the team into making turn-overs. Riley did manage to tally 17 points while holding his opposing centerman, Stan Krebs, to just 10, but it wasn't enough as the Robbins cruised into the semi's.

South St. Paul then crushed Park Rapids, 97-61, in the final quarterfinal game. The Packers' trio of Brian Peterson, Mark Steve and Kurt Virgin, who scored 36, 26 and 18 points, respectively, showed why they were the tournament favorites coming in.

The opening semi saw Sherburn's Jeff McCarron go absolutely nuts by scoring 37 points and grabbing 24 rebounds against Marshall. Sherburn opened up a convincing 53-35 third quarter lead and hung on from there. Marshall rallied late on Rick Manke's 16 points, but came up on the short end of a 71-60 ball-game. The Sherburn Raiders were headed to the Finals.

Then, in the other semi, South St. Paul came on strong late in the game to upend Robbinsdale, 68-54. The Packers' big three of Steve, Peterson and Virgin, played solid two-way basketball, but unheralded Guard Steve Jancaric was the real hero of the day, scoring 16 points off the bench and scorching the Robins' defense with his smoking hot outside touch.

The Finals were now set, and it was yet again another case of little David against big Goliath, with unbeaten Sherburn, of course, playing the part of Dave. The entire southwestern Minnesota town of Sherburn was seemingly in attendance this Saturday night, complete with their "Hicks from the Sticks" buttons and all. The game got underway with Sherburn's six-foot-four swing-man extraordinaire, Tom Mulso, catching fire. He hit for 24 first-half points and scorched the Packers to the tune of 37 points on 18 for 38 shooting. South St. Paul stayed cool though, and rallied back. By the fourth quarter they had trailed only 49-47, and were poised to do some damage. Their half-court trap had gotten them a bunch of steals and they knew that if they could tire them out, the Raiders did not have a very deep bench. Then, early in the fourth, South St. Paul's Kurt Virgin fouled out and Sherburn, behind Jeff McCarron's 19 points and Pete Eiden's 15, got hot. Coach Dennis Christofferson then employed his aggressive 2-3 zone and the Raiders were back in business. From there they rebounded hard and stayed out of foul trouble, cruising to an amazing 78-62 victory. The crowd erupted in a scene very "Hoosier-esque" indeed.

Sherburn's improbable win would signify the end of an era, however, as the tournament switched to a two-class format that next year. It was a controversial move, and one that the large schools, particularly in the Twin Cities, opposed. The new system meant that only two teams would represent the entire metro area, which comprised over half of Minnesota's population. On the other hand, however, many of the small schools from rural areas were tired of having to compete in district and regional play with schools that were three, four and even five times larger. Throw the Cinderella Edgertons and Sherburns of the world into the mix and it was a real mess.

After much heated deliberation though, here's how it all went down: Each of the 486 member schools was allowed to cast four separate ballots, one each from the basketball coach, the athletic director, the principal and the superintendent. When the votes were counted, they overwhelmingly chose to create a two-class plan which would be implemented as a two-year experiment. As a result, the 68 largest high schools in the state would be considered "AA" teams while all others were given "A" status. The new tourney, which would now be spread out over four days, would also feature a new twist — a play-off game at Williams Arena between the "AA" and "A" champions that following week to determine a single out-right champion.

1971: Class A: Melrose vs. Red Wing

In the opening Wednesday quarterfinal contest of the "new" tourney, Melrose got balanced scoring from Butch Moening (20 points), Ron Maus (19) and John Thelen (17), to edge a very tough Two Harbors squad, 70-66. Scott McDonald, who later played at the University of West Virginia, scored 20

First Row: Frank Sheldon (Ass't. Coach), Tom Walz, Tom Herges, Dave Schneider, Paul Meyer, Marty Meyer, Ken Rausch, Del Schiffler (Ass't. Coach).
Second Row: John Thelen, Ron Maus, Rick Beuning, Randy Douvier, Mike Hertzog, Herb Ehlert, Dean Westendorf, Dave Linehan (Coach).
Third Row: Don Rademacher (Student Manager), John Herkenhoff, Butch Moening, Neil Thelen, Bruce Schulzetenberg (Student Manager).

The 1971 State A Champs from Melrose

points in the loss. East Grand Forks rallied back from a 41-29 deficit to top Albany, 63-49, in Game Two. Future Minnesota Vikings star Kurt Knoff led the charge by scoring 19 points for East Grand Forks, while Albany, which shot a dismal 28% in the game, was led by Joe Hasbrouk's 19-point effort. Now, on Thursday night after rotating with AA), Renville stayed undefeated thanks to the combined 26-point scoring efforts of both Doug Wertish and Larry Mulder, in their 74-55 win over Luverne. Mike Ahrendt and Bill Boehlman led Luverne with 18 and 17 points respectively. Then, in the last quarterfinal, Red Wing, on Steve Bombach's 22 points and Dan Meyers' 20, beat Rosemount to advance into the semifinals.

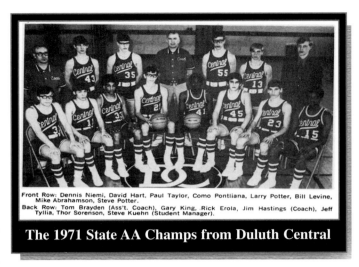

Front Row: Dennis Niemi, David Hart, Paul Taylor, Como Pontliana, Larry Potter, Bill Levine, Mike Abrahamson, Steve Potter.
Back Row: Tom Brayden (Ass't. Coach), Gary King, Rick Erola, Jim Hastings (Coach), Jeff Tyllia, Thor Sorenson, Steve Kuehn (Student Manager).

The 1971 State AA Champs from Duluth Central

Red Wing opened the first semifinal by jumping out to a commanding 47-33 lead against Renville. Renville, however, on Larry Mulder's 23 points, rallied big-time in the second half and even took a 61-59 lead with 5:51 to go in the game. But the Wingers, behind Dan Meyers' 33 points and Steve Bombach's 19, didn't panic. They instead worked their zone press defense and played fundamental basketball en route to pulling it out down the stretch, 76-65.

It was strength versus finesse in Melrose's thrilling win over East Grand Forks in the second semi. Melrose, behind Ron Maus' 19 points and John Thelen's 14, rallied to edge the Green Wave down the stretch, 54-53. Kurt Knoff had 17 points while his teammate, Rip Thompson, added 12 in the loss

The inaugural Class A title game wasn't as lopsided as the 64-53 score might indicate. Sure, Melrose outshot Red Wing 59% to 36%, and out-rebounded them, 40-19, but the Wingers, with their infamous zone press, hung around until the end and made it interesting. Melrose's Ron Maus had defended Red Wing's Dan Meyers tough all game, and even held the speedy swing-man scoreless until late in the third quarter. Meyers would come on strong in the second half though, scoring 19 points to lead a late rally. It was too little too late however, as the Dutchmen, behind John Thelen's 23 points and Butch Moening's 12, pulled away down the stretch, 64-53.

1971: Class AA: Duluth Central vs. North St. Paul

Minneapolis Central Guard Emmanuel Rogers tallied 33 points and was all over the floor in leading his Pioneer squad to a 79-76 win over the Mankato Scarlets in Game One of the AA quarterfinals. The North St. Paul Polars, with their big front line, crushed Alexander Ramsey, 67-42, in Game Two. Ron Adams scored 16 points and Jim Petrich added 15 for the winners, while Don Carlson had 22 in the loss for Ramsey. Duluth Central then topped Hopkins Eisenhower in the first evening game as Paul Taylor drained his first eight shots and six-foot-nine Center Como Pontliana dominated the boards en route to scoring a game-high 26 points. Then, in the last quarterfinal of the evening, Brainerd got past Robbinsdale, 67-56, on six-foot-five Forward Larry Bunnell's 17 points.

Duluth Central's Como Pontliana scored 34 points en route to leading his club past Brainerd in the opening semifinal game, 63-59. Wally Larson led Brainerd with 14 points while Larry Bunnell and Mickey Timmons had 11 apiece.

Then, in the final semifinal, Tom Bock's 23 points were the big difference in North St. Paul's 69-58 victory over Minneapolis Central. Jim Petrich added 20 for the Polars, while Emmanuel Rogers scored 21 of his own in Central's loss.

The Class AA title game was a real slug-fest as Duluth Central pounded North St. Paul, 54-51. The Polars', led by Jim Petrich's 22 points, had a game plan they wanted to stick to right out of the gates. They wanted to rattle Pontliana, and initially it worked. They double-teamed the big center and held him to just 18 points, but Central's other star, Larry Potter, picked up the slack and popped in 14 points of his own to lead Duluth to its first ever state title.

1971 Playoff: Duluth Central (Class AA) vs. Melrose (Class A)

The inaugural championship playoff game that next week between Duluth Central and Melrose was closer than the 54-43 final score appeared. In fact, Melrose, behind some balanced scoring from John Thelen, Ron Maus and Butch Moening, jumped out to an early lead and even held a nine-point lead late in the third quarter. But Central, behind Como Pontliana's 26 points, closed the gap. Their full court press got the best of Melrose, which turned the ball over too much down the stretch run. The six-foot-nine Pontliana, who dominated the boards, was also a huge factor in the game, towering over Melrose's tallest player, who was just six-foot-four. Central shut-out Melrose in the last four minutes of the game and cruised from there to take the playoff title.

With that, the first two-class tourney was put to bed. By all accounts it went well and the fans enjoyed it. Of course, in years to follow, many changes would be made. Smaller schools would join forces with neighboring schools to join the Class AA ranks, while "declining enrollment," would, conversely, put some of the AA schools into the A column. In addition, the tournament would also later be held at multiple locales, with both classes competing not only at the U of M's Williams Arena, but also at the St. Paul Civic Center and Bloomington's Met Center as well.

1972: Class A: St. James vs. Melrose

St. James got by a very determined St. Paul Murray squad in the opening round and moved into the semi-finals with a 57-51 victory. Murray actually led in this one, 51-49, with just over a minute to play but Jim Chalin's 25-footer tied it and a pair of ensuing free-throws by Mark Vanderbilt put the Saints on top for good. Chalin led St. James with 18 points, while Walt Johnson and Paul Healy each posted 18 and 17 points, respectively, for

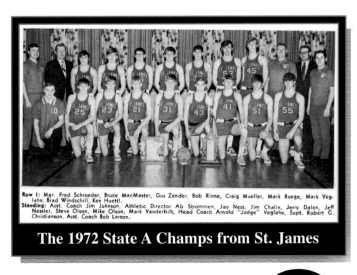

Row 1: Mgr. Fred Schroeder, Bruce MacMaster, Gus Zender, Bob Rinne, Craig Mueller, Mark Runge, Mark Veglahn, Brad Windschill, Ken Huettl.
Standing: Asst. Coach Jim Johnson, Athletic Director Ab Strommen, Jay Ness, Jim Chalin, Jerry Dalen, Jeff Nessler, Steve Olson, Mike Olson, Mark Vanderbilt, Head Coach Arnold "Judge" Veglahn, Supt. Robert G. Christianson, Asst. Coach Bob Larson.

The 1972 State A Champs from St. James

The 1972 State AA Champs from Mounds View

Front Row: Rick Pederson, Bryan Beggin, Kent Pletscher, Scott Moen, Steve Hage, Jim Berg, Brian Pletscher, Mike McEwen.
Back Row: Phil McManus (Asst. Coach), Jim Horn (Asst. Coach), Don Stevenson (Student Manager), Tom Kranz, Graydon Held, Al Jones, Mark Landsberger, Gary Nast, Paul Haskins, Paul Swenson, Mike Dietsch (Student Manager), Zig Kauls (Coach).

Murray.

Steve Broughton's 30-footer with time running out sent the Red Wing-Proctor quarterfinal game into overtime. There, Broughton scored three of his game-high 22 points to lead the Wings to a 66-59 victory. Gary Egerdahl led the Rails with 23 points of his own.

Howard Lake survived a late-game surge by Renville to post a 71-64 win in the third quarterfinal contest. Joel Pettit led the Lakers with 30 points while Center Larry Mulder canned 32 points for the Indians.

Then, in the last game of the day, the defending state champs from Melrose rolled over Littlefork-Big Falls, 69-45. Leading the charge for the Dutchmen was six-foot-five Forward Randy Douvier, who led all scorers with 28 points. Tom Morris posted 16 for Littlefork-Big Falls in the loss.

Howard Lake's undefeated season came to a screeching halt when Melrose spanked them in the first semifinal, 64-58. The Dutchmen played solid defense, eluded the press and shot 52% from the field in the big win. Leading the charge once again was Randy Douvier, who tallied 28 points for Melrose, while Dale Burau hit 15 for Howard Lake.

In the other semifinal St. James jogged to an easy 82-57 victory over Red Wing to advance to the state championship game. The Wingers couldn't keep up with the high flying James Gang, and crumbled down the stretch. Leading the charge for St. James were Jeff Nessler, who scored 31 points, and Jim Chalin, who added 16.

The Class A Final was a thriller to say the least. With 13 seconds left in the game, the defending champs from Melrose appeared poised to repeat. They had a 55-54 lead and the ball out of bounds. That's when St. James' speedy swing-man Mike Olson jumped in and stole the ball, only to get fouled in the process. From there he calmly stepped up to the line and hit a free throw to tie it up. Incredibly, the Saints then intercepted a long Melrose pass down court. That's when Jeff Nessler grabbed the ball and heaved up a 40-foot prayer which banked off the back-board and somehow found the back of the net as the buzzer was sounding. The Melrose bench stood in silence, while the Saints went absolutely nuts. Leading the way for the Saints was Jim Chalin, who scored 19 points, while future Gopher star Mark Olberding led the Dutchmen with 13.

1972: Class AA: Mounds View vs. Austin

Bloomington Lincoln, led by Dan Houck's 23 points and Denny Toles' 19, opened the AA tourney by beating White Bear Lake, 67-56. White Bear was led by Craig Tweedale's 22 points in the loss.

In Game Two North St. Paul rallied back from a 28-23 half-time deficit to beat Brainerd, 51-42. The Polars' defense stepped it up big-time in the second-half, holding Brainerd to just five total buckets. Chuck Petrich and John Hattenberger scored 15 apiece for the Polars while Brainerd's John Straka had 12 in the loss.

The tourney's first upset came in Game Three as Austin shocked Minneapolis North, 69-52. The Packers, led by Jim Riles' 24 points and Kal Kallenberger's 21, used a stifling defense to shut down North, and earn themselves a trip to the semi's.

Mounds View needed not one, but two overtimes to finally knock off the tourney favorites, Duluth East, 65-63. Mark Landsberger was the hero in this one as he nailed a pair of free-throws with just seven seconds left to ice the game. Landsberger, a future Gopher star, was huge in the game, scoring 26 points and grabbing 20 rebounds in the big win. In addition, Paul Haskins scored 18 for Mounds View, while Dennis Lund led East with 20 points.

Mounds View, behind Landsberger's 17 points, kept it rolling in the first round of semifinal action. There, they beat Bloomington Lincoln, 44-41, while holding the Bears to just 29% shooting. Dennis Toles had 15 points for Lincoln in the loss.

Then, in the other semi, Austin got 31 points from Kal Kallenberger en route to beating North St. Paul, 67-62. The Polars, behind Chuck Petrich and Dennis Auge, who scored 14 points apiece, did rally late, but came up short. The Pack played solid defense throughout the contest and nailed their free-throws when they were called upon down the stretch.

The Finals were all about Mounds View's Mark Landsberger, who dominated play en route to scoring 24 points and hauling in 15 rebounds, as his club beat Austin, 62-55, to win the AA championship. Austin did press late and mounted a rally midway through the fourth, behind Jim Riles' 21 points and Kal Kallenberger's 18, but ran out of juice in the finale.

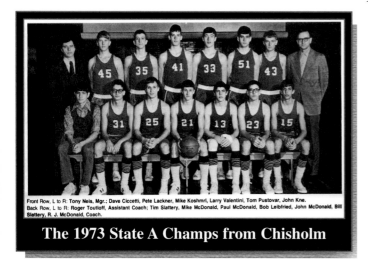

Front Row, L to R: Tony Neis, Mgr.; Dave Ciccetti, Pete Lackner, Mike Koshmrl, Larry Valentini, Tom Pustovar, John Kne.
Back Row, L to R: Roger Toutloff, Assistant Coach; Tim Slattery, Mike McDonald, Paul McDonald, Bob Leibfried, John McDonald, Bill Slattery, R. J. McDonald, Coach.

The 1973 State A Champs from Chisholm

1972 Playoff: St. James (A) vs. Mounds View (AA)

A crowd of 13,452 fans showed up at Williams Arena that next Tuesday to watch undefeated St. James battle Mounds View in the A vs. AA playoff. There, the Saints played a tough 1-2-2 defense and focused on shutting down Mark Landsberger. Their strategy worked, as they started out strong and finished strong for a 60-52 win. Protecting their lead late in the game, St. James played a tremendous slow-down game, frustrating Mounds View, and even forcing them into making turn-overs. Mounds View, behind Landsberger's 17 points and 19 rebounds, had the rebounding advantage throughout the game, but couldn't get their offense going. Offensively, St. James was led by Jeff Nessler's 22 points, Jim Chalin's 15 and Mark Vanderbilt's 10.

1973: Class A: Chisholm vs. Melrose

Windom forced a Mound into committing a state tournament record 32 turn-overs but still came up on the short end of a 58-53 ball-game in the Class A quarterfinal opener. Mound, led by John Luse's 20 points and Jerry Gibbs'

14, shot an amazing 69%, while Doug Miller led Windom with 19 points in the loss.

In Game Two Mark Olberding was simply unstoppable. The big-man dominated play by scoring 36 points, grabbing 29 rebounds and blocking four shots en route to leading his Melrose club past Preston, 70-44.

Chisholm, led by Tim Casey's 22 points, started off slowly in the first evening game but came back with a vengeance, out-scoring Mahnomen, 50-16, to cruise to an easy 74-43 win. Incredibly, Mahnomen broke the state tournament record for turn-overs, with 35, which had just been set in Game One by Mound!

Then, in Game Four, Gaylord suffered its first defeat of the year when it fell to Brooklyn Center, 52-48. After being knotted at 30-30, Brooklyn Center, behind Smith's 21 points and Arnie Barland's 16, broke it open in the fourth to get the big win.

Both semifinal games were yawners, as Chisholm, led by Mike Kochevar's 23 points and Tim Casey's 20, crushed Mound, 70-44. The Bluestreaks outscored Mound 46-26 in the second half en route to gaining entry into the Finals.

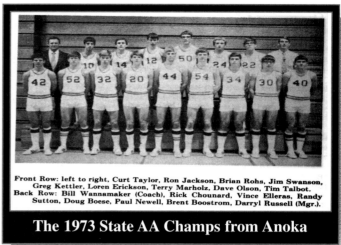

Front Row: left to right, Curt Taylor, Ron Jackson, Brian Rohs, Jim Swanson, Greg Kettler, Loren Erickson, Terry Marholz, Dave Olson, Tim Talbot. Back Row: Bill Wannamaker (Coach), Rick Chounard, Vince Elleras, Randy Sutton, Doug Boese, Paul Newell, Brent Boostrom, Darryl Russell (Mgr.).

The 1973 State AA Champs from Anoka

Then, in the other semifinal, Mark Olberding came out and once again posted some insane numbers, this time scoring 33 points and hauling in 16 rebounds, as his Melrose club smashed Brooklyn Center, 63-44.

Then, in the Finals, for the second ironic year in a row, the Dutchmen had sweet victory snatched away from them in the final moments of the game. The match was back and forth throughout the entire first half, with Melrose going up in the second. Chisholm then rallied back and won the game in dramatic fashion on Mike Kochevar's jumper in the lane with just five seconds left on the clock to seal the dramatic 53-52 victory. Melrose, behind Mark Olberding's 24 points and solid defensive play, out-rebounded Chisholm 33-18, but once again, had too many turnovers — this time 20, which proved to be the difference. Tom Kochevar led the way for the Bluestreaks, scoring 24 points in the big win.

1973: Class AA: Anoka vs. Richfield

Big Mark Landsberger tried to pick up where he left off in the 1973 Class AA playoffs, but was held to just 14 points by Rochester John Marshall, as they upset Mounds View, 63-52, in Game One. John Marshall's front line of Craig Hovland, Wayne Hegland and Dave Terhaar simply shut down Mounds View and cruised to the easy victory. In Game Two St. Cloud Apollo went on a 17-2 run in the fourth quarter and cruised to a 62-51 victory over St. Paul Park. Gary Frericks led the way for Apollo with 14 points, while Park was led by sophomore Glen Bourquinn's 18. Anoka, on Bryan Rohs' 20 points, went on a 13-4 run in the second quarter and never looked back in their 55-42 Game Three defeat of Duluth East. The final quarterfinal then saw Richfield roll over Edina West, 64-49, on Brian Denman's 21 points. Jeff Beebe added 18 for West in the loss.

Richfield kept it going in the opening semifinal, rallying back from an 11-point deficit to beat Rochester John Marshall, 52-47. Steve Bender led the way for Richfield with 18 points and 8 rebounds, while Dave Terhaar had 16 points for John Marshall in the loss.
The Anoka Tornadoes topped St. Cloud Apollo, 59-40, in the other semi as their tandem of big men, Greg Kettler and Loren Erickson, scored 18 and 17 points, respectively. Brad Akason had 16 for Apollo in the loss.

Now, in the championship game, Anoka rallied to beat Richfield, 58-54, in a game which had plenty of end-to-end action. Anoka started out slowly in this one and came back to fend off a late Richfield push. Their defense worked like a champ though, as they held Richfield at bay, never letting them get closer than four points in the fourth quarter. Six-foot-eight Loren Erickson scored 18 points and Bryan Rohs and Greg Kettler each added 12 in the big win, while Brian Denman had 16 points and Steve Bender added 15 for Richfield.

1973 Playoff: Anoka (AA) vs. Chisholm (A)

The overall championship game played that Monday did not feature the much-anticipated Olberding vs. Landsberger match-up, but it did pit two formidable foes against one-another in Anoka and undefeated Chisholm. Anoka, whose starters averaged six-foot-five, was simply too tough for Chisholm, which averaged just five-foot-eleven per man. The Iron Rangers got off to a quick start in this one though, forcing six Tornado turnovers with their full-court press. But Anoka stayed calm and went inside to their big men early and often, opening up a commanding 15-2 first quarter lead. Chisholm rallied to make it 23-16 at the half but Anoka increased its margin to 41-31 after three before going on to win, 63-56. Loren Erickson led the Tornadoes with 26 points and Greg Kettler followed suit with 19 of his own, while Tim Casey scored 18 points and Mike Kochevar added 17 for Chisholm.

1974: Class A: Melrose vs. Mound

Waseca kicked off the Class A tournament at the St. Paul Civic Center by beating Thief River Falls, 60-53. Gene Glynn scored 21 points for Waseca while six-foot-eight Center Wayne Peterson scored 18 for the Prowlers. In the second game of the afternoon, Mound, behind six-foot-seven Jerry Gibbs' 27 points, overcame leads of 14-2 and 28-15 to beat Simley, 66-49. Incredibly, in Thursday night's first game, Chisholm trailed in the second half for just the first time all year, 43-39 in the fourth quarter, but rallied to beat the former state champs from St. James, 53-47. The Bluestreaks were led by the amazing brother tandem of Paul and Mike McDonald, who scored 18 and 12 points, respectively. Marshall, behind Dave Scheele's solid play, jumped out to a 12-7 lead and held it until half-time against Melrose. The

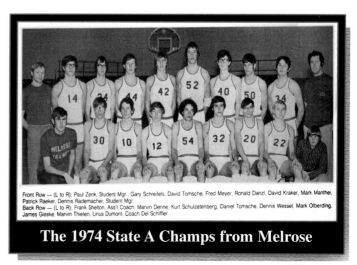

Front Row — (L to R): Paul Zenk, Student Mgr., Gary Schreifels, David Tomsche, Fred Meyer, Ronald Danzl, David Kraker, Mark Manthei, Patrick Raeker, Dennis Rademacher, Student Mgr.
Back Row — (L to R): Frank Shelton, Ass't Coach; Marvin Denne, Kurt Schulzetenberg, Daniel Tomsche, Dennis Wessel, Mark Olberding, James Gieske, Marvin Thielen, Linus Dumont, Coach Del Schiffler.

The 1974 State A Champs from Melrose

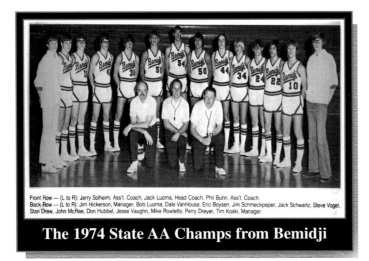

Front Row — (L to R): Jerry Solheim, Ass't. Coach, Jack Luoma, Head Coach, Phil Buhn, Ass't. Coach.
Back Row — (L to R): Jim Hickerson, Manager, Bob Luoma, Dale VanHouse, Eric Boysen, Jim Schmeckpeper, Jack Schwartz, Steve Vogel, Stan Drew, John McRae, Don Hubbel, Jesse Vaughn, Mike Rowlette, Perry Dreyer, Tim Koski, Manager.

The 1974 State AA Champs from Bemidji

second half, however, was an entirely different story altogether as Mark Olberding took over and scored 31 points en route to a convincing Melrose victory.

Jerry Gibb's 18-foot jumper at the buzzer was just what Mound needed to squeak by Waseca, 47-45, in the opening semifinal contest. Waseca led 30-22 at the half but Mound came back in the second on Huff's 19-point effort. Six-foot-six Forward Steve Cunningham led the charge for Waseca by tallying 14 points in the loss.

Chisholm then suffered its first loss in the other semi, a 63-54 defeat at the hands of undefeated Melrose. It was Mark Olberding, who hit for 25 points and grabbed seven rebounds, who did most of the damage in this one as Melrose exacted a little revenge over the team which dramatically eliminated them from the playoffs the previous year.

With that, Melrose finally won that ever-elusive state title by edging Mound, 38-32, in the Finals. Mound rallied in the fourth quarter behind Jerry Gibbs' 11 points, but Mark Olberding, who finished with 26 points and 13 rebounds, played great defense down the stretch to seal the deal for the Dutchmen. They had finally won their championship!

1974: Class AA: Bemidji vs. Richfield

Bemidji, behind Steve Vogel's 18 points and 11 rebounds, and guards Don Hubbell and Perry Dryer's 16 and 15 points, beat a very tough Alexander Ramsey team, 67-53. Craig Johnson led Ramsey with 16 points in the loss. Rochester Mayo rallied from a 23-13 deficit to edge Anoka, 52-51, in the second afternoon game. Mark Brandenberg scored 18 points for Mayo, while Bob Foss added 13 for the Tornadoes.

Washburn topped Hopkins Lindbergh in overtime, 58-56, in the first evening contest. Bill Molzahn's jumper got Hopkins into the extra session, but buckets by Randy Williams and Ross Baglien, who scored 18 and 16 points in the game, respectively, gave the Millers the thrilling victory. Then, in the last quarterfinal contest, a very physical Richfield squad spanked Willmar by the final score of 68-52. Brian Denman scored 25 points and Paul Meisner added 16 for Richfield, while Joel Jacobson scored 19 for the Cardinals.

Steve Vogel scored 20 points and Stan Drew added 18 as Bemidji kept it going in the first semifinal, easily beating Rochester Mayo, 66-51. Mayo, which started out strong, only to fall behind in the second half, was led by Brandenberg and Weisner, who each scored 12 apiece in the loss.

The other semifinal then saw Richfield fly past Minneapolis Washburn, 68-56. The game was closer than the score would indicate, however, as Washburn stayed in it up until the fourth quarter, when turn-overs and poor defense did them in. Paul Meisner had 22 points and Brian Denman added 15 for the Spartans, while Randy Williams dropped in 22 of his own for Washburn.

The AA championship game was a thriller as Bemidji, which shot 50% from the floor, fended off a late Richfield rally to come out on the good end of a 52-50 ball-game. Bemidji played solid defense and got balanced scoring from Steve Vogel, who tallied 16 points, as well as from Stan Drew and Don Hubbell, who each added 12 apiece, and Jack Schwartz, who chipped in 10 for the champs. Paul Meisner and Steve Bender each scored 14 points for Richfield, which shot just 34% in the loss.

1974 Playoff: Melrose (A) vs. Bemidji (AA)

Bemidji and Melrose then met that following Monday night as Bemidji tried to find a way to stop the unstoppable Mark Olberding. In the end, however, they simply could not, as Olberding blasted the Jacks for 30 points and 14 rebounds in a 58-42 Melrose win. Melrose which jumped out to an early 19-6 advantage and upped it to 27-17 at the half, watched Bemidji shoot a paltry 29% from the field.

1975: Class A: Chisholm vs. St. Paul Mechanic Arts

Fulda opened the Class A tourney by beating Mahnomen, 60-45, thanks to 25 points from Arvid Kramer and 21 more from Kevin Fury. Then, in Game Two, St. Paul Mechanic Arts edged Barnesville,50-49, in overtime, on Charles Petain's clutch rebound basket and free throw as time was running out. Waseca's 25-game winning streak was ended by Dave Herzan and De LaSalle in the first evening game, 49-45, while Chisholm topped New Ulm, 66-55, behind Paul McDonald's 24 points and his brother Mike's 16. Ken Haag scored 24 for New Ulm in the loss. The opening semifinal match then saw Mechanic Arts top Fulda, 34-33, in a real defensive battle, while Chisholm got past De La Salle, 80-73,

giving the Bluestreaks a one-way ticket into the Class A championship game. There, behind Paul McDonald's game-high 18 points, Chisholm started strong and finished strong en route to beating Mechanic Arts, 41-33. Elmer Bailey led Mechanic Arts with 15 in the tough loss.

1975: Class AA: Little Falls vs. Robbinsdale

The Class AA opener saw Mankato West, behind the strong inside play of Greg Briggs and Jim Northenscold, knock off Alexander Ramsey, 55-43. Game Two was much closer as a pair of Lake Conference foes hooked up. Robbinsdale came out on top in this one though, as they upset Bloomington Jefferson on Scot Stainer's 23-foot jumper at the buzzer, 55-53. The third quarterfinal was equally as exciting as Little Falls, led by Frank Wachlarowicz's 19 points, rallied late to beat Hibbing, 48-46. John Retica scored 20 points for the Blue Jackets, while a young forward by the name of Kevin McHale added 10. Unheralded Robbinsdale Cooper then knocked off St. Paul Highland Park, 47-36, in the last game of the day to earn themselves

Front Row: Tom Pustovar, Tim Slattery, Paul McDonald, Bob Leibfried, Mike McDonald, Capt., Larry Valentini. Back Row: Joe Kruchowski, Mgr., Mike Palmquist, Jon Kne, Bob McDonald, Coach, Roger Toutloff, Assistant, Jim Prelesnik, Ken Perry, Richard Clochetto, Mgr.

The 1975 State A Champs from Chisholm

a trip to the semi's

There, Robbinsdale, behind Tom Fix's fine all-around play, raced by Mankato West, 66-52, in Game One, while Little Falls rallied to beat Cooper, 58-53, in Game Two.

In the Class AA Finals that Saturday night at the St. Paul Civic Center, Little Falls edged Robbinsdale, 54-49, on Frank Wachiarowicz's 28 points and 15 rebounds. His scoring, combined with the Flyers' ability to dominate on defense proved to be the difference in this one. Meanwhile, Tom Fix scored 22 points for the Robins in the loss.

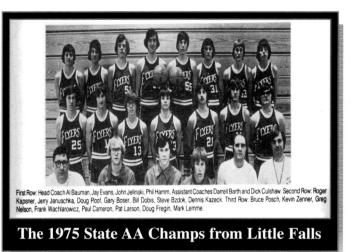

First Row: Head Coach Al Bauman, Jay Evans, John Jelinski, Phil Hamm, Assistant Coaches Darrell Barth and Dick Culshaw. Second Row: Roger Kapsner, Jerry Januschka, Doug Ploof, Gary Boser, Bill Dobis, Steve Bzdok, Dennis Kazeck. Third Row: Bruce Posch, Kevin Zenner, Greg Nelson, Frank Wachiarowicz, Paul Cameron, Pat Larson, Doug Fregin, Mark Lemme.

The 1975 State AA Champs from Little Falls

1975 Playoff: Little Falls (AA) vs. Chisholm (A)

Little Falls and Chisholm met in what proved to be the fifth and final Class AA vs. Class A playoff game that Monday night. The two unbeaten teams kicked off the action in front of just 4,537 fans who braved one of the worst blizzards to ever hit Minnesota. It was worth it though, as the two teams played a dandy. Chisholm jumped out to an early lead in this one but couldn't hang on in the end. The Flyers, and their tough 2-2-1 zone-press, matched up well with Chisholm's disciplined full court press, and were able to get through it in the end. Things were going well through the first three quarters for Chisholm, but when their star, Paul McDonald, fouled out with just a couple minutes to go, it was all over. That's when Little Falls found an unlikely hero in five-foot-seven Guard Doug Ploof, who came out of nowhere to score 22 huge points and rally the Flyers to a thrilling 54-50 victory.

1976: Class A: Marshall University vs. Mankato Wilson

Class A action kicked off with Montevideo fending off Mahnomen, 53-51, as Brad Olson scored 19 points and Gary Vien hit for 15. Meanwhile, Myron Kersting scored 16 and Paul Muckinhirn added 14 in the loss for Mahnomen. Windom, behind Dan Carpenter's 27 points, rallied to beat Winona Cotter, 72-63, in Game Two, while Marshall University crushed Breckenridge, 77-54. The Cardinals were led by Rodney Hargest's 29 points, while Brady Lipp popped in 24 for Breckenridge. Mankato Wilson then snuck by Orr, 58-56, in the final quarterfinal contest. Mike Westland and Paul Biewen had 14 apiece for Wilson, while Orr's Nate Dahlman had 23 points and 13 rebounds in the loss.

Seated on Floor L to R: Dindo Dawis, Steve Zerby, Peter Slettehaugh, Kevin Smith.
2nd Row: Walt Whittaker, Rodney Hargest, John Greene, Nick Puzak, Jesse Gray, Ronnie Henderson, Jeffy Morley.
3rd Row: Jon Starr, Claude Madsen, Steve Newby, Jim Ludgate, Ronnie Hadley, Jeff Hager, Coach Ed Prohofsky.
Not pictured: Asst. Coach Bill L'Herault.

The 1976 State A Champs from Marshall U.

Windom came out of the gates smoking in the first semi, hitting 15 of their first 19 shots. But Marshall University hung tough and found themselves up at the half by the score of 46-34. From there Windom, behind Dan Carpenter's 26 points, rallied, even out-rebounding the Cardinals and committing fewer turnovers. But Marshall, led by their speedy guard, Ronnie Henderson, who dished out 14 assists, had four players scoring in double figures and was too tough down the stretch, winning 76-67.

The other semifinal contest then saw Mankato Wilson overcome an 18-8 first quarter deficit to beat the Montevideo Mohawks, 64-48. Wilson, which scored 15 points during the last four minutes of the game, was led by Paul Biewen's 23 points. Montevideo, on the other hand, was led by Brad Olson, who tallied 15 in the loss.

Nearly 13,000 fans showed up at the Civic Center that Saturday afternoon to watch the evenly-matched Marshall University vs. Mankato Wilson title game. This one was worth the wait as both teams battled all game long before Wilson, on Paul Biewen's 21 points, rallied late in the game to score 10 straight to take a 52-46 lead. Marshall then came back and tied the game, even forcing an overtime. There, in the extra session, Ronnie Henderson led Marshall's attack. The undefeated Cardinals quickly took the lead and never looked back, beating Wilson in a thriller, 64-59.

1976: Class AA: Bloomington Jefferson vs. Hibbing

Little Falls, which was riding a 35-game winning streak, had little problem with Stillwater in the Class AA opener, beating the Ponies by the final score of 55-44. Milo Backowski scored 12 points, Brian Silbernick added 11 and Gary Walters pitched in 10 for the Flyers, while the big seven-footer Chris Engler, who would go on to star in the NBA, led Stillwater with 14 points.

Game Two was a dog fight between a pair of undefeated squads in Bloomington Jefferson and Prior Lake. Jefferson would come out on top in this one though, forcing Prior Lake into making 25 turnovers en route to a 61-51 victory. Al Hutchinson led the Jaguars with 23 points while Steve Lingenfelter, Brent Knight and Dave Bratland all hit for double digits as well. Meanwhile, Prior Lake's duo of Doug and Brian Pederson scored 18 and 16 points, respectively, in the loss.

Cretin rallied from an early deficit to beat New Prague in the first evening game, 58-56, on Dave Herzan's 24 points, while Ron Schoenecker scored 16 points for New Prague.

Kevin McHale made his presence felt in the quarterfinal finale by

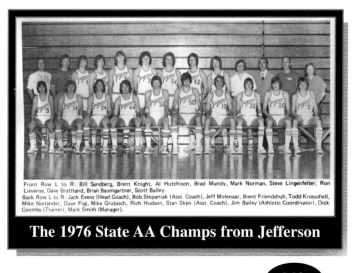

Front Row L to R: Bill Sandberg, Brent Knight, Al Hutchison, Brad Mundy, Mark Norman, Steve Lingenfelter, Ron Lievense, Dave Brattland, Brian Baumgartner, Scott Bailey.
Back Row L to R: Jack Evens (Head Coach), Bob Stepaniak (Asst. Coach), Jeff Molenaar, Brent Friendshuh, Todd Krosschell, Mike Norlander, Dave Figi, Mike Grubisch, Rich Hudson, Stan Skjei (Asst. Coach), Jim Bailey (Athletic Coordinator), Dick Coombs (Trainer), Mark Smith (Manager).

The 1976 State AA Champs from Jefferson

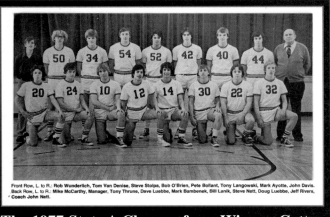

Front Row, L. to R.: Rob Wunderlich, Tom Van Denise, Steve Stolpa, Bob O'Brien, Pete Bollant, Tony Langowski, Mark Ayotte, John Davis. Back Row, L. to R.: Mike McCarthy, Manager, Tony Thrune, Dave Luebbe, Mark Bambenek, Bill Lanik, Steve Nett, Doug Luebbe, Jeff Rivers, Coach John Nett.

The 1977 State A Champs from Winona Cotter

torching Minneapolis North for 21 points en route to leading his Hibbing Blue Jackets to a 64-41 victory.

Hibbing exacted a little revenge in the AA semifinals, beating the defending champs from Little Falls, 41-39, on McHale's 16 points, 9 rebounds and 7 blocks. The Flyers, which had beaten the Jackets in 1975, had taken an early lead in this one, only to see McHale tally eight fourth quarter points en route to leading his club into the Finals.

Then, in the other semi, Bloomington Jefferson, behind Steve Lingenfelter's 21 points, rolled over Cretin, 69-51. The Jags were too tough down in the paint in this one as they started out strong and finished strong to advance to the title game. Al Hutchinson and Dave Bratland added 14 and 11 points, respectively, for Bloomington, while Gary Koop and Dave Herzan each scored 18 points apiece for Cretin in the loss.

Then, in one of the most highly anticipated match-ups in Minnesota state high school basketball history, undefeated Bloomington Jefferson met Hibbing before 14,307 fans.

In what was hyped as "McHale and Lingenfelter," it would go down as the best battle between two big men in tourney history. Hibbing took an early lead in this one as McHale got hot early. In fact, his 12 points, 10 rebounds and five blocked shots were good enough to give the Blue Jackets a 32-25 half-time lead. From there, however, the Jags rallied back. Lingenfelter, who had scored eight first-half points, but had several shots blocked by McHale, decided to pull out the old hook-shot in the second half. He taunted McHale with the shot, and because McHale had some early foul troubles, he had to play him honestly — giving him plenty of room to maneuver. Before long, Jefferson had the lead, and Hibbing, perhaps still weery from their tough quarterfinal win over Little Falls, started to look tired. Lingenfelter poured it on from there, scoring 18 second-half points, 14 alone in the fourth quarter, to lead the Jaguars to an impressive 60-51 victory. For McHale, who finished with 21 points, it was a game he will always remember.

"It was kind of a David vs. Goliath game, with us being the small Iron Range town playing the big school from the Twin Cities," said McHale. "I remember having the lead at half-time and then they pressed the heck out of us in the second half, which caused us to turn it over quite a bit down the stretch. I picked up my third foul midway through the third and it seemed like we just couldn't get our offense going after that. From then on I couldn't be as aggressive defensively and that really hurt us. Overall, it was a good game but I thought we were probably a better team overall. But hey, their trap got us and they deserved to win that night."

"The Minnesota State High School Basketball Tournament was a great experience and about as fun as it gets in sports," added McHale. "The Civic Center was a pretty new building back at that point and to get down there with your family and friends was a real thrill. Every kid from the Range dreams of playing in the tournament, and when you make it, you're playing there with teammates you've known your entire life. The entire experience was such a good time for me."

1977: Class A: Winona Cotter vs. Pelican Rapids

Glencoe, behind Scot Phifer's 17 points and 17 rebounds, beat Twin Valley, 56-41, in the opening game of the Class A tourney. Glencoe's towering front line even grabbed a record-setting total of 65 rebounds in the big win.

Winona Cotter doubled-up Redwood Falls, 70-35, in Game Two as the Ramblers got 23 points from Doug Luebbe and another 17 from Steve Nett.

The tourney's first upset came in Game Three, as Silver Bay bumped off Marshall University, 69-66. Incredibly, Marshall's 53-game winning streak came to a screeching halt on Dave Trost's 26 points for Silver Bay. (Sadly, Mankato Wilson, a private school, was forced to close its doors after that season when the state legislature and Mankato State College decided to discontinue the school's funding.)

The final contest of the day featured Pelican Rapids beating tiny Wellcome Memorial, 68-61, behind 34 points from Jim Knutson. Dan and Tim Wasinger scored 20 and 17 points, respectively, for Welcome in the tough loss.

The first Class A semifinal saw Winona Cotter, behind super sophomore Mark Bambanck, who scored 18 points and grabbed 18 rebounds, top Glencoe, 48-37. Scot Phifer and Rick Witthus each scored a dozen apiece for the Ramblers as well.

Pelican Rapids then edged Silver Bay, 54-50, as the Vikings held Silver Bay's star, Dave Trost, to just eight points. Jim Knutson pumped in 20 points and Pete Restad added 10 for the Rapids, while Tom Frericks and Kasey Frank led Silver Bay with 17 and 15 points each.

Winona Cotter came out strong in the Class A Final, beating Pelican Rapids fairly soundly, 60-47. Cotter, the first private school ever to win the MSHSL title, led 26-25 at the half, and simply pulled away down the stretch. Steve Nett scored 17 points in the big win, while Pelican Rapids was led by Jim Knutson and Pete Restad, each of whom scored in double digits.

1977: Class AA: Prior Lake vs. Duluth Central

Prior Lake opened the Class AA tournament by edging a very tough Highland Park squad, 52-50. Leading the charge for the Lakers were a pair of outstanding big men in six-foot-seven Brian Heise and six-foot-eight Brian Pederson, who scored 20 and 12 points, respectively.

Game Two then saw Little Falls' stifling defense shut down Minneapolis Central, 74-59. Gary Wolters led the Flyers with 34 points and Paul Cameron added 18, while Andra Griffin got 25 for Central in the loss.

Duluth Central, led by Rich Perkins' 19 points and 13 rebounds, whipped Bloomington Kennedy, 68-48, in the first evening game, while Stillwater closed out the quarterfinals by eking out a very tough 56-55 win

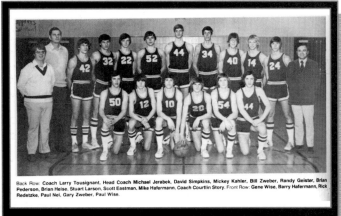

Back Row: Coach Larry Tousignant, Head Coach Michael Jerabek, David Simpkins, Mickey Kahler, Bill Zweber, Randy Geister, Brian Pederson, Brian Heise, Stuart Larson, Scott Eastman, Mike Hafermann, Coach Courtlin Story. Front Row: Gene Wise, Barry Hafermann, Rick Redetzke, Paul Nei, Gary Zweber, Paul Wise.

The 1977 State AA Champs from Prior Lake

over Rochester Mayo thanks to seven-foot Center Chris Engler's two clutch free-throws with just 12 seconds to go in the game.

Prior Lake kicked off the Class AA semi's by man-handling Little Falls, 66-53. The Lakers just beat the Flyers with solid defense and fundamental rebounding. Brian Pederson led the Lakers with 23 points while Brian Heise added 21 in the big win.

In the other semi, Duluth Central spanked Stillwater, 70-55, thanks to their superior speed and quickness. Rich Perkins led the way for Central with 21 points while Buck Easterling added 18 as well.

Then, in the AA Finals, Prior Lake rallied from an early deficit to upset Duluth Central, 52-49. Central cut the Lakers' lead to one point on several occasions, but came up short at the free-throw line, going just 3-8 in the second half. Brian Pederson, who posted 18 points and 23 rebounds for the Lakers, was all over the floor though, and made a huge difference in the game's final outcome. Mark Hall scored 17 to lead Central, while Rich Perkins and Greg Downing each added 12 in the loss.

Row 1 — Left to right — Front: Jay Packman - Manager, Joe Russell, Bill Anderson, Boyd Snyder, Chip Comadoll, Craig Powers, Scott Swanson, Sid Hegseth, Dean Spring - Manager. Row 2 — Left to right — Back: Jerry Snyder - Head Coach, Pat Kennedy, Randy Swanson, Steve Willers, Randy Breuer, Steve Haeska, Don Hanson, Carl Weinmann, Mike Augustinson, Leo Fausch - Assistant Coach.

The 1978 State A Champs from Lake City

1978: Class A: Lake City vs. Breckenridge

The Class A tourney got underway at the St. Paul Civic Center with a pair of unbeatens doing battle. But this one wasn't even close as Butterfield-Odin shot 66% from the floor and pummelled Clara City, 80-52. Kyle Myers led Butterfield-Odin with 29 points, while his teammate, Brad Flater dished out a state tournament record 12 assists in the win.

Game Two saw Lake City, behind Center Randy Breuer's 18 points and 19 rebounds, rally from an early deficit to beat Glencoe, 48-42. Paul Edwards and Rick Witthus had 12 apiece for Glencoe in the loss.

Then, in the first evening game, Howard Lake-Waverly beat a pesky McIntosh-Winger team, 67-60. Ken Kutz and Mark Wackler led HLW with 20 and 19 points, while Tim Rolf and Larry Haugen had 26 and 18 points for McIntosh-Winger.

Tim Olson hit for 24 points en route to leading his Breckenridge Cowboys past Breck, 49-42, in the last quarterfinal. Breckenridge's balance cancelled a fine offensive performance by Orr's Tim Olson as the Cowboys won, 49-42. Stan Ekren's 15 points led Breck in the loss.

In addition to grabbing 13 rebounds and blocking seven shots, Randy Breuer scored 36 of his team's 49 points in leading Lake City to a 49-32 win over Butterfield-Odin in the first semifinal contest. Kyle Meyers and Brian Langeland had 12 points apiece for Butterfield-Odin, but could simply not find a way to stop the future NBA star.

The other semifinal game was all about defense, as Breckenridge held Howard Lake-Waverly to just 32% shooting for the game. Breckenridge, led by Tim Olson's outstanding two-way play, even went on a late-game offensive binge, outscoring the Lakers 21-2 en route to posting an easy 47-32 win.

The much-anticipated Class A Finals between the Lake City Tigers and Breckenridge Cowboys turned out to be a blow-out, as Randy Breuer once again played like a man among boys. Lake City opened up a 22-17 lead at the half and then cruised from there. The Cowboys focused simply on double and triple-teaming the big man, and as a result, Lake City forward Bill Anderson had open looks at the net all day. He scored 16 points in the 60-44 win, while Breuer added 14 as well. Scott Lipp played solidly for Breckenridge in the loss, scoring 17 points and playing outstanding defense.

1978: Class AA: Prior Lake vs. St. Louis Park

In the first round of Class AA quarterfinal action, which was held at the Met Sports Center in Bloomington, Rosemount edged Cambridge, 47-44. Cambridge opened up a 39-24 lead after three quarters, but was outscored down the stretch. Steve Oxborough scored 14 points in the win for Rosemount, while Brian Nelson had 12 for Cambridge.

Doug Jones' dramatic game-winner with time running out proved to be the difference in Prior Lake's 44-43 Game two win over St. Paul Tartan. Jones dropped in 20 points for the Lakers, while Kit Carson and Mark Balding added 12 points apiece for Tartan.

The undefeated Bemidji Lumberjacks, and their star Jim Jensen, who hit for 30 points and 15 rebounds, were upset in Game Three by St. Louis Park, 59-58, behind Dave Rosengren's 22 points.

Then, in the last quarterfinal of the day, Wally Hicks emerged as the hero when his short jumper at the final horn got Washburn past Woodbury, 57-56. Dave Hart and Lance Berwald led Washburn with 16 and 14 points, respectively, while Woodbury's back-court tandem of Bruce Kaupa and Casey Ramm each scored 20 points in the loss.

The first semifinal featured St. Louis Park barely edging Washburn, 49-47, as the Millers saw their title hopes die when their last-second game-tying shot clang off the rim at the buzzer. Washburn out-rebounded, out-shot and even committed few turn-overs than did the Millers, but still came up short. Bill Bosley's 14 points and Daryl Bittman's 11 led St. Louis Park while Lance Berwald and Al May had 16 and 14 points, respectively, for Washburn.

The other semifinal then saw Prior Lake, and its smothering defense, crush Rosemount, 41-25, to gain entry into the coveted championship game. The Lakers started out strong and never looked back in this one, cruising past Rosemount with ease. Scott Eastman led Prior Lake with 15 points while Doug Jones added 14 of his own in the big win.

Prior Lake started out slowly and kept it going until the end in their 44-33 victory over St. Louis Park in the Class AA title game. The Lakers' defense was again outstanding as it held St. Louis Park scoreless throughout

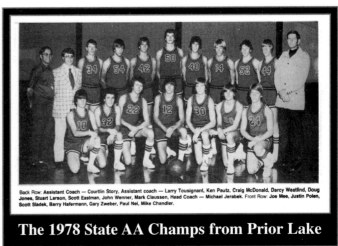

Back Row: Assistant Coach — Courtlin Story, Assistant coach — Larry Tousignant, Ken Pautz, Craig McDonald, Darcy Westlind, Doug Jones, Stuart Larson, Scott Eastman, John Wenner, Mark Claussen, Head Coach — Michael Jerabek. Front Row: Joe Mee, Justin Polen, Scott Sladek, Barry Hafermann, Gary Zweber, Paul Nei, Mike Chandler.

The 1978 State AA Champs from Prior Lake

The 1979 State A Champs from Lake City

Front Row, L. to R.: Manager: Dean Spring, Norman Hadeler, Scott Swanson, Glen Roberson, Todd Kieffer, Joe Russell, Dan Tackmann, Sid Hegseth, and faculty rep. Henry Dison. Back Row L. to R.: Coach Jerry Snyder, Boyd Snyder, Chip Comadoll, Pat Kennedy, Randy Breuer, Steve Haeska, Richard Dahman, Jim Roschen, Paul Schreiber, Assistant Coach Leo Fausch.

much of the entire third quarter. From there Prior Lake built up a 37-25 lead, fended off a late Park rally with under four minutes to go, and cruised home from there. Barry Hafferman led the Lakers with 18 points while six-foot-eight Forward Doug Jones added 12 of his own in the big win. Meanwhile, the Orioles were led by a sophomore phenom by the name of Jim Petersen, a big, rugged center who would go on to NBA stardom in the years to come.

1979: Class A: Lake City vs. Howard Lake Waverly

The 1979 Class A tourney kicked off at the Met Center with Randy Breuer picking up right where he left off. The big-man was on fire in this one, tallying unbeaten Lake City's first 10 points en route to scoring 42 points and 18 rebounds in the Tigers' 77-39 onslaught over Morgan Park.

Warren beat Breckenridge, 39-35, in Game Two thanks to Bob Lubarski's game-winning jumper with just under a minute to go. Breckenridge had an early lead in this one but the Ponies rallied behind Rob Norman's 12 points and Mark Turgeon's 10 in the win.

Thursday night's opening game came down to overtime as Howard Lake-Waverly edged Danube, 74-72, on Mark Decker's last-second shot with time running out. Decker had 26 points for Howard Lake-Waverly, while Ron Lippert scored 31 for Danube.

Then, in Game Four, Larry Withus scored 17 points in leading his Glencoe club to a 71-52 victory over Mapleton. Ken Starkey scored 16 points in the loss for Mapleton.

Lake City kept it going in the opening semifinal, beating Warren, 50-33. The Tigers blanked the Ponies 10-0 in the first quarter and led 21-11 at the half. Warren, clearly intimidated by Randy Breuer's inside presence, shot only 7% into the early part of the second quarter of the game. Breuer finished with 30 in the game, while Mark Turgeon and Dan Brekke had nine apiece for Warren.

Howard Lake-Waverly then downed Glencoe, 53-49, in the other semi. Mark Wackler, who was a member of the prestigous 1,500-point club, scored 19 points for Howard Lake-Waverly, while Ken Kutz added 16 points and 14 rebounds as well. Meanwhile, Larry Witthus scored 21 points for Glencoe in the loss.

Howard Lake-Waverly came out smoking in the Class A Finals, and found themselves in a unique situation at half-time. You see, they were actually ahead of Lake City, something that occurred for just the first time all season. Lake City rebounded back though, behind, you guessed it, Randy Breuer, who tossed in 22 of his game-high 41 points in the second half to lead his team to their second straight state championship, 63-50. (The seven-footer's three-game total of 113 points had broken the previous record of 109 set by New Prague's Ron Johnson back in 1956.)

1979: Class AA: Duluth Central vs. St. Paul Central

The Class AA quarterfinals opened at the St. Paul Civic Center that Thursday, March 8th, with St. Louis Park, behind its star center, Jim Petersen, beating Winona, 55-41. Petersen was unstoppable in the low post and when Winona did defend him, he stepped back and fired hook-shots. He wound up scoring 22 points in the game, but defensively, helped in holding Winona to just 29% shooting.

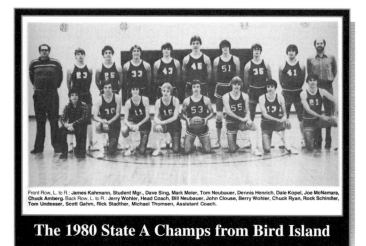

The 1979 State AA Champs from Duluth Central

Front Row, L. to R.: Asst. Mgr. Garland Joseph, Terry Taylor, Steve Dailey, Capt. Greg Downing, Tim Rock, Prinne Curry, Paul Nordvall, Warren Mitchell. Back Row, L. to R.: Coach Tom Braden, Head Coach Jim Hastings, Charles Fricke, Dan Micheau, Randy Micheau, Kevin Belchler, Richard Kelly, Gary Madison, Coach Bob Kunze, Len Olson, missing, Andre Wright.

A very quick St. Paul Central team forced 26 turn-overs en route to blowing by Mounds View, 80-69, in Game Two. Ricky Suggs and Davie Givens combined for 45 Central points in the big win, while Mounds View's star Van Troup had 22 in the loss.

Game Three then saw Duluth Central down Brainerd, 67-55, on Greg Downing's amazing 26-point, 15-rebound outing. His monster dunks were the difference in this one as Central cruised to an easy victory. In addition, Central's defense was stiffling as they held the Trojans' six-foot-ten star, Ron Falenschek, to just seven points — and scoreless in the first half.

Rocori then upset Minneapolis Central, 88-75, in the last quarterfinal of the day. Ricky Bell scored 27 points and Todd Swanson added 23 for Rocori, while Pedro Perkins added 31 for Central in the loss.

Duluth Central kept rolling in the first semifinal of the day, shooting 57% from the field, en route to a convincing 65-56 win over Rocori. After trailing 41-32 in the third, Duluth rallied back to put on a 23-4 exhibition to ice the game late in the fourth. Greg Downing had 22 points, and Gary Madison and Dan Micheau each added 12 for Central, while Ricky Bell led Rocori with 15 of his own.

St. Paul Central shut down Jim Peterson in the other semifinal to edge St. Louis Park, 66-63. The Orioles, behind Dave Hennessey's 30-point effort, jumped out to a commanding 39-30 half-time lead, but couldn't hold up down the stretch. Ricky Suggs led a balanced St. Paul Central attack with 17 points in the big win.

In what was billed as the "Battle of the Centrals," Duluth Central started out strong and finished strong in its impressive 62-54 win over St. Paul Central, giving Coach Jim Hastings his third state title. The Trojans shot 54% in this one and got some clutch shooting from Gary Madison and Greg Downing, who scored 22 and 18 points, respectively. Brian Dungy had 15

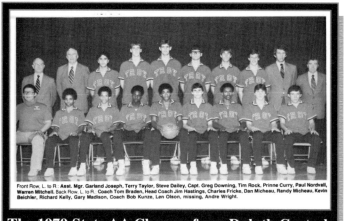

The 1980 State A Champs from Bird Island

Front Row, L. to R.: James Kahmann, Student Mgr., Dave Sing, Mark Meier, Tom Neubauer, Dennis Henrich, Dale Kopel, Joe McNamara, Chuck Amberg. Back Row, L. to R.: Jerry Wohler, Head Coach, Bill Neubauer, John Clouse, Berry Wohler, Chuck Ryan, Rock Schindler, Tom Undesser, Scott Gahm, Rick Stadther, Michael Thomsen, Assistant Coach.

points and Ricky Suggs added 12 in the loss.

1980: Class A: Bird Island-Lake Lillian vs. Lake of the Woods-Baudette

Guard Dave Gilreath scored 12 points en route to leading his Marshall University Cardinals past Windom in the first quarterfinal, 46-44, at the St. Paul Civic Center. Bird Island-Lake Lillian showed why they were one of the top teams in the state in 1980 when they knocked off Danube in Game Two, 70-65, behind Guard Barry Wohler's 23 points. Scott Nelson scored 20 and Rahn Hagberg added 19 more as Kenyon rallied to beat Morris in Game Three, 55-47, giving the Vikings a trip to the semifinals. The final game of the day then saw Baudette-Lake of the Woods edge a very tough Pine City team, 54-53, thanks to John Koller's game-winning jumper with eight seconds left in the ball-game.

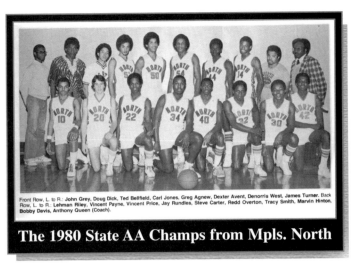

The 1980 State AA Champs from Mpls. North

Barry Wohler's 15-foot jumper with just two seconds left on the clock proved to be the game-winner in Bird Island-Lake Lillian's thrilling win over Marshall University, 54-52. The Cards had led by as many as eight points in the third quarter, but when their star, David Gilreath, got into foul trouble, Bird Island took over.

Baudette-Lake of the Woods then topped Kenyon, 49-43, in the other semi. Baudette-Lake of the Woods started out strong and ended strong as John Koller led the way with 16 points. John Oren and Tom Omerza also added 11 apiece for the winners, while Rahn Hagberg's 22 points and Scott Nelson's 16 led Kenyon in the tough loss.

The Class A championship tilt proved to be the highest scoring game in 10 years as Bird Island-Lake Lillian out-dueled Baudette-Lake of the Woods, 78-74, to take the crown. In what was billed as the "Wohler and Koller Show," Barry Wohler led Bird Island-Lake Lillian with 25 points, while John Koller added 33 of his own for Baudette-Lake of the Woods. This one went back and forth with the lead being exchanged throughout the entire contest. Both teams played great and seemingly matched each other shot for shot. In the end though, Bird Island-Lake Lillian's Barry Wohler and teammate John Clouse, who hit for 23 points in the game, took over in the final quarter by scoring their team's last 25 points. John Oren paced Koller with 15 points while Brad Troxel added 11 in the defeat.

1980: Class AA: Minneapolis North vs. St. Cloud Tech

St. Louis Park kicked off the 1980 Class AA tourney by topping St. Paul Central, 52-51. Guard John Anderson was the hero in this one as he stole an Oriole in-bounds pass and scored on a lay-up with just three ticks on the clock. Center Jim Petersen scored 17 points, grabbed 12 rebounds and added six blocked shots in the big win. Minneapolis North, with their amazing quickness and solid defense, then downed Stillwater, 64-53, in the other afternoon game. Redd Overton led the charge for the Polars by scoring 16 points. It took overtime, but St. Cloud Tech finally edged Rochester Mayo in Game Three, thanks to Tim Anfenson's 23 points and Phil Schroeder's 21. Duluth East then pummelled Mankato West in the last quarterfinal contest of the evening, 62-44. Brian Hanson led the way for the Hounds, netting 17 of his game-high 25 points in the first-quarter to lead his club to a 24-6 lead. From there East simply put it into overdrive and cruised into the semi's

St. Cloud Tech upset Duluth East, 61-55, in the first semifinal game. After trailing at the intermission, 34-20, Tech outscored the Hounds by a 41-21 margin in the second half to rally back into the game. Brian Hanson scored 21 for East, but couldn't get his club over the hump in the final period. Leading the charge for Tech was Bob Bohlig, who tallied 28 points in the game, while Chris Biggins added 16 of his own as well.

The other semifinal was also an upset as Minneapolis North beat St. Louis Park, 58-53. The Polars jumped out to a commanding 32-18 lead in this one, only to see the Orioles rally back to tie it up at 45-45 when Guard John Anderson scored a pair of his game-high 28 points. Then, when Park's star, Jim Petersen, fouled out with just under five minutes in the game, it was all over. Without Petersen, who had scored 14 points and grabbed eight rebounds, the Orioles had no presence underneath. From there, North, behind Redd Overton's 21 points and 12 rebounds, cruised into the Finals.

The Class AA Finals pitted Minneapolis North vs. St. Cloud Tech in a doozy. The Polars led 27-21 at the half but Tech rallied back to tie it at 33-33 early in the third. That's when Center Redd Overton took over down in the low post and started banging bodies. His 19 points and 13 rebounds proved to be the difference in this one as North hung on from there and glided to a 60-53, victory — their first title in 23 years. Troy Smith added 23 points and seven rebounds for the Polars, while Tech was led by Bob Bohlig's 17 points and Chris Biggins' 13.

1981: Class A: Bird Island-Lake Lillian vs. Winona Cotter

Bird Island-Lake Lillian edged Albany, 56-53, in the Class A opener. Tom Neubauer led Bird Island-Lake Lillian with 16 points, while Barry Wohler and Rock Schindler each added 11 in the win. Meanwhile, Albany Center Tom Schneider dumped in 28 points in the tough loss.

Ruthton, complete with a student-body of 75 souls, then topped Staples, 64-40, in a battle of unbeatens. Dick Stensgaard led the way with 23 points, while Doug Heidebrink and Bob Vos added 19 and 11 as well.

Winona Cotter's defense was the big story in its big 54-39 win over previously unbeaten Warren. The Ramblers held the Ponies scoreless throughout the first half of the opening quarter and cruised from there, shooting 65% along the way. Mark Wiltgen led Winona with 16 points, while Mark Czaplewski, Dennis Luebbe and Pat Flemming added 10 points apiece. Warren, on the other hand, got 16 points from Dan Carlson and another 12 from Mike Brekke in the loss.

The 1981 State A Champs from Bird Island

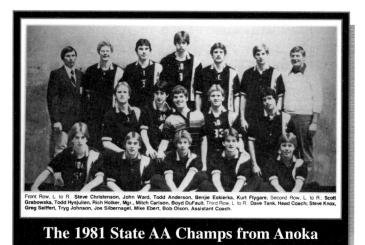

The 1981 State AA Champs from Anoka

Front Row, L. to R. Steve Christenson, John Ward, Todd Anderson, Benjie Eskierka, Kurt Flygare. Second Row, L. to R.: Scott Grabowska, Todd Hysjulien, Rich Holker, Mgr., Mitch Carlson, Boyd DuFault. Third Row, L. to R.: Dave Tank, Head Coach; Steve Knox, Greg Seiffert, Tryg Johnson, Joe Silbernagel, Mike Ebert, Bob Olson, Assistant Coach.

Tom McDonald scored 25 points and Paul Sentieri added 23 in leading the Chisholm Bluestreaks past Storden-Jeffers in the final quarterfinal of the day, 73-62. Curt Erickson and Brad Witt paced Storden-Jeffers with 20 and 18 points, respectively.

All-Stater Barry Wohler had 19 points, eight rebounds and five assists en route to leading his Bird Island-Lake Lillian club past Ruthton, 61-49, in the opening Class A semifinal. Chris Stensgaard had 18 points and 10 rebounds in the loss for Ruthton.

Then, in the other semi, Winona Cotter rallied back from an 18-12 first quarter deficit to take a 30-22 half-time lead over a very solid Chisholm club. From there, Cotter got 15 points apiece from both Dennis Luebbe and Matt Czaplewski, en route to playing a very physical second half. Their defense hung tough though as they hung on and cruised to a 48-46 win. Tom McDonald led Chisholm with18 points while teammate Paul Sentieri added 15 in the loss.

The Class A title game was a classic. This one came down to not one, but two overtimes, as Bird Island-Lake Lillian was able to get yet another heroic performance out of their star guard, Barry Wohler. In the first overtime, Cotter controlled the ball for nearly the entire three minutes, but when Mark Wiltgen's jumper clanged off the rim at the horn, it was time for another extra session. There, Wohler's 23-foot jumper gave Bird Island-Lake Lillian a thrilling 49-47 win over an extremely tough and well-disciplined Winona team. Wohler finished with 28 points in the ball game, while Mark Wiltgen paced Cotter with 22 of his own.

1981: Class AA: Anoka vs. Austin

The 1981 Class AA tourney kicked off from the Civic Center with Chaska topping Moorhead, 62-53. Dave Dahlke was the star in this one, scoring 27 points and hauling in eight rebounds, while Jim Driscoll scored 16 points for Moorhead in the loss.

The second game of the day saw unbeaten Austin upset Minneapolis North, and its gaudy 41-game winning streak, 62-53. The defending champs led 31-24 at the half, thanks to Redd Overton's game-high 21 points and nine rebounds, but couldn't keep it going in the second.

The Pack came out and made an 8-0 to take the lead and pulled away down the stretch behind Joe Longueville's 18 points and Bruce Anderson's 16, to roll into the semi's.

Game Three had Anoka edging Bloomington Jefferson, 50-46, as the Jaguars hit just 25% of their shots from the field. Anoka Forward Greg Seiffert scored 17 points and grabbed 13 rebounds in the win, while Center Tryg Johnson blocked eight shots as well. Meanwhile, Dennis Kingsley led the Jaguars with 15 points in the loss.

Then, in the final quarterfinal of the evening, St. Paul Central crushed Duluth East, 57-38. Rick Smith led the Minutemen with 19 points, while Joel Hansen added 17 in the big win. For the Hounds, however, their seven-footer, Brad Dudek, shot just 4-15 from the floor and was pretty well contained by Central's smothering defense.

Austin edged a very tough Chaska team in the opening semifinal, 57-52, behind Bruce Anderson's 17 points and Joe Longueville's 12. Austin shot nearly 60% in this one and played tremendous defense, holding Chaska's star, Dave Dahlke, who had been averaging 21 PPG, to just 14.

The other semifinal contest featured Anoka beating up on St. Paul Central, 61-45, behind Tryg Johnson's outstanding 28-point effort. Joe Silbernagel added 12 in the win, while Joel Hansen paced Central with 17 points.

Now, in the Class AA Finals, Anoka kept it going by beating Austin, 61-53, before 13,432 fans. The Tornadoes started strong and ended strong in this one, nailing 14 of 28 first-half shots and then opening up a 10-point lead into the third quarter. From there they got balanced scoring from Joe Silbernagel, who posted 23 points, and Tryg Johnson, who added 21. Lee Aase paced the Packers with 20 points, while teammate Joe Longueville added 12 in the tough loss.

1982: Class A: Winona Cotter vs. Chisholm

The 1982 Class A state tourney kicked off on March 25th at the St. Paul Civic Center with Montgomery-Lonsdale beating Staples, followed by Winona Cotter crushing Aitkin, 52-36, in Game Two. Westbrook kept its undefeated record alive by downing Argyle, 43-38, in Game Three, while Chisholm rounded out the quarterfinals by rolling over Ortonville to advance into the semi's.

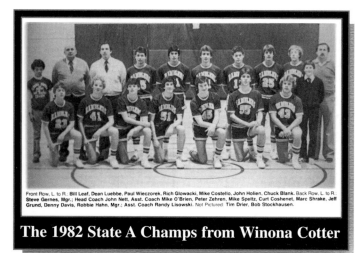

The 1982 State A Champs from Winona Cotter

Front Row, L. to R.: Bill Leaf, Dean Luebbe, Paul Wieczorek, Rich Glowacki, Mike Costello, John Hollen, Chuck Blank. Back Row, L. to R.: Steve Gernes, Mgr.; Head Coach John Nett, Asst. Coach Mike O'Brien, Peter Zehren, Mike Speltz, Curt Coshenet, Marc Shrake, Jeff Grund, Denny Davis, Robbie Hahn, Mgr.; Asst. Coach Randy Lisowski. Not Pictured: Tim Drier, Bob Stockhausen.

The opening semifinal contest pitted Montgomery-Lonsdale versus Winona Cotter. Cotter jumped out to a 21-15 half-time lead in this one and rallied back from a 31-27 fourth quarter deficit to take a 44-38 victory. Mike Costello nailed three big ones late and Paul Wieczorek iced the game on four straight free-throws with just a few seconds left in the game. Wieczorek led Cotter with 12 points in the win, while ML's Choudek had 16 in the loss

Game Two saw Chisholm edge Westbrook, 72-69, in an overtime thriller. Tom McDonald entered the game with a record 38 points per game average, and despite his "paltry" 17 points, was able to lead his club into the semifinals. After all, it was his two free-throws with just seven seconds left in the game that put his team over the top. Picking up the slack for McDonald, however, was six-foot-five Forward Paul Sentieri, who led all scorers with 26 points. Westbrook rallied late in this one and tied it up on Steve Elzenga's 25-footer with just over a minute to go, but came up short in the end. Tim Boeck led the Wildcats with 20 points, while Elzenga added 18 in the loss.

Winona Cotter then stepped it up huge in the Finals by beating a very tough Chisholm club, 48-46, to take home the hardware. The No. 1 ranked Blue Streaks were the favorites going in but came up just one bucket short. The had a 38-37 lead going into the fourth quarter in this one and kept it until Luebbe hit a lay-up with under a minute to go to give the Ramblers a 46-44 lead. Reserve Guard Jeff Grund then nailed a pair of free-throws after being intentionally fouled with just six seconds left to ice it for Cotter, giving Head Coach John Nett, the state's winningest ever, his second state title. John Hollen led the Ramblers with 15 points and 10 rebounds.

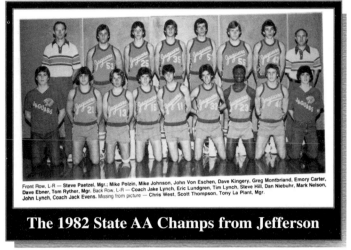

Front Row, L-R — Steve Paetzel, Mgr.; Mike Polzin, Mike Johnson, John Von Eschen, Dave Kingery, Greg Montbriand, Emory Carter, Dave Ebner, Tom Ryther, Mgr. Back Row, L-R — Coach Jake Lynch, Eric Lundgren, Tim Lynch, Steve Hill, Dan Niebuhr, Mark Nelson, John Lynch, Coach Jack Evens. Missing from picture — Chris West, Scott Thompson, Tony La Plant, Mgr.

The 1982 State AA Champs from Jefferson

1982: Class AA: Bloomington Jefferson vs. Duluth East

The Class AA version of the 1982 State Basketball Tournament got going with Chaska taking Austin in Game One, followed by the Duluth East Greyhounds beating the Stillwater Ponies in the second quarterfinal of the day. In Game Three St. Cloud Tech beat St. Paul Central, while Bloomington Jefferson had no problem with Minneapolis North in the last game of the day, winning 60-50, to advance into semifinal action.

In a battle of the top two ranked teams, Duluth East edged Chaska in the opening semifinal, 72-70, in what turned out to be a real classic. No less than three overtimes were needed to resolve this one as East's man-child, seven-foot Center Brad Dudek, out-dueled Chaska's Dave Dahlke in the end. Dudek tallied 36 points in the game, while Dahlke added 24 in the loss. For Chaska, it was just the team's second loss — with the other coming at the hands of those very same Greyhounds, 49-48, earlier in the season.

Bloomington Jefferson beat St. Cloud Tech, 46-43, in the other semifinal. Tech kept it close throughout the entire game, but were hampered by the loss of six-foot-two senior Forward Phil Johnson, who suffered a knee injury in the quarterfinals. Tech's Dave Imbolte picked up the slack by scoring 15 points while Dan Johnson added 12 in the loss. The Jaguars were led by John Lynch's 11 points while Steve Hill and Greg Montbriand added 10 each in the big win.

Bloomington Jefferson then came out and edged Duluth East, 59-51, in the Finals. The champions of the Lake South Conference and Region 6AA, the Jags used a balanced offensive attack and played solid defense in defeating the Hounds. East, led by seven-foot Brad Dudek, and his twin brother, six-foot-seven Brian, had come into the game ranked No. 1 for the third straight year, but came home empty handed yet again. They did force the Jag's to shoot from the outside though, and that is exactly what they did. Guard Greg Montbriand's 10 straight free-throws in the final 1:21 iced it for Jefferson down the stretch. John Lynch led the Jags with 20 points while Montbriand added 18 in the victory. Bloomington rallied in this one but took the lead for good with three minutes to play when Montbriand stripped Dudek of the ball and drove the length of the court for a dramatic lay-up. The Jaguars zone-press defense held the Hounds at bay down the stretch as they cruised to their second state title.

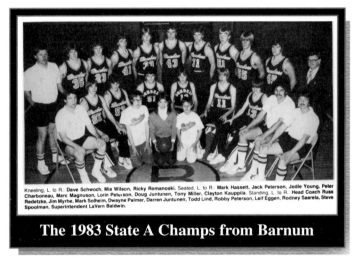

Kneeling, L. to R.: Dave Schwoch, Mia Wilson, Ricky Romanoski. Seated, L. to R.: Mark Hassett, Jack Peterson, Jodie Young, Peter Charboneau, Marc Magnuson, Lorin Peterson, Doug Juntunen, Tony Miller, Clayton Kauppila. Standing, L. to R.: Head Coach Russ Redetzke, Jim Myrhe, Mark Solheim, Dwayne Palmer, Darren Juntunen, Todd Lind, Robby Peterson, Leif Eggen, Rodney Saarela, Steve Spoolman, Superintendent LaVern Baldwin.

The 1983 State A Champs from Barnum

1983: Class A: Barnum vs. Luverne

Clara City opened the 1983 Class A tourney by defeating Littlefork-Big Falls. Game Two then saw Luverne, behind their star, Gordie Hanson, beat Lake City. The first evening contest featured Staples upsetting Minneapolis De LaSalle, while tiny Barnum took care of Brooklyn Center in the final game of the day, 58-47.

Barnum came out smoking in the opening semifinal contest, eliminating Staples, 56-53. The Bombers rallied from a 17-12 first quarter deficit to win the tight game. With 20 seconds to go in the fourth quarter, Darren Juntunen stepped up to the line and nailed an insurance free-throw to ice it. Leading the charge for Barnum were Todd Lind, who tallied 15 points, and Robbie Peterson, who added 14 in the big win. Forward Kevin Dosmann led Staples with 14 points and seven rebounds in the loss.

Luverne, behind Gordie Hansen's 30 points, rolled over Clara City in the other semi, 59-43. Hansen came out and scored the first 10 points in this one to set an early tone. Clara City kept it close and were only down by three at the half, but couldn't get their offense going in the second as Luverne opened the third by going on a 16-2 run. Luverne's patient half-court attack coupled with a strong defense made all the difference in this one as the Cardinals advanced into the Finals.

Little Barnum, which was playing in its first-ever MSHSL state team-sponsored tournament (in any sport), came out and conquered Luverne in the championship game, 53-47, to take the Class A title. Located just 30 miles southwest of Duluth, Barnum became the smallest community (population 382) to win a state title, and did it in style by going undefeated as well. The game got underway with Barnum playing smart basketball: running when they could and waiting for their shots when they came available. They jumped out to a 16-11 lead and made it 30-22 at the half. From there they never looked back. The Cardinals rallied late, getting it to 50-46, on Tim Vink's rebound tap-in, but could get no closer than that. Todd Lind and Robbie Peterson again led they way, scoring 18 and 15 points, respectively.

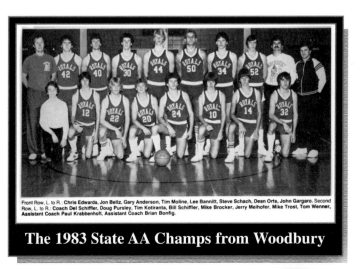

Front Row, L. to R.: Chris Edwards, Jon Beltz, Gary Anderson, Tim Moline, Lee Bannitt, Steve Schach, Dean Orts, John Gargaro. Second Row, L. to R.: Coach Del Schiffler, Doug Pursley, Tim Kotiranta, Bill Schiffler, Mike Brocker, Jerry Meihofer, Mike Trost, Tom Wenner, Assistant Coach Paul Krabbenhoft, Assistant Coach Brian Bonfig.

The 1983 State AA Champs from Woodbury

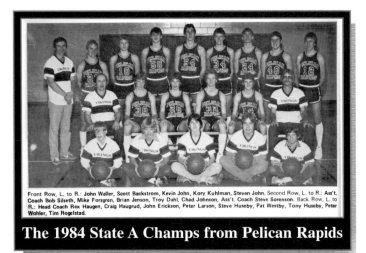

Front Row, L. to R.: John Waller, Scott Backstrom, Kevin John, Kory Kuhlman, Steven John. Second Row, L. to R.: Ass't. Coach Bob Silseth, Mike Forsgren, Brian Jenson, Troy Dahl, Chad Johnson, Ass't Coach Steve Sorenson. Back Row, L. to R.: Head Coach Rex Haugen, Craig Haugrud, John Erickson, Peter Larson, Steve Huseby, Pat Westby, Tony Huseby, Peter Wohler, Tim Rogelstad.

The 1984 State A Champs from Pelican Rapids

Gordie Hanson led Luverne with 22 points and 12 rebounds, but was held in check by Barnum's quick defense.

1983: Class AA: Woodbury vs. Coon Rapids

The Class AA tourney opened with Chisago Lakes, and its star, Keith Hasselquist, upsetting Minneapolis North in Game One, followed by Woodbury downing New Prague, 59-42, in Game Two. From there Willmar edged Edina, 51-47, while Coon Rapids upended St. Cloud Tech, 52-33, in the final quarterfinal of the evening.

In the opening semifinal, Woodbury, behind Bill Schiffler's 13 points, topped a tough Chisago Lakes club, 45-35, to extend its winning streak to 23 games. Woodbury rallied from a four-point half-time deficit and made just one turn-over the rest of the way en route to their big win. Chisago's Center, Keith Hasselquist, played out of his mind in this one, scoring 18 points and grabbing 14 rebounds in the defeat. The Trojans led by one point going into the final quarter but ran out of gas down the stretch — scoring just six points in the final eight minutes of the game.

The other semi then saw Coon Rapids defeat Willmar, 59-50, in a game which featured two of the top-rated players in the state — Willmar's seven-foot Center, Paul VanDenEinde and Coon Rapids 6-foot-10 Center, Tom Copa. Not since the Steve Lingenfelter vs. Kevin McHale matchup between Jefferson and Hibbing back in 1976 had their been so much hype over a couple of big men. Copa would ultimately finish with 23 points in this one while VanDenEinde tallied 23. And, while the two big fellas battled it out underneath, Kevin Treanor picked up the slack for the Cardinals by scoring 16 points, 13 rebounds and four blocked shots. Guard Matt Wirman also added 10 points in the win, while Greg Nelson added 15 points for Willmar.

Woodbury then came through in the clutch by narrowly grabbing a thrilling 56-50 overtime triumph over a very strong Coon Rapids club in the title game. The game marked the first time since 1942 that two teams had entered the contest with unblemished records, and this one was as entertaining as any in previous history. Eight free-throws in the final 1:43 of overtime proved to be the difference in this one. Woodbury's Bill Schiffler had tied the game at 46-46 on a 20-footer with just under a minute to go and when the Cards got called for an over-and-back penalty, Woodbury had a chance to win it. Schiffler's 30-footer came up short though, and this one went to sudden death. There, Tom Copa, who scored 24 points in the game, got Rapids the lead on a short jumper, only to see Mike Brocker even it back up with a pair of free-throws. Schiffler and Jerry Melhofer added a pair each down the stretch as well as Woodbury cruised to the title.

1984: Class A: Pelican Rapids vs. Winona Cotter

St. Anthony Village opened the Class A tourney by eliminating Warren, 51-39. Mike Howey scored 10 of the last 13 points for the Huskies, finishing with a total of 17 in the win. Winona Cotter, thanks to Tom Paskiewicz's game-winning jumper, edged Sanborn, 47-45, in Game Two, while Pelican Rapids topped Wells-Easton, 46-44, in Game Three. The Vikings got a pair of clutch free-throws from Pat Westby with just three seconds in the game to ice it. Then, in Game Four, St. John's Prep beat tiny Orr (just 99 students!) by the final score of 61-58. Tulio Suarez nailed three straight baskets late in the game en route to tallying a game-high 20 in the big win.

Winona Cotter got past St. Anthony in the opening semifinal game, 61-57. John Nett, the state's winningest all-time coach put together a solid game-plan for his Ramblers, as they rallied to beat the Huskies in the game's final moments. Jim Galkowski was the hero in this one, hitting the tying basket with just over 30 seconds left and then icing the game by nailing three straight free-throws down the stretch. Cotter came back late in the game on Center Jim Glowacki's eight points in a 10-1 run that gave the club a 52-48 lead. St. Anthony regained the lead when John Wilson scored six of his game-high 21 points (on 10 of 10 shooting nonetheless) down low in the paint, but couldn't hang on late in the game.

Pelican Rapids, behind Pat Westby's 26 points, edged St. John's Prep, 59-58, in the other semi. Pete Larson could've iced the game for Rapids with just 25 seconds left, but missed both and gave the Johnnies a chance to get back into it. He did grab 10 rebounds, however, and also hit the go-ahead jumper with 5:07 left in the fourth to get his club the lead. Johnnies' Guard Tulio Suarez, who tallied 28 points in the loss, couldn't connect on his last-second shot which clanged off the rim, as Pelican Rapids hung on for the thrilling victory.

It's somewhat ironic that when Pelican Rapids made its first ever appearance in the tournament back in 1971, the Vikings lost to Winona Cotter, 60-47, in the championship game. Revenge is sweet though, as this time the Vikings beat the Ramblers, 57-55, to take the title. Pat Westby capped off a terrific tournament by draining a clutch 18-footer from the right of the lane with just seven seconds left to give his Vikings club a thrilling come-from-behind victory. Rapids had been playing for the last shot with 1:20 remaining thanks to Center Steve Huesby's steal down low. Westby, who hit for 22 points in the game, was the obvious choice to take the last shot, since he had just made eight of his previous 14 from the floor. Cotter tried to rally, but after a time-out, came up short when Jim Galkowski, who led Cotter with 19 points, put up a 20-footer that fell short.

1984: Class AA: White Bear Lake vs. Minneapolis North

Bloomington Kennedy beat North Branch in Game One, 54-41, on senior point guard Mike McCollow's 16 points. In addition, senior Guard Steve Rushin (now a regular writer for Sports Illustrated) added 14 points and 12 rebounds as well. Top-ranked Minneapolis North struggled to get past Fergus Falls in Game Two, but rallied from a third quarter stalemate to take a 60-54 victory. Fergus tried to come back late on Steve Thom's 26 points,

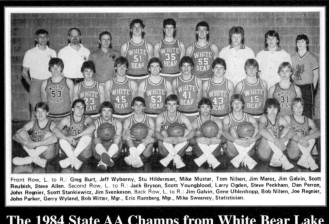

Front Row, L. to R.: Greg Burt, Jeff Wyborny, Stu Hilderman, Mike Mustar, Tom Nilsen, Jim Mares, Jim Galvin, Scott Reubish, Steve Allen. Second Row, L. to R.: Jack Bryson, Scott Youngblood, Larry Ogden, Steve Peckham, Dan Perron, John Regnier, Scott Stankiewicz, Jim Svenkeson. Back Row, L. to R.: Jim Galvin, Gene Uhlenhopp, Bob Nilsen, Joe Regnier, John Parker, Gerry Wyland, Bob Witter, Mgr., Eric Ramberg, Mgr., Mike Sweeney, Statistician.

The 1984 State AA Champs from White Bear Lake

but were no match for the Polar brother duo of Bronson and Brett McNeal, who scored 22 and 10 points, respectively in the win. White Bear Lake's sound defense was enough to get past Rochester John Marshall, 47-38, in the first evening game. The Bears jumped out to a 24-14 lead at the half and cruised from there. St. Paul Central then edged Mankato East, 43-42, on the game's final shot. Allen Lankford was the hero for the Minutemen in this one as his hanging jumper in the final seconds proved to be the game-winner.

Undefeated White Bear Lake reached the title game by crushing St. Paul Central, 58-37. Joe Regnier was the work-horse in this one, leading the Bears with 17 points and 12 rebounds. White Bear jumped out to a 10-4 lead at the quarter, expanded it to 27-17 at the half, and led 37-29 going into the final frame.

Minneapolis North then topped Bloomington Kennedy, 59-52, in the other semifinal to advance to the Finals. North started slowly and finished like a thoroughbred in this one as they came back from a 9-2 early deficit to finish strong. By the half the Polars were up 27-23 and they rolled from there. In the fourth Kennedy began to self-implode, committing five costly turn-overs and were outscored 13-4 over one span alone. Doug Carter led the way for North with 20 points while Brett McNeal added 10 in the win.

The Class "AA" Finals featured a pair of top-rated, undefeated clubs in Minneapolis North and White Bear Lake. The Bears rallied hard in the second half of this one and overcame a strong Minneapolis North defense en route to taking a 51-47 triumph. A pair of huge free-throws by junior Forward John Parker with just nine seconds to go in the game broke a 47-47 stale-mate and the Bears rolled from there on Mike Mustar's ensuing steal and lay-up. North had leaped out to a commanding 40-30 lead in the third, but suffered several turn-overs late to come up short. The Bears then came back to post a 9-0 run on baskets by Joe Regnier, Larry Ogden and Mustar. North's Bronson McNeal made it 43-43 but two free-throws by Tom Nielson gave White Bear a 45-43 edge. Doug Carter answered to tie it again, but Regnier responded. Brett McNeal made it 47 apiece, but with 14 seconds left, Parker's free-throws gave the Bears the final lead and they never looked back.

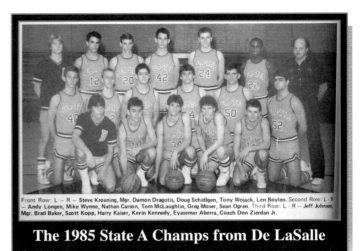

Front Row: L – R – Steve Kroening, Mgr. Damon Dragotis, Doug Schidlgen, Tony Wojack, Len Boylen. Second Row: L – R – Andy Longen, Mike Wynne, Nathan Carson, Tom McLaughlin, Greg Moser, Sean Ogren. Third Row: L – R – Jeff Johnson, Mgr., Brad Baker, Scott Kopp, Harry Kaiser, Kevin Kennedy, Eyasemer Aberra, Coach Don Zierdan Jr.

The 1985 State A Champs from De LaSalle

1985: Class A: Minneapolis De La Salle vs. Winona Cotter

The top-rated De La Salle Islanders lived up to their season-long billing as the team to beat in Class A by eliminating Twin Valley, 50-46, in the opening round thanks to Mike Wynne's last-second steal and ensuing game-winning free-throws.

Tiny Ceylon, with an enrollment of just 45 souls, beat Cedar Mountain-Morgan in Game Two, 53-44, thanks to their big-man, six-foot-ten Center Rich Saggau, who posted 24 points and 10 rebounds.

Winona Cotter, behind Guard Matt Maley's nine points, employed a tough man-to-man defense and a solid slow-down offense in rolling over Le Sueur in Game Three, 39-27. It was the lowest scoring game in Class A history.

Greenway then topped Glenwood, 62-59, in the final quarterfinal of the day. Mike Petrich scored 14 of his game-high 26 points in the second quarter and fended off a couple of late Glenwood rallies en route to leading his club into the semi's.

Winona Cotter crushed Greenway in the opening semifinal contest, 70-43, to cruise into the title game. It was the Glakowski and Glowacki show in this one as the two combined for nearly 50 points en route to leading Cotter back to the big dance. Mike Petrich played solid two-way basketball for Greenway, scoring 10 fourth quarter points, but couldn't get it done down the stretch.

De La Salle downed Ceylon, 62-51, in the other semifinal. Ceylon Center Rich Saggau came out and scored early and often, but couldn't get his club past a very tough De La Salle team. The Islanders jumped out to a 33-22 lead at the half and thanks to Damon Dragotis' marksmanship, cruised through the second half and into the Finals. Saggau scored 11 points in the fourth quarter alone and got his club to within five points with under two minutes to go, but Dragotis answered by scoring eight of his own points in the final frame to preserve the win.

De La Salle kept it going in the Finals, beating Winona Cotter, 56-46. For the Islanders, who used to dominate the Catholic State Tournament, it was their first MSHSL title. Damon Dragotis tallied 24 points for the victors and played some amazing defense to boot, holding Cotter's ace Jim Galkowski to just five points. De La Salle's full-court-press was stifling, and caused Cotter to commit several turn-overs in the second half. Jeff Glowacki score two of his 23 points midway through the third to give his club a 23-22 lead, but that was as close as they would get. Dragotis took over down the stretch and led his club to victory.

1985: Class AA: White Bear Lake vs. Minneapolis North

The defending state champs from White Bear Lake beat Willmar, 55-47, in Game One as Joe Regnier scored 18 points and Larry Ogden added 14 points in the big win. Willmar, behind Mark Harvey's 16 points, got to within one point on several occasions in the fourth but couldn't get it done.

Minneapolis North crushed St. Thomas Academy in Game Two, 83-54, on Doug Carter's 23 points and Bobby Walker's 18.

The first evening quarter then saw Jefferson hammer Bemidji, 75-57, thanks to 6-foot-7 swing-man Shawn Day's 28 points and 10 rebounds.

Then, in the final quarterfinal of the evening, Duluth Central jumped out to an early 34-22 lead and cruised past Rochester John Marshall, 59-50, as Jeff Everett led a balanced Trojan attack with 19 points.

Minneapolis North then beat Duluth Central in the first semifinal game, 70-60. North's Bronson McNeal scored six early points in this one as the Polars took a 39-25 lead at the half and never looked back. McNeal and Doug Carter each scored 16 points in the win, giving North their second

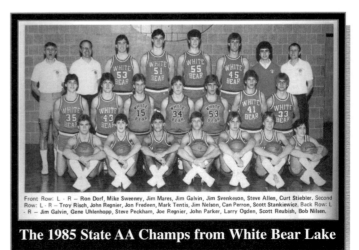

Front Row: L – R – Ron Dorf, Mike Sweeney, Jim Mares, Jim Galvin, Jim Svenkeson, Steve Allen, Curt Stiebler. Second Row: L – R – Troy Risch, John Regnier, Jon Fredeen, Mark Tentis, Jim Nelson, Can Perron, Scott Stankiewicz. Back Row: L – R – Jim Galvin, Gene Uhlenhopp, Steve Peckham, Joe Regnier, John Parker, Larry Ogden, Scott Reubish, Bob Nilsen.

The 1985 State AA Champs from White Bear Lake

Front Row, L to R: Student Manager Randy Oscarson, Dean Guthrie, Perry Wiest, Don Tonseth, Bill Schaffer, Jerry Meger, Tim Nelson, Dan Evans, Student Manager Chris Heidelbauer. Back Row, L to R: Head Coach Tim Dittberner, Assistant Coach John Laabs, Scott Ruud, John Ross, Peter Welter, Brian Krenik, Jim Elvestrom, Brad Narveson, Erik Allen, Terry Obele, Assistant Coach Terry Turek.

The 1986 State A Champs from LeSueur

straight trip to the Class AA championship game.

White Bear Lake then edged Bloomington Jefferson in the other semi-final, 41-39, thanks to Larry Ogden's five straight points in the game's final two minutes. Shawn Day was big in this one, scoring the Jags final two baskets of the game, but couldn't get them over the hump in the final seconds.

White Bear Lake then went ahead and completed its second consecutive undefeated season, by beating North in the Finals, 67-62, to run their winning streak to 52 games, fourth longest in state history. White Bear Lake rallied in the second half to upend the Polars in this one, thanks to Ogden and Parker's key free-throws in the game's final 30 seconds. North opened up a 36-26 half-time lead in this one only to watch it slip away midway through the fourth quarter. That's when Dan Perrin's jumper gave the Bears the lead for good at the 4:50 mark, at 53-51. Doug Carter scored five of his 18 points in the final 30 seconds but was unable to get his Polars over the top. Joe Regnier led the Bears with 23 points and 10 rebounds, while Perrin added 19 of his own in the win.

1986: Class A: LeSueur vs. Staples

Staples beat a tough Paul Thompson-led Norman County West club in the opening game of the 1986 tourney, 55-46. The Cardinals trailed early in this one but rallied behind Matt Nelson's 19 points and Greg Gorton's 16, to win it going away. Springfield roughed up Watertown-Mayer, 71-58, in Game Two. Troy Raitz had 23 points, while Tim Shively and Randy Sturm added 20 and19 points, respectively in the big win. The "Cinderella" Peterson Tigers, with just 50 students, topped Eveleth in Game Three, 55-46, thanks to Jim Hildebrand's 22 points. Le Sueur then eliminated Southwest Minnesota Christian (Edgerton) in the final quarterfinal of the day, 63-45, on Scott Ruud's 16 points and Tim Nelson's 14.

Le Sueur defeated previously unbeaten Peterson, 42-40, in the opening semifinal game. This one was a battle from the get-go as both teams played extremely physical basketball. The game was tied four times in the fourth quarter alone in this one, and just one basket was made in the final 2:14 of the final quarter. That occurred when Giants Forward Bill Schaffer, who led the squad with 12 points, grabbed a rebound and heaved it three-quarters of the way down the court to an awaiting Tim Nelson, who made an easy lay-up with just 14 ticks on the clock. Peterson's wild ride had finally come to an end.

Staples then upended Springfield in the other semifinal, 62-56, thanks to Chad Walthall's 19 points and Greg Gorton's 17. The Cardinals out-hustled Springfield in this one and used a pressure defense that forced the Tigers to cough up the ball 21 times throughout the contest. The Cards led early on but could never put Springfield away. The Tigers rallied late and got to withing three points on several occasions in the fourth, but couldn't make the key shots they needed. Free-throws hurt the Cards, but they stayed strong and wound up with a ticket to the Finals.

Le Sueur kept it going in the Finals, downing Staples, 55-43, to capture their first ever state title. The Cardinals played excellent defense and got some clutch shooting in the big win. They started out hot as well, rolling to a quick 9-0 lead, and extending that an impressive 28-14 lead at the half. Bill Schaffer was all over the court in the Finale, scoring 14 rebounds and adding five rebounds in the victory. He also held Staples Center Mark Nelson to just 13 points as well, a key factor in the outcome. Every time Staples' "Iron-Five" tried to make a run, the Cards slowed it down and played solid defense — forcing them to take low-percentage shots. It worked, as they cruised to their first state crown.

1986: Class AA: Bloomington Jefferson vs. Duluth Central

St. Paul Central, behind Gary New's 14 points, edged Mounds View in Game One, 44-42, at the Metrodome. Mounds View self-destructed late in the game by missing key shots and letting Central back into this one. Derrick Rummels was the hero, scoring a pair of free-throws late to give Central the lead for good. Bloomington Jefferson beat Faribault in Game Two, 42-40, thanks to Cory Otterdahl's tie-breaking free-throw late in the fourth. Then, with time running out, Kevin Lynch intercepted Bill Bardell's attempted alley-oop pass to Scott Gutzmann to end the game. Lynch, the last of four brothers to play for the Jag's, scored 10 points and added eight rebounds in the win. Duluth Central topped Fergus Falls in Game Three, 59-49. The Trojans jumped out to a 10-0 lead in this one and cruised to victory behind Tim Radosevich's 21 points and 17 rebounds. Minneapolis North eliminated Mankato East, 59-55, in the last quarterfinal of the day thanks to a trio of sophomores: Marvin Singleton, who tallied 16 points, Derek Reuben, who added 11, and Mark Riley, who sank a pair of free-throws in the last seconds to seal the deal for the Polars down the stretch.

Bloomington Jefferson topped St Paul Central in the opening semi, 59-34, on Kevin Lynch's 15 points and 12 rebounds. The Jags jumped out to a quick 14-3 lead and never looked in the rear view mirror. Their zone-defense was stifling and it caught Central off guard. The Minutemen shot just 34% and committed 19 turn-overs in this one and just couldn't get it going, never trimming the deficit to less than 14 points in the fourth quarter. Troy Jackson led the Minutemen with 11 points in the loss.

Duluth Central edged Minneapolis North, 51-50, on Tim Radosevich's dramatic spinning lay-up at the buzzer. North Guard Tim Bellfield missed the front end of a one-and-one free-throw attempt with just 13 seconds left to set up the thrilling ending which saw Central's Tom Pearson grab the rebound and heave it to Radosevich, who finished the game with 20 points. Central went on an 11-0 run in the second quarter and turned the momentum in their favor for the stretch run. North, behind Dan Bannister's 15 points, regained the lead in the fourth but ran out of gas down the stretch. For Coach

Front Row, L to R: Trainer Jim Colehour, Matt Stilwell, Chrys Wykle, Jeff Monson, Kevin Lynch, Tom Batta, Chad Jurgens, Manager Doug Lundahl. Middle Row, L to R: Coach Lynch, Jeff McArthur, Jim Berg, John Walker, Dave Flick, Cory Otterdahl, Dale Foerster, Coach Evens. Back Row, L to R: Mike Jenson, Tom Jasper, Mike Scherer, Robb DeCorsey, Dan Nerud.

The 1986 State AA Champs from Bloomington Jefferson

Tony Queen's Polars, it was their seventh straight trip to the big dance, and a bitter pill to swallow.

Bloomington Jefferson then escaped top-rated and previously undefeated Duluth Central, 52-51, in the championship game that Saturday evening at the St Paul Civic Center. John Walker's two free-throws with just 11 ticks on the clock secured the Jaguars title hopes and sent the boys from Duluth back to Lake Superior. Jefferson rallied in this one and finally took a four-point lead at the 3:56 mark when Walker nailed a base-line jumper to make it 48-44. The Trojans scored the next five points though, behind Tim Radosevich's outstanding play. The Jag's grabbed the lead for good, however, when Dan Nerud tipped in a rebound with just under two minutes to go. Jim Hastings, the state's No. 2 winningest all-time coach with more than 500 wins, finished his illustrious 31-year coaching career at Duluth Central with three state titles and a whole bunch of state tournament wins.

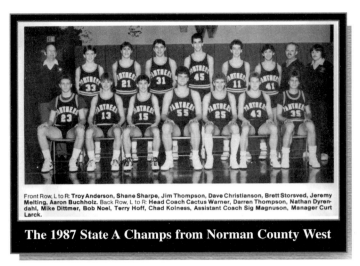

Front Row, L to R: Troy Anderson, Shane Sharpe, Jim Thompson, Dave Christianson, Brett Storsved, Jeremy Melting, Aaron Buchholz. Back Row, L to R: Head Coach Cactus Warner, Darren Thompson, Nathan Dyrendahl, Mike Dittmer, Bob Noel, Terry Hoff, Chad Kolness, Assistant Coach Sig Magnuson, Manager Curt Larck.

The 1987 State A Champs from Norman County West

1987: Class A: Norman County West vs. Crosby Ironton

Crosby Irnonton opened the 1987 state tournament by defeating Jackson in the opener, 63-54. Guard Mike Nagorski scored 25 points and Center Mike Gindorff added 20 in the win, while Wade Wacker tallied 30 in the loss.

Undefeated Hawley, behind Steve Molstre's 24 points and Randy Kragerud's 22, beat Waseca in Game Two, 64-61.
Norman County West side-lined Aurora-Hoyt Lakes, 62-47, in Game Three. Dave Christianson led the way for the speedy Panthers by scoring 24 points and 15 rebounds while Troy Anderson added 20 points of his own.

Minnesota Valley Lutheran of New Ulm, and their star center, Dave Begalka, topped Tracy-Milroy, 61-59. Begalka provided most of the Chargers' potent scoring punch by draining 29 points, while Tim Lenz and Dana Fischer got the game-tying and game-winning buckets at the end.

Norman County West breezed by Minnesota Valley Lutheran in the first semifinal, 45-37. The Panthers used speed and good defense to beat MVL. The game's two big men: six-foot-nine center Dave Christianson of NCW and the six-foot-eight Begalka of MVL battled down low all night and neutralized one another in the paint, each scoring 11 points and grabbing 11 rebounds for their respective teams. Forward Troy Anderson led the Panthers with 15 points while Senior Guard Brett Storsved added 14 in the win.

Hawley, the only un-defeated team, fell to Crosby-Ironton by a 53-52 margin in the other semi. Mike Nagorski was again the hero in this one, as his driving 10-foot bank-shot with just seven seconds left in the game proved to be the game-winner. Hawley had a six-point lead deep into the fourth quarter, but the Rangers got it close when Forward Wade Stangel converted on a reverse lay-up. Nagorski had 20 points and Mike Gindorf added 14 in the win, while Steve Molstre, who nearly drained a game-winner of his own a mili-second after the buzzer, added 17 in the loss.

Norman County West kept it going in the Finals, topping Crosby-Ironton, 70-58, to take the Class A championship. Dave Christianson and Brett Storsved each topped the 1,000-point plateau's for their careers in the game, giving the Panthers their first title since 1948. NCW led 27-18 at the half and never looked back from there. Crosby-Ironton tried to put together a couple of late rallies behind Mike Nagorski's 25 points, but couldn't get it in gear when it mattered. The Panthers spread out their offense in the second half and shot a lot of free-throws en route to keeping the Rangers at bay. Storsved finished with 19 points while Christianson added 16 points and 14 rebounds in the big win.

1987: Class AA: Bloomington Jefferson vs. Blaine

Moorhead jumped out to an 11-0 lead but had to fend off a late rally to edge Rosemount in the opener, 49-47. Rosemount's Rob Phenix kept his club in it late, but the Spuds went ahead for good on Scott Arnseth's three-point play in the final minute to ice it. Mike Bjelland's 18 points, led the way for Moorhead.

The Blaine Bengals, led by their dunking machine, Jeff Wirtz, who tallied 27 points and 11 rebounds, beat Park Center in Game Two, 58-50.

The defending champs from Bloomington Jefferson crushed previously unbeaten Woodbury, 59-38, in Game Two. The Jags took a 29-14 half-time lead and cruised on Tom Batta and Kevin Lynch's 17 and 16-point efforts.

Duluth East, behind sophomore Dann Hanson's 21 points, cruised past Willmar in the last quarterfinal of the day, 63-51. Dave Zollar almost tallied a triple double in the win as well, posting 16 points, 11 rebounds and nine assists in the win.

Bloomington Jefferson beat Duluth East 44-39 in the opening semifinal contest, thanks to Kevin Lynch's 12 points, six rebounds and three assists. The Jags, which led by as many as seven points in the first, fell behind in the fourth. They rallied behind 8-12 free-throw shooting and pulled it out down the stretch. East kept alive behind the outstanding play of Dave Zollar, who scored 10 of his 15 points in the fourth quarter, only to come up short in the final stretch. The Jags took the lead for good with just over two minutes to go, thanks to Lynch's jumper, but committed a couple of potentially deadly turn-overs late. Luckily for Bloomington, however, the Hounds couldn't capitalize on them.

Blaine, meanwhile, reached the title game by winning the longest game in the 75-year history of the tournament. The Bengals finally out-lasted Moorhead, 62-56, in five overtimes — shattering the previous record of just three. Tim Remme's buzzer-beater got the Bengals into the first overtime, and from there it was a wild one. Mark Arzdorf's two free-throws coupled with Bjelland's turn-around jumper got the Spuds into the second OT.

Front Row, L to R: Tom Jasper, Dale Foerster, Dan Nerud, Kevin Lynch, Tom Batta, Chad Jurgens, Mike Scherer. Middle Row, L to R: Assistant Coach Jake Lynch, Rob DeCorsey, Mike Jensen, Steve Cole, Mike Kirhorst, Todd Concavage, Pete Johnson, Head Coach Jack Evens. Back Row, L to R: Players Joel Daniels, Dave Larson, Aaron Topper, Scott DeBolt, Brad Pawek.

The 1987 State AA Champs from Bloomington Jefferson

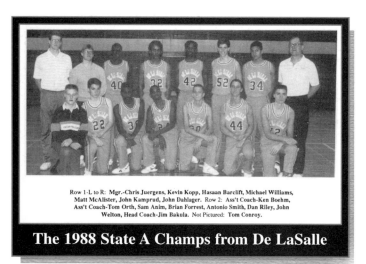

Row 1-L to R: Mgr.-Chris Juergens, Kevin Kopp, Hasaan Barclift, Michael Williams, Matt McAlister, John Kamprud, John Dahlager. Row 2: Ass't Coach-Ken Boehm, Ass't Coach-Tom Orth, Sam Anim, Brian Forrest, Antonio Smith, Dan Riley, John Welton, Head Coach-Jim Bakula. Not Pictured: Tom Conroy.

The 1988 State A Champs from De LaSalle

After conservative play in the next three extra sessions, including a pair of scoreless ones in the third and fourth periods, Moorhead Center Mike Bjelland blocked Jason McKay's driving jumper early in the fifth OT. From there Arzdorf picked up the rebound though and scored at the 2:40 mark to put his Bengals ahead for good. Wirtz, Arzdorf and Remme each had 14 points apiece in the historic win.

Bloomington Jefferson, the state's only undefeated team with a perfect 26-0 record, won its 34th straight game that Saturday night by blowing out Blaine, 54-37, in the Class "AA" championship game at the St Paul Civic Center before 13,407 fans. The Jaguars' defense was the big story in this one as they held the Bengals to just 37 points and forced them into way too many turn-overs throughout the contest. Bloomington jumped out to a 19-6 lead in the second, even holding Blaine's star, Jeff Wirtz to just two first-half points, and never looked back. Remme's outside shooting kept the Bengals alive in the second, but Lynch and Jurgens were too much down the stretch as they led their club to its second straight title with ease.

1988: Class A: Minneapolis De La Salle vs. Russell-Tyler-Ruthton

The 1988 tournament welcomed the addition of the three-point play, an offensive tactic put to good use by Russell-Tyler-Ruthton's Bob Schueller, who nailed a trio of early three's en route to leading his Knights to a commanding 69-47 victory. Jeff Brosz scored 19 points and Troy Bouman added 14 in the win, while Paul King tallied 16 points in the loss.

Crookston then edged Waseca in Game Two, 62-59. Steel Senske scored 17 of his 24 points in the first-half for the Pirates, while Bob Holder got the game-winner with under a minute to go on a dramatic under-handed scoop-shot.

No. 2 ranked De La Salle topped No. 1 rated Le Sueur, 86-73, in Game Three. Brian Forrest led the Islanders with 30 points while Sam Anim added 19 and a banged up Tom Conroy chipped in 18. Eric Allen played great two-way basketball for Le Sueur, but came up short in the end.

Bigfork edged SW Minnesota Christian of Edgerton in the last quarterfinal of the day, 83-81, thanks to Scott Chiabotti's lay-up with just 38 seconds to go in the game. Chiabotti had 28 points in the win while Scott Spronk, who rallied his Eagles back from a 17-point deficit, added 30 in the loss.

De La Salle rallied from a three-point half-time deficit to roll over Bigfork, 80-55, in the opening semifinal. Bigfork came out strong in this one and jumped to a 37-34 lead, only to see the Islanders dominate the second half. Their defense was smothering and forced several key turn-overs down the stretch. Sam Anim's tip-in just 29 seconds into the third quarter gave De La Salle the lead and from there they never looked back. John Dahlager led the way for the Islanders with 26 points while Brian Forrest added 19 in the big win.

Russell-Tyler--Ruthton then beat Crookston in the other semifinal, 48-45, in overtime. This one was a wild one that went down to the wire. Crookston took an early 24-21 half-time lead in this one, only to see RTR rally back to take a 31-30 lead early in the fourth quarter on Jeff Brosz's reverse lay-up. Then, with just 10 seconds to go, and RTR down by two, Brosz hit a clutch 17-foot jumper from the corner to tie it up and send it to overtime. There, Wendell Buysman got the go-ahead free-throw and the Knights never looked back.

De La Salle then came out and steam-rolled Russell-Tyler-Ruthton in the Finals, 58-36, to take the title. RTR was big up front, but Islanders were quick, and in the end quickness won out. Sam Anim scored 14 points and grabbed 12 rebounds en route to the Isle's jumping out to a 17-2 lead early on. Anim opened the fourth quarter with a huge dunk and from there they played smart basketball down the stretch. Troy Bouman tried to rally his club late, scoring 13, but came up short in this one. De La Salle shot 47% in the game and had four players in double figures: Anim, Conroy, Dahlager and Forrest.

1988: Class AA: Cold Spring Rocori vs. Robbinsdale Armstrong

Game One saw No. 1 ranked Cold Spring-Rocori beat Willmar, 63-60, in overtime. Craig Ehrlichman scored 18 points, including the tie-breaking three-pointer in overtime, to give Cold Spring-Rocori it's third win over Willmar that season. Brian Akervik led Willmar with 19 in the loss. Cloquet beat St. Thomas Academy in Game Two, 43-42, on Mark Lindquist's three-pointer and ensuing two free-throws in the final 1:37. Osseo topped Apple Valley in the third quarterfinal of the day, 67-62. Osseo's high-pressure defense held future Gopher and NBA Center Bob Martin to a mere 25 points in this one en route to advancing to the semi's. The Orioles went on a 19-4 run in the second quarter on Jeff Jones' 15 points.

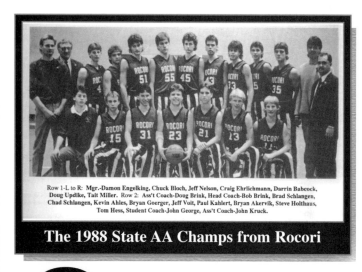

Row 1-L to R: Mgr.-Damon Engelking, Chuck Bloch, Jeff Nelson, Craig Ehrlichmann, Darrin Babcock, Doug Updike, Tait Miller. Row 2: Ass't Coach-Doug Brink, Head Coach-Bob Brink, Brad Schlangen, Chad Schlangen, Kevin Ahles, Bryan Goerger, Jeff Voit, Paul Kahlert, Bryan Akervik, Steve Holthaus, Tom Hess, Student Coach-John George, Ass't Coach-John Kruck.

The 1988 State AA Champs from Rocori

Robbinsdale Armstrong beat up on Forest Lake, 56-41, in the last quarterfinal. Jason Johnson started out slow but came on strong in the end, finishing with 19 points in the big win.

Cold Spring-Rocori topped Cloquet in the opening semifinal, 62-50. Cloquet rallied back from a 14-16 first quarter deficit to take a 33-30 lead at the half. Tim Giacomini had the hot hand for the Lumberjacks early on, scoring 19 first-half points. But Cold Spring-Rocori came back to take a 44-41 third quarter lead on Jeff Voit's jumper. Voit was tough down the stretch as he scored 21 points en route to leading his club into the Finals.

Robbinsdale Armstrong then narrowly edged out Osseo, 65-64, in the other semifinal. Osseo opened the game by springing to a quick 8-0 lead, only to see Robbinsdale Armstrong rally back to make it 27-32 at the half. From there it went back and forth with Robbinsdale Armstrong taking the lead for good at the 6:13 mark of the fourth when Jay Kirchoff nailed a pair of three pointers. Osseo rallied back late and got to within a basket on Herman's three-pointer with under two minutes to go, but the Falcons hung on and got the "W."

Cold Spring-Rocori beat Robbinsdale Armstrong, 66-56 in the Finals. Craig Ehrlichman was again the hero in this one as he rallied his team from a 47-42 deficit to get Coach Bob Brink an undefeated state title. Ehrlichman answered Scott Janckila's fourth quarter bucket by draining six free-throws over a two minute span to give his club the lead. He later added another pair with 2:12 left to give his club a commanding 57-46 advantage. The Falcons tried to rally back on Johnson's late three-pointers, but were held in check by a smothering Spartan's defense. Jeff Voit led the way with 22 points for Rocori, while Ehrlichman added 14 and Akervik chipped in 13 as well.

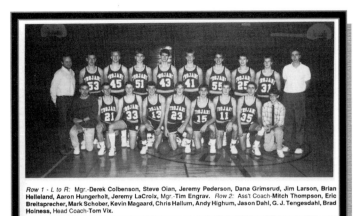

Row 1 - L to R: Mgr.-Derek Colbenson, Steve Oian, Jeremy Pederson, Dana Grimsrud, Jim Larson, Brian Helleland, Aaron Hungerholt, Jeremy LaCroix, Mgr.-Tim Engrav. Row 2: Ass't Coach-Mitch Thompson, Eric Breitsprecher, Mark Schober, Kevin Magaard, Chris Hallum, Andy Highum, Jason Dahl, G. J. Tengesdahl, Brad Holness, Head Coach-Tom Vix.

The 1989 State A Champs from Rushford

1989: Class A: Rushford vs. Russell-Tyler-Ruthton

Warren opened the 1989 Class A tourney at Williams Arena by beating Pipestone, 59-50, thanks to Trevor Monroe's 23 points off the bench. Rushford crushed Crosby-Ironton in Game Two, 68-46, on Dana Grimsrud's 25 points. Russell-Tyler-Ruthton rolled over Rush City in Game Three, 63-43, behind Lee Rood's 18 and Troy Bouman's 15-point efforts. Staples-Motley then knocked off Mankato Loyola in the final quarterfinal of the evening, 67-59, as Arden Beachy scored six of his 17 points in the final moments of the game to get his club into the semi's. His two brothers also got into the act as well, with Collin and Ryan scoring 13 and 10 points, respectively.

Rushford kept it going and romped past Warren, 71-46, in the opening semifinal. Dana Grimsrud was again the star, scoring 19 points, while his back-court partner, Aaron Hungerholt added 14 in the win. The Trojans jumped out to a 28-6 lead in this one, highlighted by an impressive 17-0 first-half run. Trevor Monroe led the Ponies with 10 points.

RTR side-lined a good Staples-Motley entry, 50-43, in the semifinals. RTR jumped out to a commanding 23-12 half-time lead in this one and never looked back from there. Staples-Motley rallied late but came up short thanks to some great defense. Sophomore Forward Todd Bouman (the future Minnesota Vikings back-up quarterback) led the Knights with 17 points, while Lee Rood added 10 in the win. Collin Beacy scored 12 while his brother Ryan added 10 in the loss.

Unranked Rushford surprised most of the experts and completed a 26-2 season ny winning the Class A state tournament by virtue of a 64-52 victory over No. 1 rated Russell-Tyler-Ruthton. After 25 winning seasons, Rushford finally came home with the hardware as Andy Highum scored 17 points and added 15 rebounds en route to leading his club to glory. The back-court tandem of Dana Grimsrud and Aaron Hungerholt also did their part, scoring 20 and 17 points, respectively. Rushford played great defense, out-rebounding the Knights 40-32 and caused several key turn-overs down the stretch. The last three minutes of the first half saw Rushford go on a 16-2 run, and they never looked back after that. RTR made a run of their own in the final quarter, cutting the gap to 46-37 on Todd Bouman's rebound lay-up with 6:34 left. The Trojans, however, responded with a 7-0 run of their own to put it away for good. The Bouman brothers, Troy and Todd, scored 17 and 16 points each in the loss.

1989: Class AA: Owatonna vs. Robbinsdale Armstrong

Owatonna eliminated Eden Prairie in the Class AA opener at the Civic Center, 46-37, thanks to junior Center Chad Kolander, who tallied 15 points and hauled in 17 rebounds in the win. Stillwater edged Hibbing in overtime, 69-66, in Game Two. Center Daren Danielson, also an All-State football player, had 32 points and 13 rebounds, as well as six points in sudden death, en route to leading his Bluejackets to the semi's. Scott Koenig tied it on a turn-around jumper with 49 seconds left for the Ponies, but they got out-hustled in the extra session. Robbinsdale Armstrong rolled over Minneapolis South in the third game of the day, 86-60. Solid defense and quickness were the keys to the Falcons victory as Guard Jason Johnson led the way with a game-high 31 points. St. Paul Central then topped Rocori in the last quarterfinal, 76-75, thanks to David Hollman and Metro Player of the Year Juriad Hughes. They combined for 55 points in this one and held off a late Rocori rally, highlighted to Tom Hess' trio of three-pointers, to advance into the semi's.

Owatonna held off Stillwater in the first semifinal contest, 45-43, to move into the Finals. Chad Kolander's pair of free-throws with just 35 seconds left proved to be the game-winners in this one. The Ponies came out and tried to play an up-tempo game against the Indians, and take Kolander out of the game. Owatonna hung tough though and rallied to finish strong. The Ponies forced 13 turn-overs and pushed the ball inside to Daren Danielson and Scott Koenig, who scored 13 points apiece in the loss. Kolander, however, finished with 19 points and 9 rebounds in the win.

Robbinsdale Armstrong eked past St. Paul Central, 76-75, in the other semifinal match-up. Mike Moen was the hero in this one as he grabbed Dan Nabedrick's rebound and put it back in the basket as the buzzer sounded to give his club a thrilling victory. The Minutemen played a stifling pressure defense in this one and were in it up until the very end. Moen led all scorers with 22 points, while Juriad Hughes and David Hollman combined for 49 points and 16 rebounds in the loss.

Owatonna, who was appearing in only its second state tourney, and first since 1924, then completed a 24-1 campaign by winning the championship game over Robbinsdale Armstrong, 45-43, in over-time. Armstrong made an impressive first-half showing in this one, holding the Indians scoreless for more than five minutes in the second quarter to take a 24-13 half-time lead. Matt Nigon's 17-foot jumper at the buzzer highlighted the first half for the Falcons, as they looked poised to do some damage in the second half. Owatonna cut the deficit to 27-33 on Kolander's jumper in the lane

Row 1 - L to R: Dan Olson, Mike Iserman, Matt Holland, Mike Nill, Chad Kolander, Mike Broich, Charley Hackenson, Mike Ebert. Row 2: Ass't Coach-Dan Meier, Ass't Coach-Harv Golberg, Mgr.-Gregg Feuerstein, Wayne Robke, Mark Randall, Than Johnson, Jason Westra, Kyle Paulson, Mike Tacheny, Corey Ihrke, Scott Armstrong, Ass't Coach-Brad Larson, Coach-Len Olson.

The 1989 State AA Champs from Owatonna

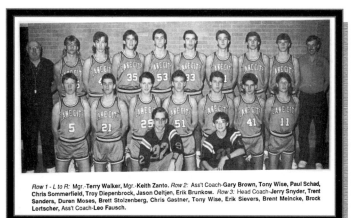

Row 1 - L to R: Mgr.-Terry Walker, Mgr.-Keith Zanto. Row 2: Ass't Coach-Gary Brown, Tony Wise, Paul Schad, Chris Sommerfield, Troy Diepenbrock, Jason Oeltjen, Erik Brunkow. Row 3: Head Coach-Jerry Snyder, Trent Sanders, Duren Moses, Brett Stolzenberg, Chris Gastner, Tony Wise, Erik Sievers, Brent Meincke, Brock Lortscher, Ass't Coach-Leo Fausch.

The 1990 State A Champs from Lake City

with just a few ticks remaining in the third, and then tied it up at 40-40 when Kolander hit another jumper with just 57 seconds to go in the game. Jason Johnsen could've won it for Armstrong at the horn, but his shot fell short and the game went to overtime. There, Holland got Owatonna on the board first, only to see Janckila answer with a jumper of his own. But Randall's lay-up with 22 seconds left followed by his ensuing free-throw proved to be the game-winner in this one as the Indians hung tough and won it as Johnsen's three-point "Hail-Mary" clanked off the rim at the final buzzer.

1990: Class A: Lake City vs. Mankato Loyola

De LaSalle beat Russell-Tyler-Ruthton in the opener, 66-53, as they rallied back from a 12-point half-time deficit to advance into the semi's. The trapping Islanders stymied RTR down the stretch, cruising to victory on Charles Maddox's 19-point effort. Lake City led from the opening gun and went on to rout Staples-Motley in Game Two, 60-47, as Tony Heise and Brent Meincke each scored 17 apiece in the big win. Mankato Loyola beat East Central, 72-53, behind Dan Ward's spectacular triple-double of 20 points, 11 assists and 10 rebounds. Chad Germann, meanwhile, drained an impressive 36 points in the losing effort. Fairmont then crushed Mahnomen in the last quarterfinal of the day, 76-47. Coach Ron Hested, a Cardinal legend who produced three stud basketball sons: Tim, Mike and Bradley, got his club into the semifinals for the first time in history that night thanks to Bradley Hested's 12 points and Lee Baarts' 11. Dan Engelby and Cory Kalheim each added nine in the big win for the Cards.

Lake City made it to the Class A final with a 46-36 semifinal victory over De La Salle. Tony Heise made six of eight free throws in the final 69 seconds as Lake City hung on to beat the Islanders and advance to the title game. Heise had 17 points and nine rebounds en route to leading his club to victory.

Mankato Loyola then upset Fairmont, 75-72, in overtime, to advance to the Finals. Loyola's Eric Holmstrom, who finished with 26 points in the game, nailed a huge three-pointer at the end of regulation to send this one to overtime. There, Holmstrom got his Crusaders on the board first on a 12-footer, for a 70-68 lead. Rick Theuninck then stole the ball and made a lay-up for a four point lead 40 seconds into the extra session. Fairmont tied it at 72-72 on six-foot-eight Center Dan Jacobson's short turn-around, followed by a Brad Hested jumper from the lane. But Loyola hung tough and got a big basket from Mac Johnson with under a minute to go. Theuninck added an insurance free-throw with 18 ticks on the clock to ice it. Lee Baarts then heaved a desperation shot at the buzzer, but it fell short, giving the Crusaders the big win. (The Cards did go on to win the third-place trophy with a 72-69 victory over De La Salle.)

The Lake City Tigers then went on to edge Mankato Loyola, 52-51, in the 1990 tournament finale. Senior Guard Tony Heise finished with 15 points in this one, but none was bigger than his clutch free-throw with just 37 seconds left that broke a 51-51 tie and iced the game for his Tigers. Trailing by one point with time running out, Loyola's Dan Ward, who finished with 21 points, dribbled down the left side of the lane and pushed up a shot that at first appeared destined to be the game-winner, but instead the ball rolled around the rim and came off — leaving the Crusaders high and dry.

1990: Class AA: Owatonna vs. Minneapolis North

Minneapolis North, behind Forward David Dennis' 25 points, rallied back to take a 60-54 victory over Cretin--Derham Hall in the opener. Cretin jumped out to a 12-0 lead in this one, but couldn't keep up with the speedy Polars down the stretch. Fergus Falls edged Bloomington Jefferson in Game Two, 49-48, on sophomore Kevin Pearson's game-winning lay-up with just 11 seconds to go in the match. Dan Sternberg added 20 in the thrilling win. Chaska crushed St. Francis in the third game of the day, 76-61, as Nate Streed scored 16 of his game-high 27 points in the third quarter alone. Owatonna then rolled over previously unbeaten and top-ranked Mounds View in Game Four, 72-58, behind 26 points from Mike Broich, while soon-to-be-Gopher Chad Kolander added 18 in the win.

The Minneapolis North Polars followed suit with a 49-48 semifinal victory against Fergus Falls. The Polars got the game-winner from David Dennis, who nailed a clutch jump-shot with just 11 seconds to go. The Otters tried to rally but saw Kevin Pearson's attempted game-winner fall short at the buzzer.

Owatonna then beat Chaska in an extremely tight semifinal contest, 35-34. Mike Broich popped in a pair of free-throws with 22 seconds left and the Indians held on to take the dramatic win. Chaska, which led for most of the game, got off two desperation shots in the final six seconds, with both missing their mark. Chad Kolander played tough defense all night and led the Indians with 16 points.

Then, in the Class AA title game, Minneapolis North was simply no match for an outstanding Owatonna Indians squad, losing big-time, 72-26. By the half it was 34-9 and this thing was over. The Polars struggled from the opening tip-off, shooting just 20% on the afternoon, and just couldn't get it in gear. Owatonna, on the other hand, shot 54% from the floor, 85% from the line, and hauled in 48 rebounds en route to their second straight state championship. Mike Broich finished with 20 points while Chad Kolander, who was in foul trouble early, added 10 in the huge win.

1991: Class A: Chisholm vs. Westbrook-Walnut Grove

Westbrook-Walnut Grove beat the Rushford-Peterson Chargers in the first round of the Class A tourney, 63-61, thanks to Juhl Erickson's late three-pointer and five free-throws down the stretch. Dawson-Boyd beat Argyle in Game Two, 56-51, behind Jeff Nordgaard's 17 points and 20 rebounds. The

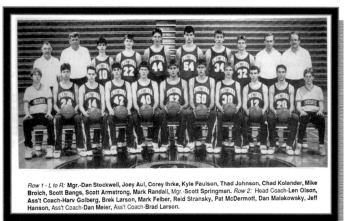

Row 1 - L to R: Mgr.-Dan Stockwell, Joey Aul, Corey Ihrke, Kyle Paulson, Thad Johnson, Chad Kolander, Mike Broich, Scott Bangs, Scott Armstrong, Mark Randall, Mgr.-Scott Springman. Row 2: Head Coach-Len Olson, Ass't Coach-Harv Golberg, Brek Larson, Mark Felber, Reid Stransky, Pat McDermott, Dan Malakowsky, Jeff Hanson, Ass't Coach-Dan Meier, Ass't Coach-Brad Larson.

The 1990 State AA Champs from Owatonna

Chisholm Bluestreaks got by Gibbon-Fairfax-Winthrop, 59-51, thanks to the efforts of Joel McDonald's 26 points. Becker then crushed Long Prairie in the last game of the day, 62-44, on Jeremy Karpinske's 23 points and Justin Hegna's 21.

Chisholm then routed Becker, 88-56, in the first semifinal. Ted Krize was the hero in this one, scoring a career-high 36 points en route to leading the No. 1 ranked Bluestreaks into the championship game. Joel McDonald had an "off-night," scoring a mere 30 points in the blow-out victory.

The Westbrook-Walnut Grove Chargers beat Dawson-Boyd in the opening semifinal, defeating them 80-66 to advance to the title game. The Chargers were ahead by just one point late in the third quarter, but they went on a 17-4 after that and coasted from there. Jason Bakke led that charge by scoring 24 points and grabbing 13 rebounds, while Jeff Nordgaard added 27 in the loss for Dawson-Boyd.

The championship game between Chisholm and Westbrook-Walnut Grove was a dead-heat through three quarters, with the both teams beginning the fourth period tied at 50-50. But Chisholm 14-point fourth-quarter streak proved insurmountable for the Chargers as they rolled to a commanding 77-61 victory — their fourth overall and first since 1975. Joel McDonald, who scored 30 points in the win, established a new all-time career scoring mark for any Minnesota high school athlete with 3,292 points. For Coach Bob McDonald, the winningest coach in Minnesota history whose two other sons, Paul and Mike, led the Streaks to titles in 1973 and 1975, it was an emotional night.

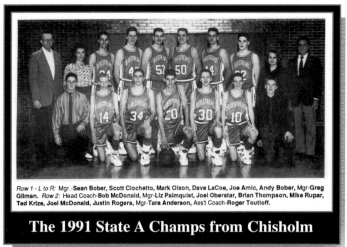

Row 1 - L to R: Mgr.-Sean Bober, Scott Ciochetto, Mark Olson, Dave LaCoe, Joe Amic, Andy Bober, Mgr-Greg Gilman. Row 2: Head Coach-Bob McDonald, Mgr-Liz Palmquist, Joel Oberstar, Brian Thompson, Mike Rupar, Ted Krize, Joel McDonald, Justin Rogers, Mgr-Tara Anderson, Ass't Coach-Roger Toutloff.

The 1991 State A Champs from Chisholm

1991: Class AA: Cretin Derham Hall vs. Minneapolis Roosevelt

Mounds View beat Brainerd, 48-43, in the opening quarterfinal game thanks to Brad Johnson's game-winning jumper — his only bucket of the day. The Minneapolis Roosevelt Teddies rolled Cambridge in Game Two, 66-44, as Forward Don Phillips led the way with 26 points. The Cretin-Derham Hall Raiders, behind Arvesta Kelly's 23 points, ended Owatonna's two-year reign as state champs by edging out a 76-72 win. The Raiders went on a 10-0 run late in the first half to take a 40-23 half-time lead, and held off a late Owatonna rally fueled by Mark Randall's 41 points. Mankato West upset Edina in the last quarterfinal of the day, 62-56, thanks to a 16-point second quarter run which put them up 32-21 at the half. Pat Coleman was the star in this one, scoring 23 points and grabbing 16 rebounds en route to leading his club into the semi's.

Cretin-Derham Hall beat Mankato West, 63-53, in the opening semifinal contest. Johnny Tauer scored 21 points and grabbed seven rebounds en route to leading his Raiders to the Finals. Tauer opened the second half of this one by draining a clutch three-pointer which gave his club a 35-28 lead. The Raiders expanded that lead to 49-39 into the fourth, and then held off a Scarlett rally which fell short.

Roosevelt beat Mounds View in the other semifinal, 40-39. Don "Tex" Phillips made the second of two free-throws with 16 seconds left in what proved to be the game-tying and game-winning points. This one was tied at 39-39 with 2:56 left on the clock, as both teams battled for position down the stretch. Mounds View had the last shot, but Dusty Becker's 16-foot turn-around jumper fell short at the buzzer. Wayne Charles led the Teddies with 12 points, while Mark Hronski had 15 for the Mustangs in the loss.

The Cretin-Derham Hall Raiders and Minneapolis Roosevelt Teddies battled early and often in this one, trading the lead throughout the AA Final. Arvesta Kelly, Matt McDonagh and Isreal Moses led a third quarter rally for the Raiders, rallying them into the lead. It was the Teddies, however, behind Tex Phillips' three-pointer, who came back from a four-point deficit in the waning seconds of the fourth quarter to force the overtime period. There, the Teddies got a three-pointer just seven seconds into the extra session from Johnny Tauer, who tallied 25 in the game, to take the lead for good. His teammates added eight more free-throws from there as they cruised to a very lop-sided 74-62 victory.

1992: Class A: Austin Pacelli vs. Minneapolis De La Salle

Rocori of Cold Spring blew out Chisholm 61-31 in the first quarterfinal game. Dan McMahon scored 20 while Luke Froehle added 14 as the Spartans cruised into the semi's. Minneapolis De La Salle scored early and often in defeating Clearbrook-Gonvick-Trail, 80-66, in the second quarterfinal game. The Islanders shot 63% in this one as Darren Dearring had 26 points and Adrian Patterson added 18 in the big win. Austin Pacelli, making their first tournament appearance, beat Lac qui Parle Valley, 55-51 in Game Three. The Shamrocks made eight straight free-throws in the last 44 seconds to seal the deal in this one. Bobby Beck, who became the state's No. 4 all-time leading scorer in the game, led Pacelli with 24 points in the win. Game Four was a doozy, with Minnewaska Area of Glenwood defeating Gibbon-Fairfax-Winthrop, 49-47, in overtime. Ryan Shea, who tallied 16 points in the match, was the hero in this one, as his three-pointer with three seconds left proved to be the game-winner.

De La Salle edged out a very tough Rocori squad in the first semifinal contest, 54-53, thanks to freshman Adrian Patterson's 19 points, including three free-throws in the final 18 seconds to propel his Islanders into the Finals. Darren Dearring also added 19 points, including 11 in the first quarter alone, during which the Islanders made of 10 of 14 shots from the field. Senior Forward Dan McMahon led the Rocori club with a tough 16 points in the loss.

Austin Pacelli then beat Minnewaska Area, 60-52, in the other semifinal. The Shamrocks made 14 of 18 free-throws in the fourth quarter and 21 of 28 throughout the game en route to earning a trip to the Finals. Steve Rogne was the hero for the Shamrocks, dumping in 25 points and playing outstanding defense. Pacelli, on the other hand, was led by Forward Jacob Nelson, who tallied 20 points.

Row 1 - L to R: Steve Rosga, John Salmen, Diallo Gant, Matt McDonagh, Arvesta Kelly, Jr. Row 2: Israel Moses, Johnny Tauer, Nick Tamble, Josh Krieger, Chris Walsh, Dave Schlatty, Head Coach-Len Horyza.

The 1991 State AA Champs from Cretin

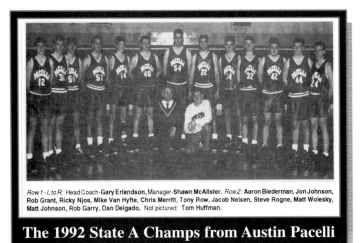

Row 1 - L to R: Head Coach-Gary Erlandson, Manager-Shawn McAlister. Row 2: Aaron Biederman, Jon Johnson, Rob Grant, Ricky Njos, Mike Van Hyfte, Chris Merritt, Tony Row, Jacob Nelsen, Steve Rogne, Matt Wolesky, Matt Johnson, Rob Garry, Dan Delgado. Not pictured: Tom Huffman.

The 1992 State A Champs from Austin Pacelli

Austin Pacelli kept it rolling in the title game, shooting an amazing 69% from the field en route to a 68-62 win over De La Salle. The Shamrocks opened up a 15-point half-time lead and fended off a late Islanders run to win this one going away. The Islanders regrouped at the half, but Pacelli, behind Jacob Nelson and Steve Rogne, who combined for 51 points, was just too much down the stretch. Darren Dearing, who led the Islanders with 20 points, fouled out with six minutes to go, and Austin held freshman sensation Adrian Patterson to just 13 points — both huge factors in the outcome. It was Pacelli's first title in its first-ever trip to the state tournament — not too shabby.

1992: Class AA: Anoka vs. Cretin Derham Hall

Eden Prairie and Duluth Central brought identical 19-6 records to their quarterfinal contest, but Duluth Central, behind Todd Hanson and David Berntson's 14-point efforts, proved to be too strong in this one, winning by a 53-40 margin. Anoka overcame a 47-39 fourth quarter deficit to top Rochester John Marshall in the second quarterfinal contest, 56-55. Dan Novotny's tap-in at 1:11 followed by Bryan Doughty's free-throw with 24 seconds proved to be the go-ahead and game-winning shots. Defending champion Cretin-Derham Hall knocked off No. 1 Chaska in Game Three, 63-52. Arvesta Kelly scored 31 points en route to leading his Raiders on a 17-0 fourth quarter rally to seal the deal in this one. Moorhead then defeated Minneapolis South 71-61 in the final quarterfinal game. Corey Zimmerman scored a game-high 31 points for the Spuds, while Patrick Williams scored 19 to lead the Tigers.

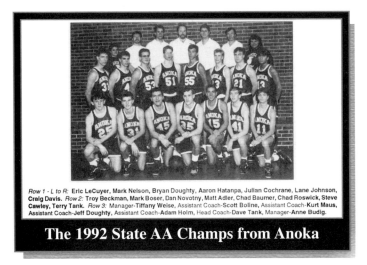

Row 1 - L to R: Eric LeCuyer, Mark Nelson, Bryan Doughty, Aaron Hatanpa, Julian Cochrane, Lane Johnson, Craig Davis. Row 2: Troy Beckman, Mark Boser, Dan Novotny, Matt Adler, Chad Baumer, Chad Roswick, Steve Cawley, Terry Tank. Row 3: Manager-Tiffany Weise, Assistant Coach-Scott Boline, Assistant Coach-Kurt Maus, Assistant Coach-Jeff Doughty, Assistant Coach-Adam Holm, Head Coach-Dave Tank, Manager-Anne Budig.

The 1992 State AA Champs from Anoka

The first semifinal saw Anoka and Duluth Central tangling in a defensive battle, with Anoka emerging as the victor, 49-35. Bryan Doughty's 16 points, including seven during a critical juncture in the second quarter, were the difference in this one. The Tornadoes turned it on in the second half and got a big boost from Aaron Hatanpa's break-away bucket to seal the deal. Todd Hanson led the Trojans with 11 points, but it wasn't enough as Anoka advanced on to the Finals.

Cretin-Derham Hall and Moorhead played an entirely different kind of semifinal game, with the run-and-gun Raiders emerging on the winning side of an 82-69 ball-game. The Spuds led 22-18 after the first, and 25-22 into the second before the Raiders, behind five-foot-six speedster Myron Taylor, rallied and took a 44-39 half-time lead. The Raiders led 70-62 with three minutes to go in this one, and finally slowed it down just enough at that point to coast to victory. Arvesta Kelly led the Raiders with 22 points, while Jason Kline added 21 and Steve Rosga chipped in 18.

Anoka then came out and played smart basketball en route to beating Cretin Derham-Hall in the championship game, 50-47. Anoka took a three-point half-time lead behind Bryan Doughty and Aaron Hatanpa's outstanding play, only to see the Raiders rally in the third quarter to take a 2-point lead. Then, Doughty suffered a facial cut, which took him out of the lineup for a while — ultimately holding him scoreless in the second half. Now, with just 12 seconds left in the game, Dan Novotny, who had 12 points in the game, missed the front end of a one-and-one try. Cretin rebounded and Arvesta Kelly, who led the Raiders with 14 points, walked it up the court. With four seconds left, Kelly launched a three-pointer from the top of the key, but the ball clanked off the front of the rim. Game over.

1993: Class A: Maple River, Mapleton vs. Bethlehem Academy, Faribault

Maple River opened the Class A tourney with a 58-46 defeat of Storden-Jeffers. Chad Ostermann, an 1,800-point career scorer, led the Cardinals with 24 points in the big win. Clearbrook-Gonvick edged Delano in Game Two, 63-61, on Dylan Goudge's dramatic three-pointer at the buzzer. Crosby-Ironton defeated Pelican Rapids, 51-48, in the third quarterfinal. Jamie Haskins and Mike Davis scored 12 and 11 points, respectively, en route to leading Crosby-Ironton into the semifinals. Bethlehem Academy of Faribault, then defeated DeLaSalle, 52-46, in Game Four. Jim Lovrien scored 20 points and drained four clutch free-throws in the final moments of the game to lead his club to victory.

Maple River rallied behind an amazing 22-4 run in the final eight minutes of their semifinal contest with Clearbrook-Gonvick to eke out a 54-52 victory. Matt Sohre's lay-up tied the game at 52-52, and then senior Bob McGregor scored the game-winner on a five-foot bank-shot with just three seconds left to ice it for Maple River. Chad Ostermann and Mark Lancaster each had 17 points in the win.

Bethlehem Academy, making its first tournament appearance, advanced to the title game with a 52-40 defeat of Crosby-Ironton. This one was close for the first three quarters but then the roof caved in on Crosby-Ironton. The Eagles went on a 13-1 run to kick off the fourth quarter and pulled away behind Jim Lovrien and Tim Schlaak's 17-point efforts. Center Bruce Holmvig led the Rangers with 11 points in the loss.

Then, in what turned out to be the lowest-scoring championship game since boys' basketball was split into two classes, and also the lowest total of

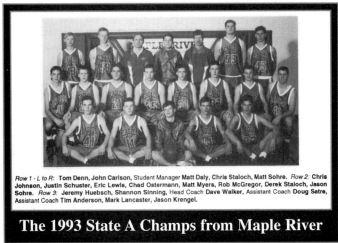

Row 1 - L to R: Tom Denn, John Carlson, Student Manager Matt Daly, Chris Staloch, Matt Sohre. Row 2: Chris Johnson, Justin Schuster, Eric Lewis, Chad Ostermann, Matt Myers, Rob McGregor, Derek Staloch, Jason Sohre. Row 3: Jeremy Huebsch, Shannon Sinning, Head Coach Dave Walker, Assistant Coach Doug Satre, Assistant Coach Tim Anderson, Mark Lancaster, Jason Krengel.

The 1993 State A Champs from Maple River

any championship contest since 1942, Maple River took home the championship trophy with a 33-29 victory over Bethlehem Academy. Maple River took a 30-25 lead in the low-scoring contest, and fended off a late Eagle rally, led by Jason Krengel's 10 points, to take the crown. Mark Lancaster led the Cardinals down the stretch, scoring seven of his team's final eight points in this one. The six-foot-eight center played huge, recording 12 points, nine rebounds and seven blocks on the day.

1993: Class AA: Cretin Derham Hall vs. Anoka

Cretin-Derham Hall opened the 1993 state tournament quarterfinals with a 65-47 pounding of Totino Grace. Elk River then eliminated Hopkins, 57-46, in Game Two, while Duluth Central had little trouble in getting past Rochester John Marshall, 57-45, in Game Three. Then, in the final quarterfinal of the day, Anoka topped Chaska, 53-46, to advance into the semifinals.

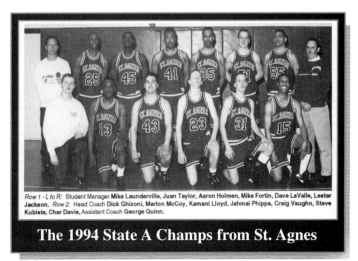

Row 1 - L to R: Jeff Cragg, Tim Rosga, Sean Benton, Kevin Adrian, Myron Taylor, Buzz Hannahan, Andrew Johnson, Scott Heather. Row2: Aaron Macke, Matt Birk, Jeff Ellens, Jarvis Archibald, Jerry Kline, Arvesta Kelly Jr., Sana Anetipa, Rene' Rodriquez, Joel Pederson, Head Coach Len Horyza.

The 1993 State AA Champs from Cretin

It took a pair of overtime periods for Cretin-Derham Hall to dispose of Elk River in the first semifinal game. The Raiders hung tough though and eked out a thrilling 72-69 victory. Raiders' five-foot-eight guard Myron Taylor sank two free-throws with 10 seconds to go to clinch the victory in this one, bringing the sell-out Civic Center crowd to its feet. After a slow first OT, the Raiders' Jeff Ellens was fouled with just two seconds to go. He then stepped up to the line and iced it for Cretin. Then, with just a second to go, Elk River's Skipp Schaefbauer, who scored 34 points, including 13 of the Elks' 14 points in the two extra sessions, heaved a 50-foot Hail-Mary which fell short to end the game.

Anoka then knocked off Duluth Central in the other semifinal, 66-54, to advance to the championship game. The defending champions from Anoka played a physical brand of basketball in this one, wearing down the undefeated Trojans throughout the game. Matt Adler led the Tornadoes with 18 points, while Bryan Doughty and Craig Davis added 17 and 15 points, respectively, in the win. Central rallied from an early 59-44 deficit though, and got it to within seven points on Justin Black's three-pointer with just over a minute to go. But that was as close as they would get, as they were forced to foul and try desperation three's the rest of the way.

Cretin-Derham Hall, playing in its third straight title tilt, kept it going into the Finals, beating Anoka, 56-44, for all the marbles. It was sweet revenge for the Raiders, who lost to the Tornadoes in the 1992 state championship game. Jarvis Archibald scored a team-high 13 points in leading the Raiders, and made a pivitol play late in the game which turned out to be huge. With the Raiders leading 47-39, Archibald grabbed a Jerry Kline missed free-throw and got fouled in the process. He stepped up and made them both, however, giving his club the cushion it would need for the stretch run. Anoka trailed throughout the entire game as Cretin played a tough defense all night. Anoka's Terry Tank nailed a three to get it to 15-12 in the first, but that was as close as the Tornadoes would get. Arvesta Kelly also played a solid game for Cretin, scoring 11 points in the big win.

1994: Class A: St. Agnes vs. Morris Area

St. Agnes dethroned the defending champion Maple River Eagles in the opening quarterfinal contest, 63-56, behind Kamani Lloyd's rebound basket with 27 seconds left. Bethlehem Academy of Faribault knocked out previously unbeaten Bigfork in the second quarterfinal, 51-36, behind Guard J.J. Korman's 12 points. Morris Area pummelled newcomer Climax-Fisher in Game Three, 61-37, on Zach Witt's 16 points and six assists. Westbrook-Walnut Grove eliminated New London-Spicer, 68-55, in the final game of the day. The Chargers went on a 22-7 third quarter run, highlighted by Guard Nate LeBoutillier's 21 points.

St. Agnes ousted Westbrook-Walnut Grove in the opening semifinal game, 66-53. St. Agnes jumped out to a quick 11-0 lead in this one only to see the Chargers, behind Jeff DeBates' two three-pointers, rally to tie it up at 18-18. The Aggies were up 30-24 at the half, and never looked back from there though. Lester Jackson led the Aggies with 19 points and punctuated the big win with a 180-degree slam-dunk on a break-away with just under two minutes to go. Marlon McCoy, who played great defense on DeBates, added 12 points and eight rebounds as well.

Morris Area then defeated Bethlehem Academy in the other semi, 52-40. Kevin Loge, a six-foot-eight center, scored 16 points in this one, as his Tigers remained undefeated and cruised into the Finals. The Cardinals put together a nice second half rally though, getting it to 45-42 with 1:18 left on the clock. But the Tigers hung tough and spread it out down the stretch to advance into the title game.

First-time qualifier St. Agnes won the Class A tournament by beating previously unbeaten Morris Area, 78-71. The momentum went back and forth between the Aggies and Tigers. The Aggies let a 19-point second half lead evaporate to just two in less than eight minutes, but stayed calm and regrouped. Their full-court press worked well and they were able to force several key turn-overs down the stretch. Morris' Kevin Loge was again solid in this one, scoring 12 of his game-high 24 points in the first quarter, while Cory Schmidgall added 16 and Zach Witt put in 13. The Aggies, however, were led by Lester Jackson, who tallied 20, while Jahmai Phipps added 19 and Marlon McCoy chipped in 18 as well.

1994: Class AA: Minneapolis Washburn vs. Hopkins

The 1994 tourney kicked off with Minneapolis Washburn edging Worthington in overtime, 72-71. The previous year's champion, Cretin-Derham Hall, was then upset in the second quarterfinal by Mounds View, 48-43. Moorhead eliminated Forest Lake in Game Three, 71-60, while Hopkins, behind Justin White's 32 points, took care of Apple Valley, 67-59, in the last quarterfinal of the day.

Minneapolis Washburn defeated Moorhead, 69-59, in the first semifinal match-up. Eric Minea was a monster inside, raking the boards for 15

Row 1 - L to R: Student Manager Mike Launderville, Juan Taylor, Aaron Holmen, Mike Fortin, Dave LaValle, Lester Jackson. Row 2: Head Coach Dick Ghizoni, Marlon McCoy, Kamani Lloyd, Jahmai Phipps, Craig Vaughn, Steve Kubista, Char Davis, Assistant Coach George Quinn.

The 1994 State A Champs from St. Agnes

The 1994 State AA Champs from Washburn

rebounds and adding five blocks as well. Akeem Carpenter was equally impressive from the outside, tallying 18 points in the win. The Millers struggled at the free-throw line, however, making just 14 of 32, but made up for it in the rebounding department — where they hauled in 21 offensive boards. Sean Greenwaldt led the Spuds with 20 points in the loss.

Hopkins then beat Mounds View in its semifinal contest, 63-51, en route to shooting a very solid 48% from the field. Mounds View tied it at 25-25 at the half, but then came up short in the second. The Royals went on a 7-0 run mid-way through the third and then a 6-0 run early in the fourth. James Ware scored 19 and Shawn Granner added 15 to lead the Royals into the Finals. James Ware scored 19 points while Shawn Granner added 15 in the big win.

Minneapolis Washburn kept it going in the Finals, winning the Class AA title in thrilling fashion. This one had the Civic Center fans on the edge of their seats for the entire game. This one was a back and forth affair, with both teams shooting nearly 50% from the field. Finally, with just 11.9 seconds to go, Washburn's Aaron Boone stepped up to the free-throw line. With his Millers trailing 65-63, Boone made the first, but missed the second. That's when six-foot-eleven Eric Minea grabbed the rebound and tried to stuff it in. It too bounced off, and with just five ticks on the clock, Byron Suttles grabbed the ball out of mid-air and put it home to the win the game, 66-65. Suttles led the Millers with 17 points while Boone added 13 in the win. Matt Arnold recorded 15 for the Royals before fouling out in the fourth.

1995: One Class Format: Minneapolis North vs. Staples Motley

In 1995 the MSHSL, in an effort to to increase interest and attendance, decided to change its two-class format into a singular, one-class "Sweet 16" tournament. The change, which would now be more favorable to seeing a big, inner city school versus a small, rural school match-up, would last just two years, before changing again in 1997 to a four-class system. The one common denominator, however, of the one-class tournament was Minneapolis North, which took home the hardware in both seasons.

In the first-round, where all teams played within their own class, tournament favorite and 25-0 Minneapolis North met White Bear Lake in a rematch of the 1985 Class AA title match. The Polars got their revenge in this one though, easily defeating the Bears, 84-64.

In the other opening round match-ups, Cretin-Derham Hall beat Robbinsdale Armstrong, 48-41; New London-Spicer rolled over St. Peter, 73-46; and Monticello lost to Duluth East, 47-55.

In the other games, Staples-Motley, behind Blaine Joerger's 24 points, defeated Caledonia, 69-63; Lakeville beat Rocori, 60-58; St. Agnes eliminated Redwood Valley, 64-53; and Chisholm had no problem with Fertile-Betrami, 65-51.

Then, in mixed class quarterfinal action, the Staples-Motley Cardinals, behind Blaine Joerger's 31 points and 11 rebounds, pounded Lakeville, 82-65.

Chisholm topped St. Agnes, 58-56, in overtime, thanks to Forward Chad Trembath's tip-in at the buzzer. Trembath scored seven of his 16 points in the extra session.

The Duluth East Greyhounds got 25 points from senior Center Josh Quigley in their big win over New London-Spicer, 61-45.

Minneapolis North, behind Jabbar Washington's 20 points, then edged Cretin-Derham Hall, 51-48, in the last quarterfinal contest. Center Elbert Wall came up with a pair of big steals and a rebound basket late in the game to get his Polars into the Semifinals.

Guard Erik Kelly's base-line jumper with only four seconds left on the clock lifted the Staples-Motley Cardinals to a thrilling 46-44 semifinal victory over Chisholm. Blaine Joerger once again led the Cardinals in scoring, dumping in 17 in the win.

The undefeated Polars kept on rolling in the other semifinal, eliminating Duluth East 48-41. Albert Green's three-pointer late in the third quarter gave the Polars a six-point lead and they cruised from there. Ozzie Lockhart added 14 points in the big win, including a clutch steal-turned-layup in the final 13 seconds to ice it.

The Staples-Motley Cardinals, with an enrollment of just 445, then met mighty Minneapolis North in the Finals. This one was a barn-burner, full surprises — one of them coming when two of North's starting guards were named academically ineligible for the big game. The Cardinals jumped out to an early 17-5 lead in this one, and then extended it to 23-9 on Cy Bestland's three-pointer. But North's pressure defense kicked in and the Polars scored the next 11 points. North trailed 41-36 in the second-half, but took its second lead of the game after going on a 6-0 run. The final minutes of the fourth quarter then produced some good drama. With the score see-sawing back and forth, North's Khalid El-Amin took a shot and missed, but Kavon Westberry, on the other side of the basket, grabbed it and put the ensuing rebound back in with just three seconds left to give the Polars a thrilling 54-52 victory. El-Amin led North with 17 points, while Blaine Joerger led the Cards with 28 in the loss.

The 1995 State Champs from Minneapolis North

1996: One Class Format: Mpls. North vs. Fertile-Beltrami

In first-round action, where all teams played within their own class, Staples-Motley downed MACCRAY, 55-48; Monticello edged Rocori in a double-overtime thriller, 69-67; Janesville-Waldorf-Pemberton beat Cromwell, 67-55; and Fertile-Betrami beat Caledonia, 58-49. St. Thomas Academy then topped Duluth East in yet another double-overtime thriller, 62-56; Minneapolis North rolled over Rochester Mayo, 73-53; Minneahaha Academy topped No. 1 New London-Spicer, 62-51; and Eden Prairie edged out Blaine, 55-48.

In quarterfinal action, a Khalid El-Amin three-pointer (his record ninth of the game) at the buzzer gave Minneapolis North a dramatic 67-65 win over St. Thomas Academy. El-Amin's 41 points helped the Polars rally back from a four-point deficit, with just 12 seconds remaining to advance to the semi's.

Minnehaha Academy, led by Marc Johnson's 19 points, defeated the No. 1 ranked Class AA Eden Prairie Eagles, 55-50.

Junior center Chris Heier's 28 points and 11 rebounds helped the Staples-Motley Cardinals defeat Rocori, 70-57.

Fertile-Beltrami, behind Aaron Thompson's 18 points, knocked off undefeated Janesville-Waldorf-Pemberton, 58-52.

Now, in the semifinals, Minneapolis North rolled over Staples-Motley, 62-41, to advance back to the Finals. North out-rebounded the Cardinals 30-18 and played a stifling brand of pressure defense. Khalid El-Amin, Jabbar Washington and Ozzie Lockhart had 21, 18 and 17 points, respectively, in this one as the Polars started out strong and rolled to an easy victory. Chris Heier led the Card's with 20 points in the loss.

Fertile-Beltrami remained unbeaten with a 61-58 victory over Minnehaha Academy in the other semifinal game. The Falcons played sound defense and were 25 of 30 from the charity stripe in this one. D. J. Motteberg nailed a pair of free-throws with 10 seconds to go in this one to ice it for the Falcons down the stretch. Senior Guard Aaron Thompson had 21 points while junior Forward Ryan Solie added 20 in the win.

It was just what the doctor ordered for the Finals, city vs. out-state. But the "city" in this case was the defending champs from Minneapolis North — and that spelled trouble for the previously unbeaten Fertile-Beltrami Falcons, who were crushed in this one, 80-47. The Falcons took an early 3-2 lead before North took over and simply dominated. The Polars jumped out to a 38-20 half-time lead and never looked back. North's junior forward Jabbar Washington scored 28 points and had eight rebounds in the game, while teammate Khalid El-Amin added 17. The win gave North back-to-back state titles over a stretch which saw them rack up an amazing 56-1 record.

That next year the MSHSL decided to abandon the "Sweet 16" format, and instead institute a new four-class system which would allow many more teams to appear in the state tournament.

Row 1 - L to R: Khalid El-Amin, Jason Spellmon, Jerome Hubbard, Ozzie Lockhart, Jabbar Washington. Row 2: Terry Hinton, Duane Slaughter, Kavon Westberry. Row 3: Coach Ingram, LaMont Scott, Alvarez McKendall, Kerek Taylor, Coach Brown, Andrew Lemmie, Jerry Hinton, Andre Gray, Coach Gray

The 1996 State Champs from Minneapolis North

1997: Class A: Hancock vs. Wabasso

The Class A tourney kicked off with the Hancock Owls beating Norman County West of Halstad, 62-48, in the quarterfinals and Minnesota Valley Lutheran of New Ulm, 78-46, in the semi's. Justin Thielke scored 22, while Ryan Jepma and Chad Nuest each added 18 and 17, respectively, in the semi-final win. With the win, the Owls met up with Wabasso in the Finals.

The Wabasso Rabbits followed a tougher path. After beating Trinity at River Ridge of Bloomington, 99-64, in their quarterfinal contest, the Rabbits went on to make history in their semifinal game against Red Lake. This one was a barn-burner, literally, as the Rabbits set several records in finally beating Red Lake, 117-113, in overtime, to advance to the Finals. Derrick Jenniges had 31 points for Wabasso while Brady Brau had 25 in the win. Gerald Kingbird had 37 for Red Lake and Delwyn Holthusen added 30 in the loss. (The game will be recorded in Minnesota state record books as the highest scoring game in history, with tournament records also set for the most points scored by the winning team and the losing team. Red Lake also broke records for most field goals, 48; most field goals attempted, 87; most points in one quarter, 43; and most three-point field goals, 11.)

In the title game, Hancock, making its first state tournament appearance since 1923, edged the Wabasso Rabbits, 60-58. Rob Moore's three-pointer with just over a minute to go tied it and Chad Nuest's 12-footer with four seconds on the clock sealed the deal as Hancock hung on to take the crown. Tony Thielke led the Owls with 24 points while Justin Thielke added 12.

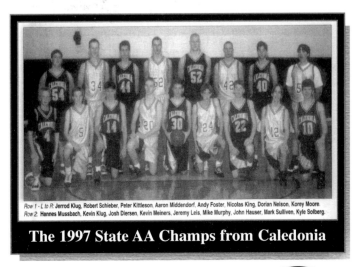

Row 1 - L to R: Student Manager Kirby Marquart, Student Manager Kameron Berget. Row 2: Jeremy VerSteeg, Tony Thielke, Chad Nuest, Justin Thielke, Andy Charles. Row 3: Assistant Coach Randy Thielke, Nate Christie, Ryan Jepma, Jeff Harmsen, Austin Wartner, Dan Bolluyt, Head Coach Dave Schoeck.

The 1997 State A Champs from Hancock

1997: Class AA: Caledonia vs. Minneapolis De La Salle

Caledonia opened the AA tourney by beating Janesville-Waldorf-Pemberton in the quarterfinals, 71-66. From there the Warriors, behind Neil Austin's 14 points, eliminated Albany in the semifinal game, 65-44. Meanwhile, Minneapolis DeLaSalle beat Redwood Valley, 57-49, in its quarterfinal match-up, and then edged out a very tough Staples-Motley club, 63-61, in two overtimes, in the semi's. Ben Johnson, who finished with 31 points, nailed a dramatic 14-footer in double-OT to seal the deal in this one as the Islanders surged into the Finals.

The Class AA championship game then featured Caledonia against DeLaSalle, and this one was all Caledonia. The Warriors finished their perfect 29-0 season behind Aaron Middendorf's amazing 45-point effort, only five points shy of the state record. This one was over before it really began as the Warriors, who never let the Islanders cut their lead to less than 15 points in the second half, cruised to a 69-47 victory.

Row 1 - L to R: Jerrod Klug, Robert Schieber, Peter Kittleson, Aaron Middendorf, Andy Foster, Nicolas King, Dorian Nelson, Korey Moore. Row 2: Hannes Mussbach, Kevin Klug, Josh Diersen, Kevin Meiners, Jeremy Leis, Mike Murphy, John Hauser, Mark Sulliven, Kyle Solberg.

The 1997 State AA Champs from Caledonia

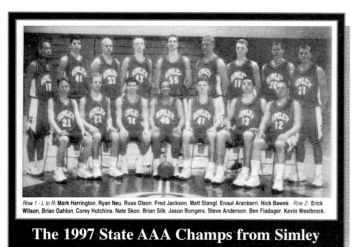

Row 1 - L to R: Mark Harrington, Ryan Neu, Russ Olson, Fred Jackson, Matt Stangl, Enaut Aranbarri, Nick Bawek. Row 2: Erick Wilson, Brian Gahlon, Corey Hutchins, Nate Skon, Brian Silk, Jason Bongers, Steve Anderson, Ben Fladager, Kevin Westbrock.

The 1997 State AAA Champs from Simley

1997: Class AAA: Simley vs. New Prague

The AAA tourney opened with the Simley Spartans pounding Chisago Lakes Area, Lindstrom, 65-38, in the quarterfinals. From there they advanced into the semifinals against Alexandria, where the Spartans escaped with a thrilling 51-50 win. Leading the way for Simley were Brian Silk, who tallied 23 points, and Enaut Aranbarri, who added 14 in the win.

New Prague, meanwhile, making its first state tournament appearance since 1983, opened up their bracket by beating Marshall, 53-49, followed by Minneapolis Roosevelt in the semi's, 72-57, to advance to the title game. Six-foot-eight Center Brian Giesen led the way for the Trojans by scoring 20 points and grabbing 19 rebounds in the big win. Corey Sheplee was also instrumental in the victory, as the speedy guard distributed the ball well and tallied 16 points to boot.

The championship game then featured Simley topping New Prague, 61-47. Matt Stangl scored 14 of his game-high 26 points in the first half en route to leading the Spartans to the title. Simley built a 19-point lead in this one and then had to fend off a late Trojan rally for the win. In fact, New Prague was within three points with just over four minutes to go, but thanks to Brian Silk's 13 points, the team went on a late scoring binge and cruised from there. Center Brian Giesen led the Trojans with 20 points and 12 rebounds in the loss.

1997: Class AAAA: Minneapolis North vs. Stillwater Area

The Minneapolis North Polars' road to the championship began with a 73-59 quarterfinal win over Rochester Mayo. From there they topped

Row 1 - L to R: Head Coach Robin Ingram, Assistant Coach Clifford Brown. Row 2: Ozzie Lockhart, Kevin Holley, Terry Hinton, Kerek Taylor, Andrew Lemmie, Jerry Hinton, Kenji Torrance, Wendell Johnson, Jabbar Washington, Khalid El-Amin.

The 1997 State AAAA Champs from Minneapolis North

Hopkins, 59-48, in the semifinals, thanks to 23 points from Khalid El-Amin and another 18 from Jabbar Washington. Ozzie Lockhart was also instrumental in the win, playing outstanding defense while holding Hopkins' star Jared Nuness to just 12 points.

Stillwater, meanwhile, opened up their bracket with a 52-49 quarterfinal win over Roseville. Then, in the semi's, the steam-rolled Elk River, 65-48, on junior Guard Drew Carty's 20 points. The Ponies opened up a 21-4 lead in this one and cruised from there, shooting a gaudy 58% along the way. Adam Runk added 13 points and six rebounds in the win, while Jake Maros led the Elks with 14 in the loss.

The championship game then pitted the Minneapolis North Polars against the Stillwater Ponies, and this one was all North. Khalid El-Amin's 26 points and Ozzie Lockhart's 15 points led the Polars as they started out strong and rolled to an impressive 61-53 victory. For El-Amin, who would go on to lead U-Conn to the NCAA championship and later play in the NBA, he had solidified himself as one of Minnesota's greatest prep players of all-time. It was the Polars' third consecutive title, tying Edina's 29-year-old record for most consecutive championships. Over that span North posted an amazing record of 81-4.

1998: Class A: Noman County East, Twin Valley vs. Carlton

The Class A state tournament kicked off with the Noman County East, Twin Valley Eagles outscoring Red Lake 5-1 in overtime to beat the Warriors 69-65 at Concordia College in Moorhead to advance to the semifinal round. There, the Eagles edged the Rushford-Peterson Trojans, 57-54, to advance to their first championship appearance. Eagles' Guard John Gullinsrud joined the prestigious 1,000-point club after scoring 20 points in this one, while James Carrier, whose three game-tying attempts in the final seconds each came up short, added 28 points in the loss.

The Carlton Bulldogs, meanwhile, advanced to the championship game after winning their quarterfinal win over Hancock, 65-52. From there the Bulldogs advanced to the semifinals, where they topped Sleepy Eye Saint Mary's, 63-47. The Eagles took the early lead in this

Row 1 - L to R: Kyle Olson, Brandon Stueness, Mike Syverson, Nate Andersen, Dan Pinske. Row 2: Assistant Coach Keith Hanson, Assistant Coach Mike Sather, Rick Kraft, John Gullingsrud, Jeff Plattner, Adam Broers, Head Coach Kevin McKeever.

The 1998 State A Champs from Norman County West

one, only to fend off a late Bulldogs rally. Carlton's Sam Pearsall led the charge in this one with 21 points, while Center Judd Walter led St. Mary's with 15 points and 14 rebounds in the loss.

Norman County East of Twin Valley kept it going in the Finals by winning its first state title ever in defeating Carlton, 75-48. The Eagles jumped out to a 12-5 lead in this one only to see Carlton come back to take the lead. But the Eagles rallied back and regained a 29-21 lead at the half. Carlton ran out of steam in the second half though and Norman County East of Twin Valley cruised from there. Kyle Olson and John Gullingsrud led the Eagles with 16 and 14 points, respectively, in the win. Norman County East, however, had no starters score in double digits.

1998: Class AA: Minneapolis De La Salle vs. Long Prairie–Grey Eagle

The Class AA tournament began with Minneapolis De La Salle defeating Martin County West, Sherburn, 57-43 in the quarterfinals. Ben Johnson led the Islanders with 26 points and five steals. The Islanders then won their semifinal game in a blow-out, defeating Sibley East, 75-44. Ben Johnson teamed up with Dominique Simms for 46 points in this shalacking.

In the other bracket, Long Prairie-Grey Eagle defeated Sauk Centre, 51-44, in the quarterfinals. From there the Thunder then edged Kenyon-Wanamingo, 53-50, in the semifinals. (Unranked Kenyon-Wanamingo got to the semi's by upsetting No. 1-ranked Redwood Valley 55-47.) Steve Ruda sparked the Thunder's rally in this one as the center took over late in the game. Todd Lisson and Adam Gustafson each made free-throws in the final 30 seconds as well to life the Thunder to victory.

De La Salle then edged a very tough Long Prairie-Grey Eagle club in the Finals, 53-52, to earn its third state championship.

The Long Prairie-Grey Eagle Thunder had a 14-12 lead at the start of the second quarter and held a 46-42 lead heading into the final frame. But this one came down to the final 4.8 seconds, when Ben Johnson, who led all scorers with 35 points, hit a clutch free-throw to break a 52-52 tie and give his Islanders their first lead since the opening quarter. From there the Islanders played tough defense and held on as the Thunder's desperation, buzzer-beating half-court shot fell short.

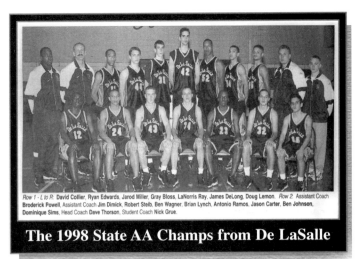

Row 1 - L to R: David Collier, Ryan Edwards, Jarod Miller, Gray Bloss, LaNorris Ray, James DeLong, Doug Lemon. Row 2: Assistant Coach Broderick Powell, Assisstant Coach Jim Dimick, Robert Steib, Ben Wagner, Brian Lynch, Antonio Ramos, Jason Carter, Ben Johnson, Dominique Sims, Head Coach Dave Thorson, Student Coach Nick Grue.

The 1998 State AA Champs from De LaSalle

1998: Class AAA: St. Thomas Academy vs. Minneapolis Patrick Henry

The Class AAA tournament opened with Saint Thomas Academy beating Faribault, 53-40, in quarterfinal action. From there the Cadets topped Monticello in the other semifinal, 59-47. S.T.A. held Monticello's seven-foot Center Joel Przybilla to just two second half points in this one en route to earning a trip to the Finals. Przybilla, who would go on to star with the Gophers and later the NBA's Milwaukee Bucks, scored 17 points in the first half, but was held in check in the second. Ben Pearson scored 25 points for St. Thomas Academy in the big win.

Meanwhile, Minneapolis Patrick Henry crushed Cloquet in the other quarterfinal, 72-47. From there the Patriots reached the Finals for the first time since winning it all back in 1945 by upsetting fourth-ranked Totino-Grace, 60-55, in the semifinals. Darius Lane, who would go on to star at Seton Hall University, scored 30 points for the second game in a row, but it wasn't enough as Patrick Henry cruised to victory. Mike Pettis led Patriots by scoring 16 of his 18 points in the second half.

Then, in the championship tilt, Saint Thomas Academy used its superior inside strength in defeating Minneapolis Patrick Henry, 60-49, to win its first state championship. This one was closer than it looked as the

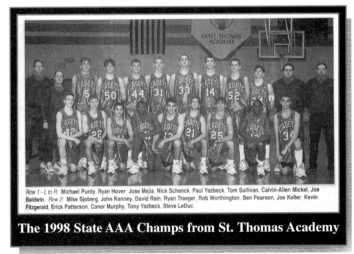

Row 1 - L to R: Michael Purdy, Ryan Hover, Jose Mejia, Nick Schenck, Paul Yazbeck, Tom Sullivan, Calvin-Allen Mickel, Joe Baldwin. Row 2: Mike Sjoberg, John Kenney, David Rain, Ryan Traeger, Rob Worthington, Ben Pearson, Joe Keller, Kevin Fitzgerald, Erick Patterson, Conor Murphy, Tony Yazbeck, Steve LeDuc.

The 1998 State AAA Champs from St. Thomas Academy

Cadets built an eight point lead over the Patriots midway through the fourth and never looked back. The Patriots tried to rally, but the Cadets' defense was too tough down the stretch. Kevin Fitzgerald led the Cadets in scoring with 13 points, while Center Rob Worthington added 10.

1998: Class AAAA: Minnetonka vs. Eagan

The Class AAAA tourney began with Minnetonka edging Elk River, 68-65, in the quarterfinals. From there the Skippers knocked off the three-time defending state champs from Minneapolis North, 55-54, in the final seconds of a truly wild semifinal game. Here's how it went down. Shane Schilling found Big Jake Kuppe, a future Gopher Football Tackle, under the net with just 6.3 seconds left. Kuppe, bloody lip and all, was then intentionally fouled. So he stepped up to line and drained a clutch free-throw to ice it. The Skippers led the entire game but watched the Polars get to within one when Jerome Hubbard, who scored a game-high 26 points, drain a jumper with 14 seconds left.

Eagan held both its quarterfinal and semifinal opponents to 59 points each. The Wildcats defeated Tartan of Oakdale, 74-59, in the quarterfinal game before beating Eden Prairie, 78-59, in the semifinals. Anthony Scott had a game-high 21 points against Tartan en route to leading his club to to the Finals.

There, Minnetonka claimed its first boys' basketball tournament championship since 1965 by topping Eagan, 65-57. Minnetonka was led by future Gopher Shane Schilling who had 26 points and played solid defense. The Skippers led 34-23 at half-time and fended off several Eagan rallies, including a third-quarter run that closed the gap to 40-39. The Skippers nailed seven of eight free-throws in the final minute though, as they cruised to the big win. Kyle Stirmlinger finished with 20 points for Eagan in the loss.

1999: Class A: Southwest Minnesota Christian of Edgerton vs. Hillcrest Lutheran Academy

The Class A tournament began with Southwest Minnesota Christian beating tournament-newcomer New Ulm Cathedral, 66-42, in quarterfinal play. The Eagles, behind Cody Kuipers 16 points and five rebounds, then went on to defeat Rushford-Peterson, 57-49, to make their third consecutive appearance

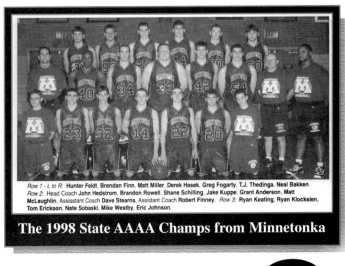

Row 1 - L to R: Hunter Feldt, Brendan Finn, Matt Miller, Derek Hasek, Greg Fogarty, T.J. Thedinga, Neal Bakken. Row 2: Head Coach John Hedstrom, Brandon Rowell, Shane Schilling, Jake Kuppe, Grant Anderson, Matt McLaughlin, Assisstant Coach Dave Stearns, Assistant Coach Robert Finney. Row 3: Ryan Keating, Ryan Klocksien, Tom Erickson, Nate Sobaski, Mike Westby, Eric Johnson.

The 1998 State AAAA Champs from Minnetonka

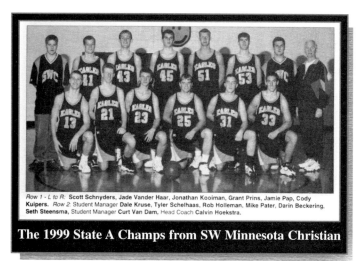

Row 1 - L to R: Scott Schnyders, Jade Vander Haar, Jonathan Kooiman, Grant Prins, Jamie Pap, Cody Kuipers. Row 2: Student Manager Dale Kruse, Tyler Schelhaas, Rob Holleman, Mike Pater, Darin Beckering, Seth Steensma, Student Manager Curt Van Dam, Head Coach Calvin Hoekstra.

The 1999 State A Champs from SW Minnesota Christian

in the semifinals. Tied at 42-42 late in the game, Tyler Schelhaas iced it for the Eagles when he drained a pair of three-pointers.

In the other bracket, Hillcrest Lutheran Academy of Fergus Falls topped Red Lake, 68-51, in its opening quarterfinal match-up. From there the Comets took care of Carlton, 62-50, in the semifinals to advance to the title game against Hillcrest Lutheran Academy of Fergus Falls. Six-foot-three Center Nick Hanson, a ninth grader, led the Comets in this one, scoring 22 points and grabbing 10 rebounds.

Southwest Minnesota Christian met another newcomer in the championship game when they faced Hillcrest Lutheran of Fergus Falls. The Comets led 19-18 at the end of the first quarter in this one, only to see the Eagles' Robbie Holleman score five consecutive points in the second quarter to give his Eagles squad a 28-27 lead at the half. In the third, it was Hillcrest Lutheran's turn and Dan Scheid scored seven straight points to put the Comets ahead 37-31. From there the Eagles outscored the Comets 21-9 into the fourth quarter and won the game by the final of 63-50. Cody Kuipers, Robbie Holleman and Tyler Schelhaas each scored 15 points for the Eagles in the big win.

1999: Class AA: Minneapolis De La Salle vs. Watertown-Mayer

The Class AA tournament saw the defending champs from De LaSalle roll over Rochester Lourdes in the quarterfinals, 49-32. From there the Islanders squared off against Belle Plaine in the semifinals. With seven seconds remaining in the game, De LaSalle pulled ahead by six points when Ben Johnson drained a pair of free throws. The Tigers tried to rally but wound up on the losing end of a 64-60 ball-game. Johnson finished the game with 32 points for the Islanders, while Drew Carlson tallied 30 for Belle Plaine.

The other bracket saw Watertown-Mayer beat Long Prairie Grey Eagle, 56-45, in the quarterfinals. Next, the Royals rolled over St. Cloud Cathedral, 87-58, in the semifinals to advance to the title game. Derek Boll led the Royals with 22 points while Wade Hokenson added 17 in the win — surpassing the coveted 1,000-point plateau in the second half as well.

Row 1 - L to R: Ronald Richard, David Collier, Lucas Kaster, Doug Lamon. Row 2: Edwin Huff, Robert Steib, Ben Johnson, Arthur Gardner, Dominique Sims, Mitch Nelson, Assistant Coach Dan Rubishko. Row 3: Head Coach Dave Thorson, Jared Newberry, Chris White, Derreck Robinson, David Coyle, Ben Wagner, Assistant Coach Broderick Powell.

The 1999 State AA Champs from De LaSalle

The Islanders and Royals then hooked up in the Class AA championship game. DeLaSalle jumped out early and took a four-point lead at the end of the first quarter, but Watertown-Mayer shot 55% in the first half and rallied to make it 27-27 at the half. The Islanders went on a 7-0 run in the opening minutes of the third quarter though, and never looked back. The Royals cut the lead down to two points with 15 seconds remaining in the game, but DeLaSalle's David Collier made four free throws down the stretch to give his Islanders a 50-44 victory, and their second state title in as many years. Ben Johnson finished the game with 15 points and six rebounds, while Dominique Sims added 13 as well.

1999: Class AAA: Highland Park vs. Rocori-Cold Spring

The Class AAA tourney kicked off with Highland Park cruising past Mankato East, 80-67, in the quarterfinals. From there the Scots went on to defeat North St. Paul in the semifinals, 59-47. Leading the charge for the Scots in that game were Thomas Miley, who had 18 points, Maurice Hargrow and Mark Wingo, who added 14 and 13 points, respectively.

In the other bracket, Rocori-Cold Spring edged out Minneapolis Henry in overtime, 60-57, to advance to the semi's. There, the Spartans crushed Monticello, 68-38. Mason Thelen scored nine of his 17 points in the first quarter en route to leading his squad into the Finals. The Magic fell behind 33-17 at the half and shot just 25% in this one as they came up short. Steve Kron also added 17 points for the Spartans, while Center Shawn McGuire led the Przybilla-less Magic with 10.

The championship game featured the Highland Park Scots against Rocori-Cold Spring Spartans, with the Scots coming out on top, 56-48. Highland Park took a 30-20 lead at the half and rolled to its first title from there. Steve Kron's three-pointer got it to 44-41 with just over four minutes to go, but the Scots, behind Mark Wingo's late buckets, hung tough and played great defense down the stretch. It was the first St. Paul public school crown in more than 50 years. Wingo led the Scots with 17 points and nine rebounds, while Terrance Stokes added 14 points as well.

1999: Class AAAA: Mounds View vs. Minnetonka

The Class AAAA tournament began with Mounds View eliminating the 1998 runners-up of Eagan in their quarterfinal game by the final score of 70-52. Then, in the semifinals, Mounds View beat Minneapolis North, 61-51. Leading the charge for the Mustangs were Duke University recruit Nick Horvath, who finished with 18 points and 12 rebounds, as well as Cal Ecker and Mickey Anderle, who each added 14 apiece.

On the other side of the bracket the defending champions of Minnetonka were cruising along. The Skippers opened the tourney by

Row 1 - L to R: Tony Burns, Joshua Watson, James Bradford, Terrance Stokes, Marcus Rogers, Josef Mathews. Row 2: Assistant Coach Fernando Horton, Jamaal Diaz-Cruz, Maurice Hargrow, Thomas Miley, Geoffrey Brown, Daniel Lee, Mark Wingo, Head Coach Charles Portis. Not Pictured: Robin Jackson, Aaron Howard.

The 1999 State AAA Champs from Highland Park

spanking the Moorhead Spuds, 85-65. From there the Skippers took care of rival Hopkins, 63-52, in the semifinals to advance to the title game. Shane Schilling led the Skippers with 26 points in the big win.

Mounds View, behind Nick Horvath's 31-point effort, then came out and beat the defending champions of Minnetonka in the championship game. The Mustangs led by two points at half-time, only to trail by one going into the fourth. But, when Cal Ecker drained a three-pointer with 7:43 remaining to give the Mustangs a 52-50 lead, it was money in the bank. Horvath scored eight of the team's next 10 points and Mounds View cruised to the title, 69-64. Minnetonka's Adam Boone, who would go on to play at the University of North Carolina, was equally impressive in the game, scoring 26 points and keeping his squad in it until the very end. He nailed a pair of late buckets to make it interesting, but with Shane Schilling on the bench, having already fouled out, it was just too little too late.

Row 1 - L to R: Student Manager Matthias Scholz, Ryan Hatteberg, Matt Pilon, Aaron Slindee, Cal Ecker, Trent Perry, Josh Fernholz, Matt Howard, Demetrius Charles. Row 2: Coach Dave Leiser, Coach Steve Pieterick, Mike Leach, Scott Karpe, Adam Weizenegger, Nick Horvath, Mickey Anderle, Scott Nelson, Drew Brodin, Brian Pramann, Coach Zig Kauls, Coach Mark Sembrowich.

The 1999 State AAAA Champs from Mounds View

2000: Class A: Southwest Minnesota Christian of Edgerton vs. Win-E-Mac, Erskine

The Class A tourney began with the defending champs from Southwest Minnesota Christian of Edgerton eliminating Mayer Lutheran, 59-45, in their quarterfinal game, thanks to Robbie Hollemans's 29 points. Then, in the semifinals, the defensive-minded Eagles, behind Holleman's 21 points, frustrated the Rushford-Peterson Trojans into committing 26 turnovers en route to a 51-37 win.

In the other bracket, Win-E-Mac of Erskine rolled over Mountain Iron-Buhl in the quarterfinals, 81-67. From there the Patriots edged Ortonville, 70-67, to advance to the Finals. The Trojans rallied back from a 15-point deficit in this one and got to within one point, 68-67, on Jordan Botker's three-pointer with 44 seconds left. But the Patriots hung tough and iced it on Matt Tradewell and Steve Bradley's free-throws. The duo, by the way, tallied 20 and 16 points, respectively, in the win.

Then, in the championship game, Southwest Minnesota Christian jumped out to a commanding 23-point lead after three quarters, only to see Win-E-Mac rally to score 29 points in the final quarter. The Patriots came up short though, losing 72-61. Win-E-Mac's Matt Tradewell hit a three-pointer with 1:07 to play to bring the Pats to within five, but the Eagles hit six of eight free throws to put it away down the stretch. Mike Pater led the way with 17 points and 17 rebounds in the big win.

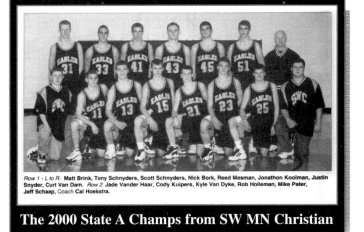

Row 1 - L to R: Matt Brink, Tony Schnyders, Scott Schnyders, Nick Bork, Reed Mesman, Jonathon Koolman, Justin Snyder, Curt Van Dam. Row 2: Jade Vander Haar, Cody Kuipers, Kyle Van Dyke, Rob Holleman, Mike Pater, Jeff Schaap, Coach Cal Hoekstra.

The 2000 State A Champs from SW MN Christian

2000: Class AA: Litchfield vs. Waterville-Elysian-Morristown

The Class AA bracket began with Litchfield, which returned to the tournament after an 81-year absence, spanking St. Cloud Cathedral in the quarterfinals, 84-41. Alex Carlson, John Carlson and Mike Patten each scored 19 points for the Dragons in the win. From there the Dragons topped a very tough Staples-Motley squad in the semifinals, 59-45. Alex Carlson led the Dragons with 23 points while his brother, John, finished with 16 in the win.

Waterville-Elysian-Morristown opened the other bracket by edging Rochester Lourdes in the quarterfinals, 50-49. From there the Buc's upset the two-time defending state champs from De LaSalle, 51-46, to advance into the Finals. The Bucs jumped out to a 11-1 lead and made it 35-25 at the half. From there the Islanders rallied behind Anderson and Simms, but came up short in the end. Guard Gabe Hauer led W-E-M with 21 points, while Cory Hackett, the school's all-time leading scorer, added 12.

Undefeated Litchfield got off to a slow start in the championship game, falling behind 11-3 early on. But the Dragons tallied nine straight points to start the second and went on a 13-2 run. Then, with just three minutes to go, Mike Patten sank three straight lay-ups, and Alex Carlson nailed four free throws to lead Litchfield to a 42-28 victory. Mike Patten finished with 16 points and Alex Carlson added 10 in the big win.

2000: Class AAA: Minneapolis Patrick Henry vs. St. Thomas Academy

The Class AAA tournament saw Minneapolis Patrick Henry crush Totino-Grace of Fridley in their quarterfinal game, 87-48, and then easily handle Cloquet in the semi's, 76-46. Guards Greg Patton and Terry Pettis led Henry with 17 and 14 points, respectively, in this one. In addition, Center Johnnie Gilbert, who would go on to attend Oklahoma University, had a solid all-around game by scoring 13 points, seven rebounds and five blocks.

Meanwhile, in the other bracket, St. Thomas Academy of Mendota Heights beat Shakopee in their quarterfinal contest, 63-47. From there the Cadets, behind Vern Simmons' 17 points, edged a very tough Mankato East club, 70-68, to advance to the Finals. Joe Thomas' two free-throws with just three seconds left iced it for St. Thomas Academy. Mankato East Forward Bryan Wolle, who tallied 25 in the game to raise his career total to 1,004, saw

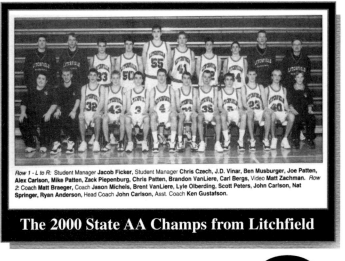

Row 1 - L to R: Student Manager Jacob Ficker, Student Manager Chris Czech, J.D. Vinar, Ben Musburger, Joe Patten, Alex Carlson, Mike Patten, Zack Piepenburg, Chris Patten, Brandon VanLiere, Carl Bergs, Video Matt Zachman. Row 2: Coach Matt Braeger, Coach Jason Michels, Brent VanLiere, Lyle Olberding, Scott Peters, John Carlson, Nat Springer, Ryan Anderson, Head Coach John Carlson, Asst. Coach Ken Gustafson.

The 2000 State AA Champs from Litchfield

The 2000 State AAA Champs from Henry

his desperation Hail-Mary heave at the buzzer fall short.

In the Finals, top-ranked Minneapolis Patrick Henry, making its third consecutive tournament appearance, scored the first 11 points of the game, only to see the St. Thomas Academy Cadets roar back to outscore the Patriots in the second quarter, 23-10. Down by five at the half, the Patriots came out and scored 13 straight points to open the second and took a commanding 34-26 lead. They never looked back from there as they cruised to a 59-45 win. Patrick Henry finished with four players in double figures; Tony Travis had 14, Johnnie Gilbert finished with 12, Edwin Huff pitched in 11, and Greg Patton added 10. The 2000 tournament marked the third championship in five appearances for the Patriots. They won consecutive titles back in 1944 and 1945.

2000: Class AAAA: Tartan vs. Maple Grove

The Class AAAA tournament featured Tartan of Oakdale beating Bloomington Jefferson in the quarterfinals, 75-63. Then, in the semifinals, the Titans easily handled Apple Valley, 80-56, as Jake Sullivan started slow but got hot in the second to score 26 points. Erik Crawford added 23 points while Mark Meerschaert chipped in with 10 as well.

The other bracket saw Maple Grove top White Bear Lake in the quarterfinals, 56-52, and then go on to eliminate Moorhead in the semifinals, 74-58. Brent Lawson led the Crimson with 27 points as his team shot an amazing 62% in this one.

Tartan kept it going into the Finals, beating first-timer Maple Grove, 62-51, to take the crown. Maple Grove trailed by only one point at half-time, but couldn't ever get command of the game. The lead continued to teeter back and forth throughout the second quarter before Tartan pulled away with a seven-point lead at the end of the third. The Crimson crept to within three points when Brent Lawson hit a lay-up at 5:39 in the fourth, but the Titans went on a 6-0 run to extend their lead back to 54-45. They played tough defense from there and cruised to the win.

The 2000 State AAAA Champs from Tartan

Tartan's Jake Sullivan, a three-time All-Stater, scored 18 of his game-high 28 points in the second half. With just over six minutes to play in the game, Sullivan, who was a career 90% free-throw shooter, hit a jumper from the right base-line to score the 3,000th point of his high school career. (Joel McDonald of Chisholm, who finished with 3,292 points in 1991, is the only other boy in Minnesota history to accomplish that same feat.) In addition, Crawford finished with 19 points and 13 rebounds for the Titans, while Lawson was the top scorer for Maple Grove, finishing with 19 points and ten rebounds.

2001: Class A: Southwest Minnesota Christian of Edgerton vs. Christ's Household of Faith

The 2001 state basketball tournament moved from Williams Arena, on the University of Minnesota's campus, to its luxurious new St. Paul home, the Xcel Energy Center. There, the Class A tourney saw Southwest Minnesota Christian of Edgerton winning it all.

The Eagles defeated Rushford-Peterson, 48-38, in the quarterfinals, behind Junior Center Jeff Schaap's 11 points, seven rebounds and three blocks. The score was tied at 31-31 heading into the fourth quarter, but the Eagles finished with a solid 15-2 run down the stretch to ice it.

Then, in the semifinals, the Eagles cruised past Cass Lake-Bena, 56-43. Southwest Minnesota Christian had an 11-point lead going into the fourth quarter and followed that up by outscoring the Panthers 16-14 in the final eight minutes. Schaap once again led the way, finishing this time with 18 points and 15 rebounds in the big win.

The Eagles then went on to win their third consecutive Class A tournament by beating the first-time qualifiers from Christ's Household of Faith of St. Paul, 65-55. The three-peat was only the third in the 89-year history of the tournament, along with Minneapolis North and Edina. After a back-and-forth first quarter, the Eagles took control when they hit a barrage of three-pointers and stepped up their smothering defense.

The 2001 State A Champs from SW Minnesota Christian

It was 34-23 by the half and thing appeared to be looking good for Southwest Minnesota Christian, but the Lions went on a 13-4 run midway through the fourth quarter to make it 57-54. That's when Eagles' Center Jeff Schaap took over and nailed a bank-shot from the lane to kill the run. Daniel De Witt then sealed the victory for the Eagles when he blocked a key shot and added an insurance lay-up in the final minute. Schaap finished the game with 22 points and 14 rebounds, while De Witt, Reed Mesman, and Justin Snyder all scored 10 points apiece. Neal Harms led Christ's Household of Faith with 17 points and eight rebounds in the loss.

2001: Class AA: Kenyon-Wanamingo vs. Hayfield

Kenyon-Wanamingo, which returned to the tournament after a two-year absence, captured its first Class AA title with a 53-30 victory over Hayfield. The Knights crushed Minnewaska Area of Glenwood, 54-32, in the quarterfinals thanks to Joe Evert's solid play. Evert started the festivities with a monstrous game-opening dunk and finished the game with 13 points, three rebounds, and three blocks.

The Knights continued their winning ways in the semifinals when they spanked Staples-Motley, 47-28. Kenyon-Wanamingo made 17-of-27 shots, and went 8-for-10 in the second half in this one. Brent Lurken led the Knights with 20 points and seven rebounds en route to guiding the team into the Finals.

There, Kenyon-Wanamingo beat Hayfield, 53-30, to capture the state crown. The Knights jumped out to a quick start in this one, taking a 28-14 lead at the half. From there they played great pressure defense, showed their inside muscle and shot an impressive 59% from the field. Hayfield, on the other hand, shot just 26% from field goal range and finished with a season-low in points. Brent Lurken and Joe Evert scored 17 and 16 points, respectively, for the Knights, while also finishing with six rebounds apiece as well. Korey Holtan led the Vikings with 12 points and four rebounds in the loss.

Row 1 (L-R): Manager Dan Hjermstad, Allen Froyum, Wesley Freiberg, David Jacobsen, Justin Stevenson, Erik Sviggum, Kiel Berg, Dan Dodds. Row 2: Coach Jerry Wieme, Curt Peterson, Kirby VandeWalker, Brent Lurken, Joe Evert, Anders Haugen, Chris Metcalf, Nick Myran, Luke Redfield, Asst. Coach Josh Wieme.

The 2001 State AA Champs from Kenyon Wanamingo

2001: Class AAA: Patrick Henry vs. St. Thomas Academy

For the second consecutive year, Minneapolis Patrick Henry and St. Thomas Academy reached the Class AAA title game. Patrick Henry opened the tourney by defeating Duluth Denfeld in its quarterfinal game, 66-55, thanks to Zerek Knight's 22 points and 13 rebounds. From there the Patriots eliminated Shakopee, 67-52, in the semifinals. Terry Pettis led the Patriots with 15 points, while Forest Bryant and Zerek Knight added 14 apiece.

In the Finals it was Minneapolis Patrick Henry rolling over St. Thomas Academy for the second straight season. The Patriots jumped out to a quick 24-13 lead in the first quarter, only to see St. Thomas Academy rally back to keep the lead to single digits throughout most of the second half. The Cadets made it interesting late in the third quarter, however, when they went on a 10-1 run to get the score at 52-48. Zerek Knight of Patrick Henry stepped up his game at that point though and nailed a clutch three-pointer along with a short pull-up jumper to put the Patriots back up by nine heading into the fourth quarter. Then, with just over two minutes to go, a pair of dunks by Knight and Lawrence McKenzie stretched the Patriots lead to 73-55, and put the game out of reach.

All five of Minneapolis Patrick Henry's starters finished the game in double figures. Zerek Knight scored 15 points, Edwin Huff had 14, Forest Bryant chipped in 12, Lawrence McKenzie added 11 and Terry Pettis 10 for the top-ranked Patriots. Carl Spande, meanwhile, was the leading scorer for the Cadets, finishing with 20 points and 11 rebounds in the 74-61 loss.

Row 1 (L-R): Walter Power, Gerald Bryant, Forest Bryant, Charles Clark, Cedric Bates. Row 2: Zach Deming, Zerek Knight, Rodney Thompson, Lawrence McKenzie, Bryan Politte. Row 3: Head Coach Lawrence McKenzie, Sr., Coach J.D. Deloney, Asst. Coach Chris Johnson, Tyrell Thorton, Steven Neal, Edwin Huff, Terry Pettis, Tyrell Sledge, Asst. Coach Jerry Williams, Coach Mike Shelton.

The 2001 State AAA Champs from Patrick Henry

2001: Class AAAA: Osseo vs. Duluth East

The Osseo Orioles came out and won their first Class AAAA title with a 73-48 victory over Duluth East. Osseo jumped out to a fast start in the quarterfinals against Elk River and grabbed a 20-5 lead late in the first quarter and cruised to an 82-61 win behind 18 points from Zack Kiekow. In the semifinals, the Orioles topped Cretin-Derham Hall, 88-82, behind Bryan Foss' 29 points and Kiekow's 21 points and seven rebounds. Osseo played great team defense in this one and won it down the stretch despite the fact that Cretin nailed 17 three-pointers in the game.

In the championship, the top-ranked Orioles knocked off a very tough Duluth East squad, which was making its 10th overall appearance at the tournament, 73-48. The Orioles got off to a fast start when Keenan Jones scored seven points in the first three minutes. But East's star Center, Rick Rickert, a McDonald's All-American and Gophers prize recruit, got hot and kept his team close by scoring 15 of the Greyhounds' 25 first-half points. The Orioles led 32-25 at halftime, and looked as if they might pull away after an 8-0 run early in the third quarter. But Rickert and Greg Anderson answered with three-pointers to keep the game close. It wasn't until the fourth quarter, when the Orioles went on a 13-2 run, that the game got out of reach. From there Osseo's relentless press wore down Rickert every time he got near the ball.

Three Oriole players finished the game in double figures: Keenan Jones with 25 points and five steals; Josh Cadwallader with 19 points; and Kiekow with 10. Rickert led Duluth East with 26 points, nine rebounds and five blocks in the loss. The Orioles ended their spectacular season with a 30-1 record, with their only loss coming from Oak Hill Academy of Virginia — the No. 1 team in the country.

Well, there it is. The abbreviated history of our beloved state tourney. It has been a wild past century to say the least, and one can only hope that the next 100 years are half as much fun as the last. The bottom line is this: our high school kids can match up with any in the country, and the proof is in the pudding. In the past couple of decades Minnesota has been churning out Division I, II and III talent on a consistent basis. From our administrators to our officials and from our coaches to our kids, things are looking good and are only going to get better. (Oh, by the way, keep your eye on Hopkins' six-foot-eight junior phenom, Kris Humphries, who is something special!)

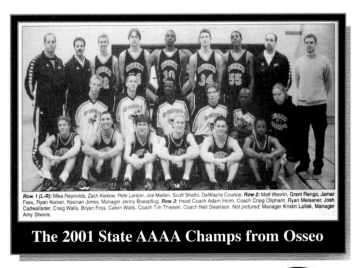

Row 1 (L-R): Mike Reynolds, Zach Kiekow, Pete Larson, Joe Mallen, Scott Shatto, DeWayne Counce. Row 2: Matt Wavrin, Grant Rengo, Jamar Foxx, Ryan Kocker, Keenan Jones, Manager Jenny Boespflug. Row 3: Head Coach Adam Holm, Coach Craig Oliphant, Ryan Meissner, Josh Cadwallader, Craig Walls, Bryan Foss, Calvin Walls, Coach Tim Thiesen, Coach Neil Swanson. Not pictured: Manager Kristin Lallak, Manager Amy Stwora.

The 2001 State AAAA Champs from Osseo

Minnesota Basketball Coaches Association Hall of Fame

1984
Ove Berven — Austin
Clarence Fortier — Bemidji
Lloyd Holm — St. Louis Park
John Nett — Winona Cotter
Jack Peck — Little Falls Media
Hartvik Strand — Moorhead
Lloyd Stussy — Wells

1985
Odis LeGrand — Fergus Falls Radio/TV
Russell Maetzold — Hopkins
Mario Retica — Hibbing
Harvey Roels — Chisholm
Louis Todnem — Mankato

1986
Jerry Dahlberg — Crookston Media
Glenn Hanna — Moorhead
Jim Hastings — Duluth Central
Fred Kellett — Brainerd
Herman Woock — Crosby-Ironton

1987
Ted Peterson — Minneapolis Star Tribune
Bill Selisker — Sauk Centre, Crosby
Jack Stackpool — Glenwood
Walt Williams — Minneapolis Southwest

1988
Rod Black — Danube
Ralph Boline — Fosston
Loran Eickhoff — Brooklyn Center
Hugo H. Goehle — Hills-Beaver Creek

1989
Irv St. John — Duluth East
Larry Selk — East Grand Forks
John (Blackie) Varriano — Dilworth
Allan Wold — Rochester John Marshall, Faribault

1990
Ralph Anderson — Detroit Lakes Media
A. J. Kramer — Roseau
Steve Lipp — Breckenridge
Bob McDonald — Chishoim
Angelo "Angie" Pergol — Cloquet, Hibbing, Duluth

1991
Ralph Anderson — Detroit Lakes Newspapers
Duane Baglien — Edina, Fergus Falls
Bruce Bennett — Duluth News Tribune
Lloyd Carlson — McIntosh/Winger
Ken Fladager — South Saint Paul

1992
Gerald Keenan — Saint Paul Harding
Marsh Nelson — KDAL Radio/KDLH TV, Duluth
Steve Kerzie — Gilbert
Bill Wanamaker — Anoka

1993
Russ Adamson — Willmar
Manny Beckmann — Waseca
Wayne Courtney — Minneapolis Roosevelt
Rex Haugen — Pelican Rapids

1994
Leonard M. Espeland — Granite Falls
Jack Evens — Bloomington Jefferson
Len Horyza — Cretin-Derham Hall
Bill King — Orr

1995
Walter Chapman — Minneapolis Marshall
Larry Holverson — Alexandria
George Embretson — Montgomery
M. Kenneth Novak — Hopkins

1996
Bob Erdman — Roseville Area
Richard Olson — Edgerton, Virginia
Jack Kelly — Windom
Dick Jonckowski — Shakopee/Chaska Radio

1997
Denny Anderson — Frazee
Dick Beetsch — Red Wing
Ron Cadwell — Columbia Heights
L. C. "Whitey" Thoreson — Minneapolis Central
Laurel "Baldy" Waldahl — Verndale, Wadena

1998
Bob Brink — Rocori, Cold Spring
Jerry Chiabotti — Bigfork
Ed Prohofsky — Marshall-University, Minneapolis
Joe Odonovich — Crosby-Ironton, Alexander Ramsey
Richard Wiebusch — Zumbrota-Mazeppa

1999
Oscar Haddorff — Austin
Darrell Kreun — Sibley East
Steve Kjorness — Westbrook-Walnut Grove
Ron Hested — Fairmont
Mike Morrissey — Faribault KDHL Radio

2000
Louis C. Deere — Kittson County Central in Hallock
Del Schiffler — Melrose, Woodbury
Jerry Snyder — Lake City
Ray Stinar — Mahnomen, East Grand Forks
Tom Critchley — Hawley, Roseville

2001
Brother Mike Glidden — Onamia Crosier
Warren Keller — Argyle/Warroad
Ted Pelzl — New Richland-Hartland-Ellendale-Geneva
Gary Schuler — Warren/Fergus Falls
Dave Tank — Anoka

The Catholic and Independent Schools State Tourney

In addition to the MSHSL's annual tournament, there was the Catholic School Tournament as well as the Private or Independent School Tourney. Both held annually in early March at various sites throughout the Twin Cities, usually at the St. Paul Auditorium and later at the Minneapolis Armory, drawing eight regional winners from around the state. The two ran separately but then merged in 1971 to play a combined tournament. Form there they played for three more years, at the Minneapolis Auditorium, before merging into the MSHSL in 1974.

(In the early days of the Catholic League, there was a National Catholic High School Tournament which was held annually in Chicago. In 1931 DeLaSalle, led by a Native American Center named Ray Buffalo, became the first and only Minnesota team to win the tourney, when they defeated Jasper, Ind., 23-21, in the Finals. For their efforts the Islanders were awarded the Cardinal Mundelein Trophy, named after the head of the Chicago diocese, Cardinal George Mundelein.)

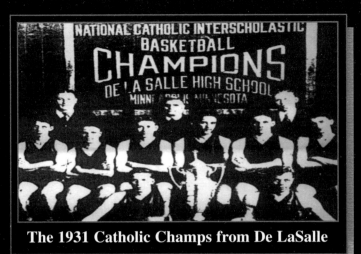

The 1931 Catholic Champs from De LaSalle

Some of the catholic schools which participated in the Tourney included: Austin Pacelli, Benilde, Bird Island St. Mary's, Chaska Guardian Angel, Cretin, Currie Immaculata, De LaSalle, Duluth Cathedral, East Grand Forks Sacred Heart, Faribault Bethlehem, Fridley Grace, St. Paul Hill, Iona St. Columbia, Mankato Loyola, Marshall Central Catholic, New Ulm Holy Trinity, New Ulm Cathedral, Owatonna Marion, Pierz Memorial, Rochester Lourdes, Sleepy Eye – St. Mary's, Adrian St. Adrian's, St. Agnes, St. Boniface, St. Cloud Cathedral, St. John's Prep, St. Thomas Academy, Wabasha St. Felix, Wabasso St. Anne's, Waseca Sacred Heart, Winona Cotter and Winsted Holy Trinity

In addition, some of the schools which participated in the Independent & Private School Tourney included: Benilde, Blake Academy, Breck Academy, Concordia, Edgerton Southwest Christian, Mayer Lutheran, Minneapolis Lutheran, Minnehaha Academy, Prinsburg Central Christian, Faribault Shattuck, St. Paul Academy

Catholic Tourney Championship Games
1937 -- Winona Cotter 28, Austin St. Augustine 26
1938 -- Austin St. Augustine 22, Mankato Loyola 16
1939 -- Austin St. Augustine 32, Winona Cotter 19
1940 -- Austin St. Augustine 23, Wabasha St. Felix 19
1941 -- Duluth Cathedral 26, Cretin 21
1942 -- Cretin 38, Duluth Cathedral 34
1943 -- Cretin 35, Winona Cotter 28
1944 -- DeLaSalle 32, Cretin 28
1945 -- Mankato Loyola 37, Cretin 31
1946 -- DeLaSalle 48, Winona Cotter 30
1947 -- St. Cloud Cathedral 55, Winona Cotter 44
1948 -- Cretin 38, St. Thomas Academy 31
1949 -- St. Thomas Academy 63, Cretin 45
1950 -- St. Thomas Academy 52, Winona Cotter 41
1951 -- St. Thomas Academy 37, DeLaSalle 30
1952 -- Winona Cotter 70, DeLaSalle 57
1953 -- St. Thomas Academy 61, St. Cloud Cathedral 59, (2 OT)
1954 -- DeLaSalle 34, Duluth Cathedral 25
1955 -- DeLaSalle 57, Duluth Cathedral 33
1956 -- DeLaSalle 51, St. Thomas Academy 48
1957 -- DeLaSalle 67, Winona Cotter 41
1958 -- Austin Pacelli 44, Winona Cotter 43
1959 -- DeLaSalle 59, Cretin 46
1960 -- St. Thomas Academy 71, St. Cloud Cathedral 60
1961 -- DeLaSalle 74, Duluth Cathedral 58
1962 -- DeLaSalle 67, St. Thomas Academy 40
1963 -- Benilde 32, St. Thomas Academy 29
1964 -- Benilde 52, Austin Pacelli 49
1965 -- Austin Pacelli 86, Winona Cotter 56
1966 -- Rochester Lourdes 64, DeLaSalle 43
1967 -- Rochester Lourdes 67, Cretin 64
1968 -- Rochester Lourdes 67, St. Cloud Cathedral 64
1969 -- St. Cloud Cathedral 64, Benilde 47
1970 -- St. Thomas Academy 63, Benilde 38

Independent & Private School Tourney Championship Games
1946 -- Shattuck 41, Minnehaha Academy 27
1947 -- Concordia Academy 36, Pillsbury 35
1948 -- Minnehaha Academy 41, Shattuck 35
1949 -- Shattuck 29, Minnehaha Academy 23
1950 -- Minnehaha Academy 43, Shattuck 40
1951 -- Minnehaha Academy 54, Concordia Academy 35
1952 -- Minnehaha Academy 81, Shattuck 46
1953 -- Minnehaha Academy 52, Blake 43
1954 -- Blake 60, Minnehaha Academy 59
1955 -- Blake 51, Concordia Academy 50
1956 -- Shattuck 48, Breck 45
1957 -- Concordia Academy 60, Minnehaha Academy 52
1958 -- Minnehaha Academy 69, Concordia Academy 53
1959 -- Minnehaha Academy 69, Concordia Academy 54
1960 -- Minnehaha Academy 60, St. Paul Academy 48
1961 -- Blake 55, Concordia 49
1962 -- Minnehaha Academy 44, Shattuck 43
1963 -- Minnehaha Academy 50, Blake 46
1964 -- Minnehaha Academy 65, Wessington Springs (S.D.) 42
1965 -- Blake 68, Hillcrest 53
1966 -- Shattuck 60, Concordia Academy 36
1967 -- Edgerton SW Christian 61, Prinsburg Central Christian 57
1968 -- Shattuck 86, Mayer Lutheran 68
1969 -- Shattuck vs. Prinsburg Central Christian
1970 -- Shattuck 47, Minnehaha Academy 30 (Shattuck was now riding a 65-game winning streak, the longest in state history.)

Combined Independent High School Basketball Tourney (Catholic and Independent School's Combined)
1971 -- Cretin 52, Shattuck 50
1972 -- Fridley Grace 63, DeLaSalle 42
1973 -- Rochester Lourdes 47, Edgerton SW Christian 46
1974 -- Cretin 50, Rochester Lourdes 33

After four years of combined play, the tournament ended here, with all the teams assimilating into either Class A or AA of the MSHSL.

YEAR	CHAMPIONS and RECORD	REGION/SECTION	RUNNERS-UP	REGION/SECTION	SCORE
1913	Fosston (14-1)	8	Mountain Lake	2	29-27
1914	Stillwater (14-2)	4	Winona	1	30-4
1915	Red Wing (15-1)	4	Mountain Lake	2	30-18
1916	Virginia (13-2)	7	St. Paul Mechanic Arts	4	20-9
1917	Rochester (11-2)	1	Mountain Lake	2	19-8
1918	Waseca (13-0)	1	Duluth Central	7	29-10
1919	Albert Lea (17-0)	1	New Ulm	3	37-8
1920	Red Wing (15-2)	4	Mankato	2	21-10
1921	Minneapolis Central (13-1)	5	New Ulm	3	19-15
1922	Red Wing (19-0)	4	Madison	3	34-27
1923	Aurora (17-2)	7	Austin	1	24-14
1924	Two Harbors (21-2)	7	Minneapolis South	5	21-12
1925	St. Paul Mechanic Arts (17-1-1)	4	Buffalo	5	20-8
1926	Gaylord (20-3-1)	3	Gilbert	7	13-9
1927	Minneapolis South (12-5)	5	Excelsior	5	32-13
1928	Moorhead (19-3)	6	Minneapolis Edison	5	29-16
1929	Moorhead (24-3)	6	Red Wing	4	20-16*
1930	St. Paul Mechanic Arts (22-2)	4	Moorhead	6	23-13
1931	Glencoe (16-3)	3	Buffalo	5	22-14
1932	Thief River Falls (23-0)	8	Chisholm	7	21-15
1933	Red Wing (22-3)	4	Minneapolis North	5	16-13
1934	Chisholm (21-2)	7	St. Paul Mechanic Arts	4	29-27
1935	Austin (16-6)	1	Glencoe	3	26-24*
1936	Bemidji (21-4)	8	Wadena	6	26-20
1937	Minneapolis Edison (15-1)	5	Virginia	7	37-24
1938	Thief River Falls (27-0)	8	Minneapolis North	5	31-29
1939	Mountain Lake (23-1)	2	Minneapolis Marshall	5	37-31
1940	Breckenridge (28-3)	6	Red Wing	4	43-40
1941	Buhl (26-3)	7	Red Wing	4	31-29
1942	Buhl (28-0)	7	Marshall	3	30-29
1943	St. Paul Washington (22-2)	4	Alexandria	6	52-33
1944	Minneapolis Patrick Henry (24-1)	5	Crosby-Ironton	6	51-42
1945	Minneapolis Patrick Henry (24-1)	5	Ely	7	66-35
1946	Austin (22-3)	1	Lynd	3	63-31
1947	Duluth Denfeld (23-3)	7	Crosby-Ironton	6	46-44
1948	Bemidji (28-3)	8	Hopkins	5	38-29
1949	St. Paul Humboldt (19-5)	4	Mankato	2	47-35
1950	Duluth Central (24-3)	7	Robbinsdale	5	42-40
1951	Gilbert (26-1)	7	Canby	3	69-52
1952	Hopkins (25-1)	5	South St. Paul	4	42-29
1953	Hopkins (23-0)	5	Hibbing	7	58-47
1954	Brainerd (23-3)	6	Bemidji	8	49-47
1955	Minneapolis Washburn (22-1)	5	Austin	1	67-58
1956	Minneapolis Roosevelt (20-3)	5	Blue Earth	2	101-54
1957	Minneapolis Roosevelt (27-0)	5	Red Wing	4	59-51
1958	Austin (20-3)	1	Brainerd	6	68-63
1959	Wayzata (23-4)	5	Carlton	7	55-41
1960	Edgerton (27-0)	2	Austin	1	72-61
1961	Duluth Central (27-0)	7	Bemidji	8	51-50
1962	St. Louis Park (22-2)	5	South St. Paul	4	62-57
1963	Marshall (25-1)	3	Cloquet	7	75-74
1964	Luverne (20-5)	2	Rochester	1	72-66
1965	Minnetonka (22-4)	5	Faribault	1	71-60
1966	Edina (26-0)	5	Duluth East	7	82-75*
1967	Edina (27-0)	5	Moorhead	6	72-55
1968	Edina (26-1)	5	Moorhead	6	70-45
1969	Rochester John Marshall (23-1)	1	Duluth Central	7	58-42
1970	Sherburn (26-0)	2	South St. Paul	4	78-62
1971 A:	Melrose (24-3)	6	Red Wing	1	64-53
AA:	Duluth Central (23-1)	B	North St. Paul	G	54-51
Playoff:	Duluth Central	B	Melrose	6	54-43
1972 A:	St. James (29-0)	2	Melrose	6	57-55
AA:	Mounds View (21-5)	F	Austin	A	62-54
Playoff:	St. James	2	Mounds View	F	60-52
1973 A:	Chisholm (27-1)	7	Melrose	5	53-52
AA:	Anoka (24-2)	G	Richfield	E	58-54
Playoff:	Anoka	G	Chisholm	7	63-56
1974 A:	Melrose (27-0)	6	Mound	5	38-32
AA:	Bemidji (22-3)	B	Richfield	E	52-50
Playoff:	Melrose	6	Bemidji	B	58-42
1975 A:	Chisholm (27-1)	7	St. Paul Mechanic Arts	4	44-33
AA:	Little Falls (26-1)	C	Robbinsdale	F	54-49
Playoff:	Little Falls	C	Chisholm	7	54-50
1976 A:	Marshall-University (28-0)	5	Mankato Wilson	4	65-59*
AA:	Bloomington Jefferson (27-0)	6	Hibbing	7	60-51
1977 A:	Winona Cotter (25-2)	1	Pelican Rapids	6	60-47
AA:	Prior Lake (24-4)	2	Duluth Central	7	52-49
1978 A:	Lake City (25-1)	1	Breckenridge	6	60-44
AA:	Prior Lake (24-1)	2	St. Louis Park	6	44-33
1979 A:	Lake City (26-0)	1	Howard Lake-Waverly	5	63-50
AA:	Duluth Central (22-3)	7	St. Paul Central	3	62-54
1980 A:	Bird Island-Lake Lillian (23-3)	4	Lake of the Woods, Baudette	8	78-74**
AA:	Minneapolis North (23-2)	5	St. Cloud Tech.	8	60-53
1981 A:	Bird Island-Lake Lillian (16-10)	4	Winona Cotter	1	49-47**
AA:	Anoka (21-4)	4	Austin	1	61-53
1982 A:	Winona Cotter (23-2)	1	Chisholm	7	48-46
AA:	Bloomington Jefferson (23-1)	6	Duluth East	7	59-51
1983 A:	Barnum (26-0)	7	Luverne	2	53-47
AA:	Woodbury (24-0)	3	Coon Rapids	4	56-50*
1984 A:	Pelican Rapids (24-2)	6	Winona Cotter	1	57-55
AA:	White Bear Lake (26-0)	4	Minneapolis North	5	51-47
1985 A:	DeLaSalle, Minneapolis (26-2)	5	Winona Cotter	1	56-46
AA:	White Bear Lake (26-0)	4	Minneapolis North	5	67-62
1986 A:	LeSueur (26-2)	4	Staples	6	55-43
AA:	Bloomington Jefferson (23-4)	6	Duluth Central	7	52-51
1987 A:	Norman County West, Halstad (26-2)	8	Crosby-Ironton	5	70-58
AA:	Bloomington Jefferson (26-0)	6	Blaine	4	54-37
1988 A:	DeLaSalle, Minneapolis (26-1)	5	Russell-Tyler-Ruthton	3	58-36
AA:	Rocori, Cold Spring (26-0)	8	Robbinsdale Armstrong	6	66-56
1989 A:	Rushford (26-2)	1	RTR (Russell-Tyler-Ruthton)	3	64-52
AA:	Owatonna (24-1)	1	Robbinsdale Armstrong	6	45-43*
1990 A:	Lake City (26-2)	1	Mankato Loyola	2	52-51
AA:	Owatonna (23-2)	1	Minneapolis North	5	72-26
1991 A:	Chisholm (29-1)	7	Westbrook-Walnut Grove	2	77-61
AA:	Cretin-Derham Hall (27-1)	3	Minneapolis Roosevelt	5	74-62*
1992 A:	Austin Pacelli (19-11)	1	DeLaSalle, Minneapolis	4	68-62
AA:	Anoka (25-3)	4	Cretin-Derham Hall	3	50-47
1993 A:	Maple River, Mapleton (29-1)	2	Bethlehem Academy, Faribault	1	33-29
AA:	Cretin-Derham Hall (28-1)	3	Anoka	4	56-44
1994 A:	Saint Agnes, Saint Paul (25-5)	4	Morris Area	6	78-71
AA:	Minneapolis Washburn (27-1)	5	Hopkins	6	66-65
1995	Minneapolis North (30-0)	5AA	Staples-Motley	6A	54-52
1996	Minneapolis North (26-1)	5AA	Fertile-Beltrami	8A	80-47
1997 A:	Hancock (26-2)	5A	Wabasso	3A	60-58
AA:	Caledonia (29-0)	1AA	DeLaSalle, Minneapolis	4AA	69-47
AAA:	Simley, Inver Grove Heights (25-3)	3AAA	New Prague	1AAA	61-47
AAAA:	Minneapolis North (25-3)	2AAAA	Stillwater Area	3AAAA	61-53
1998 A:	Norman County East, Twin Valley (27-2)	6A	Carlton	7A	75-48
AA:	DeLaSalle, Minneapolis (24-3)	4AA	Long Prairie-Grey Eagle	8AA	53-52
AAA:	Saint Thomas Academy (22-6)	3AAA	Minneapolis Patrick Henry	5AAA	60-49
AAAA:	Minnetonka (25-2)	5AAAA	Eagan	1AAAA	65-57
1999 A:	Southwest MN Christian, Edgerton (24-1)	3A	Hillcrest Lutheran Academy	5A	63-50
AA:	DeLaSalle, Minneapolis (21-3)	4AA	Watertown-Mayer	5AA	50-44
AAA:	Saint Paul Highland Park (24-2)	3AAA	Rocori, Cold Spring	8AAA	56-48
AAAA:	Mounds View (21-3)	4AAAA	Minnetonka	5AAAA	69-64
2000 A:	Southwest MN Christian, Edgerton (28-1)	3A	Win-E-Mac, Erskine	8A	72-61
AA:	Litchfield (29-0)	5AA	Waterville-Elysian-Morristown	2AA	42-28
AAA:	Minneapolis Patrick Henry (28-1)	5AAA	Saint Thomas Academy	3AAA	59-45
AAAA:	Tartan, Oakdale (26-1)	3AAAA	Maple Grove	5AAAA	62-51

* Overtime ** Double Overtime

The "50 Point" Club

70	Norm Grow, Foley, 1-28-58
69	Ron Johnson, Starbuck, 2-17-53
62	Carl Johnson, Balaton, 1-21-66
61	Greg Lens, Marshall Central Catholic, 12-11-62
61	Brian Jamros, Moose Lake-Willow River 1-28-00
60	Ron Johnson, New Prague, 1956
60	Ben Paxson, Meadow Creek Christian, 2-1-00
58	Jonas Holte, Starbuck, 12-19-19
57	Phil Berg, Hanley Falls, 1-26-54
56	Norm Grow, Foley, '56
56	Mike Esaw, Minneapolis North, 1-16-79
56	Dave Cekalla, Cloquet, Dec. 1991
56	Aaron Chaput, Red Lake County Central, 1996
55	George Borgerding, Belgrade, 1946
55	Gary Hagemeyer, Clara City, 1966
55	Mike Peterreins, Lamberton, 1972
54	Joel McDonald, Chisholm, Feb. 1991
53	Murton Boyum, Peterson, Dec. 1964
53	Andra Griffin, Minneapolis Central, Feb. 1977
53	Brian Wiersma, Bethany Academy, 1999
53	Jibrahn Ike, St. Anthony Village, 1999
52	Jibrahn Ike, St. Anthony Village, 1999
52	Ron Johnson, New Prague, 1956
52	Jon Hagen, Belview, 1957
52	Murton Boyum, Peterson, Nov. 1964
52	Mel Homuth, Spring Grove, 1965
52	Leland Christensen, Atwater, 1982
52	Michael Bauer, Hastings, Dec. 1996
51	Gene Volz, Janesville, 1956
51	Ron Craigmile, Canby, Dec. 1958
51	Larry Maurice, Danube, 1966
51	Tom McDonald, Chisholm, 1982
50	Dean Zachow, Gaylord, 1972
50	Jimmy Jensen, Bemidji, 1978
50	Rodney Helgas, McIntosh, 1984
50	Tim Piechowski, Raymond, 1984
50	Glen Simes, Grand Meadow, 2-10-89
50	Daniel Fischer, Bagley, 1995
50	Ryan Iverson, Eden Prairie, 1998

McDonald's High School All-Americans

Year	Name	High School
1980	Jim Petersen	St. Louis Park
1997	Khalid El-Amin	Mpls. North
1998	Joel Przybilla	Monticello
2001	Rick Rickert	Duluth East

The "1,000 Rebound" Club

1,417	Norm Grow, Foley
1,304	Julian Greer, Brooklyn Center
1,243	Johnnie Gilbert, Minneapolis Patrick Henry
1,239	Justin Bessler, Laporte
1,134	Paul McDonald, Chisholm
1,132	Nate Holmstadt, Monticello
1,096	Chris Neumann, Mahnomen
1,091	Joel Przybilla, Monticello
1,061	Chad Nelson, Rothsay
1,051	Ted Krize, Chisholm
1,049	Ben Kipp, Janesville-Waldorf-Pemberton
1,042	Chad Henke, Sibley East
1,016	Bob Winzenburg, Fairmont
1,013	Jeff Nordgaard, Dawson - Boyd
1,013	Sam Jacobson, Park of Cottage Grove
1,011	Josh Ziemke, Janesville-Waldorf-Pemberton
1,003	Kelly Nelson, Rothsay
1,001	Joel McDonald, Chisholm

The "2,500 Points" Club

1.	3,292	Joel McDonald, Chisholm, '91
2.	3,013	Jake Sullivan, Tartan, '00
3.	2,852	Norm Grow, Foley, '58
4.	2,805	Mitch Ohnstad, Faribault, '96

State Tournament All-Time Records

Single Game:
Most Points: 50, Jimmy Jensen, Bemidji (Vs. Woodbury) - 1978
Most Free Throws Made: 19, Tom Nordland, Minneapolis Roosevelt - 1957
Most Rebounds: 32, Bob Laney, Proctor - 1964
Most Assists: 14, Ronnie Henderson, Marshall-University - 1976
Most Three-Point Field Goals: 9, Khalid El-Amin, Minneapolis North (Vs. St. Thomas), - 1996

Three-Game Tournament:
Most Points: 113, Randy Breuer, (Lake City) - 1979
Most Free Throws Made: 37, Martin Norton, (Minneapolis Central) - 1921
Most Assists: 28, Jay Black, (Danube) - 1979
Most Rebounds: 69, Bob Laney, (Proctor) - 1964
Most Three-Point Field Goals: 16, Steven Bradley, (Win-E-Mac, Erskine) - 2000

"Mr. Basketball Minnesota"

2001	Rick Rickert - Duluth East
2000	Adam Boone - Minnetonka
1999	Nick Horvath - Mounds View
1998	Darius Lane - Totino Grace
	Joel Przybilla - Monticello
1997	Khalid El-Amin - Mpls. North
1996	Mitch Ohnsted - Faribault
1995	Robert Mestas- Mpls. Roosevelt
1994	Sam Jacobson - Park Cottage Grove
1993	Skipp Schaefbauer - Elk River
1992	Brett Yonke - Eagan
1991	Joel McDonald - Chisholm
1990	Chad Kolander - Owatonna
1989	Tom Conroy - De La Salle
1988	Derek Reuben - Mpls. North
1987	Kevin Lynch - Bloomington Jefferson
1986	Steve Scholtthauer - Mounds View
1985	Brett McNeal - Mpls. North
1984	Tim Hanson - Prior Lake
1983	Tom Copa - Coon Rapids
1982	Robb Shelquist - Irondale
1981	Redd Overton - Mpls. North
1980	Jim Petersen - St. Louis Park
1979	Randy Breuer - Lake City
	Greg Downing - Duluth Central
1978	Jim Jenson - Bemidji
1977	Brian Pederson - Prior Lake
1976	Kevin McHale - Hibbing
1975	Gene Glynn – Waseca

Minnesota's All-Time State Basketball Records

Ind. Game Records	Stat	Player
Points Scored	70	Norm Grow, Foley, (1-28-58)
Rebounds	38	Carl Johnson, Balaton, (1-21-66)
Assists	20	Joshua Wallendorf, All.Christian, (12-21-00)
Steals	17	Pat Driscoll, Moorhead, (12-9-66)
Steals	17	Mark Anderson, Gonvick, (12-4-84)
Blocked Shots	20	Nate Holmstadt, Monticello, (3-18-95)
Overall Fg Made	32	Ron Johnson, Starbuck, (2-17-53)
Free Throws Made	22	Joel McDonald, Chisholm, (12-27-90)

Ind. Season Records	Stat	Player
Points Scored	1,157	Joel Mcdonald, Chisholm, '91
Rebounds	513	Norm Grow, Foley, '58
Assists	300	Drew Carlson, Belle Plaine, '98
Steals	202	Mark Buri, Trinity, '98
Blocked Shots	267	Joel Przybilla, Monticello, '97
Overall Fg Made	403	Joel McDonald, Chisholm, '91
Free Throws Made	248	Joel McDonald, Chisholm, '91
3 Point Fg Made	105	Matt Dittberner, Hinckley-Finlayson, '92

Ind. Career Records	Stat	Player
Points Scored	3,292	Joel Mcdonald, Chisholm, '91
Rebounds	1,417	Norm Grow, Foley, '58
Assists	1,066	Drew Carlson, Belle Plaine, '99
Steals	467	Drew Carlson, Belle Plaine, '99
Blocked Shots	694	Joel Przybilla, Monticello, '98
Overall Fg Made	1,183	Joel McDonald, Chisholm, '91
Free Throws Made	703	Jake Sullivan, Tartan, '00
3 Point Fg Made	349	Ryan Giehler, Bigfork, '94

"The Top-10"
(1914-1980)

On Sunday, March 2nd, 1980, the Minneapolis Tribune selected who they felt were the best 10 players to play in the state tournament:

PLAYER	SIZE	TEAM	YEARS
Bob Zender	6-7	Edina Morningside	1966-68
Dave Tschimperle	6-3	Hopkins	1951-53
Greg Downing	6-3	Duluth Central	1977-79
Tom Nordland	6-2	Minneapolis Roosevelt	1956-57
Mark Olberding	6-8	Melrose	1972-74
Mark Landsberger	6-6	Mounds View	1972-73
Ron Johnson	6-7	New Prague	1955-56
Hal Haskins	6-4	Alexandria	1943
Willie Warhol	6-0	Minneapolis Edison	1935-37
John Klarich	6-2	Buhl	1941-42

Among those being left off the list, as reported in Joel Krenz's 1982 book entitled: "Gopher State Greatness" included: Randy Breuer, Kevin McHale, Bill Davis, Ray Cronk, Bryan Grohnke, Jimmy Hill, Bob Bruggers, Dean Veenhof, Chet Anderson, LeRoy Gardner, Kurt Knoff, Andra Griffin, Jerry Butler, Bob and Dick Peterson, Jimmy Jensen, Brian Pederson, Paul McDonald, Jim McIntyre, Mike Forrest, Terry Kunze, Steve Lingenfelter, Tom Kezar and Jimmy Brown. (It is interesting to note that during this era, Kevin McHale, Mark Landsberger, Mark Olberding, Chris Engler and Randy Breuer, among others, all went on to play in the NBA.)

Hey, this list doesn't even include the top players from the last 20 years

Women's basketball in Minnesota has a long and storied tradition. In fact, it can be traced all the way back to before the turn of the century when a gentleman by the name of Max Exner, a former roommate of Dr. James Naismith (the inventor of basketball from Springfield, Mass.), moved to Minnesota to teach at Carleton College back in 1893. While there, he quickly saw the wintertime void left in the wake of football and baseball, so he decided to introduce the game to the women of Northfield.

Now, Naismith had already spread the gospel about his new game throughout the country by this time, via a national YMCA publication that explained the rules and formalities. It caught on in some places, but struggled in others. In many instances, men thought the game wasn't "manly" enough, and chose instead to let the women play. And that is exactly what they did. Carleton's first rivalry was, of course, with the U of M, where the game was rapidly becoming very popular on campus. Let's start there.

The Lady Gophers

Believe it or not, the University of Minnesota's Gopher Women's Basketball program was, at one point, one the nation's most dominant. OK, we have to go back quite a ways for this — about a 100 years to be exact, but the ladies were indeed all the rage back on campus at that time. That's right, Gopher Women were the buzz of college basketball back in the day, fully 75 years prior to anyone even having a clue about the term Title IX. But it was a short-lived existence, however, because after just eight seasons of playing in the spotlight, the game disappeared altogether at the U of M and wouldn't return for another 65 years, when it was again reintroduced in 1973.

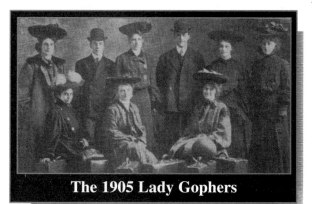

The 1905 Lady Gophers

To fully understand the evolution of the women's basketball program at the University of Minnesota, however, we have to go back to 1897. It was at that point that about 90 Gopher co-eds formed a women's basketball association. Over the next several years the team would play intramurally, on campus, but before long they began to play other college and university clubs, as well as several local high school teams which also started programs.

By 1899 the game had become increasingly popular and with that, drew its share of critics. Now, even though the ladies played in huge wool skirts and formal tops, to stay "lady-like," many felt that the sport was just too violent and unfeminine for women of that era. The game went on though, and that next year, on Feb. 24, 1900, the University of Minnesota women's varsity team played its first game against an outside opponent — defeating Stanley Hall, a Minneapolis prep school for young women, by the final score of 12-6.

Before long, the Lady Gophers had built themselves into one of the best teams in the entire nation. They began to travel throughout the Midwest, taking the train to such exotic locales as Nebraska and North Dakota. They dominated their opponents, often playing to packed houses at the Armory gymnasium on campus, which had seating for nearly 1,000 fans.

Over the next eight years, the Lady Gophers would go on to win an incredible 46 of their 51 games, even posting an amazing 36-1 stretch along the way. Perhaps the best season came in 1902-03 though, when the U, captained by Emily Johnston, went 9-0 and was proclaimed as the state champion.

The University of Minnesota Alumni Weekly publication praised the title team, commenting: "Perhaps there has never been a team representing the University in any line of sport that has shown such finished team work through so much of the season. The great beauty of the seasons work has been the fact that five young women on the team always played as though controlled by a single purpose, to make the best showing possible."

Yep, those were the glory days of Gopher Hoops. Not only did the ladies have an outstanding team, but the men weren't doing so bad either — posting a perfect 15-0 record just the year before en route to being named as the national champions by the Helms Athletic Foundation.

By 1906 the opposition to women playing intercollegiate sports was mounting though. College football was getting increasingly barbaric, and as a result, the ladies were being singled-out to not be a part of games

The Evolution of Women's Basketball Rule Changes

1906	Five to nine players on a side
1908	Placing one hand on a ball held by an opponent is a foul
1908	Double teaming a shooter is a foul
1910	Dribbling is outlawed
1913	Officiating first appeared in guides
1913	Single dribble returns, but ball must bounce knee high
1916	No coaching is allowed from the sidelines during game (except halftime)
1916	No time-outs, no substitutions
1918	Basket with open bottom instead of closed basket with pull chain becomes official
1918	Bounce pass legalized
1918	Substitutes may be used, but they cannot re-enter the game
1925	Goals scored by one-hand overhand throw, two-hand underhand throw, shot-put throw, and throw with back to the basket count as one point
1932	All field goals count as two points
1956	Three seconds in the lane is a violation
1962	Each team is permitted two players to roam the court
1962	Player allowed to "snatch" the ball from another player
1966	Continuous unlimited dribble becomes official rule
1971	Five-player, full-court game and 30-second clock become official
1987	Three-point field goal is introduced to collegiate basketball

Linda Roberts

Linda Roberts was one of the best players ever to perform in Gold Country. She still holds 11 Gopher records, the most of any athlete to play for the Gophers. Linda, who played from 1977 to 1981, competed in 129 games during her career, starting 126 of them, the most of anyone in Gopher history. She also holds the career records for most free throws made (426) and most rebounds (1,413). In 1977-78, Roberts pulled down a team record 387 rebounds and also attempted a team record 254 free throws that same year. The next season, Linda sank 21 of 25 free throw attempts against Rhode Island, both team records. Roberts was twice nominated for the coveted Wade Trophy, was a three-time recipient of the team's MVP award, and three times won the Minnesota Gopher Award. In 1996 Roberts was rewarded for all of her accomplishment when she was inducted into the Minnesota Women's Athletics Hall of Fame. Currently she works in the Women's Athletics Department at the University of Minnesota as an administrative assistant.

which involved any sort of physical violence. Soon, parents were forbidding their daughters from taking part in the game, and the American Athletic Union, the national body which governed sports outside of high schools and colleges, even declared that it would never permit girls to take part in basketball in public places because "such displays spawned undesirable traits and led to the exploitation of women."

As a result, the 1908 season would be the last for the lady hooptsters at the U of M. That April they lost what proved to be their final game, 9-3, to Nebraska. Shortly thereafter, in response to the concerns of faculty members who considered the activity to be "inappropriate," the schools' Board of Regents voted to abolish intercollegiate athletics for women. It would be a truly sad day for the future of women's sports as a whole.

And, while there was no formal reason given as to why the school decided to hand women's athletics this death sentence of sorts, there were several theories that surfaced which helped to explain why. Among them included excuses ranging from travel expenses (the team required chaperones when it traveled) to finances, to dealing with the logistics of an already overcrowded Armory gymnasium. For whatever the reason, women's basketball was gone, and it wouldn't come back, on a varsity basis at least, for another six and a half decades.

The game did stick around on campus at both the intramural and "club" levels, but it wasn't the same as big-time college basketball — the way it should've been. A separate women's gymnasium named Norris Hall was later built in 1915, but it didn't help to get the game back into the big-time like many had hoped for.

This trend of opposition to women playing sports also continued with younger-aged girls as well, but did not hamper the prep game altogether. In fact, the game was flourishing at the high school level and was even growing in popularity during this era, giving girls from around the state the opportunity to play the game at a higher level. Over the next several decades, however, the girls game would struggle. There were a few shining stars like "Babe" Didrikson (Zaharias) and Nera White, who were early pioneers of women's basketball, but the game wouldn't gain the respect if deserved for decades to come. The war hit in the late 1930s and things changed from there on out. Women didn't experience a great movement with regards to basketball, and even sports in general, until the early 1970s — when things finally began to change.

So, let's fast-forward to this era, when basketball made its triumphant return to Gold Country, and try to dissect what went down. By the early 1970s a rapid series of developments gave birth to the modern game of women's hoops. The first change, in 1971, was the adoption of a five-player full-court game, which finally made the women's game look like the men's. The next change was the big one, however, and that was the enactment of Title IX in the Education Act of 1972. This law essentially required colleges and universities to provide the same opportunities for women as they provided for men with regards to sports. This ultimately made schools everywhere completely revamp their policies and procedures for women's athletics. Women would now be given the chance to play big-time college sports, and they would also be given athletic scholarships for their efforts.

Laura Coenen

With 2,044 points, Laura Coenen was the all-time leading scorer among both men and women at the University of Minnesota. What's even more impressive is the fact she did it all while overcoming a thyroid problem that limited her to just 299 points during her junior season. Coenen still holds five Gopher single-game, season, or career records. She scored in double figures in 91 of 102 games and had 10 or more re-bounds in 53 games. She earned first team All-American honors in 1983 and 1985, and was also a District IV Kodak All-American.

In 1983, as a sophomore, Laura was named the Big Ten MVP, and in 1985 she was named the Comeback Player of the Year by Women's Basketball News Service. She also was a Wade Trophy finalist as a senior. In 1986 the women's basketball program made her number 44 the first jersey ever to be officially retired. She was also inducted into the Minnesota Women's Athletics Hall of Fame in 1996. Upon graduation, Coenen played professionally in Germany. Then, wanting to try something different, she returned to the United States and competed on the gold medal winning U.S. handball team at the 1987 Pan Am Games and at the 1988 and 1996 Summer Olympics.

The newly empowered women quickly took charge and the rest is history. Before long first wave of female superstars arrived on the scene, and started to attract national attention for the women's college game and really began to give the sport a lot of credibility. With that, in 1973 the first University of Minnesota basketball team hit the hard-court. The Lady Gophers, under Coach Linda Wells, finished their inaugural season with a modest 3-10 record. They lost their first five games before finally edging Minnesota-Duluth, 38-37, in what proved to be the first victory in the modern era of Gopher Basketball history.

Jenny Johnson took over the young Minnesota program in its second season and directed the Gophers to an improved 7-12 record. Though not a part of a conference schedule of any kind, the Gophers beat their first future Big Ten opponent, Illinois, 53-50, for the season's first win. Denise Erstad led the Gophers in scoring with 11.5 points and 15.8 boards per game.

Minnesota posted its first winning season in 1976 with a 14-11 record. Erstad led the Gophers for the second consecutive season, scoring 11.4 points and grabbing 10.8 rebounds per game. That next year the team went 15-14, to post its first back-to-back winning season. The team also played in the Sixth Annual AIAW (Association for Intercollegiate Athletics for Women) Basketball National Tournament. (The NCAA, which didn't recognize women's sports at the time, finally hosted a women's national tournament in 1982.) The Gophers competed by virtue of hosting the event, but lost to defending AIAW champion Delta State and then were eliminated by Missouri-Columbia.

The 1977-78 campaign was one of the best-ever for the Gophers. First-year Coach Ellen Mosher's club posted a 14-game winning streak en route to finishing with a 24-10 record and advancing to the AIAW National Tournament. Elsie Olm, who averaged 16.5 points a game, was named as a AIWA all-American, while Rachel Gaugert earned AIAW All-Region Six honors as well.

Deb Hunter

Many consider Deb Hunter to be the greatest all-around player in Gopher women's basketball history. Known for her quickness, Deb was always quick to steal the ball and unselfishly dish it to her teammates for the bucket. She owns nine Minnesota records including most career assists and steals. She also holds the Minnesota record for most assists in a game (15), most assists in a season (241), most steals in a game (12), and most steals in a season (139). She holds the Minnesota records for best field goal percent-age in a season (.600), best career field goal percentage (.519), and best career free throw percentage (.829).

The guard could also shoot the ball with great accuracy, as evidenced by her career-high 34 point outburst against Purdue in 1983. In 1983, the two-time team MVP received first-team All-Big Ten honors. In 1982 she received honorable mention All-American honors, and in 1983 she was named as a Kodak Region IV selection. Currently she owns a private business in Austin, Texas.

The team kept it going that next year, placing fifth in the 1979 National Invitational Tournament to end the season with a 17-15 record. Center Linda Roberts scored 15.5 points and grabbed 11.8 rebounds per game en route to team MVP honors while Laura Gardner was named as an AIWA All-American. Roberts then led the Gophers to an a 18-11 record in 1980, en route to being named as a Wade Trophy nominee, which recognizes the nation's top player.

Things couldn't have gotten much better for the Gophers that next year as they cruised to an outstanding 28-7 record behind the amazing play of three-time MVP and future hall of famer, Linda Roberts. She led the Lady Gophers to the AIAW National Tournament, only to watch her squad get upset by both Kansas and Jackson State to round out the season. Roberts was again nominated for the Wade Trophy after leading the team in scoring with 12.4 points and 10.3 rebounds per game. She finished her illustrious career at Minnesota as the all-time career scoring and rebounding records as well with 1,856 points and 1,413 rebounds. Additionally, teammates Marty Dablen, Deb Hunter and Mary Manderfeld were selected to the AIAW All-Region Six squad.

The 1981-82 Gophers, behind Laura Coenen and Debbie Hunter, who both earned All-American honorable mention honors, recorded their highest post-season finish in history by advancing all the way to the quarterfinal round of the AIWA National Tournament before losing to Rutgers.

That next year proved to be the first season of Big Ten Women's basketball. Minnesota, which finished with a 20-7 overall record, placed third with a 13-5 conference mark. Leading the way for the Gophers, however, were Big Ten Player of the Year, Laura Coenen, and two-time team MVP, Deb Hunter, who formed one of the program's best one-two-punch combo's in history. (Coenen and Hunter shared the distinction of being the first Gophers honored as all-Big Ten first-team selections. Coenen scored 24.2 points per game that season, while Hunter added 17.7 points as well. Hunter finished her brilliant Gopher career with all-time records in assists, with 633, steals, with 413, and second on the all-time scoring list, with 1,363 points.)

Minnesota slipped to 12-15 overall in 1983-84, recording the only losing season in Ellen Mosher Hanson's 10-year coaching stint with the Gophers. That next season the Gophers improved to finish with an 18-10 record and a third-place showing in the Big Ten. Leading the way was Laura Coenen, who, following the season, had her No. 44 officially retired. An All-American, two-time all-Big Ten first-team selection and Wade Trophy finalist, Coenen set 11 of her 13 Minnesota school records during her final season. After averaging an impressive 20 points per game in each year of her collegiate career, Coenen became the Gophers' all-time leading scorer with 2,044 points.

With Coenen gone, the Gophers limped to an 8-20 overall record, good for just ninth in the

Carol Ann Shudlick

Apple Valley's Carol Ann Shudlick is arguably the greatest women's basketball player ever to come from Minnesota. One of the most highly recruited prep stars in state history, luckily for us she opted to stay put at the University of Minnesota. By the time she finished her tenure in Gold Country, she owned eight school records and became the Gophers' all-time leading scorer with 2,097 points. During her senior campaign in 1994, Shudlick became Minnesota's first-ever winner of the Wade Trophy, awarded to the nation's most outstanding senior basketball player.

The three time all-academic Big Ten selection was also the first Gopher ever to be named as a first team Kodak All-American. To top it off she was named as the Big Ten's Player of the Year, the Sports Channel-Chicago Player of the Year, and the Chicago Tribune Silver Basketball Award winner. The Patty Berg Award honoree also received the Big Ten Medal of Honor Award and was also named to every all-tournament team that she participated in that season.

After graduating with a journalism degree, Carol Ann played professional basketball overseas in Madrid, Spain and also with the upstart Columbus franchise of the ABL. She later signed with her hometown WNBA Minnesota Lynx, but was later cut.

Big Ten standings. Molly Tadich became the team's "go-to" player, gathering 18.3 points per game, while senior Forward Carol Peterka earned all-Big Ten honorable mention honors after posting 14.3 points and 7.9 rebounds per game. Peterka, who played in all 110 games during her four-year career and started 96, scored 1,441 career points to rank third on Minnesota's all-time scoring list.

The 1987 Gophers, winners of just nine games, said good-bye to one of its best all-around players when senior Forward Molly Tadich, who averaged 19.5 points and 9.6 rebounds per game that season, graduated. A three-time all-Big Ten second-teamer, Tadich finished as Minnesota's all-time leader in blocked shots with 192, second in career rebounding with 1,135 and third in career scoring at 1,706.

LaRue Fields took over in 1987-88 and led the squad to yet another nine-win season. Sophomores Lea Blackwell and Ellen Kramer led the way as they each were accorded all-Big Ten honorable mention honors. Things got worse from there though, as the team finished in the Big Ten cellar in its next three seasons. In 1990 Linda Hill-MacDonald took over as the team's coach, and things slowly began to improve. At the end of the 1991 season Forward Ellen Kramer wrapped up her career in Gold Country by being named as an All-Big Ten second-teamer. In addition, she finished fifth on the Minnesota career scoring and rebounding lists with 1,371 points and 728 rebounds.

Sophomore Forward Carol Ann Shudlick, from Apple Valley, emerged as the Gophers' "go-to" player in 1991 as the local star posted a team-high 20.3 points per game average. Shudlick even shattered the team's single-game scoring record when she poured in 44 points against Marquette. That next season the team finished with a 14-12 overall record, its first winning campaign in eight years. With 22.6 points per game, Carol Ann Shudlick earned honorable mention all-America honors, as well as being named as an All-Big Ten first-team selection. One of the highlights, er... lowlights, of the season came in a win against Michigan State, which killed an ugly 38-game Big Ten road losing streak that spanned four years.

The Gophers, who won their first nine games in their newly remodeled home, the Sports Pavilion (the former Mariucci Arena), finished the 1993-94 season with a much improved 18-11 overall record. The 10-8 Big Ten record and fourth-place conference tie was also the best for a Gopher team in nine years. But the best was yet to come for these Gophers, who received their first-ever invitation to the NCAA Tournament. There, Senior Forward Carol Ann Shudlick, who averaged 23.6 points per game that year, led the No. 10-seeded Gophers to their first-ever NCAA Tournament victory over Notre Dame, in South Bend. The Gophers led 31-30 at the half and opened up a 68-65 lead with 7:14 to play. The Irish rallied to pull within six in the closing minutes, but the Gophers hung on and drained seven of eight free throws down the stretch to ice the win. Minnesota then lost to #12 ranked Vanderbilt in the second round, 98-72, to conclude the most exciting season in Gopher history.

Carol Ann Shudlick was rewarded with several honors at season's end, including the Wade Trophy Award, honoring the nation's top senior collegiate women's basket-ball player. Shudlick also garnered Kodak All-America, All-Big Ten and Big Ten Player of the Year honors as well. She finished her four-year career at Minnesota as the school's all-time leading scorer with 2,097 points, a total which was the third-highest in Big Ten history. She would go on to play professionally with the ABL's Columbus Quest, and eventually playing briefly with her hometown Minnesota Lynx.

Coming off the best season in Minnesota history, the Gophers took a nose dive in 1994-95, finishing seventh with a 7-9 conference mark and a 12-15 record overall. Seniors Cara Pearson and Shannon Loeblein were the big guns in the Gopher lineup finishing one-two in scoring at 15.4 and 14.5 points per game, respectively. The highlight of the season came as the Gophers opened their Big Ten schedule with three consecutive wins, including a weekend which Coach Linda Hill-MacDonald termed the "greatest in the history of Minnesota basketball." In it, the Gophers captured a 71-56 upset of No. 7 Penn State, as well as a 68-67 buzzer-beater over No. 19 Purdue.

From there things got even uglier in 1995-96 as the Gophers suffered their worst season since 1973, the inaugural year of Gopher women's basketball. The Gophers posted a 4-23 overall record and went winless in 16 Big Ten contests. The solid play of Cheri Stafford and Angie Iverson were the lone bright spots on an otherwise dismal season. The next two seasons were only a little bit better as the team won just one Big Ten game in each season. One bright spot came in 1997, when the team rebounded to post a first-round victory in the now-annual Big Ten Tournament over Wisconsin, 80-75, in the opening round. They did lose to Illinois in Round Two, however, to end their season at 4-24.

That off-season the team brought in Cheryl Littlejohn to serve as its new coach. Expectations were high for Littlejohn, who had learned the game under the tutelage of Tennessee coaching legend, Pat Summitt. An assistant at both North Carolina State and Alabama, Littlejohn entered a program in disarray. Her 1998-99 Gophers finished in the Big Ten cellar yet again after posting just seven overall wins. The team improved in 1999-00 to post a 10-18 overall record, thanks to the efforts of Erin Olson, Lindsay Lieser, Cassie VanderHeyden and Brandy Pickens, who all played good basketball for the Gophers. Minnesota then finished the 2000-01 season with an identical 10-18 overall record, but went just 1-15 in the Big Ten to finish 10th yet again.

Following the 2001 season Coach Littlejohn, who compiled a 29-81 record in four years with the program, was fired after allegedly committing 12 NCAA violations. She was replaced with Brenda Oldfield, formerly the head coach at Ball State University. Oldfield, 31, agreed to a five-year contract with a base salary of $130,000 annually, a $10,000 media package, and a whole bunch of incentives and bonuses that could bump the total to about $200,000 a year.

Oldfield inherits a program that has only seven Big Ten victories over the past four years. She also inherits a program in financial trouble. The program generated just $43,000 in revenue in 1999-2000, almost $1.1 million less than it spent.

Lady Gophers All-Time Records

Total Points
1.	2,097	CarolAnn Shudlick	1991-94
2.	2,044	Laura Coenen	1982-85
3.	1,856	Linda Roberts	1978-81
4.	1,706	Molly Tadich	1984-87
5.	1,441	Carol Peterka	1983-86

Total Rebounds
1.	1,413	Linda Roberts	1978-81
2.	1,135	Molly Tadiech	1984-87
3.	1,029	Laura Coenen	1982-85
4.	848	Angie Iverson	1995-98
5.	744	Carol Peterka	1983-86

Total Assists
1.	633	Debbie Hunter	1981-83
2.	314	Debbie Hilmerson	1985-88
2.	314	Holly Thompson	1989-92
4.	276	Nikki Coates	1990-94
5.	255	Laura Coenen	1982-85

Total Blocks
1.	192	Molly Tadich	1984-87
2.	128	Diane Kinney	1985-88
3.	102	Laura Coenen	1982-85
4.	84	Carol Ann Shudlick	1991-94
5.	47	Dana Joubert	1989-92

Total Steals
1.	290	Laura Coenen	1982-85
2.	173	Carol Ann Shudlick	1991-94
3.	161	Molly Tadich	1984-87
4.	149	Shannon Loeblein	1992-95
5.	147	Carol Peterka	1983-86

(Incidentally, Tennessee made almost $2 million over expenses that same year.)

But she has shown in the past that she can coach. She has some good players returning in Guard Lindsay Whalen, and she has recruited some solid talent for the future in Blue Earth's Shannon Schonrock and Marshall's Shannon Bolden. Oldfield has a great reputation, is a proven winner, and seems to be well on her way to turning this program around in the years to come.

The Women's MIAC

While the Minnesota Intercollegiate Athletic Conference was first created back in 1921 for men's sports, the ladies would have to wait another 60 years to compete for MIAC titles. Sure, many of Minnesota's college and universities began playing the sport in as far back as the 1890s, but most of them were playing on an informal, intramural or club basis. Augsburg, for instance, finished second in the 1926 national tournament at Charleston, S.C., while other local teams toured the Midwest for competition as well. Through the years women's college hoops have grown in popularity. Teams played independent schedules, however, but still found ways to play games against one another on a consistent basis.

Carleton's 1900 Team

In 1973 non-scholarship Division III officially became a part of the NCAA when the association switched from a two division to a three-division format.
By the mid-1970s many of the current MIAC schools were playing on a regular basis. Some were affiliated with the Minnesota Association of Intercollegiate Athletics for Women (MAIAW), a very competitive local conference, while others simply scheduled intramural contests for competitive outings. One of the more successful local college conferences, located in Northern Minnesota and western North Dakota, was the Minn-Kota, which featured eight teams, including: Moorhead State, UM Morris, Bemidji, Concordia, UND, NDSU, Valley City and Mayville.

Augsburg's 1926 Lady Free-Throws

It wasn't until 1981 though that the MIAC officially recognized and sponsored women's basketball on a full-time basis. Today the MIAC is one of the strongest NCAA Division III athletic conferences in the nation and its top teams are seemingly always nationally ranked. The MIACs' 12 member institutions for women's basketball include: Augsburg, Bethel, Carleton, Concordia, Gustavus, Hamline, Macalester, St. Benedict, St. Catherine, St. Mary's, St. Olaf and St. Thomas.

St. Ben's 1993 Final Four Team

The inaugural MIAC title for the 1982 season was won by the Lady Cobbers from Concordia University in Moorhead. They rolled to a perfect 8-0 record that season and were justly rewarded with the first-ever conference crown. (For Concordia, however, which had been playing organized women's hoops for quite some time, in the Minn-Kota Conference, this wasn't their first taste of success. In fact, in 1979 the Cobbers, led by Kathy Meyer, Mary Schultz and Coral Beske — the school's first All-American, made an appearance in the Region 6 tournament of the Association of Intercollegiate Athletics for Women, which was held in Missouri. Concordia, behind Center Sue Ekberg, then added a third place finish at the Division III MAIAW state tournament in 1980, as well as another third in the AIAW regional tournament after losing to champion Mount Mercy of Cedar Rapids, Iowa, in the semifinals.)

There was a three-way tie for the MIAC title in 1983 as Concordia, St. Olaf and St. Thomas all finished with identical 8-1 records. Concordia was then selected as the site for the Minnesota AIAW Division II and Division III tournament, which would decide the state championship. After winning in the first round, the Cobbers faced St. Thomas in the semifinals and

All-Time Ladies MIAC Champions

1981-82	Concordia
1982-83	Concordia
	St. Olaf
	St. Thomas
1983-84	St. Thomas
1984-85	St. Mary's
1985-86	Concordia
	St. Mary's
1986-87	Concordia
1987-88	Concordia
1988-89	St. Benedict
1989-90	Concordia
1990-91	St. Thomas
1991-92	St. Thomas
1992-93	St. Benedict
1993-94	Bethel
1994-95	St. Benedict
1995-96	St. Thomas
1996-97	St. Thomas
1997-98	St. Thomas
	St. Benedict
1998-99	St. Benedict
1999-00	St. Thomas
2000-01	St. Thomas

Gustavus' All-Time Leading Scorers:

1. L. Erickson	1,399	1983-87
2. J. Ree	1,252	1984-88
3. B. Wannarka	1,098	1980-84
4. P. Mickow	1,079	1982-86
5. J. Peik	960	1991-95

UST's Laurie Trow

lost 70-64. St. Thomas went on to take the state title, followed by UM-Morris in second place and Concordia in third. Because of their third-place finish, the Cobbers did not expect to continue in postseason play. However, they were nonetheless invited to host and play in the National Collegiate Athletic Association Division III West Region tournament, where they beat Pomona-Pitzer College of Claremont, Calif., 75-60. Then, in the next round, the Cobbers, behind their star JoDee Bock, played hard but lost to Morris, 69-68, on a heart-breaker with just 17 seconds to play.

The 1999 St. Ben's National Runner-up's

Meanwhile, the Lady Toms, who began their program in 1978, were led by Ruth Opatz, Mary Tomsche and Mary Asenbrenner, while St. Olaf put together an amazing run considering they were playing without the recently graduated Karen Stromme, who had just ended her career in Northfield as the program's all-time leading scorer with 1,449 points.

St. Thomas made it two in a row in 1984 and kept on going from there, right into the NCAA Division III West Regional Playoffs, held at St. Thomas. There, the 18-2 Lady Toms lost to Bishop College in round one, 71-67, but rebounded back to beat Pomona-Pitzer, 63-59, to round out the tourney. Ruth Opatz, Mary Asenbrenner and freshman Jane Tschimperle led the Lady Toms that season.

St. Mary's took the fourth ever MIAC championship in 1985 when they posted an impressive 19-1 conference record that season, fully four games ahead of Concordia, which took second. From there the Lady Cardinals advanced to the Regional tourney, held in California that year, ultimately losing to in the playoffs. The Lady Cards were led by two-time All-American Mary Schultze, who remains as the school's all-time leading scorer, with 1,989 points, as well as the all-time leading rebounder, with 1,001 boards.

St. Mary's, which at one point was ranked No. 3 in the nation, made it two in a row in 1986, sharing the MIAC crown with Concordia that season. Leading the charge for St. Mary's was the school's all-time assists leader, Lisa Janikowski, who dished the ball off to Mary Schultze early and often that season. Led by seniors Cynthia Bogatzki, Janet Peterson and Kim Sternhagen, Concordia, on the other hand, was just getting warmed up. Coming off a 17-game winning streak, the Lady Cobbers advanced to the NCAA Division II Regional Tournament, where they beat St. Mary's, 67-63, before falling to Bishop College of Dallas, 90-86.

Bethel's All-Time Leading Scorers:

1. Allison Rostberg	511	1990-91
2. Kitri Peterson	498	1995-96
3. Beth Johnson	475	1997-98

From there the Lady Cobbers would go on to post a pair of 21-1 records over the next two seasons en route to back-to-back MIAC titles. But they didn't stop there. Coach Duane Siverson's Lady Cobbers were about to go on a roll which was unprecedented in Minnesota women's basketball history. In 1987 not only did they win the MIAC, they also went on to make a serious post-season run in the NCAA national playoffs and ultimately finished second in the nation. In post-season play the Lady Cobbers defeated California State-Stanislaus, 77-64, and Pomona-Pitzer, 68-46, to win the West Regional title. From there Concordia beat the nation's No. 1 team, Rust College of Holly Springs, Miss., in a home game, winning 72-62 to reach the Final Four. Then, after downing Kean College, Union, N.J., 74-69, the Cobbers fell just short of the national championship by losing to Wisconsin-Stevens Point, 81-74. A finalist for Player of the Year, Cobber star Jessica Beachy was named to the NCAA Division III All-America First Team by the Women's Basketball Coaches Association.

In 1988, meanwhile, they repeated as MIAC champs, but they were intent on winning that elusive D-III National Championship that had come so close the year before. With that, the Lady Cobbers, who played tournament host, entered the post-season right in their own back yard. From there they cruised to five straight wins. The big finale came in front of an overflow crowd as the Lady Cobbers won their 40th consecutive Division III home game and met their ultimate goal with style and grace, beating the previously undefeated, No. 1-ranked St. John Fisher College (Rochester, N.Y.), 65-57. Following the historic event, the Women's Basketball Coaches Association selected Staples native Jessica Beachy as the Outstanding Player of the Year for Division III women's basketball and named her to the all-America basketball team as well. The WBCA also honored Coach Siverson as Coach of the Year as well. In addition to Beachy, Jillayn Quaschnick and Michelle Thykeson were also named to the final four all-tournament team, while New York Mills native Mary Lee Legried, the school's all-time assists leader, was named as a second-team All-American. (The Lady Cobbers also earned a cumulative 3.51 grade point average that year!)

St. Olaf's Marty Suek

The 1989 season saw St. Ben's make their mark, earning their first conference crown by posting a tremendous 19-1 record. The Blazers, under long-time Head Coach Mike Durbin, then qualified for the NCAA Division III West Regional Tournament, where they went on to win four more games en route to claiming Final Four runner-up honors. Belgrade's Joyce Spanier, who led the team in scoring with an average of 17.2 points per game, along with Glencoe's Patty Mayer and Shakopee's Mickey Jurewicz all earned All-MIAC honors for the squad.

Concordia came back to claim its sixth MIAC crown in 1990, this time posting a 19-1 tally en route yet another trip to the post-season. And this time the Lady Cobbers, led by senior

Carleton's All-Time Leading Scorers:

1. Katherine Frewing	1,712	1988-92
2. Lisa Nordeen	1,649	1986-90
3. Laurie Peterson	1,306	1996-00
4. Denell Downum	1,011	1990-94
5. Anna Bandick	1,003	1986-90

point guard Becky Ehnert and All-American Michelle Thykeson, then went on to capture their third National Collegiate Athletic Association West Region title in four years with a thrilling 81-77 overtime victory over MIAC runner-up St. Thomas in the Cobber gym. The championship put the Lady Cobbers in the nation's top eight Division III schools, but a 70-65 road loss in the NCAA's quarterfinal game to Centre College of Danville, Ky., ended Concordia's 24-5 season.

The next two seasons of MIAC lady hoops were all St. Thomas, as they captured the 1991 and 1992 crowns. So tough were the Toms during this stretch, that from January 1991 to March 1992, they won an amazing 40 consecutive games (and 56 of 57), breaking an NCAA Division III record in the process. (They had even won 16 straight games just prior to the streak beginning as well!) The 1991 campaign was special though, as the Tommies went on to win an NCAA championship, playing all five of their NCAA tournament games in the comfort of Schoenecker Arena. Led by All-American Laurie Trow and Tonja Englund, UST claimed the title with a 73-55 win over Muskingum, the second- biggest margin of victory ever in an NCAA title game. Along the way the Toms beat St. Ben's, 76-62, UW-Oshkosh, 87-63, Concordia, 76-62, and Eastern Connecticut, 91-55.

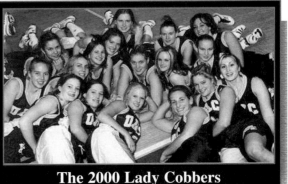

The 1951 Auggiettes

Macalaster's All-Time Leading Scorers:

1.	Jane Ruliffson	1,762	1989-92
2.	Jane O'Brien	1,349	1982-85
3.	Amy Amundson	1,215	1995-98
4.	Janis Ratz	1,060	1995-88
5.	Mary Moriarty	1,052	1983-86

Then, in 1992, the Lady Toms became the first MIAC school to go undefeated, when they posted an amazing 20-0 record. From there they pounded St. Olaf in the first round of the playoffs, 89-60, before being edged in the West/Central Section Finals in Waverly, IA, by Luther, 61-60. Laurie Trow, who simply rewrote the STU record books, once again led the way as she went on to become the first Minnesotan ever to be named as the WBCA National Player of the Year.

St. Ben's got back on top in 1993, taking their second MIAC title. The Blazers were coming off an extraordinary season in 1992, when they advanced to the "Sweet 16" round in Waverly, Iowa, where they ultimately lost to Wartburg College in the sectional tournament. In 1993, however, CSB made their first-ever appearance in the NCAA Division III Women's Basketball National Championships. The Blazers won their first 28 games of the season, which included a 25-0 record during the regular season and an unbeaten MIAC mark of 20-0. Then, after cruising through three straight home sellouts in the NCAA Tournament, the squad traveled to the Final Four in Pella, Iowa, only to lose in the semifinals to Central College, 60-59, on a last second buzzer-beater. The Blazers then lost the third place game to Scranton College (pa.) 89-69 to finish fourth in the nation. It was an amazing season, however, as Sacred Heart's Kelly Mahlum became CSB's second All-American, and the Blazers second all-time leading scorer.

Bethel won its first MIAC title in 1994. The Royals, led by Kim Carlson and Jennifer Egge — both members of the 1,000-point club, posted a 17-3 conference mark and then went on to win four more post-season games to round out their season at 21-4. They edged the Lady Cobbers, who finished as the conference runner-ups, in the first round of the NCAA Tourney and made a very nice playoff run.

The Blazers found their way back to top of the conference leader board in 1995, capturing their second conference title in three years, and their

St. Olaf's All-Time Leading Scorers:

1.	Karen Stromme	1,449	1978-82
2.	Sue Grack	1,039	1990-93
3.	Michelle Pederson	1,035	1988-92
4.	Jill Anderson	874	1990-94
5.	Betsy Anderson	841	1991-95

third championship in seven seasons. From there the ladies of St. Ben's advanced to the "Sweet 16" round of NCAA Tournament for the fourth year in a row, and after advancing to the "Elite Eight" came within two points of returning to the "Final Four." The big win which catapulted the Blazers into the big dance came after winning at Concordia-Moorhead, when they knocked off Aurora College by 34 points. Leading the way for CSB was the Division III Women's Athlete of the Year, Tina Kampa, who registered 1,000 kills in volleyball and 1,000 points in basketball in her illustrious career. In addition, Danielle Guse was also named as the MIAC Player of the Year as well.

St. Thomas returned to the conference summit in 1996, and wouldn't step down again until 1999. That '96 season saw the Lady Toms post a perfect 20-0 record en route to another brilliant post-season run which saw them make it all the way to the Final Four. UST kicked off the playoffs by beating St. Ben's, 68-52, followed by UC-San Diego, 66-42, Marymount 67-62 in the West Sectionals, and Bethel, 65-57. Then, in the Final Four, the Lady Toms were topped by Mount Union, 71-57. They did rebound to take third though, when they beat NYU, 75-51.

St. Thomas made it back-to-back undefeated seasons in 1997, becoming the first and only MIAC basketball team — men or women — to post consecutive 20-0 records in conference play. From there the Lady Toms went on to crush Luther, 89-47, in opening round play, followed by St. Ben's, 95-67, to advance to the West Sectional Playoffs in Defiance (Ohio). There, they were beaten by Capital, 70-64, to round out their tremendous season.

UST's Missy Pederson

The 2000 Lady Cobbers

UST's Molly Hayden

In 1998 St. Thomas and St. Ben's shared the conference honors as they each finished with identical 21-1 records. These two seemed destined to get it on from the get-go. The Blazers began the season by winning their first 21 games, which included a decisive 10-point victory at St. Thomas, 60-50, snapping a 65-game Tommie winning streak over MIAC

opponents, and giving UST its first loss at home in 41 games. Under the direction of 12th-year head coach Mike Durbin, St. Ben's returned to the NCAA Tournament for the 10th straight season. There, the Blazers advanced to the NCAA "Sweet 16" round of the tournament after receiving a first-round bye and then pummeling UC-San Diego, 73-47, at Claire Lynch Hall. The Lady Toms, meanwhile, behind their star, Kirsten Vipond, beat Central, 85-56, in their opener, followed by DePaw, 80-61, in the West Sectionals. From there STU then lost a heart-breaker in the Elite Eight to Mount Union, 67-64, to finish their season.

The Blazers made it two in a row in 1999, this time edging St. Thomas in the final standings with a 21-1 conference record. From there it was historic as the team went on to the NCAA Finals, where they took second place in the nation. They opened their historic season by winning the National Catholic Tournament and then claimed their second straight MIAC crown from there. Then, in their 11th straight post-season appearance, St. Ben's rolled to a couple of big home playoff wins over St. Thomas, DePaw (Ind.), and Pacific Lutheran, en route to advancing to the NCAA Final Four on the campus of Western Connecticut State University. There, they beat up on Salem State (Mass.), 74-54, before losing in the championship game to Washington University (St. Louis, Mo.), 74-65.

In 2000 the Lady Toms got back on top of the MIAC and haven't looked back since. Long-time assistant Tricia Dornisch took over as the Lady Toms head coach in 1998-99 and wasted little time in making a name for herself. The former UST guard led UST to a 28-2 overall finish that year, including an NCAA Final Four berth and third-place national finish. It all began with a first round home win over Pacific Lutheran, 64-45, in round one, followed by wins over George Fox (OR), 76-64, and Hardin-Simmons, 68-56, to make it to the national semifinals. There, the Toms, led by two-time All-American Molly Hayden, played tough but lost to Southern Maine, 49-42. They did manage to battle back, however, to beat Scranton, 66-56, for third place honors.

St. Thomas made it back-to-back conference titles in 2001 thanks to the efforts of National Player of the Year, Missy Pederson. She led UST back to the NCAA Tournament, where they first beat Claremont-Mudd Scripts, 69-59, followed by George Fox, 64-52, in the Sweet 16. From there the Toms lost in the Elite Eight to Washington University, 65-85, to end their season.

It is also important to note that in 2000-01 the first-ever MIAC Playoff was held with Carleton beating St. Thomas, 61-58, in the inaugural conference title game. The second place Knights, behind Renée Willette, arguably the school's best player since 1992 All-American Katherine Frewing, then went on to earn their first ever NCAA Tournament bid.

The Women's NCC

Sarah Howard

St. Cloud State University

Women's basketball at SCSU has evolved from the Campus Lab School to Halenbeck Hall, from the AIAW to the NCAA, and from the Northern Sun Conference to the North Central Conference. Through it all it has been one of Minnesota's strongest women's programs, continually producing some of the state's elite players from top to bottom.

Founded in 1896, St. Cloud State University was once known primarily as a teacher's college. And, while the Lady Huskies have been playing basketball on an informal basis for many, many years, the first school-sponsored non-club-based team hit the hardcourt in 1968-69 under coach Linda Ochs. In 1970, the regular season was extended to eight games and post-season play was initiated in Minnesota. The women played two regional tournaments divided into northern and southern regions. St. Cloud State finished as the consolation champion in the Northern Regional Tournament and ended the season with a 5-7 overall record under new coach Joan Payne. Following the season SCSU officially recognized the lady hoopsters as an intercollegiate basketball team.

By 1976 the Lady Huskies played a 16-game schedule and finished that season with a 10-6 record. From there they went on to the state tournament and

Jan Niehaus
AWSF
All-American 1989-90

Sarah Howard
AWSF
All-American 1986-88

Toni Jameson
AWSF
All-American 1989-90

Brenda Meyer
NCC MVP 1996

Julie Eisenschenk
AWSF
All-American 1987

St. Cloud's All-Americans

finished second, losing to Dr. Martin Luther College, 62-60. The second-place finish qualified the Huskies for the large college Association for Intercollegiate Athletics for Women (AIAW) Region 6 tournament though, where SCSU ended fifth in the region. That next year the state divided into large and small college divisions with the Huskies wining the MAIAW's Division I championship.

The Huskies notched 9-12 and 19-10 records in 1978 and 1979, respectively, garnering second-place finishes both years in the MAIAW Division I tournament behind the University of Minnesota. A key player during these years was Sue Wahl, who became the first women's collegiate basketball player in Minnesota to both score 1,000 points and grab 1,000 rebounds.

In 1979 the Huskies joined the Northern Sun Conference along with: Bemidji State, Mankato State, Moorhead State, Southwest State, St. Cloud State, University of Minnesota-Duluth, University of Minnesota-Morris and Winona State. Diane Scherer, a five-foot-nine guard from St. Cloud Apollo, exploded onto the scene that year, leading Coach Gladys Ziemer's Huskies to a 15-13 record — good for third in the MAIAW Division II tourney, but tied for first in the Northern Sun Conference.

Jeanne Burnett, who wound up her illustrious career in St. Cloud with 1,394 points — third in school history — led SCSU to a 15-12 record in 1982. Then, in 1983, the Huskies posted an amazing 31-4 tally and won another NSIC title en route to advancing to the quarterfinal round of the NCAA Division II playoffs, where they lost a 65-63 heart-breaker to Central Missouri State. All-American Diane Scherer, who averaged 21.4 ppg that season, finished her incredible career that year as well with 2,349 points, a Minnesota women's basketball record that stood until 1991.

The 1984 squad continued their amazing success, winning a school-record 26 consecutive games and once again capturing Northern Sun and NCAA II North Central Region titles before advancing to the NCAA II quarterfinals, where they ultimately lost to Dayton. That next year the Huskies jumped over to the North Central Conference, where they finished in a second-place tie with a 10-4 record. The Huskies, led by Bonnie Henrickson, who finished her

St. Cloud State's All-Americans

1998	Christine Williamson
	Tina Schreiner
1996	Brenda Meyer
1991	Simona Samuelson
1990	Jan Niehaus
	Toni Jameson
1989	Jan Niehans
	Toni Jameson
1988	Sarah Howard
1987	Sarah Howard
	Julie Eisenschenk
	Jan Niehaus
1986	Sarah Howard
	Julie Eisenschenk
1985	Ramona Rugloski
	Dawn Anderson
	Linda Nelson
1984	Ramona Rugloski
	Dawn Anderson
1982	Diane Scherer

Tina Schreiner

The North Central Conference (NCC)

Widely regarded as one of the top NCAA Division II leagues in the country, the North Central Conference has consistently received national honors in many sports for women's athletics. While the league originally began back in 1921, for men's athletics, representatives began discussing the formation of a women's conference in the spring of 1979. At that time, eight institutions: Augustana, Morningside, the North Dakota, North Dakota State, Nebraska-Omaha, Northern Colorado, South Dakota and South Dakota State, became charter members. In 1982, both Morningside and Northern Colorado disbanded from the league (only to rejoin again in 1989), while Minnesota State, Mankato and St. Cloud State were added in 1982 and 1984, respectively, as well. From then on the league has been one of the top in the nation with regards to quality of play and talent produced.

NCC Women's Basketball Champs:

1982	Nebraska-Omaha
1983	South Dakota
1984	South Dakota
1985	South Dakota
1986	Minnesota State, Mankato
1987	North Dakota State
1988	North Dakota State
1989	St. Cloud State
1990	North Dakota
1991	North Dakota
1992	North Dakota State
1993	North Dakota State
1994	North Dakota
1995	North Dakota State
1996	North Dakota State
1997	North Dakota State
1998	North Dakota
1999	North Dakota
2000	North Dakota State
2001	North Dakota

Diane Scherer
1979-83
Leading Scorer

Sue Wahl
1975-79
Leading Rebounder

Dawn Anderson
1981-85
Steals/Assists Leader

Teri Watkins
1995-99
3pt. Field Goal Leader

Bonnie Henrickson
1981-85
Free Throw Leader

St. Cloud's All-Time Leaders

Christine Williamson

Tami Jameson

Willmar native and former St. Cloud State star Bonnie Henrickson (a three-time all-conference selection from 1983-85), is now a top NCAA Division One basketball coach at Virginia Tech. She led the Hokies, a national top-10 program, to the Atlantic 10 title in 1998, and in 2000 and 2001 she led the Hokies to the NCAA Tournament.

career as the second leading scorer in SCSU history with 1,731 points, finished the season with a 24-6 overall mark and advanced yet again to the quarterfinals of the NCAA Division II National Championship where they lost to Cal Poly-Pomona. Ramona Rugloski and Dawn Anderson repeated as AIAW All-America selections while Linda Nelson earned All America Honorable Mention honors as well.

In 1987 SCSU got back into post-season play, this time after posting a 21-8 overall record — good for third place in the NCC. The Huskies, led by All-American Guard Sarah Howard and All-NCC Forward Julie Eisenschenk, then received a bid to compete in the NCAA II North Central Region Tournament, where they recorded a 68-60 win over Nebraska-Omaha in the first round and then lost to North Dakota State 67-65 in the Finals.

The 1989 edition of SCSU women's basketball was perhaps its best yet. Despite losing three-time All-American and second all-time leading scorer, Sarah Howard, to graduation, the Huskies still found a way to dig deep and make a little history. After posting their 14th consecutive winning season, the Lady Huskies went on to capture their first ever NCC title en route to making a fourth appearance in an NCAA Division II quarterfinal game. In NCAA play, SCSU polished off NDSU in the North Central Regional by a score of 87-80 before losing in the quarterfinals to Central Missouri State, 87-71. (All-NCC star Julie Eisenschenk tore her achilles tendon the night before the quarterfinal game, something that definitely didn't help the team's morale going in.)

In 1990 it was more of the same for St. Cloud State as they completed the season 23-5 overall and placed third in the NCC with a 14-4 mark, and for the seventh time in eight years, the Huskies advanced to the NCAA Division II post-season play-offs. In addition, Coach Ziemer captured her 300th win, while All American Guard Jan Niehaus finished her illustrious career ranked third in all-time scoring with 1,776 points. Tami Jameson, the twin sister of Toni Jameson, also received All America honors as well. (The Jameson sisters would later be named to 1992 US Olympic team as members of the team handball squad.)

That next season Clearwater native Simona Samuelson averaged nearly 19 points and 10 rebounds per game en route to becoming an All-America selection. She ended her four-year career as the all-time NCC leader in blocked shots, with 132. Then, in 1992, Gladys Ziemer stepped down as SCSU's head coach. She posted a solid 321-212 record during her tenure, won five conference titles and advanced to the NCAA tournament seven times.

In 1994 Lori Ulferts was named as the

St. Cloud State's All-Time Leaders:

St. Cloud State's All-Time Scoring Leaders

1. Diane Seherer	1979-83	2,349
2. Sarah Howard	1984-88	1,812
3. Jan Niehaus	1986-90	1,776
4. Bonnie Henrickson	1981-85	1,731
5. Ramona Rugloski	1982-85	1,604

St. Cloud State's All-Time Rebounding Leaders

1. Sue Wahl	1975-79	1,074
2. Toni Jameson	1986-90	1,046
3. Bonnie Henrickson	1981-85	955
4. Jeanne Burnett	1978-82	919
5. Brenda Meyer	1992-96	863

St. Cloud State's All-Time Assists Leaders:

1. Dawn Anderson	1981-85	705
2. Emily Van Gorden	1992-96	442
3. Jan Niehaus	1986-90	407
4. Sarah Howard	1984-88	393
5. Katie Shea	1995-99	363

head coach at SCSU and guides her Huskies to 14-13 finish. All-American Forward Brenda Meyer averaged 21.5 ppg and 10.4 rpg that season, while being named the NCCs MVP. That next year both Tina Schreiner and Christine Williamson were both named to D-II All-American team. In 1999 and 2000 the Huskies recorded back-to-back 18-win seasons. Christine Williamson, Jessica Forsline and Jennifer Higgins were all named to the AII-NCC squad over that span. In 2001 the Husky women, led by All-Conference Forwards Tina Schreiner and Christine Williamson, posted a 21-9 record, and made their 8th NCAA Playoff appearance, their first since 1990.

Minnesota State University, Mankato

In 1868 Mankato Normal School first opened its doors in the picturesque river valley town of Mankato, with its primary role being to train teachers for work in rural schools throughout Southern Minnesota. In 1921 the school became Mankato State Teachers College and was authorized by the State to offer a four-year curriculum.

MSU was originally a member of the Northern Teachers College Conference (NTCC) back in the 1930s. In the late 1970s the team played briefly in affiliation with the Northern Intercollegiate Conference (NIC) and then in 1980 they joined the North Central Conference (NCC), where they have been ever since.

Minnesota State, Mankato began playing organized women's basketball on a non-club basis in 1966 against such opponents as St. Olaf, Carleton, Winona State, Southwest State, Pillsbury Academy, UW-River Falls, South Dakota State, UM-Duluth and even the University of Minnesota. Their first coach was Mary Willerscheidt. For the next three seasons the Mavericks played six-man basketball, not changing to the now-common five-man format until the 1969 season. That year saw the 10-1 squad won the Southern Minnesota Regional Championship as they beat St. Olaf in the one-game playoff, 43-24. In 1971 the Mavs added St. Cloud State to their schedule, beating the Huskies 49-35 en route to finishing second in the post-season that year after losing to Gustavus, 35-31.

Lynn Peterson

In 1972 MSU won the MAIAW state championship. After posting a 10-6 record, the team went on to make a nice play-off run, beating St. Olaf, Southwest State, Dr. Martin Luther, Carleton, UM-Duluth and then Dr. Martin Luther in the Finals, this time winning, 42-35, for the title. They repeated as MIAIW state champs that next season as well, this time edging Valley City College in the Finals, 43-42. The 1974 Mavs finished as runner-ups, losing to Dr. Martin Luther in the title game, but they rebounded in 1975 by beating by beating both South Dakota State and Dickinson State in the Final Four to reclaim their (All-Division) MAIAW championship.

In 1976 the school went through some major changes, going from College status to an official University, and even decided to get politically correct by changing their mascot from the "Indians" to the "Mavericks." (In the late 1990s the school also changed its name from Mankato State University to Minnesota State University.) That year the team lost to Bemidji in the Finals, and the next year they finished third, losing to St. Cloud State in the Final Four. That 1977 season saw the Mavs now playing in the newly created Division One category of college hoops.

Lisa Walters

The next two seasons would see the Lady Mavericks play some pretty good basketball. In 1979 the team took third, losing to St. Cloud State and North Iowa in the Final Four. Then, in 1980, the team joined the Northern Sun Intercollegiate Conference (NSIC). In 1982 the Mavs made a jump to become members of the North Central Conference (NCC). They played well, finishing with an impressive 21-11 record over some very tough Midwest teams. All-American Lynn Peterson averaged nearly 25 points per game that season and even lit up a solid UMD squad with 43 points as well. They made it to the post-season that year, beating Bemidji State in the opening round, only to fall to St. Cloud State in round two, 74-63. MSU had several early stars from this era that went on to play professionally with the local Minnesota Fillies of the late 1970s and early 1980s. Among them include: Cheryl Engel, Elsie Ohm, Lynn Peterson and Mary Manderfeld.

The 1983 season saw the Lady Mavs post a 21-win season, only to lose to UM-Duluth in the playoffs. That next year might very well

Minnesota State's All-Time Scoring Leaders:

Minnesota State's All-Time Points Leaders

1. Lisa Walters	2,072	1984-88
2. Rhonda House	1,654	1980-84
3. Pat Burns	1,524	1982-86
4. Lynn Peterson	1,518	1978-82
5. Brenda Stachowski	1,416	1996-00

Minnesota State's All-Time Assists Leaders

1. Ann Christopherson	575	1982-86
2. Carla Bronson	537	1992-96
3. Pat Burns	444	1982-86
4. Karyn Valentino	396	1990-94
5. Kendra Carter	369	1988-91

Minnesota State's All-Time Rebounding Leaders

1. Lisa Walters	1,074	1984-88
2. Julie Cink	1,025	1982-86
3. Lynn Peterson	865	1978-82
4. Mary Manderfeld	812	1977-79
5. Pat Burns	802	1982-86

Ann Walker

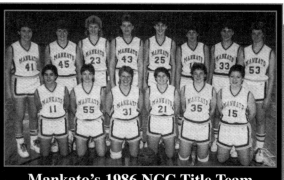

Mankato's 1986 NCC Title Team

have been the most talented in school history. The 1984 Mavs featured the top-four scorers in the program's history — a record which still stands today. Lisa Walters, Rhonda House, Pat Burns and Lynn Peterson, all of whom are members of the 1,500-point club, made up one of the best lineups in college basketball history. On the court, however, the team produced just an 18-8 record. They went 20-8 in 1985, and in 1986 history was finally made on the campus of Minnesota State University. That off-season Mary Willerscheidt, who had racked up nearly 250 career wins behind the Maverick bench, stepped down as the team's first and only coach, and was replaced with Sarah Novak. Novak, meanwhile, wasted little time in making a name for herself.

The 1986 Lady Mavs went 25-4 and won what would prove to be their only NCC title in school history. All-American Lisa Walters, who would finish her illustrious career as the school's only 2,000-point scorer, led the charge this year as the team simply dominated. The team started out with 16 straight wins that year before finally dropping a close one to Grand View, 80-78. The rounded out that dream season with a few highs and a few lows. The highs came in a pair of late wins over UM-Morris, 104-44, and St. Cloud State, 87-63, while the lows came in a pair of close losses in the final two games of the season to both South Dakota and South Dakota State. Joining in on the action were Ann Christopherson, the school's all-time assists leader, and Julie Cink, who is No. 2 all-time in rebounds behind only Lisa Walters.

The club went through a couple of bad years following that big conference title season. They went 16-12 in 1987, and then 11-15 in 1988. Then, in 1989, Coach Novak was replaced midway through the season by Susan Buntin. The team finished at just 6-21 that year under Joan Anderson, who was hired as the team's new coach, and followed that up with a 10-17 tally in 1990. In 1991 the team opened the season strong by winning the Hamline Tournament, but faded late to finish at 13-15.

The Mavs went through a couple more rough seasons in the early '90s before getting back on track in 1994, when they finished at 17-10. The team was led by a pair of guards during this era in Karyn Valentino and Carla Bronson, both of whom would finish their careers ranked in the top-five for all-time career assists. MSU then posted three straight losing seasons from 1995-97, only to rebound in 1998, behind their star, Brenda Stachowski, with another 17-win season. Paula Buscher was brought in as the new coach that year and made an immediate impact.

The team dropped off, however, that next season by going 8-19. It got just marginally better from there as they produced a 9-18 mark in 2001 under new coach Ann Walker, a former assistant coach at Creighton University. Walker was ushered into her new job with the team now playing in the new 5,000-seat Taylor Center, which was a result of Minnesota State University alum Glen Taylor's original $8 million donation. Taylor, who also owns the Minnesota Timberwolves, has been the program's biggest supporter.

The 2001 Mavs went just 8-20 and 5-13 in the NCC. There are some bright spots though, with Center Jenny Groom, and Guards Kim Curtis and Kelli Freeman leading the way. Things will only get better for these Lady Mavericks. Walker, who came into a program in a rebuilding phase, has vowed to keep it simple. "Never be satisfied...it is about the constant desire to improve, as an athlete and a person, in order to reach your fullest potential," she said. "We attain this by focusing on commitment to oneself and others, respect, pride, effort, and a desire to learn. And we try to surround all of these things with an attitude of having fun!"

Lady Mavs in the Pros:

1. Cheryl Engel (Minnesota Fillies, 1977-79, 1981)
2. Elsie Ohm (New Orleans Pride, Minnesota Fillies)
3. Lynn Peterson (Minnesota Fillies, 1981)
4. Mary Manderfeld (Minnesota Fillies, 1981)
5. Lisa Walters (Sweden)

The Women's NSIC

UMD's Diana Kangas

Long recognized as one of the premier athletic unions in the Upper Midwest, the Northern Sun Intercollegiate Conference has roots which can be traced back all the way to 1932. Over the course of seven decades, the NSIC has since undergone several make-overs, but throughout numerous additions and departures, it has remained one of the strongest conferences in women's college basketball.

What originally started as the original Northern Teachers College Conference back in the heart of the Great Depression, the then all-men's circuit featured six original charter members: Bemidji State, UM-Duluth, MSU-Moorhead, Mankato State, St. Cloud State and Winona State. In 1947 the conference was renamed as the Northern Intercollegiate Conference (NIC). (Mankato State and St. Cloud State would later defect the North Central Conference.)

In 1979 the Northern Sun Conference (NSC) was created as an all-women's circuit to compliment the NIC. With that, the Northern Sun Intercollegiate Conference was later formed by a merger in the spring of 1992 of the NIC, which was the men's conference, and the NSC, which was the women's conference. The new NCAA-sanctioned conference included the following member schools: Bemidji State, UM-Duluth, St. Cloud State, UM-Morris, Moorhead State, Northern State, Southwest State, and Winona State.

Another significant change was implemented in 1995, when the NSIC became a solely NCAA Division II conference, after previously being affiliated with the National Association of Intercollegiate Athletics (NAIA). Additionally, in 1999 Concordia University-St. Paul, UM-Crookston and Wayne State (NE) all joined the NSIC to increase the league's membership to 10.

The first championship for women's basketball, however, was held in 1979-80 with Southwest

State, St. Cloud State and Bemidji State sharing the inaugural league crown. For the next seven years, those three schools — Bemidji State (1985-87), St. Cloud State (1981-84) and Southwest State (1981) — along with MSU-Moorhead (1981 and 1985), UM-Duluth (1985) and UM-Morris (1981) brought home championship trophies to their respective schools. Since the 1987-88 season, the NSIC title sweepstakes has involved just three schools, UM-Duluth (1988-91, 1993, 1995-96 and 1998-2000), Northern State (1988, 1992, 1994-95, and 1997) and Southwest State (2001). Here's the breakdown:

The inaugural 1979-80 NSIC championship for women's basketball featured a trio of teams sharing the title with 5-2 records — Southwest State, St. Cloud State and Bemidji State. Southwest State, under the tutelage of Coach Carmen KeKoster, was led by a quartet of stars in Nancy Trebbensee, Judy Schreifels, Ann Pryor and Mary Becker. The Mustangs went on to the MAIAW tournament that year and after beating Moorhead State, Bemidji State and Mankato State, lost to UN-Omaha in the Finals, 61-41. St. Cloud State, under Coach Glady Ziemer, and led by Diane Scherer, Sue Wahl and Jeanne Burnett, then went on to beat Mankato State and Bemidji State in the MAIAW D-II State Tournament. Bemidji State, meanwhile, was led by All Conference Guard Sherry Hill, who averaged 17 points per game during her illustrious career in Bemidji. It was the first title for the Beavers, who were on the verge of creating their own little mini-dynasty in 1986-87.

In 1981 it was all Southwest State University as head Coach KeKoster once again led her Mustangs to their second straight NSIC title. Led by Mary Becker, who averaged 14.6 points and 9.2 rebounds per game, and Judy Schreifels, who dished out 3.1 assists per game that season, SSU went on to advance to the MAIAW State Tourney & Region 6 Tournament. There, they beat UM-Duluth, 64-52, and St. Cloud State, 68-56, only to fall to Southwest Missouri State in the Finals, 65-58.

It was another trio of teams sharing the NSIC crown in 1982 as UM-Morris, Moorhead State and St. Cloud State all laid claim to the title with 10-4 records. UM-Morris, which won the 1979 Minn-Kota Conference championship, was adjusting just fine to life in the NSIC. Led by All-Conference Forward Cindy Lonneman, who went on to become the school's all-time leading scorer, with 1,949 career points, as well as the school's leading rebounder, with 1,447, and Darcy Rheingans, this would be the lone Cougars conference championship. Next was Moorhead State, who, under the tutelage of Coach Bobby Daniels, was led by All-American Karen Card, as well as All-NSIC stars Becky Ailts and Kelley Owen. Finally, the St. Cloud State Huskies were once again led by Diane Scherer that season, as she tallied 21.4 points per game and became the school's first-ever AIAW All-America selection. The Huskies then went on to edge Southwest State, 56-55, in the opening round of the MAIAW D-II Tournament, only to fall to Bemidji State, 67-59, in round two.

In 1983 it was St. Cloud State all by their lonesome. All-American Diane Scherer graduated that season as the Huskies all-time leading scorer with 2,349 points. The 31-4 Huskies then went on to win the North Central Regional playoff game over Texas A&I to advance to the NCAA Elite Eight. There, they were edged out by Central Missouri State by the final score of 65-63 to end their tremendous season.

The Huskies did it again in 1984, this time finishing with a 27-3 overall record. Led by All-Americans Ramona Rugloski, Dawn Anderson and Linda Nelson, they went on to beat South Dakota in the NCAA regions, 66-55, before falling to Dayton in the NCAA quarterfinals. It would be St. Cloud's last as a member of the NSIC as they defected to the North Central Conference following that season.

UMD's Sue Fiero

Mustang All-American

Lillie Brown is the only Mustang to take home All-American honors. Lillie was named NCAA II third team as a junior in 1995 and honorable mention as a senior in 1996.

SWSU's Lillie Brown

UMD's Karen & Dave Stromm

Northern Sun Conference Members:

1. Bemidji State University
2. Concordia-St. Paul University
3. Moorhead State University
4. Northern State University
5. Southwest State University
6. University of MN-Crookston
7. University of MN -Duluth
8. University of MN-Morris
9. Wayne State College
10. Winona State University

Year-by-Year Champs

1980	Southwest State
	St. Cloud State
	Bemidji State
1981	Southwest State
1982	Minnesota-Morris
	Moorhead State
	St. Cloud State
1983	St. Cloud State
1984	St. Cloud State
1985	Minnesota-Duluth
	Moorhead State
1986	Bemidji State
1987	Bemidji State
1988	Northern State
1989	Minnesota-Duluth
1990	Minnesota-Duluth
1991	Minnesota-Duluth
1992	Northern State
1993	Minnesota-Duluth
1994	Northern State
1995	Minnesota-Duluth
	Northern State
1996	Minnesota-Duluth
1997	Northern State
1998	Northern State
	Minnesota-Duluth
1999	Minnesota-Duluth
2000	Minnesota-Duluth
2001	Southwest State

All-Time Titles

	No.	Last
UM-Duluth	10	2000
Northern State	6	1998
St. Cloud State	4	1984
Bemidji State	3	1987
Southwest State	3	2001
MSU Moorhead	2	1985
UM-Morris	1	1982

UMD's Stacy Nelson

The 1985 campaign saw both UM-Duluth and Moorhead State share the NSIC title with identical 7-3 records. The UM-Duluth Bulldogs, under first-year coach Karen Stromme, went 13-12 overall that season en route to capturing its first conference crown.

The Lady Bulldogs were led by a trio of All-NSIC forwards in Chris Beal, Sarah Halsey and Amy Jaeger, who led the bunch with 11.3 points and 9.7 rebounds per game. Meanwhile, the Moorhead State Dragons were led by 1,000-point club member Karen Card, as well as All-NSIC players Deb Meyer and Krista Rolland. It was the second conference championship in just four seasons for the Lady Dragons.

In 1986 Bemidji State re-entered the mix and kept it going for two straight NSIC championships. Several Beaver players emerged as stars during this era of Bemidji dominance. Leading the way were Laurie Peterson and Kim Babula, a pair of All-Conference picks who teamed up to created one of the league's most powerful offensive attacks. Also helping out was Kris DeMaris, Mona Muelken, Jill Haverly and Sonia Stehr, who each made major contributions throughout the two-year reign. The Beavers went on to make a couple of decent post-season appearances in those two seasons, and built the foundation for one of the NSIC's top programs.

Following Northern State's conference win in 1988, UM-Duluth officially became a dynasty when they took the next three straight NSIC titles from 1989-91. Karen Stromme's Lady Bulldogs went 26-6, 24-7 and 26-6 over that three year span, taking no prisoners along the way. Also included in the streak were three successive appearances in the NAIA National Tournament. In 1989 the Dogs beat Moorhead State in the opening round of the NIAI District 13 Midwest Regional Playoffs, 87-50, followed by Bemidji State, 81-68, and then UW-Plattesville, 101-88, in the Bi-District Finals. From there they advanced to the NAIA National Tourney, where, after beating Wayland Baptist (TX), 72-70 in overtime, they lost to Arkansas Tech in the second round, 65-63. (The 1989 Bulldogs also won a school record 15 games at home!)

In 1990 UMD beat Winona State, 71-65, in the first round, followed by Southwest State, 81-75, and then Cardinal Stritch (WI), 62-49, in the Bi-District Finals to make it two in a row. Then, it was back to the NAIA National Tourney, where this time they lost to Simon Fraser (BC) in the first round, 79-56. In 1991 UM-Duluth opened up the post-season by beating St. Scholastica, 57-47, followed by Bemidji State, 82-68, to advance yet again to the NAIA National Tourney. There, after beating St. Joseph's (ME), 82-66, in round one, they lost a tough one to Wayland Baptist (TX), 58-51, to round out the season. The Dogs were led by several big-time hoops stars during this reign of terror, including a trio of All-NSIC first-teamers. Among them were three-time All-American Center Dina Kangas, the school's all-time leading scorer with 2,810 career points; Kelli Ritzer, who ranks No. 2 on that same list with 1,887 career points; and Denise Holm, UMD's all-time assists leader.

Northern State added their second conference title in 1992, only to see Minnesota-Duluth jump right back into the fold by winning their fourth championship in five years. The Dogs went 11-1 in conference play en route to an impressive 22-8 overall record which brought them deep into the post-season. Leading the charge this time for Duluth were Center Julie Coughlin and Forward Amy Erickson, both All-NSIC first-team selections. In the play-offs that year UMD beat Winona State in the opening round of the NAIA tourney, 71-42, followed by Moorhead State in round two, 70-66, to advance to the NAIA National Tourney in Jackson (TN). There, the Dogs beat Carson-Newman (TN) in round one, 62-49, but lost in the semi's to Southern Nazarene (OK), 72-61.

It was Northern State yet again in 1994, to make it three titles in seven years for the Wolves of Aberdeen, South Dakota. They would share the title again that next season as well with UM-Duluth, each finishing with identical 11-1 conference marks. That year the Bulldogs, who were led by a trio of All-Conference stars in Guards Sara Belanger and Stacy Sievers, and Center Jodi Lerino, went 20-8 overall and this time instead of advancing on to the NAIA Nationals in the post-season, went on to the NCAA Division II Playoffs in Greeley (CO). That's because that year the NSIC received full membership in the National Collegiate Athletic Association (NCAA). There, the Bulldogs beat Northern Colorado, in the first round by the final score of 77-72. Next up was North Dakota State, and this time, their luck ran out as NDSU spanked the Dogs, 98-61, to round out their season.

UMD would rebound to take yet another conference crown in 1996 though, finishing this time with an undefeated 12-0 conference mark and 23-5 overall. Once again, the team, this time led by Christy Roberts and Sadie Suomala, both All-NSIC picks, headed back to the post-season. There, in the NCAA D-II Playoffs, the Dogs beat Northern Colorado in round one, 65-60, only to lose again to North Dakota State in the semis, 61-50.

Northern State added their fifth title in 1998, sharing it yet again with you know who, UM-Duluth, of course, as each finished with 10-2 records. These two teams had developed quite a rivalry at this point, which was helping the conference to establish its competitive identity. For the 21-7 Bulldogs, however, who were led this time around by the NSIC Player of the Year, Stacy Nelson, it was another great season. They missed the post-season that year, but were poised to get back in 1999. And that was exactly what they did. In fact, they didn't stop there, and just kept on winning until they had three in a row through the 2000 season. In 1999 the Lady Dogs, led by the now two-time NSIC Player of the Year, Stacy Nelson, got back to the post-season. This time, however, they edged Nebraska-Kearney in the first round of the NCAA D-II Playoffs, 66-65, in overtime. But, like in years past, they just couldn't get past NDSU in round two as they lost that one, 61-50, to end another tremendous season. The Lady Bulldogs

Bemidji's Jen Ohme

came back strong in 2000 though. Led by the All-Conference duo of Forward Sue Fiero and Center Kate Madrinich, UMD won an amazing 25 games en route to another post-season run in the NCAA's, this time held in Fargo. There, they got past Northern State in the opener, 82-67, only to lose to their old nemesis, NDSU, 77-72. For Coach Stromme, a Duluth Central High School grad who later starred at St. Olaf College, it was official — she was now the NSIC's top coach — bar none. (By the way, the Dogs finally beat NDSU, 81-73, in the 2000 playoffs!)

In 2001 Southwest State concluded their long climb back to the top of the conference standings, despite losing to UMD, 53-49, in the NSIC Tournament championship game at Concordia University's Gangelhoff Center. The team ultimately lost to St. Cloud State in first round of the NCAA II Regional Tournament, but still had a great season. After posting a 25-5 record, the Mustangs won the program's third conference championship and first since 1981 en route to earning its first ever Top 25 national ranking. Senior Forward Andrea Schreier was named the NSIC Player of the Year, while SSU head coach Kelly Kruger was named as the NSIC Coach of the Year for the second straight season.

In 2002 Winona State and the city of Rochester will again shine as they serve as the hosts for the NCAA Division II Women's Elite Eight Basketball Championships. Some 48 teams from around the country will take part in eight regional tournaments, and the winners of the regional events will converge on Rochester's Mayo Civic Center for the national championship.

UMD's Kelly Ritzer

The Evolution of the Women's Pro Game

Believe it or not, women's pro basketball's roots can be traced back for several decades in Minnesota. Several major events in the world of women's equality helped to lead the way for this. The first, which came in 1964, was the Equal Pay Act, and the other was the formation of Title VII of the Civil Rights Act, which greatly expanded the rights of women in America. By 1968 the National Organization of Women (NOW) was lobbying for an Equal Rights Amendment and before long women everywhere were burning bras in symbolic gestures of gender equity — jump-starting the Women's Liberation Movement. In addition, the American Medical Association, which had previously cautioned against strenuous competition for girls, began endorsing vigorous physical activity in the form of sports. Physical fitness, which was emphasized by President Kennedy, was also being boosted within schools and varsity sports were finally emerging for girls at the high school levels as well.

Pat Montgomery & Marie Kocurek

Then, with the advent of Title IX legislation in the early 1970s, women everywhere now had the chance to play big-time college basketball. With those opportunities came a whole crop of annual graduates who now wanted to play the game after their collegiate careers. For years the only outlet for these women was to go overseas, to Europe, where women's pro basketball was emerging as a legitimate entity. By 1976, however, women's basketball had made its Olympic debut and two years later the pro game found its way to America when the eight-team Women's Professional Basketball League (WPBL) was formed. All of these factors played roles in the explosion of women's sports, and basketball was on the front-burner ready to take off.

Before long many of these newly empowered women began to take charge of their destinies and decided that the time was right for there to be a pro league of their own. The first wave of superstars to arrive on the scene included: Ann Meyers, Nancy Lieberman-Cline, Lynette Woodard, Molly Bolin, Carol Blazejowski and Lusia Harris, who had all attracted national attention at the collegeiate level. Some even began to cross over the lines into the world of men's pro hoops — as was the case in 1979, when Ann Meyers was invited to the NBA's Indiana Pacers training camp.

In 1982 Cheryl Miller, the sister of Indiana Pacers All-Star Reggie, arrived at USC. Miller, the first basket-ball player—male or female—to be a four-time high school All-American, went on to become the only three-time winner of the Naismith Award, given annualy to the best women's collegiate player in the country. Two years later Miller led the U.S. Olympic women's team to its first gold medal in Los Angeles — an event which truly ignited the game for the ladies on their own home turf.

The captain of that team was four-time All-American University of Kansas star, Lynette Woodard, who was nothing short of amazing. A year after winning the gold medal, Woodard became the first woman to play for the famed Harlem Globetrotters — an event which signalled a major breakthrough for women's hoops.

Then, in 1986 Nancy Lieberman-Cline, herself a collegiate star with Old Dominion University, played for the USBL's Springfield Fame and became the first woman to play in a professional men's league. She would later go on to play opposite Woodard as a member of the Washington Generals, the fictitous nemesis of the Globetrotters.

In 1988 Team USA won their second gold medal at the Seoul Olympics, and in 1992 the Americans were upset in the semis leaving them with a bronze medal at the Barcelona Olympics. They

Coach Terry Kunze

Donna Wilson

rebounded in 1996, however, to recapture the gold medal at the Centennial Olympics in Atlanta, and then followed that up with yet another gold at the 2000 Summer Games in Sydney. Incredibly, Teresa Edwards was a member of all of those teams, competing in her fifth Olympics that year — truly carrying the torch for women's basketball.

Then, just over a century after the first women's game, the sport grabbed the spotlight when the University of Connecticut Huskies, led by their "All-American-All American" star, Rebecca Lobo, went 35-0 en route to winning the 1995 national championship. Husky-mania spread like wildfire and before anyone knew it, women's basket-ball was suddenly cool. Fans, men and women alike, started to tune in to watch it on ESPN, and before long rumors spread that the NBA might start a pro league for women. The result was actually for formation of two rival leagues: the American Basketball League (ABL), which opened shop in 1996, and the WNBA, which opened a year later. Of course, the ABL would soon go broke, leaving the WNBA to rule the roost. Today, the WNBA operates a franchise in Minnesota called the Lynx, which, coincidentally, is not Minnesota's first pro team. Here's the deal:

Before we get into the Lynx, let's go back to Minnesota's first professional women's team, the Fillies, who played for three seasons in the upstart Women's Professional Basketball League. From 1978-79 to 1980-81 the WPBL gave countless women from around the world an opportunity to play the game professionally. Sure, they didn't make a lot of money, but they were doing what they loved and serving as real pioneers for countless generations of future lady hoopsters.

The WPBL was launched on October 11, 1977, when Bill Byrne and Dave Almstead decided to create a new pro women's league. After a lengthy investigation of potential markets, which included 750 applications for franchises, available talent and logistics, the league selected eight teams: Minnesota, Iowa, New Jersey, Milwaukee, Chicago, Dayton, New York and Houston.

The league's first annual draft was held on July 18, 1978 at the Essex House Hotel in New York City. Franchise holders selected 80 of the top college seniors and free agents, including All Americans and Olympians from around the world. Try-out camps followed with rosters being finalized for the opening tip off on December 9, 1978, with the Milwaukee Does hosting the Chicago Hustle before an audience of 8,000 enthusiastic fans.

Minnesota's contingent, the Fillies, was owned by local businessman, Gordon Nevers, who served as the Vice-President & General Manager of Werness Brothers Funeral Chapels. Nevers also played professional baseball for three years in the Kansas City Athletics (now Oakland) system following his collegiate career at the University of Missouri. A passionate fan and long-time supporter of the University of Minnesota Men's Basketball program, Nevers also worked for a local sports management and promotion consulting corporation prior to his purchasing the WPBL franchise.

Led by No. 1 draft pick Center Katrina Owens, from Fayetteville State University, the Fillies went 17-17 that first year, providing Minnesota fans with a high calibre of talent. Marie Kocurek was the big star, being named to the All Pro Team. The freshman club, which played its games at the Minneapolis Auditorium, wasn't without its share of growing pains though, as it went through no less than four coaches that first season. The Houston Angels won the inaugural WPBL championship.

The team had a solid core of players to begin the 1979-80 season, but they needed a big-time disciplined coach to lead them. With that, Nevers went out and hired Terry Kunze. Kunze, who led the Duluth Central Trojans to the 1961 state high school championship, went on to play at the University of Minnesota. From there he played for a short period of time with the St. Louis Hawks of the NBA, and later with the now defunct Minnesota Muskies of the ABA. Then, after three years of serving as an assistant coach at the University of Minnesota and a year at East Carolina, Kunze came home again to coach the upstart Fillies.

The league expanded, perhaps too aggressively, that next year with several colorful new teams joining the mix, including: the California Dreams, Dallas Diamonds, New Orleans Pride, Philadelphia Fox, San Francisco Pioneers and Washington D.C. Metros. Realignment was then necessary shortly in to that second season due to financial difficulties suffered by Philadelphia and Washington DC.

Kunze's Fillies hit the hardcourt that year with some solid leadership. The team was led by leading scorer Marie Kocurek, Guard Donna Wilson, Scooter DeLorme and Kathy DeBoer. In addition, the team got a lot of productivity from draft choices Pat Montgomery and Janet Timperman. They also acquired Deb Mason from New York and Denise Sharps from Chicago, giving the club a new guard and small forward combination that was needed to make a playoff run.

The team fared well in 1979-80, ultimately finishing the regular season with a 22-12 record — good for second place in the Midwest Division. With that, the Fillies qualified for the playoffs, where they defeated the New Orleans Pride at Williams Arena in the best-of-three quarterfinal series. Then, in the semifinals, the rival Iowa Comets came to town. The Fillies, full of talent and hustle, won Game One with ease, 108-87. Iowa took the next two games, however, 128-111 and 95-92, ending the team's bid for the championship. The New York Stars finally captured the title. For Minnesota though, there was some good news. Pat Montgomery and Marie Kocurek were both named to the All Star team and Kocurek was named for the second year to the All Pro Team.

Nessie Harris & Scooter DeLorme

Four teams folded that next year though, including New York, Houston, Iowa and Milwaukee, while California moved to Omaha, and New England got an expansion franchise. Through all of that though, the Fillies hit the courts in search of that first title. Led by five-foot-four fireball, Marie "Scooter" DeLorme, who signed a one-year contract as a player and assistant coach, the Fillies looked good for their third season.

"This is probably the most challenging thing I've ever done," said DeLorme.

"When you're a player, you always want to play But it was an opportunity I couldn't turn down. And I want to be in a capacity to best help the Fillies."

DeLorme dished out a team-high 157 assists and averaged 10.7 points per game that year, and also gave the Fillies a much-needed voice on the bench. The Fillies finished strong in the Central Division that season, only to find out that the league would fold shortly thereafter. It was a nice run, but travel costs and low attendance finally did in the start-up league in the end.

Our state's next professional team were the the Minnesota Stars, which played in the newly formed Women's Basketball Association in 1995. The WBA, which began in 1993 with eight clubs, was originally started as a summer league for elite women's players. The WBA played a 15-game schedule and achieved a moderate level of success, with franchise located primarily throughout the Midwest.

The Stars finished with a 5-10 record in 1995, good for third place in the WBA's American Conference — which also featured the Chicago Twisters, Nebraska Express and Oklahoma Flames. The Stars folded after just one season though, but were replaced two years later by the Minnesota Heat, which joined the WBA in 1997. It was a short-lived existence, however, as the league disbanded later that year. From there, Minnesota was blessed with the creation of the WNBA. Here's that story:

The Minnesota Lynx

The WNBA, a Brief History

While there have been several start-up women's basketball leagues that have come and gone over the past couple of decades, there is no question that the most successful of these incarnations has been the Women's National Basketball Association, or WNBA. The impetus behind it came as a result of the U.S. women's dream team winning the gold medal at the 1996 Atlanta Olympics. The league, which was to be owned and operated by the NBA, was launched that next year with eight teams — each of which was an affiliate of an existing NBA franchise. They included: The Charlotte Sting, Cleveland Rockers, Houston Comets and New York Liberty in the Eastern Conference and the Los Angeles Sparks, Phoenix Mercury, Sacramento Monarchs and Utah Starzz in the Western Conference.

The league also decided to play its games in the summer, when the sports calendar was less crowded, and also to avoid a direct confrontation with its NBA parent. That move not only allowed the teams to play in the same large arenas used by NBA teams, but also afforded them the opportunity to have their games televised in prime time on a consistent basis by a trio of networks: NBC, ESPN and Lifetime. (Incredibly, more than 50 million viewers in over 25 countries and in 11 languages tuned in to watch that first year.) With that, the league began to formalize the logistics of filling up its rosters and getting on the business of playing basketball. The first stars to sign on were, of course, the Olympians.

That October of 1996, Sheryl Swoopes, Rebecca Lobo, Ruthie Bolton-Holifield, Lisa Leslie and Cynthia Cooper all joined teams, and were joined shortly thereafter by a frenzy of women from around the globe who came out to show their stuff. To ensure balance, however, 16 of the world's best players were assigned to teams (regional interests were considered in this in order to create an instant fan-base), and a draft was then held in February of 1997 to fill out the remaining rosters.

Lennox, Smith & Van Gorp

The New York Liberty beat the Los Angeles Sparks, 67-57, in the WNBA's first-ever game on June 21, 1997, before a crowd of 14,284 in the Great Western Forum. It was the beginning of something wonderful in the world of women's sports. Little girls from coast-to-coast were coming out in droves to see their new heroes and as a result, the league's attendance averaged nearly 10,000 fans during that first season. That next year both the Detroit Shock and Washington Mystics joined the WNBA, and in 1999 the Minnesota Lynx and Orlando Miracle were added. In 2000 the league expanded to 16 teams, adding the Indiana Fever, Miami Sol, Portland Fire and Seattle Storm.

Now, the WNBA was not without its fare share of healthy competition right out of the gates. That's because another rival league also opened up shop that same inaugural season, the American Basketball League. The ABL, however, chose to play its games during the winter, in the midst of all the other competition. At first, the two league's co-existed peacefully, with each capturing its own niche in separate markets throughout the country. But eventually, the ABL, without its strong affiliation with the NBA, couldn't make it financially and folded.

The result was an even better WNBA, with more talent and exclusive market-share of the entire world of women's professional basketball. Before long, even the best Europeans were migrating across the pond to suit up with America's best. In addition, it was great to see college basketball

Minnesota Lynx All-Time Leading Scorers

2001 Leading Scorers

	Avg.
1. Katie Smith	23.1
2. Svetlana Abrosimova	13.2
3. Betty Lennox	11.0
4. Erin Buescher	5.7
5. Lynn Pride	5.3

2000 Leading Scorers

	Avg.
1. Katie Smith	20.2
2. Betty Lennox	16.9
3. Kristin Folkl	7.6
4. Grace Daley	5.8
5. Andrea Lloyd Curry	5.4

1999 Leading Scorers

	Avg.
1. Brandy Reed	16.1
2. Tonya Edwards	14.8
3. Katie Smith	11.7
4. Andrea Lloyd Curry	6.7
5. Kristin Folkl	4.9

Katie Smith

players finally having an opportunity to make a career in professional basketball. The pay wasn't even close to what the men were making, but it did allow them to play hoops for a living and open the door for other women's pro sports as well.

(In addition to receiving health-care, shared autos and housing, WNBA players average between $35,000 and $55,000 per season in salary... or about roughly what Timberwolves' star Kevin Garnett makes while playing in one quarter of one game! Some players are making as little as $28,000 in salary for the three-month-long season, while superstars such as Rebecca Lobo, with marketing deals, can earn up to $200,000.)

The big story early on in the WNBA was the absolute domination of one team, the Houston Comets. Led by the league's first MVP, Cynthia Cooper, as well as Sheryl Swoopes, the first female player to have her own line of Nike Shoes, the Comets won the first four WNBA championships. It wasn't until 2001 that another team could break through, as the Los Angeles Sparks, behind their star, Lisa Leslie, finally captured the league crown by sweeping the Charlotte Sting in the Finals.

From the get-go the league wanted to be different and build its own identity. So, they created their own unique orange and white striped ball, which was one inch smaller than the NBA's regulation ball. The league also instituted a 30-second shot-clock, two 20-minute halves, and also a three-point-line which measured 19-feet, nine-inches — all moves intended to make the ladies' game both exciting and fan-friendly.

In addition, the league embraced women's issues and focused its community outreach initiatives primarily towards breast cancer research and also to encourage young girls to lead physically active lifestyles while practicing good sportsmanship. All of these moves helped to grow the league into a legitimate sports power. Since its inception several millions of fans have seen games in person and countless millions more have tuned in on TV to catch the action. With their now-infamous motto: "We Got Game," the WNBA is truly "fan-tastic."

The Minnesota Lynx

When the WNBA decided to expand its then eight-team league in 1998, Minnesota was an obvious choice. Women's basketball has achieved a great deal of success through the years and has only grown in popularity since the inception of Title IX, at the collegiate level, and with gender-equity issues, at the high school level — both of which have provided many more opportunities for young girls in the world of sports. As a result, a very knowledgeable and loyal fan-base was already in place for the upstart league's decision to come to the Land of 10,000 Lakes. They would be affiliated with the NBA's Minnesota Timberwolves, and share much of the same infrastructure with regards to marketing and public relations front-office work. They also shared the same blue, silver and green team colors as the Timberwolves, making them an obvious brother-sister partnership.

"This is a great honor for Minnesota and the Twin Cities," said Timberwolves Owner Glen Taylor. "We are excited to be one of the newest additions to the very successful WNBA. Basketball fans throughout the Upper Midwest will get a chance to see some of the greatest female athletes in the world and experience one of the fastest growing professional sports."

Maylana Martin

So, after unveiling their new mascot and logo, the Lynx then secured the league-mandated 5,000 season-ticket deposits required for admission. With that, the team announced the signing of their first coach and GM, Brian Agler, who had just led the now-defunct Columbus Quest to a pair of ABL championships. Agler, who had compiled an impressive 67-17 record with Columbus, then brought in a pair of very competent assistants in Kelly Kramer, an assistant with the Quest, as well as Heidi VanDerveer, who was the former head coach of the WNBA's Sacramento Monarchs.

The new franchise then also signed its first player, Forward Kristin Folkl from Stanford University. From there they rounded out their roster by adding Brandy Reed (Phoenix Mercury), Kim Williams (Utah Starzz), Octavia Blue (Los Angeles Sparks) and Adia Barnes (Sacramento Monarchs) through the 1999 Expansion Draft, while also signing Tonya Edwards (Columbus Quest), Trisha Fallon (WNBL, Australia) Andrea Lloyd (Columbus Quest), Sonja Tate (Columbus Quest) and Angie Potthoff (Columbus Quest), through the annual collegiate draft. In addition, the WNBA also allocated former Columbus Quest Forward Katie Smith to the team — giving them one of the league's biggest stars right out of the gates.

Kate Paye

After that they held open tryouts at Concordia University, where more than 180 women participated — approximately 70% from out of state. A few reserves were picked up from there, but no real big names. With that, the team opened training camp and set out to hit the hardcourt as members of the six-team Western Conference, which included Houston, Los Angeles, Phoenix, Sacramento and Utah.

On June 4th, 1999, the team played its first exhibition game in Mankato, losing to Orlando, 80-76, but came back to win its regular season opener a week later with a 68-51 victory over the Detroit Shock at Target Center. More than 12,100 fans showed up to watch Tonya Edwards score the franchise's first-ever points en route to the thrilling victory. They went on to beat Utah just a few nights later to become the first expansion team in WNBA history to start the season 2-0. That came to an abrupt end, however, when the two-time defending WNBA Champion Houston Comets came to town on Jane 19th. In a battle of the only two unbeatens, the Lynx fell short, losing 69-55 for their first loss of the season.

The season had its shares of ups and downs, but overall it was respectable. Along the way

Minnesota had several highlights, including setting a WNBA record for most three-point field goals made in a game when they connected on 14 three's against the Utah Storm on June 26th. Another was the team's three-game winning streak in mid-July which featured wins over New York, Sacramento and Charlotte. Soon after they produced an impressive 17-point win over Phoenix at home to bring its Target Center record back to the .500 mark. They dropped their next four though and ended their regular season home schedule with a three-point overtime loss to Orlando. They rebounded though to close their inaugural season with a win at Washington the very next day, ending a six-game road losing streak. The team finished at 15-17, and out of the post-season.

Brandy Reed paced the team with 16.1 ppg, while Tonya Edwards added 14.8 and Katie Smith chipped in with 11.7. Other key members of the team included Andrea Lloyd Curry, who, in addition to averaging nearly seven points per game, emerged as one of the team's biggest fan-favorites, and Kristin Folkl, who scored in double-figures in four of Minnesota's last five games.

During that off-season the Lynx did some wheeling and dealing. In addition to losing Angela Aycock and Charmin Smith, who were allocated to Portland in the Expansion Draft, the team traded Forward Brandy Reed to Phoenix for a first round pick in the 2000 draft. They also traded Center Marlies Askamp to Miami for several draft picks as well. Then, in the 2000 WNBA Annual Draft, the Lynx acquired: Grace Daley (Tulane), Betty Lennox (Louisiana Tech), Maylana Martin (UCLA), Maria Brumfield (Rice), Keitha Dickerson (Texas Tech), Phylesha Whaley (Oklahoma), Jana Lichnerova (St. Joseph's) and Shanele Stires (Columbus Quest).

Lynn Pride

Training camp opened that season on May 3rd as the team kicked off its second season. Leading the way were rookie Guard Betty Lennox and Forward Katie Smith, who, after averaging nearly 23 points per game, was named as the WNBA's Player of the Week for games played June 12-18. That July both Smith and Lennox were selected to play in the 2000 WNBA All-Star Game at America West Arena in Phoenix. Later that month, Smith became the WNBA's single-season record-holder for three-pointers. (She would finish with 88 trés on the season, while averaging 20.2 overall points per game as well.) The team played well, but once again finished out of the playoff hunt with a modest 15-17 record. One bright spot was the play of Lennox, who was named as the 2000 WNBA Rookie of the Year after leading all first-timers with nearly seven points per game.

Svetlana Abrosimova

That off-season the Lynx selected five players in the 2001 WNBA Draft: Svetlana Abrosimova (Connecticut), Erin Buescher (Master's College), Janell Burse (Tulane) Tombi Bell (Florida) and Minnesota's very own Megan Taylor, the state's all-time leading scorer from Roseau (Iowa State).

(On a separate but related note, it is important to acknowledge that Rochester natives and identical twins Kelly and Coco Miller, who starred for the University of Georgia, were both drafted in the first round as well. Kelly was taken No. 2 overall by the Charlotte Sting, while Coco was the No. 9 overall selection of the Washington Mystics. The Millers, who led Rochester Mayo to a pair of state championships in the late 1990s, would play on different teams for the first time ever. In the world of basketball, these two are the real "Minnesota Twins!")

The Lynx's third training camp opened on May 2nd, with the team feeling more optimistic than ever. The season got underway with Katie Smith emerging as a real superstar in the world of women's basketball. She tore it up and put Lynx basketball on the map, big-time. On June 18th of that season Smith scored a career and franchise-record 40 points as the Lynx beat the Detroit Shock, 71-63. Smith and Houston Comets All-Star Cynthia Cooper were now the only players in league history to score 40 or more points in a WNBA game. Then, on July 9th, she scored 45 points in a 100-95 loss to the Los Angeles Sparks, breaking the league's single-game scoring record. Finally, on August 11th, the agile Forward scored 22 points in a 65-51 win over the Seattle Storm to break the WNBA's single-season scoring record. The WNBA's top scorer in 2001, with 23.1 ppg, Smith also set league records in minutes played and free throws.

Despite the tremendous efforts of Smith, Brian Agler's Lynx struggled the entire season. After finishing 15-17 in each of their first two seasons, they were a disappointing 12-20 in 2001. Agler assembled a team heavy on promise but low on talent and experience. He counted heavily on Smith and Lennox, who performed well, but what he didn't get was tremendous productivity from everyone else. Injuries had taken their toll. Lennox went down early in the season with a bum hip and missed 20 games; Point Guard Kristi Harrower, who spent the 2000 season training with the Australian national team, suffered an early season-ending knee injury; and Whiting-Raymond, who had given birth in March, faded early on. With that, the team struggled and even went through 14 different starting lineups. Opponents double-and triple-teamed Smith, and shut down the team's offense — which shot a league-worst 37% and committed 15.8 turnovers a game.

There were some bright spots though, including the progress of six-foot-two rookie Center Svetlana Abrosimova, the two-time Connecticut All-American from Russia, who showed great promise by averaging 13.3 points per game and finished with a team-record six double-doubles. Who knows? With Smith, Lennox and Abrosimova providing a potential "Big Three Combo," the Lynx could be a playoff caliber team in the future. They have a decent fan-base, although it has shrunk steadily through the years, and they are providing tremendous sports entertainment for families everywhere. Little girls have real sports role models now that are good people, and that is a wonderful thing.

Betty Lennox

As we look to the future of women's professional basketball, however, there are some genuine concerns about the its future. While the Lynx can feel good about providing a great product to countless girls throughout the Gopher State, they are also scrambling to hold on to their season ticket base in an already overcrowded and fickle Twin Cities sports marketplace. The economics of the league are coming into question, and that has some concerned. Attendance has steadily dipped for the Lynx, having gone from averaging over 10,000 fans per game in 1998 to less than 5,000 in 2001. In an effort to increase ticket sales, the team has aggressively sought out corporate sponsorship and even enlisted its players to help market the team. At least they've got the backing of their owner though, who is committed to making it work.

"Operating the Lynx is the right thing to do in this market," said Team Owner Glen Taylor, who's Wolves have signed a long-term deal with the NBA to operate the Lynx through 2008. "But our hope is that if we stick with this, that it will be a solid business deal. Not this year or next year, but in the long haul."

Some of the reasons for the league's decline include good competition. Not from other summer basketball leagues, but from the new women's pro soccer league, the Women's United Soccer Association. Like the women's Olympic gold medal basketball run of 98', women's soccer also enjoyed a revival of sorts following its amazing World Cup victory. Each got huge television ratings and each is still hoping to capitalize on those events. Whether or not they can parlay that into long-term success still remains to be seen on both sides.

For whatever the reason, the league is at a cross-roads. But with solid management and a good product, this thing can work. It has already proven most of the critics wrong and that is tremendous for women's basketball. In the end though, it's just like what Oakland Raiders' Owner Al Davis said, "Just win baby." If they win, then all of their grass-roots marketing tactics and advertising dollars won't really matter, because the fans will come out to watch a winner. They have embraced Minnesota, giving time and respect to women's causes far and wide, and have reached out to everyone from the Girl Scouts to the Twin Cities lesbian community. Their message is positive, their product is great, and their people are good. For that we should all go out and support these ladies. They are the real-deal.

The Girls State Tourney

While Minnesota's Girls State High School Basketball Tournament officially began in 1975, our ladies' prep hoop history goes back much, much further. In fact, it goes back nearly 100 years, to 1903, when records show that girls' basketball was being played between high schools throughout the state. Between 1903-1942 girls basketball was a statewide program in Minnesota which featured more than 200 teams. The genesis of this wonderful game is an amazing one to say the least. Let's take a trip down memory lane, shall we?

The game of basketball, which was invented by Dr. James Naismith in 1891, was still a relatively new game by the turn of the century across America. In Minnesota, however, the game had already been played by the boys for several years. The ladies were no exception either as the Lady Gophers as well as the ladies from Carleton were playing as early as 1893. By 1900 many of those teams opponents were local high school squads, who scrimmaged the college gals on occasion. From those humble beginnings the prep game so began in the Land of 10,000 Lakes, and, although there have been a few disruptions along the way, it has been a real wild ride ever since.

The game as we know it today was nothing like it was back in the day. Back then the rules were sketchy at best and most of the teams played with some variations of their own local "house" rules. Some of the teams had five players and played the full-court game, while others played a variety of multiple-court games. There were also variances with regards to how many players would play against one another, as well as the number of dribbles a player could make before having to pass the ball. (Usually there were six players per team on the court — three on defense and three on offense, and they never crossed the centerline. Additionally, the rules of the day allowed the players no more than three dribbles before they had to pass.)

The game itself was also somewhat controversial as well, as many thought that such a barbaric sport was not suitable for young "ladies" who might be too delicate physically and emotionally to play this rough-and-tumble game. Not to mention the fact that bloomers were considered scandalous and even distasteful attire for young ladies at this time in history. (Bloomers were long split skirts created so girls could ride bicycles — a relatively new invention at that time.)

Uniforms also changed greatly during the early years of the game. At first the ladies started out wearing formal "lady-like" wool bloomers and middies, which were World War I sailor-tops, but by the late 1920s teams began to change over to shorts and short-sleeved tops. The girls of this era often-times had to make their own uniforms, and as a result, they were very feminine and oftentimes included such accessories as decorative bows and ribbons. The knee-high socks always matched something, while the sneakers were usually black or white.

The game played on though, and with it came some great rivalries between girls basketball teams from neighboring communities. One such rivalry, according to historian Marian Johnson in her article: "Celebrating the roots of girls' interscholastic basketball in the early 1900s," was Jordan, Montgomery, New Prague and Belle Plaine — who played for district championships as early as 1928. Teams would travel to nearby towns by any means possible back then, including riding sleighs, bobsleds and even hay-wagons. But the most popular mode of transportation was the train, which, during the dead of the winter, was often a challenge to say the least.

These ladies were not tomboys though, but rather real-life pioneers. They suffered through all the adversity just for the opportunity to play the game and did it with far fewer advantages than that of the boys. Often, girls had to walk home after evening practices as far as three miles, in freezing temperatures and in the dark. They did it though, so that the women of today can simply play the game of basketball.

At away-games, the girls would often times stay overnight in the homes of their opponents. With that came many lasting friendships, however, many of which lasted for decades to come. Sometimes, banquets and dances, before and after the games, were held with great community involvement. Competitive conferences were soon created by the schools that resided along the same railroad lines, making the travel logistics more convenient for

An early team from the turn of the century

everybody.

The gymnasiums of the day were also quite an adventure. In fact, many of the girls' games weren't even played in gyms, rather in such locales as ball rooms, opera houses, lodges and even in church basements. Many times the ceilings were too low, and the floors were often riddled with cracks. Some of the venues were heated with a potbellied, wood-burning stove off in one corner, where spectators would have to stand by in order to protect a player from being burned if she got too close. The baskets were another story. Some were mounted on the walls, while others were hung by wires — either one made for some interesting bounces.

One story about what it was like can be found in the 1909 Grand Rapids High School yearbook: "It was with great impatience that we awaited the coming of the 6th day of February the date set for the great double game, boys and girls — to take place at Cass Lake. A jolly crowd, numbering about 20 in all started out from the depot. We were shown about the village during the afternoon, and were entertained at different homes for supper. The girls played first. The game was close, but we finished eight points to the

The 1913 Sauk Centre High School Squad

good. The boys' game followed ours immediately, and resulted in another decisive victory for the Rapids. After the game we were invited to "trip the Light Fantastic" to strains of sweet music. After the dance we returned to the high school, where a sumptuous banquet was prepared for us."

Another entry, this one from the 1923 Cloquet High School yearbook, tells of the travails of winter travel: "On a cold, bitter night, the basketball team went to Lincoln in a sleigh. It turned out to be a cold ride, but the girls score warmed us up. The score was 32 to 12 in favor of Cloquet. The teams also went to Carlton in a sleigh, and several other sleighs followed with the rooters. The last game of the season against Coleraine, and the teams traveled by train and over 700 people attended, the largest crowd ever assembled for a basketball game on the Range."

By the late 1930s World War II was in full gear and women of the day were being called upon to do their duty. As a result, the ladies prep game was left without many coaches and administrators. In addition, in 1939 the Minnesota State Education Department sent out a letter to all high school superintendents demanding that they stop sponsoring interscholastic sports competition for high school girls — especially basketball and swimming, which were viewed as "unlady-like" and "too strenuous." As a result, schools gradually began to drop their teams. Less than three dozen teams remained by this point, as most opted to terminate their programs. What ensued was a 30-year hiatus of the game, which did not again resume until the early 1970s. Over that time frame, the ladies did play on a intramural and recreational basis, but there was no official governing body to speak of. (Some programs sought sponsorship and guidance via the Girls' Athletic Association, but they were few and far between.)

The biggest casualty of that death-sentence might have been the ending of our state's greatest winning-streak, otherwise known as the "Grand Meadow Decade of Dominance." The first dominant prep team in state history was without question, Grand Meadow High School, which practiced as much as four times per week. So good was Grand Meadow that for 10 years, from 1929-1939, they never lost a single game. Never! They won 94 consecutive outings over that incredible span, racking up 3,634 points, while yielding just 1,138 — for an average score of nearly 39 to 12. In 1929 alone, Grand Meadow, which occasionally saw some of its girls score 40 or more points in a single game, outscored its 14 opponents by a total of 591-153, and pounded its competition along the way. Some of the more memorable games included a 68-8 dubbing of Lyle, a 51-6 pasting of Adams and a 52-8 shellacking of LeRoy. There's no telling just how far the streak would've grown to had the state not stepped in and terminated the sport with one fell swoop.

The Attire of 1920s

In 1969 the second era of girls' basketball officially began in Minnesota, when the Minnesota State High School League established girls' interscholastic athletics, thus opening the door for the development of a sports program on par with the longtime boys' athletics program. Over the next five years a seemingly special chapter of girls' basketball history was written. During this era, both girls' volleyball and girls' basketball teams became competitive and found themselves vying for both gymnasium space as well as respect.

No statewide season for either sport had been established, and as a result, some schools played girls' basketball in the fall while others played in the winter. Finally, in 1974, the Minnesota State High School League Board of Directors established a fall season for girls volleyball with the first state championships being conducted in November of that same year. The girls' basketball situation was a little more tricky, however, so the Board decided to conduct a one-time seasonal playoff — one for the 220 teams playing in the Fall and another for those playing in the Winter.

In that inaugural Fall playoff on Nov. 23, 1974, eight schools came together at St. Cloud State's Halenbeck Hall to do battle. There, Wadena advanced to the championship round with a decisive 43-14 quarterfinal victory over Roseau, followed by a closer 50-41 win over Litchfield. Meanwhile, in the other bracket, Glencoe advanced to the title game by beating Granada-Huntley in the quarterfinals, 76-51, followed by Kasson-Mantorville in the semifinals, 76-36. Nearly 2,500 fans then showed up to witness this first Minnesota girls' basketball Finals where Glencoe capped its perfect 21-0 season by spanking Wadena, 46-29.

Then, just three months later, on Feb. 22, 1975, eight more teams battled for the right to show up at Bloomington Kennedy High School to play in the Girls Winter

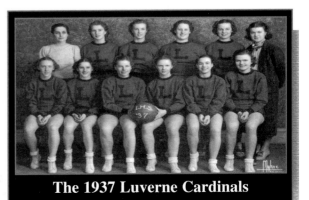
The 1937 Luverne Cardinals

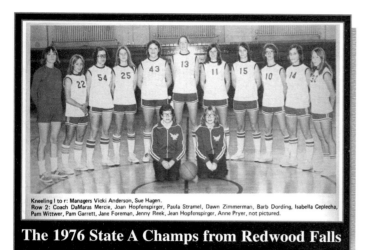

Kneeling l to r: Managers Vicki Anderson, Sue Hagen.
Row 2: Coach DaMaras Mercie, Joan Hopfenspirger, Paula Stramel, Dawn Zimmerman, Barb Dording, Isabella Ceplecha, Pam Wittwer, Pam Garrett, Jane Foreman, Jenny Reek, Jean Hopfenspirger, Anne Pryer, not pictured.

The 1976 State A Champs from Redwood Falls

Kneeling L to R: Michael Adams, Linda Roberts, (Co-capt.) Steve Studer (Coach), Teresa Tierney (Co-capt.), Davvie Mims. Standing L to R: Teri Weber (Manager), Kimberly Weber, Yolanda Bruce, Bon Lubben, Deb Krengel, Keylene Thompson, Rita Burch, Sue Smith, Mickey McNeil, Lisa Lissimore, Weller Johnson, Dolly Pugh (Chaperone). Not pictured: Gwen Crowe, Kim Miller, Diane Farrell, Georgetta Hawkins, Barb Strong.

The 1976 State AA Champs from Central

Row 1—L to R: Brenda Rudolph, Carmen Sundeen, Marianna VonRuden, Tina Rutten, Cindy Koste, Lisa Hagel. Row 2: Kim Salathe, Laura Rud, Janice Becker, Jenny Miller, Janet Karvonen, Mary Rutten. Row 3: Sally Patron-Manager, Carol Wilkowski-Assistant Coach, Kathy Lervold-Head Coach, LuAnne Tellers-Manager.

The 1977 State A Champs from NY Mills

Row 1—L to R: Dotti Piotrowski, Chris Engler, Suzanne Sienkiewicz, Karen Peterson, Anne Abicht. Row 2: Terri Wisdorf, Joyce Detlefsen, Sue Kavanaugh, Kris Haugen, Jane Abicht, Karin Orson. Row 3: Coach Judy Johnson, Patti Motzko, Kathy Hetterick, Laurie Callstrom, Kris Orson, Christa Meier, Amy McDermott, Donna Peterson, Ass't. Coach Harlan Eernisse.

The 1977 State AA Champs from Burnsville

Basketball Finals. This time more than 3,000 fans showed up to watch the Academy of the Holy Angels beat LeSueur for the state crown. The Academy of the Holy Angels kicked off the tourney with a 36-33 quarterfinal victory against Mayer Lutheran, followed by a close 38-36 win over Crookston in the semifinals. LeSueur, on the other hand, advanced to the Finals by beating Luverne in the quarterfinals, 62-43, followed by Rochester Lourdes, 37-33, in the semis. In the title game the Academy of the Holy Angels got a pair of clutch free-throws with just 43 seconds left in the game to take the thrilling 39-37 victory.

Following the conclusion of those winter playoffs, the Board voted unanimously to establish girls basketball as an official winter activity — becoming just the 10th sport designated as a MSHSL-sponsored sport for girls. With that, some 489 high school girls basketball teams from across the state prepared to do battle in district and sub-region playoffs. What followed was the first ever official Minnesota State Girls' Basketball Tournament that February 18-21, 1976, at the Met Center in Bloomington, where more than 10,000 fans showed up to watch St. Paul Central win the Class AA title and Redwood Falls take the Class A crown. Here's how it all went down:

1976: Class A: Redwood Falls vs. Glencoe

The 1st annual Class A State Tournament kicked off at the Met Center in Bloomington with eight teams vying for the right to be called state champion. In the end, however, Redwood Falls, which beat Rochester Lourdes, 55-42, the quarterfinals, and Southwest Minnesota Christian, 53-37, in the semifinals, went on to beat a very tough Glencoe team, 41-28, in the title clash.

1976: Class AA: St. Paul Central vs. Benilde-St. Margaret's

The AA tourney then saw St. Paul Central defeat the Wadena Indians, 42-34, in their first game, followed by a 43-36 win over Austin in the semis. From there the Minutemaids squared off with Benilde-St. Margaret's, which had topped Hill-Murray in the other semi, 41-29. In the Finals Central was tough. Led by a pair of future Gopher stars Linda Roberts and Lisa Lissimore, the Minutemaids edged the previously unbeaten Red Knights, 49-47, thanks to Krengel's last-second free-throw to ice the game.

"The state tournament provided an opportunity for people throughout the state to see a group of dedicated, respectable young women working together to achieve a common goal — not only on the court but in life," recalled Lisa Lissimore, now an associate director at the Minnesota State High School League.

1977: Class A: New York Mills vs. Mayer Lutheran

Led by Janet Karvonen, arguably the greatest women's basketball player ever to ever hail from Minnesota, New York Mills made it to the Finals by beating Buhl and Marshall-University in the quarters and semi's. There, they beat a very tough Mayer Lutheran squad, 40-39, to take the Class A crown. Coach Kathy Lervold's squad ended their exciting campaign with an outstanding 25-1 record.

1977: Class AA: Burnsville vs. St. Cloud Apollo

After beating both St. Paul Central and Benilde-St. Margaret's in the opening two rounds, Burnsville won the second Class AA title by defeating St. Cloud Apollo, 46-41. Coach Judy Johnson's winning Braves squad finished the season with an equally outstanding 25-1 record.

One of the highlights of the 1977 state tourney was the fact that for the first time ever, a portion of the tournament was carried live on local television. Its popularity was growing as evidenced by the fact that some 45,370 fans showed up to watch the four-day event, fully 11,163 more than the last year's tourney.

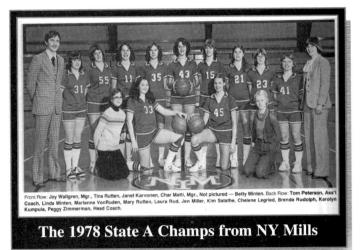

Front Row: Joy Wallgren, Mgr., Tina Rutten, Janet Karvonen, Char Matti, Mgr., Not pictured — Betty Minten. Back Row: Tom Peterson, Ass't Coach, Linda Minten, Marianne VonRuden, Mary Rutten, Laura Rud, Jen Miller, Kim Salathe, Chelene Legried, Brenda Rudolph, Karolyn Kumpula, Peggy Zimmerman, Head Coach.

The 1978 State A Champs from NY Mills

1978: Class A: New York Mills vs. Redwood Falls

New York Mills successfully defended its Class A championship in the third annual MSHSL State Girls' Basketball Tournament held at the St. Paul Civic Center and Met Center.

After an unbelievable 22-1 regular season record, the defending champions from "the Mills" went on to beat the Perham Yellowjackets, 78-58, at the Sauk Centre gym to win the Region 6A title. In that game, Karvonen, then a sophomore, scored 51 points, pulled down 16 rebounds, and was totally unstoppable. Next, it was off to the St. Paul Civic Center and the State High School Tournament for the Eagles, where they took on the Fertile-Beltrami Falcons in the first round. Behind Janet's 31 points, New York Mills crushed Fertile-Beltrami, 80-33.

Next up were the Minnesota Lake Lakers, and the Eagles waltzed to a 59-40 victory behind Janet Karvonen's 21 points. At 6:43 of the first period, she made history when she hit a soft 15-footer to pass Morton's Mary Beth Bidinger and take over the all-time girls scoring record with 1,474 points. She was averaging around 30-points per game and she was only 15-years-old! It was back to the Finals for the Eagles, where they would meet the undefeated Redwood Falls Cardinals, who had won the title two years earlier.

The Cards jumped out to a 14-9 lead after the first period, only to see the Mills score 16 straight points to start the second quarter and gain a 33-20 halftime lead. "I knew we were going to come back," said Janet. "Everyone on the team was hitting really well. I think that's the best we've played all year, in the second and third quarters." Led by six-foot-one Center Jenny Miller, who grabbed 21 boards, the Rutten sisters, and all-state point guard Kim Salathe (who would later go on to become the school's head coach), the Eagles increased their lead to 52-36 after three periods. The Cardinals trimmed that lead to nine at one point, but the Eagles were too tough down the stretch. They went on to win the game, 64-55, earning their second title in as many years. New York Mills out-rebounded their opponents 46-20, and she set up a zone-defense that forced the Cards to shoot from long range.

"We knew how to stop them," said Karvonen, "and we did." Jean Hopfenspirger led the Cards with 19 points while her sister Joan added 10. The 7,000-plus fans were in awe of "Janet the Great," as the six-foot forward scored a game high 24-points and added 10 rebounds. The team also set a tournament record, by scoring 203 points.

Front Row: Ann Tsuchiya, Barb Bailey, Doreen Gill, Laura Gardner, Wendy Wolfe, Pat Hanke, Sue Mooney and Betsy Mooney. Second Row: Head Coach Don Kuzma, Lisa Kallberg, Kim Sether, Becky Johnson, Sara Lokensgaard, Lorraine Woldum, Kari Jacobsen, Sue Bailey, (Mgr.) Wendy Miller, Asst. Coach Mac Redmond.

The 1978 State AA Champs from Jefferson

Front Row, L. to R.: Char Matti, mgr., Karolyn Kumpula, Linda Keskitalo, Brenda Rudolph, Betty Minten, Ann Rutten, Linda Minten, Darla Bauck, Joy Wallgren, mgr. Back Row, L. to R.: Peggy Zimmerman, Head Coach, Laura Rud, Sue Miller, Janet Karvonen, Jen Miller, Kim Salathe, Mary Rutten, Chelene Legried, Tom Peterson, Asst. Coach. Not Pictured: Jen Rud.

The 1979 State A Champs from NY Mills

1978: Class AA: Bloomington Jefferson vs. Regina

The 1978 Class AA titlist was Bloomington Jefferson, which, after three straight tries, won their first state championship. The Jaguars, led by senior Forward Laura Gardner, who scored a record 78 points in the tourney, edged

Front Row, Kneeling, L. to R.: Rosie Burch, Jean Tierney, Dana Watts. Middle: Joyce Hueller, Mgr. Back Row, L. to R.: Susie Strong, Barbara Moore, Lynne Foss, Roxanne Lissimore, Coach Lou Kanavati, Stacy Durand, Carol Kraus, Twyla Mitchell, Laurie Grahek.

The 1979 State AA Champs from Central

The 1980 State A Champs from Albany

Front Row, L. to R.: Julie Budde, Mgr., Julie Lane, Kelly Skalicky, Carol Oehrlein, Bev Schleper, Carol Thelen, Sue Schleper, Linda Weisbrich, Mgr. Back Row, L. to R.: Kay Kronebusch, Ass't. Coach, Peg Thelen, Darlene Statz, Laurie Desautel, Lori Cigelske, Pat Statz, Shelly Linz, Liz Allen, Linda Konsor, Nancy Way, Head Coach.

The 1980 State AA Champs from Little Falls

Front Row, L. to R.: Asst. Coach Lynn Halstead, (Co-Capt.) Tina Keller, (Co-Capt.) Peggy Urbanski, Coach Jerry Cool. Back Row, L. to R.: Marie Banick, Anita Miller, Mary Vosen, Betty Spillum, Shelly Chisholm, Leeanne Grosso, Melanie Melby, Karen Johnson, Barb Lehn, Marj Hill, Mary Jo Filippi, Bridget Fabian, Kathy Thielen.

The 1981 State A Champs from Heron Lake

Front Row, L. to R.: Mary Egge, Deb Kirsch, Pat Burns, Lynette Rients, Cindy Garoutte, Cathy Baumgard, Lois Mathias. Back Row, L. to R.: Assistant Coach Wayne Rasche, Amy Christians, Ruth Henkels, Chris Ferguson, Lori Sontag, Janeen Rasche, Jane Wolff, Cindy Seydel, Head Coach Les Knutson.

The 1981 State AA Champs from Coon Rapids

Front Row, L. to R.: Assistant Coach Sharen Keller, Assistant Coach Jeff Wolfe, Head Coach Penny Stiles. Back Row, L. to R.: Sandy Gallagher (manager), Kathy Cordes, Beth Wik, Lynn Weyek, Jodi Thorson, Cindy Nelson, Amy Jaeger, Sandra Sparks, Lisa Neuman, Colleen Schroer, Caryl Parks, Caren Jund, Dawn Anderson, Tracy Cronin, Jeana Cullen, Al Huebsch (manager).

Cloquet in the quarterfinals, 49-45, followed by St. Paul Central in the semi's, 54-53. From there the Jags downed Regina, 53-40, en route to the title. Coach Don Kuzma's squad finished the season with a perfect 24-0 record.

1979: Class A: New York Mills vs. Albany

The two-time defending champs from New York Mills made it three in a row in the Class A tourney as they opened the tourney with a 50-36 victory over Austin Pacelli in the quarterfinals, followed by Archbishop Brady of West St. Paul, 70-50, in the semi's. Then, in the Finals, the Eagles downed Albany, 61-52, to make it a three-peat.

Leading the charge once again was junior forward Janet Karvonen, who had already accumulated 2,284 points in her prep career — the most ever by a girl in Minnesota. Janet set numerous tournament records yet again during this tourney, most noteworthy were most points in a game (38) and most points in a tournament (98).

1979: Class AA: St. Paul Central vs. Northfield

St. Paul Central, which won the state title back in 1976, and had been a qualifier in each of the four years the tourney has been conducted, kicked off the Class AA tournament by eliminating Minneapolis North, 60-50, in the quarterfinals. From there the Minutemaids crushed Melrose in the semifinals, 57-33, and kept on rolling in the Finals by beating previously unbeaten Northfield, 55-46, for their second state championship.

The three-day tournament, televised for the first time on all three days, attracted a record 53,702 persons — 7,275 more than the record total of 1978.

1980: Class A: Albany vs. Austin Pacelli

The three-year reign of New York Mills came to an abrupt end in the Class A semifinals when upstart Austin Pacelli upset the Eagles. (Senior Janet Karvonen, the National Player of the Year who averaged nearly 33 points per game that season, went on to become Minnesota's all-time leading scorer, boys or girls, by tallying an amazing 3,129 points.) Pacelli went on to get trounced in the Finals though, 56-25, by last year's runner-up, Albany, who this year rolled to a state title with a perfect 26-0 record. Albany made it to the big game with wins over Warren in the quarterfinals, 64-39, and then East Chain, 61-41, in the semi's.

1980: Class AA: Little Falls vs. Hill Murray

First time entrant Little Falls made a memorable state tournament debut by eliminating Proctor, 47-40, in the quarterfinals, and Hopkins Lindbergh, 58-53 in the semifinals. From there the Flyerettes, holders of a 24-1 overall record, knocked off Hill-Murray, 50-42, in the Class AA title game.

1981: Class A: Heron Lake-Okabena vs. Moose Lake

Heron Lake-Okabena went 26-0 en route to taking the 1981 Class A title. Heron Lake-Okabena beat Bagley, 55-28, in the first round, and then took care of Austin Pacelli 52-42, in the semi's. From there Heron Lake-Okabena won the championship game, convincingly, 62-46, over Moose Lake.

One of the highlights of the tourney was the outstanding play of Albany scoring whiz, guard Kelly Skalicky, who set a new tournament scoring record by tallying 102 points in the tourney — breaking Janet Karvonen's old mark of 98, set back in 1979. Skalicky also broke Karvonen's single-game scoring mark of 40 when she lit up Bagley for 45 points.

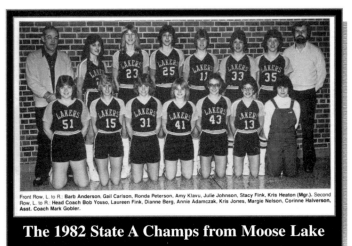

Front Row, L. to R.: Barb Anderson, Gail Carlson, Ronda Peterson, Amy Klavu, Julie Johnson, Stacy Fink, Kris Heaton (Mgr.). Second Row, L. to R.: Head Coach Bob Youso, Laureen Fink, Dianne Berg, Annie Adamczak, Kris Jones, Margie Nelson, Corinne Halverson, Asst. Coach Mark Gobler.

The 1982 State A Champs from Moose Lake

1981: Class AA: Coon Rapids vs. St. Paul Harding

The Coon Rapids Cardinals completed a perfect 25-0 season by defeating St. Paul Harding, 60-42, in the Class AA title game. Making their second tournament appearance, Coon Rapids advanced to the Finals with victories over Minneapolis Washburn, 61-42, in the quarterfinals, and defending champion Little Falls, 57-56, in semi's. There, Coon Rapids outscored the Flyers by a 6-0 margin in the final 28 seconds to advance to the championship game.

Front Row L. to R.: Kam Mohs, Danna DeZiel, Heidi Miller, Tammy Champa, Jane Williams, Lynn Lembeck, Linda Carlson. Back Row, L. to R.: Assist. Coach Curt Mark, Deanne Sand, Debi Lucas, Karen Foy, Carol Peterka, Terri Deaton, Kelly Thomas, Teri Foy, Kristin Dragland, Sue Hampton, Dana Dykstra, Head Coach Donna Mark.

The 1982 State AA Champs from St. Cloud Apollo

1982: Class A: Moose Lake vs. East Chain

Favored Moose Lake completed its 26-0 undefeated season en route to winning the seventh Class A State Girls' Basketball Tournament. The 1981 runner-up first beat Lester Prairie, 67-47, in the quarterfinals, followed by New York Mills, 60-44, in round two. Then, in the title game, the Moose edged East Chain, 52-49, to take the crown. (Leading the way for Moose Lake was "Miss Basketball Minnesota," Annie Adamczak, who went on to become an All-America volleyball player at Nebraska, was named Big Eight Female Athlete of the Year and later played pro volleyball for the Minnesota Monarchs.)

The tournament's leading scorer was Lester Prairie's Kay Konerza, who, after scoring 75 points in her three tournament games, finished her illustrious career second on the all-time scoring list behind New York Mills' Janet Karvonen, with 2,715 points.

Front Row, L. to R.: Brenda Brenke, Mary Trimbo, Michele Murphy, Janet Reiter, Janelle Trimbo. Second Row, L. to R.: Vicki Chadwick, Cindy Brenke, Teresa Kahlow, Ellen Heinz, Stephanie Felix, Tamie Fossum. Third Row, L. to R.: Head Coach Ryan Bremmer, Amy Byrne, Lisa Walters, Jane Pieper, Cheryl Walters, Stu. Mgr. Lori Haggenmiller.

The 1983 State A Champs from Henderson

1982: Class AA: St. Cloud Apollo vs. Rochester Mayo

St. Cloud Apollo completed its perfect 25-0 season by not allowing any opponent to come closer than nine points of defeating them. The Eagles opened the tourney by beating Chaska, 53-32, in the quarters, and Duluth East, 50-35, in the semi's. From there the Eagles topped Rochester Mayo, 53-44, to take the Class AA title.

1983: Class A: Henderson vs. Lake City

In its first ever state tournament, undefeated 26-0 Henderson, with an enrollment of just 96 students, became the smallest school to win the Class A title.

Front Row, L. to R.: Carol Thelen, Julie Budde, Ann Wellenstein, Terri Kuhn, Lori Pierson. Back Row, L. to R.: Coach Dick Cady, Ass't Coach Pat Schleper, Peggy Linz, Kim Tamm, Carol Oehrlein, Lori Radamacher, Sandy Thelen, Mgr. Barb Baggenstoss. Not Pictured: Cindy Mackedanz.

The 1983 State AA Champs from Albany

Front Row, L. to R.: Amy Gornick, Mgr., Missy Putkonen, Leslie Powers, Judy McDonald, Candy Novoselac, Kathy Fredeen, Mgr. Back Row, L. to R.: Mike Ciochetto, Coach, Michelle Samsa, Mary Zgonc, Laura Lackner, Lynda Hill, Kim Olson, Heidi Amistadi.

The 1984 State A Champs from Chisholm

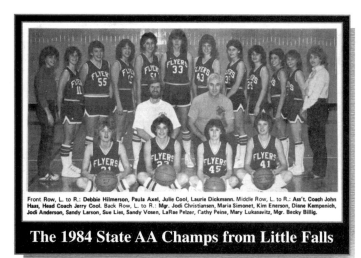

Front Row, L. to R.: Debbie Hilmerson, Paula Axel, Julie Cool, Laurie Dickmann. Middle Row, L. to R.: Ass't. Coach John Haas, Head Coach Jerry Cool. Back Row, L. to R.: Mgr. Jodi Christiansen, Maria Simonet, Kim Enerson, Diane Kempenich, Jodi Anderson, Sandy Larson, Sue Lies, Sandy Vosen, LaRae Pelzer, Cathy Peine, Mary Lukasavitz, Mgr. Becky Billig.

The 1984 State AA Champs from Little Falls

Front Row: L - R — Donna Botelho, Kristi Anderson, Darci Peterson, Ramelle Beachy, Stu. Mgr. DeAnne Blanchard. Second Row: l - R — Coach Ron Beachy, Tosha Martell, Kris Borash, Tricia Bates, Deanne Olander, Coach Dale Hausmann. Back Row: L - R — Renata Glaser, Kari Wolhowe, Kristi Wolhowe, Kyra Odden, Karla Howard.

The 1985 State A Champs from Staples

Front Row: L - R — Mgr. Michelle Patnoude, Kris Jackson, Sandy Vosen, LaRae Pelzer, Kathy Peine, Maria Simonette, Ass't Coach John Haas. Back Row: L - R — Coach Jerry Cool, Maarja Aalgaard, Sue Lies, Sandy Larson, Jodi Anderson, Diane Kempenich, Ass't Coach Ron Hennenkamp.

The 1985 State AA Champs from Little Falls

The Region 4A champions breezed past Waubun, 53-38, in quarterfinal play, and followed that up by beating the previously unbeaten and heavily favored Chisholm Bluestreaks, 44-36. Then, in the Finals, the Tigers defeated Lake City, 52-31, to take the state crown.

1983: Class AA: Albany vs. Edina

Albany became the first school in tourney history to win both the Class A and AA championships. A Class A school by enrollment prior to this year, the Huskies captured the title in 1980. Then, three years later, Albany took the AA crown by edging a very tough Edina squad, 41-39, in overtime. Albany advanced to the big game by virtue of victories over Derham Hall, 60-56, in the quarters, and unbeaten Rochester John Marshall, 45-36, in the semi's.

1984: Class A: Chisholm vs. Eden Valley-Watkins

Making its second tournament appearance, No. 1 Chisholm eliminated Staples, 59-48, in the opening round, and then roughed up Glencoe, 80-55, in semifinal action. The 27-0 Bluestreaks then went on to win the state title by beating Eden Valley-Watkins, 55-41. Led by its tough defense, Chisholm's closest game all season was the seven-point triumph over Staples in the quarterfinals.

1984: Class AA: Little Falls vs. Burnsville

Undefeated Little Falls became the first Class "AA" school in the tournament's history to win a second state championship, with the first one coming back in 1980. The Flyers kicked off the tourney by beating Stillwater, 75-39, in the opener, and Minneapolis Washburn, 59-48, in Game Two. Then, in the Finals, Little Falls outlasted Burnsville, 45-43, in one of the event's most exciting championship games ever.

1985: Class A: Staples vs. Milroy

Top-ranked Staples completed its perfect 28-0 season with first and second round victories over East Grand Forks, 60-43, and Southwest Minnesota Christian of Edgerton, 45-43. In the title game, Staples beat the darling of the tournament, tiny Milroy — enrollment 47. It was closer than the score looked, but the Cardinals started strong and finished strong en route to beating Milroy, 49-39, to earn its first crown.

1985: Class AA: Little Falls vs. Mankato East

The defending champs from Little Falls became the first AA school to capture three state championships when they beat Mankato East, 48-43, in the title game. The Flyers gained entrance to the title tilt by virtue of victories over Totino Grace, 47-27, in first round action, and top-ranked Duluth East, 51-50, in the semifinals.

Front Row, L to R: **Student Manager Carmen Kleene, Statitician Jill Mattson, Student Manager DeVonna Kimpling.** Middle Row, L to R: **Shaun Bodin, Rhonda Harguth, Jaci Geurtz, Dayna Rethlake, Deb Kattevold, Dee Randt, Christy Moen.** Back Row, L to R: **Assistant Coach Mary Lou Lanes, Kellie Thein, Shannon Groothuis, Julie Thein, Heidi Hubel, Shannon Knapper, Deb Olson, Stacey Freeze, Head Coach Brad Atchison.**

The 1986 State A Champs from Midwest Minn.

1986: Class A: Midwest Minnesota vs. East Grand Forks

Midwest Minnesota, a cooperative sponsored team made up of players from Clara City and Maynard High Schools, took home the hardware in the Class A tourney. The champions from Region Three edged Le Sueur, 50-49, in the opener at the Minneapolis Auditorium, and then sidelined perennial Class A power New York Mills, 54-43, in semifinal action. Then, in the title game against East Grand Forks, the Rebels cruised to a 54-38 victory.

1986: Class AA: St. Louis Park vs. St. Paul Highland Park

The heavily favored St Louis Park Orioles went on to win their first ever state title by virtue of a 61-55 triumph over St Paul Highland Park. St Louis Park got to the Finals by beating Bemidji, 58-46, in the quarterfinals, and Burnsville, 53-40, in the semifinals.

Front Row, L to R: **Julie Anderson, Jen Winters, Marla Detache, Stefanie Oberts, Michele Anderson.** Middle Row, L to R: **Assistant Coach Corinne Melmer, Assistant Coach Deb Wold, Julie Kelly, Sally Gannon, Laurie Bannick, Kathy Blair, Sarah Henriksen, Anne McInerney, Sue Brynteson, Cindi Aarsvold, Head Coach Phil Frerk.** Back Row, L to R: **Amy Davidson, Karla Johnson, Barb Eide, Deanne Hop, Michelle Skaug, Ellen Hanson, Meg Stoneking.**

The 1986 State AA Champs from St. Louis Park

1987: Class A: Rochester Lourdes vs. Wheaton

Rochester Lourdes went on to win its three games in the Class A tournament by a grand total of just 10 points. The Eagles topped Marshall County Central of Newfolden, 40-36, in the quarterfinal round and then eliminated New London-Spicer, 48-44, in the semi's. From there they edged the tourney-favorites from, Wheaton, 33-31, in the title game.

Front Row, L to R: **Heather Harens, Lisa Petricka, Nora Breckle, Sara Friedt.** Back Row, L to R: **Coach Myron Glass, Manager Patty Ward, Sue Erickson, Kim Rowekamp, Laurie Decker, Katie Cooney, Catherine Restovich, Martha Macken, Managers Jill Mahon, Denys Erickson.**

The 1987 State A Champs from Roch. Lourdes

1987: Class AA: Mankato East vs. Rocori, Cold Spring

Top-rated Mankato East lived up to its pre-tournament billing as the favorite by going on to win its first ever state girls title by virtue of a 50-47 victory over Rocori of Cold Spring. The 25-1 Cougars recorded impressive tourney victories over Osseo, 53-47, in the quarterfinals, and Hill-Murray, 47-46, in the semifinals.

1988: Class A: Tracy-Milroy vs. Storden Jeffers

Tracy-Milroy opened the tournament at Williams Arena, where they handed Esko its first loss, winning 55-50. Then in semifinal action that Friday at Met Center, Tracy-Milroy beat another undefeated club in New London-Spicer, 57-50. Then, in the championship game, they edged their third unbeaten team, Storden-Jeffers, 47-35, to take the title.

Front Row, L to R: **Sarah Maschka, Kendra Carter, Kristin Maschka, Tammy Shain, Karla Wolthuis, Connie Fitzloff, Shelly Vokal, Kristin Petersen.** Back Row, L to R: **Statistician Angie Jacobson, Manager Christy Long, Head Coach Cliff Woodford, Beth Benzkofer, Maggie Schwamberger, Liz Tolzmann, Shelly Fredrickson, Jodi Chamberlain, Angie Hansen, Assistant Coach Mark Schmiesing, Assistant Coach Pat Burns.**

The 1987 State AA Champs from Mankato East

Row 1-L to R: Ass't Coach-Terry Culhane, Mgr.-Carmine VanDeWiele, Kristin Campbell, Pam Lenertz, Susan Williams, Mary Jo Miller, Mona Schreier, Jenny McCoy, Mgr.-Sara Engen, Ass't Coach-Bill Bolin.
Row 2: Ass't Coach-Paul Soupir, Stacy Lamfers, Jenny Nackerud, Jill Vroman, Tonja West, Gaylene Van Gelderen, Rachel Williams, Elaine Eischens, Karen Hicks, Laurie Horsman, Head Coach-Shorty Engel.

The 1988 State A Champs from Tracy-Milroy

Row 1-L to R: Cathy Gashe, Becky Sladek, Sue Reicoff, Suzanne Weeks, Lesley Flaten, Jackie Moe.
Row 2: Coach-Doug Galligher, Ingrid Podnieks, Kate Riley, Liz Zeller, Ass't Coach-Marty Dahlen, Ass't Coach-Mike Peterson. Not Pictured-Missy Perry.

The 1988 State AA Champs from Edina

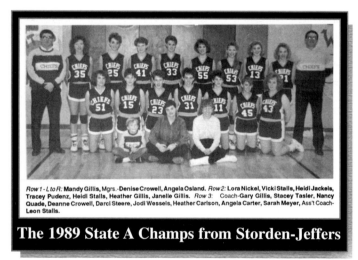

Row 1 - L to R: Mandy Gillis, Mgrs.-Denise Crowell, Angela Osland. Row 2: Lora Nickel, Vicki Stalls, Heidi Jackels, Tracey Pudenz, Heidi Stalls, Heather Gillis, Janelle Gillis. Row 3: Coach-Gary Gillis, Stacey Tasler, Nancy Quade, Deanne Crowell, Darci Steere, Jodi Wessels, Heather Carlson, Angela Carter, Sarah Meyer, Ass't Coach-Leon Stalls.

The 1989 State A Champs from Storden-Jeffers

Row 1 - L to R: Amy Ruuska, Shane Hilton, Jennie Youngquist, Dawn Rattray. Row 2: Trisha Krone, Nancy Umnland, Amy Walker, Kari Wraspir, Jodi Grzeskowiak, Billeye Gladen, Heather Peterson. Row 3: Ass't. Coach-Tim Teas, Brenda Lingen, Alissa Brodin, Kelly Geistler, Jessica Fiebelkorn, Kari Olson, Kris Juntunen, Lisa Sadler, Coach-Dave Thorpe.

The 1989 State AA Champs from Osseo

1988: Class AA: Edina vs. Rosemount

The opening round of the Class AA tourney had Edina fighting off a strong St. Paul Harding team in overtime, 57-54. From there the Hornets ousted Stillwater, 62-55, in Game Two, before capturing the championship with a 41-33 win over Rosemount.

1989: Class A: Storden Jeffers vs. Eden Valley-Watkins

The 1988 state runner-ups from Storden-Jeffers kicked off the tourney by beating Rochester Lourdes, 63-49, in the first game, and then defeating the defending state champs from Tracy-Milroy in the semi's by the final score of 57-41. From there the Chiefs, rated No. 1 all season long, posted a 76-52 victory over Eden Valley-Watkins to take the state title.

1989: Class AA: Osseo vs. Little Falls

The Osseo Orioles defeated Burnsville, 57-49, in the quarterfinal round, followed by International Falls, 69-46, in day two. From there Osseo rallied back to beat a very solid Little Falls club, 54-50, to take the state championship at the Met Center in Bloomington.

1990: Class A: Rochester Lourdes vs. Storden Jeffers

Rochester Lourdes avenged its 1989 quarterfinal loss to Storden-Jeffers as the Eagles coasted to the 1990 championship game with a 45-point win against Virginia and a 28-point win against MACCRAY (Maynard-Clara City-Raymond). There, Lourdes beat the Storden-Jeffers Lady Chiefs, who were riding a gaudy 53-game winning streak, to take the title.

1990: Class AA: St. Louis Park vs. Elk River

The Class AA contest was a classic confrontation between unranked Elk River, making its first ever tournament appearance, and St. Louis Park. There was a sea of red in the stands on one side and an ocean of orange on the other side when the two squared off at the Met Center. St. Louis Park hung tough though, and played solid defense in beating the Elks, 60-50, to take the crown.

1991: Class A: Rochester Lourdes vs. New London Spicer

Owners of an outstanding 57-1 record over the previous two consecutive state championship seasons, Rochester Lourdes beat MACCRAY and St.

Peter en route to advancing to the title game. There, the New London-Spicer Wildcats were overshadowed by the Eagles' solid defense, being held to just eight first-half points followed be a mere 20 in the second half. Rochester Lourdes won this one in a rout, 53-28, to take the crown.

Row 1 - L to R: Stacy Sievers, Angela Weinschenk. Row 2: Mary Schwieters, Nicole Hines, Darla Erickson, Jolene Amundson. Row 3: Mgr.-Pam Zeimetz, Lori Lawler, Shawn Sivly, Amy King, SeAnn Sivly, Maggie O'Connor, Mgr.-Jenny Campbell.

The 1990 State A Champs from Roch. Lourdes

1991: Class AA: Burnsville vs. St. Paul Harding

After beating Mankato East and Osseo in the quarterfinals and semifinals, Burnsville faced off with St. Paul Harding in the title tilt. There, the Braves took a one point half-time edge, only to fall behind by four with just two minutes to play. That's when a pair of free-throws by Burnsville sent the game into overtime at 54-54. In the extra session, Harding's star player, Shannon Loeblein, who had tallied 26 points on a whole bunch of three-pointers for the Knights, fouled out. With that, Burnsville's Sheila Roehl and Tiffany Trenkle took over by nailing five clutch free throws to ice the game for the Braves, 59-54.

Row 1 - L to R: Mgr.-Angie Martinson, Jenny Seim, Lisa Schuetz, Jenny Peacock, Leah Mason, Jill Anderson, Jenny Combs, Cathy Roe, Nicol Claymon, Ass't Mgr.-Tove Jensen. Row 2: Ass't Coach-Bruce McLean, Head Coach-Phil Frerk, Barb Motzko, Sarah Foulkes, Kate Henriksen, Barb Gordon, Rita Henriksen, Jenny Keeley, Rita Gerhardson, Ass't Coach-Darold Wold.

The 1990 State AA Champs from St. Louis Park

1992: Class A: Tracy Area vs. New London-Spicer

Tracy Area cruised to a 66-56 victory over St. Peter in the opening round of the Class A tourney, and then followed that up with an impressive 63-49 victory over New Prague in the semifinals. From there the Panthers hooked up with undefeated New London-Spicer in the championship game. There, New London-Spicer jumped out to an early two-point lead in the first quarter, only to see the quick-striking gals from Tracy go on an unanswered 14-point run which gave the Panthers a 10-point halftime lead. The Wildcats rallied in the second half to draw within nine points, but came up on the short end of a 61-52 ball-game.

Row 1 - L to R: Missy Decker, Anita Sadler, Tracie Breckie, Nerissa Gander. Row 2: Patti Reardon, Kate Lawler, Stacy Sievers, Leslie Whiting, Patti Yanish, Angela Weinschenk, Sara Sievers, Krissy Campbell. Row 3: Jenny Campbell, Sara Atkinson, Amy King, Erin McEvoy, Lori Lawler, Jenny Pehler, Maggie O'Connor, Julie Mullany.

The 1991 State A Champs from Roch. Lourdes

1992: Class AA: Burnsville vs. Mounds View

Burnsville was the only team from the 1991 field to return to the 1992 tournament, and this time it was personal. The Braves first dismantled the Willmar Cardinals in the opening round, 60-46, and then advanced to the Finals by beating the Roseville Raiders in the semifinals, 49-41. There, the Braves opened up a 28-18 half-time lead and cruised from there, out-scoring Mounds View, 17-10 in the final frame to cruise to a 53-36 win and their first state title.

1993: Class A: Rochester Lourdes vs. New London-Spicer

The girls state tournament switched to a four-day format this year, with Rochester Lourdes winning its fourth Class A title over New London-Spicer. Rochester Lourdes breezed through its first two games, first defeating Esko, 62-28, in the quarters, followed by Cimax-Fisher, 65-30, in the semi's. Then, in the Finals, Rochester and New London-Spicer, both undefeated, prepared to do battle. This one was tight all the way through with Lourdes taking an early seven-point lead at half-time. New London-Spicer shaved the lead to four points in the third quarter, but could not outscore Lourdes in the fourth

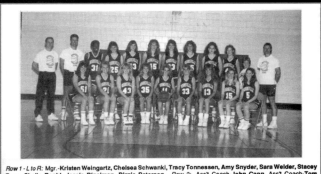
Row 1 - L to R: Mgr.-Kristen Weingartz, Chelsea Schwankl, Tracy Tonnessen, Amy Snyder, Sara Welder, Stacey Dove, Sheila Roehl, Jessie Rigelman, Bizzie Peterson. Row 2: Ass't Coach-John Cann, Ass't Coach-Tom Robison, Gehmelle Johnson, Christie Johnson, Stacie Suneson, Tiffany Trenkle, Joe Ward, Tricia Wakely, Kenya Samuels, Mgr-Jenny Wernecke, Head Coach-Doug Bos. Not pictured: Mgr-Julie Rodewald.

The 1991 State AA Champs from Burnsville

Row 1 - L to R: Manager-Angela Vandendriessche, Manager-Kim Weedman. Row 2: Bridget Smith, Malynnda Olson, Mandy Coquyt, Sandra Zwach, Terry Retzlaff, Nicki Heinrich, Kathy Ankrum, Teri Pruszynski. Row 3: Assistant Coach-Dave Anderson, Assistant Coach-Paul Soupir, Jenni Dold, Susan Van Moer, Hilary Ludeman, Amy Christian, Chris Brink, Melissa Snobl, JoAnn Lanoue, Head Coach-Terry Culhane.

The 1992 State A Champs from Tracy Area

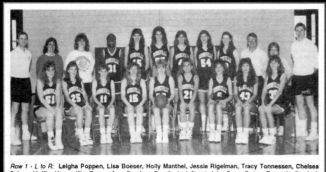

Row 1 - L to R: Leigha Poppen, Lisa Boeser, Holly Manthei, Jessie Rigelman, Tracy Tonnessen, Chelsea Schwankl, Kim Hearn, Kim Deyoe, Amy Snyder. Row 2: Ass't Coach-John Cann, Trainer-Renee Ledin, Ass't Coach-Sharon Roos, Gehmelle Johnson, Stacie Suneson, Tricia Wakely, Jeanna Eck, Janel Warmka, Bizzle Peterson, Ass't Coach-Pat Feely, Mgr-Jenny Wernecke, Head Coach-Doug Boe.

The 1992 State AA Champs from Burnsville

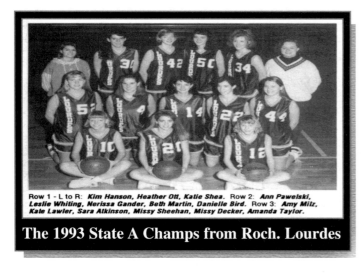

Row 1 - L to R: Kim Hanson, Heather Ott, Katie Shea. Row 2: Ann Pawelski, Leslie Whiting, Nerissa Gander, Beth Martin, Danielle Bird. Row 3: Amy Milz, Kate Lawler, Sara Atkinson, Missy Sheehan, Missy Decker, Amanda Taylor.

The 1993 State A Champs from Roch. Lourdes

Row 1 - L to R: Sue Nicholson, Mary Kate Fretheim, Joanne Ebeling, Stacey Nicholson. Row 2: Teri Witcraft, Kjersten Miller, Jessica Johnson, Eryn Bartels, Ana Davis. Row 3: Assistant Coach Ron Cordes, Alicia Cordes, Missy Kane, Colleen Polzin, Becky Timm, Allison Derck, Head Coach Terry Hunst. Not pictured: Amber Luckie, Student Manager Dawn Caliguri, Student Manager Nikki Seibert.

The 1993 State AA Champs from Jefferson

period and finished as the runner-up yet for the third consecutive year by the final score of 48-43.

1993: Class AA: Bloomington Jefferson vs. Roseville Area

Bloomington Jefferson made its first tournament appearance since 1978, the same year the school captured the Class AA title. The Jags road to the championship featured victories over Forest Lake and Rochester Mayo in the quarters and semi's, which then set up a date with Roseville in the Finals. There, Jefferson fell behind early, but rallied back to outscore the Raiders by a two-to-one margin in the second quarter to take a three-point half-time lead. From there the Jaguars rolled, playing solid defense and cruising to a 42-34 victory.

1994: Class A: Blake vs. New London-Spicer

The Blake School, a first-time tournament qualifier, finished its perfect 30-0 record en route to taking the Class A title at the newly constructed Women's Sports Pavilion at the University of Minnesota. Blake had a close one in its first quarterfinal game, but defeated Red Rock Central, 68-61. Then, in the semifinals, the Bears eliminated the Fosston Greyhounds, 57-47. Now, in the Finals, Blake hooked up with New London-Spicer, where the Bears took a three-point lead with just 13 seconds to go and held on for the big win. The Wildcats heaved a 30-foot prayer late, but it came up short as Blake won the defensive battle, 39-36. For New London-Spicer, it was their fourth time finishing as the tournament's runner-up in as many years.

1994: Class AA: Bloomington Jefferson vs. Osseo

Bloomington Jefferson went into the 1994 state tournament looking to defend its 1993 title and succeeded. The Jags returned with the experience of five juniors and seven seniors this time as they first topped Bemidji in the quarterfinals, 45-30, before edging Apple Valley in the semi's, 55-52, to advance into the Finals. There, the Jaguars met Osseo, a team which they had beaten earlier in the season. Jefferson jumped out to an 11-0 lead in this one, but Osseo rallied its way back to get to within five points at half-time. The Jaguars took over in the third quarter though, and went on an impressive 20-2 run en route to taking their second straight state crown, 73-50.

1995: Class A: Rochester Lourdes vs. St. James

It was an all Rochester state tournament in 1995 as Rochester Lourdes and Rochester Mayo brought home the hardware in each of their respective classes. Rochester Lourdes won the A title by defeating its first two opponents by 32 and 18 point margins, respectively, before going on to beat St. James in the Finals. Katie Shea led the way for Lourdes in the title game as she scored 12 of her game-high 20 points in the first half en route to leading her club to a 35-24 lead at the intermission. From there Lourdes put it into overdrive and cruised to a 65-39 victory — giving them an amazing 5-0 record in state championship games.

1995: Class AA: Rochester Mayo vs. St. Cloud Apollo

The Rochester Mayo Spartans, led by the fabulous Miller twins, also brought home the title when they beat St. Cloud Apollo in the Finals. The two-time runner-ups opened the tournament by rolling past Apple Valley in Game One, 68-40, followed by Tartan, 73-44, in the semifinals. Then, in the championship game, Mayo, led by Coco Miller's 32 points and her twin sister Kelly's 12 points, steam-rolled St. Cloud Apollo, 74-49, to take the title.

The Spartans exceptional pressure defense provided many opportunities for the offense, which, coincidentally, set a tournament record for most points in a three-day tournament, with 220.

Row 1 - L to R: Teresa Henriksen, Linara Washington, Laura Bellafronto, Liz McDonald, Catherine Bellafronto, Brooke Anthony. Row 2: Kimberly Gill, Kelly McAnnany, Kinesha Davis, Katy Herwig, Nora Anderson, Zumari Chatham, Sara Grudnowski. Row 3: Head Coach Ray Finley, Lisl Von Steinberge, Carolyn Moos, Tiffany Willard, Kristin Henderson, Assistant Coach Faith Johnson.

The 1994 State A Champs from Blake

1996: Class A: Tracy-Milroy vs. Blake

The Tracy-Milroy Panthers won their third state basketball title in 1996, defeating the Blake Bears, 40-38, in a real thriller. The Panthers did their best to neutralize the Bears' six-footer, Carolyn Moos, and led 23-17 at half-time. Then, with 1:56 remaining, Kinesha Davis scored to give the Panthers a 39-36 lead. After some back and forth play, a quickly steal gave Blake the last shot opportunity with 36 seconds left. Moos missed a 16-footer with 10 seconds remaining on the clock and Tracy-Milroy regained possession. But Brandt was fouled and went to the line with 4.9 seconds remaining. She made one and missed one to give the Panthers a 40-38 lead. Now, at the buzzer, the Bears' Katie Herwig, heaved a desperation three-pointer which came up short. The Panthers, despite shooting just 33%, came away with the championship.

Row 1 - L to R: Kari Meyer, Nicki Seibert, Kiersten Miller, Jessica Johnson, Stacey Nicholson, Nancy Nelson, Michelle Engebretsen. Row 2: Coach Terry Hunst, Amy Gentz, Jenny Dolland, Missy Kane, Maren Walseth, Alicia Cordes, Joanne Ebeling, Ann Maurice, Kael Brown, Coach Ron Cordes. Not Pictured: Ann Hultgren, Kara Jackels.

The 1994 State AA Champs from Jefferson

1996: Class AA: Hastings vs. Osseo

Hastings, making its first state appearance, opened the 1996 Class AA tourney by beating Burnsville in the quarterfinals, 54-44, followed by Shakopee, which was led by the Sames sisters, 53-48, to advance to the Finals. There, Hastings held off the No. 1 ranked Orioles to win the championship. Despite missing the first eleven shots of the game and the first 10 shots of the second half, the Raiders still found a way to get it done. With the score tied at 25-25 at the half, Osseo came out and took a nine point lead late into the third quarter. The Raiders rallied though, behind six-foot junior forward Erin Ditty's 22 points. Ditty's short jumper in the last minute of regulation gave Hastings a 53-51 lead. Osseo's Erica Haugen then nailed a free-throw to get it to within one. Then, after a double-dribble call against the Raiders, Osseo got the ball back for one last shot. But, Haugen's three-pointer clanged off the rim. Ditty added a free-throw and hung on for the thrilling 54-52 victory.

Row 1 - L to R: Statistician Brita Johnson, Bridget Garry, Lisa Graf, Katie Shea, Courtney Benda, Rachel Horgen, Kelly Schwanke, Student Manager Chantel Beaulieu. Row 2: Statistician Sara Sherman, Katie Griffin, Denise Kruse, Evelyn Molloy, Missy Sheehan, Laura Rogness, Johanne LeTendre, Marnie Bowen, Marie Wiater, Statistician Vanessa Woodcock.

The 1995 State A Champs from Roch. Lourdes

1997: Class A: Hancock vs. Red Lake Falls

The girls state tournament changed is format in 1997 to a four-class system, providing even more teams with the opportunity to appear in the big dance. Hancock opened the Class A tourney by pounding Northland-Remer, 55-31, in the quarterfinal round, and then eliminating Chatfield, 61-41, in the semifinals, on Gwen Greiner's 28 points. From there the Owls edged Red Lake Falls, 56-50, for the title. Tammy Larson led the way for Hancock by scoring 14 points, while Greiner, who is the state record-holder for career three-pointers, added 13, and Terry Nohl chipped in with 12.

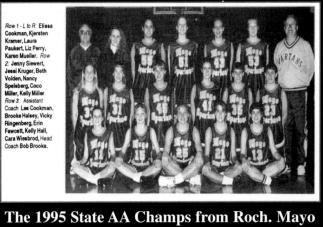

Row 1 - L to R: Elissa Cookman, Kjersten Kramer, Laura Paukert, Liz Perry, Karen Mueller. Row 2: Jenny Siewert, Jessi Kruger, Beth Volden, Nancy Spelsberg, Coco Miller, Kelly Miller. Row 3: Assistant Coach Lee Cookman, Brooke Halsey, Vicky Ringenberg, Erin Fawcett, Kelly Hall, Cara Wiesbrod, Head Coach Bob Brooks.

The 1995 State AA Champs from Roch. Mayo

Row 1 L-R: Manager Amanda Bassett, Nancy Ankrum, Sonja Kamrud, Denise Marks, Sarah Hayes, Nadine Brandt, Alison Walling, Monica Peterson, Manager Amy Hengel. Row 2: Head Coach Terry Culhane, Assistant Coach Deanna Garbera, Kris DeRuyck, Chris Brink, Holly DeSmet, Dacia Verlinde, Shannon Christensen, Jamey Erbes, Leah Ladehoff, Alyssa Ladehoff, Principal John Rokke, Assistant Coach Paul Soupir.

The 1996 State A Champs from Tracy-Milroy

Row 1 - L to R: Katy Hertel, Bessy Talalous, Jenny Ring, Michaela Burr, Jenny Lawrence, Heather Mace, Tracey Heggen, Jodie Dibble. Row 2: Head Coach Nikki Scholl, Coach Pete Zak, Leslie Nicholis, Molly Weber, Erin Ditty, Lesley Miller, Katie Larsen, Kim Sellner, Rachel Reuter, Coach Gary Burr, Manager Ken Augustine.

The 1996 State AA Champs from Hastings

Row 1 - L to R: Megan Grunig, Jolyn Thielke, Alexis Gramm. Row 2: Leah Messner, Corrine Hoffman, Lindsay Gramm, Leah Christie, Tara Stettner, Jenny Wartner. Row 3: Head Coach Dennis Courneya, Gwen Greiner, Tammy Larson, Tonya Nohl, Tracy Thielke, Terri Nohl, Assistant Coach Ken Grunig.

The 1997 State A Champs from Hancock

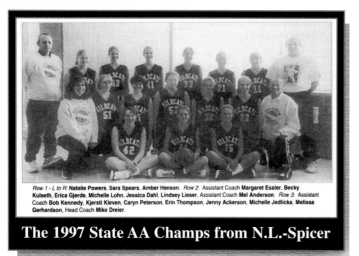

Row 1 - L to R: Natalie Powers, Sara Spears, Amber Hanson. Row 2: Assistant Coach Margaret Essler, Becky Kulseth, Erica Gjerde, Michelle Lohn, Jessica Dahl, Lindsey Lieser, Assistant Coach Mel Anderson. Row 3: Assistant Coach Bob Kennedy, Kjersti Kleven, Caryn Peterson, Erin Thompson, Jenny Ackerson, Michelle Jedlicka, Melissa Gerhardson, Head Coach Mike Dreier.

The 1997 State AA Champs from N.L.-Spicer

1997: Class AA: New London-Spicer vs. Minnewaska Area, Glenwood

After four consecutive runner-up finishes in the early 1990s, New London-Spicer finally got its first state championship in 1997. The Wildcats beat Albany Area, 60-52, in their quarterfinal, followed by Kasson-Mantorville, 60-47, in the semifinals, thanks to Sara Spears 19 points. From there New London-Spicer was able to edge a very tough Minnewaska Area squad in the championship game. The Wildcats built up a 19-4 lead in the first half, only to see Minnewaska Area rally to tie it up in the fourth quarter. The Cats hung tough though and thanks to Amber Hanson's 17 points, were able to eke out a 55-51 win.

1997: Class AAA: Alexandria vs. Minneapolis North

Fully 10 years removed from its first state tournament appearance, Alexandria won its first title by taking the first-ever Class AAA crown. Alexandria edged Hibbing, 62-61, in its quarterfinal contest, and then beat the Fridley in the semifinals, 49-39, on Sarah Ekdahl's 19 points. The Cardinals then hooked up with Minneapolis North in the Finals. There, the Lady Polars jumped out to a 21-10 lead, only to see the Cardinals rally back to post a 52-43 win. The Card's scored their last 11 points from the free-throw line and got some great shooting from Ekdahl, who posted 19 points and Shelly Schoeneck, who added 15 of her own in the win.

1997: Class AAAA: Rochester Mayo vs. Woodbury

In its fourth state appearance in five years, the undefeated Rochester Mayo Spartans won the 1997 Class AAA state girls' basketball championship. Mayo easily won its quarterfinal contest against tournament-newcomer Robbinsdale Armstrong, 85-60. Then, in the semifinals, the Spartans got an amazing 50-point effort out of the Miller sisters to edge out a very solid Bloomington Jefferson squad, 78-70. In the Finals it wasn't even close, as the Spartans beat up on the Woodbury Royals, 78-57, to take yet another title. The Spartans jumped out to an 8-1 lead by half-time, and never looked back. Leading the charge, of course, were the fabulous Miller sisters, who scored "only" 49 points in this one.

(The Miller twins, Coco & Kelly, became the first two players to share Minnesota's "Miss Basketball Award" (in 1997) after each scored more than 2,000 points during their five-year varsity careers.)

On a side-note, it is interesting to note that the Class of 1997 might have been the best-ever for Minnesota. Several players from that era went on to do us proud. Blake's Carolyn Moos went to Stanford, twin sisters Coco and Kelly Miller of Rochester Mayo went to Georgia, and Bloomington Jefferson standout Maren Walseth who went on to play at Iowa State. In addition, Roseau's Megan Taylor went to Iowa State and Edina's Kelly Siemon led Notre Dame to the National Championship in 2001. Osseo's Erica Haugen also went to Iowa State, Park Center's Janelle Jonason went to UW-Milwaukee, and Armstrong's Heather Haanen attended Colorado State. Osseo's six-foot-five Center Erin Skelly went to Michigan State, and Blake's Kinesha Davis went to Western Illinois and then UNLV. Anoka's Theresa LeCuyer went to the University of Minnesota and then UND, Woodbury's Lindsey Huff went to University of San Francisco, Tracy-Milroy's Nadine Brandt went to Northern Iowa, Owatonna's Lisa Bird went to Wisconsin, Blaine's Heather Bantz went to the University of Mississippi and Shakopee's Melissa Sames played at Creighton.

1998: Class A: Christ's Household of Faith vs. Red Lake Falls

Christ's Household of Faith of St. Paul won its first state championship in five tourney appearances by beating Red Lake Falls in the Finals. The Lions beat tournament-newcomer Bethlehem Academy of Faribault, 43-37, in the quarterfinals, and then went on to beat another first-timer in McGregor, 53-34, in semifinal play. Monica Palenschat led the Lions in scoring with 20 points in that game. The Lions then went on to beat Red Lake Falls, a very good team which was playing in its second consecutive title game. Despite the difference in experience, however, Christ's Household of Faith played great and beat the Eagles, 45-36. The Lions took a 25-21 lead at the half and cruised to the title behind Palenschat's 17 points and Ellen Jacox's 13.

Row 1 - L to R: Melissa Forster, Jessica Tvrdik, Shannon Diedrich, Janelle Spoden. Row 2: Jessica Anderson, J. J. Steinhorst, Head Coach Wendy Kohler, Leah Schultz, Katie Heydt, Carly Spencer, Paul Peterson. Row 3: Jenna Staples, Sarah Ekdahl, Assistant Coach Tim Zupfer, Shelly Schoeneck, Janelle Lynch, Sarah Engstrom.

The 1997 State 3A Champs from Alexandria

1998: Class AA: Blake vs. Caledonia

After finishing in second place in 1996 and then third in 1997, The Blake School finally got it right in 1998. The Bears edged St. James in the quarterfinals, 62-60, and then cruised past Glencoe-Silver Lake in the semi's, 49-32. Leading the charge for Blake in that game were Kristin Ambrose and Leslie Dolland, who scored 15 and 13 points, respectively. Then, in the Finals, the Bears took care of Caledonia, 73-57. Caledonia jumped out to an early 6-0 lead, only to see Blake rally to take a 37-24 half-time edge. They blew it open in the second half thanks to the efforts of four players who scored in double figures: Kristin Ambrose, 23 points; Leslie Dolland, 16 points; Kate Baumann, 13 points; and Melissa Marcotte, 11 points.

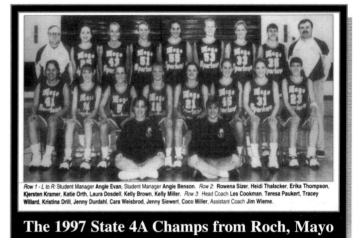

Row 1 - L to R: Student Manager Angie Evan, Student Manager Angie Benson. Row 2: Rowena Sizer, Heidi Thalacker, Erika Thompson, Kjersten Kramer, Katie Orth, Laura Dosdell, Kelly Brown, Kelly Miller. Row 3: Head Coach Les Cookman, Teresa Paukert, Tracey Willard, Kristina Drill, Jenny Durdahl, Cara Weisbrod, Jenny Siewert, Coco Miller, Assistant Coach Jim Wieme.

The 1997 State 4A Champs from Roch, Mayo

1998: Class AAA: Minneapolis North vs. Chaska

In their third state appearance, the undefeated 29-0 Minneapolis North Polars won their first state title. The Polars first beat St. Francis, 69-23, in the quarterfinals, followed by Mankato East, 69-54, in the semifinals — thanks to Tamara Moore's 18 points. The championship game then saw Minneapolis North crush Chaska, 66-33, to take the crown. After racing to a 32-12 half-time lead, the Lady Polars coasted in the second half behind Tamara Moore's 26 points.

Row 1 - L to R: Stephanie Rower, Ellen Jacox, Rebecca Tschida, Tanya Otten, Elizabeth Scheeler. Row 2: Student Manager Justina Person, Adella Alsbury, Avis Gustason, Holly Harms, Head Coach Deborah Harms, Monica Palenschat, Colette Okerstrom, Gretchen Geerdes, Student Manager Benita Alleman. Not pictured: Hanna Bratzel, Jayne Bluhm, Marion Okerstrom.

The 1998 State A Champs from C.H.O.F.

1998: Class AAAA: Bloomington Jefferson vs. Cretin Derham Hall

Playing in its seventh state tournament, Bloomington Jefferson won its fourth state championship by beating rival Cretin-Derham Hall. The Jaguars beat tournament-newcomer Grand Rapids in the quarterfinals, 49-37, followed by Rochester John Marshall, 46-42, in the semifinals. From there the Jag's spanked the Cretin-Derham Hall Raiders in the Finals by the gaudy score of 70-41. Leading the charge for Bloomington Jefferson were: Janel Palbicki, 15 points; Jamie Whitcomb, 12 points; and Megan Kane and Becky Hilgert, 11 points each.

Row 1 - L to R: Melissa Marcotte, Jane Manning, Marie Herwig, Kelly Holschuh, Molly Holschuh, Melissa Anderson, Jenny Gill, Katherine Townsend. Row 2: Assistant Coach Lea Blackwell, Head Coach Ray Finley, Jenny Fields, Maren Leuer, Leslie Dolland, Kate Bauman, Andrea Kay, Marissa McGuire, Kristin Ambrose, Assistant Coach James Williams II.

The 1998 State AA Champs from Blake

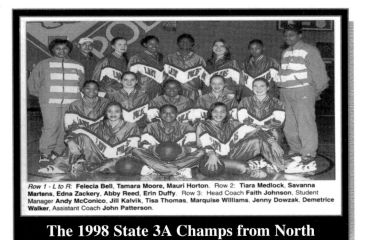

Row 1 - L to R: Felecia Bell, Tamara Moore, Mauri Horton. Row 2: Tiara Medlock, Savanna Martens, Edna Zackery, Abby Reed, Erin Duffy. Row 3: Head Coach Faith Johnson, Student Manager Andy McConico, Jill Kalvik, Tisa Thomas, Marquise Williams, Jenny Dowzak, Demetrice Walker, Assistant Coach John Patterson.

The 1998 State 3A Champs from North

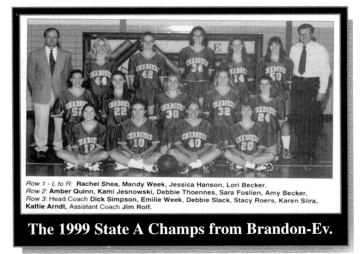

Row 1 - L to R: Becky Hilgert, Kristin Lofgren, Dara Jeffers, Alissa Thorsland, Amy Seibert, Julie Hary. Row 2: Tiffany Meek, Jamie Whitcomb, Jill Peck, Courtney Van Bockel, Lisa Kroog, Brionne Johnson, Ann Dyste. Row 3: Assistant Coach Terri Whitcraft, Assistant Coach Ron Cordes, Rachel Meier, Janel Palbicki, Kelly Have, Alissa Case, Megan Kane, Assistant Coach Todd Johnson, Head Coach Terry Hunst. Not pictured: Rachel Friberg.

The 1998 State 4A Champs from Jefferson

Row 1 - L to R: Rachel Shea, Mandy Week, Jessica Hanson, Lori Becker.
Row 2: Amber Quinn, Kami Jesnowski, Debbie Thoennes, Sara Foslien, Amy Becker.
Row 3: Head Coach Dick Simpson, Emilie Week, Debbie Slack, Stacy Roers, Karen Siira, Kattie Arndt, Assistant Coach Jim Rolf.

The 1999 State A Champs from Brandon-Ev.

Row 1 - L to R: Melissa Anderson, Melissa Marcotte, Jenn Yedoni.
Row 2: Assistant Coach Jason Shantz, Jane Manning, Kristin Ambrose, Jenny Fields, Marie Herwig. Row 3: Head Coach Lea Favor, Maren Leuer, Leslie Dolland, Kate Bauman, Andrea Kay, Marissa McGuire, Junior Varsity Coach James Williams Jr.

The 1999 State AA Champs from Blake

1999: Class A: Brandon-Evansville vs. Red Rock Central, Lamberton

The Brandon-Evansville Chargers defeated No. 1-rated Red Rock Central, Lamberton, 61-46, in the championship game — winning the title in its first appearance at the state tournament. The Chargers first beat Red Lake Falls, 44-39 in the quarterfinals, followed by Waubun, 54-43, in semifinal play. Rachel Shea led the Chargers' attack with 17 points in that game. Then, in the Finals, the Chargers took care of Red Rock Central, 61-46. Brandon-Evansville jumped out to an early lead over the Lady Falcons and cruised from there. Rachel Shea once again led the Chargers with 16 points while Debbie Slack added 15 as well.

1999: Class AA: Blake vs. Minnewaska Area, Glenwood

The Blake School of Minneapolis won its second consecutive and third overall state title in five years. The Blake School opened the tourney with a 48-39 victory over Rochester Lourdes, and then, behind Kristin Ambrose's 19 points, defeated Morris Area / Chokio-Alberta, 62-51, in the semifinals. The Bears then went on to beat Minnewaska Area, Glenwood, in the Class AA championship game. The Bears took a 14-10 lead at the end of the first quarter and extended it to 27-18 by half-time. From there they got some balanced scoring and good defense en route to a 53-44 victory. Leslie Dolland and Kate Bauman led they way with 15 and 13 points, respectively.

1999: Class AAA: Minneapolis North vs. Owatonna

Minneapolis North made it two in a row in 1999 as they opened up the tourney by beating Alexandria, 54-35, in the quarterfinals, followed by Cambridge-Isanti, 70-28, in the semifinals. The Polars then went on to plaster the Owatonna Huskies in the Finals by the score of 72-44. Tisa Thomas led the Polars to a 16-point lead at the half with 11 points and nine rebounds, and the Polars won it going away. Leading the charge for the Lady Polars were a quartet of players in double figures: Tiara Medlock, 20 points; Mauri Horton, 14 points; Abby Reed, 13 points; and Thomas, 11 points.

1999: Class AAAA: Cretin-Derham Hall vs. Moorhead

Cretin-Derham Hall claimed its first state title in 1999 by defeating the previously unbeaten and No. 1-ranked Moorhead Spuds, 62-45, in the championship game. The Raiders beat Woodbury in the quarterfinals, 52-48, followed by Mounds View, 55-41, in the semi's. Then, in the title game against the Spuds, the Raiders took a 32-17 half-time lead and cruised to the championship. Kate Townley finished the game with 27 points, while Jackie Bye added 16 points and 12 rebounds in the big win.

2000: Class A: Fosston vs. Minnesota Valley Lutheran, New Ulm

In its second overall appearance, Fosston won its first state title in the Class A tournament. The Greyhounds first defeated the Duluth Marshall Hilltoppers, 83-56, in the quarterfinals, and then the Rothsay Tigers, 75-47, in the semis. From there the Greyhounds defeated Minnesota Valley Lutheran of New Ulm 64-50 in the championship game. Fosston's Kelly Roysland scored 30 points, while Casey Francis added 12 points and pulled down 13 rebounds in the big win. Leah Morgan and Sarah Gronholz scored 16 and 15 points, respectively, for the Chargers in the loss.

Row 1 - L to R: Abby Reed, Tisa Thomas, LaRaea Starr, Edna Zackary. Row 2: Tiara Medlock, Mauri Horton, Krystal Taylor, Jill Kalrik. Row 3: Savanna Martens, Erin Duffy, Assistant Coach John Patterson, Veronica Harris, Marquise Williams, Demetrice Walker, Barbara Rundles, Head Coach Faith Johnson, Angela Hutchinson.

The 1999 State 3A Champs from North

2000: Class AA: Rochester Lourdes vs. Sibley East, Arlington

In the Class AA tournament Rochester Lourdes won its sixth championship in its 11th overall appearance. In quarterfinal action, the Eagles defeated the first-time qualifiers from Hayfield, 46-35, and then upset the two-time defending champions from Blake, 50-35, in the semi's. Then, in the Finals, the Eagles defeated Sibley East of Arlington, 57-25. Monica Hake led the Eagles with 19 points while and Michelle Melquist added 14. Tera Bjorklund led the Wolverines with 16 points and six rebounds in the loss.

Row 1 - L to R: Kristin Greenwood, Brie Valento, Chris Hayden, Maggie Skrypek, Mary Dienhart. Row 2: Leah Gautschi, Kate Garvey, Kelly Heather, Michelle Fowler, Kari Laliberte. Row 3: Head Coach Tom Cody, Katie Skaar, Rachel Connelly, Chrissy Melander, Jackie Bye, Kate Townley, Assistant Coach Amy Bellus.

The 1999 State 4A Champs from Cretin

2000: Class AAA: New Prague vs. Minneapolis North

In the opening round New Prague defeated the first-time qualifiers from Simley of Inver Grove Heights, 81-43. Then, in the semifinals, the Trojans defeated Marshall, 58-49, behind 17 points from Morgan Proshek and 14 from Randie Wirt.

Now, in the Finals, a blocked shot at the buzzer by New Prague's Wirt stopped the two-time defending champions from Minneapolis North from claiming a third straight title. The Polars led the Trojans 38-25 at half time, only to see New Prague rally back in the second half. Then, with just 7.9 seconds remaining and the score tied at 62-62, Morgan Proshek nailed a pair of clutch free throws to give New Prague the 64-62 lead. The Lady Polars then immediately in-bounded the ball to Jill Kalvik, whose last-second shot was block by Wirt to end the thrilling game.

Row 1 - L to R: Kate LaVoi, Emily Swendon, Tiffany Pearson, Amy Christen, Robin Goldsmith, Chelsea Badurek. Row 2: Student Manager Ruth Carlson, Kara Mageissen, Student Manager Lindsay Miller, Kelly Roysland, Student Manager Megan Sundbom. Row 3: Asst. Coach Scott Antonutti, Tara Erdmann, Kris Sather, Nicole Sundbom, Casey Francis, Head Coach Rochelle Horn.

The 2000 State A Champs from Fosston

2000: Class AAAA: Osseo vs. East View (Apple Valley)

Osseo, which twice earned runner-up honors, returned to claim its second championship in its ninth overall appearance. Osseo dominated the Class AAAA tournament, first beating North St. Paul in the quarterfinals, 67-45, followed by Blaine, 51-35, in the semifinals. From there the Orioles defeated the first-time qualifiers from Eastview of Apple Valley, 80-53, to take the title. The Orioles jumped out to a 37-23 half-time lead and cruised from there behind Hana Peljto's 34 points and 18 rebounds.

Row 1 - L to R: Statistician Katie Mueller, Statistician Abbie Fleischman, Marina Johnson, Sarah Jensen, Laura Nigon, Leah Kodet, Cari White. Row 2: Student Manager Quyen Nguyen, Katherine Kisabeth, Nicole Taylor, Ellen Hake, Monica Hake, Danielle Vlazny, Michelle Melquist, Courtney Williamson, Holly Wiste.

The 2000 State AA Champs from Roch. Lourdes

The 2000 State 3A Champs from New Prague

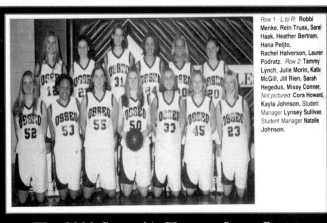

The 2000 State 4A Champs from Osseo

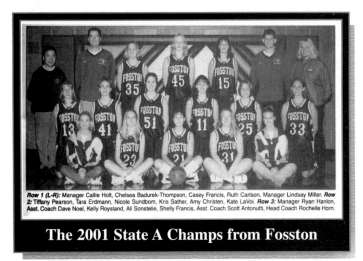

The 2001 State A Champs from Fosston

The 2001 State AA Champs from St. Michael

2001: Class A: Fosston vs. Eden Valley-Watkins

The undefeated Fosston Greyhounds, behind Kelly Roysland's 19 points, defeated Hawley, 56-39, in the quarterfinals. Roysland's 22 points again led the Hounds in the semifinals, where they knocked off Kenyon-Wanamingo, 60-38, to advance to the Finals. There, Fosston won its 51st consecutive game and second consecutive Class A title with a 50-45 victory over Eden Valley-Watkins. The Greyhounds trailed by nine points in the first half, but rallied back behind Roysland, who nailed a pair of three-pointers in the fourth quarter and then made two free throws to put the Greyhounds up for good, 46-45. Eden Valley-Watkins' Tammy Schrammel missed a three-point attempt as the clock was winding down, but the Hounds hung on to take the big win. Roysland finished with a game-high 25 points, while Nicole Sundbom added 14 points and 11 rebounds. Katie Huschle led Eden Valley-Watkins with 16 points and seven rebounds.

2001: Class AA: St. Michael-Albert. vs. New London-Spicer

The St. Michael-Albertville Knights, behind Rachel Jobes' 26 points, defeated Pelican Rapids, 59-38, in the quarterfinals. From there the Knights went on to beat the first-time qualifiers from Winona Cotter, 67-47, in semifinal action. Jenna Stangler led St. Michael-Albertville with 23 points and 17 rebounds in the win.

Now, in the Finals, St. Michael-Albertville rallied from an 11-point deficit to claim its first title in its fist state tournament appearance. The Knights beat the perennial qualifiers from New London-Spicer, 63-59, in an overtime thriller. The Wildcats, who were making their 10th overall tourney appearance, took an early lead in this one, only to see the Knights rally behind the shooting of Jenna Stangler and Rachel Jobes. They combined for 26 second half points to tie it up and send it to overtime. There, Stangler scored back-to-back baskets to put the Knights up 61-59. Then, with 30 seconds remaining in the game, Jobes added two clutch free throws to ice it. Jobes finished the game with 21 points and 14 rebounds while Stangler added 16 points and five rebounds. Kellie Heinen was the top scorer for New London-Spicer, finishing with 21 points and 10 rebounds.

2001: Class AAA: Marshall vs. North Branch

Marshall, behind Shannon Bolden's 21 points, defeated the first-time qualifiers from Orono, 49-43, in opening round action. From there the Tigers beat the Minneapolis North Polars in the semi's, 55-37, behind 17 points from Sascha Hansen.

Then, in the Finals, the Tigers jumped out to an early lead 15-1 lead over North Branch and never looked back. Bolden scored the first 11 points of the game, and the Tigers led 26-21 at the half. Trailing 41-21, North Branch rallied to score the last eight points of the third quarter, but Bolden's jumper was the first of three straight Tiger buckets that killed the Vikings' comeback hopes. Marshall went on to outscore North Branch 15-9 in the final quarter as Bolden finished the game with 21 points in the 56-39 victory.

2001: Class AAAA: Lakeville vs. Elk River Area

The Lakeville Panthers fought off a late rally and got a clutch lay-up from Liz Podominick to win their quarterfinal match-up against the Woodbury Royals, 53-52, in overtime. Then, in the semi's, Podominick and Tasha Martin, who scored 16 and 14 points, respectively, led the Panthers past Bemidji and into the Finals against Elk River.

There, Lakeville, which had made two previous tournament appearances, returned to claim its first state title. Elk River started out strong but ran out of gas in the end. Martin, who played on the varsity for five years, led the Panthers with 10 consecutive points in the final two minutes of the championship game to ice it. Lakeville took a 37-31 lead with one minute remaining in this one and shut down the Elks from there. Podominick led Lakeville with 18 points and 11 rebounds in the 42-31 victory.

No photo identification provided.

The 2001 State 3A Champs from Marshall

Row 1 (L-R): Chelsea Whitcomb, Angie Brown, Kristin Vivant, Chantele Melgaard, Megan Kehrer. Row 2: Katy Slater, Jenny Ford, Asst. Coach Kate Brexler Booth, Head Coach Andy Berkvam, Asst. Coach John Sheehan, Tasha Martin, Amy Thompson. Row 3: Kelsey Becker, Sarah Rieland, Alexis Thoms, Cassie Marks, Krista Mateffy, Liz Podomonick, Michelle Akkerman, Alana Wahl, Mandy Adelmann.

The 2001 State 4A Champs from Lakeville

Janet Karvonen: The Pride of New York Mills

Considered by many to be Minnesota's best-ever female basketball player, Janet Karvonen grew up in New York Mills, a small Finnish community of 800 people near Wadena, about 180 miles northwest of Minneapolis.

Janet loved to play basketball, and her father often took her to Milwaukee to see the NBA's Bucks play. She soon began to take the game very seriously, attending summer camps and, with a lot of hard work, made the varsity basketball team in 1976 as an eighth grader. Then, in 1977, as a freshman, Janet led the Eagles past Mayer Lutheran High School by one point in the title game to win the state championship. It was an amazing feat for the small town, but the Eagles didn't stop there. They won it all the next year against Redwood Falls and just kept on rolling. In 1979, New York Mills would three-peat as state champs, this time beating Albany, 61-52. Karvonen scored 98 points for the tournament, a new record. As a senior, the Eagles again went to the state tournament to defend their title, only this time it would not have the same outcome. In 1980, New York Mills was upset by Austin Pacelli in the semifinals, 55-43. Although they rebounded to beat East Chain, 59-54, for third place honors, it signified the end of one of Minnesota sports' greatest dynasties. Karvonen set the single season scoring record her senior year with 845 points, averaging nearly 33 points per game.

Janet single-handedly put the tiny town of New York Mills on the map. It was a special time for New York Mills during those four years. Just like in the movie "Hoosiers," Janet recalled how the town "emptied out at tournament time," with many of the local farmers driving more than three hours back home from St. Paul every night to milk their cows.

When it was all said and done, Janet had completely rewritten the record books. She had scored 3,129 points over her high school career, the most ever scored by either a boy or girl in the history of Minnesota basketball. Norm Grow of Foley had previously held the all-time career scoring record with 2,852 points, back in the 1950's. To top it all off, she was her class valedictorian.

Along with being named to the all-state team for her fourth consecutive year, Karvonen was named to the Parade All-American first-team and was named as the United States High School Player of the Year. She even got to appear on the Good Morning America TV show as a guest with O.J. Simpson.

After sifting through more than 150 college offers, Karvonen opted for perennial women's basketball powerhouse, Old Dominion University. Old Dominion had just won back-to-back national championships behind one of the greatest female basketball players of all-time, Nancy Lieberman (Cline), who had just graduated. The pressure was on, as some felt that Janet was pegged to be her heir-apparent. In 1981, the Lady Monarchs made it all the way to the NCAA Division I Women's Finals — it was a wild ride to say the least.

After two years at Old Dominion, Janet decided to make a change, and left the school to enroll at ODU's biggest rival, Louisiana Tech University. She eventually cracked the starting line-up at LTU, and in 1984, she played a solid role in leading the school all the way to the Women's Final Four, where Tech ultimately lost to USC.

Janet graduated with a B.A. in Journalism from LTU in 1985 and then came home to Minnesota. For a while, she worked as a reporter at a Duluth television station, and later worked in the legislature for then Minnesota Commerce Commissioner Mike Hatch. All the time, Karvonen was doing some soul-searching and somehow wanted to combine her love of basketball with her newly-found love of public speaking.

"I felt on a gut level that there was a need for female motivational speakers," Janet said. "There were voids that could be filled."

So, in 1988, Karvonen went into business for herself as a public speaker and basketball-camp director — ironic for someone who had dropped out of her college speech class because she was "scared to death" of public speaking. She then established her own educational and sports-oriented company called, Janet Karvonen, Inc. She even established a joint-venture with Reebok and began one of the most successful dual careers on the local sports scene.

As a national public speaker and leadership workshop director, Janet appears in school, corporate, and civic engagements focusing on areas of drug-free choices, self-esteem, and motivation. She also runs the largest girls basketball camps in the Upper Midwest, appropriately called the Janet Karvonen Basketball Camp. In addition, she has become a household name serving as a television analyst for state high school basketball tournaments as well as Women's Big Ten Basketball games.

"I want to be a friend to youth, a great mother, and someone who leads the way and opens doors for more young women for them to discover their worth," she said. "I want to help girls in their teens as they struggle with sense of self, with issues such as suicide, eating disorders, alcohol and drug abuse, and teen pregnancy. In my speaking, I am able to make a difference, and that's been rewarding."

Today, Janet is recognized as one of the all-time great female basketball players. She has spent the better part of her life playing and promoting the game of basketball and has a significant role in giving the fledgling girls' tournament credibility in Minnesota. From the French braided naive teenager that Minnesota fell in love with, to the mega-powerful, successful businesswoman today, she is a wonderful role-model for young girls everywhere. Because of that, she has become one of the most widely sought after speakers in the state.

"My philosophy is that we're developing young women and young women's skills in life," said Janet of her camps. "We're not just limiting it to girls basketball. We want to them feel good about themselves and send them home feeling more confident, ready to take on new challenges and start applying themselves. Academics are really the foundation, but athletics enhance who you are."

Who knows? Had the Minnesota Lynx come along a decade earlier, maybe Janet would've become the Michael Jordan of women's basketball. Regardless, Janet Karvonen is one of the greatest athletes to ever hail from Minnesota and is the modern matriarch of women's basketball in our state.

At six-foot-seven and 230 pounds, Vern Mikkelsen cleaned the boards and scored down low in the paint with such a reckless abandon that he was considered by many to be pro basketball's first real power forward. A rock-solid defender, "Big Mik" was also beloved by his teammates for his relentless work effort. The ultimate team-player, he became a fixture on one of the game's greatest all-time front-lines alongside the likes of fellow Minneapolis Laker Hall of Famer's, George Mikan and Jim Pollard. A gentleman in every sense of the word, Vern Mikkelsen is truly a Minnesota basketball legend.

The original "Great Dane," Arild Verner Agerskov Mikkelsen was raised in the tiny town of Askov, a small Danish community of just 300 souls, nestled halfway between Minneapolis and Duluth in northeastern Minnesota. The son of a Lutheran minister, Mikkelsen got his first taste of basketball in the seventh grade, when he saw his first schoolyard pickup game and decided to jump in and join the fun. He grabbed the ball and ran down the court as fast as he could and stopped only when the kids screamed that he was traveling. "Traveling? What was traveling?," said the lanky 12-year-old. And so began his indoctrination into the game of basketball. Oh sure, that dribbling thing would come along just fine later, and the rest they say, is history!

As an eighth grader he was a substitute, and by his freshman year he was a force to be reckoned with. But, because World War II had taken most all of the young men out of town, the kids on Askov's high school team had to do it all on their own. The superintendent helped out by serving as the team's coach, but the players weren't sure if he'd ever even seen a basketball before. Vern grew as a player throughout his prep career though and even led Askov to the District 25 Finals during his senior year of 1945, only to lose to rival Pine City, 41-36.

Vern, who also participated in baseball and track, went on to graduate that Spring. "I was ranked No. 4 in my graduating class, but still finished out of the upper third," he said jokingly of his eight other classmates. By now though the three-time All-Conference Center had grown to six-foot-five and had inklings of playing college ball. He thought about giving the University of Minnesota a shot, but reconsidered when he found out that All-State Center Jim McIntyre, who had just led Minneapolis Henry to two straight state titles, had just signed up to play for the Gophers.

Then something happened that forever changed Vern's life. That summer, Al Holst, a Hamline professor who used to travel the rural Minnesota countryside to check out basketball recruits for Coach Joe Hutton, was on his way up to the Iron Range to check out a hot prospect. As luck would have it, on his way up north he got a flat tire in Askov. So he pulled into the local Chevy dealership where Elmer Morgansen, who just happened to be a Mikkelsen family friend, got to visiting with him while he was fixing his flat. When Al explained to him that he was a basketball recruiter, Elmer said that as long as he was here that he might as well check out Askov's star player. Al obliged and with that, set out to find Vern, who was working that afternoon in his neighbor Chris Hendricksen's rutabaga field. (During the war rutabaga's became an important food staple for the troops, so many Askov farmers grew them to support the effort.)

"I can still remember seeing him pull up in his 1936 Buick," recalled Vern. "We all knew that he had to be someone important because nobody in our town had a car like that." Sure enough Al found his way there and before he knew it, wound up coming back to the Mikkelsen's home for dinner. There, he was going to try to work his magic and sign up the Piper's next prized recruit.

"Back in those days my parents didn't have a lot of money," said Vern. "My father's income came mostly in kind from the church and also through contributions from things such as chickens, eggs and even an occasional load of coal for our furnace. Sure, my parents really wanted me to go on to college but simply didn't have the resources to do so. So, when this guy shows up for dinner and says he can arrange to have my tuition paid for and even get me a campus job to pay for my room and board, my Lutheran father, himself an accomplished gymnast back in his native Denmark, quickly overlooked the fact that Hamline was a Methodist school. It was an opportunity of a lifetime and something that almost seemed too good to be true. It was as if I had hit the lottery!"

With that, at just 16, Vern enrolled at Hamline University, where he was about to play basketball under legendary coach Joe Hutton. Now, although Hamline was considered a small college (back then there were no Division I, II or III classifications), the school played a big-time national schedule against many colleges and universities which would be considered Division One powers by today's standards.

The highlight of his freshman year came at Chicago Stadium during the Windy City Tournament, where Hamline played DePaul University in front of some 21,000 fans. The fans were all there to root for one guy, Blue Demon All-American senior Center, George Mikan, the nation's best player — bar none. That would be Vern's first real assignment, to try and stop big George.

"If that wasn't baptism by fire, then I don't know what was!," chuckled Vern. "The biggest crowd I had ever played to before that was just six months prior, in front of about 400 people in the Askov Gymnasium. I mean I was just learning the game at that point and was really intimidated to just be out there. I even apologized to George when I finally scored a basket on him. I had no business scoring on him! He was my boyhood idol for goodness sakes and it just didn't seem right. I can still remember running up the court after that and seeing George turn to me to say: 'That's OK kid, you won't score any more...' And he was right!"

Also a Piper track and field standout, Vern would go on to become one of college basketball's finest players, leading his Pipers to three straight MIAC conference titles along the way. During his sophomore year of 1947 he led the Pipers to the NAIA tournament, where they lost in overtime to Indiana State, and their fiery young coach, John Wooden. (The 32-team NAIA tournament, held annually in Kansas City, was a big deal back in the days when the NCAA and NAIA were rival leagues.) It would be the first of three straight NAIA appearances for Hamline, who, after losing to powerful Louisville in the 1948 Finals, went on to win the 1949 NAIA national championship by beating Regis College of Colorado.

By his senior year Vern, who was averaging better than 17 points per game, had grown to be six-foot-seven and weighed in at 235 pounds. He quickly became one of the most coveted NBA recruits in the nation. So, with his Physical Education degree nearly in hand, Vern, who would graduate with honors, was now ready to take that next step into the world of pro hoops, and as luck would have it, his hometown Lakers wanted him badly. By this time the Lakers, who had already won the 1948 NBL and 1949 BAA crowns, were a basketball dynasty. They were on a roll, and saw Vern as the perfect compliment to their star center, George Mikan. With that, the Lakers then used their "territorial draft choice" (which allowed teams to select a local player from its own 50-mile area in the first round by substituting their regular draft position) to select Vern.

"I remember meeting with (GM) Max Winter to go over my first contract," recalled Mik, "and I told him that because I was a center, I was concerned about my playing time with big George around. Max went on to sell me on the notion that George was all set to retire that next season. Well, he was only off by five years! My dad then drove up to meet with Max and I to sign the contract, because I wasn't yet 21 years old. We got it done though and it felt great knowing I was going to be a part of big time professional basketball in Minnesota."

The rest, they say is history for the man who would go on to become basketball's first true "power forward." Known as the Lakers' "Iron Man," Mikkelsen went on to play in 699 games out of a possible 704 — a stretch which included an amazing run of 642 consecutive games played. For 10 glorious seasons, which included four NBA championships and a pair of runner-up spots, the "Great Dane" was a Laker fixture. He played on six NBA All-Star teams, was named All-Pro four times and served as the team's captain for five years, ultimately finishing with 10,063 career points (14.4 ppg) and 5,940 rebounds (8.5 rpg). (Vern was only the sixth player in NBA history to reach the prestigious 10,000 point club.)

He also added 1,141 points (13.4 ppg) in 85 playoff games as well. His amazing achievements still rank him among the all-time leaders in nearly a dozen Lakers statistical categories, right alongside fellow Hall of Famers Wilt the Stilt, West, Kareem, Magic and Shaq. (Just how tough was Big Mik? He even still holds the NBA record for most game disqualifications, with 127!)

Vern ultimately decided to hang up the sneakers after the 1959 season, when it was announced that the team had been sold to a group in Los Angeles. He clearly had the ability to keep playing (just two months before he retired he hit for a career high 43 points against Cincinnati), but wanted to leave the game on his own terms.

Laker owner Bob Short tried to convince him to stay on as a player/coach, even offering him a whopping $25,000 salary and 25% ownership of the team. Vern passed on the offer though because he wanted to devote more time to his family and his aspiring insurance business. Five years later he can still remember coming down to breakfast and having his wife Jean show him the newspaper headline revealing the news that Short had sold the Lakers to Jack Kent Cooke for a whopping $5 million. Said Vern jokingly, "She knew exactly what 25% of five million dollars was!"

Following his NBA retirement, Mikkelsen, who later got his masters degree in Educational Psychology from both the Universities of Minnesota and Oslo, in Norway, built a very successful insurance business. But, in 1967, he got that basketball itch one more time and accepted the offer to become the GM of the upstart Minnesota Muskies of the American Basketball Association. The team got into some financial problems later that season though and wound up moving to Florida. That following summer, George Mikan, who was the commissioner of the league, called Vern to tell him that the defending ABA champion Pittsburgh Pipers were in financial trouble and were moving to Minnesota. They needed a GM, and once again Vern reluctantly agreed. But, like the Muskies, the team lasted just one season and wound up moving back to Pittsburgh.

And, other than a brief stint as Breck High School's basketball coach, Vern's affiliation with the game has evolved into a purely fun one. He still continues to do fundraising work for his beloved Hamline University, and also does some public speaking. His most recent achievement was to help coordinate the 2001 George Mikan Gala at the Target Center which included the presentation of a life-size bronze statue and tribute honoring his long-time friend and teammate. Proud grandparents, Vern and his wife Jean have two sons, Tom and John, and currently reside in Wayzata.

The ultimate honor for Vern finally came on May 15, 1995, when he became the first Minnesota player ever to be enshrined into the Naismith Memorial Basketball Hall of Fame. Escorted down the red carpet by fellow Hall of Famer and friend, Bob Pettit, of the St. Louis Hawks, Mik would later say of his former rival: "That was the longest time I ever spent with Bob without having him score a point against me!"

So who better than to talk about the next 100 years of basketball in the Land of 10,000 Lakes, than the man who seemingly did it all — our very own living legend, Vern Mikkelsen:

"I think overall the state of the state of Minnesota basketball looks great," said Vern. "More and more kids, boys and girls, are getting the chance to play college ball and that is fabulous. I also think that more and more people outside of Minnesota are becoming aware of the talent we are producing here. There has been a steady influx of recruiters coming here to scout local talent and that bodes well for the future of the game."

"We have a lot of basketball history here, and I am glad to see that much of it will come to life in this new book. I think everyone should know about the glorious history that our Lakers had, and celebrating the achievements of all those players is something long overdue. I was also so pleased to see professional basketball return to Minnesota when the Timberwolves were born in 1987. The Lakers left in 1960 and it had just been too long to go without an NBA team. I follow the Wolves very closely nowadays and am very pleased to see that they are making some progress. Sure, they have some problems out on the court, but with guys like Kevin McHale steering the ship, they will address them and get better. They are really a first-class organization from top to bottom. I still root for the Lakers, but when they come to Minneapolis to play the Wolves I gotta say that I like to pull for the hometown team.

"All in all the game is growing and thriving at every level nowadays and I think that all starts with parenting. Sure, I was blessed with some God-given physical gifts, but having supporting and loving parents will always play a huge part of a kid's success in sports. I was lucky too, but I think you have to be able to be in a position to capitalize on that luck when it hits you.

"I also think it is tough for kids nowadays in regards to playing sports. It seems like a lot of them don't want to pay the price for success, and that price gets higher and higher all the time. I grew up in a small town and played all kinds of sports, not to mention drama and band, so I don't know how high school kids today can be happy just focusing in on playing one activity. It seems like so many of them are encouraged by their parents and coaches to not participate in anything else and as a result our kids aren't getting a very well rounded education into the world of sports. There are all-star games and summer camps and it seems like it has all gotten way out of hand, but today is a different era I suppose. I just want kids today to be happy and have fun. Basketball is a great game and it has been such a big part of my life for so long that I wish everyone could be lucky enough to share the things that I got to do.

"As far as the high school game goes, I think it has also come a long way. Some of the old-timers complain about the fact that we have all of the different classes now, and many of them want to go back to the old eight-team format. Sure, that was a fun time, and everyone thought it was great when the Edgertons and Sherburns of the world could come down to the Twin Cities and win it all. But nowadays I think it is great to have so many kids playing in the state tournament and experiencing all of those wonderful memories. So I would like to think that those kids are getting more chances to go on to the next level as well, which, again, is good for the game.

"Overall, I just think that the people here in Minnesota have treated me so wonderfully, and for that I can't thank them enough. I have been able to live my life in peace and raise my family in such a great environment and we just love it here. The fans have always been so respectful of me and have given me just so much support through the years. Even back in our hey-days when we were winning championships it seemed like people were never really that interested in hounding us for autographs and what not, they were just happy to meet you and shake your hand. Most people would rather talk about the weather than what it was like to play the Celtics in the NBA Finals, and that has been wonderful. I even think that is why a lot of pro athletes enjoy living here today, because they can live in peace and enjoy all of the things, like the outdoors, that make Minnesota such a wonderful place. I feel that professional sports adds so much to our quality of life and our whole family environment. It has been such a big part of my life and I couldn't be more thankful. It is so neat to see that even though I played the game 45 years ago, I am still having an impact and really making a difference.

"I feel truly blessed to be able to say that I played for Askov, Hamline and the Lakers. They were all special in their own way. As far as Hamline goes, I just couldn't have found a better place to have started my amazing journey. Joe Hutton was such a great coach and a real friend. He gave me an opportunity to play and learn this wonderful game and for that I will always be grateful. Being a Piper meant the world to me. Being in that small college atmosphere felt like being around family. I even sang for three years with the Hamline Acappella Choir. It was fabulous, I mean to travel around the country with a bunch of beautiful young ladies was a heck of a lot more fun than riding the bus with a bunch of old guys!

"And the Lakers, hey what can I say? It was the best time of my life. To win all those NBA titles was so amazing and something I will never forget. Who knows? I probably could've made more money had I gone elsewhere, but I wanted to play here in Minnesota where it was my home. Being a Laker is who I am.

"Playing basketball has been such a pleasure. It has been a wonderful part of my life and in looking back I really wouldn't change a single thing. So thanks to all the folks in Minnesota who have been so kind to me through the years and who have participated with me in this truly great adventure.

No. Thank <u>you</u> Vern… the pleasure has been all ours.

INDEX

Aakhis, Chuck: 128
Aamodt, Steve: 110,111
Aanstad, Lloyd: 123
Abel, David: 131
Abel, Skip: 136
Abrosimova, Svetlana: 189,191
Ackerman, Tam: 30
Ackland, Bob: 134
Adair, Roger: 130
Adamczak, Annie: 197
Adams, Ron: 139
Adamson, Russ: 168
Addington, Gordie: 67
Adler, Matt: 159
Aese, Lee: 148
Agler, Brian: 190,191
Ahrendt, Mike: 139
Ailts, Becky: 185
Ajax, Warren: 12,17,67
Akason, Brad: 141
Akason, Jim: 129
Akervik, Brian: 154
Allen, Eric: 154
Allen, Jerome: 60
Allen, Ray: 55,60
Ambrose, Kristin: 205,206
Anderle, Mickey: 164
Anderson, Al: 115
Anderson, Betsy: 179
Anderson, Bill: 145
Anderson, Bruce: 148
Anderson, Chet: 133, 172
Anderson, Dale: 132
Anderson, Dan: 100,101
Anderson, Dawn: 181,182,185
Anderson, Dean: 132
Anderson, Denny: 168
Anderson, Ernie: 100,101
Anderson, Greg: 167
Anderson, Jill: 179
Anderson, John: 115,147
Anderson, Mark: 172
Anderson, Mel: 137
Anderson, Oscar: 123
Anderson, Ralph: 168
Anderson, Sheldon: 137
Anderson, Tony: 153
Anderson, Troy: 153
Anderson, Welsey: 122
Anderstrom, Bob: 130
Andrades, Tom: 108
Andruski, Walt: 124
Anfenson, Tim: 147
Anim, Sam: 154
Aranbarri, Enaut: 162
Archibald, Jarvis: 159
Arlich, Don: 132
Arnold, Matt: 160
Arnsseth, Scott: 153
Arzdorf, Mark: 153
Asenbrenner, Mary: 178
Ash, Jeff: 135
Askamp, Marlies: 191
Aswumb, Tom: 135
Auerbach, Red: 20
Auge, Dennis: 140
Austin, Dan: 136
Austin, Neil: 161
Avery, William: 58,60
Aycock, Angelo: 191
Baarts, Lee: 156
Babula, Kim: 186
Backberg, Bruce: 136
Backowski, Milo: 143
Baggenstoss, Vern: 114
Baglien, Duane: 168
Baglien, Ross: 142
Bailey, Elmer: 142
Bailey, Thurl: 47,49
Baker, Dave: 107,108
Bakke, Jason: 157
Balding, Mark: 145
Bandick, Anna: 178
Banks, Bill: 30
Banks, Dick: 127
Bannister, Dan: 152
Bantz, Heather: 204
Bardell, Bill: 152
Barger, John: 124
Barland, Arnie: 141
Barnbanek, Mark: 144
Barnes, Adia: 190
Barrett, Phil: 40
Batta, Tom: 153
Bauer, Michael: 94,95, 171
Bauman, Kate: 205,206
Bauman,, Bruce: 128
Baxter, Chuck: 136
Bay, Rick: 82
Baylor, Elgin: 30,32-35,37
Beachy, Arden: 155
Beachy, Collin: 155
Beachy, Jessica: 178
Beachy, Ryan: 155
Beal, Chris: 186
Beasley, Andre: 109
Beck, Bobby: 157
Becker, Mary: 185
Beckmann, Manny: 168
Beebe, Jeff: 141
Beeson, Brett: 109
Beetsch, Dick: 168
Begalka, Dave: 153
Behagen Ron: 74,75,77,92-93
Belanger, Sara: 186
Bell, Bobby: 71,72
Bell, Ricky: 146
Bell, Tombi: 191
Bellfield, Tim: 152
Belmont, Frank: 109
Benda, Johnny: 104
Bender, Steve: 141,142
Bennett, Bruce: 168
Bennett, Charles: 128,129
Bennett, Travarus: 96
Benson, Doug: 105
Berg, Mike: 108
Berg, Phil: 171
Berger, Ben: 14,15,30,31,45
Bernabei, Paul: 105
Berntson, David: 158
Berven, Ove: 168
Berwald, Lance: 145
Beske, Coral: 177
Bessler, Justin: 171
Bestland, Cy: 160
Beyer, John: 135,136
Bickerstaff, J.B.: 92,95,96
Bidinger, Mary Beth: 195
Biebel, Bob: 106
Bierman, Bernie: 66
Biewen, Paul: 143
Bigalke, Troy: 105
Biggins, Chris: 147
Billups, Chauncey: 58,59
Bird, Lisa: 204
Bittman, Daryl: 145
Bjelland, Mike: 153,154
Bjorklund, Bob: 104
Bjorklund, Jim: 101
Bjorklund, Tera: 207
Black, Jay: 171
Black, Justin: 159
Black, Rod: 168
Blackwell, Lea: 176
Blair, Bill: 49,50
Blakeslee, C.P.: 112
Blanchard, Dave: 104
Bloom, Mike: 20
Blue, Octavia: 190
Bock, JoDee: 178
Bock, Tom: 139
Boeck, Tim: 148
Bogatski, Cynthia: 178
Boger, Chad: 102
Bohlig, Bob: 147
Bolden, Shannon: 177,208
Boline, Ralph: 168
Boll, Derek: 164
Bombach, Steve: 139
Bond, Walter: 84,86,87
Bongard, Don: 123
Bonicelli, Orlando: 125
Boone, Aaron: 160
Boone, Adam: 165, 172
Borgerding, George: 171
Bosley, Bill: 145
Boston, McKinley: 94
Botker, Jordan: 165
Boucinovich, John: 107
Bouman, Todd: 116,155
Bouman, Troy: 154,155
Bourquinn, Glen: 141
Boyum, Murton: 171
Bradley, Steve: 165, 171
Brandenberg, Mark: 142
Brandon, Terrell: 55,57,58,60
Brandt, Nadine: 204
Bratland, Dave: 144
Brau, Brady: 161
Brekke, Dan: 146
Brekke, Mike: 147
Breuer, Randy:45,47,79-81,84,93-95,145-46,171-72
Brewer, Jim: 73-75,77,78, 92-93
Brewster, Louis: 67
Briggs, Greg: 142
Brink, Bob: 155, 168
Brix, Walt: 126
Brocker, Mike: 150
Brockmeyer, Bill: 135
Broich, Mike: 156
Bronson, Carla: 183,184
Brooks, Roland: 81
Brooks, Scotty: 46
Bros, Tony: 93
Brosz, Jeff: 154
Brougton, Steve: 140
Brown, Bill: 124
Brown, Garfield: 65, 92
Brown, Hector: 125
Brown, Jim: 132, 172
Brown, Lillie: 185
Brown, Myron: 60
Brown, Tony: 111
Bruggers, Bob: 134, 172
Brumfield, Maria: 191
Brundige, Matt: 109
Brunstring, Carl: 128
Bryant, Forest: 167
Bryant, Kobe: 14,20
Bucacher, Erin: 191
Buckley, Dick: 127
Buescher, Erin: 189
Buffalo, Ray: 169
Bulka, Rick: 137
Bullock, Louis: 60
Bunnell, Larry: 139
Buntin, Susan: 184
Burau, Dale: 140
Buri, Mark: 99, 172
Burich, Gordon: 123
Burich, Pete: 123
Burk, Dick: 124,125
Burke, Tony: 137
Burleson, Kevin: 95,96
Burnett, Jeanne: 181,182,185
Burns, Pat: 183,184
Burroughs, Tim: 60
Burse, Janell: 191
Burton, Willie: 82-86, 93-95
Buscher, Paula: 184
Butler, Jerry: 131,132, 172
Butterwick, Fay: 121
Buysman, Wendell: 154
Bye, Jackie: 206
Cabalka, Tom: 137
Cadwallader, Josh: 167
Cadwell, Ron: 168
Cady, Ron: 135
Cameron, Paul: 144
Campbell, Tony: 45-48
Card, Karen: 44,185,186
Carlin, Mark: 111
Carlson, Alex: 165
Carlson, Dan: 147
Carlson, Don 15,17,21-23,67
Carlson, Don: 139
Carlson, Drew: 164, 172
Carlson, John: 165
Carlson, Kim: 179
Carlson, Lloyd: 168
Carlson, Tom: 103
Carpenter, Akeem: 160
Carpenter, Dan: 143
Carrier, James: 162
Carson, Kit: 145
Carter, Doug: 151,152
Carter, Kendra: 183
Carter, Randy: 86-88, 95
Carty, Drew: 162
Casey, Tim: 141
Castellani, John: 18,34,35
Castle, Pete: 128
Catron, Kevin: 114,115
Cekalla, Dave: 171
Cervi, Al: 12
Chalfen, Maurice: 14,15,35
Chalin, Jim: 103,139,140
Chamberlain, Wilt: 14
Chapman, Walter: 168
Chaput, Aaron: 171
Charles, Wayne: 157
Chiabotti, Jerry: 168
Chiabotti, Scott: 154
Christensen, Leland: 171
Christensen, Tony: 105
Christiansen, Ray: 65,96
Christianson, Dave: 153
Christofferson, Dennis: 138
Christopherson, Ann: 183,184
Chubin, Steve: 44
Cink, Julie: 183,184
Clark, Archie: 72,73, 95
Clark, Curt: 113
Clark, Dick: 40
Clark, Jim: 113
Clark, Kevin: 82,91-93
Clark, Pat: 127
Cleve, Frank: 14
Clouse, John: 147
Coatta, Jay: 103
Cochran, Shorty: 128
Coenen, Laura: 174, 175
Coffey, Richard: 83-86, 95
Coleman, Pat: 114,157
Collier, David: 164
Colvard, Jack: 103
Connor, Bill: 126
Conroy, Tom: 172
Conroy, Tom: 154
Cooke, Louis: 65,66
Copa, Tom: 150, 172
Corbin, Ty: 45-47
Cordes, Jason: 110
Costello, Mike: 148
Coughlin, Julie: 186
Courtney, Wayne: 168
Cowles, Ozzie: 16,32,67,68,70,102
Craigmile, Ron: 171
Crawford, Erik: 166
Critchley, Tom: 168
Crittenden, Hosea: 88
Cronk, Ray: 70,71,131,132, 172
Cross, Irv: 105
Cumbura, Raymond: 125
Curley, Bill: 51
Curtis, Kim: 184
Czaplewski, Mark: 147,148
Dablen, Marty: 175
Dahlager, John: 154
Dahlberg, Jerry: 168
Dahlke, Dave: 148,149
Dahlman, Nate: 143
Dale, Don: 128,129
Daley, Grace: 189,191
Daly, Joe: 126
Daniels, Bobby: 185
Daniels, Mel: 37,40
Daniels, Preston: 125
Danielson, Daren: 155
Daugherty, Dave: 135
Dave Tank: 168
Davis, Bill: 133, 172
Davis, Craig: 159
Davis, George: 123
Davis, Kinesha: 203,204
Davis, Mark: 45,60
Davis, Mike: 158
Davis, Tommy: 80,81, 95
Day, Shawn: 151,152
Dean, Everett: 101
Dean, George: 131
Dearring, Darren: 157,158
DeBates, Jeff: 159
Deckers, Mark: 146
Deere, Louis: 168
DeKoster, Steve: 136
DeLapp, Myrvin: 124
DeLorme, Scooter: 188,189
DeMaris, Kris: 186
Denman, Brian: 141,142
Dennis, David: 156
Deon, George: 131
Devlin, Corky: 31
DeWitt, Daniel: 166
Dick, John: 124
Dickerson, Keitha: 191
Dickson, Judge: 72
Diebold, Marshall: 102
Dienhart, Mark: 94
Ditty, Erin: 203
Ditty, Tom: 115
Dolland, Leslie: 205,206
Dornisch, Tricia: 180
Dosmann, Devin: 149
Doughty, Bryan: 158,159
Doumer, Charles: 134
Douvier, Randy: 140
Dow, John: 135
Downing, Greg: 145-147, 172
Downum, Denell: 178
Dragotis, Damon: 151
Drew, Stan: 142
Driscoli, Tom: 137
Driscoll, Jim: 148
Driscoll, Pat: 137, 172
Dryer, Perry: 142
Dudek, Brad: 148,149
Dudek, Brian: 149
Duke, Greg: 109
Dukes, Walter: 31
Dungy, Brian: 147
Dungy, Tony: 77
Dunphy, Mike: 129
Durbin, Mike: 178,180
Dutcher, Jim: 77-79,81,83,103
Dvoracek, Dennis: 72
Dwan, Jack: 13,18,19
Eastman, Scott: 145
Ecker, Cal: 164,165
Eddy, Steve: 121
Edwards, Leroy: 17
Edwards, Paul: 104,145
Edwards, Tanya: 189-91
Egerdahl, Gary: 140
Egge, Jennifer: 179
Eha, Doug: 137
Ehnert, Becky: 179
Ehrlichman, Craig: 154,155
Eickhoff, Loran: 168
Eiden, Pete: 138
Eisenschenk, Julie: 181,182
Eisley, Howard: 60
Ekberg, Bill: 125
Ekberg, Sue: 177
Ekdahl, Sarah: 204
Ekren, Stan: 145
El-Amin, Khalid:58,160-62,171-72
Ellens, Jeff: 159
Ellingson, Jim: 103
Ellis, Alex "Boo": 32
Ellis, LaPhonso: 56,59,60
Elzenga, Steve: 148
Embretson, George: 168
Emerson, John: 132
Engel, Cheryl: 184
Engelby, Dan: 156
Engler, Chris: 143,145, 172
Englund, Tonja: 179
Epp, Henry: 125
Epp, Ruben: 125
Erdmann, Bob: 103, 168
Ereun, Darrell: 133
Erickson, Amy: 186
Erickson, Bill: 41,134
Erickson, Curt: 148
Erickson, Darrell: 131
Erickson, Dick: 71
Erickson, Juhl: 156
Erickson, L.: 177
Erickson, Loren: 141
Erstad, Denise: 175
Esaw, Mike: 171
Espeland, Leonard: 168
Evens, Jack: 168
Everett, Dean: 102
Everett, Jeff: 151
Evert, Joe: 166, 167
Exberg, Jerry: 127
Exel, Ken: 12,14,17
Exel, Larry: 131
Exner, Max: 11,101,169
Falenschek, Ron: 146
Falk, Dennis: 136
Fallon, Trisha: 190
Faubush, Lee: 133
Feely, Tom: 99,124
Ferrin, Arnie: 20,26
Fiedler, Bill: 137
Fiedler, Tim: 135
Fiero, Sue: 185,187
Fischer, Dana: 153
Fischer, Daniel: 171
Fisher, George: 160
Fitch, Bill: 16,45
Fitch, Bill: 72,73
Fitzgerald, Kevin: 163
Fitzpatrick, Dennis: 99
Fix, Tom: 133
Fjerstad, Willie: 130
Fladager, Ken: 168
Flater, Brad: 145
Flemming, Pat: 147
Folkl, Kristin: 189-191
Ford, Perry: 111
Forman, Don: 20
Formanek, Frank: 126
Forrest, Brian: 154
Forrest, Mike: 134,135, 172
Forsline, Jessica: 183
Fortier, Bun: 131,133,136
Fortier, Clarence: 168
Foss, Bob: 142
Foss, Bryan: 167
Foust, Larry: 23,31,32
Francis, Casey: 207
Frank, Kasey: 144
Fredrickson, Mark: 136
Freeman, Don: 39,40
Freeman, Kelli: 184
Frericks, Gary: 141
Frericks, Tom: 144
Freund, Bob: 131
Frewing, Katherine: 178,180
Fritsche, Jim: 30,98,128
Fritz, Harry: 111
Fritz, Steve: 99
Fritze, Gary: 136
Froehle, Luke: 157
Frost, Jack: 111
Frost, Rich: 136
Fundingsland, Larry: 134
Fury, Kevin: 142
Gaffney, Ray: 82,83
Gagliardi, John: 104
Galkowski, Jim: 150,151
Gallivan, Phil: 12
Galloway, Norman: 124
Gardner, Earl: 20
Gardner, Laura: 175,195
Gardner, LeRoy: 135, 172
Garmaker, Dick:27,31-35,69,70,92
Garnett, Kevin: 48,50-60
Garrett, Dean: 51,55
Garrick, Tom: 47
Gary Schuler: 168
Gaugert, Rachel: 175
Geibman, Jerry: 126
Gelle, Bob: 69
Gentile, Jim: 129
George, Devean: 100,102
Gerber, Bob: 17
German, Darryl: 131
Germann, Chad: 156
Gerry, Ryan: 105
Gervais, Bernie: 126
Getzlaff, Dennis: 112
Giacomini, Tim: 154
Gibbs, Jerry: 140-142
Giehler, Ryan: 172
Giel, Paul: 73,74
Giesen, Brian: 162
Gilbert, Johnny 165, 166, 171
Gilbert, Wally: 12
Gilbreath, Dave: 114
Gilcud, Dennis: 77
Gillen, Harold: 66, 92
Gilles, Tom: 98
Gilreath, David: 147
Gindorf, Mike: 153
Glass, Gerald: 47,60
Glowacki, Jeff: 151
Glynn, Gene: 141, 172
Goehle, Hugo: 168
Gorton, Greg: 152
Goudge, Dylan: 158
Govig, Bruce: 103,104
Granner, Shawn: 160
Grant, Bud: 16,18,21,22,25
Grant, Bud: 68,69
Grant, Paul: 60
Graphenteen, LeRoy: 133
Green, Albert: 160
Green, Mario: 85,86
Greenwaldt, Sean: 160
Greer, Julian: 171
Greiner, Gwen: 203
Griffin, Andra: 144, 171-72
Griggas, Bob: 71
Grim, David: 88,89
Grimsrud, Dana: 155
Grodahl, Walt: 126
Grohnke, Bryan: 135, 172
Groholz, Sarah: 207
Groom, Jenny: 184
Grover, Charles: 128
Grow, Norm: 171-72, 209
Grund, Jeff: 149
Gugliotta, Tom: 50,55-58
Guidinger, Jay: 107,108
Guiot, Jeff: 112
Gullinsrud, John: 162
Gunlin, Glenn: 124
Gunther, Dave: 112
Guse, Danielle: 179
Gustafson, Adam: 163
Gutzmann, Scott: 152
Haag, Ken: 142
Haanen, Heather: 204
Haaven, John: 129
Hacket, Cory: 165
Haddon, Bill: 137
Haddorff, Oscar: 168
Hafferman, Barry: 146
Hagberg, Rahn: 104,147
Hagemeyer, Gary: 171
Hagen, Dan: 115,116
Hagen, Jon: 113, 171
Hake, Monica: 207
Halbakken, Wally: 109
Halbert, Greg: 111
Haldorson, Burdett: 129
Haldorson, Mike: 103
Hale, Bruce: 12,13
Hall, Hugh: 130
Hall, Mark: 79,80,145
Hall, Stan: 171
Hall, Ted: 99
Hallman, Dick: 124,125
Halmrast, Cliff: 121
Halsey, Sarah: 186
Halvorsen, Dan: 104
Hamilton, Steve: 32
Hanna, Glenn: 168
Hansen, Brian: 80
Hansen, Joel: 148
Hansen, Larry: 133
Hanson, Amber: 204
Hanson, Art: 123,124
Hanson, Brian: 171
Hanson, Dann: 153
Hanson, Don: 135
Hanson, George: 73
Hanson, Gordie: 149,150
Hanson, Jim: 135
Hanson, Mark: 103,138
Hanson, Nick: 164
Hanson, Paul: 137
Hanson, Roger: 133
Hanson, Stuart: 131
Hanson, Tim: 82,83, 172
Hanson, Todd: 110,111,158
Harding, Jim: 41,43
Hargest, Rodney: 143
Hargrow, Maurice: 96,164
Harlan, Kevin: 46
Harris, Eric: 89-93, 95
Harrison, Bob: 21,22,27
Harrower, Kristi: 191
Hart, Dave: 145
Hart, Jim: 137
Hartman, Dave: 134
Hartman, Sid: 12-19,24,26-30,49
Harvey, Mark: 151
Harvey, Red: 132
Hasbrouk, Joe: 139
Haskins, Clem: 82-86,89-92,103
Haskins, Hal: 13,98,126, 172
Haskins, Jamie: 158
Haskins, Paul: 140
Hasselquist, Keith: 150
Hastad, Doug: 137
Hastings, Jim: 137,146,153, 168
Hasz, Herb: 134
Hatanpa, Aaron: 158
Hattenberger, John: 140
Hauck, Dan: 103
Haugen, Erica: 203,204
Haugen, Larry: 145
Haugen, Rex: 168
Haverly, Jill: 186
Hawkins, Connie: 38,41-44,211
Hawkins, Dick: 135
Hawkins, Tam: 30
Hawks, Gordy: 127
Hayden, Molly: 180
Hayek, Pete: 129
Hayes, Jim: 132
Haynes, Marques: 19
Headley, Dick: 13
Healy, Paul: 139
Hedenstad, Howard: 124
Hegland, Wayne: 141
Heglund, Paul: 137
Hegna, Gerald: 132,133
Hegna, Justin: 157
Heidebrink, Doug: 147
Heier, Chris: 161
Heinen, Kellie: 208
Heise, Brian: 144,145
Heise, Tony: 156
Heiss, David: 112
Helgas, Rodney: 171
Hemer, Don: 123
Henderson, Ronnie: 143, 171
Hendricks, Greg: 99
Henke, Al: 131
Henke, Chad: 171
Hennessey, Dave: 146
Henrickson, Bonnie: 182
Hermsen, Clarence: 12,21
Hermsen, Kleggie: 20
Herwig, Katie: 203
Herzan, Dave: 142-144
Hested, Bradley: 156
Hested, Mike: 156
Hested, Ron: 156, 168
Hested, Tim: 156
Heyman, Art: 42-44
Hicks, Wally: 145
Hidlen, Dick: 126
Higgins, Jennifer: 183
Higgins, Larry: 133
Highum, Andy: 155
Hildebrand, Jim: 152
Hilgert, Becky: 205
Hill, Chuck: 129
Hill, Eric: 72,73
Hill, Jim: 136, 172
Hill, Sherry: 185,186
Hill, Steve: 149
Hiller, Jack: 126
Hill-MacDonald, Linda: 176
Hinzman, Jon: 114,116
Hiti, Charles: 108
Hoffman, Don: 130
Hoganson, Howard: 135
Hokenson, Wade: 164
Holder, Bob: 154
Holland, Chris: 63
Holland, Zeke: 111
Hollander, Dave: 137,138
Holleman, Robbie: 164, 165
Hollen, John: 149
Hollman, David: 155
Holm, Denise: 186
Holm, Lloyd: 168
Holman, Eddie: 40
Holman, Jerry: 96
Holmes, Gary: 79-81
Holmgren, Dave: 82
Holmstadt, Nate: 171-72
Holmstrom, Eric: 156
Holmvig, Bruce: 158
Holquist, Gary: 107
Holstein, Jim: 161
Holtan, Korey: 167
Holte, Jonas: 171
Holthusen, Delwyn: 161
Holtquist, Bill: 123
Holverson, Larry: 168
Homuth, Mel: 171
Hoover, Tom: 43,44
Hopfenspirger, Jean: 195
Hopkins, Dave: 107
Horton, Mauri: 206
Horvath, Nick: 164,165, 172
Horyza, Len: 168
Houck, Dan: 140
House, Rhonda: 183,184
Hovde, Fred: 66
Howard, Dan: 133
Howard, Sarah: 180-182
Howell, Zebedee: 81
Howey, Mike: 150
Hronski, Mark: 147
Hubbard, Jerome: 163
Hubbell, Don: 142
Hubert, Gaylord: 129
Hudson, Lou: 71-73, 92-95
Huesby, Steve: 150
Huff, Edwin: 166,167
Huff, Lindsey: 204
Hughes, Juriad: 155
Hull, Warren: 114
Hundley, "Hot Rod": 31,32,35
Hungerholt, Aaron: 155
Hunt, Claude J.: 117
Hunter, Deb: 175
Hunter, Les: 40
Huntington, Omer: 124
Huschle, Sarah: 208
Huselid, Charlie: 130
Hutchins, Dave: 111
Hutchinson, Al: 143,144
Hutton Jr., Joe: 26,30,98,114
Hutton Sr., Joe:15,16,98,102,105, 210-211
Hutton, Tom: 98
Idstorm, Tom: 131
Ike, Jibrahn: 171
Imbolte, Dave: 149
Ingram, McCoy: 31
Inniger, Irv: 38,40
Isaman, Richard: 137
Iverson, Angie: 176
Iverson, Ryan: 171
Ives, Bucky: 135,136
Jackson, Bobby: 59,89-93
Jackson, Dana: 86
Jackson, James: 79
Jackson, Lester: 159
Jackson, Phil: 109
Jackson, Troy: 152
Jacobson, Don: 127
Jacobson, Ed: 127
Jacobson, Joel: 142
Jacobson, Sam: 88-95, 171-72
Jaeger, Amy: 186
Jahr, Jim: 106
James, Courtney: 89,91
James, Karnell: 99
Jameson, Tami: 186
Jameson, Toni: 181,182
Jamros, Brian: 171
Jancaric, Steve: 138
Janckila, Scott: 155
Jaros, Tony: 12,15,20,67
Jenkins, Birman: 108
Jenniges, Derrick: 161
Jensen, Craig: 138
Jensen, Jim: 145, 171-72
Jepmam Ryan: 161
Jerisek, Chuck: 128
Jersak, Daryle: 129
Jessen, Del: 135,136
Jobe, Rachel: 208
Joerger, Blaine: 160
Johnson, Arnie: 111
Johnson, Ben: 161-164
Johnson, Ben: 96
Johnson, Bobby: 103,112
Johnson, Carl: 103, 171-72
Johnson, Charlie: 15,31
Johnson, Dan: 149
Johnson, Dick: 132,135
Johnson, Gary: 137
Johnson, Gus: 110
Johnson, Jack: 125
Johnson, Jason: 154-156
Johnson, Jenny: 174
Johnson, Judy: 195
Johnson, Magic: 14
Johnson, Marc: 161
Johnson, Maynard: 69,70
Johnson, Nicky: 107
Johnson, Phil: 149
Johnson, Roger: 70
Johnson, Ron: 70-72, 92-95, 131, 146, 171-72
Johnson, Steve: 45
Johnson, Tryg: 148
Johnson, Vic: 124
Johnson, Walt: 139
Johnston, Emily: 173
Joldersma, Eric: 102,104
Jonason, Erica: 204
Jonckowski, Dick: 39,43, 168
Jones, Doug: 145
Jones, Jeff: 154
Jones, Keenan: 167
Jones, Shelton: 46
Jones, Tom: 136
Jordan, Reggie: 57
Jorgensen, Johnny: 20
Juntunen, Darren: 149
Jurewicz, Mickey: 178,180
Kachan, Whitey: 20
Kaess, Dick: 126
Kagol, Steve: 135
Kaighn, Ray: 65,97,98
Kalafat, Ed: 26,30,69,70
Kalheim, Cory: 156
Kalland, Guy: 102
Kallenberger, Kal: 140
Kampa, Tina: 179,180
Kane, Megan: 205
Kangas, Diana: 184,186
Kapitan, Jim: 109
Karpinske, Jeremy: 157
Karsten, LeRoy: 122
Karvonen, Janet: 194-197,209
Kasch, Warren: 114
Kaupa, Bruce: 80,145
KeBoer, Kathy: 188
Keenan, Gerald: 168
Keenan, Joe: 106
KeKoster, Carmen: 185
Keller, Gary: 40
Kellett, Fred: 168
Kelly, Arvesta: 41,44,157-159
Kelly, Erik: 160
Kelly, Jack: 168
Keogan, George: 24,98
Kerman, Kenneth: 122
Kernan, Ed: 129
Kersting, Myron: 143
Kerzie, Steve: 168
Kettler, Greg: 141
Kezar, Tom: 132, 172
Kiedrowski, Jay: 136,137
Kiekow, Zack: 167
Kietzer, Curt: 105
Kindall, Jerry: 69
King, Bill: 168
King, Paul: 154
Kingbird, Gerald: 161
Kingsley, Dennis: 148
Kingsley, Norman: 66
Kipp, Ben: 171
Kirchoff, Jay: 154
Kjorness, Steve: 168
Klarich, John: 126, 172
Klasna, George: 126
Kline, George: 70
Kline, Jason: 158
Kline, Jerry: 159
Knezovich, Milan: 128
Knight, Bobby: 73-75
Knight, Paul: 135,136
Knight, Zerek: 167
Knoff, Kurt: 139, 172
Knutson, Dick: 128
Knutson, Jim: 144
Kochevar, Mike: 141
Kochevar, Tom: 141
Kocurek, Marie: 187,188
Koenen, Scott: 109,155
Koepnick, Brian: 113,114
Kolander, Chad:87-89,155,156,172
Koller, John: 147
Kondla, Tom: 72,74, 92-95
Konerza, Kay: 197
Koop, Gary: 144
Kopetka, Frank: 111
Korman, J.J.: 159
Korsmo, Ed: 128
Kosmoski, Dan: 103
Kovach, Frank: 107
Kowalkowski, Norb: 104
Kragerud, Randy: 153
Kramer, A. J.: 168
Kramer, Arvid: 142
Kramer, Ellen: 176
Kramer, Kelly: 190
Kramer, Scott: 111
Krampf, Fred: 120
Krebs, Jim: 30,34,35
Krebs, Stan: 138
Krengel, Jason: 159
Kreun, Darrel: 133, 168
Krize, Ted: 171
Kron, Jason: 115,116
Kron, Steve: 164
Kruger, Kelly: 187
Kuipers, Cody: 163
Kukar, Bernie: 104
Kulbitski, Vic: 125
Kumlin, Dick: 103
Kundla, John: 12,14-18,21,22,24-26,31-34,66,67,70-72,93,99,210
Kunze, Bob: 137
Kunze,Terry:40,71,72,133,188,172
Kunze, Tom: 136
Kupla, Jack: 132
Kuppe, Jake: 163
Kurtz, Mike: 134
Kutz, Ken: 145,146
Kuzma, Don: 196
LaCuyer, Theresa: 204
Laettner, Christian: 48,50,51,60
Lancaster, Mark: 158,159
Landsberger, Dave: 105
Landsberger, Mark: 77,140, 172
Lane, Darius: 163, 172
Lanen, Van: 127
Laney, Bob: 101,135, 171-72
Lang, Andrew: 51
Langeland, Brian: 145
Lankford, Allen: 151
Larson, Greg: 131,132

Larson, Jim: 128
Larson, Pete: 150
Larson, Tammy: 203
Larson, Wally: 139
LaRusso, Rudy: 35
Laumaun, Bill: 103
Lawler, Frank: 65, 92
Lawson, Brent: 166
Leaf, Mike: 110
LeBoutillier, Nate: 159
Lee, David: 111
Lee, Mitch: 82
Lee, Roy: 124,125
Leggett, Sam: 109
Legler, Tim: 62
LeGrand, Odis: 168
Legried, Lee: 178
Lehman, Paul: 70
Lenard, Voshon: 82,86-88,93-95
Lennox, Betty: 189,191
Lens, Greg: 171
Lenz, Tim: 153
Leonard, Bob: 30-32,35
Leonard, Gary: 46,60
Lerino, Jodi: 186
Lervold, Kathy: 194
Lewis, Connell: 84,85
Lewis, Hershel: 110
Lewis, Quincy: 88,89,92,93-95
Lichnerova, Jana: 191
Lieser, Lindsay: 176
Lightly, John: 130,131
Lind, Todd: 149
Lindquist, Mark: 154
Lindsley, Buck: 70
Lingenfelter, Steve: 79,82,143,144, 150,172
Lipp, Brady: 143
Lipp, Scott: 145
Lipp, Steve: 168
Lippert, Ron: 146
Lissimore, Lisa: 194
Lisson, Todd: 163
Littlejohn, Cheryl: 176
Littler, Bliss: 122
Lloyd, Kamani: 159
Lloyd-Curry, Andrea: 189-191
Lockhart, Osborne: 36,77-79,95
Lockhart, Ozzie: 160-162
Loeblein, Shannon: 176,201
Loewen, Leroy: 129
Loge, Kevin: 159
Lohaus, Brad: 45,46
Londgren, Duane: 127
Longley, Luc: 47,48,60
Longueville, Joe: 148
Lonneman, Cindy: 185
Lopez, Felipe: 59,60
Lovellette, Clyde: 28-31
Lovrien, Jim: 158
Lowe, Sidney: 46,49
Lubarski, Bob: 146
Luebbe, Dennis: 147,148
Luebbe, Doug: 144
Luering, Fred: 66
Lund, Dennis: 140
Lundell, Dick: 133
Lurken, Brent: 167
Luse, John: 140
Luther, Cal: 73
Luymes, Les: 115
Lynch, George: 115
Lynch, John: 149
Lynch, Kevin:84-87,95,152-54,172
Lynch, Red: 114
Lysaker, Pete: 109
MacIver, Doug: 110
Mackay, Harvey: 73
MacKinnon, George: 66
MacLeod, Larry: 108
MacMillan, Dave: 15,210
Maddox, Charles: 156
Madison, Gary: 146
Madrinich, Kate: 187
Maetzold, Butsie: 130
Maetzold, Jim: 125,126
Maetzold, Russell: 168
Magdanz, Eric: 71
Mahlum, Kelly: 179,180
Mahorn, Rick: 45,46
Maley, Matt: 151
Malmar, Steve: 132
Malone, Gordon: 60
Malosky, Jim: 127
Manderfeld, Mary: 175,183,184
Manke, Rick: 138
Mantel, Dave: 109
Marbury, Stephon: 50-52,55-57
Marcotte, Melissa: 205
Margenthaler, Matt: 114
Mariucci, John: 69
Marmeczak, Frank: 123
Maros, Jake: 162
Marquart, Jerry: 135,136
Marshall, Donyell: 50,60
Marshall, Jason: 108
Martin, Bob: 86-88,95,154
Martin, Maurice: 45
Martin, Maylana: 190,191
Martin, Slater: 16,21,23,25-31
Martin, Tasha: 208
Martins, Wes: 72
Mason, Deb: 188
Masterson, Tom: 137
Matchinsky, Dick: 104,105
Mattke, Glenn: 134
Mattson, Bill: 108
Mattson, Don: 125
Mattson, Red: 125
Matyas, John: 120
Mauer, Kenny: 13
Maurice, Larry: 171
Maus, Ron: 138,139
Maxey, Marlon: 60
May, Al: 145
Mayasich, John: 71
Mayer, Patty: 178
McCarrell, Dan: 113,114
McCarron, Jeff: 138
McCloskey, Jack: 48,50
McCollow, Mike: 156
McCormick, Frank: 68
McCoy, Marlon: 159
McDermott, Steve: 103
McDonagh, Matt: 157
McDonald, Ariel: 86-88,95
McDonald, Bob: 157,168
McDonald, Joel:116,157,166,172
McDonald, Mike: 141,142,157
McDonald,Paul:141-43,157,171-72
McDonald, Scott: 138
McDonald, Tom: 148, 171
McGregor, Bob: 158
McGuire, Shawn: 166
McHale, Kevin: 46-55 57,59-61,78 80,85,93,142,144,150, 172,211
McIntyre, Jim:67,70,92,95,127,172
McKay, Jason: 154
McKenzie, Lawrence: 167
McKinney, Billy: 45,48
McLagen, John: 134
McMahon, Dan: 157
McMillan, Dave: 16
McNamara, Bob: 70
McNeal, Brett: 151,171
McNeal, Bronson: 151
McSweeny, Elisha: 113
McWaters, Dick: 125,126
Mealey, Bob: 127
Means, Dick: 69
Medlock, Tiara: 206
Meerschaert, Mark: 166
Meincke, Lance: 110
Meisner, Dave: 110,134,135
Meisner, Paul: 142
Melby, Si: 100
Melhofer, Jerry: 150
Melquist, Michelle: 207
Mencel, Chuck:19,30,69-71,92-95
Mernik, Joe: 124
Mesman, Reed: 166
Mestas, Robert: 172
Metcalf, Rob: 86
Meyer, Brenda: 181-183
Meyer, Deb: 186
Meyer, Josh: 107
Meyer, Kathy: 177
Meyer, Maynard: 129
Meyer, Ray: 15,16,24,27
Meyer, Ronald: 134
Meyer, Terry: 131
Meyers, Dan: 139
Meyers, Kyle: 145
Miasek, Stan: 13
Michaelan, Dave: 131
Micheau, Dan: 146
Mickelson, Allen: 134
Mickow, P.: 177
Middendorf, Aaron: 161
Mikan, George: 12-24,26 31,37,38, 44,67,72,73,210,211
Mikan, Larry: 74,95
Mike Glidden: 168
Mikkelsen, Vern:12-14,16,18,21-23-28,30-37,41,43,97-98,210-11
Mikkelson, Ervin: 129
Miles, Tim: 109,110
Miley, Thomas: 164
Millen, Dick: 132
Miller, Coco: 191,203,204
Miller, Darrell: 131
Miller, Dick: 69
Miller, Doug: 141
Miller, Jenny: 195
Miller, Kelly: 191,203,204
Miller, Virgil: 128
Miller, Wendell: 129
Mills, Gordon: 122
Mills, Sherron: 60
Minea, Eric: 159,160
Mitchell, Darryl: 79-82,95
Mitchell, Sam: 46-51,56,59,60,62
Mitchell, Wes: 67
Moen, Mike: 155
Moening, Butch: 138,139
Moes, Mike: 104
Mohr, Max: 67
Moir, John: 125
Molstre, Steve: 153
Molzahn, Bill: 142
Monroe, Gerrick: 102
Monroe, Trevor: 155
Monson, Dan: 93-96
Monson, Rudy: 108,128
Montbriand, Greg: 149
Montgomery, Pat: 187
Moore, Doxie: 13,17
Moore, Rob: 161
Moore, Tamara: 205
Moos, Carolyn: 203,204
Moren, Ray: 129
Morgan, Leah: 207
Morris, Bill: 113
Morrissey, Karen: 186
Morrissey, Mike: 168
Moses, Israel: 157
Mosher, Ellen: 175
Moss, Randy: 112
Mottteberg, D.J.: 161
Movold, Ralph: 117
Mrkonich, Joe: 136
Muckinhirn, Paul: 143
Muelken, Mona: 186
Mueller, Don: 132
Mulder, Kevin: 109
Mulder, Larry: 139,140
Mullin, Duane: 103
Mulso, Tom: 138
Murphy, Bob: 73
Murphy, Dennis: 37
Murphy, Tod: 46,47
Musselman,Bill:45-48,58,62,73-78
Musser, Harry: 134
Mustar, Mike: 151
Myers, Kyle: 145
Myrum, George: 103
Nabedrick, Dan: 155
Nace, Paul: 127,128
Nagorski, Mike: 153
Naismith,James:9-11,65,66,97,101, 117,173,192
Nefstead, John: 134
Nelson, Brian: 145
Nelson, Chad: 171
Nelson, Dave: 135
Nelson, Dick: 126
Nelson, Edor: 100
Nelson, Jacob: 157,158
Nelson, Kelly: 171
Nelson, Linda: 181,182,185
Nelson, Mark: 152
Nelson, Marsh: 168
Nelson, Matt: 152
Nelson, Scott: 147
Nelson, Stacy: 186
Nelson, Tim: 152
Nelson, William: 52
Nerud, Dan: 153
Ness, Norman: 128
Nessler, Jeff: 140
Nestande, Pete: 131
Nesterovic, Rasho: 58-60
Nett, John: 149,168
Nettleton, Jake: 108
Neubauer, Tom: 147
Neumann, Chris: 171
Nevers, Gordon: 188
Newbern, Melvin: 83-87,95
Niehaus, Jan 181,182
Nigon, Matt: 155
Nix, Bob: 73,74,77
Nohl, Terry: 203
Nordeen, Lisa: 178
Nordgaard, Jeff: 156,157,171
Nordland, Tom: 131,132,171-72
Nordly, Dr. Carl: 67
Nordly, Oliver: 102
Norlander, Gene: 128
Norlander, Johnny: 98
Norman, Rob: 146
North, Fred: 132
North, Ron: 132
Northenscold, Jim: 142
Northway, Mel: 71,72,95
Norton, Martin: 119,171
Novak, Ken: 115,168
Novak, Sarah: 184
Novotny, Dan: 158
Nuest, Chad: 161
Nuness, Jared: 162
Nydahl, Molly: 66
Nylund, Ed: 125,126
Nzigamasabo, Ernest: 88
O'Neal, Shaquille: 14
O'Shea, Kevin: 30
Ochs, Linda: 180
Odonovich, Joe: 168
Ogden, Larry: 151,152
Ohm, Elsie: 184
Ohman, Eddie: 132
Ohme, Jen: 186
Ohnstad, Mitch: 171-72
Olberding, Mark:77,79,93,140-42, 172
Oldfield, Brenda: 176
Olin, Elsie: 175
Olsen, Lute: 91,100
Olson, Brad: 143
Olson, Don: 127
Olson, Erin: 176
Olson, Jerry: 130,131
Olson, Kyle: 162
Olson, Mike: 109
Olson, Noel: 115
Olson, Norm: 107
Olson, Paige: 180
Olson, Richard: 168
Olson, Richie: 133
Olson, Tim: 145
Olson, Wilburn: 122
Omerza, Tom: 147
Opatz, Ruth: 178
Oren, John: 147
Orr, Townsend: 63,86,95
Osborne, Manly: 132
Osgood, Stacy: 17
Oss, Arnie: 67,92-93
Osterkorn, Wally: 13
Ostermann, Chad: 158
Ostrom, Taffy: 180
Otterness, George: 66
Overskei, Larry: 72
Overton, Redd: 147,148,172
Owen, Kelley: 185
Owens, Katrina: 188
Oxborough, Steve: 145
Palbicki, Janel: 205
Palenschat, Monica: 205
Palmer, Erol: 38,40
Parker, John: 151
Parkhurst, Ronald: 118
Parks, Cherokee: 56
Paskiewicz, Tom: 150
Pater, Mike: 165
Patten, Greg: 165-66
Patton, Mike: 165
Patterson, Adraian: 157,158
Patterson, Andrae: 60
Patterson, Bill: 103
Patterson, Mike: 108
Patzwald, Johnny: 103
Paxson, Ben: 171
Paxson, Jim: 30
Paye, Kate: 190
Payne, Joan: 180
Pearsall, Sam: 162
Pearson, Ben: 163
Pearson, Cara: 176
Pearson, Kevin: 156
Pearson, Richie: 137
Pearson, Tom: 152
Peck, Jack: 168
Pederson, Brian: 80,143-145,172
Pederson, Doug: 143
Pederson, Michelle: 179
Pederson, Missy: 179
Pederson, Ron: 104
Peeler, Anthony: 51,56,57,60
Peik, J.: 177
Peljto, Hana: 207
Pennington, Dick: 137
Pepelnjak, Nick: 124
Pergol, Angelo: 168
Perkins, Reggie: 36,114-116
Perkins, Rich: 144,145
Perpich, Rudy: 44
Perrin, Dan: 152
Perry, Ron: 39,40
Person, Chuck: 48-50
Petain, Charles: 142
Peterreins, Mike: 171
Petersen, Jim: 45,80,81,95,146-47,171-72
Peterson, Billy: 125
Peterson, Bob: 101,104,136,172
Peterson, Brian: 138
Peterson, Dick: 101,136,172
Peterson, Janet: 178
Peterson, Laurie: 178,186
Peterson, Lloyd: 107
Peterson, Lynn: 183,184
Peterson, Robbie: 149
Peterson, Ted: 168
Peterson, Wayne: 141
Petrich, Chuck: 140
Petrich, Jim: 139
Petrich, Lou: 127
Petrich, Mike: 151
Pettis, Mike: 163
Pettis, Terry: 165,167
Pettit, Bob: 31
Pettit, Joel: 140
Pfepsin, Ed: 133
Pheips, Jack: 133
Phenix, Rob: 153
Phifer, Scot: 144
Phillips, Don: 157
Phipps, Jahmai: 159
Pickens, Brandy: 176
Piechowski, Tim: 171
Pierson, John: 132
Pineovich, Mike: 124
Pivec, Don: 123
Plandon, Dennis: 134
Platou, Erling: 66,92-93
Ploof, Doug: 143
Podoloff, Maurice: 20,23
Podominick, Liz: 208
Pollard,Jim:12-19,21-30,35,40,102
Polomny, Mike: 109
Pontliana, Como: 139
Porter, Jerry: 133
Porter, Terry:51,56,59,116,134,135
Porter, Willie: 44
Potter, Larry: 139
Potthoff, Angie: 190
Presthus, Paul: 72
Price, Spencer: 133
Pride, Lynn: 189,191
Prohofsky, Ed: 168
Proshek, Morgan: 207
Pryor, Ann: 185
Przybilla, Joel: 91-95,163,171-72
Quaschnick, Jillayn: 178
Queen, Tony: 152
Quigley, Josh: 107,160
Race, Dale: 107
Radosevich, Tim: 152,153
Raitz, Troy: 152
Rakocevic, Igor: 60
Ramm, Casey: 145
Rancik, Rado: 116
Randall, Mark: 157
Rasey, Black: 66
Rashad, Ahmad: 47
Rasmussen, Don: 129
Rasmussen, Doyle: 129
Ratner, Harvey: 44,45,49,56
Ravenhorst, Dick: 127
Ray, Del: 104
Raymond, Butch: 113
Redman, Alan: 134
Reed, Abby: 206
Reed, Brandy: 189-191
Reed, Clayton: 133
Regnier, Joe: 151,152
Reiger, Bob: 128
Reimer, Don: 128
Reiten, Dave: 101
Remme, Tim: 153
Restad, Pete: 144
Retica, John: 142
Retica, Mario: 168
Reuben, Derek: 152,172
Rheigans, Darcy: 185
Richardson, Harper: 127
Richardson, Pooh: 44,46-48,50,60
Richardson, Tom: 129
Rickert, Rick: 96,167,171-72
Rider, Isaiah: 49,50,60
Riles, Jim: 140
Riley, Dennis: 138
Riley, Mark: 152
Ritzer, Kelli: 186,187
Rivers, David: 45
Robbin, Buck: 124
Roberts, Christy: 186
Roberts, Linda: 174,175,194
Roberts, Loren: 60
Roberts, Stanley: 56
Robinson, James: 51
Robs, Bryan: 115
Rodgers, Jimmy: 47-49
Roefil, Sheila: 201
Roels, Harvey: 168
Rogers, Emmanual: 139
Rogloski, Ramona: 181
Rogne, Steve: 158
Rohs, Bryan: 141
Rolando, James: 127
Rolek, Marty: 67,92
Rolf, Tim: 145
Rolland, Krista: 186
Romano, Ralph: 108
Rood, Lee: 155
Rooks, Sean: 51
Rosengren, Dave: 145
Rosga, Steve: 158
Rosier, Bob: 99
Roth, Scott: 46
Roysland, Kelly: 207,208
Ruda, Steve: 163
Rugloski, Ramona: 181,182,185
Rulifson, Dave: 125,126
Rummels, Derrick: 152
Runk, Adam: 162
Rupp, Adolph: 17
Rushin, Steve: 150
Russell, Bill: 30
Ruud, Melvin: 125
Ruud, Scott: 152
Ryan, Frank: 32,34,35
Rychart, Dusty: 93,95,96
Sabourin, Wes: 128
Saggau, Rich: 151
Salathe, Kim: 195
Salmi, Walt: 124
Salscheider, Karl: 111
Sames, Melissa: 204
Samuelson, Simona: 181,182
Sanden, Kyle: 91
Santleman, Lawrence: 122
Saul, Pep: 26
Saunders, Flip: 50-61,77,79,95
Schaap, Jeff: 166
Schaefbauer, Skipp: 159,172
Schaeffer, Herm: 17,19-21
Scheele, Dave: 141
Scheid, Dan 164
Schelhaas, Tyler: 164
Schellhas, Kurt: 136,137
Schellhase, Dave: 109
Scherer, Diane: 181, 182,185
Schiffler, Bill: 150,152
Schiffler, Del: 168
Schilling, Shane: 95,163,165
Schilling, Tim: 104
Schindler, Rock: 147
Schlaak, Kyle: 110
Schlaak, Tim: 158
Schlagel, Kevin: 115
Schmeising, Izzy: 114,115
Schmidgall, Cory: 159
Schmidt, Luke: 102,103
Schmiesing, Joe: 134
Schneider, Tom: 147
Schnittker, Dick: 30
Schoeneck, Shelly: 204
Schoenecker, Ron: 143
Scholthauer, Steve: 172
Schonrock, Shannon: 177
Schrammel, Tammy: 208
Schreier, Andrea: 187
Schreifels, Judy: 185
Schreiner, Tina: 181,183
Schroeder, Dennis: 135
Schroeder, Phil: 147
Schueller, Bob: 154
Schultz, Howie: 12,23,26,98
Schultz, John: 113
Schultz, Mary: 177,178
Schwanke, Dave: 134
Schwanke, Don: 134
Schwartz, Jack: 142
Scott, Anthony: 163
Scroggins, Steve: 161
Sealy, Malik: 58,59
Seeback, Dick: 123
Seiffert, Greg: 148
Selisker, Bill: 168
Selk, Larry: 168
Seltz, Rollie: 13,98
Senkse, Gary: 108
Senske, Steel: 154
Senst, Tom: 138
Sentieri, Paul: 148
Severson, Jim: 111
Severson, Red: 115
Sexton, Bill: 104,105
Seymour, Paul: 12
Shaffer, Dennis: 77
Shannon, Ollie: 72,73,77
Sharps, Denise: 188
Shasky, John: 81,82,95
Shea, Katie: 182,202
Shea, Rachel: 206
Shea, Ryan: 157
Sheeran, C.L.: 98
Sheets, Duane: 135
Shelquist, Robb: 172
Sheplee, Corey: 162
Shields, Larry: 40,41
Shikenjanski, Jim: 83-86
Shively, Tim: 152
Short, Bob: 211
Short, Robert: 14,31,32,35
Siemon, Kelly: 204
Sievers, Stacy: 186
Silbernagel, Joe: 148
Silbernick, Brian: 143
Silk, Brian: 162
Simes, Glen: 171
Simmons, Terrance: 95,96
Simmons, Vern: 165
Simms, Dominique: 163
Simonovich, Bill: 69,129
Sims, Dominique: 164
Singleton, Marvin: 152
Siverson, Duane: 101,178
Skalicky, Kelly: 197
Skelly, Erin: 204
Skoglund, Steve: 126
Skoog, Rod: 130
Skoog,Whitey:16,26-31,68,93,103
Skyberg, Dale: 137
Skyberg, Kennard: 123
Slack, Debbie: 206
Sladum, Arnold: 123
Smed, Roger: 131
Smith, Charmin: 191
Smith, Chris: 60
Smith, D.L.: 103
Smith, Don: 12,14,17,128
Smith, Jim: 104,105,128
Smith, Joe: 50,56-59
Smith, Katie: 189-191
Smith, Kevin: 82,83
Smith, Ron: 128,129
Smith, Sam: 40
Smith, Troy: 147
Smock, Wes: 124
Snyder, Andy: 129
Snyder, Jerry: 168
Snyder, Justin: 166
Sohre, Matt: 158
Solie, Ryan: 161
Solien, Wally: 126
Sonnarborg, Ken: 128
Spande, Carl: 167
Spanier, Joyce: 178,180
Spears, Sara: 204
Spencer, Felton: 47,50,51,60
Springer, Jim: 103
Spronk, Scott: 154
St.John, Irv: 168
Stachowski, Brenda: 183,184
Stackpool, Jack: 168
Stadsvold, Francis: 66,92
Stadum, Jim: 136
Stadum, Loren: 125
Stafford, Cheri: 176
Stainer, Scot: 142
Stanbra, Gene: 125
Stangel, Wade: 153
Stangl, Matt: 162
Stangler, Jenna: 208
Stanglund, Herb: 132
Stanley, Chris: 108
Stark, Johnny: 66
Starkey, Ken: 146
Stauber, Aaron: 90
Stehr, Sonia: 186
Stein, Bob: 46
Stemen, Greg: 110
Stensgaard, Chris: 148
Stensgaard, Dick: 147
Stephan, John: 128,129
Stephens, Scott: 72
Sternberg, Dan: 156
Sternhagen, Kim: 178
Stinar, Ray: 168
Stires, Shanele: 191
Stirmlinger, Kyle: 163
Stoeve, Mark: 138
Stokes, Terrance: 164
Storsved, Brett: 153
Straka, Cliff: 103
Strand, Hartvik: 168
Strand, Shocky: 137
Stromer, Ray: 123
Stromm, Dave: 185
Stromme, Karen:178,179,185,186
Stussy, Lloyd: 168
Suarez, Tulio: 150
Sue, Grack: 179
Suek, Marty: 178
Suggs, Ricky: 146
Sullivan, Jake: 166,171-72
Sundborn, Nicole: 208
Sundin, Gordie: 131
Suomala, Sadie: 186
Sutor, George: 44
Suttles, Byron: 160
Sutton, Jim: 136
Sutton, Matt: 126
Svenningson, Al: 110
Swanson, Todd: 146
Sweeney, Pat: 131
Swenson, Ron: 135
Syring, Dick: 134
Szczerbiak, Wally: 50,55,58-60
Tadich, Molly: 176
Tank, Terry: 159
Tanner, Robert: 66
Tarver, Miles: 89,93
Tate, Sonja: 190
Tatum, Goose: 19
Taube, Mel: 102
Tauer, Johnny: 157
Taylor, Corky: 73-75,77
Taylor, Bob: 137
Taylor, Charlie: 109
Taylor, Fred: 74
Taylor,Glen:49-59,114,184,190-92
Taylor, Harold: 66
Taylor, Megan: 204
Taylor, Myron: 158,159
Taylor, Paul: 139
Ted Pelzl: 168
Teist, George: 134
Terhaar, Dave: 141
Thalberg, Curt: 132
Theis, Dave: 106
Thelan, John: 138,139
Thelen, Mason: 164
Theuninck, Rick: 156
Thielke, Justin: 161
Thielke, Tony: 161
Thom, Steve: 150
Thomas, Carl: 128
Thomas, Charles: 89,91
Thomas, Joe: 165
Thomas, John: 88-91,93
Thomas, Tisa: 206
Thomforde, Chris: 104
Thompson, Aaron: 161
Thompson, Chester: 122
Thompson, David: 107,108
Thompson,Mychal:78-85,88,92-95
Thompson, Owenn: 129
Thompson, Rip: 139
Thompson, Tuffy: 123
Thone, Greg: 135
Thoren, Skip: 40
Thoreson, Whitey: 168
Thornley, Stew: 13
Thorre, Ben Van: 105
Thurnblad, Jack: 102
Thurston, Orieon: 115
Thykeson, Michelle: 178,179
Timmons, Mickey: 139
Tobin, Mike: 109
Todnem, Louis: 168
Toles, Dennis: 140
Tomsche, Mary: 178
Totushek, Ross: 136
Townley, Kate: 206
Tradewell, Mat: 165
Traham, John: 124
Tranz, Pete: 129
Trebbensee, Nancy: 185
Trembath, Chad: 160
Trenkle, Tiffany: 201
Trent, Gary: 60
Trewick, Mike: 115
Trochil, Bennett: 134
Troland, Greg: 137
Trost, Dave: 144
Troup, Van: 146
Trow, Laurie: 178-180
Troxel, Brad: 147
Tschemperie, Dan: 129
Tschemperie, Dave: 129,130,172
Tschimperle, Jane: 178
Tubbs, Nate: 87
Tuck, George: 65,92-93
Tucker, Trent: 79-82,85,92-95
Tunstall, Marvin: 106
Turgeon, Mark: 146
Turner, Clyde: 73-75,77
Turnquist, Dale: 104
Ullman, Vern: 34
Ulness, Vern: 125
Vacendak, Steve: 44
Valentino, Karyn: 183,184
VanDenEinde, Paul: 150
Vanderbilt, Mark: 139,140
VanderHeyden, Cassie: 176
VanDerveer, Heidi: 190
Vanek, Jerry: 120
VanGorden, Emily: 182
Varriano, John: 168
Vaughn, Chico: 41,42,44
Veenhof, Dean: 133,172
Ventura, Jesse: 56
Verdoes, Dean: 133
Vink, Tim: 149
Vipond, Kirsten: 180
Virgin, Kurt: 138
Vogel, Steve: 142
Voit, Jeff: 154,155
Volz, Gene: 171
Vos, Bob: 147
Voss, Roger: 132
Vujovick, Nick: 125
Wachlarowicz, Frank: 104,142,143
Wacker, Wade: 153
Wackler, Mark: 145,146
Wade, Jack: 130
Wager, Clint: 106
Wagner, Bob: 130
Wahl, Sue: 181,182,185
Wahl, Tim: 113
Waldahl, Laurel: 168
Walker, Ann: 183,184
Walker, John: 153
Wall, Elbert: 160
Wall, Ray: 127,128
Wallendorf, Joshua: 172
Wally, Chuck: 131
Walseth, Maren: 204
Walter, Judd: 162
Walters, Gary: 143
Walters, Lisa: 183,184
Walthall, Chad: 152
Walton, Jayson: 86-88
Wanamaker, Bill: 168
Wandmacher, Mark: 102
Ward, Dan: 115,156
Ward, Jeff: 137
Ware, James: 160
Warford, John: 135
Warhol, Bill: 12,123,124,172
Warmath, Murray: 37,72
Warner, Erwin: 108,109
Warren Keller: 168
Washington, Jabbar: 160,161
Washington, Tom: 41-44
Wasinger, Tim: 144
Weaver, Tom: 135,136
Webb, Spud: 51
Weisman, John: 114
Weiss, Travis: 105
Wells, Jeff: 136
Wells, Linda: 174
Wendorff, Laura: 180
Wentworth, Dennis: 103
Wertish, Doug: 139
West, Doug: 46,48,49,56,60
West, Jerry: 14,37
Westberry, Kavon: 160
Westby, Pat: 150
Western, Ralph: 109
Westland, Mike: 143
Westlund, Dave: 115
Westlund, Roger: 115
Westrum, Rod: 130
Whalen, Lindsay: 177
Whaley, Phylesha: 191
Whilook, Ira: 110
Whitaker, Walt: 109
Whitcomb, Jamie: 205
White, Eric: 46
White, Justin: 159
White, Malcolm: 108
White, Maurice: 12,13,15,17
White, Ron: 103
White, Rory: 63
Whiting, Jack: 130,131
Wholer, Barry: 115
Wiebusch, Richard: 168
Wieczorek, Paul: 148
Wiersma, Brian: 171
Wildenborg, Ryan: 95
Wilhelm, Josh: 102
Wilkinson, Bud: 12
Willard, Tom: 136
Willberg, Russ: 126
Willerscheidt, Mary: 184
Willette, Renee: 180
Williams, Bob: 30
Williams, Charles: 42-44,108
Williams, George: 82
Williams, Henry: 68,69
Williams, Jimmy: 74,103
Williams, Michael: 48-50
Williams, Patrick: 158
Williams, Randy: 142
Williams, Ray: 78,79,92-95
Williams, Walt: 168
Williamson, Christine: 181-183
Wilson, Donna: 188
Wilson, John: 150
Wilson, Marc: 81-83,95
Wiltgen, Mark: 147,148
Winey, Dave: 79
Winfield, Dave: 74-77
Wingo, Mark: 164
Winston, Maury: 14,15
Winter, Max: 15,17,22-29,35,210
Winter, Trevor: 88-90
Winzenburg, Bob: 171
Wirman, Matt: 150
Wirt, Randie: 207
Wirtz, Jeff: 153,154
Witham, Jim: 113
Withaus, Larry: 146
Witt, Brad: 148
Witt, Forrest: 116
Witt, Zach: 159
Witte, Laura: 180
Witte, Luke: 74
Witthus, Rick: 144,145
Wittman, Randy: 58,60
Wohler, Barry: 81,147,148
Wold, Allan: 168
Wolfenson, Marv: 44,45,49,56
Wolle, Bryan: 165
Wollin, Rick: 138
Wolters, Gary: 144
Woock, Herman: 168
Wooden, John: 66,68,71,98
Woods, Loren: 60
Worthington, Rob: 163
Wright, Jeff: 136
Wynne, Mike: 151
Yates, Don: 72
Yonke, Brett: 171
Young, Gus: 43,102,103
Young, Keith: 73,74,77
Young, Roscoe: 110
Zachow, Dean: 171
Zahn, Fred: 136
Zanna, Mark: 134
Zebedee, Howell: 81
Zender, Bob: 136,137,172
Ziemer, Gladys: 181,185
Ziemke, Josh: 171
Zimmerman, Corey: 158
Zollar, Dave: 153
Zurcher, Kim: 83

List of Works Cited:

1. Ross Bernstein: Interviews from over 50 Minnesota sports personalities and celebrities
2. "Fifty Years o Fifty Heroes" A Celebration of Minnesota Sports, by Bernstein, Mpls., 1997.
3. "Frozen Memories: Celebrating a Century of Minnesota Hockey," by Bernstein, Mpls., 1999.
4. "Hubert H. Humphrey Metrodome Souvenir Book": compiled by Dave Mona. MSP Pubs., Inc.
5. "Remember Bronko, Bernie, Bud and Bruce?," by Jay Walljasper, Minnesota Mag, Sept. 1979.
6. "ESPN Outtakes," by Dan Patrick, Hyperion Books, NY, 2000.
7. "Gustavus Athletics," by Lloyd Hollingsworth, Gustavus Adolphus Press, St. Peter, MN., 1984.
8. "Sid!" by Sid Hartman & Patrick Reusse - Voyager Press, 1997
9. "Minnesota Trivia," by Laurel Winter: Rutledge Hill Press, Nashville, TN, 1990
10. "NCAA Championships": The Official National Collegiate Champs & Records, by the NCAA. 1996.
11. The Star Tribune Minnesota Sports Hall of Fame insert publication
12. "Can You Name That Team?" by David Biesel
13. "Scoreboard," by Dunstan Tucker & Martin Schirber, St. John's Press, Collegeville, MN, 1979.
14. "Awesome Almanac Minnesota," by Jean Blashfield, B&B Publishing, Fontana, WI, 1993.
15. "The Encyclopedia of Sports," by Frank Menke, AC Barnes Pub., Cranbury, NJ, 1975.
16. "My lifetime in sports," by George Barton, Stan Carlson Pub., Minneapolis, 1957.
17. "Professional Sports Teams Histories," by Michael LaBlanc, Gale Pub., Detroit, MI, 1994.
18. "The Encyclopedia of North American Sports History," by Ralph Hickock, 1992.
19. "Minnesota State Fair: The history and heritage of 100 years," Argus Publishing, 1964.
20. "Concordia Sports - The First 100 Years" by Vernon Finn Grinaker, Concordia Website.
21. "Sports Leagues & Teams," by Mark Pollak, McFarland and Co. Pub., Jefferson, NC, 1996.
22. Minnesota Almanacs - (various 1970s)
23. "Season Review": ESPN Sports Almanac by Jerry Trecker, Total Sports Publications, 1983.
24. "Before the Dome," by David Anderson: Nodin Press, 1993.
25. "On to Nicollet," by Stew Thornley, Nodin Press, 1988.
26. MSHSL Media Guides (various 1950-2001)
27. Minn. Timberwolves Media Guides (various)
28. University of Minnesota Men's Athletics Media Guides (various 1950-2001).
29. Media Guides: Bemidji State, Moorhead State, UM-Duluth, Minnesota State, Mankato, St. Cloud State, Augsburg, Bethel, Carlton, Concordia, Hamline, Macalaster, St. John's, St. Mary's, St. Olaf, St. Thomas
30. "The Official NBA Encyclopedia," by Jan Hubbard, Doubleday Pub., NY, 2000.
31. "The Lakers: A Basketball Journey," by Roland Lazenby, St. Martin's Press, NY, 1983.
32. "The History of Minnesota State High School Basketball Tournaments," by Ed Simpkins, 1964.
33. "A Century of Women's Basketball," by Joan Jult & Marianna Trekell, Reston, VA, 1991.
34. "Duluth Sketches of the Past," by Bruce Bennett.
35. "Pioneers of the Hardwood," by Todd Gould, Indiana University Press, 1998.
36. "The Minneapolis Lakers: A Pictorial Album," by Stan Carlson, Olympic Press, Mpls., 1950.
37. St. Paul Slam Media Guide, 1996-97
38. "Lakers Collectors Edition," by Joe Hession, Foghorn Press, San Francisco, 1994.
39. "Kevin Garnett," by John Torres, Lerner Sports Publishing, Minneapolis, 2000.
40. "Basketball's Original Dynasty," by Stew Thornley, Nodin Press, 1989.
41. "Corporate Report Minnesota," November 1991; June 1993.
42. "Minneapolis-St Paul City Business," September 18, 1992.
43. "Sports Illustrated," June 26, 1989; November 6, 1989; February 25, 1991; May 6, 1991.
44. "Basketball's Great Dynasties: The Lakers," by Jack Clary, Brompton Books, NY, 1992.
45. "Championship NBA," by Leonard Koppett, Dial Press, NY, 1970.
46. "The Lakers: A Basketball Journey," by Roland Lazenby, St. Martin's Press, NY, 1993.
47. "The Encyclopedia of Pro Basketball Team Histories," by Peter Bjarkman, Carrol & Graf Pub, NY, 1994.
48. "The NBA Finals: A 50 Year Celebration," by Roland Lazenby, Masters Press, Indy, 1996.
49. "Minneapolis Lakers match up with L.A. team," by Sid Hartman, June 17, 2001.
50. "Mikkelsen, Askov 's finest, named a Hall of Famer," By Howard Voigt, MSHSL Program, '95.
51. "Helping with Lakers provided memories to always cherish," by Sid Hartman, Star Tribune, Oct. 29, 1989.
52. "Unstoppable," by Joe Oberle...
53. "The Biographical History of Basketball," by Peter Bjarkman, Masters Press, Chicago, 2000.
54. "Mr. Basketball: George Mikan's Own Story," by Bill Carlson, Greenburg Pub., New York, 1951.
55. "The Roots: Early Professional Leagues," by Robin Deutsch and Douglas Stark.
56. "George Mikan: The First Icon," by Dan Barriero, "The Official NBA Encyclopedia," Doubleday Pub., NY, by Jan Hubbard, 2000.
57. "Obsession: Timberwolves Stalk the NBA," by Bill Heller, Bonus Books, Chicago, 1989.
58. "Cages to Jumpshots," by Robert Peterson, Oxford Univ. Press, NY, 1990.
59. "Gopher Glory," by Steve Pearlstein, Layers Publishing, Minneapolis, 1995.
60. "Winfield: A Players Life," by Dave Winfield.
61. "The Living Legend: Ray Christensen," by Brad Ruiter, Fast Break Magazine, March 4, 2001.
62. "This is Gold Country," by Bob Utecht, Piper Publishing, Blue Earth, Minn., 1977.
63. "The Minneapolis Lakers: A Pictorial Album," by Stan Carlson, Olympic Press, MN, 1951.
64. "Timberwolves sign Garnett to six-year deal," by Steve Aschburner, Tribune, Oct. 2, 1997.
65. "How Kevin Garnetted the NBA," by John Rosengren, World Traveler, Dec. 2000, Pgs. 44-50.
66. "Minnesota's Rising Star," by Troy Young, 2000-2001 T-wolves Yearbook, 2001. Pgs. 73-76.
67. "Minnesota's Rising Star," by Troy Young, 2000-2001 T-wolves Yearbook, 2001. Pgs. 73-76.
68. "Garnett puts Wolves first," by David DuPree, USA Today, March 7, 2001. Pg. 8.
69. "Wolves win, in," by Robbi Pickeral, Pioneer Press, April 11, 2001, Pg. 1D.
70. Bjarkman, Peter C. The History of the NBA. NY: Crescent Books, Random house, 1992.
71. Strasen, Marty (et. al.). Basketball Almanac, 1993—94. NY: Publications International, 1994.
72. "The Encyclopedia of Pro Basketball Team Histories," by Peter Bjarkman, Carrol & Graf Pub, NY, 1994.
73. "Minn. Timberwolves," by Richard Rambeck, Creative Education Pub., Mankato, 1993.
74. "Minnesota Timberwolves," by John Nichols, Creative Education Pub., Mankato, 1998.
75. "The Guiding Force," by Lisa Helgeson, Timberwolves Tonight, April 8, 2001. Pgs. 14-16.
76. "Wolves, Saunders agree to contract extension," by Sid Hartman, Star Trib, June 20, 2001.
77. "Lone Wolf," by John Millea, Sporting News, Nov. 27, 2000, pp.10-12.
78. "T-wolves History," Timberwolves.com, 2001.
79. "The Ultimate Vet," by David Brauer, Timberwolves Tonight, April 8, 2001. Pgs. 14-16.
80. "Red, White and Blue: The ABA," by Terry Pluto, Official NBA Encyclopedia, NBA Properties, NY, 1994.
81. "Minnesota Muskies," By Stew Thornley.
82. "Minnesota Pipers," By Stew Thornley.
83. "Welcome the Minnesota Pipers," By Jim Kaplan, Minneapolis Star, Pipers Program, 1968.
84. "The Connie Hawkins Story," By Bob Fowler, St. Paul Pioneer Press, Piper's Program, 1968.
85. "Gopher State Greatness," by Joel B. Krenz, Richtman's Publishing, 1984.
86. "Minnesota Basketball News" various publications throughout past decade.
87. "Minnesota High School Basketball Records: Web-Site," by Matthew Pederson, Starbuck, Minn.
88. Bjarkman, Peter, "Hoopla: A Century of College Basketball," 1996.
89. Naismith, James, "Basketball: Its Origin and Development," 1996.
90. Salzberg, Charles, "From Set Shot to Slam Dunk: The Glory Days of Basketball in the Words of Those Who Played it," 1998.
91. Wolff, Alexander, "Sports Illustrated 100 Years of Hoops; A Fond Look Back at the Sport of Basketball," 1995.
92. "HickokSports.com," Web-Site, 2001.
93. "The Association for Professional Basketball Research," Web-Site, 2001.
94. "They Were No. 1: The History of the NCAA Basketball Tournament," by Robert Stern.
95. "Celebrating the roots of girls' interscholastic basketball in the early 1900s," By Marian Johnson, MSHSL Program, 1999.
96. "20 years ago basketball became a girls sport too," By Jill Lorentz, MSHSL Program, 1996.
97. "In the 1930s, These Girls Never Lost," By Bruce Brothers, MSHSL Program, 1992.
98. "Minutemen Girls Made History in '76 With First State Tournament Title," by Jess Myers, MSHSL Program, 1993.
99. "WNBA: Stars of Women's Basketball," by James Ponti, Pocketbooks, NY, 1999.
100. "A WNBA primer," Star Trib, May 20, 2001.
101. "The Lynx and WNBA at a crossroads as 2001 season approaches," by Jay Weiner, Star Tribune, May 20, 2001.
102. "WNBA: Stars of Women's Basketball," by James Ponti, Pocketbooks, NY, 1999.
103. "J. Gordon Nevers President," by Lynnette Sjoquist, Fillies Program, 1980.
104. "Basketball Is bouncing In Minnesota," by Greg Carlson, Fillies Program, 1980.
105. "Scooter Does It All," by Greg Carlson, Fillies Program, 1980.
106. "Progress in the WBL: Fact or Fiction," by Lynnette Sjoquist, Fillies Program, 1980.
107. "The History of the Fillies," by Lynnette Sjoquist, Fillies Program, 1980.
108. "J. Gordon Nevers President" by Lynnette Sjoquist, Fillies Program, 1980.
109. "Dr. James A. Naismith," by Robin Deutsch and Douglas Stark.
110. "The Roots: Early Professional Leagues," by Robin Deutsch and Douglas Stark.
111. "Gustavus Athletics: A Century of Building the Gustie Tradition," by Lloyd Hollingsworth, Gustavus Adolphus Press, 1984.
112. "Coach Bill Musselman Dies at 59," by Landon Hall, Associated Press, May 5, 2000.
113. Website: www.harlemglobetrotters.com.
114. "Loose Balls : The Short, Wild Life of the American Basketball Association," by Terry Pluto
115. "Scandals of '51 : How the Gamblers Almost Killed College Basketball,"
116. "FOUL! Connie Hawkins: Schoolyard Star, Exile, NBA Superstar," by David Wolf, H-R-W Publishing, 1972.
117. "Minnesotans in the NBA," by Dan Bell, MSHSL Program.
118. "The Husky Tradition," by John D. Kasper, 1980.
119. "SCSU Women's Athletics 25th Anniversary Brochure," 1993.
120. NSIC Web-Site & Corresponding Member Web-Pages (Men's & Women's)
121. NCC Web-Site & Corresponding Member Web-Pages (Men's & Women's)
122. MIAC Web-Site & Corresponding Member Web-Pages (Men's & Women's)
123. Minnesota History Center Online Archives
124. Steve Dimitry's Extinct Sports Leagues
125. MN High School Basketball Records
126. Association for Professional Basketball Research web-site
127. Naismith Memorial Basketball Hall of Fame
128. wnba.com
129. gophersports.com
130. nba.com
131. remembertheaba.com
132. mshsl.com
133. usoc.org
134. usabasketball.com
135. hoophall.com
136. umdbulldogs.com
137. startribune.com
138. pioneerplanet.com
139. espn.com
140. mscsports.com
141. Concordia University Web-Site
142. augsburg.edu
143. varsityonline.com
144. cnnsi.com
145. miac-online.org
146. ncc.com
147. northernsun.org
148. dickscourtroom.com
149. hickocksports.com
150. iba.org
151. cba.com
152. channel4000.com
153. "The Clock Ran Out," MN Mag., Dec. 2000.

Here's to the Next 100 Years...

About the Author

Ross Bernstein is the author of several regionally best-selling coffee-table sports books, including: **"Pigskin Pride: Celebrating a Century of Minnesota Football," "Frozen Memories: Celebrating a Century of Minnesota Hockey"** and **"Fifty Years • Fifty Heroes: A Celebration of Minnesota Sports."**

Ross Bernstein

Bernstein first got into writing through some rather unique circumstances. You see, after a failed attempt to make it as a walk-on to the University of Minnesota's Golden Gopher hockey team, he opted to instead become the team's mascot, "Goldy." His humorous accounts as a mischievous rodent, back at old Mariucci Arena, then inspired the 1992 best-seller: **"Gopher Hockey by the Hockey Gopher."** And the rest, they say... is history!

Bernstein also writes children's and young-reader sports biographies as well. Among these books include bio's about such superstars as: Seattle Supersonics All-Star Point Guard **Gary Payton**, Minnesota Vikings All-Pro Wide Receiver **Randy Moss**, Minnesota Timberwolves All-Star Forward **Kevin Garnett** and Minnesota Vikings All-Pro Quarterback **Daunte Culpepper**. (Garnett and Culpepper are due out in 2002.)

In addition, Bernstein also writes an annual book for the U.S. Hockey Hall of Fame, entitled: **"The Hall: Celebrating the History and Heritage of the U.S. Hockey Hall of Fame."** Proceeds from the sale of the book, which chronicles and updates the history of the Eveleth, Minn., based museum and its more than 100 world-renouned enshrinees, go directly to the Hall of Fame.

Today the Fairmont native works as a full-time sports author for several Midwest and East Coast publishers. He is also the co-founder and Contributing Editor of a start-up life-style based hockey magazine entitled: **"Minnesota Hockey Journal."** A sister publication of USA Hockey's **"American Hockey Magazine"** — the nation's largest hockey publication, the **"Journal"** has a regional circulation of nearly 50,000 Minnesota hockey households.

Ross and his wife Sara, along with their sock-snarfing Jack Russell Terrier, "Herbie" (named in honor of local hockey legend Herbie Brooks), presently reside in Oakdale. *(Oh yeah, his new coffee-table book celebrating the history of Minnesota Baseball will be out in the Fall of 2002. Stay Tuned!)*

To order additional signed and personalized copies of any of these books, please send a check to the following address: *(**Ross Bernstein • P.O. Box 280201 • Oakdale, MN 55128-9201**)* (*Prices include tax and bubble-packed U.S. Priority-Mail shipping.) *Thank you!*

1.) "Hardwood Heroes: Celebrating a Century of Minnesota Basketball" — $30.00
2.) "Pigskin Pride: Celebrating a Century of Minnesota Football" — $30.00
3.) "Frozen Memories: Celebrating a Century of Minnesota Hockey" — $28.00
4.) "Fifty Years • Fifty Heroes: A Celebration of Minnesota Sports" — $25.00
5.) "Gopher Hockey by the Hockey Gopher" — $18.00
6.) "The Hall: Celebrating the History and Heritage of the U.S. Hockey Hall of Fame" (Class of 2000) — $18.00
7.) "The Hall: Celebrating the History and Heritage of the U.S. Hockey Hall of Fame"(Class of 2001) — $18.00
8.) "Gary Payton: Star Guard" — $25.00
9.) "Randy Moss: Star Reciever" — $25.00
10.) "Kevin Garnett: Star Forward" (Due out in 2002) — $25.00
11.) "Daunte Culpepper: Star Quarterback" (Due out in 2002) — $25.00

To learn more about any of these books, as well as about future titles and book-signing information, please check out Ross' web-site at: www.bernsteinbooks.com

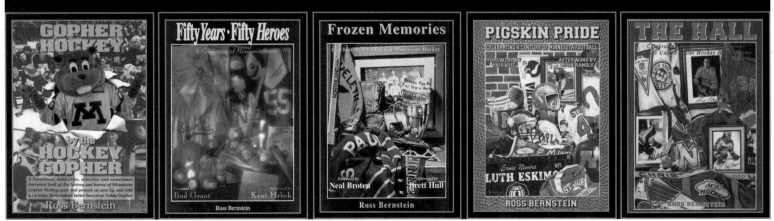